NEPAL
HANDBOOK

NEPAL
HANDBOOK

SECOND EDITION

KERRY MORAN

MOON
PUBLICATIONS INC.

NEPAL HANDBOOK
SECOND EDITION

Published by
Moon Publications, Inc.
P.O. Box 3040
Chico, California 95927-3040, USA

Printed by
Colorcraft Ltd., Hong Kong

ISBN: 1-56691-041-2
ISSN: 1085-2689

Editor: Pauli Galin
Copy Editors: Elizabeth Kim, Sharon Brown
Production & Design: Carey Wilson
Cartographers: Bob Race, Brian Bardwell
Index: Nicole Revere

Front cover photo: Lou Corbett: *Nepali resident seated next to masks typically reproduced for the tourist trade.*
All photos by Kerry Moran unless otherwise noted.

Distributed in the U.S.A. by Publishers Group West
Printed in Hong Kong

Please send all comments,
corrections, additions,
amendments, and critiques to:

**NEPAL HANDBOOK
MOON PUBLICATIONS, INC.
P.O. BOX 3040
CHICO, CA 95927-3040, USA
e-mail: travel@moon.com**

Printing History
1st edition — October 1991
Reprinted — May 1992
2nd edition — April 1996

For Chris

CONTENTS

MAPS

MAP SYMBOLS

INTERNATIONAL BOUNDARY
ROADS, HIGHWAYS (NOT ALL ARE PAVED)
UNPAVED ROADS
FOOT PATHS
BRIDGE
RAILROAD
PASS
GLACIER
RIDGE LINE

WATERFALL
WATER
MOUNTAIN
GATES
STUPAS

o   TOWNS / VILLAGES
O   CITIES
●   ACCOMMODATIONS
■   POINT OF INTEREST
♣   TEMPLES (PAGODAS)
GOMPAS (MONASTERIES)

CHARTS AND SPECIAL TOPICS

ABBREVIATIONS

a/c—air-conditioning
ACAP— Annapurna
  Conservation Area Project
AMS—acute mountain sickness
BDP—Bhaktapur Development
  Project
CIWEC—Canadian
  International Water and
  Energy Consultants
d—double occupancy
GI—gastrointestinal illness
GNP—gross national product

GPO—general post office
HAN—Hotel Association of
  Nepal
HRA—Himalayan Rescue
  Association
KEEP—Kathmandu
  Environmental Educational
  Project
KPH—Kilometer Per Hour
OW—one-way
NGO—nongovernmental
  organization

NP—national park
RNAC—Royal Nepal Airlines
  Corp.
Rs—Nepali rupee
RT—roundtrip
s—single occupancy
STOL—short takeoff and
  landing (airstrip)
TAAN—Trekking Agents
  Association of Nepal
WR—wildlife reserve

IS THIS BOOK OUT OF DATE?

Things change fast in Nepal: hotels open and close, new destinations emerge, transportation hopefully improves, and prices inevitably rise. To keep up with it we plan a complete revision of this book every three years. We'd appreciate comments based on your own experiences in Nepal—suggestions for good hotels, retaurants, travel agents and trekking companies; trekking and trail advice; accounts of harrowing and pleasant experiences; compliments and complaints. Please send your comments to:

> NEPAL HANDBOOK
> Moon Publications
> P.O. Box 3040
> Chico, CA 95927-3040, U.S.A.
> e-mail: travel@moon.com

ACKNOWLEDGMENTS

This book is the result of 10 years of meetings, travels, conversations, and experiences in Nepal. It would be impossible to list everyone who has contributed to it, but special thanks to those who contributed to this update: Miriam Corneli, Bidur Dangol, Lorne Goldman, David DeWit, James DeCoo, Carroll Dunham, Matthew Fassberg, Sallie Fischer Limbu, Frances Higgins, J.P. Lama, Kim Larsen, Siobhan Maderson, Rick Nacius, Paul Osborne, Eric Shapiro, Peter Shankland, Amy Shavelson, Christa Skerry, Vince Spucces, and Michel van Dam.

Most of all, thanks to my husband, Christopher Gamm, for getting me here in the first place and making our life in Nepal fun throughout. His sensible advice and constant support have contributed much to this book. Finally, warm thanks to all the Nepalis who have welcomed, fed, and entertained me, making me feel at home, and helping me to understand their compellingly complex country.

INTRODUCTION

BOB RACE

INTRODUCTION

The kingdom of Nepal packs more into its 147,181 square km than most countries 20 times its size. Crowned by eight of the world's 10 highest mountains, Nepal's landscape compresses lush tropics and arctic tundra into an amazingly small span. Altitude ranges from near sea level to 8848 meters above it—the summit of Mt. Everest, the highest piece of the planet.

This wild altitudinal variation fosters an incredible variety of ecosystems: steamy jungles and terraced valleys, forested hills, frozen peaks and high-altitude deserts. Tropical flowers frame views of not-so-distant snow peaks; tigers and rhinos roam lush jungles while less than 150 km north, snow leopards prowl barren mountain slopes. Whatever you say about Nepal is bound to be true—somewhere.

The natural diversity is only the beginning. Nepal's rugged terrain has preserved a kaleidoscope of linguistic, ethnic, and cultural traditions rivaled by few nations. Dozens of different ethnic groups live among its hills, each with their own language, costumes, customs, and beliefs. The Kathmandu Valley, a fertile green bowl set in the midst of Himalayan foothills, is an oasis of magnificent art, and the home of the ancient and sophisticated Newar culture.

Once isolated by suspicious rulers, Nepal only opened its borders to the outside world in 1951. At the time barely 200 Westerners had ever visited the country. Few had ventured far beyond the Kathmandu Valley. Today, over 300,000 tourists come to Nepal each year to explore the spectacular landscape, rich culture, and harmony of a traditional way of life. In terms of statistics Nepal is one of the least developed countries in the world, but it's rich with humor, warmth, and natural beauty. Visitors are drawn here by the amazing landscape, but they leave remembering the friendliness of the people.

> *Nature alone makes it one of the most fascinating countries in Asia: a confusion of mountains and hills, almost as if the Himalayas, in an attempt to reach the heavens, had crumbled back down to earth.*
>
> —GIUSEPPE TUCCI,
> JOURNEY TO MUSTANG

THE LAND

Dramatic, extreme, verging on the outrageous, mountains shape Nepal's reality, molding its culture, history, economy, and politics. For 80% of the country, vertical is the main orientation, and up-and-down is the determining fact of life. The rugged topography is both a blessing and a curse. The spectacular landscape is world-famous, and the isolation enforced by mountains has preserved age-old cultures and traditions. But for a nation attempting to modernize, those breathtaking ranges are nothing but trouble.

Nepal is less than 900 km long from east to west and only 150-200 km wide north to south. You could drive the length of the country in a day, if only there were a decent level road. As it is, the East-West Highway traversing the flat southern portion of the country takes several agonizingly bumpy days, and it takes several months to cross central Nepal end to end on foot, a tough journey few would care to make. The mountainous terrain makes the country far larger than its actual size in terms of trans-

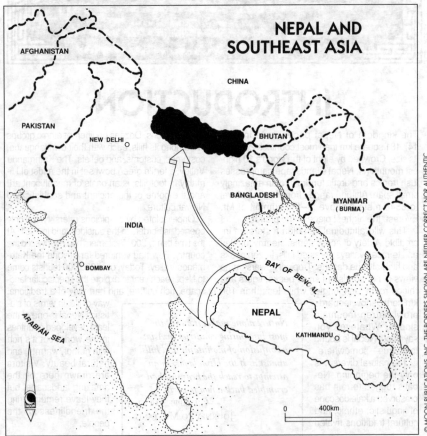

NEPAL AND SOUTHEAST ASIA

AFGHANISTAN

CHINA

PAKISTAN

NEW DELHI

BHUTAN

BANGLADESH

MYANMAR (BURMA)

INDIA

BOMBAY

BAY OF BENGAL

ARABIAN SEA

NEPAL

KATHMANDU

0   400km

portation and development. It's said if Nepal's landscape could somehow be detached from the rugged terrain and stretched out flat, it would approximately equal the area of the United States.

Borders

The eastern section of Nepal's long northern border with Tibet runs along the crest of the Himalaya Mountains. West of Kathmandu the border is delineated by the Tibetan Marginal Range, a slightly lower series of mountains rising up about 30 km north of the Himalayan crest. This range also defines the region's watershed, between Tibet's great Tsangpo River to the north and India's sacred Ganges to the south. In the small high valleys between the Himalaya and the Marginal Range, tiny pockets of Tibetan culture have been preserved from the Chinese influence which has devastated Tibet itself.

Nepal's remaining borders are shared with India: the protectorate of Sikkim in the east, the states of Bihar and Uttar Pradesh to the south and west. Sandwiched between China and India, Nepal is in a ticklish spot, geopolitically speaking. Consider India is 22 times larger in area than Nepal—and China is over three times as big as India. *Then* think about the population differences! An 18th-century Nepali ruler succinctly described his kingdom's location: "like a yam between two rocks."

The northern barrier of the Himalaya mutes Chinese and Tibetan influence on Nepal, but the open southern border has always been a gateway to India. The latter plays an important role in modern Nepali politics, economics, and culture,

Nepali women planting rice

though sovereign Nepal remains sensitive about India's unofficial, if indisputable, influence.

THE THREE REGIONS

Nepal can be roughly divided into three geographic regions, each with its own distinctive environment, peoples, economy, customs, and culture. Different landscapes have shaped different lifestyles. Flying over Nepal, you get a bird's-eye view of the dramatic extremes: the level lush fields and jungles of the Terai rise into the crumpled, corrugated landscape of the Hills, patchworked with fields and forests and ribboned by streams. These in turn rise up—and up, and up, into the highest of all mountains, the Himalaya, floating on the northern horizon like a dream.

The Terai

This narrow strip of land running along the southern border averages only 20 km in width and constitutes less than one-fifth of Nepal's total

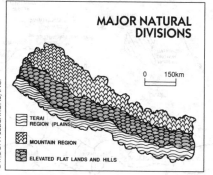
MAJOR NATURAL DIVISIONS

0   150km

TERAI REGION (PLAINS)
MOUNTAIN REGION
ELEVATED FLAT LANDS AND HILLS

© MOON PUBLICATIONS, INC.

area. Yet the flat, fertile Terai contains virtually the only reasonable farmland in Nepal and supports nearly half of the population. Seventy percent of the country's arable land is in the Terai; over 60% of its grain is grown here.

> *Upon what gigantic scale does Nature here operate!*
>
> —BOTANIST/NATURALIST
> JOSEPH HOOKER,
> SPEAKING OF THE HIMALAYA

The hot lowland Terai is a geographic extension of Northern India's Gangetic Plain, and Indian influences have shaped its cultures and societies. Traditional Terai dwellers (Madeshi) are either indigenous tribal people or Hindus speaking Sanskrit-based dialects. The open border with India allows people, influences, and goods to move across freely. Despite its enormous wealth and potential, the Terai is looked down upon by the "true" Hill Nepalis who set the standards for mainstream culture; Terai dwellers in turn tend to feel snubbed.

Through the 1950s, much of the Terai was uninhabited jungle. Even a single night spent in the area could prove fatal during the fever season, April-Oct., when malaria-carrying mosquitoes appeared. Except for a few indigenous tribes with a natural immunity, malaria kept out

everyone—Nepalis, Indians, and foreigners alike. It was the perfect natural defense for Nepal's vulnerable southern flank. A British historian noted: "Sundown in the Terai has brought an end to more attempted raids into Nepal and has buried more political hopes than will ever be known."

Beginning in the mid-'50s intensive DDT spraying sponsored by WHO and the U.S. opened the region for settlement. Hundreds of thousands of Nepali farmers poured down from the hills to settle on the new land, joined by landless Indians from the neighboring state of Bihar. Today the Terai is the major agricultural and industrial region of Nepal. Most of the country's roads and industry are found here, as well as virtually all the urban centers outside the Kathmandu Valley.

The Hills

Nepal's heartland is the Hills, a rugged region of deep valleys and terraced ridges covering about half its total area. The name is misleading. Nepal's "Hills" would rank as mountains anywhere else,

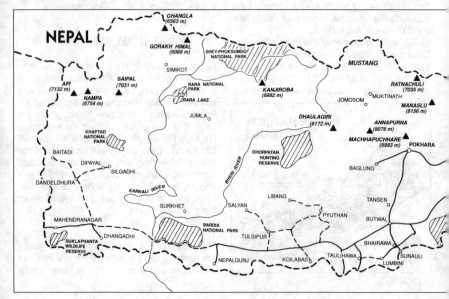

THE WORLD'S 8000-METER PEAKS

1. Everest	8848 meters	Nepal/Tibet
2. K-2	8760 meters	Pakistan/China
3. Kangchenjunga	8586 meters	Nepal/India
4. Lhotse I	8516 meters	Nepal/Tibet
5. Makalu	8463 meters	Nepal/Tibet
6. Lhotse II	8440 meters	Nepal/Tibet
7. Cho Oyu	8201 meters	Nepal/Tibet
8. Dhaulagiri	8167 meters	Nepal
9. Manaslu	8163 meters	Nepal
10. Nanga Parbat	8126 meters	Pakistan
11. Annapurna I	8091 meters	Nepal
12. Gasherbrum	8068 meters	Pakistan/China
13. Broad Peak	8046 meters	Pakistan/China
14. Gosainthan (Shishapangma)	8012 meters	Tibet

mensity of this land. Trails ascend 2500 vertical meters, plunge down to a river valley, and rise again, crossing what seems to be an endless ocean of land frozen into huge breakers.

This rugged region is the cradle of Nepali identity and nationalism. While a bare majority of the population now lives in the flat Terai, the Hills are still identified with genuine Nepali culture.

The Mountains

The Himalaya welds the Indian subcontinent to Asia, extending over 3,800 km in a great arc from the Hindu Kush range of Afghanistan to eastern Tibet. Twice the height of the Alps, it's the undisputed king of mountain ranges, claiming the world's 86 highest peaks before another range manages to interject a contender.

The cream of the Central Himalaya, nearly one-third of the range's total length, falls in Nepal. Here rise eight of the world's 10 highest mountains, nine of its 14 8000-meter-plus peaks, two

and they would almost certainly be uninhabited. Few people would care to climb down 1000 vertical meters to fetch water and then haul it back up even once, but for many Nepalis it's part of daily life. About 45% of the population lives in this up-and-down region, farming terraced fields patiently carved out of hillsides by generations of farmers. Only by walking can you appreciate the true im-

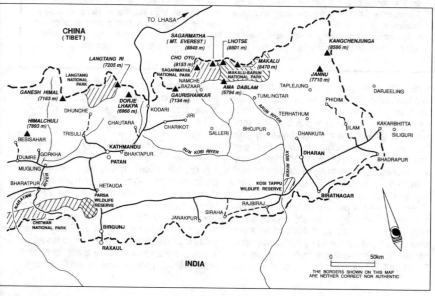

© MOON PUBLICATIONS, INC.

THE MONSOON

"There is more joy in the rainy monsoon than there is in any other season, with happiness the rains begin, and with happiness the rains end."

—NEPALI POET LEKHNATH POUDYAL

The annual summer monsoon is welcomed across the Indian subcontinent as a joyous period of renewal following the dry spring. The summer rains sweep into eastern Nepal each year at the beginning of June, bringing water to nurture fields of sprouting rice, and reaching the Kathmandu Valley by mid-June. The monsoon diminishes in intensity as it moves gradually west. By the time it reaches the great barrier of Dhaulagiri west of the Kali Gandaki River, most of its force has been spent; as a result, western Nepal is much drier than the eastern portion of the country, reflected in its sparse vegetation and low crop yields.

The seasonal rains are orchestrated as precisely as a symphony, climaxing slowly to a crescendo in July and early August, then tapering off. About 80% of the year's total precipitation falls between June and September. The amount of rainfall varies wildly. The village of Lumle just west of Pokhara got a torrential one meter of rain one July, while Jomosom, less than 70 km north, recorded a bare four cm.

The monsoon cycle begins each spring as the blazing sun sucks up moisture from the Bay of Bengal, creating masses of heavy moist air. These low-lying clouds are drawn northeast by the temperature differential between the central Asian landmass and the sea. Soon they collide with the great barrier of the Himalaya, which forces the clouds upwards. As they rise the air cools into water vapor and condenses into rain. Most falls on the lower southern Himalayan slopes, watering the lush rainforests of Sikkim, Bhutan, and Nepal.

The clouds have dumped most of their moisture by the time they reach higher altitudes, and few make it across the Himalaya, explaining the rain-shadow effect that freeze-dries the Tibetan Plateau. In Nepal, north-south mountain ranges like Langtang Himal and Annapurna Himal have a similar effect. Their western flanks remain relatively dry throughout the summer, making them good destinations for monsoon trekking.

The monsoon is not the continual dreary downpour imagined by many outsiders. Rain falls in predictable patterns, either a 30- to 45-minute shower during the morning and afternoon, or more typically a brief daytime shower followed by a long, soaking night rain. Only one or two weeks of the year does it pour all day; when it does it's time to wade barefoot into the streets and celebrate.

A monsoon visit is worth considering if for no other reason than you'll have Nepal virtually to yourself. Tourist arrivals bottom out May-Sept. and the country's trails, temples, and streets regain their tranquillity. The rainy season shows the Kath-

dozen 7000-meter-plus giants, and several hundred peaks over 6000 meters—nobody has ever bothered to count them all. The Nepal Himalaya is not an unbroken line of peaks, but an assortment of smaller chains or *himal* divided by river tributaries or lower ridges. Individual ranges branch off into a maze of spurs and ridges, many of them nameless even today despite the interest of Western cartographers. To local people, giant mountains are nothing special.

Less than eight percent of Nepal's population lives in this rugged region, in permanent settlements which at up to 4000 meters are among the highest in the world (temporary summer herding settlements are found even higher). The Mountain region's culture and religion are closely linked to Tibet's, and the traditional economy was, and sometimes still is, based on trans-border trade with its northern neighbor.

THE HIMALAYA

Figures alone don't convey the overwhelming presence of the 45-km-wide swath of mountains dominating Nepal's northern skyline. Ancient Hindus called the range "The Abode *(alaya)* of Snows *(him)*" and revered it as the home of gods and saints, and as a place of pilgrimage. Even today local people worship certain peaks as the abode of the area's protective spirits, an ancient belief predating both Hinduism and Buddhism.

mandu Valley at its loveliest. Fields of sprouting rice carpet the land in vivid, electric green, and sunsets are long, lingering displays of spectacular cloud-caught light. The rice transplanting of June and July is hard work, eased by merriment, song, and mud-flinging. From August on the later monsoon is marked by a flood of colorful festivals— Gai Jatra, Janai Purnima, Krishna Jayanti, Teej— which continue into the great harvest celebrations of autumn.

Monsoon Trekking

Monsoon trekking is a secret enjoyed by a handful of souls who prefer to have the trails to themselves. The atmosphere is gentle and blessedly warm even at high altitudes. The mountains are carpeted with greenery and tiny wildflowers, caressed by mist rather than rain. Mountain peaks are veiled in clouds, but reveal themselves in breathtaking, unexpected glimpses. Best of all, the local people are their friendly, relaxed, normal selves, enjoying socializing after the hectic rush of tourist season. Summer is a time for weddings, festivals, and celebrations, as well as the season to graze livestock in the highest pastures.

Monsoon trekking is not completely idyllic. Trails may be treacherously slippery and rivers dangerously high, while the highest passes can be blocked by fresh snow. Leeches emerge, disease is rampant, and there's always the chance of a week of solid rain. Preparation and patience can minimize these problems, however, as can selecting a relatively dry area like the upper Kali Gandaki, Manang, or Khumbu. When planning your schedule, make allowances for high rivers, washed-out roads, and cancelled flights.

Rainy Season Survival

High-tech raingear can be useful, but a US$250 jacket is not essential to survival. The best protection is the classic black Asian umbrella, which shelters from rain and sun alike and doubles as an emergency walking stick on slippery slopes. Heavy plastic bags or sheeting from the bazaar will keep backpacks dry; rubberized ponchos from trekking goods shops are good for cyclists. If a downpour catches you unprepared, don't be shy about ducking beneath the nearest eaves. It's a great excuse to sit and watch the world, and to meet people you otherwise never would.

Shoes inevitably become wet and muddy. Leather repels water longer than cloth sneakers, but takes longer to dry and will be ruined after a few good soakings. Washable, quick-drying plastic sandals are the best solution for Kathmandu's muddy streets, but avoid flip-flops that fling mud up your backside. Bring strapped rafting sandals (cheap local knockoffs are sold in Thamel), or get a pair of Chinese-made galoshes in Boudhanath.

The monsoon season is definitely hazardous to your health. All the waste deposited over the winter is washed into rivers, seriously contaminating the water supply. Hepatitis, typhoid, and intestinal parasites abound, and you must be scrupulous about food and water. Infection is also a problem; the smallest cut or scratched mosquito bite can take weeks to heal in this season if your resistance runs down, so keep breaks in the skin clean and protected.

It's easy to see why the Himalaya has made such a deep impression upon the people dwelling in its shadows. Its jagged ice-capped peaks crown the horizon; its snows water the region's great rivers; its massive bulk serves as the weather-maker for much of Asia. The range serves as a great climactic divide between the lush foothills to the south and the arid Tibetan Plateau to the north, and the range of vegetation and wildlife covering its lower flanks is among the richest in the world.

Geology

The birth of the Himalaya is an epic saga played out in slow motion over an inconceivably long period of time. Fifty million years ago, Eurasia and India lay floating atop slowly moving tectonic plates, separated by the tropical Sea of Tethys. About 45 million years ago the Indian plate slammed into the Eurasian and the colliding edges crumpled upwards to form the Himalaya. The Sea of Tethys drained out as its bed was pushed up, leaving ocean fossils embedded in mountain rock. Sculpted by erosion and polished by the slow slide of glaciers, the Himalayan peaks emerged in their present spectacular form, more sharply defined than other, older mountains.

India continues to push under the edge of the Eurasian plate even today, and the mountains keep growing at the rate of one cm a year. That works out to around 30,000 feet per million years—a tremendously high growth rate in geological terms. The Himalayas are growing faster, and on a larger scale, than anywhere else in the world, a fact signalled by Nepal's regular earthquakes and the frequent landslides and erosion.

Rivers

Nepal's major rivers are a geographic anomaly, rising on the north side of the Himalaya and running southwards to eventually join India's Ganges River and empty into the Bay of Bengal. These rivers actually preceded the Himalaya; as the mountains emerged, the rivers were strong enough to simply cut through them, creating tremendously deep transverse gorges. The passages they carved through the maze of hills have been used for millennia as trade routes between Tibet and India, and most Hill settlements are concentrated along rivers and their tributaries.

Three major river systems drain Nepal: the Kosi in the east, with seven main tributaries; the Narayani in the central portion; and the Karnali in the far west. These rivers also create an enormous hydropower potential, largely untapped as of now. If it could somehow be accessed, it would catapult the nation ahead in terms of development.

CLIMATE

On the same date you can be sweltering in subtropical valleys, basking in the temperate Kathmandu Valley, or shivering atop a frozen summit.

Visitors expecting Nepal to be nonstop snowy mountains are often surprised by the fierceness of the sun. Remember that at 26°-30° north of the equator, Nepal's latitude is similar to that of central Florida and Cairo. The highly varied terrain creates dramatic climactic differences, however: it might be better to speak of microclimates rather than one particular climate. The following generalities broadly apply.

Seasons are typical of the Northern Hemisphere: hot April-Aug. and cold Nov.-Jan., with two brief warm periods in Feb.-March and Sept.-October. Regional variations on this basic theme are distinct. The humid, tropical Terai receives the most monsoonal rain and records the country's highest temperatures (over 39°C in Nepalgunj in May). The lower Hills (900-2700 meters), including the Kathmandu Valley, are subtropical, with hot summers and moderate winters with only occasional frost. The higher Hills (2700-4000 meters) are more temperate. Because clouds frequently rest at this level, the Hills tend to get plenty of rain, fog, and frost. Above 4000 meters, the Mountains have a cooler, drier alpine climate; daily temperatures vary wildly depending on sunshine, wind, and altitude. Generally speaking, temperatures drop 6°C for every 1100 meters ascended.

Seasons

Set at an altitude of 1300 meters, the Kathmandu Valley has a near-ideal climate, reflected in its

AVERAGE MONTHLY TEMPERATURES

	MEGHAULI (TERAI)		KATHMANDU (HILLS)		NAMCHE BAZAAR (MTNS.)	
	MAX. °C	MIN. °C	MAX. °C	MIN. °C	MAX. °C	MIN.°C
Jan.	23	8	17	2	6	-6
Feb.	28	11	21	3	6	-4
March	33	17	25	9	8	-1
April	37	19	27	11	11	1
May	37	22	28	16	14	3
June	34	23	28	19	15	7
July	33	25	28	20	16	8
Aug.	32	24	27	20	16	8
Sept.	32	24	26	19	15	7
Oct.	31	19	25	12	11	1
Nov.	27	14	21	8	8	-3
Dec.	24	8	19	3	7	-4

lush vegetation and beautiful gardens. Residents distinguish six distinct seasons:

Sheet: From mid-Dec.-Feb. a chilly mist rises from the moist fields at dawn, swaddling the Valley in white until the midmorning sun burns through. Farmers call the fog "milk" because it nourishes their fields in the dry winter season. Winter afternoons are clear, crisp, and pleasantly warm in the sun, but nights can be quite cold in Kathmandu's unheated buildings. Snow falls in the Valley only once in a generation, but occasionally the surrounding hilltops are dusted with a light snowfall, and Valley residents rush out to marvel at the phenomenon.

Basanta: The festival of Basant Panchami in late January celebrates the official first day of spring, but it usually takes a few more weeks for the weather to follow suit. When the morning fog no longer appears, spring is on its way. Fruit trees and mustard fields blossom in February. The air remains clear but the bite of winter is gone, though nights may still be chilly. This season is a very pleasant time to visit the Valley and explore the surrounding hills.

Grisma: From April-May heat and dust are on the rise and the sun is increasingly fierce. Winter wheat and mustard are harvested in April, and across Nepal and India the remaining stubble is burned to fertilize the earth with ashes.

The smoke combines with dust to form a murky brown haze blurring distant views, though higher altitudes rise above it. Spring is the second most popular trekking season: nearly 25% of trekkers head out in March-April. By May, temperatures in the low river valleys and Terai are sweltering, flies and mosquitoes are everywhere, and disease is on the rise. May and early June are the hottest months, but things cool down after the monsoon arrives.

Barkha: See special topic "The Monsoon."

Sharad: The monsoon departs with a final burst by mid-October. Skies are clear, the air crisp, the sun warm, and the Himalaya appears in the north beneath a fresh coat of snow. The second week of October is the unofficial start of the trekking season, and overnight Kathmandu fills with tourists. Autumn is popular for good reason. The dry, sunny days are exhilaratingly clear, with moderate temperatures and splendid mountain views, and the year's greatest festivals take place at this time.

Hemanta: Early winter continues the clear fresh air of autumn, edging slowly into colder temperatures by November. Late November to early December is a good time to avoid trekking crowds while keeping clear views and good weather. The only drawback is that nights above 3500 meters start to get quite cold.

FLORA

The Himalaya compresses a wider range of vegetation into a smaller area than possibly anywhere else in the world. Like nearly everything else in Nepal, flora is classified in vertical terms. Long bands of tropical, temperate, and alpine vegetation zones ribbon the country from east to west, but the rapid increase in altitude compresses them into extraordinarily narrow areas. As an example, in North America, coniferous forests extend nearly 1400 km north before giving way to tundra. In Nepal, on the other hand, conifers appear in a narrow band extending only one vertical km. The tremendous range of altitudes and microclimates creates an extraordinarily high biodiversity in which many different types of vegetation appear within a small area.

Forests
Through the '50s the Terai's tropical deciduous forests were among Nepal's greatest natural resources, protected by the malaria-carrying mosquitoes that kept the region nearly uninhabited. Over the last 40 years much has been cut, both for timber and to clear land for settlement. The straight-trunked sal trees *(Shorea robusta)*, which grow up to 30 meters in height, yield top-quality hardwood used to build temples, houses, railway sleepers, and bridges. The exquisitely carved sal wood pillars and beams of the Valley's temples have endured for hundreds of years. Woodcarvers say sal wood can be immersed in water for a thousand years, be exposed to air for another thousand, and still remain intact.

Intermixed with Terai forests grow dense stands of grasses, over 50 different species, some of which reach up to six meters tall. Local people use it for thatching roofs and building walls. It's commonly called "elephant grass," either because elephants eat it or because it can only be crossed by elephant-back.

Moving north, subtropical wet hill forests appear in the lower Hills, typified by the broad-leaved *chilaune,* bamboo, and tree rhododendron. Upper Hill regions are covered by temperate moist montane forests which mix conifers, oaks, bamboo, and rhododendrons. Forests of this type once blanketed the entire southern side of the Himalaya until villagers and farmers cut down vast amounts to clear land. Clouds, rain, and mist are all common at this altitude, and in some pockets the moisture nurtures luxuriant cloud forests of moss-draped trees, orchids, and ferns.

Above 4000 meters plantlife dwindles to tough grasses, alpine plants, and dwarf varieties of rhododendron, juniper, and birch. Beyond the alpine zone vegetation virtually disappears, leaving only the colorful, hardy lichen. Treeline is typically around 4500-5000 meters, lower in dry rain-shadowed valleys. Permanent snowline begins at about 5330 meters.

Plants and Flowers

At least 6,500 species of flowering plants appear in Nepal. Orchids are abundant in the moist hills, appearing in more than 18 different forms. Nearly every variety of garden flower flourishes in Kathmandu's beneficent climate. Many have been introduced from Europe, Africa, or the Middle East, including the ubiquitous marigolds *(sayapatri)* which are strung into garlands for the great autumn festivals. Many of the ornamental trees in the Kathmandu Valley, like blue-blossomed jacaranda, bottlebrush with its bristling red flowers, silver oak, eucalyptus, and silk oak, were also introduced from abroad.

The gods have their favorite plants and flowers too. Holy basil *(tulasi)* is sacred to Vishnu because it incarnates his consort Lakshmi, and is worshipped in homes and temples. All the goddesses love the bright-red poinsettias *(lalpate)* that blossom in the subtropical winter here. The lotus is an ancient sacred symbol of purity, representing the pure mind of enlightenment rising untainted from the mud of earthly concerns. Deities are often depicted holding a lotus or seated atop one. The goddess Lakshmi is especially associated with it, praised as lotus-eyed, lotus-colored, and decked with lotus ornaments.

PIPAL TREES AND *CHAUTAARA*

The endless steep climbs of Nepal's hill trails are mercifully interrupted by stone platforms built beneath giant trees, providing cool resting places for weary travelers. These *chautaara* are built and maintained by individuals as a public service and a means of earning religious merit. A *chautaara* is most often shaded by a pipal tree *(Ficus religiosa),* the same tree under which Buddha gained enlightenment. Often a multi-trunked *baar* or banyan *(Ficus bengalensis)* stands alongside. Its round leaves represent the female principle, the pointed-leaved pipal the male.

The village *chautaara* is the local meeting place, the rural Nepali equivalent of a Parisian sidewalk cafe or the American coffeeshop. It rivals the water tap as a place for flirting and romance. Even Kathmandu has its pipal tree: the Pipal Bot on New Road is the place to buy newspapers, have one's shoes shined, and catch up on political gossip.

More than a social center, the pipal is the residence of the gods. Village deities live beneath some *chautaara,* embodied in sacred stones. The goddess Lakshmi is said to visit the pipal on Sundays; others say her husband Vishnu comes every Saturday. Hindu women honor the tree by pouring water or milk on the roots and anointing the trunk with vermilion powder, rice, and flowers. Pipal worship is a remedy for infertility and a way to nullify the evil omen of widowhood appearing in a bride's horoscope. Astrologers may advise those whose horoscopes are mis-aspected by Saturn to girdle a pipal tree in a network of red thread.

The banyan tree is sacred to Shiva and is also revered. Both trees are considered supernatural and nearly immortal and are never cut—to do so would bring bad luck. The pipal in particular is associated with spirits; so much so that its leaves are said to rustle not because of the wind, but from the movements of invisible beings like *yaksha* and the celestial musicians, *gandharva.*

RHODODENDRONS

Nepal's national flower, the tree rhododendron (R. arboreum), is the world's tallest species, with an average height of 7-14 meters. Some specimens in wet eastern Nepal may grow to 20 meters in height. Rhodies flourish across the eastern Himalaya, with 50-60 species appearing in Nepal, Sikkim, and Bhutan, some 30 in Nepal alone.

They grow right up to timberline, most commonly on exposed slopes and ridgelines between 1800-4000 meters. Rhododendrons thrive in harsh conditions and help anchor soil to steep slopes, but their soft wood makes them a favorite of woodcutters. Unlike most trees, they can form a pure forest with no other species intermixed; they often intermix with oak as well. The rhodie forests of Eastern Nepal are a sight to behold in springtime when they're in full bloom.

Between February and May, depending on altitude, clusters of trumpet-shaped blossoms appear in a spectacular display of scarlet, pink, and white, the paler colors appearing higher up. Nepalis love laligurans, especially the red ones, which come out in full display in March. Women tuck the blossoms in their hair, woodcutters place them atop their loads, devotees offer them to the gods. Rhododendron flowers are kept on hand in homes as a folk remedy for a bone stuck in the throat.

Rhodies have their bad side too. Raw honey made from their flowers may contain a potent neurotoxin that can cause nausea, vomiting, and loss of consciousness. Susceptible people may fall into a coma after consuming a small amount, while their companions remain unaffected. There is no guarantee that local honey is cooked. Beware of rhododendron honey on your breakfast pancake.

BOB RACE

The Himalaya is home to all kinds of rare medicinal plants (jadibuti) that are used in ayurvedic and pharmaceutical preparations. Sacks of leaves, roots, stems, and flowers are collected by peasants and sold for a pittance, to be taken into India where they are compounded into lucrative preparations. The annual trade is estimated to be worth tens of millions of dollars, but it proceeds unregulated, and many rare and delicate species are being threatened with disappearance.

Ganja
Cannabis sativa grows like the weed it is all through the Hills and Terai. Before the arrival of foreigners who made a big fuss about it (and eventually caused it to be declared illegal), ganja was no more than a respected herb, said to have been one of the gifts that emerged from the mythic Churning of the Ocean. Older men still meet in the evening to relax with some hashish (charas) to fuel their singing and conversation. Traditional medicine prescribes charas for many ailments, including headaches, tetanus, malaria, even insanity. Ganja itself is said to cure insomnia; there is also bhang, a potent brew of marijuana sticks and stems that can leave you reeling for days. Ganja is sacred to Shiva, Lord of the Yogis, who is said to consume prodigious amounts as an aid to meditation. On the festival of Shiva Ratri hundreds of Hindu sadhu gather at the Pashupatinath Temple to pay homage to Shiva with prayer, singing, and austerities, all fueled by massive doses of ganja.

FAUNA

Nepal is a veritable Noah's Ark, embracing snow leopards and rhinoceroses, crocodiles and mountain goats, over 500 species of butterflies, and 800 species of birds. Located in the heart of Asia at the juncture of two great biogeographical regions, Nepal harbors species from both. Distinct zones are determined by altitude; species also vary from east to west as the land becomes progressively drier and less forested.

Himalayan wildlife in general was a scientific mystery until the 19th century. Credit for exploring it goes to Brian Hodgson, a consumptive clerk for the British East India Company who had been given the rather grim choice of dying in England or in a hill post. He chose the unknown and was shipped off to Kathmandu in 1821 to serve as assistant to the British Resident. The Valley suited Hodgson: he thrived on the exotic culture, plunging into scholarly studies and producing stacks of research papers. He eventually succeeded the British Resident, stayed a total of 22 years in Nepal, and finally died in England at the age of 95.

Tibetan yak

In spite of the ban on travel outside the Kathmandu Valley, Hodgson managed to assemble the world's first major collection of Himalayan species, over 900 mammals and 9,500 birds, which he finally presented to the British Museum. Working entirely on his own, he published over a hundred papers on 563 Nepali species, 150 of them previously unknown. His work laid the foundations for the study of Himalayan natural history, till then an unexplored field.

DOMESTIC ANIMALS

Domestic animals are vital to the economy of rural Nepal but the Western concept of pets is practically unknown. Cats are shunned as familiars of witches and most dogs are ownerless scavengers who become yapping nuisances after dark. They bark a lot but are generally too cringing to bite. In a few city neighborhoods dog packs harass late-night cyclists and pedestrians. A couple of well-aimed stones will disperse them. The dog to watch out for is the big black Tibetan mastiff, bred to sink its teeth into unannounced visitors. Originally trained to protect the tents of nomadic herders, it's now a popular guard dog for homes; Bhotia villagers sometimes keep them as well, so be cautious.

Livestock

Just about every Hill family has at least a few goats and chickens. A cow or water buffalo is expensive to purchase, but supplies a small cash income from the sale of milk. Nepal's livestock population equals or exceeds its human population, and is an essential component in the hardscrabble agricultural economy. The meat, milk, hides, and wool are essential for farming families, but are obtained at a major cost to the environment. Herds of sharp-hooved goats and sheep graze grassy slopes into dust, earning the nickname "hooved locusts." Good pasture is scarce, but a water buffalo needs two large loads of grass and leaves each day. Altogether, Nepal's livestock is estimated to consume over 50 million tons of green fodder a year—a major cause of deforestation.

Yaks

Larger, stronger, and shaggier than domestic cattle, the yak is uniquely adapted to heights, thriving at altitudes above 3000 meters. This is due to specialized adaptations like an exceptionally heavy coat and very few sweat glands, which allows it to conserve heat but makes it impossible for the yak to survive in lower climates. A yak sent to the London Zoo soon died—of malaria, the Sherpas explained. Another ingenious adaptation involves its oxygen-bearing red blood cells, which are half the size of those of other bovines, and thus pack in more per unit of blood volume.

As in Tibet, yaks are an essential part of Nepal's high-altitude economy, serving as pack

SACRED COWS

Serene in their sanctity, cows rule Kathmandu streets, flopping down in the middle of rush-hour traffic to ruminatively chew their cud amid honking horns. They make the city's hazardous driving conditions even worse, but for every motorist who silently curses a cow, 10 passersby will reverently touch it, then lift their fingers to their foreheads in a blessing.

The cow is Nepal's national animal, the symbol of fertility and prosperity and the giver of the "five gifts": milk, yoghurt, ghee (clarified butter), dung, and urine (the latter considered a medicinal remedy). The worship and protection of cows is an ancient Hindu tradition. Anthropologists speculate the wise men of Vedic India realized the cow's milk, manure, and draft power were essential to agriculture. To protect this valuable beast from being turned into hamburger, they proclaimed a taboo on beef. When I repeated this pragmatic theory to a Nepali friend, he was horrified. "No, no; cows are sacred because they are such kind and gentle creatures!" he protested.

As the giver of milk, the cow is revered as humanity's second mother. Cow manure is an equally precious gift. It fertilizes fields and in dried form is burned as fuel; a purifying mixture of cow dung and mud is smeared daily on the floors and walls of orthodox Hindu homes, and a cow dung poultice is the traditional remedy for cuts and wounds. Not surprisingly, orthodox Brahmans refuse to harness such a revered beast to the plow.

Cow worship is believed to have the power to nullify an unlucky horoscope, and one day a year, a cow is said to lead the souls of the dead across the great river blocking their entry into heaven. Cow worship reaches its peak on the third day of the festival of Tihar, when wandering bovines are washed, fed, and adorned with *tika* and garlands.

Beef-eating is abhorrent to nearly all Nepalis, and *gai khaane maanche* or "cow-eater" is an impolite epithet for foreigners. (If you want to shock somebody, tell them about McDonald's.) Water-buffalo meat, "buff" on local menus, is the rather tough, stringy substitute served in most tourist restaurants. More expensive restaurants serve chateaubriand flown in from India, where Muslims do the butchering, to foreigners and a few daredevil Nepalis.

During the Malla era, killing a cow was one of the five great sins, ranked just behind murdering a Brahman, woman, child, or relative. A century ago cow slaughter was the legal equivalent of murder, punishable by death. Today the penalty is a Rs20,000 fine or two years' imprisonment: killing a cow is taken very seriously, and the street scene will not be pretty if you run into a cow while driving.

Buddhist mountain people eat yak and yak-cattle crossbreeds, a practice frowned upon by Hindus. The yak's status has always been flexible. A century ago, Nepali troops were starving in the snow during a campaign against Tibet. Prime Minister Jung Bahadur Rana then suddenly "discovered" that yak were not cattle, but deer. He persuaded the Raj Guru, the ultimate Hindu authority, to go along with his revelation, and his soldiers got a supply of meat.

the "wish-fulfilling cow," Kamdhenu

and plough animals and providing milk, meat, and wool. In the Sherpa language a female yak is a *nak,* giving rise to the old saw, "There's no such thing as yak milk." Yak or *nak,* the milk is wonderfully rich, and yak/*nak* yoghurt is deliciously creamy. To preserve it, highlanders turn it into butter (which they mix liberally into tea) and the rock-hard dried cheese called *churpi.* The long, coarse outer hair is made into ropes and tents; the soft underwool is used in blanket-weaving, while the tanned hides are used to make belts, saddlebags, boot soles, even boats. Before the advent of synthetics, fluffy white yak tails were the main source of Santa Claus beards in the U.S. They are still in demand as ceremonial fly whisks for Hindu temples.

Sixteen different words in Nepali and Tibetan describe all possible crossbreeds of yaks and lowland cattle. A *nak* bred with a regular bull produces a *dzum* (female) or *dzopkio* (male). These slightly smaller and less shaggy crossbreeds combine the stamina of the yak with the tractability and higher milk production of the cow. *Dzopkio* make excellent pack animals, unlike purebred yak, which are temperamental beasts equipped with wicked upward-curving horns. Long trading caravans still cross the Himalayas, taking rice, tea, and sugar up and bearing rock salt and bales of wool down.

WILDLIFE

Terai Wildlife

The jungles and forests of the Terai were once rich in game, but widespread resettlement has drastically altered habitats and populations. Less than 50 wild Asiatic elephants *(hatti)* remain in small scattered groups along Nepal's southern border. A remnant population of fierce, strong wild buffalo *(arnaa)* are huddled in a wildlife refuge on the small island of Kosi Tappu Wildlife Preserve in southeast Nepal. The Terai is also home to the gaur *(gauri gai),* the world's largest wild cattle, standing 1.8 meters at the shoulder and weighing over 900 kg. The Narayani River, on the western boundary of Chitwan National Park, harbors a quarter of the world's remaining *gharial* population. This fish-eating crocodile is hunted for its hide and the reputed aphrodisiac power of its long, slender snout.

The one-horned rhinoceros *(gaidaa)* has a semi-magical aura. A rhino skin bracelet is said to protect against evil spirits; rhino dung acts as a laxative and rhino urine cures stomach pains and tuberculosis. Rhino horn, most coveted of all, fetches up to US$17,000 per kg in China, where it's used as a fever remedy. Poaching has reduced the world's population of *Rhinoceros unicornis* to 1,800. About 400 of these live in Chitwan National Park. With armor-plated skin and stubby legs, rhinos are shortsighted and must rely on hearing and smell to target a victim. Antisocial and unpredictable, they can charge without provocation; contrary to popular belief they are quite agile. Every year during grass-cutting season, rhinos trample several villagers.

Chitwan and the adjoining Parsa Wildlife Reserve provide one of the world's best remaining tiger habitats, harboring about 140 Royal Bengal tigers *(bagh).* In 1972 it was set aside with Suklaphanta and Bardia wildlife reserves as part of the World Wildlife Fund's "Operation Tiger." Probably around 300 tigers are left in all of Nepal. See the "Chitwan National Park" section for more on Terai wildlife.

Monkeys *(Bandar)*

Halfway between domesticated and wild, bands of rhesus monkeys roam Kathmandu temple grounds, sliding down banisters, swinging from power lines, and begging or stealing food. The largest communities are at Swayambhunath and Pashupatinath, where they are protected by religion and tradition. Believe it or not, several scientific studies have been done on Kathmandu's monkeys. All conclude these monkeys have lost their natural fear of humans and can be exceptionally aggressive, especially when they're eating. Look out for simian thieves who snatch your lunch or your camera. Monkeys can carry rabies, so any bite breaking the skin should be treated.

Langur monkeys, larger than rhesus and always wild, are handsome gray-furred creatures with distinctive white heads and black faces. Even their feet are equipped with "thumbs" for grasping at tree branches. They're regarded as sacred and never killed, even if they raid crops, because in the Ramayana an army of langur monkeys fought under the direction of the Monkey King Hanuman to rescue the kidnapped maiden Sita. They inhabit the sal forests of the Terai and the conifer forests of central Nepal, and can be spotted on some main trekking routes.

Hill and Himalayan Wildlife

Because the Hills are so densely populated you're not likely to spot much wildlife on a trek. Local people may hunt wild pigs and game like the tahr, argali, blue sheep, and Himalayan ibex. The leopard, a bold and intelligent cat still common in midland Nepal, lives off game, livestock, and village dogs. A few lurk in the forested hills surrounding the Kathmandu Valley.

The snow leopard's habitat is the remote mountains of central Asia. These stocky, strong creatures are so elusive nobody has managed to determine how many dwell in northwest Nepal, despite years of research—the best guess is approximately 1,200. Despite their evocative name they dwell on cliffs and rock outcroppings, using their dusty spots as a natural camouflage. Their numbers are dwindling due to trapping and hunting. Although the animal is supposed to be protected, it's easier to find a snow leopard-skin coat in the exclusive shops on Durbar Marg than a live snow leopard in the wild. The same goes for the skins of the clouded leopard, another endangered and supposedly protected species. Kashmiri fur merchants are largely responsible for this illegal trade, upon which the Nepali government recently clamped down.

BIRDWATCHERS' PARADISE

Tiny Nepal has less than one percent of the world's land mass, but 10% of its birds—801 species. The huge range is due to its tremendous diversity of altitudes, and therefore vegetation. The names alone will entertain the armchair naturalist: plumbeous redstart, satyr tragopan, Himalayan tree pie, hoary barwing, coal tit. More than half the total can be found in the Kathmandu Valley. The area around the Royal Botanical Gardens at Godavari is especially rich: on the four-hour walk from Godavari to the summit of Phulchowki it's possible to spot 100 different species. The wooded summits of Nagarjun and Shivapuri and the area around Thankot on the Valley rim are other good sites.

Chitwan National Park, with its wide range of natural environments, hosts over 400 bird species. The Feb.-March spring migration season brings the most sightings. Another prime spot is the marsh and reed beds of Kosi Tappu Wildlife Reserve in eastern Nepal, which is on the spring migration route for thousands of waterfowl.

Trekking greatly increases the variety of sightings, offering birds like the Impeyan pheasant or *danphe,* the gorgeously colored national bird of Nepal which prefers high altitudes. One of the better birdwatching treks is the western side of the Annapurna Circuit. The Kali Gandaki Valley is a migratory route for waterfowl, and the trail spans terrains from subtropical Pokhara to the dry highlands beyond Jomosom, where species typical of the Tibetan Plateau appear.

Serious birdwatchers should visit in spring and summer, when the birds are in full breeding plumage. An excellent field guide is *Birds of Nepal* (see Booklist), compiled by a father-and-son team of missionary doctors from 25 years of field research. With color illustrations by renowned artist Lain Singh Bangdel, it's a classic book. Salim Ali's *Indian Hill Birds* or the *Field Guide to the Eastern Himalayas* may be useful for cross-referencing. **Himalayan Birds Exploration Center,** tel. (1) 221-604, arranges birdwatching trips with veteran ornithologists to various regions of Nepal.

Kathmandu's most impressive birdwatching experience actually involves mammals. April-Dec., Thamel-bound tourists will stop dead in their tracks to stare at hundreds of giant fruit bats roosting upside down in the poplars of Kaiser Mahal. Hanging from the branches like so many ripe plums, the bats squabble and sleep during the day, then fly off at dusk in search of a dinner of fruit and flowers.

The Impeyan pheasant (danphe) *is Nepal's national bird.*

BOB RACE

Leeches

The lowly terrestrial leech is possibly Nepal's most detested creature. For most of the year it hides in an underground burrow. During the rainy season it emerges in moist, shaded forests and meadows at elevations between 1200 and 2700 meters. Sensing the body heat of a warm-blooded victim, the leech uncurls from its hideout and extends to an amazing length to attach itself. The modus operandi of a leech is fascinating to everyone but its victim. Its mouth forms an ideal suction device. Inside are three moveable internal lips, each lined with a row of teeth. The leech first secretes a local anesthetic to numb its host, then drills a hole through the skin and injects an anticoagulant to assure a continuous flow of blood—the reason why bleeding continues even after the creature is removed. Left to feed their fill, leeches swell up to 10 times their size, and can then survive several months without eating.

Tibetan charm used as protection against dog bites

The whole process is repulsive rather than painful. You might feel a twinge as the leech latches on, but probably won't notice a thing until you see blood. Leeches don't transmit disease, but a bite can easily get infected, especially during the monsoon, so treat leech bites as carefully as other small wounds.

Prevention is the first course of defense: move fast through damp, shady places. If you're traveling in single file with several companions, space yourselves out. Those at the end of a line tend to gather the most leeches. Keep as much skin covered as possible; wear long pants tucked into socks. Soaking trouser cuffs and socks in salt water might be one way to repel them. If you spot a leech inching aboard, brush it off immediately; if it's attached itself to you, it can be pulled off with a bit of determination: unlike ticks, the head won't remain embedded. It will withdraw by itself after sucking its fill; however, most victims are unwilling to play the good host. Touching the leech with a hot match tip or lit cigarette should precipitate a speedy withdrawal. So will coating it with salt, iodine, or alcohol. The Nepali method is to smear it with *kaini,* tobacco snuff available in small tins from any shop.

The Yeti

This shaggy man-ape is the most elusive of all Nepal's creatures, rumored but never proven to inhabit the remote eastern Himalaya. Reports of "hairy wild men who are believed to live among the eternal snows" date to 1832 and go back even further among Sherpas, Bhutanese, and Tibetans, who call him *Yeh Teh* ("Man of the Rocky Places"), *Kang Mi* ("Snowman"), or *Dzu Teh* ("Cattle Lifter"). The sensational term "Abominable Snowman" was coined by a popular British columnist in 1921.

Since 1950, mountaineering expeditions fueled speculation with reports of giant footprints found on uninhabited frozen slopes, bigger than those of humans but with prehensile toes. Skeptics point out footprints normally enlarge with melting snow, and a bear or similar creature walking upright can replicate a man's stride. (What a bear would be doing at 7000 meters they can't explain.) Other tantalizing scraps of evidence include tufts of strange black fur, mysterious droppings, and a piercing scream that terrified members of one expedition.

Over a dozen expeditions mounted in search of the yeti have found little beyond a few more footprints and some skins which turned out to be from other animals. Taken to the West for lab analysis, the famous yeti scalp of Pangboche Gompa was declared to be fashioned from the 200-year-old skin of a serow, a Himalayan goat-antelope.

Reports of actual sightings are equally inconclusive. Yeti are said to have an acute sense of smell that allows them to disapper when foreigners approach. Local yeti viewers always turn out to be of the "friend's cousin's wife's brother," ilk, someone who lives in a distant village and who wouldn't be there even if you did visit, because he's gone away for business. For now, at least, the yeti is shadowy symbol rather than solid fact, and will probably remain that way for a long time.

ENVIRONMENTAL ISSUES

The Himalaya may seem eternal, but it is among the most fragile ecosystems on earth. Steep slopes, poor soil, and heavy monsoon rains make its mountains vulnerable to erosion. Deforestation accelerates the process, as topsoil slides down into rivers and is washed away into the sea. What's happening in Nepal is occurring all across the Himalaya, and has been for centuries. The pace has accelerated in the last few decades due to intense population pressures. Much has been made of tourism's environmental impact, but 76,000 trekkers use only a fraction of the eight million tons of firewood burned annually by 19 million Nepalis. Tourism's biggest impact is on culture rather than the environment.

Nepal's population doubled between 1951 and 1983 and is expected to double again in 30 years. The delicate ecological balance of the Himalaya can't support many more people; even now there are signs of strain. In the Hills every available scrap of land is already cultivated. Nepali Hillpeople are skilled and sensible farmers, but growing families and shrinking plots leave them with no choice but to extend their holdings onto land better left unplowed, to graze their animals on steep slopes, and to cut down forests.

The result is frequent landslides, silted rivers, and barren hills furrowed by deep gullies. For rural Nepalis this translates into lowered crop yields, dried-up water sources, and longer walks to cut firewood and fodder as nearby forests vanish. Trees are the weakest link in the ecological chain. Demands for fuel and fodder are simply too great to allow time for natural regeneration, and aid-sponsored reforestation efforts have not made much of a dent in the damage.

Deforestation

Enormous tracts of Nepal's forests have been cut in the last century for new cropland or to fill rising demands for fuelwood, timber, and livestock fodder. Some estimates show forests are being destroyed at a rate of two to three percent yearly, far faster than the natural regeneration rate. At this pace, accessible forests could vanish in the next 10-20 years, spelling disaster

for a country where three-quarters of the energy comes from fuelwood.

So runs the doomsday scenerio put forward by some experts. Many are now willing to admit they don't know precisely how fast Nepal's forests are disappearing, since rates vary so widely from place to place. Illustrating the perils of overconfident projection, in 1980 a World Bank report warned Nepal would run out of trees by 1995. Recent satellite imagery and ground surveys indicate, however, the Terai's natural forests are far more abundant than was formerly believed.

While things might not be as grim as they are painted, it does appear deforestation has accelerated with the recent doubling of Nepal's population. Another culprit was the nationalization of forests in 1957, which wiped out the traditional community systems of controlled local forest use. Since the trees didn't belong to the people anymore, they had no reason to preserve them, and woodcutting became a grab-all-you-can-get affair.

Fuelwood consumption is frequently blamed for deforestation, but farming and overgrazing are equally, if not more, responsible. Too many goats or sheep can reduce rich pasture to barren stubble in just a few years, and grass is more important than trees to soak up excess moisture and prevent erosion. Once it's grazed bare, high pastureland is unlikely to ever recover naturally.

Erosion

According to some estimates, fertile topsoil is disappearing from Nepal at the rate of 35-70 metric tons per hectare per year—20 times the weight of the rice crop from the same area. The soil is washed into rivers that eventually deposit it in the Bay of Bengal, where islands are being created from the siltation. Rueful references are made to this new "Nepali territory" as Nepal's most precious and unpaid export. The result in the Hills is decreased soil fertility and diminishing water sources, while downstream erosion brings increased siltation and flooding.

Again, this is the standard scenario presented as gospel for over a decade, but now losing credibility. The current consensus is the situation is more complex than the neat cycle of "deforestation-erosion-Bay of Bengal" would indicate. It's now understood most catastrophic floods are due to heavy rains; that more than half of Nepal's erosion is inherent in steep, young slopes like those of the Himalaya; and that forest removal plays a relatively minor role in the process. Along with this is the realization that in a tremendously heterogeneous place like Nepal where every watershed is different from the next, it's impossible to extrapolate trends across the entire country. This doesn't deny the existence of problems, but underscores the need for thorough research at a local level, and the difficulty of prescribing any kind of across-the-board remedy.

Pollution

The Valley's ancient towns are afflicted with that plague of modern life, smog. The bowl-shaped Valley is an ideal place for thermal inversions à la Los Angeles and Mexico City. Dust particles and exhaust fumes combine with the winter mist to form murky haze. Thirty years ago the Himalayan peaks appeared crystal-clear behind the Valley rim to the north; nowadays they're frequently hidden behind a brown smudge. Public Enemy Number One for environmentalists is the coal-burning Himal Cement Factory at Chobhar. In most of Nepal the air outside is clear; pollution is hidden indoors, in poorly ventilated houses that trap smoke from cooking fires, causing eye infections and respiratory illnesses.

Gravely polluted water is a major carrier of disease. The Valley's sewage treatment and water purification plants are often out of commission; when they are working they are rendered practically useless, as low pressure and the close proximity of water and sewage pipes mean the water is dangerously fouled by the time it reaches home taps. Chemical pollution is a growing danger in the Valley, as industries pour untreated wastes directly into rivers, the traditional dumping site for all kinds of garbage.

Litter

The most visible pollution appears along trails strewn with biscuit wrappers, noodle packages, and (the exclusive mark of tourists) pink rosettes of Chinese toilet paper. Local usage of expensive packaged products is growing, and there is a complete unawareness of litter as a problem, partly because until recently everything was either natural or recycled. Feasts were served on leaf plates and clay cups, scrap paper was recycled into paper bags, old bits of metal were melted down into new cookpots. The advent of plastic has outpaced the realization that when you throw it away, it's there to stay.

A few neighborhoods in Kathmandu organize community clean-up efforts to keep trash off the streets, but the municipal sanitation office is woefully unorganized. Out in the countryside there's no official control, and everyone has someone else to blame. Group treks generate quantities of garbage from their prepackaged and canned foods, the remains half-heartedly buried at best or dumped in a river. Independent trekkers are often just as careless with their plastic water bottles and candy wrappers. The lack of local trash depots leaves no real solution to the problem, other than generating less trash. Carrying the waste back to Kathmandu shifts the problem, hopefully to a municipal garbage dump, but it doesn't solve it.

Mountaineering expeditions deserve special mention for bringing garbage to higher heights in Nepal than anywhere else in the world. The South Col of Everest, which sees at least a dozen foreign expeditions a year, is renowned as the world's highest garbage dump. Periodic clean-up expeditions haul down used oxygen cylinders, tin cans, and plastic barrels, but the supply is endless. Still, though litter is a highly visible problem, it doesn't go beyond being an eyesore. Less visible threats, like the filthy water which kills 40,000 children each year from diarrheal disease, are far more serious.

NATIONAL PARKS AND RESERVES

Nearly 14% of Nepal's total area is set aside as national parks and wildlife reserves—the purpose to conserve and manage at least a portion of the country's splendid natural heritage by protecting representative examples of threatened and unique ecosystems. Some national parks, like Chitwan and Sagarmatha, have been declared UNESCO World Heritage sites due to their unique natural and cultural environments.

Organization

Parks and reserves managed by the Department of National Parks and Wildlife Conservation (DNPWC) rely heavily on the Nepali Army to enforce its regulations. Three-fourths of the DNPWC budget goes to maintain army battalions in various national parks, which doesn't leave much left over for other activities. In 1982 a private nonprofit organization, the **King Mahendra Trust for Nature Conservation,** was founded with the purpose of protecting Nepal's wildlife wherever it may be.

The national park model inspired by the United States' vast tracts of virgin territory is ill-suited to Nepal, where people rely heavily on the natural environment to meet their basic needs. The earliest parks evicted local residents and resettled them outside park boundaries, creating widespread resentment and fear. The contemporary model, in Nepal and worldwide, is moving towards combining parks and people, based on the realization the only way to preserve remaining wild areas is to include in the process the people living in and around them.

National parks like Langtang and Sagarmatha now harbor populations of several thousand people. Villagers are legally excluded from park jurisdiction, but conservation-oriented restrictions on woodcutting, hunting, and trapping affect their lives. The resurgence of wildlife in protected areas includes wild boars, pheasants, rhinos, and other beasts fond of uprooting farmers' crops. In the past, villagers shot or trapped the offenders; now they must try to scare off the animals without harming them, or stand by and watch their crops being destroyed.

Achieving the right balance between ecological and human needs is a tricky matter. One potential model is offered by the Annapurna Conservation Area Project (see special topic "In ACAP Land"), an innovative scheme to protect the natural environment of the heavily trekked Annapurna Himal with minimal disruption to the lives of the region's 40,000 inhabitants.

Parks

Chitwan National Park, Nepal's first, is among Southeast Asia's finest wildlife reserves, protecting rhinos, tigers, and over 40 other species of mammals and 400 species of birds. Nepal's other big draw is **Sagarmatha National Park,** which encompasses Mt. Everest and a host of other great peaks, some famous monasteries, and about 2,500 Sherpa villagers. Its eastern border abuts the new **Makalu-Barun National Park,** which protects the headwaters of the upper Arun River. There is talk of linking it to a nature preserve/national park on the Tibetan side of Everest, and creating a single giant reserve. **Langtang National Park,** directly north of Kathmandu, extends from rich forests through alpine terrain up to Himalayan peaks, and encompasses Tamang and Tibetan settlements.

Remote western Nepal holds less-visited parks and reserves. The most interesting is **Bardia National Park** along the Karnali River, with wildlife and terrain similar to Chitwan's, but bigger, drier, and more remote. Tiny **Lake Rara National Park,** 370 km northwest of Kathmandu, protects Nepal's largest lake, surrounded by magnificent conifer forests. **Khaptad National Park** in the middle hills of far western Nepal encompasses forests, grassland, and the ashram of Khaptad Baba, a revered Hindu saint. **Shey-Phoksumdo National Park** is Nepal's largest, 3,555 square km of trans-Himalayan territory including forests and the high-altitude desert typical of the Tibetan Plateau.

Royal Bengal tiger

BOB RACE

Wildlife Reserves

Formerly a famous Rana hunting ground, **Parsa Wildlife Reserve** provides additional territory for the tigers of adjoining Chitwan. The grasslands of **Suklaphanta Wildlife Reserve** in extreme southwestern Nepal are a prime habitat for endangered swamp deer. **Koshi Tappu Wildlife Reserve** in the eastern Terai shelters the country's last surviving population of wild water buffalo, while its swamps and mudflats provide refuge for migrating birds. **Dhorpatan Hunting Reserve** in the Dhaulagiri Himal of west-central Nepal supports game like blue sheep, serow, *goral,* Himalayan *thar,* pheasants, and partridges—all available to hunters, for a price.

HISTORY

The history of Nepal centers on the Kathmandu Valley. Until the country assumed its present form in the 18th century, the Valley *was* Nepal, in both name and fact. Even today, Hill people heading to Kathmandu will tell you *"Nepaalma jaane"*—"We're going to Nepal." From the beginning the Valley has been the center of politics, intrigue, religion, trade, and urban civilization—in short, everything worth recording. Compared to it, life in the Hills was unremarkable, and it continued for centuries unnoted, much as it does today.

The Valley's traditional prosperity came from its fertile soil and its strategic location on the trans-Himalayan trade route between India and Tibet. Kathmandu was a pleasant place for caravans to wait out the malarial summers of the southern Terai and the winter snows blocking the northern passes into Tibet. Traders, scholars, monks, pilgrims, and envoys from many countries journeyed through the Valley, leaving a legacy of diverse ideas and influences.

Despite the constant stream of visitors, outside historical accounts are scanty, limited to a few Chinese diplomats, Christian missionaries, and the British Residents who were forcibly settled in Kathmandu in the 19th century. Local history on the other hand appears everywhere in the Valley. Royal edicts were etched in copper plates, carved onto pillars, or engraved on stone slabs. Later came manuscripts of palm leaves or handmade paper recording the stories of gods and kings, and the *Vamsavali,* chronicles blending myth and history.

These written accounts record only a fraction of Nepal's history, for much of its culture is preliterate, embodied in the oral history transmitted by storytellers, minstrels, and the old people of villages. In a still larger sense, history is encoded in the Valley's traditional art and architecture and lives on in festivals and customs, some over 1,500 years old, which act as direct links to the past.

EARLY HISTORY

Prehistory

Neolithic artifacts discovered in the Valley indicate humans have inhabited it since prehistoric times, but archaeological exploration has been hampered by a dense urban population, religious restrictions, and a shortage of funds. A treasure trove of history most certainly lies underground. Workers digging building foundations regularly uncover ancient sculptures, artifacts, and 1,300-year-old bricks from vanished palaces.

The transition from the mythic beginnings described in the Valley's creation legend to the historical era is blurred. In ancient histories the Valley seems to be floating somewhere between heaven and earth. Kings are divine and gods are remarkably human in the old chronicles, which relate that the gods themselves came on pilgrimage to the holy Valley to view the miraculous light of Swayambhunath. Many deities settled in the Valley, while kings imported others from abroad and installed them in temples placed in the four directions to protect the land. The Valley's traditional role as a Buddhist and Hindu pilgrimage site is rooted in these vague legends.

The Kiranti

Factual history begins with the Kiranti, a Mongoloid people believed to be the ancestors of

LEGENDARY BEGINNINGS

The origin of the Kathmandu Valley is recorded in the *Swayambhu Purana,* an ancient chronicle:

Long, long ago, aeons before our present epoch, the Kathmandu Valley was a holy lake 14 miles in circumference, ringed by mountains and dense forests. In its clear blue depths dwelt magical snake-like creatures called *naga;* thus the lake was called Nagavasahrada, the Lake Kingdom of the Serpents, or because of its depth, Kalihrada, "Tank of the Blue-Black Waters."

In the Golden Age the first of all Buddhas, Vipaswi, came to the sacred lake on pilgrimage. From the summit of Nagarjun mountain he tossed a lotus seed into the lake and predicted it would one day become a holy site.

Eighty thousand years later the earth quaked as the seed split open. A thousand-petaled lotus as large as a chariot wheel, with jeweled pollen and golden seeds, rose above the waters. In the middle of the flower appeared the dazzling self-created light of Swayambhu, the "self-born." Buddha Manjushri came from the north to see this marvel. Thinking to open this place to pilgrims, he circled the Valley rim until he found the lowest point. With a single stroke of his Sword of Wisdom he cleft the gorge of Kotwal and the lake waters rushed out, leaving behind the valley we know today.

Most of the resident *naga* floated out with the lake waters, but Manjushri persuaded the *naga* king Karkotaka to remain to guard the Valley's wealth. He awarded the serpent a golden palace with diamond windows, set in the bottom of a deep black pond near Chobhar Gorge.

The miraculous Swayambhu light shone upon the newly revealed valley for centuries. Finally a Buddhist priest, realizing the sinful present age of Kali Yuga was approaching, hid the magic light in a hole and covered it with a precious stone. Atop it he built a stupa, topped by a gilded spire—the Swayambhunath Stupa, among the holiest Buddhist shrines in Nepal.

This legend is a poetic and uncannily accurate rendering of historical fact. Ages ago the Valley was indeed a lake; the rich black soil called *ko* that Newar farmers dig up and spread on their fields as fertilizer is decomposed sediment left by aquatic vegetation. And Manjushri's sword represents the earthquake that split the rock cliffs of Chobhar, leaving fault marks visible on the sheer walls of the gorge.

---

the modern Rai and Limbu hill tribes of eastern Nepal. Some historians think they were indigenous to the Valley; other accounts say they swept down from the east around 700 B.C. and ruled for a thousand years. Little is known of them aside from the mention of a Kiranti king fighting in the epic battle described in the Mahabharata. During their rule Buddhism was brought from India to Nepal.

Legend says the Indian emperor Ashoka, a devout Buddhist who spread the religion throughout his vast empire, visited the Valley in the 3rd century B.C. and built Patan's five ancient stupas. They're still called the "Ashoka stupas," but his visit is pure legend. By Ashoka's time the Valley was already a thriving commercial center. An Indian chronicler of the 4th century B.C. noted Nepal's woolen blankets and carpets, and later accounts mention caravans carrying musk, yak tails (used as ceremonial fly whisks in Indian temples), iron, and red copper from the Valley to India.

Licchavi Period (A.D. 300-879)

About A.D. 300 Kiranti rule was overthrown by the Licchavi dynasty of India, which introduced the Hindu caste system and a number of social and religious traditions that endure to the present day, including the *guthi* system and the sacred cow. Nepali art and architecture was already highly developed by this time, and included Buddhist *vihara,* or monasteries, stupas and smaller *chaitya,* and exquisite stone sculptures. Recorded history begins in A.D. 467 with a lengthy inscription on a pillar erected at the temple of Changu Narayan.

Life in 7th-century Nepal is preserved in the accounts of Wang Hsuan Tse, a Chinese diplomat who journeyed several times between the Tang Court and India by way of Kathmandu. He marveled at the city's long-vanished royal palace and its seven-story copper-roofed tower inset with gems, ornamented with dragon-headed fountains and "sculptures to make one marvel." King Narendra Deva rivaled his splendid palace with his own ornaments of mother-of-pearl, rock crystal, coral, amber, jade, and gold. Some of Wang's observations remain true even today: the Valley people eat with their hands, live in carved and painted wooden houses, and build "multistory temples [so tall] one would take them for a crown of clouds."

The Chinese Buddhist Hsuan Tsang, a contemporary of Wang's, never set foot in Nepal, but during a lengthy pilgrimage in India he recorded what he had heard about the land of "Ni-Po-La": "The national character is stamped with falseness and perfidy, the inhabitants are all of a hard and savage nature; to them neither good faith nor justice nor literature appeal. . . . Their bodies are ugly and their faces are mean." But even his informants had to admit "they are gifted with considerable skill in the arts."

Transitional Period (A.D. 879-1200)

Few records survive from the next four centuries, and little is known except it was a time of turmoil. As the central rule of the Licchavi era crumbled, the Valley fragmented into petty kingdoms ruled by a succession of dynasties. Power-hungry nobles feuded with their rulers, instituting a pattern of conflict between aristocracy and royalty that would endure for centuries.

Despite the instability, religion and art flourished. The Valley became a center for Buddhist pilgrims, monks, teachers, and translators, a major channel through which the Buddhist Dharma was transmitted from India to Tibet. Its own contribution to this process is significant: King Narendra Deva sent his daughter, the princess Bhrikuti, to become a bride of the powerful Tibetan king Srongtsen Gampo. Bhrikuti, along with a Chinese princess who also wedded the king, is credited with converting her husband (and through him the Tibetan nation) to Buddhism. Even today she is revered by Newar Buddhists as Green Tara, an emanation of the female bodhisattva of mercy.

THE MALLA DYNASTY

By the 13th century the Valley was divided into the three small kingdoms of Kathmandu, Patan, and Bhaktapur, with the influential realm of Banepa-Panauti just over the eastern rim. Frequent skirmishes took place over control of the lucrative trade routes with Tibet. The Valley took on the appearance of a medieval battlefield, with walled cities ringed by moats and fortifications crowning strategic hilltops.

Out of this turmoil sprang a period of unprecedented creativity and unity that would endure for over five centuries. Historians call it the Malla period, after an honorific title Valley kings adopted around this time. Different dynasties came and went, but the Malla epoch endured for 550 years, over twice as long as the better-known Moghul and Gupta empires of India.

The era shaped the Valley's rich cultural and artistic legacy, as well as many of its festivals and social traditions. Kings poured their wealth into tiered pagodas, superb woodcarvings, sculptures, jewelry, and paintings. The most intimate reminders are the gilded images of Malla rulers that stand in each of the three Durbar Squares, kneeling atop pillars facing the palaces they inhabited centuries ago.

statue of King Bhupatindra Malla, Bhaktapur Durbar Square

The Early Malla Period (A.D. 1220-1482)

The stability of the Malla period began with Jayasthiti Malla, an orthodox Hindu outsider summoned to wed the princess of the ruling lineage of Bhaktapur. Swiftly and vigorously he consolidated his rule, until by 1382 he had won control of the entire Valley. *Sthiti* means "rule, regulation," and Jayasthiti lived up to his name by codifying existing caste restrictions and dividing the Newar population into a system of 64 occupational castes. The lowest castes were forbidden to wear sleeved garments, caps, or shoes, or to roof their houses with tiles. The king, on the other hand, proclaimed himself an incarnation of the god Vishnu, a tradition borrowed from Indian rulers that continues to the present day in Nepal. Jayasthiti's reign marked the beginning of the Hinduization process, which was to increasingly dominate religion and society.

His son Jyoti Malla and grandson Yaksha Malla followed in his footsteps. All were orthodox Hindus who worshipped Buddhist deities as well. To the Malla kings and their subjects the gods were living, active entities with the power to intervene in human affairs, and supplicants performed elaborate *puja* or ritual worship when threatened with the disasters of the time: famine, smallpox, invasions by Mithili and Muslim raiders, and horrifying earthquakes. A great quake shook the Valley nearly every century, killing up to one-third of the population and destroying cities and temples.

Yaksha Malla (1428-82) is said to have expanded his rule up to the Tibetan border in the north, the Ganges in the south, the Kali Gandaki in the west, and Sikkim in the east, though his acquisitions did not endure. One of the greatest of the Valley's kings, he lavishly patronized gods and temples and developed the Tibet trade. On his deathbed he distributed his domain among his children, expecting them to rule jointly, but they soon carved up the territory, and the Valley united only a century ago was again fragmented.

The Three Kingdoms (A.D. 1482-1767)

For the next 300 years Yaksha Malla's descendants squabbled among themselves, ignoring their common ancestry. The three cities of Kathmandu, Patan, and Bhaktapur (or Kantipur, Lalitpur, and Bhadgaon, as they were known) became rival centers of power, their territories extending far into the surrounding countryside.

Political disunity proved better for the arts than the century of harmony that preceded it. By the 15th century the Valley had entered its golden age. Much of its superb architecture, carving, and sculpture date back to this time. Rival kings vied to produce the most magnificent palaces, the tallest pagodas, the most lavish offerings. Whatever one created the others were compelled to surpass. The main battlefields for this artistic warfare were the Durbar Squares. These brick plazas adjoining royal palaces sprouted a fantastic array of temples, shrines, and statues, as the palaces themselves were ceaselessly improved and expanded.

Kings sponsored the artists who created these wonders, paying them with grain collected as taxes, and lavishing fantastic quantities of gold onto temple roofs and images. Much of the wealth came from the lucrative Tibet trade that flourished in the late Malla period. Rulers heavily taxed revenues passing through their domains, and in addition the Valley had a monopoly on Tibetan money. The Tibetan government sent the silver, and for a hefty cut, the Nepali minted it into coins—a lucrative privilege that gave the Three Kingdoms something else to squabble over.

Cultured Kings

Kings took responsibility for public and private affairs, sponsoring the construction of water tanks and taps, resthouses, and temples, and providing endowments of land to fund their perpetual maintenance. They took care of entertainment too, with royal proclamations initiating festivals like Gai Jatra, Bhaktapur's Bisket Jatra, and the chariot rides of the Kumari, the young girl who serves as a living embodiment of the goddess Durga. Wealthy nobles performed extravagant sacrifices like the *kotyhoma,* the "10 million burnt oblations" of ghee, grain, and yoghurt, which would be carried out nonstop day and night for six weeks. Only the very wealthiest could perform the *tuladana* or "scale gift," in which a donor had himself publicly weighed against a heap of gold and gems and offered the entire mound to a deity—or more likely the proxy of the gods, the Brahmans.

Malla court life was a sophisticated affair. Nobles and kings divided their time between fighting, worship, and dabbling in dance, drama, poetry, and music. Patan's King Narendra proclaimed himself on coins as "one who has crossed the ocean of music"; King Pratapa Malla of Kathmandu chose the title Kavindra, "King of Poets." His ambition culminated with a prayer to Kali he composed one day in 1654 and had inscribed on stone in 15 different languages—all of which he had supposedly studied. The inscription, which can still be seen embedded in the wall of the Kathmandu palace, is a gobbledygook of fragments, including the words *l'Hiver* and *l'Otomn,* possibly contributed by a pair of Jesuit missionaries who briefly settled in the Valley during Pratapa Malla's reign. The first Westerners to visit Kathmandu, they showed the king a telescope and several mathematical instruments which thrilled him so much he insisted they speedily return. By the time they did, though, the Malla reign had ended.

The Mallas' Downfall

The splendor of their kingdoms could not hide the fact the Mallas were quarrelsome and suspicious rulers who broke treaties as soon as it became convenient. The Three Kingdoms era saw a series of shifting alliances: one week Kathmandu and Patan would unite against Bhaktapur, then Patan and Bhaktapur would be against Kathmandu. A few months later the three cities would be proclaimed friends, then the whole round would begin again. Quarrels often centered around the lucrative trade route to Tibet, and eventually the constant fighting drove merchants' caravans to other, more peaceful, routes.

UNIFICATION OF NEPAL

While the Mallas were busy alternately beautifying and fighting over the Valley, Hindu princes and local chiefs had carved western Nepal into a number of fiefdoms and petty states. Among the most important was the Shah dynasty of Gorkha, a hilltop fortress-town midway between Pokhara and Kathmandu. The Shah kings were bold and powerful, none more so than Prithvi Narayan Shah (1723-75). The first time he stood atop the Chandragiri Pass and viewed the cities

of the Valley spread out below, he set his heart on their conquest. His wish took 26 years of planning, sieges, and battles to come true, but Prithvi Narayan Shah was blessed with an extraordinary amount of tenacity, vision, and skill.

He began by seizing the town of Nuwakot in 1744, thus gaining control of the profitable Tibetan trade route and the northern approach to the Valley. Slowly the Gorkhalis encircled the Valley, building forts on the mountaintops and winning disgruntled nobles and chieftains over to their side. By the time the Valley's kings realized the threat and dropped their quarrels to unite against their common enemy, it was too late.

Next the Gorkhalis attacked Kirtipur, a fortresslike settlement in the southeast Valley. The hilltop city was virtually impregnable, and its Newar defenders withstood two sieges before they succumbed to trickery in a third attempt in 1766. In retaliation for the death of his brother, who had been killed in an earlier siege, Prithvi

King Prithvi Narayan Shah

Narayan ordered the nose of every Kirtipur male over the age of 12 cut off—a humiliating punishment also used for adulterous women. The chronicles record that 865 men were thus mutilated, and the cut noses filled several baskets and weighed about 80 pounds. Only the players of wind instruments were spared, so they could serve as musicians for the conquering army.

With a firm foothold in the Valley it didn't take long for the Gorkhalis to mop up the remainder. Opposition was weak in any case. The king of Kathmandu raided the treasury of Pashupatinath to pay his mercenary troops and begged the British East Indian Company for military assistance, but the poorly organized English expeditionary force was wiped out by malaria and the Gorkhalis before it ever reached the Valley.

Gorkhali troops entered Kathmandu in September 1768, in the midst of the boisterous Indra Jatra festival, for which most of the town was drunk. That particular night was the occasion for the king to receive ritual *tika* from the Kumari, validating his rule for the coming year. Legend has it the Shah conqueror seated himself on the royal throne and accepted *tika* from the virgin goddess, as Kathmandu's last Malla king fled to Patan. That city fell without a struggle a few days later and the recently deposed rulers took refuge in Bhaktapur, where the three Malla kings huddled together for over a year, united at last in their downfall. When Gorkhali troops finally assaulted the city it fell easily into their hands, and thus the era of the Three Kingdoms ended.

The Anglo-Nepal War

Prithvi Narayan Shah died only seven years after his conquest. His successors continued to use his fine-tuned war machine to annex new territory, though none equaled his ruthless brilliance. By 1814 Nepal had expanded to nearly twice its present size, stretching from Kumaon in the west to Sikkim in the east. Its bold incursions into Indian territory exasperated the British East India Company, and in 1814 war was declared, which Nepal lost after some hard fighting. The 1816 Treaty of Segouli forced Nepal to relinquish much of its newly acquired domain and fixed the country's borders at their present location on the Mahakali and Mechhi Rivers.

The most painful concession for Nepal was to admit a British Resident observer to Kathmandu.

On other points the British were willing to negotiate, but they were adamant Nepal "must take either the Resident or war." Forced to concede, the Nepali government settled the unwanted Englishman in the worst piece of land in the Valley, a tract rumored to be ghost-infested and malarial. Then it steadfastly ignored him. Forbidden to venture beyond the Valley, bereft of duties save for a once-a-year meeting, the Residents were left to putter in their expansive gardens and record observations on Nepali life that today provide a window on the past.

The 1816 treaty also required Nepal's contact with Western nations be made through Britain, making it in a sense a political dependent of the Raj. Nepal, however, was never colonized or directly ruled by outsiders, a fact still cited with pride. It was lucky for Nepal it had been recently unified, otherwise the East India Company might well have absorbed it, as it did various small Indian hill states.

After Segouli, Nepal withdrew into seclusion, closing its borders to all foreigners except Indians. The power amassed by Prithvi Narayan Shah was usurped by nobles and regents who ruled in the stead of his descendants. From 1799 to 1951 the Shah kings were kept in the background as semi-revered but powerless figureheads.

The ongoing struggle for power involved brutal plotting and intrigue. From 1769 to 1846, not one of Nepal's prime ministers died a natural death; all were either assassinated or forced into suicide. Writing in the 1850s, Laurence Oliphant succinctly summarized the era's politics:

> *The power of the Prime Minister is absolute until he is shot, when it becomes unnecessary to question the expediency of his measures. . . . The ability to gain office is not talent so much as his ability in taking aim and his skill in seizing any opportunity offered by his rival of showing his dexterity in a manner more personal than pleasant.*

THE RANA ERA

The Kot Massacre

In 1844 a new player appeared on the turbulent political scene, an ambitious young soldier named Jung Bahadur Kunwar. Ingratiating him-

JUNG BAHADUR IN ENGLAND

Once he had squelched all opposition and was confident his rule was secure, Jung Bahadur turned the government of Nepal over to a few of his more trusted brothers and in 1850 sailed off to visit England and Queen Victoria. It was a courageous act for a high-caste Hindu of the era: anyone who dared to cross the great "Black Water" to Europe and take food and drink from the hands of foreigners was threatened with automatic loss of caste. But Jung Bahadur had an intense desire to see the powerful English in their own land, and he defied the warnings of the Brahman priests to become the first Hindu ruler to visit Europe.

The account of a member of his retinue, juxtaposed with British newspaper reports of his visit, makes interesting reading. The British were impressed by their foreign guest's "strange and gorgeous" attire, while he was impressed with their coal mines, horse races, and ballerinas. Newspaper reports described the "Nepaulese" prime minister's magnificent costumes of embroidered satin, gold, diamonds, and jewels: to British eyes he was the epitome of an Oriental potentate. The Nepali retinue was overwhelmed by the beautiful, fair-skinned young women who mingled freely with them at gatherings, and the women took the young and dashing Jung Bahadur to heart, though they probably would not have been nearly so thrilled had they been aware of his bloody past. Jung Bahadur was the rage of London's social season. He visited Paris as well before returning to Kathmandu a little over a year after his departure.

The journey abroad evidently made a profound impact on him. Upon his return he revised Nepal's punitive criminal code, restricted capital punishment, and tried to discourage the deep-rooted custom of sati, which required that a good high-caste wife lay herself on her husband's funeral pyre. Along with social changes came fashion fads. Nepali noblewomen stuffed their buxom figures into corsets, curled their hair into fat sausages, and draped their saris over bustles. The Ranas built columned, neoclassical palaces and furnished them with crystal chandeliers and mirrors to rival Versailles. Jung Bahadur started the trend with his Thapathali palace, where four rooms held a permanent display of English bric-a-brac.

self with an influential queen, he rose to power through a series of bloody intrigues. The final coup came on 15 September 1846. The queen's main supporter and rumored lover, the military commander-in-chief, was murdered late at night. Distraught, the queen summoned an immediate assembly of ministers and state officials to the state assembly hall (known as the Kot) to find the murderer. Exactly what happened next is uncertain, but during the course of the stormy discussion that ensued, Jung Bahadur's soldiers attacked the unarmed officials. Within a few minutes, several dozen ministers and over a hundred lower-ranking officials were dead, and the gutters of the Kot ran red with blood.

The Kot Massacre left Jung Bahadur the most powerful man in Nepal. He rapidly consolidated his hold by exiling the queen, deposing the king, and keeping the young heir apparent powerless. Changing his family name to the more prestigious Rana and adopting the title of Maharaja ("King," as opposed to the Shah ruler, who was Maharajdhiraj, "King of Kings"), he founded the Rana dynasty, a succession of hereditary prime ministers who would rule Nepal for the next century.

The Shah kings remained on the throne as powerless rulers, pampered figureheads who were indulged (some said debauched), closely guarded, and kept from sight. "One may live for years in Nepal without either seeing or hearing of the king," noted a 19th-century Englishman. It was easy enough for the Ranas to maintain the king, as an incarnation of the god Vishnu, was too holy to deal in affairs of state.

Jung Bahadur secured his power further by arranging marriages between members of his family and the upper classes—everyone from the king down to the lowest officials. With over 100 children by his five wives and numerous concubines, he had plenty of opportunities to develop connections. Intermarriage between the Shahs and the Ranas continued through each generation to the present day. The present queen of Nepal is a Rana, and her two younger sisters are married to the King's two younger brothers.

"Ranocracy"

Succession within the Rana regime was passed onto the eldest living male of the family, be he

a Rana family

cousin, nephew, brother, or son of the former prime minister. Just *who* qualified as next in succession became such a problem for the prolific Ranas that in the 1920s an "A-B-C" classification method was established to rank descendants according to the caste and status of their mothers. A-Class Ranas, born of primary wives, got the most perks, the highest military posts, and the right to rule the country. B-Class Ranas got the perks, but couldn't be king. C-Class Ranas were the numerous offspring of concubines and unofficial wives. The inequity between them and A-Class Ranas led to dissent that contributed to the system's eventual demise.

The Rana regime was the ultimate autocracy—some call it "Ranocracy." The rulers did not oppress their subjects as much as ignore them. Nepal remained in a virtually medieval state well into the 1950s, with no public medical care, transportation, or education. The one Rana prime minister liberal enough to suggest a public school system was quickly booted out of office by his brothers. A few grudging changes were made in the status quo during the Rana years. Slavery, an institution involving one percent of the population, was finally abolished in 1926, and the custom of sati or widow-burning, discouraged by Jung Bahadur, was officially made illegal in 1920.

The country was in essence the Ranas' private estate. The entire national revenue of Nepal was at their personal disposal with no need to account for how they spent it. Appropriating vast plots of land from farms and temple endowments, they built huge European-inspired neoclassical palaces. The Rana prime minister-cum-maharaja dwelt in Singha Durbar, reportedly the largest private residence in Asia. Its grounds constituted fully half the area of the city of Kathmandu; its white stuccoed wings contained anywhere from 1,000 to 1,800 rooms, up to 500 of them occupied by concubines. A British visitor in the 1920s described a ground-floor salon:

> *The walls were almost entirely covered with bad but realistic frescoes, all of them depicting past rulers engaged, in various situations calling for personal bravery, in the sport of big-game hunting, for which the Terai is still world-famous. The floor was covered in tiger-skins, so that it was necessary to walk with circumspection lest one tripped over their gaping mouths. Stuffed animals, rhinoceros, tigers, buck of every description, were ranged along the walls, giving the room the appearance of a natural history museum.*

Another visitor noted: "You passed through hall after hall, every one of them as big as a parade ground, glittering with marble and crystal and showy furniture which made anyone with good taste feel quite seasick."

The palaces overflowed with Victorian bric-a-brac: plush upholstery, bronze statues, crystal chandeliers, and Carrera marble pillars, all carried in from India by barefoot porters. Roads were another modernity sternly opposed by a government bent on isolating itself from the outside world. There were a few short, bumpy tracks within the Valley, used by the aristocracy for brief spins in their Rolls Royces. Even automobiles were carried over the hills by porters. The wheels were removed and the cars were lashed to bamboo racks, carried by relays of up to 60 men. Moving at about one km per hour, they took a month to haul their burden to Kathmandu.

Prithvi Narayan Shah's famous maxim, "First the Bible, then the trading stations, then the cannon," was taken to heart by the Ranas. The few foreign guests invited were restricted to hunting big game in the Terai. Rarely were they permitted to enter the Kathmandu Valley, and never were they permitted to venture beyond it. Even Nepalis needed a permit to leave the Valley.

The result was as late as 1948, Nepal was the largest inhabited country unexplored by Europeans. Ancient traditions, beliefs, and customs were preserved in a vital, living culture that endured nearly untouched into the '50s and still lingers on today. The last 40 years have brought tremendous changes to Nepal. In 40 more years, only traces of the past will exist. Like buried artifacts, which crumble when exposed to light and air, ancient cultural patterns are vanishing in the face of modernization.

REVOLUTION OR RESTORATION?

The changes sweeping the globe in the years following WW II came even to Nepal. The Rana regime had supported the British with troops and supplies in both World Wars. When India won its independence from Britain in 1948, the Ranas gained an enemy in the new government, which bitterly resented their previous support of Britain.

In 1947, Nepali participants in the Indian independence movement formed the Nepali National Congress Party in Calcutta. Joined by a group of young dissident Ranas and supported by the new Indian government, the opposition challenged

Rana rule, uniting behind the long-ignored king of Nepal as a symbol of promised freedom.

Heartened by the support, King Tribhuvan made a dramatic break for freedom in November 1950. He and his family set off on a routine leopard-hunting excursion to Nagarjun forest, but unknown to the guards, the picnic baskets were stuffed with the Shah family jewels. The king, driving the lead car, suddenly swerved into the grounds of the Indian Embassy. Before his guards caught up, he was granted asylum by a waiting Indian officer. In a prearranged plan the royal family was whisked to New Delhi, as Nepali Congress forces based in India attacked Nepali border towns.

The sporadic fighting ended in a stalemate by January 1951, when a compromise settlement installed a coalition Rana-Congress Party government. King Tribhuvan returned to a hero's welcome in Kathmandu on 16 February 1951. The coalition government soon crumbled and the king called on the Nepali Congress to form an interim one, which proved equally chaotic.

The political turmoil of these early years worked in the king's favor. The chaos continued after Tribhuvan died in Switzerland in 1955 and his eldest son Mahendra was crowned king. The opposite of his quiet, withdrawn father, Mahendra was a vigorous ruler who liked direct contact with the people, and direct control of the government.

Parliamentary elections held in February 1959 swept the Nepali Congress Party into power, but the fledgling democracy ended abruptly on 15 December 1960, when King Mahendra declared a state of emergency. Political turmoil had paralyzed the government, he announced, and indeed he had a point—since the 1951 revolution, Nepal had been through 10 different governments. The king dissolved Parliament and arrested leading politicians on charges of bribery and corruption. Political parties and activities were outlawed, to be replaced by a new system—the "partyless" *panchayat* system.

Panchayat means "Assembly of Five," and the concept was supposedly modeled on the traditional village council—which, if they existed at all, were of very minor significance in most areas. The four-tier system spanned village to national levels, and operated through indirect elections. Voters elected members to a village assembly, and these officials chose representatives for the district *panchayat,* who in turn selected zonal *panchayat* officials. Until a 1980 constitutional amendment established their direct election, members of the National Panchayat were also chosen indirectly.

King Mahendra died in 1972. His son Birendra, the present king of Nepal, inherited the political framework introduced by his father. The 1962 Constitution had invested the king with sweeping powers, including the right of approval on legislative bills and the power to appoint all ministers, including the prime minister.

Through the 1980s, a vague Public Security Act permitting imprisonment for up to three months without charges or trial led to the arrest of hundreds of dissident students, activists, and journalists. The 1951 revolution with its hopes for democracy had seemingly ended in a restoration of autocratic rule, exchanging the Ranas for the Shahs.

DISSENT AND DEMOCRACY

In May 1979, popular dissatisfaction with corruption, inflation, and shortages of goods erupted into demonstrations across the kingdom. To defuse the situation King Birendra announced a national referendum to determine whether to keep the *panchayat* system or change to a multiparty government. The government mounted a vigorous pro-*panchayat* campaign, while the opposition fragmented into factions. The *panchayat* system won 54% of the May 1980 vote, a victory taken as confirmation of the status quo.

Even before the referendum, the king amended the constitution to open most seats in the National Panchayat to direct election. Still, the National Panchayat remained a rubber-stamp assembly with little real power. One-fifth of its members were named directly by the king, and all representatives had to swear loyalty to the king, the royal family, and the principle of partyless politics. The real holder of power was clearly defined in the 1962 constitution, which stated: "The sovereignity of Nepal is vested in His Majesty. . . . All powers, executive, legislative, and judicial, emanate from him."

Dissatisfaction continued to simmer in urban areas. The situation came to a head with the 1989 trade embargo India slapped on landlocked Nepal. In theory the dispute involved an expired trade and transit treaty between the two countries; in reality, a major aggravation was a weapons purchase Nepal had made from China. India retaliated by closing 13 of the 15 entry points along Nepal's southern border and halting shipments of fuel. While this scarcely affected the remote interior of the country, it shut down Kathmandu. Street traffic vanished, petrol and kerosene were rationed, and people waited in lines for hours for cooking fuel, or reverted to cooking over wood fires. The fuel blockade lasted nine months, until Rajiv Gandhi's government lost the November 1989 elections and the new Indian government lifted the ban as a signal of goodwill.

On 18 February 1990, the 40th anniversary of King Tribhuvan's declaration of a multiparty democracy, Nepal's outlawed political parties announced a campaign to restore the multiparty system. The Nepali Congress and a left-wing coalition of Nepal Communist Party factions joined in a movement headed by respected Congress Party leader Ganesh Man Singh. Demonstrations and rallies spread across the country, swelling as people joined in to protest police shootings of demonstrators. By early April the movement reached a crescendo in the Valley, as normally apolitical professionals, peasants, and even women and children joined the protests.

On 6 April a huge crowd of over 200,000 rallied at Kathmandu's central Tundikhel. Joined by processions from Bhaktapur, Patan, and Kirtipur, demonstrators marched down Durbar Marg toward the Royal Palace in late afternoon, shouting

THE FIGHTING GURKHAS

Nepal's best-known export is the Gurkha soldier. In over 140 years of fighting these fierce hillmen have earned a reputation as the world's finest infantrymen. Contrary to popular belief, the Gurkhas are not a race or tribe. The term is derived from Prithvi Narayan Shah's old capital of Gorkha in central Nepal. The Gorkhali army that conquered the Kathmandu Valley was composed of Magar and Gurung soldiers, and these two ethnic groups, along with a few Chhetris and the Rai and Limbu from eastern Nepal, dominate the British and Indian Gurkhas today. All are hardy hillmen and instinctive survivors, and the determination, independence, and resourcefulness bred by the Hills are put to good use on the battlefield. The Gurkhas' good humor and loyalty are legendary; so is their bravery and their skill with their signature *khukri* knife. In the 1982 Falkland Islands conflict, Argentine forces supposedly fled at the mere news the Gurkhas were approaching, adding another chapter to the legend.

The British first encountered Nepali soldiers in the 1814-16 Anglo-Nepali conflict. Though the British won the war, they were deeply impressed by the bravery of their opponents, and even built a memorial at the site of a famous battle commending the fort's commander, "our gallant adversary . . . and his brave Gurkhas." Officers lost no time in recommending Nepali soldiers be drafted into British forces.

The long-lasting relationship was cemented when Prime Minister Jung Bahadur Rana sent 12,000 soldiers to aid Queen Victoria during the Indian Mutiny of 1857. After Nepali forces helped put down the rebellion, a grateful Britain returned a large portion of the Terai lands taken in the 1816 Treaty of Segouli. The Gurkha soldiers, in turn, paid British troops the highest compliment when they said, "The English fought almost as well as the Gurkha."

British military literature of the period is filled with pithy praise of the Gurkhas. A British major-general described them in 1893: ". . . the Gurkhas of Nepal, a small diminutive race of men not unlike the Huns, but certainly as brave as any man can possibly be. A Gurkha thought himself equal to any four other men of the hills. . . . The other men of the hills began to think that he really was so, and could not stand before him."

The Gurkhas were formally incorporated in the Indian army in 1850; formal British recruitment began in 1886. Since Nepal was closed to outsiders, an enlistment camp was set up in Darjeeling; later, recruiting centers were established near Pokhara and in Dharan in eastern Nepal (the latter was recently closed).

"Death to the *panchayat* system," and "Long live democracy." Police stationed on Durbar Marg tried to stop them with tear gas; when that failed, they fired into the crowd. The official government death toll was 10; eyewitness accounts estimated 200-300 people were killed. They have joined the ranks of other "martyrs" in Nepali folk history, though most, including a young British tourist, were simply unlucky enough to get in the way of a bullet.

The bloodiest violence recorded in modern Nepal shocked the country and provoked major changes. Several tense days later, King Birendra bowed to demands for democracy and lifted the ban on political parties; the following month he dissolved the *panchayat* system. An interim government headed by Congress Party leader K.P. Bhattarai was formed to govern the country until free elections could be held, and an independent commission was created to rewrite Nepal's constitution in a more democratic mold. The Congress Party won a majority in the elections of 1991, with the Nepal Communist Party (UML) a close second.

Over 300,000 Gurkhas fought in World Wars I and II and were highly decorated for bravery. Following Indian independence in 1947, Gurkha regiments were divided between the Indian Gurkha Rifles and the British Brigade of Gurkhas. Their impressive list of battle honors covers most of the major sites of action in this century, from Gallipoli to the Gulf War. Their courage has inspired many legends. There was the hardheaded Gurkha who deflected a bullet which then killed a British officer on the ricochet, and the Gurkha POW who found his way through a thousand kilometers of Burmese forest aided by a wrinkled, stained map—of the London subway system. Then there was the Gurkha regiment that was asked to volunteer to jump from planes behind enemy lines. Half the regiment stepped forward on the first request; the other half joined after it was explained they would be jumping *with* parachutes.

More recently, Nepali historians have been fleshing out this one-dimensional portrait of the brave and loyal brown man dying for his white master. The reality behind the romance is that of poor peasants driven into soldiery by economic necessity. The Gurkhas only become more heroic when an understanding of the suffering and fear involved in the great wars is incorporated into their image.

Gurkha soldier with his symbol, a pair of crossed khukri

BOB RACE

Kathmandu intellectuals like to criticize the Gurkhas' "mercenary" status, but the fact remains that a position in the Indian or the British military is highly coveted. Soldiery is virtually the only ticket out for young Nepali men from the Hills: it brings social status, the chance to see the world, and what by local standards is an extremely generous salary and pension. Gurkha remittances are currently Nepal's fourth-largest source of foreign currency earnings and are the biggest single source of cash in the rural economy.

Britain's recent plans to reduce its Brigade of Gurkhas to 2,500 soldiers by 1997 has only intensified the competition. Around 100,000 to 150,000 Nepalis serve in the Indian Army's Gorkha *(sic)* regiments, making the Indian military the largest single employer of Nepalis outside of the government.

Upon retirement, soldiers usually return to their village to live on a comfortable pension. Some become schoolteachers or political leaders or open teashops and trekking lodges. The Central Hills are full of old *lahurey* who like to reminisce, some in excellent English, about all they've seen and done. In the hills around Pokhara I met a Gurkha who was still laughing at the ironies of fate. "Thirty years ago in the jungles of Burma we were cutting off the heads of Japanese soldiers," he said. "Now here I am serving tea to Japanese tourists!"

GOVERNMENT

The victory of the 1990 "Movement to Restore Democracy" threw Nepal into a state of flux from which it's still emerging. Thirty years of the partyless *panchayat* system preceded by centuries of autocratic rule provide a poor foundation for democracy, but democracy is what people want. Exactly what's meant by the term is unclear. Just as the *panchayat* system has become the scapegoat for every evil, "democracy" is the code word for good. It's also used to perpetrate an "anything goes" mentality—democracy is whatever *I* want to do right now, be it engage in a lively political discussion, or get a half-day off from school, or harass young women on the street.

Nepal's government faces serious challenges, among them a horrendously low standard of living, a chronically weak economy, governmental corruption, and a burgeoning population with growing expectations. Urbanites in particular expect it to increase their standard of living, and are increasingly dissatisfied with the failure to do so. Beset with its own problems, the government is still largely unable to effectively address development issues. Many people grumble things have not gotten better under democracy: on the contrary, the standard of living is lower, crime is higher, and optimism is diminishing.

The Constitution

One positive result of the *jana andolan* or "People's Movement" was the promulgation within the year of a new constitution, which, though it doesn't please everybody, does invest sovereignty in the Nepali people. The document includes a carefully worded description of Nepal as "a multiethnic, multilingual, democratic, independent, indivisible, sovereign, Hindu, and constitutional monarchical kingdom." The "Hindu kingdom" business was retained despite the protests of non-Hindus. The king remains a constitutional monarch and a symbol of Nepali unity. He and a Council of Ministers form the executive branch; the legislative branch is composed of a directly elected 205-member House of Representatives, commonly called Parliament, and a smaller National Council.

Political Parties

Some 71 political parties registered with the Election Commission for the 1994 midterm polls, most of them tiny splinter groups struggling for a piece of the pie. Elections in a country with a 40% literacy rate take on a strange twist. Each party is assigned a symbol—fish, umbrella, sickle, plough—that can be easily recognized by illiterate voters. This leads to cryptic campaign slogans like "Vote for Plough" or "Be as Rocket, Vote for Bucket" painted on walls and buildings around election time.

Only a handful of parties have any impact. "Tree," the Nepali Congress Party, portrays itself as *the* democratic alternative, appealing to conservative and middle-of-the-road voters. "Sun," the Nepal Communist Party (United Marxist-Leninist), maintains it's the party of the oppressed and poor—a sizeable portion of Nepal's population—and promises social justice and a decent standard of living for all. Third largest is the Rastriya Prajatantra Party, composed of old *panchayat* supporters and shunned by other politicians, though it can provide a vital swing vote with its present 20 seats. The Terai-based Nepali Sadbhawana Party has only a few seats.

Sooner or later, all these diverse factions must overcome their mutual dislike to work together, but past experience is not encouraging. Nepal's previous brief fling with democracy was marred by partisan politics, providing an excuse for King Mahendra to step in and assume direct rule; the present situation is a repeat of that factional bickering. The Nepali Congress party is riven between three personalities: former prime minister Girija Prasad Koirala, aging party "Supremo" Ganesh Man Singh, and Krishna Prasad Bhattarai. This "troika" spends much of its time bickering over patronage, perks, and the placement of chairs at receptions rather than the many substantial issues facing the country.

The 1994 Elections

The lack of political cohesiveness became painfully apparent in mid-1994, when the ruling Congress party was brought down by the refusal of 36 dissident MPs to support Prime Minister G.P. Koirala. In the midterm polls of November 1994, Congress lost its majority, going down to 83 seats, while the Communists (CPN-UML) won a bare majority of 88 seats. Nepal thus became the world's first Communist Hindu monarchical democracy—an odd mix which goes down better than it sounds. The Communists are essentially misnamed social democrats, and since they've been in power they've had to work with the status quo rather than emphasize the revolutionary.

Bureaucratic Culture

Inefficiency, widespread corruption, and general public distrust are among the biggest problems facing the government; cleaning its own house will prove a major task. The civil service remains a sluggish bureaucratic mire, staffed by low-paid workers who find the best policy is doing as little as possible. The predominant malaise grinds down even the most innovative and highly educated professionals—no wonder the cream of the crop goes abroad to study and stays abroad to work. Initiative isn't rewarded; in fact it's generally discouraged as a threat to higher-ups. What matters is higher-up connections *(soras phoras)* as well as obeisance to bosses and important people. Criticism is taboo and loyalty and nepotism are valued over energy and talent.

Politics is regarded not as public service, but as a means of personal advancement. It can be argued that politicians in other countries entertain a similar attitude, but the tilt is blatant here. Personal connections are crucial to enter the civil service, and ministers often create new "temporary" posts to reward their followers, expanding the bloated bureaucracy still further. Government positions are valued primarily for their ability to make money through opportunities for bribery and corruption.

Of course honest and intelligent government officials exist, but they are stymied at every turn. And although critics blame all these problems on the *panchayat* system, the flaws lie deeply embedded within the bureaucratic culture itself, which has proven to be bigger than even democracy. As they say in Nepal, *"Ke garne?"*—"What to do?"

Worst of all, the prevailing culture has undermined the innate capacity for transformation, and the sense of responsibility for this. The highly centralized structure only serves to reinforce passivity: the purpose of regional, district, and field offices appears to be to generate paperwork for Kathmandu to shuffle, control, lose, or otherwise tie up. Minimal local participation is not just a fault of *panchayat* society, but goes all the way back to Rana days. Power is concentrated in the landed, wealthy classes: the same influential people are elected at the local level, whether the organization calls itself the local *panchayat* or the local Village Development Committee. The democratically elected Parliament remains largely ineffective: MPs sign the attendance register to get their daily allowance, but few participate in discussions. The resolutions and laws passed remain difficult to implement, due in part to a highly centralized governmental structure which routes everything through the morass of Kathmandu.

Post-Revolution Blues

Obviously, the advent of democracy has not proven a magic cure for Nepal's political problems. Much misunderstanding remains about democracy, too often equated with prosperity. It's a framework for action—and that action must be from a wide spectrum of people, not the "somebody else" everyone seems to be waiting for. The fundamental problem underlying issues like corruption and inefficiency is the lack of political will.

In place of a clear vision, petty power struggles engulf the system, and nothing gets done.

There are some encouraging points, beginning with a growing public awareness of problems and an increased expectation for the government to somehow address these. People feel freer to criticize and discuss the political system, as well as freer to express their disgust with it and vote on it. Voter apathy is not yet a problem: turnout in the last election was over 60%, remarkable in a place where most people must walk several hours to the polls. Slowly, people are beginning to realize that democracy requires work—introducing it in name is only the beginning.

The Royal Family

King Birendra is 10th in the succession of Shah kings. His full title is "Shri Paanch Maharajdiraj Birendra Bir Bikram Shah Dev." An intricate system surrounds the honorific prefix *shri*. Ordinary respectable gentlemen have a single *shri* preceding their name, the equivalent of the English "mister" (actually it translates as something like "illustrious"). Members of the royal family are *shri teen*, "three *shri*," while the king is *shri paanch*, "five-times *shri*." This is as high as the scale goes for humans, though deities like Gorakanath may be honored by 108 *shri*.

Born in 1945, the king studied for four years at Eton and a year at Harvard, though he didn't receive a degree at either. He ascended the throne in 1972 after the death of his father, though the official coronation didn't take place until 1975, due to astrological reasons. Belief in the king's status as an emanation of Visnhu has waned in Kathmandu, but many rural people remain in awe of their ruler.

In 1970, then-Crown Prince Birendra married Aishwarya Rajya Laxmi Devi Rana, the daughter of Lt. Gen. Kendra Shumsher J.B. Rana, the man who would effectively have run Nepal had the Rana domination continued. In a simultaneous ceremony the bride's two sisters married the groom's younger brothers, continuing a long tradition of intermarriage between the Ranas and Shahs. The royal couple have three children; the eldest, Crown Prince Dipendra, was born in 1971. The queen, her relatives, and the king's relatives held a considerable amount of behind-the-scenes power before the

1990 uprising, though things seem to have toned down a bit since then. The royal family and the intrigues surrounding them generate an endless supply of wild rumors for the public mill; keep your ears open for the latest.

International Relations

Foreign policy is based on nonalignment, a prudent course for a tiny buffer state between India and China. On his coronation day, King Birendra made an official proposal that Nepal be declared an international "Zone of Peace." This was accepted by 87 countries, but because China and India are not among them and probably never will be, the post-1990 government has dropped the matter.

Despite the Zone of Peace rhetoric, Nepal has a large and well-trained standing army. Relations with China are relatively formal, with the Nepali government generally careful not to do anything that might ruffle Chinese feelings, like allow the Dalai Lama to visit. Little Nepal is feistier in its relationship with India, which is frequently accused of trying to dominate Nepal or interfere with national politics. Congress's alleged kowtowing to India was an issue in the 1994 midterm elections, and the Communists have vowed to straighten things out. While India's "big brother" attitude is commonly resented, Nepal's profound economic dependence on it remains undeniable.

Relations with other countries revolve around foreign aid (see "Industry and Trade—Development and Foreign Aid" under "Economy" below). King Mahendra was particularly skilled at playing one donor against another and reaping profits from both. This relationship cuts both ways now: as funding from foreign donors grows, their opinions and input become increasingly important to Nepal's new government.

ECONOMY

Statistically Nepal ranks among the world's poorest countries. The average per-capita income is around US$170 a year, which makes it about the ninth poorest country in the world (figures vary annually). This standard reckoning of wealth, derived by dividing the GNP by the population, is largely irrelevant in a country where much of the economy is still nonmonetized. Nepal scores slightly better when incomes are measured by purchasing power (US$896 a year, 28th lowest in the world), and also according to the Human Development Index, which ranks countries in terms of lifespan, literacy, and purchasing power. Nepal is 0.17 on this scale, ahead of 20 other countries.

Most Nepalis are subsistence farmers. They manage to grow enough to feed their families and sell a small surplus, which buys a few necessities like salt, tea, and cloth. The national economy was not really born until Nepal opened to the outside world in 1951. Rana rule kept the country secluded from everything outside, including trade, industry, and roads. Economists called in to examine the situation labeled Nepal's Rana-era economy "pre-feudal."

Despite 50 years of effort and huge infusions of foreign aid, economic development has been slow and spotty, in part because geography has dealt Nepal a difficult hand. Landlocked, with the nearest seaport being Calcutta, 500 km away, it must rely on India for all imports and exports aside from the little that trickles down from China via Tibet. Nepal's economic vulnerability became painfully clear during the 1989 trade and transit treaty dispute, when India clamped an economic blockade on Nepal, halting passage of petroleum products for six months and bringing industry and transportation to a standstill.

Nepal's marketable natural resources are scanty. Mineral and metal deposits exist, but access and shipping difficulties make them too expensive to extract. Like other small landlocked countries, Nepal's greatest asset is its tremendous hydropower potential, as yet largely untapped; its exploitation is tied up in often-touchy relations with India.

AGRICULTURE

Nepali life is based on farming. Agriculture supports over 80% of the population and contributes to over half of national production, one of the world's highest rates. That a land that is four-fifths nonarable still manages to support so many people is a tribute to the skill and tenacity of its farmers. In the Hills, each cultivatable hectare must support 12-18 people, a figure rivaling

farmer plowing field
for rice planting

those of the lush delta regions of India and Bangladesh. Terracing is the only answer to this, and slopes are layered bottom to top with terraced fields patiently carved out over the centuries with simple hand tools.

The Rural Economy

Independent farmers working tiny plots are the backbone of the rural economy: an average holding is 0.4 hectares, often in scattered parcels. They use traditional systems and techniques tested over the centuries and expanded to the limits of the possible. Rice *(dhaan)* is the favorite lowland crop, grown in irrigated fields at up to 2000 meters. Maize *(makaai),* introduced from the New World early in the last century, is planted in unirrigated fields at up to 2400 meters, while wheat *(gau)* is popular in the dry winter season. At higher elevations, farmers plant millet *(kodo),* barley *(jau),* and potatoes *(aalu).* Yellow-flowering rapeseed or mustard *(tori)* is cultivated in lower regions for the oil pressed from its seeds, used for cooking and oil lamps.

The fertile, flat Terai contains 70% of Nepal's arable land and produces over half its grain, but poor transportation means much of the surplus is sold in India. Meanwhile, many families in the western Mountain and Hill districts produce enough food for only six or seven months of the year. During the lean months of spring they get perhaps a single meal a day, and must forage to supplement their diet. Devastating famines like Africa has don't occur here, but farmers constantly face the challenge of wringing a livelihood from unrelentingly vertical, often dry and usually unpromising land. It's easy for poor families to fall into a cycle of debt and exploitation which can continue through generations.

Migrant Labor

With land at a premium, people turn to livestock, foraging, and trade to supplement their livelihood. Medicinal herbs and honey are among the few local items with cash value, and portering is the most widespread means of employment. To survive the lean period, male members or entire families may migrate into the Terai and India in search of temporary labor. Shrinking farmland and growing families have forced many Nepalis to permanently emigrate in search of work; close to 500,000 are gone half the year or more.

Most go to India, where they work as menial laborers, porters, servants, or, most popular, night watchmen, using the Gurkhas' reputation for ferocious protection. Living simply, they can send back a portion of their salaries to support their families and farms. Some go further abroad, to rubber plantations and construction sites in Malaysia and Korea or as drivers and domestics in the Middle East. Kathmandu job brokers charge tremendous sums to arrange foreign employment that is seldom as lucrative as promised.

Land Reform

Under the Rana regime, portions of Nepal suffered under one of Southeast Asia's worst land tenure systems. Terai landlords commonly extracted rents of up to 80% of the annual crop from their tenants. Families found it impossible to survive on the remainder of their harvest and were forced to borrow money from the landlord, who doubled as the local moneylender. A vicious cycle of debt began, for interest could be as high as 100%, compounded annually.

The Land Act of 1964 abolished the *zamindar* system of ownership, fixed rents at 50% of production, and restricted the amount of land a single family could control. But the reform largely failed due to lax enforcement and redistribution. Though tenancy rates have dropped and most farmers are now independent, their plots are tiny. By one estimate, the bottom 50% of the population owns seven percent of the arable land, while the top nine percent of the population controls nearly half the total.

INDUSTRY AND TRADE

Domestic Trade

Nepal's rural economy is dictated by season. Monsoon is the time for planting and herding, when high rivers and slippery trails make travel unpleasant or impossible. During the dry season, Oct.-May, several million Nepalis hit the trails for travel and trade. Hill people trek to Terai markets and India on annual shopping trips, perhaps carrying homemade ghee or bamboo matting to sell for a small profit.

Landlocked Nepal's need for salt spawned an ancient trans-Himalayan trading system. Hill

PORTERS

The backbone of Nepal's internal economy and transport system, porters haul whatever needs to be moved—sacks of rice and boxes of cigarettes for a shopkeeper, wooden beams and tin roofing for a new building, tables and chairs for a trekking group, tinned food for a mountaineering expedition, cases of Coca-Cola for a tourist lodge. Just about anything can be carried in a porter's *dokko* or bamboo basket, even a sick relative bound for the health post. A trekker's backpack is a light and easy job in comparison, and earns much better money than 100-kg sacks of cement.

Loads are carried suspended from a *naamlo*, a jute headband worn over the top of the head. This arrangement evenly distributes the burden along the spine, using the weight of the head to support the load with minimal muscular strain and maximum leverage for legs—a far better arrangement than a backpack. A five-foot-tall hillman can carry well over twice his weight all day with hardly a pause, and loads up to 100 kg are common. A porter's only other piece of equipment is the *teko,* a short, T-shaped wooden stick that provides balance on slippery slopes and serves to support the load when there's no resting place. Many porters don't even have shoes, just quarter-inch-thick calluses on their feet.

A porter's movements are a study in strength, agility, and energy conservation. He climbs uphill with a steady stride, seldom pausing for breath. After a brief rest at the top, steadying his load with the *teko,* he heads downhill with quick, short steps. Any mountain man will tell you it's the descents that tear up the knees. There is little breath left to spare for talking on the trail, and communication is mostly through long, breathy whistles. At mealtimes porters leave their loads by the trail to cook their *dhiro* and relax for an hour or two. *Daal bhaat* from a teashop is an expensive luxury. At night they sleep in teahouses if they can, but more often outside under a rock overhang or in a clearing. High-altitude treks generally offer a few miserable freezing nights for the *bhariya,* who must sleep outside with only a ragged blanket and inadequate clothing.

Porters are drawn from a cross-section of society. Many subsistence farmers turn to it in the slow winter season to earn extra money, while other porters are landless laborers, doing the only work they can find. The vast majority work in the local economy: trekkers and expeditions account for only a small fraction of portering employment.

There is no question that portering is a hard life, a tremendous amount of work for the meager reward of being able to continue living at a subsistence level. Most of the porter's daily salary (currently around Rs100) goes for food. No medical studies have been done on the physical effects of long-term portering, but the wear and tear of carrying heavy loads up and down steep hills must be enormous. Porters are the unsung heroes of Nepal, unorganized and with no clout—but were they to stop walking, the entire country would grind to a halt.

dwellers walked two to four weeks north into the mountains to purchase the year's supply of salt, bartering grain for it in an annually fluctuating measure. Strategically located Bhotia peoples like the Sherpas and Thakalis acted as middlemen in the lucrative trade, obtaining salt from Tibetans and grain from Nepalis and exchanging them at a profitable rate. Long caravans of yaks, mules, even goats and sheep carried bags of the precious salt down narrow trails, the type of pack animal changing with the region.

The 1959 closure of the Nepal-Tibet frontier halted this vital trade. Later the border was reopened, but by then people had shifted to using Indian salt, made widely available with the development of a southern road network. The old system lingers in a few remote areas, but many of the traditional traders have turned their business acumen to modern businesses and trekking.

Industry and Foreign Trade

Nepal's industry is minimal. Manufacturing employs less than two percent of the population and produces less than 20% of the GNP, one of the world's lowest rates. The Tibetan carpet industry brought in US$192 million in 1992-93, over half the nation's total foreign exchange earnings, though sales have since slumped (see special topic "The Modern Carpet Industry"). Garments are the second biggest foreign exchange earner after carpets, directly employing some 50,000 workers and exporting Rs95 million in goods in 1993-94. Most factories are local offshoots of Indian producers, established to take advantage of Nepal's preferential U.S. quotas. These will be phased out over the next 10 years with the implementation of the GATT treaty, and Nepal will lose its current competitive edge.

Minor exports include goatskins, jute, oil, ginger, and pulses. Industrial enterprises like oil and grain processing mills and factories for textiles, building materials, soap, matches, cigarettes, and liquor are concentrated in the Kathmandu Valley and in Terai towns like Biratnagar and Birganj, which have ready access to Indian markets and supplies. About one-third of Nepal's exports go to India and thus don't generate desperately needed hard currency, as the Indian rupee is nonconvertible.

The import list is long: Nepal needs petroleum products, machinery, construction and industrial materials, textiles, medicine, and nearly every kind of manufactured good. Through 1987, the value of imports was three times greater than that of exports, creating a huge trade deficit. The government attempts to control the outflow with heavy import duties on imported goods like TVs, computers, motorcycles, and cars.

Hydropower

Nepal has no known petroleum deposits, though some exploratory drilling is currently going on in the eastern Terai. Over 70% of the country's energy needs is filled by wood. The bright spot is Nepal's immense hydropower potential—an estimated 83,000 megawatts (MW), about a quarter of it economically feasible to develop. The small fraction of it tapped so far is insufficient for even the 10% of the population with access to electricity, and power cuts are a twice-weekly event in Kathmandu. With demand increasing annually and no major projects on line, things will get worse before they get better.

Yet falling water is all around. A tremendous amount of water rushes down from the Himalayan heights, its power intensified by narrow gorges and monsoon rains which swell rivers up to 30 times in volume. Most of Nepal's current supply of 241 MW comes from hydropower projects built with foreign assistance. Rugged terrain, no roads, and endemic corruption have made many of these projects incredibly expensive to construct—about 20-35 times the cost of similar plants in the Indian Himalaya.

Despite this, even larger ones are being studied. The proposed US$4.7 billion Karnali Project in the Far Western Hills would be among the world's largest hydropower projects, producing enough electricity to equal the entire installed capacity of India. The Arun III project in East Nepal is another controversial proposal (for more details, see "Eastern Nepal" under "Off the Beaten Track" in the Trekking chapter). Nepal could potentially earn millions from selling electricity and irrigation water to India, but hydropolitics are a prickly matter between the two countries. Critics say donor organizations have pushed massive environmentally destructive constructions at the expense of smaller, lower-impact projects that are more practical but less glamorous.

Development and Foreign Aid

For a tiny country Nepal draws an impressive amount of foreign aid: US$320 million in 1991-92. Germany, Japan, the Asian Development Bank, the World Bank, and various U.N. organizations are the major donors. Political expedience plays a big part in this generosity, and Nepal is well aware of the advantages of its precarious location between two giant countries. As a Nepali official once described it: "We have struck political oil by our location between China and India; the result is a lasting flow of aid." Being a perennial candidate on the World's 10 Poorest Countries list doesn't hurt things either.

Foreign aid funds as much as 30% of Nepal's regular budget, and 40-65% of the development budget (the amount varies yearly). Annual per capita foreign aid works out to nearly US$20 per Nepali, but little of this reaches the people it's meant to help. Part of the problem is with poorly designed programs developed by "experts" who fly in, spend a few weeks in the field (or more frequently, in Kathmandu), make their recommendations, and depart, without ever comprehending the situation. Much of the money is diverted into private bank accounts, or swallowed by the gigantic foreign-aid mechanisms themselves.

Nepal's development problems—"constraints," in the jargon of the trade—are certainly daunting: a burgeoning population expected to double in 40 years; one of Asia's worst health situations; declining agricultural yields; a mortality rate of 12%

for children up to age five; and an adult illiteracy rate of 68%. Attempts at developing a basically medieval and largely nonmonetized economy began only in 1951, and have proceeded slowly due to Nepal's rugged terrain and tremendous cultural diversity.

Trying to jump-start a feudal economy is a massive task, of course, and compared to 45 years ago much progress has been made. Large-scale broad changes like the appearance of shoes in the countryside, or vegetables, or roads, or the ongoing dissolution of the caste structure, are difficult to measure. Still, expectations are growing far faster than development.

TOURISM: A LOOK IN THE MIRROR

From 1664, when a pair of Jesuit priests arrived in the Kathmandu Valley, all the way up to 1948, fewer than 250 Westerners had visited Nepal. The floodgates opened with 600 tourists in 1951, and things haven't been the same since. Now more than 330,000 tourists arrive yearly, a third of them middle-class Indians come to escape the summer heat and tour Kathmandu's shops. Some 800,000 foreign tourists are expected for the year 2000.

Tourism is roundly welcomed as an economic lifesaver, an industry with an apparently sky-high potential for employment and foreign exchange. Currently it's Nepal's third largest source of foreign currency, after foreign aid and exports. But as in most third world countries, at least half of the money goes back out to pay for imported goods and services demanded by tourists and unavailable in Nepal. The remaining money is focused almost exclusively in the Kathmandu Valley and a few smaller areas, and tends to pool in the coffers of a few large enterprises.

Cultural Pollution

Rather than an all-round economic panacea, tourism is proving to be a luxury export, contributing little to integrated national development. (It does, however, bring in the foreign currency.) Because tourism demands a relatively high ratio of capital to labor, it doesn't produce as many jobs as industrial development, and its employment is limited to service occupations like hotel and restaurant work, portering and guiding. The

effects of its benefits are clustered in the Kathmandu Valley, Pokhara, and Sauruha, and along a few main trekking trails. Unfortunately (or fortunately, if you manage to get beyond these places) so are the damaging effects—the resulting inflation, environmental degradation, and above all, "cultural pollution."

Over 300,000 temporarily unemployed pleasure-seeking consumers—a good working definition of tourists—pour into Kathmandu annually. With a roughly 2:1 ratio of locals to tourists, disruptive effects are bound to occur. Now consider the essence of mass tourism, which involves the sale of a country: in it, culture becomes an object, and a way of life an industry. In the words of one observer, the natives "trade cultural peculiarities for basic needs."

Forty years of tourism, though on a relatively small scale, have already deeply affected Nepal, and the negative results become more apparent each year. Social identity is diluted, behavior and values change; Rambo and Madonna replace Rama and Sita as folk heroes. This is not just the fault of tourism, of course. Education, mass media, and urbanization all contribute to the dramatic social upheaval. Modernization is an inescapable trend affecting every traditional society on earth. Tourism merely accelerates the rate of change.

Inevitably, tourists change the traditional life they've traveled so far to see. Their appearance and attitudes advertise a world of unimaginable wealth, reinforced by their expensive clothes, cameras, and outdoor gear. Their constant quest for pleasure and recreation is understandable—after all, they're on vacation—but it gives an unrealistic impression of the West as a place where everyone is rich and no one needs to work. Nearly every young Nepali man wants to go to the West, preferably the U.S., but few can cite a reason beyond "it's a rich country." For 40 years now Nepal has been told it's a poor country, and this attitude is starting to erode a once-strong identity. It's only one step from here to a hands-out mentality, typified by the begging children who line the trails in touristed areas yet are never seen off the beaten track. Pico Iyer sums up the process nicely in *Video Night in Kathmandu:* "Westerners had left Nepalis with an expanded sense of horizon, and a diminished sense of wonder."

Mutual Stereotypes

Tourism has made its biggest impression on Nepali youth, introducing clothing, behavior, and values quickly adopted by the younger generation. Unfortunately the lifestyles introduced make little sense in the local context, thus increasing the feeling of alienation.

Groups of denim-clad "punks" (that's what they're called in Nepali, too) hang out waiting for Western girls, who, even if they don't do everything they're shown doing in pornographic videos, prove far more willing than their conservative Nepali sisters. The norm in much of Asia is Western men pursuing Asian women, but Nepal's strict sexual mores reverse the roles, so it's mainly Western women who end up pursuing, or being pursued by, Nepali men.

The greatest loss is the slow erosion of the genuine hospitality and friendliness once found everywhere in Nepal, increasingly being replaced by a reserved welcome, by set stereotypes, or by a "what-can-I-get-out-of-you" attitude. Nepalis have seen so many weird foreigners their image of them is understandably skewed. Summed up, they see an unpredictable, temperamental, and very wealthy people, prone to irrational generosity, but just as frequently irrationally cheap. The fallout is apparent along the most popular trekking trails, especially among proprietors of tourist lodges—sometimes the only Nepalis independent trekkers ever contact. They're still polite and friendly, and really the professional veneer is to be expected. Someone who's catered to 8,000 tourists in the past 12 years is not going to be excited about the 8,001st.

The reassuring part is tourism hasn't penetrated into the rugged majority of Nepal, and probably never will. Transportation difficulties and meager accommodations will keep it concentrated around Kathmandu, Pokhara, and the main trekking trails for years to come. If you get out of the standard tourist rut, the Durbar Square-Mt. Everest-Annapurna circuit, and into the villages—even those of the Kathmandu Valley—you will find traditional society and its hospitality still flourishing.

"Quality" Tourism

Nepal's tourism industry has lurched along with little guidance or planning from the government. While the country has enormous natural appeal, few efforts have been made to develop or maintain destinations beyond the Kathmandu Valley, Chitwan, and Pokhara. Government policy is influenced by big hotels and travel agencies, which have lobbied for the current emphasis on "quality tourism," a euphemism for big bucks. Budget travelers, who constitute perhaps 20% or 30% of non-Indian visitors, get little official respect. The government views them with a jaundiced eye, a leftover of Kathmandu's hippie days.

Surely if a quality tourist does exist, he or she is determined not by an open wallet but by an open mind. He is sensitive and unobtrusive, is aware of cultural nuances, is responsive to and truly interested in the people whose country he is visiting. How much money he spends is beside the point: while he doesn't expect the same level of comfort he has at home, he's not compelled to slum it, either. Tourism is an inevitable part of the modern age, and it must be hoped bringing people together in new and unusual combinations will ultimately be of mutual benefit. Right now it's up to each of us to make it so.

THE PEOPLE

The Gorkha king Prithvi Narayan Shah called Nepal "a garden for all types of people." Its steep mountains and isolated valleys preserve a complex mixture of ethnic groups, castes, and tribes—exactly how many depends on how closely you look. The national census lists 60 different groups, but ethnologists estimate there are more than 100, many of the smaller ones unknown even to most Nepalis.

This striking diversity is the result of centuries of intermingling between two main types of peoples: Indo-Aryans from the south and west and Mongoloid peoples from the north; or put another way, Hindu rice growers and Buddhist herders and barley farmers. These two distinct types remain in their purest forms along Nepal's northern and southern borders. In the middle of the country they've met and intermingled, creating an enormous variety of Hill ethnic groups.

Hindu caste groups tend to dwell in lowland settlements up to 1800 meters, growing rice in irrigated paddies. The settlements of ethnic groups are located on higher ridges, surrounded by fields of millet, corn, barley, and wheat. Each culture has its own typical type of dwelling, farming method, diet, and costume, all tailored to the natural environment. Constant trade and contact between the two assures that ideas as well as goods are exchanged. Each predominates in a certain region, but all move and mix to an extent, creating the many small pockets of different cultures scattered across the country. Atop this basic strata, successive waves of immigrants have overlaid their cultures, from the medieval Rajputs fleeing the Muslim conquest of India to the recent Tibetan exodus. Even Nepal's dominant Brahman-Chhetris are immigrants to the country, descendants of the Khasa people of the Western Himalaya who came from the 10th century on and spread slowly eastward, eventually dominating the Kathmandu Valley as the Gorkhalis of Prithvi Narayan Shah.

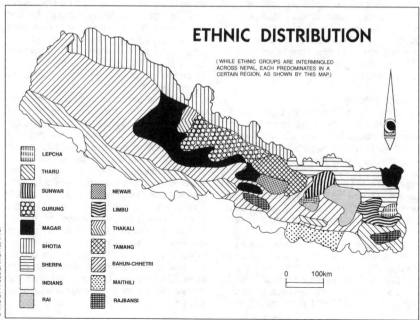

ETHNIC DISTRIBUTION

(WHILE ETHNIC GROUPS ARE INTERMINGLED ACROSS NEPAL, EACH PREDOMINATES IN A CERTAIN REGION, AS SHOWN BY THIS MAP.)

LEPCHA
THARU
SUNWAR
GURUNG
MAGAR
BHOTIA
SHERPA
INDIANS
RAI

NEWAR
LIMBU
THAKALI
TAMANG
BAHUN-CHHETRI
MAITHILI
RAJBANSI

0   100km

© MOON PUBLICATIONS, INC.

Nepal's bubbling ethnic stew reaches full boil in the Kathmandu Valley, which adds its own indigenous people, the Newars, to the blend. An astonishing variety of features and costumes appear on city streets. Picking out Tamang from Limbu, Chhetri from Newar is an endlessly fascinating game, and it reveals to what extent Nepal remains a mixing rather than a melting pot.

Several forces are working to homogenize the country's native ethnic diversity, however. Anthropologists have long noted the process of "Sanskritization," in which ethnic peoples seeking to increase their status in Nepal's Hindu-dominated society adopt the values and practices of high-caste Hindus as they make their way up the social scale. Though in theory Hinduism allows no converts—a Hindu is born, not made—in practice it's simple enough for many Nepalis to make the change. The process of change is two-way: Nepal's Hindu castes are mellowed by their contact with the ethnic peoples who form a third of the population, and are more tolerant regarding rituals and prohibitions than their more orthodox Indian brethren. Most significantly, both are being modernized by the increasing influences of modernization, transmitted by tourists, economic development, and the inevitably changing times. The result is old ethnic-oriented values of family and religion are being replaced with an increasing emphasis on material wealth and individuality.

National Identity

In many ways the Tharu hunter, Chhetri farmer, and Bhotia yak-herder have less in common than the inhabitants of three different European countries. Only since Nepal's 18th-century political unification have they shared even a nominal nationality; a distinct cultural and political character didn't emerge until after 1950. The government now cultivates a sense of national unity through mass media and public education, but old customs die hard, and in most villages ethnic affiliations remain more important than the vague concept of national identity.

The keynote of Nepali identity is struck by the inhabitants of the middle Hills, the Brahman and Chhetri castes who are the original Nepali speakers. They constitute a quarter of the population, but form 70-80% of the trained manpower, and most of the politicans, army officers, and upper-level government officials. The Newars and some Bhotia groups like the Sherpas and Thakalis may rival them in wealth, and the Newars have a foothold in the civil service as well, but Hindu castes have always held political power in Nepal, and the "official" values of Nepal are high-caste Hindu values.

Only since the revolution have ethnic differences been acknowledged by the government. The new constitution provides somewhat of a base for cultural pluralism, but ethnic aspirations vs. national integration remains a touchy issue, and many Nepalis remain either unaware of the tremendous diversity of their nation, or disinclined to respect it.

Characteristics

Describing a people as diverse as Nepal's is difficult, but a distinctly Nepali character becomes apparent when you compare Nepal with India. In religion, culture, and social practices the two nations share much in common, but Nepal is a world apart from India's brand of intensity. Crossing the border, you feel a palpable sense of relaxation in the air on the Nepal side, and immigration officials may actually smile at you. Despite the growing pressures of modern life there's still plenty of time in Nepal—at once a frustrating and a charming trait. Things take longer to get done, but if you keep some patience and humor, you can have a lot of fun in the process.

The Nepali approach to caste restrictions and religious rules is more relaxed than that of orthodox Indian Hindus, an inevitable result of cultural intermingling. Nepalis are generally easygoing, willing to overlook a mistake or faux pas, but a deliberate insult may arouse a surprisingly fierce pride. British officers have long marveled at the bravery of the Gurkha soldiers recruited from Nepali Hill tribes, as well as their loyalty, stamina, and constant good humor. Life in Nepal is people-oriented, not run by technology, and there is still time to sit and talk—indeed, that's one of the main pleasures of life. Villagers may have few material goods, but they possess an innate dignity that can't be bought. Nepal is a poor country in terms of money, but in spirit it's among the wealthiest there is.

Population

The 1991 census tallied Nepal's population at 18.5 million; by 1995 this was estimated to have grown to 19.4 million. The census estimate of an annual population growth rate of 2.08% a year was unexpectedly low; many experts peg the rate at around 2.5%, meaning the population is doubling every 40 years. This will place an intolerable burden on the fragile Himalayan environment. In the Hills, natural resources and arable land are already stretched to their limits, and the "pressure valve" provided by new Terai land is disappearing as the plains fill up.

The imbalance in population distribution only exacerbates these pressures. Much of Nepal is uninhabitable mountains: the rugged northern region is virtually deserted, while the Kathmandu Valley has an urban density double that of New York City. The rural population density of 500-700 per square mile is equalled only by those of monsoon Asia and a few areas in Africa.

Population growth isn't likely to decrease anytime soon: nearly half of all Nepalis are under the age of 15 and have yet to enter their childbearing years. The contraceptive usage rate is estimated at 24%, a tremendous improvement from the past, but popularizing and delivering family planning methods is a difficult task. Like all rural peoples, Nepalis value large families for the help children can give in farming and household chores, as well as for their own sake. In a materially poor society, children are among the greatest joys in life.

Of every 1,000 babies born, 102 die in the first year of life. An additional 26 will die before reaching age five. Given these grim statistics, couples feel they need plenty of kids to ensure that some will reach adulthood. The average Nepali woman bears six children in her lifetime, of which one or two die in early childhood.

CASTE

Nepali society is based on the Indian caste system, introduced and reinforced by successive waves of immigrants. The country's ethnic diversity has molded it into a unique form. Popular belief has it the caste system was introduced in the Kathmandu Valley by King Jayasthiti Malla (A.D. 1382-1422), who classified his Newar subjects into 64 different occupational categories. While he did codify numerous regulations, right down to details like forbidding outcaste sweepers to wear shoes, he was strengthening existing patterns that were already centuries old. Records from the Licchavi Era (A.D. 300-879) document the existence of a caste system based on the classic fourfold Indian division: the priestly Brahmans, the warrior/ruling class of Kshatriya or Chhetri, the trading and farming Vaishya, and the menial Sudra, servants and laborers.

The old occupational caste divisions were incredibly specific. Among the Newars, dyers of red cloth belonged to one caste, dyers of blue cloth to another, and there were separate divisions for wound-dressers, musicians, and the men who painted the eyes on the wheels of the Machhendranath chariot. Modern occupations and the demise of old ones have somewhat confounded the traditional system, which is still adapting—taxi drivers are from low castes, computer operators from high ones.

Legal punishment for violating the caste system was eliminated in the early '60s, but caste is still very much alive in Nepal, determining who can marry who, or who can eat, drink, or even smoke together. Some of these old taboos are loosening, but caste still serves to indicate political and economic status, uniting some people and dividing others.

Understandably, high-caste members take the matter most seriously. Brahmans and Chhetris look down upon the lesser Hindus, who in turn can still feel superior to the yak-eating (i.e., cattle-eating) Bhotia, who rank just above outcastes in the scheme. These casteless Buddhists can ignore the system, but the lower castes and outcastes can't—they are still an inseparable part of the society which discriminates against them.

A literal "waterline" runs through society, dividing the pure and impure castes, illustrated in the Nepali terms *paani chaalne jaat,* "water-touching caste," and its negation, *paani nachaalne jaat.* A high-caste man will lose caste if he accepts food from a member of a lower caste, or food or water from an outcaste, a threat which can only be remedied by ritual purification. To have the issue revolve around as basic a daily need as water illustrates how deep these divi-

three young Nepali boys sporting the official national dress

ALISON WRIGHT

sions run. Well into this century, Nepali traders returning from non-Hindu lands had to undergo this ceremony and have it legally certified before being admitted back to "clean" society. Strict Brahmans cannot accept food or drink from anyone except another Brahman—a restriction which kept Kathmandu's potential restaurant customers near zero until the advent of tourism.

Hindu Caste Groups

These people are the mainstay of the middle Hills, particularly in western Nepal, where they constitute 80% of the population. Brahman and most Chhetri men wear the *janaai* or sacred thread diagonally across their chest, symbolizing their ritual purity and the "twice-born" state of the upper castes. Lower castes and ethnic groups sometimes disparage it with the slang term "buffalo's intestine."

Bahun or Brahmans sit at the top of the heap. Traditionally they serve as priests and moneylenders, earning a bad reputation for usury; nowadays they're also found in government, education, and commerce. They tend to dominate society, though many rural Brahmans are no wealthier than other peasants. In exchange for receiving the social privileges of the highest caste, orthodox Brahmans are supposed to honor a number of ritual prohibitions—they shouldn't eat onions, garlic, or tomatoes, drink alcohol, or harness cattle to ploughs—but these taboos are increasingly ignored.

Chhetris are the largest Hindu caste, traditionally specializing in military and political affairs. The Shah dynasty and the powerful Rana family are members of an aristocratic Chhetri subcaste called **Thakuri.** Many Chhetris are descended from the long-ago union of Brahman immigrants and Nepali Hill women, awarded the honorary rank of Chhetri to strengthen the caste system. Their features may thus resemble those of ethnic groups more than "pure" Brahmans. Following tradition, they are prominent in the military and police, but most are small farmers scattered throughout Nepal.

The traditional middle-caste slots are vacant in Nepal, filled instead by ethnic groups. At the bottom of the totem pole, below the ritual "waterline," are the occupational castes: the **Kami** or blacksmiths, **Sarki** or cobblers and leatherworkers, and **Damai** or tailors who moonlight as musicians in out-of-tune wedding bands. Often landless, they live within an elaborate system of patron/client, in which they provide the rich with services and labor and receive a share of the harvest in exchange. Outcaste sweepers, butchers, and executioners form the poorest strata of society.

ETHNIC GROUPS

Terai Peoples

About a quarter of Nepal's people belong to one of the Indo-Aryan groups of the Terai, but few visitors come in contact with them as the Terai is not a major destination except for Chitwan.

Tharu: One of Nepal's few indigenous tribal peoples, as opposed to ethnic groups descended from later waves of immigrants, the Tharu are based in the midwestern Terai in forested land along the southern base of the Siwalik Range. They were among the few people who could live here, having a limited natural immunity to malaria. They claim to be descendants of Rajputs, but are probably of Dravidian stock. They are an exceptionally large population of some 1.2 million but possess little power or influence; because their introverted agricultural society had little contact with the outside world, it was easily taken advantage of by latecomers, and many of the traditional Tharu lands were lost during the land registration programs of the 1950s. Modern Tharus are often landless sharecroppers; in Western Nepal they may be subject to a system of bonded labor which passes debts on through generations from father to son.

Maithili: Of Indo-Aryan stock, these people take their name from Mithila, the capital of a rich and highly advanced culture which greatly influenced the Malla rulers of the Kathmandu Valley. According to census data they're Nepal's largest single ethnic group, at nearly 12% of the population.

Hill Ethnic Groups

These peoples predominate in the higher Hill regions between 1800 and 2700 meters. Though most speak Nepali as well, their mother languages are Tibeto-Burman dialects. Many share close linguistic and cultural links but have developed in different directions according to local environment and history.

Newar: The indigenous inhabitants of the Kathmandu Valley, the Newars now make up a little less than half of its population and less than six percent of the national total. Shrewd traders, expert farmers, and superb craftspeople, they produce art that ranks among Asia's finest and their old cities are masterpieces of urban planning. Originally Buddhist, the Newars are now predominantly Hindu; more precisely, their beliefs are an impossibly tangled mixture of both. Their language, a Tibeto-Burman offshoot, has its own alphabet (now largely replaced by Devanagari script) and an ancient literary tradition. Newar society is divided into 64 occupational castes and hundreds of subcastes, with parallel systems for Buddhists and Hindus. Among the largest of these groups is the **Jyapu,** peasant farmers clustered in Bhaktapur and Patan, who faithfully support the old traditions, festivals, and religious beliefs.

Tamang: One of the largest Hill ethnic groups (5.5% of the national population), the Tamangs are concentrated in the Hills surrounding the Kathmandu Valley. In many ways they form an "invisible community," poor and low-profile. The Ranas used them as porters; today they work as *tempo* drivers, rickshaw pullers, carpet and *thangka* makers, servants, and in the lower rung

smoke break for a hard-working porter

ALISON WRIGHT

children in Bhaktapur

of the trekking trade. Those in the Hills remain farmers and porters. Their Tibeto-Burman language is vaguely related to Newari; more than the Newars they have retained their Buddhist beliefs, blended in their case with animistic folk religion. The Tamangs are relatively recent arrivals from the northeast; according to one account their ancestors were Tibetan horse traders or cavalry who eventually settled in Nepal, hence the name *Ta-mi,* "Horse People."

Gurung: The Gurung homeland is in the foothills of the Lamjung and Annapurna Himal, a region they've intensively farmed and covered with a network of trails paved with precisely cut and fitted stone blocks. Gurung villages of neat stone houses are some of the largest in Nepal, and their standard of living is relatively high. They speak an unwritten language, again Tibeto-Burman, which appears in at least three main dialects. In higher regions, Gurungs retain their Buddhist traditions; in lower ones they've converted to Hinduism. Many young Gurung men have become mercenary soldiers in the British or Indian armies to support their families on their shrinking farms back home.

Magar: These people live in roughly the same area as Gurungs, but farm the lower slopes. Their homeland is around the southern slopes of the Dhaulagiri Himal. Again, they speak a Tibeto-Burman language appearing in several regional dialects. Originally practitioners of animistic folk religion with a Buddhist veneer, most have switched to Hinduism. Along with Gurungs,

Magar soldiers make up the bulk of the Gurkha and Nepali armed forces. Their role as fighters goes back to their service in the army of Prithvi Narayan Shah, and even before that to the Palpa ruler Mukunda Sen's attempted invasion of the Kathmandu Valley in the 16th century. The Magar reputation as honest and hardworking (some unkindly call them "strong and stupid") make them the *sojho* or "straight" people of Nepal; they constitute seven percent of the national population.

Thakali: Natives of the Thak Khola region near Annapurna in central Nepal, the Thakali are known as shrewd and aggressive traders. Formerly they profited from their role as middlemen in the salt trade between lowland Nepal and Tibet. Originally they were Tibetan Buddhists, influenced by shamanism, but many have become Hindus in recent years. The Thakalis are quite prosperous and many have resettled in Kathmandu or the Terai for business reasons. Thakali women are famed for their spic-and-span lodges and tasty food. In the past, they had a reputation (though not documented) for seducing their guests, then robbing them as they slept.

Rai and Limbu: The Kiranti tribe, mentioned 2,300 years ago in the Mahabharata, is said to have once ruled the Kathmandu Valley. Driven out by a succeeding dynasty, they resettled in the eastern Hills. The name "Kiranti" is kept by the Rai and Limbu as a reminder of these ancestors. They're easily identified by their striking, tilted almond eyes and flat Mongolian features. Rai and Limbu each have their own related language and share a mixture of animistic, Buddhist, and Hindu beliefs. Independent and proud, they often serve in the military and tend to hold themselves a little apart from other Nepalis.

Mountain Peoples

Bhotia or Bhotey is a term used throughout the Indian subcontinent to describe northern mountain peoples with close cultural ties to Tibet. To caste Hindus this term is mildly pejorative, used to indicate a people who eat beef (or at least yaks) and drink alcohol. Bhotia dialects are Tibetan-based and their religion is invariably Tibetan Buddhist, with a sprinkling of animistic Bönpo influences.

Life in the mountains can't be supported by farming or herding alone, so these people practice both, and in addition follow an annual cycle of trade. In winter they travel south to trade and graze their flocks; in summer they move back up into the high pastures and cross the northern passes to trade in Tibet.

Many of the dozens of Bhotia subgroups go by the names of their particular regions, suffixed by "-pa," Tibetan for "people" or "man": Dolpo-pa, Lo-pa (the inhabitants of the Kingdom of Lo or Mustang), Manang-pa (renowned traders and smugglers), and the famous **Sharpa** of Solu-Khumbu, perhaps the best known of all Nepal's ethnic groups. In English "Sherpa" has become a synonym for porter or expedition worker, but properly speaking, Sherpas are people who trace their origins to eastern Tibet, from where they emigrated about 400 years ago. Their traditional life combined yak-herding, barley and potato farming, and trading with nearby Tibet. Following the Chinese invasion of Tibet in the 1950s they quickly adapted to a new role, serving as guides and expeditors for the developing trekking and expedition business. Today the "Sherpa Mafia" dominates the trekking trade, and Sherpas are among the most prosperous and successful of all Nepalis. See special topic "The Sherpas" for more details.

Tibetan Refugees

Unusual for refugees, this community retains its unique identity despite more than 30 years of exile. A strong Buddhist faith and an un-quenched hope of a return to their homeland are important factors in this, as is the leadership of the Dalai Lama's Tibetan government-in-exile in Dharamsala, India. Some 30,000 refugees arrived in Nepal following the Chinese crackdown in 1959; their numbers have increased with later refugees and with the new generation born in Nepal.

Though most refugees arrived destitute and first worked as laborers or with the help of foreign aid, many have since become prosperous through the Tibetan carpet industry or in various businesses, including tourism. While they have adapted, they have not committed to settling there permanently. Increasingly they are accepting Nepali passports to allow them to travel more easily, but they still think of themselves as Tibetan.

LIFE AND CUSTOMS

It's impossible to touch even briefly upon the diverse customs and rituals of all of Nepal's different peoples. The mores discussed here are the "standard" Brahman/Chhetri norms.

Urban and Village Life

Nepal is still an overwhelmingly rural place, but the rate of urbanization is rapidly increasing. Currently about nine percent of the population lives in Nepal's 32 cities and towns, most of these in the Kathmandu Valley or the Terai. The remainder are scattered among 80,000 or so villages and hamlets, where life has changed little over the centuries. Here people still raise their own food, build their houses from local materials, rely very little on cash, and seldom see much of the world beyond their own particular valley. This is the real Nepal, and no one who visits only the capital can claim to have understood the country. Trekking is the best way to immerse yourself in village life, but even the hamlets of the Valley provide a glimpse of the timeless rural reality.

Men's Clothing

The official national dress is the *daura suruwal:* a long-sleeved tunic closed with cloth ties over tight-legged, baggy-seated drawstring trousers (the extra material expedites squatting, which is the national posture). Worn with a Western-style suit coat, it's the official uniform of high government officials. Among most men nowadays, shirts and trousers have become the norm. The trendy punk boys of Kathmandu, arrayed entirely in denim, wouldn't be seen dead in the *daura suruwal,* nor in its accompanying *topi,* a brimless, lopsided cap that is Nepal's distinctive own.

Terai men wear Indian-style *lungi,* a long wraparound piece of printed cotton, or a *dhoti,* a length of white cloth wound between the legs and about the waist like baggy culottes. Porters and laborers wear shorts, a loincloth, or maybe just a towel wrapped about their hips, but bare-legged men are considered low class—which is why hairy-legged tourists are considered uncouth. Ethnic groups have their own clothing: for Rai hillmen it's a vest and loincloth or *langauti,* while Gurung men wear homespun, undyed cotton *khadim* or *anti bhanro.* Tamangs may wear sleeveless woolen jackets similar in weave and pattern to *radi* carpets. Bhotia men wrap themselves in Tibetan-style wool *chuba,* but modernized Bhotias like the Sherpas save

their *chuba* for festivals and celebrations, and prefer jeans and down jackets.

Women's Dress

Always more conservative than men, Nepali women are just beginning to adopt Western dress. Five years ago a woman in jeans was unimaginable, but fashionable young Nepali women can now be seen in leggings and miniskirts. Still, nothing equals the grace of the Indian sari favored by married Hindu women, a five-meter length of cloth draped over a tight, short-sleeved blouse called a *choli.* Throughout Kathmandu, brightly colored saris flutter like banners from the upper-story windows where they are hung out to dry. Wrapping a sari is an intricate process, mastered by the inexperienced with the aid of a few strategically placed safety pins.

More practical is the *shalwar kurta* or "Punjabi" borrowed from northern India and popular with young women. A dresslike top is slit up the sides to reveal matching drawstring trousers, tight about the calves but loose at the waist. A diaphanous scarf *(dupatta)* worn over the shoulders completes the ensemble. Comfortable, at-

BOB RACE

Boudhanath Stupa (Kerry Moran)

(top) Everest (Kerry Moran);
(bottom) Annapurna from the Annapurna Sanctuary (Christopher Gamm)

tractive, and modest, Punjabis are excellent for women travelers. Shops in the bazaar sell gaudy ready-made outfits in trendy styles, the latest being bell-bottoms, or you can buy your own material and have a tailor stitch it up. Silk is especially nice, while printed cotton is durable.

Peasant women would find the flowing sari impractical for their endless round of work. They wear cotton *lungi* or the *fariya,* a length of flowered cotton wrapped into a skirt, often topped by a five-meter length of white cotton wound about their waist. This *patuka* keeps the back warm and supported, provides padding for loads, and makes a handy cache for snacks, keys, and money.

Newar Jyapu women wear a distinctive black skirt bordered in red, arranged in multiple pleats in front to allow easy walking, and hiked high in back to reveal the blue tatooes adorning their calves. (After death, it's said the woman can sell these to obtain food in the afterworld.) Newar women also favor cotton blouses block-printed in red-and-black patterns. In cooler weather they wrap themselves in patterned shawls of the same material, the colors muted by a layer of transparent muslin.

Bhotia women dress in long sleeveless wraparound dresses, tied in the back and worn over a blouse—long-sleeved and silken for festivals or a T-shirt for ordinary days. Married women top it with a striped woolen apron, which serves as a handy sit-upon, towel, and handkerchief.

Adornments

Nepali women delight in decoration, layering themselves with jewelry in carnival colors. They braid their long black hair with red cotton tassels, or twist it into a neat bun and set a flower in it. Red is considered the most beautiful color, worn by brides on their wedding day as a symbol of marital happiness. A Nepali saying goes, *Raato raamro, guliyo mitho,* "Red is beautiful, sweet is tasty."

The auspicious *tika* mark made on the forehead with red *sindhur* powder is part of daily *puja.* Special *tika* mixed with yoghurt and rice are distributed as blessings on auspicious occasions like weddings and Dasain. In a mystic sense the *tika* represents the third eye of spiritual insight; for women, it's become a cosmetic essential. Little kits of plastic stick-on *bindi* are sold in a variety of colors and shapes.

a young married woman wearing the traditional tilhari

ALISON WRIGHT

Jewelry is more than an adornment; it's an investment and a status symbol. Nobody knows the value of your bank account (and the interest rate barely keeps up with inflation) but everyone understands the value of gold. For a married woman, jewelry is one of the few possessions she can call her own. Whatever items she brings into a marriage as dowry remain hers to keep.

With the exception of Newars and Bhotias, many Nepali women have pierced noses, adorned with anything from a tiny jeweled stud to a collection of discs and rings. The larger pieces *(mundri)* hanging from the septum of some Hill women make you wonder how the wearer manages to eat. (They manage by bending their heads far over their plate.) Earrings may be a dozen tiny rings inserted along the outer rim, or huge gold or brass discs which must be put in and taken out by the goldsmith. Tharu and Tamang women wear heavy anklets of hollow silver or gold; Terai women may wear linked silver anklets. Some hill women wear necklaces of old coins; most valuable are the *kampani*, coins of the British East India Company, which contain a fair amount of silver.

Married Hindu women display their wedded state with signals as predictable as a wedding ring is in the West. Red *sindhur* powder in the part of their hair is a sure sign; ideally the powder should be mixed with a tiny portion of the *sindhur* the bride received on her wedding day. Another indication is the *tilhari,* a cylindrical golden bead set into a colorful necklace of tiny glass beads. Married women may also wear armfuls of tinkling glass bangles; widows break theirs as a sign of mourning.

Bhotia women favor big chunks of turquoise, coral, and amber, strung into necklaces, set into rings, or woven into their hair. Men and women wear all sorts of religious artifacts: amulet boxes containing blessings or holy relics, colored knotted neckcords blessed by lamas, rosaries of prayer beads *(trengwa)* for reciting mantras. Another treasure is the black-and-white *dzi* stones, said to have been created by lightning bolts. The finest cost hundreds of thousands of rupees and are worn as protection against evil spirits.

Similar protection is provided to Hindus by rosaries of the furrowed brown *rudraksha* ("eye of Shiva") seeds worn by *sadhu* and pilgrims. From the *Elaeocarpus ganitrus* tree, *rudraksha* appear in different configurations with up to 21 divisions or "faces," each combination sacred to a different god. A single-faced or *ek mukh rudraksha* is extremely rare and highly valued: it's said the mere sight of it erases sins, and the owner will be blessed by the goddess Lakshmi.

FAMILY LIFE

Society is based around the family, and loyalty to one's kin supersedes duties to caste, ethnic group, or nation. It's sometimes difficult for independent-minded Westerners to understand the extent to which an individual's identity can be submerged in social considerations. In smaller villages, virtually everyone is related some way or another. Children grow up in an extended family, surrounded by relatives. The Nepali language reflects this with dozens of detailed kinship terms. Frequently people are called by a re-

lationship word—"older brother's wife" or "little sister" rather than their personal name, which may be forgotten, or may never even be given.

Infancy and Childhood

Children are treasured in Nepali society. They help with household and field chores, support their aged parents, and bring a great deal of joy to a life with little entertainment. Not surprisingly, they're the goal of virtually every married couple. Couples without children are nearly incomprehensible to Nepalis. Whatever your explanation may be, they will secretly pity your presumed infertility (failure to bear children is always considered the fault of a woman).

Infertility is a curse for a Nepali woman, who doesn't attain full social status until she bears a child, preferably a son. Though polygamy has been outlawed, a man who has no living child after 10 years can legally take a second wife, and often does before that time. Boys are preferred for several reasons: male offspring continue the family lineage; only sons can perform the *shraddha* offerings for ancestors; and sons continue to economically support their parents after marriage, while daughters join their husbands' families.

Children are christened with a first name and clan/caste surname 11 days after birth. Hindu children are often named after deities: Shiva, Ganesh, Ram, Narayan, Lakshmi, Saraswati. Or they're given auspicious names like Kamala (Lotus), Sushil (Courteous), or Bijay (Victory). Magar and Gurung men often have Bahadur (Brave) as a middle name. Bhotia children may be named after the day they were born—Nima, Dawa, Mingma, Lhakpa, Phurbu, Pasang, and Pempa are Sunday through Saturday. The Sherpa prefix "Ang" (as in Ang Dawa, Ang Nima) is something like "junior" in English.

Given names are often replaced by a kinship term from an elaborate and extensive vocabulary. In order of birth, boys are Jetha (the eldest), Maila, Saila, Kaila, Raila, Taila, and Kancha ("Junior"). Girls are Jethi, Maili, Saili, and so on. This system covers a total of 16 children; it's highly unlikely a woman would bear more than eight of each! As children grow up to assume roles in their own families, the names change: women become *bhauju* (brother's wife) or simply "so-and-so's mother."

Mothers go about their work with their infants tied to their backs and nurse the babies for several years, sometimes until the age of six or seven. Infants are given a daily sunbath and massaged with mustard oil, said to make their skin fair and their limbs straight and supple. Toddlers wear heavy silver anklets to make their legs grow straight. Small children are considered vulnerable to evil spirits and are protected in a variety of ways: their eyes are lined with black *gajal* to avert sickness and the evil eye, while cords tied around their wrists and ankles protect against spirits. Around six months of age a baby receives its first symbolic mouthful of rice off the edge of a coin in the *pasni* ceremony, symbolizing his or her transition into a separate individual.

As soon as they can walk, children are given over to the care of an older sibling to begin a few years of intensive playing and running about. Adults keep an eye on them but rarely interfere with their games. As a result, Nepali children learn to be self-sufficient early on and never seem whiny or bored, despite their lack of conventional playthings. Every action becomes a game and every object is a toy—the rusty rim of a bicycle wheel serves as a hoop, a plastic bag is a mask, and a dead dog makes the ultimate pull toy. Children, like adults, are constantly with others in an intensely social context; privacy is a practically unknown concept.

School and Work

As children grow, they take on household tasks, especially the girls, who help their mothers with the endless round of cutting fodder for animals, fetching water and wood, and tending younger children. Boys might be sent to graze the family's livestock. Nepali boys are twice as likely to be sent to school as their sisters, at least for a few years. A girl's labor is too valuable to do without, and many parents see no point in educating a daughter who will never do more than field and housework and will soon leave them to work for her husband's family. The primary school enrollment rate is around 70% on paper, though attendance is far below that. After age 10 children start to drop out in great numbers. Few make it to the 10th and final grade; fewer still pass the exam for the School Leaving Certificate (SLC), which is the equivalent of a high school education. College may follow for those mainly urban teenagers who do pass the SLC, but the quality of education at Tribhuvan University is low, and there are very few jobs awaiting its graduates.

Rites of Passage

Sometime between the age of eight and marriage, Brahman and Chhetri boys undergo the *bartamaan* ceremony initiating them as a full-fledged member of their caste. Long ago it marked the boy's initiation as the disciple of a Hindu guru; nowadays it's purely symbolic. The boy dons the *janaai*, the triple-knotted sacred thread worn over the left shoulder as the exclusive prerogative of higher Hindu castes.

A Hindu girl reaching puberty undergoes a far less pleasant ceremony called *guphama basne*, "staying in the cave." At the onset of

boys in Kagbeni

WEDDING PROCESSIONS

November to March is prime wedding season in Kathmandu, when streets are clogged with stately, colorful processions of relatives walking behind a decorated car bearing the new couple. Leading the parade are a dozen high-stepping musicians uniformed in red jackets and oversized brimmed caps. The music they produce is raucous and almost comically off-key; nowadays the tunes are drawn from Hindi films.

Brass wedding bands were originally a Rana prerogative, but since the 1950s they have become a widespread social tradition. Musicians are drawn from the Damai or tailor caste, the traditional performers in *panchey baja* wedding bands, musical instruments being generally associated with low or untouchable castes. The inspiration for the brass band formula was India's Raj-era military bands; other countries with colonial histories have similar traditions.

Two processions are involved in every wedding, the first conducting the groom and his friends to the bride's home, where they are feasted. The marriage ceremony takes place the next day, after which the bride is carried to the car by a male relative, sobbing violently in her red-and-gold finery. Tradition demands she show her chagrin at leaving her parents' home by weeping, a scene which always draws a large and interested crowd. To tell how upset she *really* is, look at her relatives. If they seem unperturbed it's a good match, but if too many are teary-eyed as well, there's something wrong.

The gaily decorated vehicle then conducts the couple to the groom's home; in the old days the bride would have been carried on a shoulder litter, as rural brides still are. At her new home the bride is received by her mother-in-law in an elaborate ceremony which welcomes her as Lakshmi, goddess of wealth and abundance. Then she is led inside where another feast awaits.

---

menstruation she's whisked away from her home and confined in a secluded dark room, often an animal shed or a neighbor's house. The symbolic onset of female sexuality threatens her male relatives, who must avoid the sight of her. Even the sun, as the male principle, is supposed to be hidden from the girl. At the end of the allotted period she's blindfolded, ritually bathed, then brought outside for a ceremonial viewing of the sun.

The *ihi*, a mock marriage for young Newar girls, is a far more positive affirmation of femininity. Groups of girls decked out in sumptuous finery gather at a local temple, where a priest weds them to the god Narayan (a form of Vishnu), who is represented by a decorated fruit of the *bel* tree. The *ihi* ceremony can last several days and involve several dozen girls; because of the great expense it's often performed in groups. The ritual is a precaution against the social ostracism of widowhood. Even if the girl's mortal husband dies, this first marriage to the god will guarantee her status as a married woman.

Marriage

Marriage is often the greatest event in a Nepali's life, and it's celebrated with all due pomp and splendor. Poor families may go into a lifetime of debt to give their children an appropriately lavish send-off; everyone bemoans the high cost of weddings, but few do anything to limit it. A full-scale wedding involves several days of ceremonies, gift exchanging, feasting, and rituals and entails a considerable expense for both families. The bride's side must provide a dowry and feast the groom's relatives; the groom's family offers gold jewelry, the red wedding sari, and another feast.

The marriage age is slowly increasing: while the mothers of today's brides were usually wed at 14, their modern daughters wait until 17 or 18, though plenty of more youthful marriages still occur. Child marriages were banned in 1963 but still take place with children as young as six. According to orthodox Hindu beliefs, a father should arrange an early marriage; an eight-year-old girl is the ideal candidate for the "virgin gift" of a bride.

Arranged marriages remain the norm among Hindu caste groups, though love matches are on the rise in urban areas. Modern romantic ideas conveyed in movies, pop music, and magazines have a lot to do with this trend. Strangely (or perhaps predictably), many of these couples become unhappy within a few years. A traditional marriage is an economic and social partnership rather than a romantic affair, rooted in the shared goals of earning a living and raising a family. The bride and groom may only meet once before the wedding; love is obviously not a consideration, though couples will hopefully learn to care for each other. What counts in choosing a mate is social and financial standing and, to a lesser extent, character. Among ethnic groups it's more common to let the couple arrange the match themselves.

Weddings

In this family-oriented society, marriage is as much a union between families as individuals. Parents will search for a likely partner within their caste and social group. Arrangements are often made through a matchmaker hired by the bride's family. The next step is a visit to the astrologer, who determines the couple's compatibility and if all is well sets an auspicious wedding date. The month of Magh (usually January) is wedding season, and on certain lucky dates the streets are clogged by blaring brass wedding bands, followed by a procession of friends and relatives.

Rural weddings are less elaborate. The bride is borne in a palanquin to her husband's home, accompanied by family and friends. Weddings among Bhotia people are accompanied by dancing, drinking, and feasting. Among the Sherpas, matchmaking is a protracted affair. Frequently several years pass between betrothal and the actual wedding ceremony; in the interim, the couple lives together and often produces their first child.

Family Relations

Until polygamy was outlawed in the 1950s under the influence of Western morals, men who could afford to often had two or three wives. The practice continues today, especially in rural areas where such laws are rarely enforced. (Several members of Parliament have more than one wife.) Multiple wives are a sign of status and improve the odds of having sons, but bickering among co-wives often makes family life miserable, and there are often tensions between wives and children not their own.

Another fraught relationship is that between mother-in-law and daughter-in-law. The new bride is expected to serve her husband and his parents with unquestioning devotion, performing daily chores like plastering the kitchen with fresh mud, cutting grass and fetching water, and massaging her mother-in-law's and husband's feet. Her status improves over the years as she bears children, especially sons, in which case she can look forward to becoming a mother-in-law herself.

A high-caste Hindu wife is expected to treat her husband with the utmost respect. Before each meal, an orthodox woman is to wash her husband's feet and splash a little of the water into her mouth. A wife may eat only after her husband has finished, and then consumes whatever food he's left on his plate. Since the feet (the lowest part of the body) and leftover food are both *jutho*, ritually impure, these actions forcefully symbolize the complete obedience expected from a wife toward the man who, as a famous Nepali poet phrased it, is "the lord of her breath." Widowhood is a tragedy for a high-caste woman, who loses all social definition when her husband dies. Until the custom of sati was banned in the 1920s, Hindu widows were encouraged to join their husbands on the funeral pyre, a tradition imported from India in Licchavi times. Death by sati was said to earn a widow a happy rebirth, and provided an honorable escape from the ostracism of widowhood. It was especially popular among the royal and noble Nepali families. King Yoganendra Malla was joined on his funeral pyre by 33 wives, and several immolated themselves with Jung Bahadur Rana, even though he tried to ban the custom after his return from England.

Bhotia women on the other hand enjoy a remarkably independent life and equal status. Occasionally a woman may marry more than one man, a custom which originated with the long trading trips that keep men away from home for six months to a year at a time. To remedy this a woman might marry two or three brothers, who would share work, wife, and children, keeping out of one another's way with frequent travel. An added benefit of the custom is that it reduces property divisions between sons.

Old Age

On paper a Nepali's average life expectancy is among the lowest in the world: 55 years for men, 52 for women. In fact, though, if a child

NEPALI WOMEN, NEPALI MEN

It begins at birth, with the deep-rooted preference for sons that is common across Asia. A daughter is often a negative or at best neutral addition to the family, but a son is a must, since he preserves the patrilineal name and performs the essential death rituals that will allow his parents to enter the ancestral heavens. Life without a male heir is hard to accept, and couples may have seven or eight daughters in attempting to conceive a son.

Growing up, baby boys benefit at the cost of their sisters. Boys receive more and better food, are breastfed longer and weaned later, and receive more frequent and better medical attention. An ill daughter may be taken to a local healer; an ill son is more likely to be taken to a hospital or medical clinic. The results of such treatment appear graphically, in the abnormally high female mortality rates occurring in every age after the first year. Under normal conditions, males die at a higher rate than females: Nepal is one of two countries in the world where men outlive women. Part of this stems from the tremendously high maternal mortality rates and too much childbearing. The average woman bears six children, of whom at least one dies. A rural woman's endless round of hard work and poor nutrition exerts still more pressure. She often waits for her husband to finish eating before she begins her meal; in food-scarce areas this means she seldom gets her fill.

Through childhood, boys are given fewer tasks and are far more likely to go to school. Girls may attend for a few years but often are pulled out to help their mothers with the continuous round of chores. A married woman belongs to her husband's family; thus the frequently heard comment, "Why should we educate our daughter? She'll only grow up to belong to another." The national female literacy rate is 25%, less than half the rate for men.

Coming-of-age rituals for the different sexes demonstrate the disparity. Brahman boys receive the sacred thread in a proud public ceremony involving feasting and celebration. A girl reaching menarche undergoes the complete antithesis in the ritual of "sitting in a cave," isolated in a dark room for a period of one to three weeks. This vividly underscores the danger of female sexuality and introduces issues of ritual pollution and untouchability which will follow a woman the rest of her reproductive life. In orthodox Hindu families, menstruating women sleep outside, usually in the cattleshed. As small compensation for this indignity—though because they are considered ritually impure—they are not permitted to cook, giving them a break from one aspect of their chores.

Some 40% of Nepali girls still marry before the age of 16 and begin a round of childbearing far too early for their still-growing bodies. Kinship roles determine a woman's life: her place lies squarely

survives the most dangerous first five years, there's a good chance he or she will reach a respectable old age (70-80 years), which is venerated in Nepal's tradition-based society.

The Newars celebrate a reenactment of the infant's *pashni* when a man reaches the auspicious age of 77 years, seven months, and seven days. The celebrant is carried through the streets in a palanquin by his relatives during a day filled with ceremonies and offerings. From then on he is considered to have reached the first stage of divinity, and his blessing and curse take on special significance. A second ceremony is held at the "thousand-full-moon" date of 83 years, four months, and four days, and very rarely, a third celebration called "going to heaven" at the attainment of 99 years, nine months, and nine days, which earns a man semi-divine status.

Death

Death is interwoven with life in Nepal, where people die at younger ages than in the West, and usually at home. Funeral rites are handled by the family rather than undertakers, bringing home the inevitability and solemnity of death.

Death from old age or sickness is viewed as inevitable, but an untimely death is often blamed on malignant spirits or witches. A dying person may be carried to a riverbank to die with his feet in the sacred water; if this isn't possible, a continuous stream of water is poured over the feet to prevent the soul from escaping into a lower rebirth. After death, the body is wrapped in white, the color of mourning, and carried to the riverside cremation ghat on a bamboo bier. While male relatives undergo ritual purification, the body is burned. The ashes are distributed among various pilgrimage sites in the Kath-

within the family, at home, symbolized by the ritual sip of the water she uses to bathe her husband's feet, a ceremony still performed on occasion. A woman's most powerful role is as mother of a son and, later, as mother-in-law. Then she may freely dominate her son's new bride as she herself was mistreated years ago.

Contrary to the cherished popular belief of the male as provider, studies have shown that Nepali men work less, contribute less to household income, and make fewer decisions on the running of the household. This will come as no surprise to any observer of the Nepali countryside, where women haul water or bundles of fodder and fuel, tend children, weed fields, wash clothes, grind corn, and winnow grain. Rural men, meanwhile, drink tea and argue politics, activities they would no doubt define as "work" to a survey-taker.

Men *do* work hard at certain times, ploughing in the spring and harvesting in the fall, but they have the leisure to pass the time gossiping in teashops about agriculture, politics, and what should be done. Women, meantime, are busy *doing* it, spending nearly all their time in or around their homes and fields, their social life limited to a brief chat at the water tap or the rare festival. The workload for a highland woman averages more than 11 hours, compared to eight and a half hours for the average man.

Not surprisingly, discrimination is embedded in Nepali law. A son has an immediate right to inherit property from his father, but land cannot be bequeathed to a daughter unless she is unmarried and at least 35 years old; if she marries later, her share reverts to brothers. A wife's adultery is automatic grounds for divorce, but not the reverse. A man may legally take a second wife if no children exist after 10 years of marriage, regardless of where the infertility lies.

The grim picture painted above focuses on mainstream Brahman-Chhetri culture and is mitigated to some extent in the more Buddhist-influenced societies of ethnic Hill dwellers and the Bhotia. In the latter especially, women enjoy a great deal of independence and respect. And even the most orthodox Hindu women in Nepal enjoy more freedom (though also more work) than women in India, Bangladesh, and Pakistan.

Fundamental social changes need to occur in Nepal, beginning with boosting the perception of the value of women's contributions to the household economy and daily life. As in most traditional societies women create the backbone of the economy; as in most this goes largely unacknowledged. While men have a certain amount of freedom to grow, develop, and fulfill their aspirations, women remain locked into a role of unending service and support. Even the foreign-aid organizations racing to include women in their projects fall into the trap of viewing women purely as means to an end. Project documents often cite reasons to target women in their activities: "a woman's income goes to her family"; "a woman's education benefits her children"; and so on. Few acknowledge a woman's existence as a person in her own right.

mandu Valley or are tossed into the Bagmati to eventually flow into the holy Ganges.

Close relatives undergo a general mourning period of 13 days, followed by a year of mourning for the immediate family. The chief mourner, the deceased's eldest son, is expected to wear only white clothes for the period, which may be reduced by priests. Periodically he must perform *shraddha,* offerings for the spirit of the deceased. At the end of the year the spirit officially arrives in the spirit realm, the *pitorlok,* where it relies on continued offerings for its comfort. This dependency contributes to the value placed on sons, who are the only ones who may perform this rite.

Coexisting with the belief in ancestor spirits is the conviction that a soul can be reborn in many realms, according to the karma earned by its previous actions. Meditation and asceticism can liberate it from the cycle of birth and death; meritorious acts and devotion can send the deceased to *swarga,* the blissful heaven of the gods, but evil actions bring the tortures of a hell realm or rebirth as an animal.

LANGUAGES

Somewhere between 24 to 100 different languages and dialects are spoken in Nepal, depending on how closely you look; some of the more obscure are spoken by only a few thousand people. Many illiterate Nepalis are fluent in two, three, or even four languages—proof that language learning is not some kind of miraculous talent, but a skill born from the need to communicate.

Nepal's languages fall into two groups. A quarter of the population speaks one of the Sanskrit-related languages of the Terai like Maithili, Bhojpuri, and Avadhi, or the aboriginal Taru. The majority of languages are spoken by the many Mongoloid Hill tribes and belong to the Tibeto-Burman branch of the Sino-Tibetan family of languages. Gurung, Tamang, Magar, Sherpa, Rai, and Limbu tribes all have their own languages, frequently

subdivided into regional dialects; Rai alone appears in some 34 different varieties. Most are unwritten, though Newari has its own alphabet and a tradition of classical literature.

The native tongue of nearly half the residents of the Kathmandu Valley, Newari is a special case. Structurally related to Tibeto-Burman, it's absorbed much Nepali vocabulary but remains linguistically unique. Newari script faintly resembles the Tibetan alphabet, but since the advent of the printing press it's been replaced by Devanagari. During Rana rule from the mid-1800s, Newari literature was banned as subversive, and the literary tradition didn't resurface until 1946. Today the Newars proudly cling to their language as a symbol of cultural identity. In some parts of the Valley (the back streets of Bhaktapur, for instance) you can meet Newars who don't understand Nepali. Newari is a tonal language, not easy to learn, but even a few words will amaze and delight people in the Valley.

NEPALI

The official national language is Nepali, an Indo-Aryan tongue derived from Sanskrit. Like Sanskrit and Hindi, it's written in Devanagari script. It's related to Hindi about as closely as Italian is to Spanish. If you've picked up some Hindi in your travels through India, many of the nouns will be useful in Nepal, and vice versa. Nepali is also widely spoken in those areas east of Nepal: Sikkim, Bhutan, and the Darjeeling region of West Bengal.

Nepali originated from the language of the Khasa, a hill tribe that migrated east along the Himalaya and by the 14th century had established an empire in northwest Nepal. Khasa influence spread far beyond their small kingdom. Their language was officially used in the Newar courts of the Malla kings a century before the Gorkhalis conquered the Kathmandu Valley.

The Gorkhalis' rise to power solidified Nepali's role as the primary language. Today it's the mother tongue of half the population; another 30 or

Pratapa·Malla's multilingual inscription, Hanuman Dhoka, Kathmandu

NEPALI NUMERALS

ROMAN	ARABIC	NEPALI
0	०	शून्य
1	१	एक्
2	२	दुइ
3	३	तीन्
4	४	चार्
5	५	पाँच्
6	६	छ
7	७	सात्
8	८	आठ्
9	९	नौ
10	१०	दस्

quickly opens doors and hearts, and distinguishes you from the crowd.

It's not that you *have* to learn Nepali. Every Kathmanduite who deals with tourists knows some English, even if it's only the "You—how much!" of street hustlers. Staff in tourist hotels, shops, and restaurants are reasonably fluent; some speak Japanese, German, or French as well. Taxi and bus drivers are more problematic, but you can always find a bystander to help you out in a jam. Rudimentary English is taught in public schools, much to the exasperation of the traveler who finds himself endlessly greeted by gangs of children chanting "Hello-mister-how-are-you" and "Give-me-one-pen/rupee/chocolate."

Outside the Valley, lodge and teashop owners along the main trekking routes can always communicate with their foreign clientele, some quite fluently. But the Nepali-less trekker is isolated from just about every other person he or she passes on the trail. On less-traveled trails you'll need either an English-speaking guide or porter, or a basic knowledge of the language. The latter is really preferable regardless of where you're trekking.

Nepali is a nontonal, reasonably phonetic language and it's relatively easy to learn the rudiments. The hard parts are: a) understanding the voluble answer, and b) perfecting the language once you've gotten the basics down. Nepali is an exceptionally rich language with a tremendous variety of verb forms, nouns, and colorful expressions. Verbal commands change according to the social level of the person you address, ranging from the royal honorific form used only for talking with, or about, members of the royal family, through high honorific (very respectful), medium honorific (for social equals), low-grade honorific, and a *ta* form used for animals and inferior humans. For beginners the safest way to wade through all this is to use the medium-honorific *tapaai* form with adults, and try to pick up the less formal usage for children. (*Tapaai*-ing a small child for some reason seems extremely amusing to native speakers.)

On the tongue of a native speaker with a flair for rhythm Nepali is a bouncing, musical language full of syncopation and rhymes. There's a whole collection of delightfully silly-sounding words like *rungi-chungi* (multicolored), *bango-tingo* (crooked, winding), *wari-pari* (here and there), and *ukkus-*

40% speak it fluently as a second language. As the official language of government, schools, and mass media, Nepali has become the lingua franca of diverse ethnic groups. Increasingly, it's replacing these ethnic languages, the more obscure of which are slowly dying out.

Studying Nepali

Though most visitors get by with little more than *namaste* (thank you), the ability to speak even very basic Nepali is *the* single best way to enhance your stay. Even a basic knowledge

mukkus (full to bursting, said of your stomach after two plates of *daal bhaat*). The pages of a Nepali-English dictionary reveal concerns peculiar to the country: lists of special words for different types of jugs and baskets, and over four dozen precise kinship terms. Like the Eskimos with their 40 words for snow, Nepali has terms uniquely suited to its mountainous terrain: *lari-bari,* defined as "the game of rolling down a slope," and *tigre,* literally "thigh-y" or "with big thighs," meaning "well-built." (This one you'll understand after seeing the physique of a bare-legged porter carrying a 100-kg load.) But for things like radio, school, taxi and petrol, it's simply the English word with a slight alteration in pronunciation.

Studying Tips

Focus first on learning a handful of words and phrases you can use again and again. Start your basic vocabulary with greetings, farewells, and numbers, then add important nouns, verbs, and a few simple adjectives and adverbs—"good," "fast," "difficult," "expensive," "crazy"—that express feelings about an infinite number of situations. There's a big difference between book learning and actually being able to speak a language. The only way to acquire a language is to use it, practicing on everyone you meet. Don't be embarrassed by mistakes; they're part of the process. It may be difficult to find someone to practice Nepali on in Kathmandu, since everyone seems to be bent on practicing their English. A few weeks of serious study followed by a few weeks trekking will drum the basics into you; from there you can learn on your own.

Spoken "village" Nepali treats grammar casually, while the more sophisticated written and scholarly language employs a number of stylistic niceties and Sanskrit words. The informal, colloquial language is easier and quicker to learn and will serve you better than the *sanskriti khura* a well-meaning educated Nepali might teach, which, coming out of a foreign mouth at least, is virtually incomprehensible to a villager. Choose your Nepali teachers carefully, even if your lessons are informal. A taxi driver, a porter, or a six-year-old kid can be a far better instinctive teacher than someone who's hung up on "proper" speech. If you doubt the usefulness of what you're learning, emphasize you want to learn what people *say—chaltiko khura.*

The Devanagari alphabet with its 44 letters is easily learned, but there's little need to read or write in a country with a 40% literacy rate and no street signs. Studying Romanized Nepali saves time in the beginning; later you can add Devanagari if you like.

Teachers and Books

The **Experiment in International Living** in Naxal, tel. (1) 414-516, offers Nepali courses and can also arrange private teachers for Nepali and Tibetan. The smaller **Insight Nepal,** tel. (1) 418-964, offers training in Nepali and Newari and can also arrange homestays. **CAS Nepal,** tel. (1) 524-056, offers private and group tutorials by professional Nepali teachers. For serious students, Tribhuvan University's **School of International Languages** offers in-depth courses in Nepali, Newari, Sanskrit, and Tibetan starting in August every year. See "Work and Study Opportunities" under "Special Interests" in the On the Road chapter for more information.

Private tutoring is best if you're a quick learner because you can tailor lessons to your needs; for example, phrases relevant for trekking. Private lessons from an experienced teacher run around Rs200-250 an hour; small groups average Rs120 per person. There are a few excellent private teachers in town, and a lot of mediocre ones, so shop around. See "Work and Study Opportunities" under "Special Interests" in On the Road for suggestions.

The dozens of small do-it-yourself Nepali phrasebooks on the market are useless unless you get a native speaker to help you with pronunciation. If you're really intent on teaching yourself, pick up one of the lengthier books with a background in grammar. Chij Shrestha's *Basic Course in Spoken Nepali,* developed to train Peace Corps volunteers, is simple and popular, though it relies heavily on drilling. David Matthews's *A Course in Nepali* and T.W. Clark's *Introduction to Nepali* are both excellent; the latter is preferable as it uses Roman transliteration throughout. The definitive *A Practical Dictionary of Modern Nepali* compiled by the University of California-Berkeley is full of idiomatic sample usages of words. Handier is the *Basic Gurkhali Dictionary* compiled by M. Meerendonk, which is small enough to carry around in your pocket.

RELIGION

Religion is the wellspring of traditional Nepali life, inspiring art, defining culture, and regulating daily routine. The birth of a child and the symbolic "birth" of a house, the maintenance of a temple or a truck—all are influenced by religion. The term covers a range of interlacing magical, mystical, and spiritual beliefs. The multiple gods reflect the many facets of human nature. They dwell in temples, rocks, trees, rivers, homes, and most of all in the hearts and minds of their devotees, who worship them with a daily round of *puja* (ritual offering) and prayer.

Hindu and Buddhist beliefs are interwoven with tantric influences upon a background of ancient animistic cults; the many strands overlap and blend until it's impossible to separate them. Nepalis don't even try to: they simply live their beliefs, and their faith keeps the ancient gods alive. Religion provides people with something to fall back on, helping make sense of a hard life and serving as a sort of psychological social security system.

Nationwide, religion follows the pattern of Hindu lowlanders and Buddhist highlanders, with the people of the Hills exhibiting a mixture of both. The most intense intermingling of the two occurs in the Kathmandu Valley, where there is hardly a "pure" temple to be found. A single site may serve three or four different cults. A 7th-century Chinese observer noted wonderingly that "Buddhist convents and the temples of Hindu gods touch each other," and little has changed today. Shiva lingas and Buddhist *chaitya* stand side by side in temple courtyards, and Hindus and Buddhists worship the same image under different names. Everyone joins in the great festivals to worship the most popular deities—elephant-headed Ganesh, the bringer of luck; Nepal's patron god Pashupati (a form of Shiva); and the Valley's patron, Machhendranath.

Interwoven Faiths

This spirit of tolerance dates back to the Licchavi era, when the two faiths flourished side by side and kings sponsored both Hindu temples and Buddhist monasteries. With the advent of the Malla dynasty in the 13th century Hinduism became the dominant religion, increasing its hold over the centuries until today the population is declared as 86% Hindu and only eight percent Buddhist. Less than four percent of the population is Muslim, nearly all in the Terai. Nepal's vaunted religious tolerance doesn't extend to Christian missionaries, who are permitted to work in development but may not proselytize. Despite this ban there are some 50,000 local Christians in Nepal.

On paper, the Hindu/Buddhist ratio appears extreme, an indication of social realities. Hindus hold political and social power in Nepal's caste-dominated society, and many formerly Buddhist ethnic groups have converted to Hinduism in an effort to raise their social status. Actually these census figures slant the picture heavily in favor of the "Hindu Kingdom" version of Nepal. Religious

Pashupatinath crowded with worshippers at Shiva Ratri

women waiting in line to perform puja *at Kumbheswar Mahadev Mandir (Patan) during Janaai Purnima festival*

beliefs can seldom be neatly delineated as pure Hinduism or Buddhism: every community makes its own version, combining orthodox elements with animistic and local deities.

Buddhism developed out of the Hindu context of 6th century B.C. India, and the two systems share some fundamental premises. Both postulate multiple rebirths within samsara, the delusory aspect of earthly existence; both decree the soul's fortunes are determined by its previous actions, the law of karma; and both offer hope for escaping the endless wheel of samsara and achieving the liberation of release from ego-consciousness—the Hindu's *moksa,* the Buddhist's Nirvana. In the meantime, for the vast majority of followers not inclined to struggle, they offer multiple paths to please the gods and thus earn spiritual merit and its accompanying earthly rewards.

Buddhism and Hinduism are heavily influenced by animistic folk beliefs which preceded them, and both have incorporated esoteric practices and philosophies from tantra. Both religions are remarkably accommodating when it comes to recycling indigenous native deities into what they consider more acceptable forms. This results in a profusion of cults, deities, and celebrations.

WORSHIP

Deities are not a matter of faith but a matter of fact, living beings to be pleased or appeased by devotees. Westerners find it difficult to comprehend the bewilderingly large pantheon. Some are repelled by the vast number of idols and the sometimes grotesque rituals like blood sacrifice. Others are seduced by the exoticism of it all. Perhaps the best approach is to view the gods as manifold expressions of the depth, reach, and range of the human mind. Seen thus, they are transformed from superstition into archetypes, creative expressions of universal psychic forces—precisely their role in the highest Hindu and Buddhist teachings.

Probably 95% of the people, including monks and priests, are content to accept the gods literally, making offerings and supplications to ensure better circumstances in this life or the next. A small minority have a more esoteric vision, treating the gods as stepping-stones to an inner reality.

Like people, the gods have their own individual characters. They can be motherly or fierce, compassionate or wrathful, and they assume multiple forms to express their various moods. Nepal's huge pantheon encompasses all the possibilities of the human spirit and mirrors the Nepali delight in abundance, whether it be in art, religion, or feasting. As A.W. MacDonald writes: "A one-spirit or a one-god religion is as unthinkable in Nepal as a storyteller without listeners, a healer without clients, a priest without faithful."

Offerings

The gods live everywhere: in shrines and images, in sacred trees, rocks, rivers, and mountains, in the rafters, windows, and hearths of houses. There is even a god hidden in the household trash dump, uncovered and honored once a year. All these must be adored or propitiated according to their temperament: to ignore them risks misfortune, sickness, and death.

A Valley day begins with worship of household deities followed by a visit to neighborhood temples. Generally women take care of their family's religious obligations, making the rounds of temples with a tray of offerings and a small daughter in tow to learn the basics. The first stop is always the local Ganesh shrine, for he intercedes with other deities to grant requests. On Saturdays, holy days, and festivals, entire families head to more distant shrines for outings which take on a holiday air.

The basic rite of worship is *puja,* offerings meant to please divine senses. Devotees scatter flower blossoms, uncooked rice, and red *tika* powder on images, light oil lamps and incense, and ring temple bells to alert the gods to their presence. In larger shrines priests act as intermediaries between worshippers and the gods, tending to the most sacred icons as carefully as if they were living beings. Images like Machhendranath and the sacred linga of Pashupatinath are dressed, bathed, "fed," and entertained with music and prayer according to a daily schedule.

Devotion was more extravagant in the Malla era, when rich nobles sponsored the *kotyhoma,* the "10 million burnt oblations" of grain and ghee offered day and night for six weeks, and kings offered the *tuladana* or "scale gift" of their weight in gold and gems. The *Chronicles* record one king who ordered the Pashupatinath linga constantly bathed with a stream of "golden water" poured from two golden vessels, and another who nearly buried it with an offering of 125 million oranges.

Mela and Pilgrimage

On special full moons or astrologically auspicious days thousands of worshippers flock to a certain temple or sacred site to celebrate a *mela* in honor of the chosen deity. The sacred lake of Gosainkund, three days north of Kathmandu, is a well-known example, but nearly every region has its own particular holy place to be honored at an appropriate time. Part festival, part bazaar, and part county fair, *mela* are the scenes of

Kanphatta sadhu, *Pashupatinath*

great merriment. Vendors set up teashops and snack stands, peddlers spread out their wares, and flirting and drinking are as common as worship—by late afternoon, even more so.

Pilgrimages are a more personal occasion than *mela.* Hindus and Buddhists alike journey hundreds of miles, often on foot, to worship at an especially revered place like Muktinath in the Annapurna region. The temple of Pashupatinath draws thousands of Hindus from India for the festival of Shiva Ratri, while the nearby Boudhanath stupa is a magnet for Tibetan Buddhist pilgrims who prostrate themselves full-length around it.

Other means of worship include circumambulation (walking around a holy shrine or object), repeating mantras, and ritual bathing in holy rivers or springs. Fasting is a common means of purification, especially for women, but even more popular is the feasting *(bhoj)* that accompanies most Newar ceremonies and celebrations and is the happy outcome of a family's blood sacrifice.

JHANKRI: NEPAL'S THIRD RELIGION

To deal with the vast assortment of powerful and unfriendly spirits Nepalis turn to *jhankri,* faith healers rooted in an ancient tradition of shamanism. A *jhankri* is born, not made, selected by psychic abilities which usually manifest in adolescence, often in a dream state. He can come from any caste, ethnic group, or economic level, and his strange powers earn him prestige and respect, regardless of his social status.

A *jhankri* serves as a bridge, an intermediary between his clients and the threatening forces of the universe. Unlike priests, who deal with predictable events and rituals, *jhankri* deal with the unpredictable and often malevolent world of spirits. All sorts of ghosts and evil spirits are believed to manifest themselves in the human realm, in the form of illness, insanity, or possession.

The *jhankri* contacts the spirits by going into a trance state, usually signalled by uncontrollable trembling. In this state he can diagnose and cure illnesses or act as an oracle. The *jhankri's* healing ceremony may involve night-long drumming, animal sacrifice, or an incense *puja* to smoke out the evil lurking in a home. Some may administer herbal medicines or perform physical manipulations. Quite often their treatment is successful. Local people know them as contemporaries and trust them more readily than the often-unfriendly doctors at government health posts. The linkage between belief and healing which is just beginning to be explored in Western medicine is an important aspect of the *jhankri's* role.

During festivals like Holi and Indra Jatra, *jhankri* appear in full ceremonial regalia: pleated white skirt, rosaries of *rudraksha* seeds, strips of bells crisscrossed about the chest, and a headdress fashioned from braided strips of colored cloth. They circumambulate holy sites doing their hopping, twirling dance, beating the *dhyangro* (double-headed drum), which symbolizes their ability to cross between the spirit and human worlds. Their greatest festival is Janaai Purnima in August, when *jhankri* are believed to renew their power. Crowds of them gather at the holy lake of Gosainkunda and at the mountaintop power spot of Kalingchowk in Dolakha District; the best place to view them in the Valley is the Khumbeswar Mahadev temple in Patan.

Blood Sacrifice

Gentle offerings of flowers and milk are not enough for terrifying deities like Bhairab and Durga, who demand blood and alcohol. Animal sacrifice is against Buddhist tenets but remains popular among Nepali Hindus even though it's disappearing in India. Only male animals are sacrificed. Killing female animals is not only a sin but a violation of Nepali law. A water buffalo is the greatest offering, but also the most expensive and infrequent. Next-best is a black goat or sheep, then a duck or rooster. The various animals symbolize mental obscurations sacrificed by the donor: the buffalo stands for anger, sheep and goats for stupidity, roosters for desire.

Just before the sacrifice, water is sprinkled on the animal, and its consequent headshaking is taken as a sign of its assent. The balky beast which refuses gets a lifetime reprieve, but usually it's so thoroughly soaked it's forced to shake. A ritual butcher then severs the animal's jugular vein and sprays the blood over the image in offering. Traditionally the head goes to the butcher as his fee, though the horns of a water buffalo might be nailed up beneath the temple eaves in commemoration of the offering. The carcass is returned to the donor and provides a much-appreciated meat feast.

In the past certain bloodthirsty goddesses demanded human sacrifices, a tradition dating from Licchavi times which reportedly continued into this century in Kathmandu. The summer festival of the warrior god Kumar was marked with ritualistic rock-throwing battles between the inhabitants of upper and lower Kathmandu. The wounded were dragged off by the opposing sides and sacrificed at the shrines of two mother goddesses. An English writer in 1877 noted seeing the bodies of what he delicately termed "suicides" in front of Kathmandu's great Black Bhairav image, and references to "the supreme incense"—dried, powdered human flesh—and rumors of human sacrifices persist to this day. The most frequently mentioned site is the temple of Harisiddhi, a small Newar village a few miles south of Patan.

wards—the distinguishing mark of a *kichkinni*—he has a chance of escaping.

FOLK BELIEFS

Coexisting with the great religious traditions is a multitude of invisible natural forces more ancient than even the gods, with the power to affect human lives for good or ill. These mysterious local spirits or *deutaa* inhabit natural sites which instinct and tradition have labeled sacred. Regular offerings to them are thought to ensure good harvest, health, and fortune; if neglected they can cause disease and death. The Valley's ancient "curing god" shrines for toothache, paralysis, deafness, mental illness, and poxes are based on this belief. The *naga,* serpent guardians of water and underground wealth, can also cause sickness if their domain is trespassed upon by a misplaced building or well. And the ancient cult of the Mother Goddess lives on in the mother and grandmother goddesses, the often bloodthirsty Mai and Ajima of the Newars.

Ghosts and Spirits

Hordes of minor malevolent spirits also have the power to torment humans and must be placated. *Preta,* the restless spirits of dead ancestors, will harass their descendants unless satisfied with offerings. Iron nails driven into thresholds or iron rings worn on the fingers protect against *pisaach,* the malevolent spirits of suicides or violent deaths. To see the headless *mulkatta* with eyes on its chest is a certain omen of death. Cremation grounds are the abode of *bir masaan,* dangerous evil spirits which can strike a human dead on sight, while crossroads are haunted by *bhut,* a standard sort of ghost.

The belief in *boksi* or witches is widespread, and many villagers will accuse a disliked neighbor or relative of being a witch, though few are brave enough to say it to her face. Supposedly a *boksi* must sacrifice her husband or son to obtain her supernatural skills—the ability to transform oneself into an animal, fly in the air, or bring illness or death upon a neighbor. Then there is the *kichkinni,* the spirit of a woman who died in childbirth and reappears as a beautiful and insatiable young woman intent on seduction. Her unlucky lover withers away as she saps his vital energies. If he can overcome his passion enough to notice his girlfriend has her feet turned back-

TANTRA

The intricate tangle of religions is further complicated by the addition of tantra, a mystic school which emerged as a revolt against the orthodox caste restraints of 6th-century India. A technique or approach rather than a religion, tantra has influenced both Hindu and Buddhist art, meditation, and rituals. The term "tantra" refers to a vast compendium of esoteric texts. Literally it means "thread," referring to the belief that all things—humanity and the cosmos, the relative and the ultimate—are linked by the same vital energies. Tantra maps the psychic channels of the human body and teaches ritual and meditative techniques to effect a complete psychophysical transformation. Exceedingly powerful, it's a shortcut to enlightenment, a way to attain divinity in human form.

Tantra uses the senses to cultivate ecstasy instead of detachment. Orthodox religions shun worldly life, but the tantric attitude is a qualified and intense "yes." Because the energies it tries to harness can easily degenerate into self-indulgence, careful preparation is emphasized, and teachings are closely guarded. Old texts were recorded in a cryptic "twilight language" of veiled metaphors, and the most important teachings could only be obtained from a teacher capable of directly transmitting spiritual insight.

Despite an alluring reputation for "sex magic" nurtured by some risqué art, the sexual element in tantra is fundamentally symbolic, representing the union of opposites. Ritual tantric worship includes an elaborate assortment of techniques: mystic diagrams (yantra), magical incantations (mantra), symbolic gestures (mudra), and physical postures (asana).

Mantras are Sanskrit syllables imbued with mystic power which concentrate energy in the form of symbolic sound. Recited to invoke deities, to obtain certain effects, or as a form of prayer, mantras create a meditative state and earn spiritual merit. Best known are the Hindu *Om,* said to be the fundamental sound of the universe, and the Tibetan *Om Mani Padme Hum,* carved, painted, and muttered all over the

Buddhist Himalaya. Countless attempts have been made to explain the latter, but like all mantras it's inherently untranslatable. Literally rendered as "Hail, the Jewel in the Lotus," its meaning goes beyond words.

Yantras are to sight what mantras are to sound, visual patterns embodying the essence of reality in symbolic form. These concentrated diagrams of cosmic power are created for rituals in temporary form with colored powders; more permanent yantra are painted onto scrolls or encoded into the symbolic architecture of shrines and temples. Best known is the mandala, a particular type of yantra depicting the various realms and divinities of the multidimensional universe.

Mudras, ritual hand positions, encapsulate symbolic meaning in the form of gestures and are used along with mantras in rituals. Deities in sculptures and paintings can be identified by their characteristic mudras.

HINDUISM

Hinduism is a vast, all-encompassing set of beliefs, a social system as much as a religion, which explains its pervasive influence in Nepali society. Its roots go back nearly 4,000 years, to the meeting of India's Indus Valley civilization with Aryan invaders from the north. The first contributed beliefs in natural forces, fertility, and mother goddesses; the second introduced the caste system and the sacred book of the Vedas which forms the foundation for Hindu beliefs. The result blended elemental symbols like

MUDRAS

DHYANA MUDRA
The Mudra of Meditation.

VARADA MUDRA
The gesture of Charity or conferring boon or grace.

VAJRAHUNKARA MUDRA
The special mudra of Vajradhara and Samvara and most of the gods when holding their Saktis.

JNANA MUDRA
The gesture of teaching.

NAMASKAR MUDRA
The gesture of prayer.

TARJANI MUDRA
The gesture of threatening or warning.

VITARKA MUDRA
The gesture of argument.

BOB RACE

the linga and mother-goddesses with a concern for ordering society through caste and regulations. A sprawling combination of ethical teachings, theology, and metaphysics, Hinduism extends from concrete deities and defined regulations to some of the highest metaphysical subtleties the world has ever known.

Practices and Beliefs

Hinduism's ultimate goal is to break the endless cycle of life, death, and rebirth by achieving a state of consciousness described as *moksha,* "liberation" or "release." A whole range of techniques have been developed to this end, including yoga, devotion, visualization, and mantra. In the meantime, ritual worship and the fulfillment of social duties can improve conditions in one's present life and earn a better rebirth. Life is structured by *samskara* or "threshold crossings." These rituals mark significant events like the naming of an infant, the first feeding of rice, the first head-shaving for boys at age seven, investiture with the sacred thread (for higher castes only), marriage, death, and *shradda* rites for ancestors. A *sadhu,* or itinerant Hindu holy man, renounces these rituals along with his caste and family to lead a wandering life of asceticism, prayer, and sometimes just plain vagabonding. Ordinary people are guided through life by the proper *samskaras,* plus devout daily worship. Within the restraints of society and caste, an individual is left to find his or her own way. Priests officiate at certain rites, but ordinary *puja* is personal and much more essential.

The Hindu Trinity

Understanding Hinduism, the saying goes, is like shoveling mist. There are as many paths as there are believers, for a basic tenet is reality is too vast to restrict within a single set of beliefs. The ultimate source of creation is the formless Supreme Brahma, which manifests in infinite forms. Three main gods emerge, each representing a different aspect of life: Brahma the creator, Vishnu the preserver, Shiva the transformer and destroyer. However, Brahma has a very minor role among Nepalis, who worship all deities but will often select one as a special patron or *ishtadevata.*

Essentially there's no difference between the various forms of deities. The Hindu trinity is likened to the sun at dawn, noon, and sunset, or a man as an infant, adult, or elder man—varying in appearance, but fundamentally the same. Just as a drop of water eventually reaches the ocean, every act of worship ultimately reaches the Supreme Brahma. The gods are unimaginably diverse in terms of their manifestations, however. Each has his or her own special symbols, consort, animal mount for transport about the universe, mudras, and posture, all of which serve to identify him or her to worshippers.

Vishnu

Preserver of life, Vishnu, or Narayan, is the benevolent savior, adored in multiple forms. His 10 main incarnations (known as the Das Avatara) include tortoise, fish, boar, and dwarf, each associated with a different legend. Other forms have achieved a divinity of their own, like **Krishna,** the handsome flute-playing god of love, or **Rama,** the hero of the epic Ramayana. Even **Buddha** is considered an incarnation of Vishnu (though not in a complimentary sense: it's said that Vishnu assumed this form in order to delude demons with the "corrupt" Buddhist doctrine). Since the 13th century, Nepal's kings have proclaimed themselves to be avatars of Vishnu, a belief still maintained today. Vishnu's mount is the winged man-bird **Garuda,** a minor divinity in its own right; his consort Lakshmi is goddess of wealth and fortune. His symbols are the conch, mace, lotus, and disc.

Shiva

The origins of Shiva, "The Auspicious," go back 5,000 years to pre-Aryan India. Unlike Vishnu, the gentle preserver of the status quo, Shiva is the upsetter of the apple cart, an embodiment of tremendous energy who manifests in a thousand forms: Mahadev, the Great God; Nataraja, the cosmic Lord of the Dance; Yogeshvara, an ash-smeared, matted-haired ascetic. As the Great Lord, Mahesvara, Shiva appears as a family man with his beautiful wife **Parvati** seated upon his knee; the couple's sons, Ganesh and Karttikeya, are also divine. And as Pashupati, the benevolent "Lord of the Beasts," Shiva is the guardian and protector of all Nepal and a patron of Nepal's kings since the 7th century.

Shiva's fierce energy bursts forth as the fanged and fearsome **Bhairab,** the destroyer of ignorance and evil whose cult permeates Nepal. There are 64 different Bhairabs, each with an equally terrifying female consort. They may manifest in unworked stones, glaring masks, or gigantic reliefs. As the principle of locomotion, Bhairab's all-seeing eyes are painted on the wheels of festival chariots; his fierce visage painted on the fuselage of RNAC planes guards them from evil.

Shiva's cognizances are the trident, the double-headed shaman's drum, the *rudraksha*-seed rosary, and the water pot; his mount is the faithful bull, Nandi. His most ancient symbol is the cylindrical linga, a representation of many things, including masculine generative power.

Ganesh

Plump elephant-headed Ganesh is among Nepal's most popular gods, for as the creator and remover of obstacles and the bringer of luck, his worship must proceed any undertaking, including worship of another god. This portly deity seems jovial and benevolent but is known to be mischievous or downright malevolent if not supplicated. The unlucky days of Tuesday and Saturday are especially sacred to him, but each morning and evening his shrines are thronged with people bringing offerings: the blood sacrifices of tantric rites, and also flowers, incense, lights, and an array of food items. In his hands Ganesh holds a rosary, an axe, a radish (sometimes perceived as his broken tusk), and a dish of milky *laddu*, his favorite sweetmeat. He wears serpent necklaces and dancers' bells on his stubby legs. His mount is the long-nosed, short-legged shrew, an unlikely choice for the stout elephant.

Other Deities

Minor gods include **Bhimsen,** a hero of the Mahabharata who has become the patron of traders, and ancient Vedic deities like **Surya, Agni,** and **Indra,** lords of the sun, fire, and rain. Beneficient Hindu goddesses are worshipped for good fortune and wealth: **Parvati,** the lovely wife of Shiva; lotus-eyed **Lakshmi,** the consort of Vishnu; and **Saraswati,** goddess of music and learning. More compelling to the Nepalis are the fierce goddesses associated with the fearsome **Durga** or **Bhagwati,** the slayer of demons and defender of good. The subcontinent's greatest festival, Dasain, celebrates her

victory over a buffalo-demon with the sacrifice of thousands of water buffalo. As **Kali,** the "Dark One," she demands more sacrifical blood; as **Taleju,** the patron goddess of the Malla dynasty, she inspired many of the Valley's great temples. The human virgin Kumari is another manifestation of Durga-Taleju. The **Ashta Matrika** ("Eight Mothers") and the **Navadurga** ("Nine Durgas") are collective examples of Durga's multifaceted nature, each representing a different aspect of the Great Goddess.

BUDDHISM

The Buddha was born Siddhartha Gautama, a prince of the Sakya clan, in 543 B.C. in the present-day Nepal Terai. Raised in a life of luxury, he remained oblivious to the larger world until a series of outings brought him face to face with the realities of old age, sickness, and death. Shaken by the realization that all pleasure is impermanent, he abandoned his wealth and family and set out to find something of ultimate worth. Years of rigorous asceticism brought him no closer to his goal, until one day he sat beneath a pipal tree and vowed to remain there until he achieved ultimate understanding. He meditated throughout the night, undisturbed by the tempting and terrifying illusions that besieged him. When he arose the next morning he was a Buddha, one of the "Awakened Ones" who have transcended the dualistic nature of conceptual mind. For the remaining 45 years of his life, Sakyamuni (the name means "Sage of the Sakyas") taught the Buddhist path to liberation, the Middle Way between extremes.

Buddhism's fundamental tenants are austere in their simplicity. The "Four Noble Truths" state existence is suffering; suffering is caused by desire; ending desire will quench suffering; and this can be achieved by following the "Eightfold Path." In the centuries following his death Buddhism expanded beyond this bare-bones framework to embrace a vast quantity of gods and philosophies. The main schools were divided into three *yana* or vehicles. The orthodox **Hinayana** of southern Asia is based on the spoken word of the Buddha and aims at individual enlightenment. Northern Asia follows the **Mahayana,** the "Great Vehicle" whose goal is the eventual enlightenment of all beings. It includes esoteric doctrines and rituals and emphasizes transforming, rather than renouncing, desires.

Buddhism's final development was **Vajrayana,** the "Diamond Vehicle" which developed in eastern India and spread through the Himalaya and beyond into Tibet. In true Tantric fashion it tries to directly utilize the passions and physical energies as impetuses to spiritual liberation.

Vajrayana in particular proved accommodating to local indigenous deities, absorbing them into its vast pantheon. The Buddha himself didn't deny the existence of various gods nor forbid their worship: he merely noted it wouldn't lead to enlightenment. His original system dealt rather with a psychology, but over the centuries Buddhism has accumulated all the attributes of a religion. For most Buddhists, enlightenment remains a vague and distant goal. They're more interested in the present life, and propitiate an array of gods for plentiful crops, children, wealth, and good health.

Newar Buddhism

The Buddhism of the Kathmandu Valley is the world's last living remnant of medieval Indian Buddhism. Scholars speculate it held sway until Indian kings introduced Hinduism here in the 4th century. Since then Newar Buddhism has slowly waned; today it's in danger of vanishing altogether.

Newar Buddhism began as Mahayana, with an emphasis on monkhood, scholarship, and meditation. Monastery-temple complexes *(bahal)* in Kathmandu and especially Patan housed thousands of monks and served as centers of study and devotion for Nepalis, Tibetans, and even visiting Chinese pilgrims. Vajrayana influences entered soon after their origin in India, and by the 15th century had given Newar Buddhism its heavily ritualistic character.

In the process, celibate monks were gradually transformed into *barey,* married priests who inherited their caste position. Their clients were caste-based as well, organized around the formerly monastic *bahal,* now transformed into living quarters for families who shared common priests. The *barey* perform life-cycle rites for their flock just as do Brahman priests do for their

Newar puja *for Buddha, Jayanti, Swayambhunath*

Hindu clients. This preoccupation with caste and ritual, so atypical to Buddhism, helped to preserve the tradition, though it solidified it into a distinctly Hinduized form.

With the 14th-century destruction of the great Indian monasteries, Valley Buddhism was cut off from its main source of inspiration and guidance. Newar Buddhism entered a long and gentle decline, becoming more Hinduized with every century. Today it has become mainly ritual for ritual's sake. Few *barey* know the meaning of the prayers and mantras they intone, and worshippers, currently about one-third of all Newars, are decreasing as more convert to Hinduism every year.

Tibetan Buddhism

The Bhotia peoples of northern Nepal are essentially Tibetan Buddhists, a school of Vajrayana Buddhism which incorporates tantric influences and traces of the ancient indigenous Himalayan religion, Bön. (The latter lingers in a few remote mountain villages in Nepal.) Tibetan Buddhism ranges from simple superstitions to a highly developed understanding of the human mind. Esoteric teachings include complex visualization practices and meditation techniques. These attempt to realize the fundamental emptiness of all relative states of being, a term implying not blankness, but a lack of permanent and concrete existence, and the state of compassionate wisdom which constitutes enlightenment.

Most Buddhists live on a less exalted plane and ignore meditation in favor of folk rituals: burning juniper incense to drive away evil influences; spinning prayer wheels and circumambulating prayer walls carved with sacred mantras; sponsoring elaborate *puja* to invoke deities or exorcise evil. Tibetan Buddhists are exceptionally devout, and much time is spent in prayer and the pursuit of religious merit through prostrations, mantras, circumambulation, pilgrimage, and offerings. True to the Buddha's original teachings, Buddhists abhor blood sacrifices and offer ritual cakes *(torma),* incense, prayer flags, and butter lamps instead.

Monasteries and monks play an important role in Tibetan Buddhism. Tibetans differentiate between ordinary monks *(trapa)* and spiritual teachers (lamas). A relationship with the latter is essential to spiritual progress; such a master may be a monk or a yogi, layperson or married householder. Most revered are *tulku,* high-level lamas believed to be embodiments or emanations of enlightened principles, incarnated in human form to help sentient beings. Of the four major sects of Tibetan Buddhism, Bhotia tend to follow the older "Red Hat" divisions, the Nyingma and Kargyü, with their emphasis on ritual, devotion, and meditation practice.

Buddhas and Bodhisattvas

Mountain dwellers acknowledge legions of invisible forces inhabiting their land, but these are mere spirits, to be placated rather than worshipped. Devotion is directed to various divine beings who help humans achieve enlightenment. The historical Buddha is believed to be just one in a long succession of enlightened beings who appear in different aeons and realms. The five **Pancha Buddhas** (*Tathagata* or *Dhyani Buddha*) are often painted as guardians over the doorways to Newar houses. Each is associated with a different direction, color, mudra, and symbol, and each manifests a particular divine wisdom.

Bodhisattvas are compassionate semi-divinities who have deferred entry into Nirvana in order to help suffering beings. Most beloved among the Newars are the sword-wielding wisdom deity **Manjushri** who created the Valley, **Vajrapani,** and **Avalokitesvara** or Lokeswar. Tibetans revere the latter as well under the name of Chenrezig, the patron deity of Tibet (the Dalai Lama is considered an emanation of this bodhisattva). Another Tibetan favorite is the merciful female bodhisattva **Tara,** who appears in 21 forms, the best-known being Green and White Tara. These are based on actual historical figures, a Nepali-Chinese princess who married the king of Tibet in the 8th century and who together are said to have introduced Buddhism there.

The other side of reality is represented by the many terrific protective deities embodying the ferocious aspect of the peaceful bodhisattvas. They are activated whenever fierceness is required instead of gentleness, but essentially they serve the same compassionate purpose of protecting and spreading Buddhist teachings.

BOB RACE

CONDUCT AND CUSTOMS

Getting along in Nepal is a matter of common sense, a little courtesy and patience, and a large amount of observation. If you're unsure about where to put your plate or how to eat, take a cue from others. Nobody will mind if you make honest blunders; you're not expected to act like a native Nepali. But your dress, behavior, and manners are all nonverbal expressions of your attitude toward Nepal, and are read accordingly. Nepalis rarely show their displeasure with insensitive or impatient tourists. The tourists are gone soon enough, but they leave a chronic residue of mistrust.

Plunged into a world as different as Nepal, travelers often react by clinging to their own modes of behavior as a security blanket. Try instead to use the differences to provoke an exploration of the deeper cultural underpinnings these indicate. Some thoughts to ponder:

Who am I? Compare the Western concept of the individual self with the intense family-clan-caste network of Nepal. This ties into the issue of equality, where nobody is innately better than anyone else, versus the ingrained hierarchy of a more structured society into which one is slotted at birth. Consider the different usages of names, titles, and other signallers of status in this context.

Formality vs. informality: American social relationships tend to be superficially friendly and casual; in the East they are more structured—thus the different significance of gifts, invitations, and obligations.

Black-and-white, or gray? The Western mind functions by comparing and dichotomizing: things are either good or bad, progressive or backwards, and usually we believe we should *do* something about them to move things to the positive side of the equation. Nepali society is more attuned to and comfortable with the infinite shades of gray.

Humanity vs. Nature/Humanity and Nature: The two are distinctly separate in the West, where humans are considered unique because they possess a soul, or at least reason, whereas Nature is mechanistic and purely material. In the East, on the other hand, nature is profoundly alive; animals and even rocks can possess the vital essence which flows through all living things. The cycle of rebirth which funnels beings through the various realms only increases the sense of relatedness.

COMMUNICATION

With a 40% literacy rate, Nepal remains very much an oral culture, in which a contract is not nearly as important as a verbal agreement. People can, and do, talk all day long. They are fluent in gestures and expressions as well, and body language plays an important role in delivering messages.

Meetings and Conversations

The traditional greeting is *"Namaste"* ("Nah-mah-stey," evenly accented), accompanied by folded hands raised in front of the face. The greeting persists but the gesture is vanishing, though you'll find it used more frequently outside the Valley. Use the folded hands to indicate extra respect. *"Namaskaar"* is a more formal greeting, also used to indicate respect. A handshake is quite common among men but few Nepali women have adopted the custom. *"Namaste"* can also be used to bid goodbye.

When addressing people by name, you can add the polite suffix "-ji" as a mark of respect (Ram-ji, Sunita-ji). People whose names are unknown are often called by kinship terms: *daai* and *didi* are elder brother and elder sister; *bhaai* and *bahini,* younger brother and younger sister. Old couples are *baje* and *baji,* grandfather/grandmother. You can call shopkeepers *sahuji* (literally "wealthy one"), *sahuni* for women.

Out on the trail, the standard greeting is one of the multiple variations of *"Kahaa jaane?"* and *"Kahaa bata aaeko?"* ("Where are you going?" and "Where are you coming from?"). These are so widespread that even if you don't catch the words you can safely guess this is what people are asking, and call out the names of the towns in reply. Actually, they're not *that* interested in where you're going; it's just the standard slogan—just as we reflexively inquire, "How are you?"

The Western compulsion to end every interaction with a "thank you" has spread into Nepal. Originally there was no equivalent for the indiscriminate "thanks" used by Americans, which often doesn't convey gratitude but merely signals the end of a transaction. It's not that Nepali society is impolite—formalities are highly structured—but the word *dhanyabaad* was reserved for momentous occasions, not for a shopkeeper returning change. Under the influence of the ubiquitous "thank you," Nepalis are turning to *dhanyabaad* as an indigenous equivalent. Those accustomed to dealing with tourists may even *dhanyabaad* you first! It's usually better to skip the word altogether in minor transactions and do as local custom dictates, accepting change or your purchase with a nod of the head or an untranslatable "la."

Many people will automatically assume a couple is married; there's no need to disabuse them of this notion unless you're really uncomfortable with it. It's difficult to answer the next question—your lack of children—because birth control in Nepal is nearly synonymous with sterilization, and the concept of "waiting a while" is virtually unknown. You may want to say "soon" or "we're working on it" rather than "never"—a truly incomprehensible reply.

You may be surprised at the apparently intimate questions people will ask: "How much money do you earn?" is guaranteed to come up. Don't feel compelled to respond to a grilling session; either change the subject, laughingly joke them off, or start asking penetrating questions of your own—at which point the questioner often disappears.

Disagreements

As in most Asian countries, Nepalis seek to avoid conflict and preserve social harmony. It's not that disagreements and fights don't occur—but they conform to a set of unspoken rules which value cooperation over individualism. Aggressive self-assertion tends to makes people extremely uncomfortable, so try your best to solve disagreements by another means, preferably patient persistence, moving into calm expressions of displeasure if necessary. Too often travelers flip out under the pressures of operating in a different society—but angry outbursts are profoundly disturbing to all concerned, and ultimately make you lose face.

Body Language

In a ritual sense the feet are the lowest part of the body, so shoes are considered similarly impure—thus the necklaces of shoes garlanding disgraced politicians. City people often leave their shoes at the door before entering their home, a sensible practice given the filth on the ground. You should do the same when visiting someone's home. Leather shoes and handbags are forbidden in some temple compounds (a sign will indicate), while most Buddhist *gompa*s require you leave your shoes at the door. Try to ask before entering with shoes on, and wear

Trekkers coax a photo from curious Hill children.

slip-on shoes or plastic sandals if you're going on an extensive temple tour.

The degraded status of the lower portion of the body results in a whole set of cultural taboos. It's insulting to step over people seated on the ground; they won't want to step over you either, so move your legs out of the way. When you sit make sure your feet are not pointed at anyone, including a temple image; sit cross-legged or tuck your legs beneath you. The head is the highest part of the body, so don't pat or touch people on it, children included.

Nepalis typically bob their heads sideways to signal agreement, unsettling to Westerners who use the same gesture to signal no, but this all-purpose "okay" gesture becomes peculiarly comforting after some practice. The hand signals for come and go are also the opposite of what you would expect: "come" is made with the hand turned outward, "go" with it turned in. When a Nepali means "I," he points to his nose. Pointing with the finger is sometimes impolite; villagers will often point with their chins.

Because the left hand is used for cleaning after defecating, it's considered ritually impure; use only the right hand for eating or handing over an object. It's a sign of respect to give or receive an object with both hands. Extend your right hand out, and clasp the right forearm with the left hand as you offer or accept an object.

As in much of Asia, physical contact between the sexes is frowned upon in public. Even holding hands is an overly intimate act; public clinging is in very bad taste. But physical contact between the *same* sex is perfectly all right, and young men are often seen arms entwined. Regardless of what it may look like to uptight Westerners, it's all perfectly innocent, at least on a conscious level. Homosexuality certainly exists in Nepal, but it's not indicated by public displays.

TRAVELERS' TIPS

Hustlers

Kathmandu's street hustlers work hard selling trinkets, Tiger Balm, and drugs, and changing money. To judge by their weary-obnoxious demeanor, it appears harassing tourists isn't a very nice way to make a living. The veneer is not yet too thick, though. Do something unexpected,

like crack a joke or stop and actually talk to them, and the interaction might just progress to a human level.

Of course nobody has the time to do this with every hustler. There's a subtle art to handling them which is refined with practice. Don't lose your temper, but don't be excessively polite either. Be brief; act more interested in your companion's conversation or your destination than in the doodad being waved in your face. If they persist, say clearly and calmly that you don't want it, and repeat it several times if necessary, moving away. These guys have a sixth sense for misguided politeness. If you're really not interested they'll go to someone else, but if you falter for even a moment they'll be all over you, trying to pester you into buying something at exorbitant prices. The "antiques" they brandish are guaranteed fakes.

Begging

Begging is an ancient tradition that benefits both parties, earning merit for the giver and a living for the beggar. Hindu *sadhu* roam the streets with begging bowls, collecting handfuls of rice and a few coins. *Gainey* or wandering minstrels do the same thing, but they sing for their money. Tibetan Buddhist monks sit at the Boudhanath stupa reading scriptures, a cloth spread out in front to receive donations. These kinds of people are traditionally sponsored in modest ways by nearly everyone. So are the lepers, cripples, and blind and retarded people who can do little else but beg. Real beggars will seldom badger you for money; they sit and wait for whatever comes their way, and it's nice to drop them some extra change as you pass by.

The number of beggars is increasing as Kathmandu draws refugees from the countryside. Many are truly bad off, living outside and scrounging in the garbage; it's hard to turn away from them without giving a bit. A subcategory are the *khatey*, street kids as young as five, who have left their rural homes because of problems with relatives, utter poverty, or the desire for adventure. In the capital they may find work as teashop *kanchha* or ticket-takers on buses; more often they scavenge amid fetid garbage heaps and beg, sleeping outside on burlap sacking. The raggedy street kids of Thamel make quite a decent living; it's surprising more haven't set up there. The cleverest (and wealthiest) stand outside Nirula's ice cream parlor on Durbar Marg, pressing their noses wistfully against the glass in case you didn't quite get the point. If you're really concerned about their plight, it's better to encourage local efforts to help rather than to temporarily adopt an individual kid. Child Workers of Nepal, tel. (1) 271-658, in Tripureswar accepts volunteers and donations.

The *khatey* are not to be mistaken with the vast majority of child beggars, the well-dressed middle-class schoolchildren who shout out "one rupees" and await your response with interest. They do it out of curiosity, not need. Word has gotten out that Westerners give away "pen, rupee, chocolate, boom-boom (balloon)." Sometimes their mothers will even send them running after you, urging them to beg!

You can hardly blame them when you see the way some trekkers and tourists hand out pens, candy, or money, either out of guilt at the gap between rich and poor, or a simple desire to please. It can't be repeated enough: DON'T,

a small hustler and a tourist

DON'T, DON'T give to kids. Don't even hand over a rupee to the raggedy little girl with the big eyes to see her smile, or the "iskul pen" to the boy who earnestly tells you he needs it for school. It may sound coldhearted, but the impact extends far beyond one little incident. Gifts out of nowhere teach kids that you and people like you are irrationally generous, and pretty dumb to boot. Giving something for nothing is totally out of any social and cultural context; it doesn't make any sense.

This doesn't apply to people with whom you've established a genuine bond. The best gifts of all are personal: a half-hour spent playing with a child, teaching him or her a new game or song, helping a student with his English. There are plenty of ways to cross the language barrier without giveaways: blow soap bubbles, draw funny pictures, play the harmonica; show people pictures of your family, home, or country. Nepalis are always fascinated to see photos of your parents and siblings, and of your dog, car, and house too. Having a family makes you a three-dimensional person. A collection of postcards from your city or country makes a great picture show that can be replayed every evening in a different place. People also like to look at pictures of their own country—the photos in this book, for example.

Then there are the people, kids and adults, who come up to you on the street with flowers and *tika* powder, and after you accept it demand money, ruining what appeared to be a charming gesture. Another questionable category are the young men standing by a trail, soliciting money from trekkers for a new soccer field or library or school building. Skepticism is usually justified, even if they have a stack of receipts—and especially if their ledger book shows Rs1000 donations. Schoolmasters of certain villages have been known to hit up trekking groups as well; the donations seldom go to the schools.

Harassment

Sometimes kids don't beg; they just nag. They may call you names ("monkey" being a favorite) or even throw stones. The worst places for bands of screaming, shoutings urchins are north of Boudha, the area around Dhulikhel, and around Naudanda out of Pokhara. Harassing foreigners is a patently aggressive act which carries little of the threat of repercussion that would be involved with throwing stones at a Nepali. Consider it morally hygienic to teach these kids otherwise, perhaps by tracking down their parents and informing them of the actions of their offspring. Throwing stones or name-calling back will only escalate the battle.

Dress

The single biggest faux pas committed by budget tourists involves clothing. Nepalis are modest about dress, but they are also polite and tolerant. A tourist's casual wear will frequently violate the norm, but seldom will he, or, most often, she, realize it. A woman in running shorts and tank top who feels comfortable in Nepal is oblivious to the sidelong glances she's attracting, and fortunately can't understand what people are saying about her. It's only normal, since she is exposing more female flesh than most men have ever seen in their entire lives. After you stay in Nepal a while, you'll get the same shocked jolt when you see short shorts, tight tights, and bra-less tank tops. Even jeans and leggings are basically risque, though some avant-garde Kathmandu girls can be seen in these. The best choice remains loose trousers or a mid-calf length skirt, and tops which are neither tight nor revealing.

Rules for men are more relaxed but still exist: men shouldn't go about the city bare-chested. Only lower-class men (porters, laborers, peasants) go bare-legged in shorts or loincloths. Hairy Western legs only make things stranger.

Getting a fix on the dress code may be complicated by the mixed signals sent out by Nepali mores. Women commonly wear tight-to-bursting *choli,* breast-feed their children in public, and bathe topless at the public tap (it's okay for a woman who's had a child to expose her breasts). But legs are as modestly guarded as in Victorian England, and the lower half of the body is a highly charged erogenous zone. Nepali folk songs speak longingly of the brief glimpse of knee revealed by the *bahini* as she waded across the stream.

Many trekking lodges now have private bathing rooms and hot showers of a sort. If not, women can try bathing at the village water tap in baggy clothes or Nepali-style, with a *lungi* tied up underneath the arms. The same can be used for swimming. Men can get by with shorts for bathing and swimming. Nude bathing and sunbathing are shocking to Nepalis, but some trekkers like to do both these things along well-traveled trails (admittedly it's hard to find a secluded spot). A bathing suit is better than nothing for swimming, but out of the water it's pretty risqué. Once I saw a couple trekking through a village, she in a skimpy bikini, he in low-cut briefs. Locals were nearly speechless at the sight, the equivalent of parading naked through the streets.

Eating Etiquette

Caste restrictions affect the preparation and eating of food in orthodox Hindu homes, and in fact food and drink are among the most sensitive indicators of cross-caste relations. Because the kitchen is ritually sacred, lower-caste members are not permitted inside. Though technically Westerners are casteless, and thus *very* low in the hierarchy, ethnic people will generally treat them as equals. Brahmans and Chhetris tend to be more orthodox, and the liberals who invite you in the kitchen will often make a big deal about doing so. Generally it's best not to enter a Hindu kitchen unless invited. Let your host direct you to a seat: frequently the one near the fire is reserved for the head of the family or honored guests, and the rest are distributed according to hierarchy.

Strict Brahmans will not eat with members of lower castes, nor accept food or water from them. You probably won't encounter this unless you visit Western Nepal, which has a high population of orthodox Brahmans. If you ask for food from a Brahman house you may be served outside; likewise you may be sheltered on the porch, but not inside. Don't take it personally—they do the same to everyone else who's not high-caste.

Because cooked food is a primary vehicle for ritual contamination, don't touch any unless it's been given to you to eat. Any food or utensil that touches the lips or tongue is *jutho,* ritually impure, and may not be eaten by anyone else (exceptions are made for children and for a wife, who can finish her husband's leftovers). Food is dished out onto individual plates, avoiding the contamination that would result if people helped themselves Western-style from serving dishes. Whatever you take on your plate must be eaten by you or thrown out. Don't offer food from your plate to anyone once you start eating.

Your empty plate or glass is also contaminated and should be placed under the table or on the ground. Imitate what others do if you're unsure. The *jutho* concept also applies to things like tea glasses and water bottles. If you offer your porter a drink, he'll pour the water straight down his throat without touching the bottle to his lips, a method which takes some practice.

Nepalis traditionally eat with the right hand, but spoons are becoming increasingly common and most places should be able to come up with one at your request. If you choose Nepali style, wash your hands before and after with water provided in a jug. People usually eat quickly, the better to stuff down huge quantities. Leisurely mealtime conversation is unknown—eating time is for eating. A healthy belch at the end indicates pleasure with the meal.

The golden fish, sergyi nya, *symbolizes freedom from restraint, meaning in the fully emancipated Buddha state no obstacles to freedom are encountered.*

BOB RACE

ON THE ROAD

PLANNING YOUR TRIP

When to Go

Conventional wisdom maintains fall is the best time to visit and trek. The weather is indeed superb, but the huge jump in tourist arrivals in mid-October makes Thamel a crowded madhouse, and the main trails are packed. It makes sense to arrive a little earlier in order to see Indra Jatra, one of the Valley's finest festivals, and to set out on the trail by Dasain. Call a Nepali embassy for festival dates, which change yearly.

Crisp and clear sunny days make winter a remarkably good time to visit Nepal, especially if you're just planning on doing the Valley, Pokhara, and Chitwan, though lowland treks are possible too. February-March is a good choice: March-April is the second major trekking season, but things become increasingly dusty and hot. If you've only got summers off, don't rule out a monsoon visit (see special topic "The Monsoon"). It can be a gorgeous and blessedly uncrowded time to be in Nepal.

Where to Go

Kathmandu is the centerpiece, the starting and ending point of most trips—but it's not the only thing in Nepal. While the new town is an unpleasant morass of traffic, smog, and noise, the timeless old bazaar offers days of aimless wandering. Concentrate more on Patan and Bhaktapur to delve into the essential beauty of Newar civilization, and be sure to devote plenty of time to exploring the further reaches of the Valley, either through the large number of day-trips described here, or just by rambling about.

Further plans depend on your tastes, and your time. Nepal's limited road network means very few nontrekking tourist destinations lie outside the Valley; these are covered in the Beyond the Valley section. The most important in this category is **Pokhara,** a laid-back lakeside town of extraordinary beauty. An easy day's drive from either Pokhara or Kathmandu, the wildlife of **Chitwan National Park** in the Terai is the next most popular attraction. Lesser-known destinations include the hillside town of **Tansen,** historic little **Gorkha,** and **Lumbini,** the birthplace of the Buddha. Combine all these destinations into a single road trip of a week or more. A gentle **rafting** trip down the Trisuli is easily joined with a visit to Chitwan; a superb if more serious rafting trip would be 10 days down the Sun Kosi. For more information see special topic "River Rafting." Another option might be a **mountain-bike** tour, either solo or with a local company. For more information see special topic "Mountain Biking."

Trekking may sound intimidating, but a walk down the main trails is surprisingly easy, and you can take things at your own speed. There is nothing wrong, and many things right, with strolling a half-hour off the Pokhara-Baglung Highway to Birethanti and simply staying there, or perhaps moseying up to Ghandruk for a day. The essence of trekking is not plodding down a trail laden like a beast of burden but the opportunity to live in and walk through the countryside, which is not necessarily the high snowy mountains often imagined.

Where to trek depends largely on your time. One week allows a short circuit out of Pokhara or a visit to Helambu north of Kathmandu. In two weeks you can do Langtang, the Kali Gandaki Valley, Manang, the Annapurna Sanctuary, or a fly-in fly-out visit to Khumbu. Trekking intensifies over the course of time, so try to allot three or four weeks for a trek, which would allow you to do Solu-Khumbu, the Annapurna Circuit, or a thorough exploration of Langtang and Gosainund-Helambu. These suggestions cover only the major trails, which can easily be done by independent trekkers. You'll need at least two to four weeks to visit one of Nepal's lesser-known regions, many of which must be contracted through a registered agency. For more information see the Trekking chapter.

Enhancing Your Trip

It's one thing to get here and proceed through a planned trip; another entirely to get the most out of the experience. Most important, try to **put things in context**— a good trekking group with a smart leader can be better than going on your own. Read as much as you can about Nepal. Beforehand it may not make an impression, but once you've reached Nepal it will start to make sense, and there's plenty of time to read more here, given the lack of nightlife. Delving into the cultural background of a temple or the geological processes which formed a mountain will enhance your appreciation of the raw beauty. The more you know, the more you see; the more you see, the more you'll enjoy.

Incorporate people into your trip: strike up a conversation with shopkeepers, hire a porter to accompany you on your trek, sit in teashops and absorb the conversation even if you can't understand a word of it. People are remarkably friendly and easy to access in Nepal: conversation is still a lazy art here, a way of passing time.

Personalize your trip: put some thought into integrating Nepal with your life and tastes. Bring your family, or, if it's the only way you ever travel, go alone. Take botany or music or architecture or religion as the launching point for your own in-depth exploration of Nepal. Focus on a few aspects and explore them deeply rather than rushing about absorbing fragmented sights that become a blur in the end. Try to cultivate the attitude, "There is nowhere better than where I could be right now," and see what kind of experiences unfold.

Finally, a crude but crucial point is to at least occasionally **shut up and absorb.** Don't feel obligated to take photographs of everything; viewing places and people solely in terms of finding the perfect snapshot can be diminishing. The same goes for too much scribbling in journals: finding the right words for something may only place a barrier between it and you. Every so often, take time to appreciate what a trekking brochure calls "the great art of looking at mountains: quieting down, looking up."

ENTERTAINMENT AND EVENTS

FESTIVALS

In Kathmandu, "every other building is a temple, every other day a festival," an 18th-century Englishman observed. His intended exaggeration is close to the truth. Kathmandu's calendar includes more than 50 holidays totaling over 170 days, and that tally takes no account of lengthier celebrations lasting up to three months. The great festival season begins in August after the rice is transplanted and continues through early fall, climaxing with the harvest celebrations of Dasain and Tihar.

Festivals bring color and excitement to daily life, evoking magic out of thin air. Their power is waning as modern forms of entertaiment—films, television, and videos— infiltrate the culture. But the festival cycle remains a vital part of life for the Valley's farmers, rooted in the rhythms of planting and harvesting and the changing seasons.

Festivals mark every aspect of Nepali life, telling people when to clean their wells, watch out for ghosts, visit a certain temple, or worship a certain deity. The shared celebrations regulate obligations to the gods, the earth, and fellow humans, reaffirming social ties and tradition. Some rowdy festivals serve as social pressure valves, providing a rare opportunity to break out of traditional roles. All of them celebrate not just religion, but life itself. It really pays to track down whatever festivals coincide with your visit: colorful and authentic, they are a superb window into Nepali culture.

Calendars and Dates

The matter of New Year's Day is a typical example of the confusion created by Nepal's multicultural society. The official Nepali year begins in mid-April and is the most widely celebrated. But the Tibetan New Year occurs in February and the Newar New Year falls in November—while the Western date of January 1st is increasingly being acknowledged.

The standard Nepali calendar, based on ancient Indian astronomy, contains 12 lunar months of 28-32 days. Festivals take place according to the Nepali months, which bear only a faint correspondence to the Western solar calendar. Dasain usually occurs in October, but sometimes it starts in September, and sometimes it runs into November.

On a monthly basis, each date is ruled by a particular deity or being: Ganesh is the lord of the fourth, the *naga* the ruler of the fifth, and so on. Worship ebbs and flows with the phases of the moon. The 15 days following the full moon are the increasingly unlucky "dark half" *(badi)* of a month. The progressively more auspicious "bright half" of the waxing moon *(sudi)* begins the day after the new moon. Both new and full moon days *(aunshi* and *purnima)* are ritually important and are marked by major *puja* at important holy sites.

Eras

There are also multiple systems of reckoning years. Bikram Sambat, abbreviated B.S., is believed to have been founded by a semi-legendary king, Bikramditya, in A.D. 57. The Bikram era is the official reckoning used by the government and most Nepalis; B.S. 2052 began in April 1995. The Newars still follow the Nepal Sambat era, which reckons the year one as A.D. 879. This era is said to have commenced after a Newar Jyapu discovered a riverbank of golden sand and paid off all the debts of the Valley's people—a good enough reason to commemorate a new start. Finally there's the Tibetan system (similar to the

> *There are many, many religious festivals, something every week in honor of one god or another. There are very many gods, and they are all so easily offended that basically it is quite understandable that the Nepalese should be unwilling to insult any of them, and that they have festivals for them all.*
>
> —GIUSEPPE TUCCI,
> *JOURNEY TO MUSTANG*

Chinese), a 60-year cycle of 12 animals and five elements.

Finding Festivals

Since each calendar has its own set of festivals pegged to lunar dates, finding out what occurs when is not easy, especially for smaller local celebrations. Even the times of particular events may be set anew every year by astrologers searching the sky for auspicious conjunctions. To discover what coincides with your visit, ask hotel staff, shopkeepers, and friends. Older, more traditional Nepalis are more likely to be in tune with the festival cycle than younger ones. Descriptions and dates of upcoming festivals are published in the free monthly *Travellers' Nepal* available at the airport and hotels.

In addition to the great celebrations periodically sweeping the old cities, many lesser-known festivals *(mela)* are held at various temples and holy sites. Few tourists attend these but thousands of Nepalis do; it's well worthwhile to seek them out. Mary Anderson's *The Festivals of Nepal* (see Booklist) is a good resource for tracking down obscure festivals and appreciating major ones.

Festival Activities

Just about every festival honors some deity or another. Worshippers crowd around a shrine to perform *puja* until the god is buried beneath flowers, rice, and red powder. Women come decked in their finest clothing and jewelry, the bright hues creating an ocean of color, while rural families down from the surrounding Hills add their ethnic costumes to the scene.

Temple courtyards may be filled with long lines of seated people sharing a *bhoj* or ritual feast, served on sal-leaf plates. Less frequently, people, usually women, will fast for a specified period, a less joyful but more meritorious act. Ritual bathing in the sacred Bagmati is an important component of many festivals, even in the chilly winter months. The gods too are bathed, as in the annual cleansing of Seto Machhendranath.

Great processions or *yatra* wind through the streets of the old cities, sometimes accompanied by bands of Newar musicians or masked dancers. Images may be taken from their shrine and carried about on men's shoulders in a *khat* or palanquin. On other occasions the gods are

paraded in the gigantic wooden chariot-shrines unique to Nepal. These *rath jatra* honor gods like Machhendranath or the virgin goddess Kumari. For most of the year the chariot is stored in pieces beside the temple. A week or so before the festival, *guthi* members gather to assemble the parts and build the towering 15-meter bamboo spires decorating the Machhendranath chariots. For days or weeks the great carts are hauled down cobbled streets by devotees tugging on long ropes. Sometimes the chariot hits a downhill stretch and picks up speed, and everyone races out of the way. Usually an animal has been sacrificed in advance as appeasement, but occasionally a bystander is crushed under the great wooden wheels, a bad omen for the coming year.

Masked dancers appear at certain festivals, and ordinary people dance as well, though the role of women is always played by men—it's considered improper for Hindu women to dance in public except for the festival of Teej. And there's always music—bands of Newar musicians with drum, flute, and cymbals, gangs of singing children at Tihar, or groups of older men gathered to sing devotional *bhajan* with great gusto, accompanied by harmonium and drum.

Major Festivals

The following descriptions cover Kathmandu Valley annual festivals and the months in which they *usually* occur. Due to the vagaries of the Nepali calendar described above, these may occasionally fall in the preceding or following month, so check again when you reach Kathmandu.

Bisket Jatra (April)

The Nepali New Year is celebrated most jubilantly in Bhaktapur, where it combines with the 10-day local festival called Bisket. Images of Bhairab and the goddess Bhadrakali are enshrined in chariots and hauled about city streets, and a 25-meter-high "victory pole" is hoisted upright in an open field, then sent crashing down, driving away evil spirits and officially marking the New Year.

The following day the nearby village of Thimi celebrates **Bal Kumari Jatra** with a procession of palanquins bearing neighborhood deities. Later in the day crowds gather in nearby Bode to see the bizarre tongue-piercing ritual, in which priests pierce the tongue of a volunteer with large steel needles, an act of penitence said to earn great merit.

Seto Machhendranath Rath Jatra (April)

Machhendranath, "Lord of the Fishes," is the patron protector of the Valley, worshipped with equal fervor by Buddhists and Hindus. This four-day festival is a similar but milder version of Patan's Red Machhendranath celebration; in it, Kathmandu's White Machhendra is dragged about the old city in a massive chariot.

Buddha Jayanti (May)

The full moon of Baisakh is Buddha Jayanti, the auspicious triple anniversary of Buddha's birth, enlightenment, and death. Neighborhoods are decorated with paper flags, stupas are newly whitewashed, and temples get a thorough polishing and cleaning. From early morning on, Newars flock to the Swayambunath for puja. In the afternoon, crowds gather at Boudhanath to see an image of Buddha paraded atop an elephant.

Raato Machhendranath Rath Jatra (May-June)

Patan's beloved Red Machhendranath, the patron of Newar farmers and the bringer of rain, is feted with a chariot procession lasting up to three months. The deity is pulled about town to bless each neighborhood, and local people crowd into his nightly resting place with offerings, while bands of Newar musicians tootle out hymns of praise with horns, drums, and cymbals. The festival culminates with the **Bhoto Jatra,** the showing of Machhendra's tiny sacred vest to a huge crowd assembled at Jawalakhel.

Nag Panchami (July-August)

This minor festival honors the *naga,* the semi-divine snake-beings who protect water and underground wealth and who are believed to cause illness if not propitiated. Protective pictures are plastered up near doorways, and people make offerings to them.

Gunla (August)

This holy month is a time for devotion among Newar Buddhists, marking the traditional rainy season retreat founded by Buddha 2,500 years ago. Processions of worshippers make their way to Swayambunath every morning before dawn for special *puja.* A week before the full moon is Patan's **Pancha Dana,** when housewives make ritual gifts to Buddhist priests. A few days later, Buddhist *bahal* in Kathmandu and Patan display their normally hidden wealth of ancient statues, paintings, and manuscripts. Two days after full moon Patan has its **Mata Ya,** a day-long procession visiting every one of the city's hundreds of Buddhist holy places.

Janaai Purnima (August)

On the full moon of Shravan, high-caste Hindu men change their *janaai* or sacred thread; everyone else receives a protection cord from Brahman priests—a sacred yellow thread tied about the wrist. Festivities center on Patan's Kumbeshwar Mahadev temple, where thousands gather to worship the sacred linga ceremonially placed in the middle of the temple's sacred pond. Boys splash and frolic in the water, said to be connected by subterranean channel to the sacred lake of Gosainkund in the mountains north of the Valley. Hardier pilgrims trek there to join a *mela* in honor of Shiva. Janaai Purnima is also an important time for *jhankri,* who congregate at holy sites to make sacrifices and *puja.* The mountaintop temple of Kalinchowk Bhagwati in Dolakha district hosts a virtual *jhankri* convention.

Gai Jatra (August)

The "Cow Festival" is Nepal's equivalent of the Halloween masquerade, right down to its associations with death. Recently bereaved families honor their deceased by sending a cow out on parade—either a real one, elaborately adorned, or a cow effigy borne on a *khat,* or a small boy dressed as a cow. Groups of these bovine fantasies parade through the streets, accompanied by wild bands of costumed men, some dressed in drag and camping it up in rouge and saris. Bhaktapur's Gai Jatra is the most abandoned, with liberal doses of homemade alcohol and great processions following behind blaring brass bands. Political lampoons, mockery, and satire are permitted the entire week, appearing in skits and parades around Kathmandu's Durbar Square.

Krishna Astami (August)

The birth of the seductive Lord Krishna, youthful god of love, is celebrated with processions and displays of pictures narrating the events of his life. At night women gather at Patan's exquisite Krishna Mandir to chant prayers, sing hymns, and light flickering oil lamps, while at other places throughout the cities, men sing *bhajan* in praise of Krishna, worshipped as one of the many incarnations of Vishnu.

Teej-Rishi Panchami (September)

Exclusively women's celebrations, these two festivals are gay and colorful despite the solemn overtones of fasting and purification. Teej begins with a late-night communal feast as the women of a household gorge themselves in preparation for the next day's strict fast.

The fast replicates the 3,600 years of austerities the goddess Parvati performed to attract her husband Shiva, and is intended to ensure their husbands' long life. In the morning, women gather at Pashupatinath for a ritual bath in the sacred Bagmati. Then, adorned in their finest red wedding saris and gold jewelry, they dance and sing all afternoon in praise of Shiva—a mass display of flirtatiousness and female sexuality that would be unthinkable for high-caste Hindu women any other day of the year. True to Nepali propriety, men are not usually allowed onto temple grounds for the occasion. Two days later, on **Rishi Panchami,** women gather at Teku for another ritual bath and *puja,* this one meant to purify them from the sin of accidentally touching a man during menstruation.

> *It is the loveliest sight to see the groups of women sitting on the steps in a blaze of colours and flashing ornaments which turn the Kathmandu square into a superb theatrical scene under the shadow of the temples which send their darts of gold into the sky.*
>
> —GIUSEPPE TUCCI,
> *JOURNEY TO MUSTANG*

Indra Jatra (September)

The quintessential Nepali festival, Indra Jatra marks the end of the monsoon and the beginning of harvest. For eight days Kathmandu reconnects with its medieval past, with nightly performances of masked dances, *bhajan,* and costumed dramas. Ancient images of the god Bhairab, including the gigantic painted masks of Seto Bhairab at Hanuman Dhoka and Akash Bhairab in Indra Chowk, are on display for this single week.

The third day marks the beginning of **Kumari Jatra,** a festival within a festival. Thousands of brightly dressed Hill women crowd onto on the steps of Durbar Square's pagodas to view the arrival of the king and the appearance of the virgin goddess Kumari, who is carried to her gilded chariot, attended by two young boys embodying the gods Bhairab and Ganesh. For the next three evenings the three chariots are pulled about the old city. Upon their return a rowdy crowd gathers in front of the mask of Seto Bhairab at Hanuman Dhoka, and young men vie for a mouthful of the rice beer flowing from a pipe jammed between Bhairab's snarling teeth. On the final night, the King of Nepal receives *tika* from the Kumari, reaffirming his right to rule for another year.

Dasain (October)

This 10-day celebration is the year's greatest festival, a time for gifts, feasting, and family reunions. Because Dasain focuses on home and family, it presents relatively few spectacles for the visitor. Symbolically, it's both a harvest festival of thanksgiving and a bloody sacrificial reenergizing of natural powers, symbolized by the victory of the great goddess Durga over the buffalo-headed demon Mahisasura.

The weeks before Dasain are busy with preparations. Houses are scrubbed clean and replastered with mud; every family member gets a new set of clothes; special food and drink are prepared; and everyone tries to return to their family home for at least a few days. Business slows as employees take leave, and all offices are closed on the final three days.

Each of Dasain's **Navaratri** ("Nine Nights") are dedicated to a different form of the mother-goddess. On the first day, altars are established in every home and grain seeds are placed in a darkened vessel to sprout. Temples are crowded with worshippers, especially at dawn

(top) Women dressed in red crowd Pashupatinath at Teej. (Christopher Gamm)
(bottom) Bhairab's chariot smashes into a building during Bisket Jatra, Bhaktapur. (Kerry Moran)

(top left) metal statue of the Buddhist deity Vajrasattva (Kerry Moran);
(top right) seated Buddha at Swayambhunath (Kerry Moran);
(bottom) prayer wheels at Sitala Mandir, Swayambhunath (Kerry Moran)

and dusk; in the evenings, masked dance troupes perform in the Valley's three cities. On the seventh day, fruit and flowers brought from the royal family's ancestral home of Gorkha are presented to the king with a procession through city streets.

The eighth evening is **Kalratri,** "Black Night," when the great blood sacrifices commence. Every family who can afford it will offer an animal to Durga, preferably a black male goat. The offering is then transformed into a feast; for many families Dasain is one of the few occasions they get to eat meat. The sacrifices include hundreds of water buffalo slaughtered by priests in Taleju temples throughout the night, and continued by the army in the Kot courtyard behind the Hanuman Dhoka police station the morning of the ninth day. (Tibetan Buddhists, who abhor animal sacrifices, meanwhile hold special *puja* for the sacrificial victims at Boudha and Swayambu.) Sacrifices on the ninth day honor the tools of various trades. The god Bhairab is placated with blood sacrifices to protect motorcycles, taxis, even RNAC jets from accidents in the coming year.

The climax is the 10th "Day of Victory," **Vijaya Dasain,** when Durga's household shrine is opened and the sprouted grain distributed as a symbol of the goddess's blessings, along with thick, sticky *tika* made of yoghurt, uncooked rice, and red powder. Families dressed in their best clothes visit older relatives to receive their blessings, and long lines queue at the royal palace to receive *tika* from the king and queen of Nepal.

Tihar (November)

Falling two weeks after Dasain, Tihar, the Festival of Lights, is among the Valley's most beautiful celebrations, involving five days of rituals honoring Yama, the Lord of Death. The first two days honor Yama's messengers, the crow and the dog. On the third day, **Lakshmi Puja,** sacred cows are garlanded, *tika*-ed, and fed, and houses are scrubbed from top to bottom. At dusk, hundreds of tiny oil lamps are placed in doors and windows to welcome Lakshmi, the goddess of wealth and good fortune, who, drawn by the purity and light, is said to visit homes and bestow prosperity for the coming year. The pleasure of this event has been spoiled in recent years by the barrage of firecrackers which makes even walking down the street hazardous.

Lakshmi Puja is a Brahman tradition. Tihar's older roots remain in the *bhaileni/deusi rey* tradition, in which groups of young girls go door to door singing and begging for coins and sweets. On the next day (which also happens to be Newar New Year), bands of young men visit houses with rowdier improvisations. The final day is **Bhaai Tika,** when sisters perform *puja* for their brothers' long lives. Even married women return to their parents' homes for this important ritual. Brothers reciprocate with *tika* and a gift of money, and the day ends with feasting, gambling (normally illegal, but permitted during the holiday season), and playing on great bamboo swings.

Bala Chaturdasi (December)

Tamangs congregate at Pashupatinath the evening before this festival to keep an all-night vigil with bonfires and songs. Starting at dawn, they make the rounds of the temple precincts, scattering offerings of seven grains on footpaths and linga to earn merit for their deceased relatives.

Seto Machhendranath Snan (January)

Kathmandu's White Machhendranath gets a ceremonial bath in milk, oil, and water. The Kumari visits his shrine of Jana Bahal the first day of the festival. After bathing, the idol is repainted, redressed, and returned to the shrine to receive various offerings.

Basanta Panchami (February)

The first day of spring is still cold, but it's an auspicious occasion for weddings and initiation ceremonies for children (visit a Vishnu temple to view the elaborate *ihi* ceremony for little girls). The new season is welcomed in a Durbar Square ceremony attended by the king. Meanwhile, at Swayambhunath, students, teachers, artists, and musicians flock to the Saraswati stupa behind the main hillock to honor the goddess of learning whose festival this also is.

Shiva Ratri (February)

"The Night of Shiva" draws thousands of Indian pilgrims to Pashupatinath, one of the subcontinent's four great Shiva shrines. Temple grounds are transformed into a fairground with vendors, teastalls, beggars, and pilgrims huddled around campfires. A side attraction are the hundreds of Indian and Nepali *sadhu,* bearded, long-haired wandering Hindu ascetics. Some perform incredible physical austerities; others smoke quantities of ganja in imitation of Shiva, who is known to favor it. All during the day thousands visit to ritually bathe in the Bagmati and worship the temple's sacred linga; less devout young men indulge in *bhang* and ganja and by late afternoon are stumbling home red-eyed.

Losar (February)

Tibetan New Year is a time for prayer, feasting, and visits; like Dasain it's a family-oriented event. The preceding week is marked by intense rituals and *puja* in Buddhist monasteries. Public activities climax on the morning of the fourth day as hundreds of Tibetans dressed in their finest clothes arrive at Boudhanath Stupa to offer incense, string up prayer flags, and make prayers. At the right auspicious moment everyone grabs a handful of *tsampa* (barley flour), and on the count of three, tosses it into the air in a jubilant blessing. A *tsampa*-throwing free-for-all ensues, along with singing and long, shuffling Tibetan line dances. Then everyone disperses to visit

friends, relatives, and Boudha's *chang* shops for an afternoon of celebration and feasting.

Holi (March)

Spring is welcomed with Holi's riotous throwing of water and colored powder. In the past, Holi was a bacchanalian orgy; its licentious displays were toned down after Prime Minister Jung Bahadur Rana returned from Victorian England, but a distinctly sexual atmosphere still infuses the day. Roving bands of young men and boys patrol the streets, dousing passersby and vehicles with water balloons and fistfuls of brightly colored powder. Women sheltered on rooftops retaliate by dumping buckets of water. Nobody is safe, but women are favorite targets, especially young Western ones. Don't go out on Holi unless you're in the mood to "play colors," *rung khelne,* and be sure to wear old clothes.

Ghode Jatra (April)

The main event is horse racing on the Tundikhel; the drumming of hooves is said to keep down the demon Tundi for another year. Ghode Jatra coincides with the lesser-known festival of Pisaach Chautardasi, when masked dance troupes perform in the old city.

MUSIC AND DANCE

Nepali music and dance are deeply influenced by religion. They are also folk arts, pure expressions of the exuberance that infuses festivals. Festivals, especially the autumn celebrations, are the best times to witness uninhibited singing and dancing in a variety of forms. Nepal's ethnic diversity has generated a rich store of traditional songs and dances, but many of these are vanishing as ethnic languages are replaced by Nepali, and as Radio Nepal and Hindi films permeate the culture.

MUSIC

Nepal's rich musical tradition is rooted in its oral history. In the past, folk history was related in musical form—epics like the Ramayana and the Mahabharata, which could take weeks to

recite; religious tales of the exploits of Radha and Krishna; historical tales and contemporary events as well. Increasingly this tradition is being superseded by the raucous soundtracks from Indian films—screeching ballads with a pulsing backbeat that have little to do with local cultures. Kathmandu youths are turning to Western rock; the raunchier the better, and the plaintive wails of guitar solos drift over suburban neighborhoods at night. Nighttime performances of classical Indian music, both *raga* and the *git gazaal* based on Urdu poetry, are popular in Kathmandu restaurants.

Newar Music

On auspicious evenings the men of a Newar neighborhood gather at a temple's porch like resthouse to spend the night singing devotional hymns or *bhajan*. Eyes half-closed in concentration, voices rising in emotion, they sing on and on, accompanied by harmonium and cymbals and propelled by the subtle beat of the hand drum *(tabla).* Walk around the old bazaar area after dark and listen for the music. During festivals like Krishna Jayanti or the Machhendranath processions, the singing can continue all night long. The festival of Indra Jatra sees nightly performances of the Valley's best *bhajan* groups at Indra Chowk.

Bhaktapur's musical traditions are especially rich. The town has 200 or so musical groups, each with its own rituals and purposes. Most are *dhimey guthi,* percussion ensembles based around the cylindrical *dhimey* drum peculiar to Jyapu peasants and fashioned from a hollowed-out tree trunk. One of the oldest Newar instruments, it's played with cymbals during festival celebrations and religious processions.

All Newar music is linked to Nasa Dyo, the Newar god of music and dance. *Puja* to him precedes all *bhajan* and performances; often blood sacrifices are performed, and the drums, as cult objects and embodiments of the god, receive an offering of blood as well.

Folk Music

Every community has its songs, some only for certain seasons or festivals. Soldiers, Sherpas, and porters all turn to song and dance for evening entertainment. Everyone gathers in a circle by the fire; a drum *(madal)* is first idly tapped, then pounded into a hypnotic rhythm, and a sweet-voiced singer strikes up a favorite tune. Usually everyone knows it and will join in the repetitive chorus before the singer launches into yet another stanza. Sometimes an improvisation contest evolves between two singers, each tossing out increasingly risqué verses until one or the other is left speechless, to the amused derision of the listeners.

A similar singing contest *(dohari git)* sometimes determined marriages. Male and female opponents would match themselves in front of a crowd at festivals or *mela,* improvising question-and-answer verses set to a standard tune. The musical repartee might go on for hours until a contestant faltered. If the rivals were an unmarried boy and girl, the boy could claim the right to marry his opponent if he won.

Gainey

Gainey (GAI-ni) are a dwindling caste of wandering minstrels who claim descent from the celestial musicians of Hindu mythology, the *gandharva.* In pre-radio days *gainey* entertained villagers with their topical ballads accompanied by their *sarangi,* a small, violinlike instrument played with a bow. They have been called "living newspapers" for their delivery of political commentary, narrative, and news reports; in pre-radio days they were an important channel of communication. Musically their songs are repetitious, lengthy, and not very inspiring, accompanied by the drone of the *sarangi,* which is alternately plucked and bowed.

The *gainey* repertoire includes love songs and the laments of poor farmers, overworked new wives, and young widows—all the bittersweet happiness-sadness *(sukkha-dukkha)* of Nepali life. Ballads recount famous tales, like the great fire at Singha Durbar or Tenzin Norgay's conquest of Everest, with Sir Edmund Hillary being dragged to the top by the valiant Sherpa. *Gainey* provide political and sociological commentary as well. A song might detail the procedure of a coming election or criticize quarrelling political parties; development projects have also sponsored *gainey* contests to come up with a catchy family-planning song.

Gainey wander from place to place with their *sarangi* and cookpot, rewarded for their songs with a handful of uncooked rice or a few coins. Around Dasain is a common time to see them. A few still roam the suburbs of Kathmandu, and the Pokhara Valley is one of their strongholds. Some imitation *gainey* patrol Thamel, sawing out in-

Newar musicians

terminable verses of "Frere Jacques" until you're driven to pay them to stop. Others are proud of the tradition they represent and are pleased to deliver a traditional ballad for a few rupees.

DANCE

Prettied-up versions of all the following are put on in the "folk dance shows" at major tourist hotels in Kathmandu and Pokhara, but for the real thing, seek out festivals and authentic performances.

Festival Dancers

Spectacularly costumed masked dancers embodying Hindu deities perform at certain festivals, reenacting old myths with their gestures and steps. The old Newar festival of Pisaach Chautardasi features performances by entranced masked dancers believed to embody the Ashta Matrika or eight mother-goddesses, culminating with performers drinking the blood of sacrificed animals.

During Kathmandu's great Indra Jatra festival in September, eight nights of dances return the city to its medieval past. Wild-eyed, red-masked *lakhey* dancers roam the darkened streets in torchlit processions, jingling bells strapped to their legs. Other dancers include the blue-masked, long-maned Bhairab and a two-man wickerwork elephant which careens about neighborhoods searching for its master, the kidnapped god Indra. In Kathmandu's Durbar Square groups perform dance-drama pageants enacting religious themes like the 10 avatars of Vishnu. The festival of Dasain, dedicated to the goddess Durga, features performances by the Nava Durga dance troupe in Bhaktapur (see special topic Bhaktapur's "Masked Dancers" in the Bhaktapur section of the Kathmandu Vicinity chapter) and reenactments of old pageants and plays dating back to Malla times. The Ashta Matrika dances of Patan are of a similarly old cycle.

Other festivals are marked by humorous or satirical dances, like Bhaktapur's Gai Jatra with its wild costumes, and the folk-dance performances of Indra Jatra. Dancers may rhythmically beat sticks or long poles, pantomime threshing grain or pouring water from a jug. Traditional costumes display a macabre repertoire of spirits: furry *khyah,* who resemble yetis but are actually long-tongued companions to the mother-goddesses; *kowoncha* or grinning "little skeletons"; and *betal,* minor demons. The steps, costumes, and masks have been passed down from father to son for generations. Nepali women generally don't dance in public (the only permissible occasions are a son's wedding and the Teej festival), so men or young boys impersonate female roles, sometimes with hilarious results. Gai Jatra processions include lipsticked young men dressed in their sisters' saris, tight *choli* stuffed to create a bosomy figure, mincing about pantomiming feminine gestures with great gusto.

During the harvest festival season villagers may celebrate nightly with spontaneous song and dance. Someone taps a *madal* and soon others pick up the beat, clapping and singing, while a young man moves to the center of the circle to dance, though the movements now owe more to Hindi movies than authentic folk dance.

For Bhotias, song and dance are an integral part of weddings, village festivals, and New Year celebrations. Women line up on one side, the men on the other; linking arms, they sway back and forth with a shuffling step, singing the drawn-out melodies of Tibetan folk music. Celebrations may last until dawn, fueled by plentiful cups of *chang.*

Cham Dances

Cham or Tibetan religious dance is said to have been started by Guru Rinpoche, the patron of the Nyingma sect, who once danced a blessing for Samye Monastery in Tibet. Monk-dancers impersonate the gods in these costumed pageants, bringing blessings to the watchers and the community at large. They are not possessed like the Kathmandu Valley's masked dancers, but similar to the Buddhist Vajracharyas, they strive to incorporate the gods through meditation. Though *cham* dancing is profoundly religious, it's also a festive social occasion, a chance for people to picnic in temple courtyards and meet seldom-seen friends.

Tibetan *gompa* in Boudhanath often sponsor *cham* dances before or after the Tibetan New Year (Losar); check at the *gompa* of Khyentse Rinpoche or Chokyi Nyima Rinpoche. In Solu-Khumbu, festivals like Dumje are marked with *cham* dancing. Most famous here are the Mani Rimdu dances, introduced in the 1940s from Rongbuk Monastery on the north side of Mt. Everest in Tibet. Since the destruction of Rongbuk the tradition now survives only here. Tengboche Gompa's Mani Rimdu, held during the ninth Tibetan month (usually late October) is the best-known because it coincides with the main trekking season. For an equally vivid pageant less crowded with camera-wielding trekkers, visit Thami Gompa's performance during the fourth Tibetan month (usually May) and Chiwong Gompa's Mani Rimdu, held in Solu a month after the Tengboche dance. See special topic "Tengboche's Mani Rimdu" in the Trekking chapter for more on this subject.

Buddhist Ritual Dance

The Newar Vajracharya caste has an elaborate tradition of sacred ritual dance, called *charya nritya* or *cha-chaa pyakhan* in Newari. Dating back to 7th-century India and its intensely symbolic tantric rituals, the dances are at once worship, meditation, and performance. Normally they would only be performed inside temple compounds in front of initiated male members, but in recent years the secretive tradition has been opened up to public performances by dancers concerned it might otherwise fade away. One of the few traditional public performances is held on the morning of Buddha Jayanti, when five Vajracharya men dressed as the Pancha Buddhas dance at Swayambunath.

Newar temple dance is meant to be a profoundly religious experience for both dancer and audience. A singer chants out a *sadhana,* a ritual description of a deity recorded in tantric texts. Through gesture, costume, and ornamentation, the dancer acts out the words. Feet follow the rhythm of cymbals and drums as hands trace out mudras, precise symbolic gestures. The hands' movement from right to left symbolizes the energy pervading the universe; their separation symbolizes the duality of mind and body. Each movement has a symbolic significance: the tilt of the head or the flick of a wrist serves to evoke the deity; even the eyes must be perfectly controlled. Far more than art or entertainment, temple dance is a spiritual exercise, a moving prayer. It's also considered a way for the dancer to attain higher consciousness. If the dance is precisely executed and the performer's mind is perfectly concentrated, it's said the deity arises in his heart, and the dance becomes an act of worship and meditation.

The **Kala Mandapa** troupe based at the Hotel Vajra puts on excellent public performances of classical Newar temple dance. Look for their flyers, or call the Hotel Vajra, tel. (1) 271-545, fax (1) 271-695, for the dates and times of performances, which are usually twice a week during tourist season.

ART

Over the centuries the Newar artists of the Kathmandu Valley produced a wealth of sculptures, statues, paintings, and monuments dedicated to the glory of the gods. Their exquisite creations reveal a superbly developed aesthetic sense that even today makes the Valley a treasury of art and culture. Newar art is one of flowing lines, sensuous curves, and elaborate arabesques. Intricate patterns spread over every available surface like the exuberant growth of jungle creepers.

Art, architecture, religion, and life hopelessly intertwine in Newar culture, as they do throughout Nepal. The greatest example of intermingling is the Valley's old Newar cities, where exquisite stone sculptures of deities preside over neighborhood water taps, and children fly kites from the tiered steps of temples. These shrines are the dwelling places of the gods, and the laundry drying on their steps, the goats tethered to their pillars, and the grain stored beneath their eaves don't diminish their sanctity in the least.

Every element in Nepali art is imbued with symbolic significance, down to the snake twined about a pillar or the fanciful creature carved on a stone water spout. In a traditionally pre-literate culture, the rich symbolism of religious art speaks far more powerfully than the written word. It tells a story that reaffirms tradition and religion, yet manages to remain powerful and new.

Nepali art is meant for worship. A painting or sculpture can edify, terrify, or enlighten—sometimes all at the same time. Images of the gods are physical supports for a spiritual reality, and icons are treated as living entities, intimately known and adored. It's the complete opposite of the Western concept of art as something to be admired, analyzed, and isolated in sterile museums. This difference makes the ongoing theft of Nepali art doubly tragic. Torn from their settings and encased behind glass in a temperature-controlled gallery, the images are diminished, robbed of the meaning which gives them life. The marvelous technical skill remains, but without the support of adoring eyes, the faith that impelled the artist to create cannot shine through.

Cultural Influences

Living along a major Asian trade route, Newar artists drew from a wealth of cross-cultural influences to create a style they spread far beyond their Valley. Buddhist and Hindu motifs drawn from the Indian pantheon are still rendered in faithful imitation of long-vanished styles, making Nepal an art historian's dream. Artistic elements from as early as the 7th century survive as part of a living tradition here.

Having learned from India, Nepali artists went on to make important contributions to Tibetan art. In medieval times the Valley was a thriving center for Buddhist art, and Patan's small family-run ateliers produced a flood of gilded images and ritual implements. Their fame spread across Asia, and in 1250 the great Kublai Khan summoned the young Newar artist Arniko to Beijing to supervise Chinese workers. Arniko remained in China the rest of his life, earning the titles "General Director of Bronze Workers" and "Controller of Imperial Manufacturers." Other Newar artists were called into Tibet to decorate monasteries and monuments like the great Kumbum of Gyantse, a treasury of 15th-century Newar art.

The Artist's World

Painting and metalwork are caste occupations passed on from father to son. Most artists were born into the profession, though occasionally an outsider would join as an apprentice. Artists and craftspeople were among the lower-status castes. Usually their work would be commissioned by a wealthy patron, who then donated it to a temple or monastery in the hope of gaining spiritual merit. Sometimes a small image of the donor would be incorporated into a painting, or be placed near the shrine he helped to build. A piece of art might also be commissioned to commemorate a ceremony, decorate a householder's shrine, aid a meditator in visualization practice, or help speed a dead soul to a good rebirth.

Portraits of people are rare in Nepali art; those of the gods are all-pervasive. Art was a way to transmit the invisible images of divinities to worshippers, a means of providing the god with form. The artist was only an intermediary in the process. For an artist to sign his name to his work would be an act of unprecedented egoism. Nearly all Nepal's masterpieces are by unknown craftspeople.

Working in a highly traditional and formalized context, artists strove to replicate past designs rather than create new ones. Iconographic canons dictated a deity's pose, implements, dress, and

temple doors, Changu Narayan

sculpture at Teku, Kathmandu

durable, sculptures have better survived the theft which has depleted Nepal's artistic wealth, but even they are not immune.

Images and Water Taps

Stone was the first medium Nepali artists fully mastered. From the 5th century, Licchavi-era sculptors rendered classic Hindu and Buddhist themes in powerful yet graceful images influenced by the Indian Gupta school. Favorite subjects were the 10 incarnations of Vishnu, Shiva with his lovely wife Parvati perched on his knee, voluptuous goddesses, and serene Buddhas and bodhisattvas; these last were often incorporated into *chaitya*.

Mythology blends with the mundane in the form of *makara,* stone spouts carved as fantastic water serpents with water gushing from their open mouths. The spouts are set in large square sunken water taps, called *dhunge dhara,* which serve as neighborhood bath, laundromat, water source, and social center. More stone sculptures may stand in niches, transforming the *dhara* into the artistic rivals of the temple.

Stone sculpture drifted into an artistic backwater from the 9th century on, as creativity was increasingly channeled into painting, metal, and wood. With few exceptions, later stone images are pedestrian renderings, technically precise yet stocky and unexpressive. Today, stone sculpture is nearly a lost art in Nepal, apart from a few stonecutters in Bhinche Bahal on the far eastern side of Patan and Guchha Tol in Kathmandu, who chip away at commissioned works.

hues, right down to the exact proportions, taken from the "finger-measure" *(angul)* of the artist or donor. Any deviation from this code—a green Ratnasambhava or a blue-robed Shakyamuni—would have seemed absurd. Creativity was expressed within this structured framework, in the general composition and in rendering the fine details of the faces, garments, and background designs.

STONE SCULPTURE

Stone carvers have left the Valley strewn with images of deities, carved columns and pillars, delicately engraved *chaitya,* the carved relief panels adorning temples, and sacred symbols like the Shiva linga. Many are only three or four centuries old—young in the Nepali context— and are uninspired compared with earlier masterpieces, but their abundance makes the Valley an open-air museum. In few places in the world are 5th-century sculptures left unguarded in the middle of fields or even roads. Heavy and

METALWORK

Skilled metalworkers produced cast images in gilt copper and bronze, gold and silver ornaments for gods and humans, hammered reliefs for temple facades and doorways, and finely detailed accessories like temple bells, lamps, and jars. Classic Nepali metalwork ranks among the world's finest: Patan artisans were especially renowned for the ease with which they manipulated their unyielding material into fluid images which stand as masterpieces of modeling and proportion. The finest figures are supremely graceful, with a natural elegance that combines sensuality and spirituality.

Most images were made of bronze, a high proportion of copper giving it a ruddy glow. Religious images were often made of the *ashtadhatu,* a symbolically significant alloy of eight metals including copper, tin, iron, gold, and silver. More recently metalworkers have shifted to brass, a less expensive alloy of copper and zinc.

This art form peaked in the 14th and 15th centuries in richly ornamented images with sensitive, expressive features. The introduction of Tibetan tantric deities in the 16th century gave Newar artists a new opportunity to display their skills: at the very least, the multilimbed and many-headed deities locked in embrace with their consorts offered an engineering challenge. Today a few superb metalworkers remain, and temples and monasteries, especially Tibetan Buddhist *gompa* create a limited demand for fine-quality images; but most workshops produce mundane pieces sold as tourist souvenirs.

Technique

Nepal is one of the few countries to preserve the ancient technique of *cire perdue* or "lost wax" casting. The craftsperson first forms a detailed wax model and coats it with a mixture of clay and rice husks. This plaster-encased image is left to dry for several weeks, then baked to melt the wax. Molten brass or bronze is poured into the empty clay mold and left to cool. Heating the metal to the proper temperature over a charcoal fire is a time-consuming and laborious process. Usually a core is inserted at casting time to produce a hollow image and reduce the amount of metal needed. What results is a one-of-a-kind piece, for the mold must be broken to reveal the metal image, still in a rough state.

The metal is filed, polished, and engraved with the fine details of face, garments, and ornaments. The fineness of the finish and the precision of the engraving largely determines the quality of the piece. The statue, or perhaps only its face, may be coated with a thin layer of gold and inlaid with coral, agate, or turquoise. If the image is of Buddha Shakyamuni, it will probably be given a coiffure of tightly curled blue hair, a symbol of purity. Tibetans will often take newly purchased images to a lama for a consecration ceremony in which mantras, relics, or blessed grains of barley are inserted in the hollow middle and the bottom is sealed with a copper plate.

Another ancient and nearly forgotten technique preserved in the Valley is repoussé, the art of hammering metal sheets into embossed designs. This method is used to form the lavish temple ornaments, bells, and gilded sheathing for images and temple doorways. The "Golden Temple" of Patan and Bhaktapur's Golden Gate provide magnificent examples of this art, as do the dazzling inlaid and gilded crowns of Buddhist *vajracharya,* many of which are now preserved in foreign museums. Some images, like the statues of the Malla kings in the Durbar Squares, were made by combining the two techniques, using repoussé for the larger portions and *cire perdue* for the details.

Shopping for Statues

Look for a satin-smooth and flawless finish, fine engraving, a balanced pose, and a pleasing facial expression. These criteria will rule out 95% of the pieces you see. Hands and feet are a sure giveaway: they should be well proportioned and have separated fingers and toes, but in most they're a solid lump. The back of a good piece should be as carefully finished as the front.

The best and most expensive statues are found along Durbar Marg, where they can cost anywhere from Rs25,000-50,000. Well-known Patan artist Bhim Shakya is supposed to have produced many of these pieces, but it's doubtful Bhim has had the time in this life to even touch all the statues salespeople say he has. Indigo Gallery in Naxal occasionally has good pieces. More good shops are found along Ganga Path, which links Durbar Square to New Road. The most interesting place to look is Patan—either around Durbar Square (there are some excellent shops along the street north of the square) or the old metalworking quarters of Mahabuddha and Thaina to the southeast, where craftspeople in tiny dark workshops hammer away surrounded by images in all stages of completion.

PAINTING

Painting rivals metalwork as Nepal's finest art, but many of the best examples have been taken out of the country. If you want to revel in Nepali paintings, visit the Los Angeles County Museum of Art, which has a superb collection of illuminated manuscripts, artists' sketchbooks, *thangka* and *paubha*—everything but wall frescoes, which fortunately remain in Nepal.

Nepali paintings blend a potpourri of cultural influences from India, Tibet, and China, with traces of Rajput and Moghul styles thrown in. The round-faced, supple-limbed figures are portrayed in graceful postures. Color is used for its symbolic meaning rather than shading and depth, with rich red, the color of happiness, being a favorite. Paintings are characteristically devoid of perspective, compressing everything onto one plane regardless of differences in time or space. Multiple scenes may be clustered around a main image, each illustrating a different episode of the story. Paintings are stylized and symbolic rather than realistic, befitting their function of telling a religious story or embodying a deity.

Illuminated Manuscripts

Buddhist and Hindu texts copied onto palm leaves and illustrated with miniature paintings date back at least to the 11th century and were popular throughout medieval times. Ornately carved and painted wooden book covers are works of art in themselves. Many palm-leaf manuscripts have remained intact to the present day. Paper was introduced in Nepal in the 15th century from India. The most precious volumes were hand-lettered in gold or silver ink on burnished dark-blue or black paper. Itum Bahal and Tham Bahal in Kathmandu have 500-year-old volumes in this style, displayed during the festival of Gunla.

Thangka

Most paintings were done on flat scrolls, easy to roll up and transport for use in teaching, worship, decoration, or meditation. These scroll paintings are called *thangka* in Tibetan, *paubha* in Newari. Both types were produced by Newar artists, but the two show distinct stylistic differences. Tibetan *thangka* have finer lines and brighter colors, and crowd multiple figures into a small space (modern *thangka* follow a pseudo-Tibetan style). *Paubha* used more flowing, natural lines to emphasize the sensuous grace of a single deity, usually Buddhist but sometimes Hindu. Richly detailed miniatures on the border reveal minor gods and scenes of worship or court life.

Thangka are intended as supports in which a deity might be manifest.ed. A wrathful Dharmapala "protector" might be shown surrounded by an aureole of flames, decked with a garland of skulls, an apron of human bones, and a tigerskin, and brandishing an array of choppers and blood-filled skull cups—all symbols of his intense power. Or the subject might be a serene Buddha or bodhisattva, crowned, ornamented, and dressed in royal garments, hands in the boon-bestowing mudra. The same divinity can appear in fierce or peaceful form according to the situation, or he may be seated in the middle of a geometric mandala, a formalized design that serves as a meditative device. Other subjects include high

putting in the finishing details of a thangka

lamas and lineage holders of the four main Tibetan Buddhist sects, assemblies of lineage deities, or accounts of the Buddha's life.

Painting a *Thangka*

A *thangka* begins with a white cotton cloth that is stretched onto a wooden frame, treated with gesso, then sanded until smooth. The central figures are outlined first; outer scenes are then used to fill in the composition. Before the advent of synthetic colors in the 19th century, colors were ground from minerals like azurite, malachite, lapis, and cinnabar, or were obtained from plants. The expense and trouble of obtaining natural colors means tempera colors are generally used nowadays, resulting in a glossy sheen rather than the traditional smooth matte finish. As a final step, powdered 24-karat gold may be used to highlight the fine details of ornaments and robes.

As with statues, a lama may consecrate a finished painting, perhaps by painting the mantra OM AH HUNG on the reverse side behind the foreheads, throats, and hearts of the main figures, investing them with the mystic essence of Body, Speech, and Mind. *Thangka* are traditionally bordered in Chinese brocade, two contrasting strips of red and yellow followed by a broad band of blue. The first two colors form the "rainbow" separating the sacred from the mundane. A "door" of a contrasting color is sometimes inserted in the middle of the lower section. A piece of light silk stitched to the top protects the painting from dust, sunlight, and smoke, and hides secret forms from uninitiated eyes.

Watching a *thangka* painter at work is a fascinating experience; sometimes it's possible to see one in Bhaktapur or visit a workshop. Tibetan artist Karma Thupten gives lessons in *thangka* painting and takes commissions as well. Contact him through the Hotel Vajra at tel. (1) 271-545 (his studio is nearby) or try calling him at (1) 270-899.

Buying a *Thangka*

Kathmandu is flooded with new *thangka* mostly low-quality travesties cranked out for the undiscerning tourist who is looking not for a piece of religious art but for a catchy and colorful souvenir. Imitations of old pieces are painted on crumpled canvases or smoked over wood fires in an effort to reproduce the characteristic coating of soot from monastery butter lamps. Don't be fooled. If the soot was indeed from butter lamps, the smell would impregnate the fabric; in any case the painting's style (or lack thereof) is a dead giveaway. Because unvarnished *thangka* rapidly degenerate with age, old ones are seldom in good condition; those that are sell for extremely high prices. It's highly unlikely you'll come across a genuine old *thangka* outside of Durbar Marg antique shops.

The bottom line in any purchase is personal taste, but if you're interested in buying something beyond the run-of-the-mill painting, try to learn a little about quality beforehand. Study genuine old *thangka* in books, monasteries, and museums; visit shops and ask to see their very best pieces; and always ask questions.

The differences are quickly apparent. The detail work on a genuine *thangka* is fine, the figures graceful, and the background richly ornamented, not left blank. The quantity of gold paint and the type of colors are not important in themselves as long as the end result is pleasing. Some painters substitute powdered brass for the gilt, which will tarnish within a year. Check the difference by observing the direction light reflects off a gilded section. Gold diffuses light in all directions; brass shines only in one.

As in statues, look at the delicacy of the facial expressions and hands to judge quality. The subjects of the best *thangka* seem to leap off the canvas, radiating outwards in a burst of vibrant intensity. They're multidimensional rather than flat, and the eyes of the main figure may seem to follow you about the room. A handful of painters in Kathmandu know the inner meaning of their work and are capable of creating these, but their paintings must be specially commissioned. The best place to shop for *thangka* is **Indigo Gallery** above Mike's Breakfast in Naxal. Here are high-priced but beautiful quality *thangka* painted in stone-ground colors.

Paubha

The *paubha* is the purely Newar version of the *thangka,* stylistically different from its Tibetan cousins. *Paubha* can appear in the usual rectangular form, or as horizontal scrolls up to 12 meters long which are meant to be slowly unrolled to reveal the different scenes of a story.

Paubha were used for worship or recording events like festivals and temple consecrations. Surviving ones are rare; most are hidden away as temple treasures and displayed only on special occasions like Gunla.

Modern *paubha*-derived paintings use a naive, folk-art style to depict animals, minor deities, Valley landmarks, and religious practices, even contemporary events like the 1990 democracy demonstrations. To shop for these, visit **Himalayan Art and Handicrafts** off Freak Street; several shops on Bhaktapur Durbar Square; or **B.B. Thapa's Art Gallery** in Ekantakuna, Jawalakhel, tel. (1) 524-332. The latter takes commissions and will paint a custom-designed vignette of your Nepal trip—a unique souvenir.

Maithili Paintings
Colorful, vigorous paintings have been created for centuries by the women of Mithila, a former ancient kingdom centered around Janakpur in what is today the Nepal Terai. The **Janakpur Women's Development Project** supports artists who produce less-detailed but still-striking paintings rendered in tempera on handmade daphne paper, and sold in Kathmandu crafts stores like Hastakala and Mahaguthi. See "Janakpur" in the Beyond the Valley section for more details on this folk art.

Contemporary Art
Over the last decade several small Kathmandu galleries have opened to display the work of a handful of contemporary Nepali artists. The best of these painters, like M.M. Poon and Kiran Man Manandhar, render traditional ethnic-toned scenes in evocative, nontraditional styles. The popular "neo-Tibetan" style originated with Pema and Gyaltsen Sherpa, brothers from the village of Khumjung who broke away from the old *thankga* mode to paint fantastic mountain landscapes of their homeland, all fluffy yaks and floating clouds set amid stylized peaks. Former *thangka* painter Binod Moktan paints similar watercolors of Valley landscapes.

The burgeoning gallery scene gives you some idea of what's available, but you can save 50-75% by contacting the artists directly. Given Kathmandu's lack of street names and shortage of telephones, this isn't always easy. Visiting the artist's studio has several advantages besides reducing price: you can review a number of paintings (many artists keep a photo portfolio of past works) and discuss ideas for a commission. If you are willing to pay for the extra work and top-quality materials, commissioning a painting can produce superb results; don't try it if your schedule is tight, however, as it can take months.

Indigo Gallery above Mike's Breakfast in Naxal exhibits contemporary photographs and exquisitely detailed *thangka* by modern masters. The **October Gallery** at the Hotel Vajra in Bijeswari exhibits paintings by traditional and modern local artists. More are tucked away in the back room for sale, and there's a scrapbook of previous displays. **Sirjana Art Gallery** near the American Express office might also be worth a look. The **Nepal Association of Fine Arts** has an unimpressive sales gallery and occasionally hosts exhibitions. It's located in an old Rana palace in Tangal, alongside the Bal Mandir orphanage.

CRAFTS

Less sophisticated than the classical art described above, but equally appealing and certainly cheaper, are Nepal's crafts. Their charm comes from their practical nature: brass plates polished from years of use, durable hand-knotted woolen carpets, whimsical clay elephant planters. Many of the goods on the market are modern innovations created solely for the tourist. Included in this category are filigree figurines, puppets, dolls, and the prayer wheels, jewelry, and doodads sold by street vendors.

Nepal is also the international "back door" for Tibetan artifacts. China tries to restrict the export and sale of Tibetan antiques, but international art dealers still visit Lhasa to buy artifacts at low prices, then have their purchases smuggled across unguarded mountain passes into Nepal.

A similar process occurs in the restricted Himalayan kingdom of Bhutan. Buyers travel through the countryside searching for fine old embroidered garments, offering new ones and extra cash in exchange. They bring their finds to Kathmandu, where international dealers make yearly rounds and take the best examples abroad to sell for ever-increasing prices.

SHOPPING STRATEGIES

Shop in the Valley, which has the widest range of goods. The knickknacks sold along major trekking trails may be passed off as "real Tibetan prayer wheels" or "very old *thangka*," but this genre of souvenirs is cranked out in Valley workshops for the tourist trade. Prices, and mystique, simply increase with altitude. Be suspicious of all items in this category, including small statues, wood-blocks en-

a wooden puppet of the masked dancers, Kathmandu

graved with gibberish, wooden masks, and "Tibetan" bracelets inset with *Om Mani Padme Hum* written in Devanagari. Occasionally trekkers might find an authentic item to buy: an old carpet, a brass-bound *tongba* pot, an antique turquoise; or your porter may offer to part with his *khukri.*

Spend your first few days or weeks getting accustomed to the wide range of arts and crafts available in the Valley. Investigate different qualities and prices, then do your shopping all at once, after you've had time to educate yourself. The multicolored patchwork jackets that seemed appealing the first week may well seem appalling by the end of your stay.

Certain areas specialize in particular crafts: visit Thimi for pottery and masks, Bhaktapur for woodcarving, Patan for metalwork. The best bet for one-stop shopping is Kathmandu and Patan handicraft stores, which stock quality goods at fixed but very reasonable prices. Items include clothing and fabrics (including hand-loomed raw silk and cotton, and some excellent sweaters), cotton carpets, cushion covers, pottery, wooden toys, and stationery. The goods are made by underprivileged women and the handicapped, and purchases directly benefit the makers. **Dhukuti** and **Hastakala** in Kopundol on the main road to Patan are two of the best; or try **Mahaguthi,** which has branches in Kopundol, Durbar Marg, Patan Durbar Square, and Lazimpat. **Himalayan Leathers,** between Jawalakhel and Lagankhel, sells batiks and leather goods made through the Nepal Leprosy Association.

Private handicraft shops include the rather pricey **Didi's Boutique** in Thamel, next to the Potala Guesthouse; and **Koseli,**

BOB RACE

next to Hotel Himalaya in Kopundol, which has an extra-large selection.

Bargaining

Souvenirs are a luxury item and carry a tremendous markup, so you'll need to bargain practically everywhere (the above-mentioned handicrafts stores are an exception). Be ruthless with street vendors, who want, and often get, ridiculously high prices for their trashy trinkets. Don't leap into a purchase. A little research will reveal vast differences in pricing for identical items, and will ensure that you get the best for your money. Competition between merchants is heavy, especially in the off-season, so be sure to comparison-shop—especially as starting prices can vary by 300% from one shop to the next. See special topic "Bargaining" in "Money" for more advice.

METALWARE

Plastic bowls and aluminum pots may be taking over the market, but metalworkers still hammer out traditional cooking vessels and utensils of brass and copper. The north-central quarter of Patan is a major center, and the villages of **Bhojpur** and **Chainpur** in eastern Nepal produce finely finished metalware famed for its detailed decoration.

Copper may be mixed with zinc to make brass, or with tin to make bronze; the more copper, the higher the quality. Brass water pots or *ghada* are an important part of a bride's dowry. Nepali women carry them balanced on their hip, one arm wrapped about the narrow neck, in a graceful if uncomfortable pose. Smaller, more portable items include the simple water pot or *amkhora,* and the *karuwa,* a water pot with a stubby spout. *Anti* are tall slender vessels with long curved spouts used to pour *raksi* during celebrations; usually they are topped with a metal lid adorned with a bird.

An old-fashioned status symbol is the hand-hammered, tempered brass dinner plates used to feed crowds at festival and wedding feasts. These are virtually indestructible: some owners claim their plates are 200 or 300 years old, and the assembly of cooking utensils nailed up under the eaves of certain temples as offerings certainly must include plates that old.

Chainpur metalworker surrounded by his wares

ALISON WRIGHT

Finely worked ritual articles include tall incense burners, metal baskets to hold *puja* offerings, and the beautiful little *sukunda* or oil lamps used for *puja*. An image of elephant-headed Ganesh sits behind the shallow dish that holds the lamp-wick; behind him is the oil pot, guarded by five serpent deities rising up in a fan. A small spoon is used to ladle mustard oil from the pot into the dish. Another style of hanging oil lamp is trimmed with a delicate fringe of hammered metal leaves and can be seen hanging in front of the carved wooden windows of older houses.

Buying Metalware

To distinguish old pieces from artificially aged new ones, run your finger around the bottom rim. It will be smooth and worn in an older piece, sharper in a new one. Time smooths down detail work and gives a distinctive patina to the finish. Usually the quality of detail reveals the age—modern craftspeople rarely match the skill of the old ones.

The street between Asan Tol and Indra Chowk holds many modern brass shops, as does the Mangal Bazaar area of Patan. Poke around antique shops and souvenir stalls for older pieces, which may be more expensive (Rs500-2000) but are generally more pleasing. **Chainpur Brass** across from the Hotel Narayani in Patan stocks old brass and some good new pieces from eastern Nepal. Several shops clustered together in the Bhaktapur bazaar sell old pieces, along with artificially aged but attractive new ones, at ever-increasing prices.

JEWELRY

Kathmandu has a wide selection of semi-precious gems at reasonable prices. Skilled Newar silver and goldsmiths will craft a setting, or an entire piece of jewelry, for little more than the price of the metal.

Gems

Some of the gems are mined in Nepal; many others come from various parts of Asia to Kathmandu's international bazaar. Local gem mines are centered near Chainpur in eastern Nepal (tourmaline, garnet, ruby, and citrine). Recently ruby and garnet mines have been opened in central Nepal's Ganesh Himal. Usually the stones are cut, drilled, and polished in India, then returned to Nepal for sale.

Tourmaline is the principal high-quality gem: it comes in pink, rose, green, and more rarely, lemon yellow. Some crystals display several colors along their length. The facet structure should be carefully assessed before buying, as tourmaline is tricky to cut. Yellow citrine (locally and falsely called golden topaz) and purple amethyst are other good buys. Watch out for citrine or smoky quartz being passed off as topaz, a gem that is not found in Nepal.

Nepali stones tend to lack the rich coloring of the finest grade of gems. Its pale-blue aquamarines, light-red rubies, and pink sapphires are medium value on the world market, but are still good buys. Garnets from the Chainpur mines are plentiful; look for deep dark red with high luster and transparency. Most are sold in rounded, polished beads, but a few are of facetable quality.

Good buys in imported semiprecious stones include striated green malachite and lapis lazuli from Afghanistan (look for deep blue with gold in-clusions). Turquoise, coral, and amber are the mainstays of Tibetan jewelry. Artificial versions are appearing on the market as the supply of genuine quality stones dwindles. Look for sky-blue rather than blue-green turquoise; antique turquoise is darker, smoother, and more expensive. Imitation turquoise is made of plastic, or of powdered, dyed stone complete with black veins. Good coral is hard to find; it should be deep rather than light red. The coral included in ready-made necklaces is usually of inferior quality; some may even be plastic imitations.

Buying Gems

If you're serious about gem-buying, do it from a large reputable dealer. Visit several different dealers and ask them to explain the fine points of assessing quality. Most will be happy to show you varying grades of gemstones, and seeing the entire range will educate you for buying. Larger gem shops are clustered on New Road, on Durbar Marg, and inside hotels. **Himalayan Gems** has a factory at the Patan Industrial Estate in Lagankhel and an outlet on Tridevi Marg across from the immigration office.

The cut of a faceted stone can make a difference of several times in value. To judge it, hold the stone directly to the light so it reflects through the bottom towards you, and observe the percentage of internally returned light. The internal reflection should bounce off the facet angles and return an even brilliance, free of dark patches and flaws. A stone with a dark center of unreflected light or "window" is worth less.

Precious Metals

Gold and silver are sold by the *tola* (an old unit approximating 11 grams) at prices periodically set by the government. Check a local newspaper for current prices. The workmanship comes in free or nearly so. Nepalis prefer soft, pliable 24-karat gold. Only those who can't afford gold will settle for silver, but it is the most popular medium in the tourist market. Beware of "white gold," usually silver plated with rhodium.

You can choose a traditional design or pick something out of a Tiffany's catalog if you happened to bring one along with you. Good jewelers can copy from a sketch or photo. Gold-smithing is a caste occupation carried out in tiny, dark shops in the heart of the old cities.

The Buddhist Shakyas preserve traditional arts and styles, working primarily in silver filigree and deep-carved traditional designs. The best workers are found in Patan. The Hindu Sunar caste specializes in etching, *jali*-cutting, and cutout work. Both castes work with simple home-made tools, hammering the metal on tiny anvils, heating their fire with blowpipes, and often anchoring the piece with their toes as they work.

Traditional Jewelry

From Newar silverwork to the golden earrings of Magar and Gurung hillwomen and the massive turquoise necklaces of Bhotias, peasant women display an amazing amount of wealth. Gold jewelry is almost always the real thing, representing a large portion of family wealth. Instead of being put in the bank, savings go into jewelry, an investment passed on from generation to generation. Regardless of what happens to the rupee, gold is always valuable, and jewelry worn on special occasions is a bold statement of status and wealth. The finest pieces may contain US$5000 in pure gold and are saved for weddings and big festivals. A bride from a wealthy family is decked from head to foot with gold: earrings, nosepin, headpiece, necklaces, bangles, anklets, finger and toe rings, and gold-embroidered sari.

Every ethnic group has its own distinctive jewelry designs, usually dramatic and heavy. Gurung women wear impressive large golden flowers pierced through the main body of the ear, so heavy a string is looped over the top of the ear to support the weight. Tamang women wear these or large flat golden discs hanging from their earlobes. Bhotia women wear huge necklaces and hair ornaments of coral, turquoise, and amber, sacred *dzi* stones, and richly filigreed amulet boxes suspended about their necks. These pieces aren't bought in stores but are commissioned from village smiths. It's surprisingly hard to find ready-made ethnic pieces unless you buy them directly off a woman.

Boudhanath is the center for Tibetan-style jewelry of all sorts. Gold and silver work can be found or ordered in one of the many small shops in the old cities. Visit Patan for the best work. Many jewelry shops in Thamel and on Freak Street sell silver jewelry in Nepali-inspired designs. **Sadle Traders** in Thamel has a variety of interesting pieces, designed by a Canadian jeweler who incorporates a variety of Asian motifs. Other shops sell ready-made and unstrung beads and stones. You can pick through their odds and ends to find a few unique pieces and have them strung into a necklace. Hollow silver beads, sold by weight, are popular. Indian beads come shaped like fish, butterflies, shells, or tiny hearts, but the silver content is low compared to Nepali beads, which are melon-shaped, round, or diamond-cut. You can commission a silversmith to make a set of die-cast beads, or buy ready-made ones.

The Bead Bazaar

At the "Potey Pasal" behind the east side of Indra Chowk, it's Christmas year-round. Tiny stalls display shimmering, colorful strands of glass beads; it's worth walking through here just to enjoy the glittering hues. Most shops are owned by Muslim beadmakers whose ancestors were invited into Nepal in the 18th century to sell their wares. Their *potey,* necklaces of many strands of tiny colored glass beads, are an essential possession for married Hindu women. Red and green are the preferred colors, often inset with a golden *tilhari*, a ridged cylindrical ornament.

Beads come from Eastern Europe and Asia in a rainbow of colors and shapes. Prices depend on the quality of glass, color, and cutting. Czech beads are generally high quality, especially the hexagonal ones, faceted or unfaceted. Belgian beads are usually square. Japanese beads are often opalescent and come in blunt cut, round, square, diamond, or long bugle beads. Taiwanese beads offer similar colors but lower-quality cutting and correspondingly lower prices. Most elegant are beads of 18-karat gold, or with gold centers covered with faceted clear glass.

You can buy ready-made, but be sure to bargain. Or custom-order special necklaces, bracelets, belts, and earrings, choosing the color combinations and the type of closure and thread. The shopkeeper will arrange for a stringer to make your order; watch him work by anchoring the strands with his toes.

CLOTHING

Fabrics and Tailors

Kathmandu shops offer a wide variety of Nepali, Indian, Chinese, and Japanese fabrics, and tailors will stitch up a custom-made outfit in a few days. They do a reasonably good job with shirts, trousers, dresses, and skirts, even jeans. Some have Western pattern books and catalogs; better yet, bring in a favorite item to be copied.

Buy the material in the Kathmandu bazaar. The stretch from Asan down to New Road is lined with cloth shops, the more expensive silks, woolens, and shimmering gold-embroidered sari material concentrated along Sukra Path and in the Supermarket. The back street leading from Chhetrapati to Durbar Square has more exotic fabrics: raw silk from Assam, printed felt from Tibet and Ladakh, Chinese brocades and shiny silks, and Bhutanese wool woven in geometric patterns. Boudha is another good place for silks and brocade.

Ask a tailor how many meters you'll need for an item, and check the width before calculating the length. Some of the higher-priced boutiques have their own stock of special material and will sew to order. The best tailors are always busy and may need one to two weeks to finish an order. Find them by word of mouth, or look on New Road or in Bagh Bazaar. Charges are quite reasonable: perhaps Rs80 for a man's shirt, a simple dress, or a pair of trousers.

Thamel embroidery shops display T-shirts decorated with dozens of colorful motifs, anything from the Grateful Dead logo to Annapurna Circuit souvenirs and shirts proclaiming: "No Rupees. No Change Money. No Hash. No Problem." They'll also custom-make designs. The embroidery is excellent, but the T-shirt quality is often poor.

Ready-made Clothing

Ready-made items range from hand-painted crepe-de-chine ensembles, beaded evening blouses, and Rs6000 silk trousers from Durbar Marg boutiques, to cheap cotton and rayon garments sold in outdoor markets. The cotton trousers, shirts, and skirts sold all over Thamel make cheap additions to a trekking wardrobe. Poke about the more upscale shops to find overruns from local factories, including name-brand garments at a fraction of what they'd sell for in the West. Inspect each piece carefully, however, as often they are quality-control rejects with crooked seams or missing buttons.

Locals shop in the big open-air market in a corner of the Exhibition Grounds, and there are more stalls along the maze of backstreets south of New Road. Among the custom boutiques, try **Kee** in Thamel or **Wheels** and **Yasmine's** on Durbar Marg. **Mandala** on Durbar Marg, **Tara's Boutique** in Thamel, and **Dzambala** in Kopundol all stock hand-painted silks, leather goods, and silver jewelry. **Kosi Natural Fabrics** near Central Immigration has a wide range of handwoven silks and linens, and does tailoring. For remarkably cheap leather jackets visit **Human Wear Leather** on New Road.

Nepali-style ready-made clothing includes the two-piece Indian Punjabi, a comfortable and practical choice for women. The chic versions appear in ever-gaudier colors, but you can choose your own material and get one custom-made. Saris and simple cotton *lungi* are everywhere; a few shops sell Tibetan dresses in cotton, wool, polyester, and raw silk. Try **Tibet Silk Palace** in Thamel, or visit a tailor shop around Boudhanath, where lengths of cloth for *chuba* are displayed on the doors.

Hand-knitted sweaters are a popular item in Thamel, but don't be fooled by salespeople who tell you they've been knitted of yak wool by Tibetans. Most likely they've been made by women in the outlying villages of the Valley. Pick carefully, because the cheaper ones soon lose their shape and can develop huge moth holes within a year. The handicraft shops in Kopundol, particularly Dhukuti, have excellent sweaters at reasonable prices.

TEXTILES

Weaving was once a widespread cottage industry in Nepal: a spinning wheel was an essential part of a Newar bride's dowry, and every household produced its own cloth—cotton, wool, or for the poor, the durable, warm *allo* fabric woven of fiber extracted from the stinging nettle plant. The introduction of cheap foreign cloth in the '20s has practically destroyed the indigenous tradition; today, most cloth comes from India.

The clack of the fly-shuttle floor loom is still heard on the backstreets of Bhaktapur and Kirtipur, where Newar peasant women weave cotton cloth for their black, red-bordered *patasi* skirts. Cotton cloth hand-printed with wooden block patterns in red and black is popular among the Newars; a variation is overlaid with sheer muslin to mute the vivid patterns. A Hill tradition is the cotton *dhaka* cloth in colorful geometric patterns, formerly used for *topi* and shawls. Modern *dhaka* appears in a wider range of colors as placemats, neck scarves, and dress borders.

Weaving involves every member of the family. Old women sit spinning in the sun, children sort piles of yarn, men hang freshly dyed skeins up to dry, and women wind thread between bamboo poles, stretching it to reduce its bulk and prepare it for use as the warp of a loom. Though cotton is no longer widely grown, Terai men still travel from village to village twanging the string of the odd implement they use to clean and fluff the cotton filling of quilts and pillows.

Radi

Rough woolen carpets, or *radi,* in natural colors are a local craft dating back to the 4th cen-

CHRISTOPHER GAMM

woman weaving on backstrap loom, eastern Nepal

tury B.C. Hill people make them by weaving coarse, undyed wool into simple patterns on a loom. The *radi* are soaked in water, then stamped upon to make them thick and smooth. A temple just north of Indra Chowk is nearly hidden beneath a permanent *radi* display; more are sold in winter months by hillmen who wander the streets with a load, looking for buyers.

Pashmina

Pashmina is cashmere, an incredibly warm, soft wool fabric made from the silky long fleece that grows nearest the sheep or goat's skin. The real thing is light and cloud-soft, easy to distinguish from acrylic. Undyed *pashmina* in cream, white, or light brown is considered better quality than the synthetic mixed or artificially dyed material.

Shops near Indra Chowk and in major hotels sell *pashmina* shawls and scarves, but these are often mixed with wool or synthetics. The price should reflect this, but merchants may not be forthcoming about the purity of their goods. It's best to go straight to a factory outlet, like **Everest Pashmina** in Gyaneswar, which also stocks luxurious *pashmina* throws. **Nepalese Silk Products** in Balaju Industrial Estate has delicate silk-*pashmina* shawls in a range of vivid colors.

Bhutanese Textiles

Kathmandu serves as an important outlet for Bhutanese arts and crafts, as the tiny Himalayan kingdom admits only a few thousand tourists each year. Bhutan is one of the world's great weaving cultures. Craftspeople use simple backstrap looms to create inlaid designs on textiles, which are then intricately embroidered and used for garments, sashes, and blankets. Men wear a *gho,* a *chuba*-like garment, while women fold and drape an unsewn piece of cloth, usually five by eight feet, around their bodies. Unfolded, these *kira* or *thara* make unique wall hangings or bedspreads.

It takes nine months to one year to complete a single large intricate piece, woven in panels which are later stitched together. Old pieces (up to about 80 years old) are usually dark-blue or white cloth embroidered with hand-spun raw silk thread dyed in natural colors: black, blue, red, and sometimes green and yellow. They are more subtle than the new textiles embroidered with acrylic thread dyed in a rainbow of chemical hues. Modern weavers no longer spin and dye

THE MODERN CARPET INDUSTRY

Nepal's Tibetan carpet industry is a stunning refugee success story. Starting 35 years ago with nothing but their skill, Tibetan refugees created a business which today is the country's largest earner of foreign currency, its major export, and its top industrial employer. Nepal is the world's third-largest exporter of hand-knotted carpets—the best showing it makes in any international category apart from its quantity of high mountains.

The tale begins in 1961, when a Swiss foreign aid project opened a carpet production center at the Tibetan refugee camp in Jawalakhel. Additional centers developed over the next decade in Pokhara, Chialsa (in Solu), Boudhanath, and Swayambunath. In the '70s retail carpet shops opened in Kathmandu; in the '80s, European exports rocketed. As demand has grown, private entrepreneurs, both Nepali and Tibetan, have opened their own factories. Tibetans have moved up into managerial and marketing positions, until today about 80% of the weavers are Nepali, many of them Tamangs from the hills surrounding the Kathmandu Valley.

The weaving process remains largely unchanged from traditional methods. Watch it from beginning to end at the Tibetan Refugee Handicraft Center in Jawalakhel (open Sun.-Fri. 8 a.m.-noon and 1-5 p.m.). Here the raw wool is sorted by color, carded, hand-spun, then dyed with chemical or natural colors in huge copper cauldrons heated over wood fires. In the cavernous weaving room, rows of women sit before large upright looms strung with cotton warp, swiftly knotting the patterns sketched out on graph paper. Up to five weavers may work on a single carpet, each producing a portion of the pattern. As they work they talk, sing, or murmur prayers and mantras.

Tibetans are the only modern weavers to use the "senna loop" method, which can be traced back to Egyptian carpets of 2000 B.C. The weaver loops each thread around a gauge rod, the size of which determines the height of the pile. As soon as a row is finished, the knots are tamped down with a wooden mallet and slit to release the gauge rod, and a new row is begun. Weavers are paid by the square meter and can produce two simple three- by six-foot carpets per month. Most prefer the simple large designs which hide mistakes. Few weavers are willing to tackle complicated patterns like checkerboards and tiger skins, which require an exact knot count.

The finished rug is clipped with loose-hinged shears to accentuate the design's contours, then given a chemical bath to soften the wool and enhance its sheen. The latter part of the process has generated accusations of environmental pollution, as the leftover wastewater is dumped straight into the

their own thread, and rather than creating an original design they follow patterns sketched on graph paper. They work much more quickly than the weavers of the past, but the new pieces have lost some of the character of the antiques.

Prices vary with the age and condition of the piece, intricacy of the pattern, and fineness of detail, as well as the type of thread and fabric, and whether the embroidery is on both sides or only one. A new *kira* of synthetic thread on cotton is about Rs7000, while a traditional raw silk-on-cotton *kira* is Rs10,000 or more. The finest old *kira* can bring up to US$5000, but smaller old pieces, like sashes, might be around Rs1000.

Shops specializing in textiles and other Bhutanese crafts (bamboo butter boxes, arrow quivers, and woven baskets) include **Zambala** in Thamel and several places in Boudhanath. The street running from Thahiti towards Kathesimbhu Stupa is lined with interesting shops selling Bhutanese cloth and old and new embroideries.

TIBETAN CARPETS

Kathmandu is the international center for the Tibetan rug trade, both old and new. Weavers produce 500,000 square meters per year for export to Western countries, mainly Germany. Old Tibetan rugs belong to a distinctly different tradition that can't be replicated by new techniques. The limited supply of old rugs is being constantly replenished with carpets smuggled out of Tibet or brought by refugees and pilgrims to be sold for cash. Prices have skyrocketed in the last few years as dealers realized the value of these old pieces on the international market.

Valley's rivers. Recent studies indicate the carpet industry produces only a fraction of local water pollution, however. It's also been blamed for water shortages, but most of the industry's supply is drawn from tube wells rather than municipal sources.

The carpet industry's biggest impact is the vast number of people it's lured to the Valley to work. Carpet weaving is a labor-intensive industry requiring few skills, ideal for an undeveloped country like Nepal. Nobody knows how many people are employed in it: figures as high as 300,000-400,000 are often mentioned, but these include many workers involved only peripherally and/or part-time. A more reasonable guess is 100,000 full-time employees in the Valley, making the industry the Valley's largest employer and the largest modern sector employer in the country. The carpet boom, along with the garment industry, is responsible for much of Kathmandu's recent economic development, with all its benefits and accompanying social ills.

The child labor hullabaloo is similarly exaggerated: a 1994 German television segment maintaining 90% of Nepal's carpets are produced by children was way off target. To begin with, even the term "child labor" is somewhat misleading in Nepal, where kids begin working on the family farm as soon as they can walk and girls are married and often mothers themselves by age 15. The issue is further muddied by the vague definition of "child," commonly considered anywhere up to age 18 in the West, while the legal age for wage employment in Nepal is 14. Estimates of the percentage of carpet industry employees who are children thus range 5-50%, the higher figures coming from nongovernmental organizations with an interest in playing up the significance of their work.

Contrary to popular belief, children's "nimble fingers" are not preferred in the weaving of Tibetan carpets. With their high pile and low knot density, these require strength rather than dexterity. The main advantage in employing children is that they are easily exploited by unscrupulous foremen or relatives who pocket most of their wages. Most of the under-14 weavers are girls from poor agricultural households who are sent to Kathmandu to work in order to earn some money and relieve the pressure of an extra mouth to feed. Some are recruited by labor brokers, who loan a rural family money and take a child to work off the debt. It's simple enough to replace underage workers with adults, and the big factories have done so. Bad press has contributed to slumping carpet sales, however. It would be a true pity should the industry crash. Regardless of its flaws, it's provided wage employment for tens of thousands of unskilled workers, who view weaving carpets as better than the routine of backbreaking farm work they otherwise face.

Now it's nothing to pay Rs20,000-30,000 for an old carpet. The only consolation is that these pieces are one-of-a-kind creations, and prices are bound to go even higher in the future.

Sizes

Tibetan carpets are traditionally a practical art, meant to be sat on, slept on—but never walked upon. The most common size is the three- by six-foot *khaden,* big enough to cover the benches typically lining a Tibetan home's main room. Smaller square mats *(khakama)* are placed atop these as seats for honored guests. In monasteries, long runner rugs of square subsections seat assemblies of monks. The finest carpets decorate the thrones of high lamas. Matched sets of saddle rugs are used for horses: the larger rug goes under the saddle, the smaller one over it. Smaller ornamental pieces are used for pack-animal trappings, window and door coverings, and, nowadays, motorcycle and car seat covers. The carpet industry also produces room-sized rugs for the modern market.

Designs

Tibetans borrowed Chinese and Central Asian motifs to create their own distinctive designs, each with a particular meaning. Thunder is represented by an angular border, clouds by a rounded pattern, water by wavy lines. The ancient swastika design symbolizing eternity came from Buddhist India, as did the Ashta Mangal or Eight Auspicious Symbols and the lotus, a symbol of purity. Pictorial elements like flowers, dragons, and phoenixes, favored in modern carpets, are more Chinese in origin. Older designs tend to be geometric and abstract, like the medallion patterns adopted from Central Asian motifs. Tibetan carpets' cut-loop weaving technique restricts the use of curving lines and favors angular designs. Checkerboard patterns and tiger-pelt designs are more recent and popular inventions. Modern carpets tend towards less elaborate patterns: simple borders surrounding plain fields are in vogue. Dragons and tigers are among the few older patterns to remain popular, and even these have been adapted.

Color

"There are three things to consider when buying a Tibetan rug," the saying goes—"color, color, and color." Like the vivid interiors of temples, brilliant-hued carpets brightened lives and homes in barren Tibet. The modern carpet industry has altered traditional hues to suit Western tastes. Gone are the riotous colors of old rugs, replaced by muted natural hues of beige, gray, mauve, and blue.

Always known for their love of intense color, Tibetans quickly adopted chemical dyes when they were introduced in the late 19th century; these aniline dyes are more reliable than the old natural dyes distilled from roots and leaves, and produce a wide range of bright hues. The early and widespread use of chemical dyes means that an all-natural-dye traditional piece is extremely rare. Most old carpets combine synthetic and vegetal dyes or are all synthetic. Judge color not by synthetic vs. natural origins, but by the trueness of individual hues and the harmony of the overall pattern.

Weave

Tibetan rugs are not as delicately detailed as Persian carpets, which can have up to 400 knots per square inch. The average ratio for both old and new rugs is 40-60 knots per square inch, going up to 100 in top-quality new carpets.

The quality of wool means as much to a carpet as the quality of wood does to a piece of furniture. Modern sheep are bred for fine, thin wool suitable for textiles, but the best carpet wool is from aboriginal sheep, whose coarser, longer wool gives greater durability and resilience and a smoother, more lustrous surface. Wool from Tibetan sheep is high in lanolin, and carpets made with it age exceptionally well, developing a special patina with decades of use. But the Tibetan wool supply is unreliable, so weavers now blend it with cheaper, cleaner New Zealand wool. Most new carpets are an 80/20

blend of the two, the bulk being New Zealand. The handspun wool generally used in Tibetan carpets creates pleasing variations not found in more standardized Indian and Chinese rugs.

Buying Carpets

Unique, practical, and durable, Tibetan carpets are probably Nepal's most popular product. Take your time and shop around; there is a tremendous variety of designs, qualities, and prices. Color and design will determine your purchase, but there are a few basic standards to bear in mind.

A carpet's value should be determined by size, the quality of wool and dye, and the number of knots per square inch. Pure Tibetan wool carpets, if you can find them, are top quality. A few unscrupulous dealers may try to tempt you with exotic, and false, claims of yak-wool carpets.

Natural vegetal dyes have no advantage over quality chemical dyes other than their appeal to purists. The subtle hues in fashion nowadays are easy to reproduce with natural dyes or undyed wool, but properly fixed chemical dyes are equally durable. Vegetal dying is a complex art and modern production has lost some of the range of colors.

Most export carpets are in the range of 40-60 knots per square inch. Ask a salesperson to show you the knotting near an unbound corner to make the count. Top quality and price is 100 knots. Older pieces are woven with coarser wool and may have a surprisingly low knot ratio.

The best carpet-shopping area is around the old Tibetan camp in Jawalakhel. Several dozen shops in a small area make it easy to compare and bargain. A recommended outlet for quality new carpets is Pema and Chozin Karpochey's **Master Weaver.** Prices are set according to the square foot and depend on wool quality and knot ratio. You can also visit factory showrooms scattered about Kathmandu and commission a custom-made carpet, to be shipped if your visit is brief. This lets you control all the variables: design, size, color, type of wool and dye, and knot ratio.

The supply of old rugs is less predictable. Best bets are the shops on Durbar Marg (expensive: try **Ritual Art Gallery** and the Tibetan shops in the **Shakya Arcade**), Jawalakhel, and curio shops around Boudhanath. Explore, get a feel for prices and goods, then go back to review your favorites. Inexpensive local cleaning and repairs can cover tiny holes, hide unravelled edges and remove 50 years of dust, but little can be done with big holes or stains.

OTHER CRAFTS

Pottery

Unglazed red-clay pottery is one of the Valley's oldest and most practical products. Clay may be transformed into bricks and tiles, kitchen vessels, flowerpots, firepots, whimsical images, ritual masks, or various smoking devices.

In the winter months explore the streets and squares of Bhaktapur or the nearby village of Thimi to watch the production process. The potters deftly form the lump of clay on their heavy rotating wheels. Larger, heavier items like grain storage urns are shaped by hand or beaten out with small mallets. The finished goods are dried in the sun, then slowly baked in makeshift kilns made of alternating layers of straw and clay stacked up to a man's height and heaped with straw and ash. Temperatures in these improvised ovens can reach 700° C. The potter carefully watches the air flow, removing or adding more ashes to control the heat.

Traditional pottery is always unglazed, though some modern craft production centers are experimenting with simple glazes. The black pottery of Bhaktapur gets its glossy finish from the carbon left by the smoke trapped inside the kiln at the end of the firing process.

Kathmandu's pottery market is displayed on the steps of a derelict temple off Kel Tol. Go out the back door of the Seto Machhendranath temple compound to find stacks of clay pots, urns, vases, jugs, ashtrays, candleholders, and flowerpots. Look for the planters shaped like elephants, rhinos, and griffons—the smaller ones are transportable if carefully packed. Potters' Square in Bhaktapur has an even more extensive selection of items, and the handful of shops in Nikoseri, east of Thimi, generally have some unusual things.

Basketry

Light, strong, functional baskets are among the most practical items produced in village Nepal. The best-known version is the *dokko,* the backpack of Nepal, an open-weave bamboo container which appears in various forms in different regions and is used for loads up to 70 kg. Other styles of baskets are used to carry vegetables, cut grass, live chickens—even pigs. Split bamboo is also used for making winnowing trays and mats, the latter a cheap floor covering.

The women of the Terai are renowned for their basketry, woven with the dried sheaths of flowering grasses using the coil technique. Maithili basketmakers embroider vividly colored grass over the whole. Bhojpuri women use a similar method for their distinctive baskets, sized according to function: carrying temple offerings, packing food, even sifting flour. Most intricate of all are the baskets of the Tharu women, which are woven tight enough to hold water and are decorated with striking designs or with natural ornaments like freshwater shells, peacock feathers, and polished seeds. *Hastakala* in Patan carries a few examples of Tharu baskets.

Khukri

The curved Nepali knife is famed as the Gurkha soldier's weapon of choice: with it he is said to be able to split open an enemy soldier with a single stroke, prompting a British officer to marvel at "these little men . . . with the terrible *khukri."* So famous did the Gurkhas make their weapon that Bram Stoker had his hero dispatch Dracula with a *khukri,* in combination with a bowie knife.

The *khukri* is an indispensable item for hillmen, who use it to chop through the undergrowth, sharpen a stick, or lop off a goat's head with a single stroke. Elaborately decorated souvenir *khukri* may come in wooden and metal sheaths, with handles of filigree, inlaid bone, or carved wood, but these are for show rather than practical use. The genuine item is unembellished and wicked, kept in a wooden sheath. It will have a notch at the base for the blood to run off, and two smaller tools fitted into the sheath, used for smaller cutting jobs and starting fires. The best *khukri* are said to come from eastern Nepal, particularly Bhojpur. **Khukri House** near the Rum Doodle Restaurant in Thamel stocks a variety of models at reasonable prices.

Papermaking

Durable handmade *lokta* paper, often mistakenly called "rice paper," is produced from the inner fibers of the bark of the daphne shrub, a relative of the birch. The fibers are repeatedly boiled, cleaned, pounded into pulp, then mixed with water and poured into rectangular frames and dried in the sun. The result is a resilient, soft, pleasingly textured paper said to last for hundreds of years. Traditionally it was used for religious manuscripts and official documents; the modern market has turned to woodblock-printed greeting cards and cloth-bound volumes. **Bhaktapur Craft Printers** produces a range of creative greeting cards, stationery, and block-printed wrapping paper, marketed through Hastakala in Kopundol; or visit the factory in Bhaktapur.

Incense

Along with light, food, red powder, and water, incense is one of the *panchopachar,* five essential articles which should be offered daily to the gods. Traditionally it was made by the women of a household, who rolled powdered herbs into long, thin strips of *lokta* paper, creating incense sticks up to three feet long. Common fragrances include juniper, sandalwood, and jasmine root, but there are dozens of different types, each with a special function: to cure disease and cast out evil spirits, to invoke the *naga* who bring rains, or to invite Lakshmi, the goddess of riches and fortune. To cure spirit possession, *jhankri* burn special *boksi dhup,* "witch incense" made with chili, snakeskin, and the black seeds of the *lankashani* plant. The Bhotia burn dried juniper as a purifier and an offering to invisible spirits, and the pungent scent permeates Tibetan rituals.

Much of the ready-made incense sold in Kathmandu is Indian and sickly sweet. The Tibetan stick incense sold around Boudhanath is a good buy; go for the most expensive variety. Local rope incense fashioned of twisted cord is cheap and can be very fragrant.

Tibetan Antiques

Most interesting antiques are Tibetan: *thangka,* carpets, embroideries, ritual artifacts, jewelry, and household utensils like silver-lined wooden *chang* cups and copper teapots. Kathmandu shops are the first stop for artifacts smuggled out of Tibet. The most exquisite antiques are soon whisked to galleries abroad, where they command even higher prices.

The best season for shopping in this category is late winter and early spring, when highland people visit comparatively warm Kathmandu and sell off a few possessions to pay for their trip. Shops and dealers replenish their stock at this time for the autumn tourist season.

The widest selection of Tibetan goods is found in the Tibetan curio shops on Durbar Marg and in the tiny shops ringing the Boudhanath Stupa. The former are expensive, since rent on Durbar Marg is extraordinarily high. The **Ritual Art Gallery** and **Mohan's Curio Arts** are both recommended.

Indian Handicrafts

Kashmiri shopkeepers fleeing Srinagar's tourist slump are opening shop in increasing numbers in Thamel. You might first think the goods are Nepali—in fact, shopkeepers may even tell you that—but it's easy to recognize their distinctive products: leather, furs, silk carpets, chainstitch tapestries, and brightly painted papier-mâché ware. Quality Indian handicrafts, on the other hand, are in surprisingly short supply: the best place to find them is **Pasal** on Durbar Marg, which stocks beautiful printed fabrics, tableware, pottery, jewelry, toys, and furniture.

ACCOMMODATIONS

Nepali accommodations span the extremes, from palatial hotels with marble floors to mud-walled, thatched-roof huts. After a long day's trek you'll be just as happy in one of the latter as in the former—maybe even more so.

The year-round occupancy rate for Kathmandu hotels is only 45%, but the season peaks in autumn, with another minor surge in spring. You can always get a medium or low-priced room, but the top hotels are booked solid in peak seasons, as are the most popular guesthouses. Summer, on the other hand, is the season for Europeans on vacation and for Indian tourists, who come up to Kathmandu to escape the sweltering plains and shop for modern goods from Bangkok and Hong Kong. Hotel prices are usually quoted in U.S. dollars, as payment is expected in hard currency—*not* Nepali rupees.

Supplementing the official hotels are the hundreds of budget tourist lodges which have sprung up in Kathmandu and Pokhara. Everything is "Shangri-La" this or "Paradise" that, or else it's named after a famous Himalayan peak. Between these and the cheap, good restaurants, Nepal is firmly entrenched on the budget tourism circuit, with the subcontinent's friendliest and most comfortable facilities.

URBAN ACCOMMODATIONS

The cheap lodge situation is in constant flux, so when looking for a place to stay be sure to factor in word of mouth. It's easy to meet and exchange info with other travelers in lodges and restaurants, or on the trail. When looking for a place to stay in the city, be wary of potential nighttime noisemakers like dogs and radios. Only the most expensive hotels have heating, and rooms can get pretty chilly in the winter. Likewise, few places have air-conditioning or even a fan, so if you're visiting during the hot season look for a room with good ventilation, preferably not on the top floor. During mosquito season (May-July is the worst) you may need to burn Chinese-made coils or buy an electric Japanese mosquito zapper, a gadget which heats up cardboard mats of repellent. The mosquito count fluctuates with the neighborhood and the amount of surrounding greenery.

Lodges and Guesthouses

Kathmandu tourist lodges range from tiny dark cubicles furnished with a dirty hard-mattressed bed at Rs50, to spacious modern rooms from US$15 and up. A simple, clean double with shared bath averages Rs150-250; private bath is Rs300 and up. Prices are usually quoted as single or double, both of these being very bargainable. The most pleasant places (not necessarily the most expensive) have quiet courtyard gardens where you can relax in the sun—especially nice in the chilly winter months. Next best are the high-rise lodges with rooftop terraces, some with mountain views. Kathmandu street life can

hotel signboard tree, Pokhara

be overwhelming at first, and in the beginning it may be worth it to spend slightly more on a pleasant place that will serve as refuge. After you've adjusted, you can look for cheaper accommodations. The most upper-crust guesthouses will expect payment in hard currency, while the cheapest accept Nepali rupees.

Most lodges are clustered in Thamel and around the more run-down Freak Street, with a handful in more remote and tranquil neighborhoods. As Kathmandu is a relatively small town, location isn't that crucial. Accommodations are surprisingly scarce in Patan and Bhaktapur. An overnight to one or more of the growing number of lodges and hotels scattered about the Valley rim is a good way to regain peace and quiet and see something beyond the city scene.

Pokhara's lodges are even more plentiful; you can easily find a pleasant room with bath for Rs250-300. Few other towns in Nepal cater to Western tourists. Lodgings here are of a different sort: if you're lucky, there will be a cavernous cement-walled room with fluorescent lights, noisy neighbors, and a cold-water tap down the hall. In Terai towns the clientele is Indian travelers and Nepali busi-

the endless knot, pepe'u, symbolizing the interrelatedness of all things

nesspeople. Every major roadside town has a few "hotels," some of them wonderfully seedy, as well as plenty of small, extremely basic accommodations, often without even a name so just keep asking.

Hotels

At the top end of the scale are Kathmandu's half-dozen or so luxury hotels, with wall-to-wall carpeting, magnificent high-pressured showers, air-conditioning and central heating, swimming pools, restaurants, and a full range of services. Prices are slightly below international standard, around US$140 a day for a double. Outside of Kathmandu, there are few hotels of this standard.

Kathmandu also has plenty of mid-range hotels where rooms run US$60-100; some of these offer equivalent services and a more creative decor than the pricier version to boot. Hotels

may add a 10% service charge to the bill; all charge 10-14% government tax depending on their star rating, and expect the bill to be paid in hard currency.

TREKKING ACCOMMODATIONS

All the major trekking routes are lined with tourist lodges: every few hours another village appears with an assortment of lodging, so that you need never stay in a tent. In fact, the utter lack of privacy makes a tent undesirable in populated areas. Wherever there are houses, you can count on finding shelter. Nepalis themselves have always managed to travel without lodges; when you arrive in a village at nightfall, a few inquiries will always produce someone willing to feed and house a guest for a small charge.

Big new semi-luxury lodges are springing up like mushrooms along the main trails. Because the situation is changing so rapidly, this book doesn't list particular places to stay. A stroll through town will readily reveal possibilities—all the lodges are right out on the main trail—and trekkers will be happy to tell you their favorites. Don't get stuck on the hot-shower-and-cinnamon-roll circuit, however. Occasionally it's interesting to search out the little places too modest to draw foreign trekkers. Here you'll be able to stay with the family and talk to them rather than with foreign travelers—a good way to keep you grounded in Nepal.

Lodges, Inns, and Houses

Lodges in the Annapurna and Everest regions reach unexpectedly deluxe levels, offering wood-partitioned private rooms with glass windows, thick foam mattresses, sometimes even balconies, gardens, or outdoor tables with stupendous mountain views. At higher altitudes space and building materials are at a premium and facilities are simpler; often dormitories are the only accommodations. Some villages have hydropowered electricity instead of the candles and oil lamps (or lanterns) that light most lodges at night. A few even have VCRs and show nightly movies—not that you walked two weeks into the Himalaya to watch *Rambo*. Villages like Taatopani, Junbesi, and Namche Bazaar have become favorite stopping points for trekkers, and you can choose from dozens of different places. Ask passing trekkers to recommend good towns and lodges if you're interested in this type of accommodation.

These lodges are good places to meet fellow trekkers who can describe the trail ahead. Trekkers are a relaxed and friendly lot and it's easy to find social life along the trail and at night. After a while, though, the conversations may begin to sound like a rerun, and you realize these lodges are to a degree simply tourist ghettos. The only Nepalis around are the family who owns it, and it's difficult to get to know them because they're frantically busy producing more lemon tea and pancakes.

When you reach this point, you can start to seek out alternatives—the smaller, less plush and less crowded lodges. Many of these are nothing more than a local house that's been opened to trekkers. Usually the family sleeps in the kitchen, the warmest room. After a day's walking you can join them by the fire, watching the woman deftly prepare the evening meal while the children play around her and a grandmother murmurs prayers in the corner. Few trekkers seek out these kind of places, but they provide an intimate window into Nepali life.

Small settlements between big towns may have only Nepali-style *bhatti* or inns catering to local travelers, consisting of a communal sleeping room with a few wooden beds. Often the lodging is free as long as you eat your evening meal here. Water for drinking and washing comes from a stream or tap outside.

If no lodging seems forthcoming, simply ask if you can stay in a house (at this point it helps to speak a little Nepali, or have a porter). While local people may not at first believe you actually want to stay in "an old house," once you've convinced them they'll be delighted and you'll get to observe real life. In orthodox Brahman and Chhetri villages, especially in western Nepal, people may not invite you inside their houses because of caste restrictions, though they'll feed you on the porch and let you unroll your bedroll there as well.

In many places the porch is a preferable sleeping place. The big disadvantage of staying in houses is the smoke from cooking fires which often fills the main room and drifts up to the top floor. In lodges, avoid rooms directly over the kitchen. The fire may be banked when you arrive in late afternoon but cooking time will flood your room with eye-stinging smoke.

Camping

Trekking in Nepal isn't like hiking through pristine wilderness. People *live* all over these mountains, in an intimate relationship with the land. In a place like this, treating a trek like a wilderness adventure and camping everywhere makes little sense. The exception is trekking groups, which are too large to put up in villages and must be self-contained.

Even if you'd prefer to be alone, you won't find privacy no matter where you pitch your tent. Herders, grass-cutters, farmers, porters, and Nepal's ubiquitous children will find you soon enough. Kids especially will stare at your mysterious habitat for hours, making you feel like a circus act just come into town. Tents also present security problems as there's nowhere to store valuables—and valuables include your boots.

Uninhabited trekking areas are far off the beaten track and are best approached with some previous trekking experience, preferably a knowledge of Nepali, and a good guide. It seems a shame to come all the way to Nepal and miss its greatest asset, its people. **Lake Rara National Park** is probably the best-known camping-style trekking destination. Other routes (Manaslu, Makalu, Kangchenjunga) cross over high passes and require a night or two of camping. Sometimes you can find a herder's stone hut *(goth)* to shelter in at higher altitudes. Be sure to leave these places in good condition, as they are used during the summer grazing season.

Trekking agencies have developed a remarkably well-organized system providing for nearly every need. Except for firewood and a small amount of fresh food, everything is brought from Kathmandu: mattresses, tents, cooking gear, lanterns, even tables and chairs for group members to dine upon. Usually trekkers double up in tents, unless you pay a single supplement or there's an odd number of men or women in the party. If you're on a group trek without a partner, be prepared for living in intimate circumstances with a possibly messy stranger.

Toilets

Most toilets in Kathmandu are of the Asian squat variety, but all hotels and lodges with upwardly mobile aspirations have commodes. Squat toilets usually have a tap or a bucket of water alongside them, with a cup for rinsing it down after you're finished. They tend to clog with large amounts of toilet paper, so use it sparingly or follow local custom and use your left hand and water. If you're revolted by the idea, consider that Nepalis, like many Asians, consider dry toilet paper to be disgustingly unsanitary.

Finding a public toilet in the Valley can be a problem because there are hardly any, apart from the numerous empty lots and blank walls utilized by local males. You can march boldly into the marble facilities of Durbar Marg hotels if you're in the vicinity. There is one public toilet on Kanti Path, across from the General Post Office, but it is not recommended except in a dire emergency. Otherwise, ask. Even tiny hole-in-the-wall restaurants have their own *chaarpi* hidden away where you'd least expect them.

toilet, Pasang Guesthouse, Solu

CHRISTOPHER GAMM

Bus rides are a grueling experience, not least because of the scarcity of toilet facilities. When passengers agitate sufficiently, the driver will pull off the road for the men to pile out. Women will have a hard time finding a strategic roadside location unless they've thought to wear a skirt.

All but the crudest trekking lodges have their own outhouse-type *chaarpi,* which come in varying degrees of cleanliness. Most organic are the Sherpa outhouses heaped with mounds of fragrant dry leaves, a natural form of composting. Aesthetically pleasing but horrendously polluting are the outhouses built over running streams—a great way to contaminate local water sources. During the day you'll resort to the great outdoors. Trekking etiquette requires defecating off the trail well away from any water source and burying the feces. Toilet paper, if used, should be burned or buried—it's a tremendous disappointment to discover a beautiful little off-trail grotto marked with pink and white rosettes of discarded toilet paper.

Bathing

Nearly all Kathmandu and Pokhara lodges offer hot showers, though you'll pay more for one in your room. Increasingly these are heated by solar panels, saving on the rising electricity bill but not always piping hot when you want one. Early evening is the best time to bathe in a solar-heated place, or ask and see if they supplement solar with electric heaters.

On organized treks, kitchen boys bring basins of hot washing water to the tent door every morning for a quick scrub. On rest days you might be able to get extra hot water for a thorough wash. Many trekking lodges offer hot showers ingeniously improvised from oil drums and piping. Some are solar-heated or use back-burner arrangements using excess heat from wood cooking fires; others have to be heated for you. Aside from the environmental price, showers cost Rs20-50. At lower altitudes you may prefer to bathe at the village tap or in a nearby stream. At frigid high altitudes you'll find you bathe far less than usual. The dry air and intense sun dry out skin, leaving you in a freeze-dried state of preservation. You probably won't even notice your unkempt state until you descend to lower altitudes and begin to thaw out.

FOOD

Nepali food is practical rather than gourmet fare—which is not to say it isn't tasty. The national dish is *daal bhaat,* boiled rice *(bhaat)* with a thin lentil sauce *(daal),* accompanied by curried vegetables *(tarkaari)* and possibly a dab of pungent pickle *(achaar).* In rice-growing areas *daal bhaat* is eaten twice a day, the first meal at around 10:30 a.m. and the second shortly after sunset. Sweet, milky tea and snacks like beaten or popped rice, flat bread, or curried potatoes tide the hungry over until mealtime. Beyond this there isn't a tremendous variety of dishes. Ethnic groups have their own specialties, but basically it's all subsistence food. Nepalis know the value of food as fuel: trek for just a few days and you'll learn it too.

Nepali-style Dining

Apart from farmers working in the fields or porters on the trail, people almost always eat meals at home. Restaurants are a recent phenomenon sparked by tourism. Before, the only restaurants were a few *bhatti* or trailside inns serving travelers.

Most Nepalis eat with the right hand, though urban diners have adopted silverware. Metal spoons are said to ruin the flavor of food and to make you thinner—not a good thing in Nepal. Food may be served in a *thaali,* a metal plate divided into separate compartments. The method is to attack the mountain of *daal bhaat* quickly, while it's still hot. If the *daal* came in a separate bowl, pour it over the rice, breaking up chunks with your fingers as you do. Add a bit of *tarkaari* and/or *achaar,* squeeze it all together, and pop it into your mouth. Watch fellow diners to get an idea of the technique. The hand remains in constant motion until the food vanishes.

Daal bhaat is an all-you-can-eat affair. Servers make the rounds with bowls of *daal* and vegetables and will ask, somewhat dubiously, if you want more rice. Don't be afraid to request more vegetables, *daal* or *achaar* if they're not forthcoming. Westerners generally have a hard time consuming more than one plate in the beginning, but your stomach will stretch over time. A one-plate *daal bhaat* is rarely enough for a

Nepali. On the trail, watch porters fill up on three plates before heading up a hill. The distance to a mountain pass can be measured by the amount of rice it takes a porter to reach the top, as in the famous "five-*maanaa*" climb into the Kathmandu Valley. When you're finished, wash your hand with the water pitcher set on the table, either by pouring the water onto your finished plate or stepping outside the door.

The other constant feature of Nepali cuisine is milk tea, low-grade black "dust" tea boiled with milk and sugar into a sweet brew. This *dudh chiyaa* warms up cold mornings, cheers up bored office workers, and invigorates tired porters; a round of it, fetched by small boys carrying glasses in wire containers, accompanies important business transactions. Westerners often find it too sweet and prefer black or lemon tea, but trekkers should not underestimate the reviving power of milk tea. Two glasses of this potion accompanied by a packet of glucose biscuits will propel you several hours down the trail.

Rice and Grains

Grain, preferably rice, provides 90% of the calories in the national diet. Rice's fundamental role is underscored by the language: *daal bhaat* is *khaanaa,* "food," and a common greeting is *"Bhaat khaayo?"*—literally, "Have you eaten rice?"

Rice comes in many different varieties. The finest and most expensive is long-grained Basmati, which exudes a special fragrance when cooking; Pokhareli is another good-quality variety. Most people eat a mid-range rice like Mansuli or Marshi or the cheaper Tauli. After enough *daal bhaat* you will become a rice expert, noticing the distinct differences in grain and aroma.

Though rice is everywhere in Kathmandu it's difficult to find brown rice (try Bluebird Supermarket in Thapathali Lazimpat, or the organic rice from AAA Farms available in some shops). A hearty red rice grown around Jumla resembles brown rice in appearance and taste. Centuries ago it was carried down trade routes for the delectation of Malla kings.

There are dozens of ways to prepare and process rice: soaking, drying, beating, toasting, popping. Newar farmers make *hakuwa* or "black rice" by heaping harvested stalks in haystacks for 10-12 days. On cold autumn mornings these mounds can be seen steaming in the new-mown Valley fields, as heat trapped inside slowly ferments the grain. The rice is threshed, boiled, and then sun-dried, resulting in a light, digestible grain that's a favorite with children and old people.

Rice is a high-status dish and remains the favorite food in lower regions where it's plentiful. In the dry higher Hills it's often a luxury; where it is available it must be portered in and is consequently more expensive. Roasted flour *(sattu* or *tsampa)* is the staple food here, made from local grains: maize, wheat, millet, barley, buckwheat. The main food of most Hill families is *dhiro,* a cooked mush of maize or millet flour eaten alone, with fried vegetables, or with a thin soup. Grinding the family's daily flour supply on a hand-operated stone mill is one of a housewife's time-consuming tasks.

Among the highland Bhotia the staple is Tibetan *tsampa,* ground roasted barley flour, just as in Tibet. Eminently portable, it requires no cooking—just mix with tea and perhaps a little dried cheese and eat. In highland mountain regions like the Sherpa homeland of Khumbu, the staff of life is boiled potatoes, peeled and eaten with salt and a relish of pounded chilis and garlic. This is much better than it sounds, as high-altitude potatoes are marvellously tasty. Order up a kilo while you're waiting for the main meal, or make it the main course. Find a Sherpa woman to make you *rigi kur,* delicious crispy potato pancakes served with a big lump of yak butter.

Snacks *(Khaajaa)*

Chiura, beaten rice, is made by pounding soaked, uncooked rice with a heavy wooden mallet. Easy to carry and requiring no cooking, it's a popular snack with farmers and porters. Served with yoghurt, vegetable curry, *achaar,* and fried meat *(chuela),* it's an essential element of Newar ritual feasts. Try roasted *chiura,* crunchier and tastier than the plain type, mixed with yoghurt as a substitute for breakfast cereals. Roasted with butter and sugar, it rivals caramel corn. Popped rice *(bhuja)* is the Nepali equivalent of Rice Krispies, popped in a pan, in hot sand to distribute the heat evenly.

Other favorite snacks include curried potatoes *(alu daam),* dried peas in sauce *(kerau),* chewy dried meat *(sukuti),* and deep-fried triangular dumplings *(samosa).* Breads vary from fried rings of rice-flour *(sel roti)* to Gurung corn cakes and the Indian flat, thin wheat-flour disks *(chapaati)* and the smaller fried *puri.* Kathmandu's south Indian restaurants offer *dosa,* huge crispy thin pancakes of lentil flour filled with spiced vegetables and served with several sauces.

Momo, the Tibetan speciality of little steamed meat dumplings, are a big hit with Westerners and Nepalis alike. Try them dipped in tomatochili *achaar,* or Chinese-style with soy sauce and vinegar. *Thukpa* or noodle soup is another popular Tibetan dish, but it's being replaced by instant noodles, introduced in the early '80s and now as popular as blue jeans. These *chowchow* are quick, tasty, and easy to cook, though not very nutritious. Kids like to crunch on them raw. The Thai-Nepali brand Wai-Wai is the most tolerable of the lot.

Sweets are eaten for special occasions or as snacks or breakfast. Most are of the toothachingly sweet Indian variety: deep-fried orange *jelabi,* rich milk-based *barfi,* and all sorts of confections decorated with edible thin paper hammered from real silver. Try cardamom-flavored milky *rasmalaai* or warm brown *gulab jamun,* soaked in rosewater syrup.

Dairy Products

High-altitude herders turn extra milk into cheese, butter, and curd, eating some and selling the rest for a cash profit. Fresh local milk from cows, yaks, yak-cattle crossbreeds, or water buffalo is deliciously rich and makes wonderfully creamy yoghurt.

Yoghurt is widely available, called "curd" on local menus and sold in disposable clay pots in local shops. Often it picks up a smoky taste from the wood fire it's cooked on; it's best consumed in the form of a lassi or yoghurt shake sold in tourist restaurants. Bhaktapur's thick, creamy *juju dahu* or "King of Curd" is supposed to be the best available.

Excess milk is hand-churned into butter. *Mahi,* the resulting buttermilk byproduct, is eaten with *dhiro* and said to be good for digestion. Highland herders sew the butter into skins and keep it until it's bordering on rancid; mountain people use it to flavor their Tibetan-style salt tea, a substantial soupy broth which is a staple of mountain life. Farmers in lower regions boil it until the moisture vaporizes to make clarified butter or ghee (Nepalis call it *ghiu*), which they sell in Terai towns and India.

Chhurpi is dried cheese made from the solids of *mahi* or yoghurt, dried in the sun, then cut into squares and strung on cords of yak hair, rather like an edible necklace. Rock-hard at first, *chhurpi* slowly softens when boiled in soup or stew. People gnaw on chunks of it all day long as a sort of tasteless Himalayan chewing gum.

In the '60s a Swiss development project set up a chain of cheese factories in eastern Nepal to buy surplus milk from farmers and turn it into Western-style cheese. The project has boosted local incomes, though Nepalis themselves haven't really picked up on eating cheese. Today the government-owned cheese factories produce cow, yak, and buffalo cheese; private companies make buffalo-milk mozzarella, camembert, and smoked, white and pepper cheeses, not all regularly available but quite good when they are. Look for the government Dairy Development Corporation outlets in Basantapur and Lainchaur, or the private Nepal Dairy Products outlet in Thamel.

Meat

For most Nepalis, meat *(maasu)* and eggs *(phul)* are infrequent luxuries eaten on festivals and special occasions. Only male animals are supposed to be slaughtered, but the taboo is often ignored. Animal slaughter is legally prohibited on *aunsi,* the no-moon day, and the sale of meat is forbidden on *ekadasi,* the 11th of the month, which is sacred to Shiva.

"Mutton" in Nepal usually refers to goat, not sheep; it's the one meat everyone will eat. Brahmans refuse chicken, buffalo, and pork, while the strictest are completely vegetarian. Gurungs and higher-caste Chhetri shun buffalo meat, while the Newars refuse to eat pork; Limbus, on the other hand, consider it a delicacy. Meat is scarce out in the hills anyway. The best you can do many times is buy a tough, stringy, expensive chicken and have someone execute it.

Produce

The Kathmandu Valley is heaven for seasonal vegetables—immense cauliflowers, carrots, eggplants, beans, and cabbages in the winter; peppers, peas, tomatoes, spinach, and lettuce in the spring; squash, cucumbers, and many local vegetables without English names in the monsoon. Out in the hills the supply is limited to a few standards: potatoes, onion, cauliflower, giant radishes *(mula),* and various greens. The latter are often fermented and dried into a strong-tasting mess called *gundruk,* rich in vitamins, iron, and calcium.

The fruit picture is not so good. The Valley is too low for growing apples, too high for citrus. Excellent apples *(syaau)* grow in roadless north-

fruit sellers, Kathmandu

ern regions—look for them around Jomosom or Jumla or in Solu—but it's impossible to transport the crop. Small juicy oranges (suntalaa) are remarkably tasty and cheap in the winter months. Much of the fruit in the market is trucked in from India, and suffers in the process. Bananas (keraa) are available year-round in at least seven varieties; unlike other fruit, sold by the kilo, these are sold by the dozen.

Citrus fruits arrive in the winter: suntalaa and grapefruit like pomelo, plus mushy Indian apples. Spring brings luscious tropical fruits like mangoes (aap) with their sweet, sticky, bright orange flesh. The fruit of the milder-flavored papaya (mewa) is the color of orange sherbet; its black seeds are said to be a sovereign remedy for upset stomach. The addictive litchi appears in grape-like bunches in May-June: peel off the corrugated red skin to reveal the sweet white fruit, but beware of the large seeds. Peaches appear in the summer but they are almost always green. August-Sept. brings yellow-skinned guavas (ambaa), with their edible seeds and soft flesh, and more Vitamin C than oranges. The brown naspati appearing in the fall combines the flavor and color of a pear with the texture and shape of an apple.

Seasonings

Women grind their spices fresh daily on a big stone mortar, using cumin, chili, turmeric, fennel, fenugreek, mustard seed, coriander, and the mixed-spice masala. Bright orange besaar or turmeric, "poor man's saffron," gives curries their characteristic golden tint. Rubbed over the skin of butchered goats, it acts as a fly repellent and preservative.

Mustard or rapeseed is grown all over lower Nepal, carpeting fields with yellow flowers in the spring. Mustard oil is used for cooking, as well as oil lamps, temple offerings, and massage. Food is fried in mustard oil and liberally seasoned with garlic, onions, and fresh ginger. More flavor comes from a spoonful of achaar, a pickle which can be sweet, salty, sour, or hot. Try pungent mango pickle and sweet mango relish, and a simple and delicious achaar of chopped tomatoes, onion, garlic, lemon juice, and fresh cilantro.

Authentic Nepali food isn't burning hot, but it does have a distinct bite of chili pepper (koor-

sani). Restaurants and teashops catering to Westerners know by now to leave out the hot stuff, so you'll have to ask, or go off the beaten track, if you want the real thing.

Liquor

The ancient practice of home distillation manages to hold its own against modern distilleries. Commercial Nepali hard liquor is best avoided, despite names like Romanov Vodka and Bagpiper Whiskey. Often adulterated with chemicals, these can give a quick headache. Khukri Rum is a palatable exception; pack a bottle on a trek and mix it with coffee or lemon squash.

Imported liquor is available but expensive. The Nepali beer market is booming, with four local brands—not recommended—and two local licensees on the market. Tuborg and San Miguel are the best.

The finest alcohol is homemade stuff. Raksi is potent, exhilarating, and smooth as velvet; it's often mistranslated as "wine," but it's really grain alcohol. To test for good raksi, toss a small amount on a fire and see if it burns (braver or more drunken connoisseurs will dip their finger into their glass and set it aflame). Different grains produce different flavors: rice raksi is rich and smooth, kodo or millet is stronger and more fiery. Women of a household pride themselves on

---

HOMEMADE CHANG

You need four maanaa (1.65 kg) of uncooked rice and one piece of marcha, white yeast sold in Valley shops, to prepare Tibetan home-brewed beer. The better the quality of rice, the better the chang will taste, so buy Pokhareli or even Basmati. Boil the rice and let it cool slightly. When it's mildly warm but not hot, add the crumbled yeast and mix well with your hands. Place the mixture in a nonmetallic container (a plastic bucket works well), wrap snugly in plastic, pile on some blankets to retain the heat, and let it ferment in a warm place for several days to a week, depending on the weather. You can judge when it's ready by the smell. When the mash is ripe, add three times its volume of water and mix well, again with your hands. Strain and drink.

1. COLD DRINKS
2. HOT DRINKS
3. FRESH-FRUIT JUICE
4. TOAST
5. EGGS DISH
6. BRUNCH SET
7. SOUPS & MUSELI
8. CURD & MILK SHAKE
9. PANCAKE
10. CHOPUSY
10. MUSAKA
11. CHOWMEIN DISHES
12. CURRY RICE "
13. SPRING ROLLS & SALAD
14. BURGER WITH CHIPS
15. SPAGHITTIES
16. PIZZA
17. MACORANI SEIWE
18. LASSGANE SELWE
19. CHILLY DISHES

restaurant menu, Kathmandu

their liquor, and will put the most effort and time into making *raksi* for a big celebration like a wedding. At feasts and celebrations it's poured from the graceful spouted *anti* into tiny clay cups, an art which tests the grace and skill of the pourer.

Less potent is home-brewed beer of rice or millet, *jand* (Nepali) or *chang* (Tibetan), a whitish, thin drink with a refreshing sweet-sour taste. A variation served in mountain regions is *tongba*, fermented mash which is placed in a wooden container and mixed with hot water. You drink from a bamboo (or nowadays plastic) straw, sipping the liquid and avoiding the bits of millet; the hot water is refilled several times. Nursing a flask of *tongba* makes a pleasant pursuit for a cold evening.

EATING OUT

Tourist Restaurants
Since the '60s Kathmandu has been a culinary paradise for overland travelers, who, famished after the journey across Asia, stumbled into the Valley to find not only pagodas but pies—and nowadays pizzas as well. Trekkers often spend the last days of their trip fantasizing about what they're going to devour in Kathmandu. Thamel's international smorgasbord includes quiche, lasagna, enchiladas, crepes, steaks, tostadas, moussaka, soups, green salads, spaghetti, potato rosti, cheese sandwiches, and on and on and on. While these dishes are tasty and well-laced with cheese, the appropriate spices are usually missing, making Italian taste suspiciously like Mexican. Desserts fare somewhat better, and where to find the best chocolate cake and apple pie is a favorite subject among travelers. Prices are amazingly reasonable: Rs50 for a big dessert, Rs100 for a giant meal.

Restaurants and coffee shops at the main hotels provide respectable conventional fare at reasonable prices. Two can dine at Kathmandu's best restaurants for under US$15, excluding alcohol, which runs up the bill quite a bit. Another bargain is the many excellent Indian restaurants.

Local Restaurants and Teashops
Local Kathmandu restaurants are usually modest cubbyholes in the old city. Often there are no signs; you identify them by the roar of the kerosene stove or the display of food on the streetside counter. The ethnicity of the proprietor determines the food: Newar restaurants serve specialties like fried blood, lungs, and stinky fermented bamboo shoots; Tibetan stalls have *thukpa* and *momo;* Nepali *bhojnalaya* dish out *daal bhaat;* and Indian restaurants have all sorts of spicy, rich dishes.

Most pervasive is the local teashop or *chiyaa pasal.* It's the social center of a village, a place where men meet to argue and gossip over endless cups of sweet tea. Food here is limited to *daal bhaat,* instant noodles, and snacks. Again, signs seldom advertise its presence, but the plates and glasses on the shelves are a sure giveaway. Sitting in teashops is a favorite way to pass the day and meet people. Make it a point to visit them periodically if you want to stay in touch with Nepal.

On the Trail

Tourist restaurants along the trail are invariably the dining rooms of lodges. Clarify the situation beforehand if you have other plans. Most lodges have menus featuring *daal bhaat,* rice and noodle dishes, pancakes, and variations on these themes; some produce *chaapati*-based pizza and apple pies, even decent enchiladas on occasion. Don't expect too much from the cooks here, and try to consolidate your orders so the woodstove doesn't have to burn all night long. It makes a lot more sense to eat the dishes people cook well than to venture out into elaborate preparations not really suited for rural areas.

Trekkers are usually expected to eat dinner in their lodges. This is the way lodgekeepers make most of their money, and they are often understandably disturbed if a guest goes off to dine somewhere else.

During the day you may be eating in local teashops, in which case the staple is *daal bhaat* or noodles; or you might be passing through a large tourist town which has more elaborate menus. You would expect *daal bhaat* to be made by 11 a.m. or so, but it's best to ask if there's any before you order, or you can spend two hours sitting around waiting for the food to appear. Noodles are always a quick dish.

Mani Rimdu dancers, Thimi Gompa, Khumbu (Christopher Gamm)

(top left) Newar mother and daughter (Christopher Gamm);
(top right) Sherpa women viewing Mani Rimdu (Christopher Gamm);
(bottom) Newar women in Bhaktapur (Kerry Moran)

GETTING THERE

Reaching Nepal is no longer the adventurous ordeal of 40 years back, when you would be lucky just to get permission to visit. British art historian Percy Brown, who visited in 1912, described the journey from Raxaul to Kathmandu as "a materialized nightmare. . . . Before the end is reached, most known methods of locomotion and several unknown ones will have been called into requisition. Usually an elephant, two horses, several kinds of palanquin, and one's own feet, are all utilized," he wrote, going on to describe the "restful" experience of being carried in a palanquin by a team of barefoot porters, the usual means of travel for those who could afford it.

Today 90% of Nepal's visitors arrive by air. The remainder come overland through India, via one of the six border crossings open to foreign tourists, or else cross the Tibetan border at Kodari and take the Chinese-built highway to Kathmandu. Independent travelers are currently allowed to enter Nepal from Tibet, but travel the other way is often restricted to group tours.

Routing Your Trip

Few airlines fly direct to Kathmandu, and those that do may be booked months in advance for the fall season. Possible carriers from the U.S. include Thai, Singapore, Pakistan International Airlines (PIA), and Lufthansa. From Europe, try Lufthansa, Biman Bangladesh, Royal Nepal, and PIA. If reservations on direct flights are hard to come by, consider flying via Delhi, Bangkok, Dhaka, Hong Kong, or Singapore.

Nepal fits into larger Asian explorations as well. Giant India, which surrounds Nepal on three sides, is the logical destination, though India has a way of overwhelming the most ambitious of travelers. Travel to Tibet and Bhutan is restricted, but they remain possible destinations. Thailand is another country that works well into an itinerary, and basking on a Thai beach is a perfect follow-up to a trek.

AIRLINES AND FARES

Kathmandu's **Tribhuvan International Airport** is the country's single international air entry

point at the moment, though there's talk of building a second in the central Terai. Nonstop flights arrive from Delhi, Varanasi, Calcutta, and Patna in India; Dhaka in Bangladesh; Paro in Bhutan; Bangkok; and Singapore. Other popular routes include London-Frankfurt-Dubai or Karachi-Kathmandu and Hong Kong-Dhaka-Kathmandu.

Transit Tips

Travelers from the U.S. West Coast, Australia, and the Pacific Rim usually arrive in Kathmandu after overnighting in Bangkok. Those coming from Europe, the Middle East, and the U.S. East Coast arrive via Delhi. A night in the Delhi airport transit lounge is not very pleasant, and it's easy to get bumped off the Kathmandu flight. If flight distances are equal, Bangkok is preferable. You can stop off to visit Thailand en route—a two-week Thai visa is issued on arrival—or overnight in the transit area, where there's a reasonably cheap hotel. Bangkok's more upscale Airport Hotel runs around US$140 a night and requires going through customs and immigration: it may not be worth the extra hours of formalities, though it does serve a superb buffet breakfast. If you'd prefer to stay in town, ask the airport's efficient hotel reservation desk for an inexpensive hotel. Staffers will make reservations and write down directions for the taxi driver.

Airlines

The national carrier, **Royal Nepal Airlines** or RNAC, flies to over a dozen international destinations. Its limited network is supplemented by **Thai Airways International,** which flies to 60 destinations in 17 Asian countries and Australia, including Bangkok-Kathmandu five times a week. **Singapore Airlines** has repeatedly been voted the world's best airline: its network covers 54 cities, including a twice-weekly Singapore-Kathmandu flight via Dhaka.

From Europe, access is easiest via the weekly Kathmandu-Frankfurt flight on **Lufthansa German Airlines** and RNAC. Another option is the **Pakistan International Airlines** twice-weekly Karachi-Kathmandu flight, a possible hookup from the U.S. East Coast, Europe, and the Middle East. **Biman Bangladesh** flies from

DEALING WITH JET LAG

It's difficult to experience more severe jet lag than that involved in flying to Kathmandu, which is halfway around the world from the United States. Jet lag is your body's normal physical reaction to being violently wrenched across multiple time zones. The miracle of modern travel disrupts the subtle circadian rhythms that regulate physical cycles involving hormones, sleep, and body temperature. The resulting fatigue and disorientation can ruin the early days of a trip.

Apart from being a waste of precious vacation time, jet lag may cause you to function at lowered efficiency. Severe fatigue, impaired sleeping and eating rhythms, and poor vision are some of the symptoms. A rough rule of thumb prescribes 24 hours of recovery for every two hours of time difference, which means a traveler from the West Coast of the U.S. will need six days to feel up to snuff in Kathmandu.

Fortunately, much of this can be influenced by a little advance planning. Pre-departure, avoid last-minute running about and try to get enough sleep. Gradually shift your sleep patterns beginning a few days before your trip. If you're flying east, go to bed early and get up early. Westward-bound travelers should stay up late and get up late.

The efficacy of the "feast and fast" jet-lag diet has been substantiated by studies on animals, though few people are disciplined enough to follow it diligently. Starting four days before departure, "feast" on a high-protein, high-carbohydrate diet meant to induce sleep. Feast days include dairy products, beans, meat, rice, potatoes, bread, and desserts. The following day switch to a low-calorie "fast" diet (soup, fruit, toast, rice) designed to deplete the body's carbohydrate store. Continue like this for the following two days, avoiding caffeine throughout.

Once aboard the plane, move immediately into the sleeping and eating schedule of your destination. It helps to set your watch to Kathmandu time upon boarding. Some specialists recommend taking a low dosage of a mild sleeping pill to aid in-flight rest; consult your doctor before departure about this.

Compounding jet lag is the "long-haul syndrome," the punishing routine to which all airline passengers are subjected. Cabins are pressurized to the equivalent of 1500-2000 meters in altitude, a lot higher than where most of us live. The resulting reduction in oxygen can cause drowsiness and mild edema, so wear loose clothing and shoes and periodically get up to exercise and get the blood moving.

The stale, pressurized air tends to dehydrate passengers, as does the dry airline food. Drinking caffeinated or alcoholic beverages will dry you up even further. Instead, load up on water and juice and try relaxing with a wet washcloth over your nose and mouth.

After landing, move immediately into the local schedule. Most flights arrive in Kathmandu in early afternoon, so try to stumble through the day as best you can. Chaotic city streets can be especially overwhelming to jet-lagged new arrivals, so take it easy for a few days and don't feel guilty if you hang out in your hotel room a little more than you had expected at first. It may be better to avoid the urban scene until you get your feet on the ground, and to start off with some leisurely day-trips to qui-

---

Europe, Singapore, or Bangkok to Dhaka, and on to Kathmandu; it's among the cheapest international carriers.

Air India's worldwide network originates from Delhi. Its domestic division, **Indian Airlines (IA),** operates daily Delhi-Kathmandu flights, with frequent service from Calcutta, Patna, and Varanasi. However, IA is notorious for bumping passengers, and it's better to fly another airline if you have a choice. Both Indian Airlines and RNAC offer a 25% discount on Kathmandu-India flights to passengers under 30 years old.

OVERLAND FROM INDIA

Six Nepal-India border crossings are officially open to foreign tourists: Kakarbhitta, Birgunj, Sunauli, Nepalgunj, Dhangadhi, and Mahendranagar. The usual method is to take a train up to the nearest major Indian town (Gorakhpur, Muzaffarpur, Patna), then catch a bus to the Nepal border. Once across the border, day and night buses run regularly to Kathmandu.

Travel agents sell package train/bus deals

from major Indian cities to Kathmandu, but these are often scams. It's cheaper and more reliable to simply buy tickets on the spot. Most often, travelers from Delhi or Varanasi ride the train to Gorakhpur and bus to **Sunauli;** those from Calcutta take the train to Patna, India, and bus to **Birgunj. Kakarbhitta** in far eastern Nepal provides access from Darjeeling in Sikkim and the Indian town of Siliguri, though few travelers come this way as it's a long, long ride to Kath-

mandu. **Mahendranagar** in far western Nepal is similarly remote, but do-able from Delhi.

Kathmandu-bound buses depart border towns 6-9 a.m. and again at 7-9 p.m. Night buses are slightly more expensive, and also slightly faster because they stop less frequently. They're fine if you're able to sleep on them, but taller travelers will find the seats painfully cramped. Bus travel in Nepal has its own hazards and delights; see "Getting Around," below, for more on this subject. To

TRIBHUVAN AIRPORT

Tribhuvan International Airport, four km east of downtown Kathmandu, was built on a former grazing ground for the sacred cows of Pashupatinath temple; its early name, Gauchar Field, comes from *gauchar,* "grazing pasture." The international terminal opened in 1989 and can handle over 1,000 passengers per hour, a far cry from the old terminal with lines snaking out the doorway and an open-air waiting lounge.

Arrivals

Separate immigration counters process visitors arriving with visas and those applying for visas on arrival; lines for the latter can be long in season. For an on-the-spot visa, you'll need a passport-sized photo and US$15 in cash (any hard currency is accepted). The bank in the entry area and another in the main lobby will change money into rupees; rates are decent but a two percent commission is charged, so don't change much. A duty-free shop allows last-minute purchases of imported liquor and cigarettes, highly valued in Kathmandu.

Luggage and customs are downstairs: free luggage carts are available for use inside the building but it can be difficult to round up an empty one. There are no luggage storage facilities. Porters may insist on helping you with your bags, but don't feel obliged to accept their offers.

In the lobby outside customs is a booth run by the Hotel Association of Nepal (HAN), which will make reservations at some 70 middle- and upper-priced hotels and can usually arrange free transport to them. A Tourist Information Center here dispenses some very basic brochures. Pick up a free copy of the magazine *Image Nepal,* which includes a basic city map.

Getting Into Town

The transportation booth inside the lobby provides private cars for Rs200 to any destination inside the Ring Road (Rs300 at night). You'll save a little by stepping outside to the Airport Taxi Service booth, whch has cars for Rs150 (Rs180 at night). An ordinary (read: crowded) city bus shuttles between the airport and the municipal bus park. The pickup point is on the main road, and service is supposed to be every 30 minutes.

Gather your wits before you step outside into the swarm of hotel touts and taxi drivers. Touts descend upon indecisive-looking travelers—admittedly it's hard to look decisive during one's first few minutes in Nepal. Representatives from trekking companies and major hotels meet arriving guests just outside the door.

Departures

Don't get to the airport *too* early: those who arrive the recommended two hours before flight departure sometimes find the check-in counter unstaffed. One and a half hours in advance should be plenty. Anyone without an air ticket needs to purchase an Rs10 ticket to enter the airport, though this usually applies only to Nepalis. Check-in and customs are on the ground floor, while immigration, the departure lounge, and a snack bar are the second floor. The air-conditioned restaurant and the outdoor observation deck on the third floor are good places to kill time. Airport tax for international passengers is a whopping Rs700. If you have any rupees left over, you can convert them into hard currency at the ground-floor bank. You'll need to show bank exchange receipts to do so.

The domestic terminal is in a more modest building about one km north. The second-floor restaurant here is decent and quite moderately priced.

avoid grueling bus rides altogether, take a train to the Indian town of Patna and fly direct to Kathmandu for US$70. RNAC flies to Kathmandu from Terai towns like Bhairawa (US$72), Biratnagar (US$77), and Simra, near Birgunj (US$44).

Driving into Nepal, you can enter via any of above crossings. You'll need an international carnet to import a vehicle, but it shouldn't be subject to duty or taxes as long as you're staying less than three months and you take it out again.

Via Sunauli

The most popular overland crossing is the Delhi-Sunauli-Kathmandu route, involving a 16-hour Delhi-Lucknow-Gorakhpur train ride followed by a one-hour bus ride to the border. (The Varanasi-Sunauli bus takes nine hours.) Border formalities at Sunauli are usually minimal, and morning and evening buses run daily from here to Kathmandu, a nine-hour trip. See "Butwal, Bhairawa, and Sunauli" in the Beyond the Valley section for details on the town.

The route crosses the flat Terai eastwards along the Mahendra Highway, passes the town of Narayanghat on the Trisuli River (the turnoff point for Chitwan National Park), and runs up to the roadside stop of Mugling, nicknamed "Daal Bhaat Bazaar" for its many eateries. Mugling is located midway between Pokhara and Kathmandu, so it's simple to veer off here and visit Pokhara first. Visitors to Pokhara can also go direct from Sunauli on a morning bus up the bumpy 188-km Siddhartha Rajmarg.

Via Birgunj

The logical point of departure is Calcutta. Take the train to Patna (11 hours), then a four-hour bus ride to Raxaul; from here it's a half-hour rickshaw ride across the border to the Birgunj bus station. The border is open 4 a.m.-10 p.m. See "Daman and the Tribhuvan Rajpath" in the Beyond the Valley section for details on Birgunj.

Birgunj-Kathmandu buses head north up to Hetauda, passing the town of Simra, with its airstrip and frequent US$44 flights to Kathmandu. Most buses then swing west to run the faster, flatter route though Narayanghat and Mugling—longer in distance but shorter in time than the Tribhuvan Rajpath. En route they pass Tadi Bazaar, the takeoff point for a visit to Sauruha and Chitwan National Park.

The Tribhuvan Rajpath from Birgunj to Kathmandu, the original India-Kathmandu Highway, is more direct—only 200 km—but it's a slower journey as the road twists straight over the mountains. Mountain bikers usually come this way because the road is little-traveled and spectacular. Only a few buses operated by the government Sajha cooperative ply this route, climbing up and over the mountains, then down to join the main Pokhara highway at Naubise and ascend again to the rim of the Kathmandu Valley.

Via Kakarbhitta

The Indian town of Siliguri is the hub for traffic from Darjeeling, Gangtok, or Calcutta. From here it's a one-hour bus ride to Ranigunj on the Nepal/India border. Take a rickshaw across the Mechi River bridge to the Nepali border post of Kakarbhitta, a dinky little collection of teastalls and rude lodges huddled around the bus park. If you need to overnight, try the **Koshi Hotel** or the **Shere Punjab Hotel,** which has an Indian restaurant.

Buses depart daily around 4 p.m. for Kathmandu, some 600 km and 20 hours away. Try to buy a ticket a few hours before departure to guarantee a decent seat. Buses to other, closer destinations leave in the morning. You might take the opportunity to visit Kosi Tappu Wildlife Reserve, or detour 25 km down to the Hindu city of Janakpur. To avoid a lot of long, hard travel, catch a flight from Bhatrapur, a 40-minute bus ride from the border, to Kathmandu for US$99.

Via Mahendranagar

This Western Terai boomtown of some 62,000 is one of Nepal's fastest-growing municipalities. Few travelers come through here but it's only a 12-hour bus ride from Delhi. Indian immigration is in the town of Banbassa, on the banks of the Mahakali River; eight km east is Mahendranagar, usually reached by rickshaw. Kathmandu-bound buses run along the East-West Highway across the Western Terai, a long, long journey (24 hours) via Nepalgunj. The twice-weekly Mahendranagar-Kathmandu flight would be tempting; it costs US$150 and is routed via Dhangadhi. Traveling by road, it's advisable to go slowly and break the journey at several points, Nepalgunj being the most obvious, though not the most interesting. The big local attraction is Suklaphanta Wildlife Reserve just south of Mahendranagar. The highway also runs through Bardia National Park, a less-developed alternative to Chitwan.

OVERLAND FROM TIBET

The three-day overland trip from Lhasa to Kathmandu is a rugged, spectacular journey through an incredible range of terrain, from the vast, wide-open spaces of the high-altitude Tibetan Plateau down through rugged yet relatively lush Nepali farmland. It's a dusty, bumpy, cold, and unforgettable way to enter Nepal. From Lhasa, the road passes through Tibet's second city of Shigatse, crossing several 5000-meter-plus passes along the way. Near the village of Tingri the north face of Mt. Everest briefly appears. The road crests once again with the 5050-meter Lalung La pass, then suddenly drops into a seemingly endless descent. Within a few hours you've left the frigid Tibetan Plateau and entered the pine forests surrounding the dramatic river gorge of the Bhote Kosi. Nepal lies just beyond, below the border outpost of Zhangmu, also called Khasa.

Down the hill and across the "Friendship Bridge" is the small Nepali border post of Kodari. Seven km further is the larger town of Taatopani, with some natural hot springs. From Kodari it's 114 km to Kathmandu along the Chinese-built Arniko Rajmarg. The distance is relatively short but the road between Zhangmu and Barhabise is frequently blocked by landslides during the monsoon, the main travel season to Tibet, and you may have to traverse the destroyed sections on foot. Porters can be hired to carry luggage, and vehicles of some sort—buses, jeeps, taxis, or trucks—will be waiting on the other side to ferry you to Kathmandu.

LEAVING NEPAL

By Air
Don't forget to save enough rupees for the Rs700 **airport tax** (Rs600 for flights to countries like Pakistan, Bangladesh, Bhutan, and India). Outgoing flights from Kathmandu are slightly cheaper than one-way fares from the West, but are no bargain compared to the cheap fares available in Asian cities like Hong Kong or Bangkok. There are no "bucket shops" in Kathmandu, so shop around among travel agents to find the best offer. Durbar Marg is a good place to start, or try the larger agencies in Thamel, like **Mosaic Touring,** tel. (1) 418-224.

If you already have reservations out of Kathmandu, be sure to reconfirm 72 hours in advance. Competition for seats is intense in season, and it's easy to lose a seat.

Overland to India
Dozens of small travel companies in Kathmandu and Pokhara offer special bus/train pack-

a tourist agency, Pokhara

ages to Indian cities, most frequently Delhi via Sunauli and Gorakhpur. The idea is to save you the hassles of buying different tickets, and to guarantee you a seat or an a/c sleeper—but many travelers complain of being ripped off, and with such complex arrangements it's almost certain something will go wrong. Most commonly, you don't get the sleeper reservations from Gorakhpur that you paid for. A visit to the stationmaster may help turn one up, but you'll have to pay for it all over again.

Even recommended companies can turn out to be shady; the biggest problem is their clients never return to confront them. It's usually better to head off on your own and make arrangements as you go. If you do deal with these companies, double-check everything, don't leave without your tickets, and hang onto all receipts. **Student Travels and Tours** in Thamel, tel. (1) 221-348, and **Pagoda Travels** at Basantapur in Kathmandu, tel. (1) 216-871, are perhaps the most reliable of the lot. A second-class bus/train package to Delhi is Rs850, while an a/c sleeper is Rs2300; the public bus to Varanasi is Rs450.

It may also be possible to sign up on a returning overland bus to Europe—check notice boards around Thamel for flyers. These trips take six to eight weeks, passing through India, Pakistan, Iran, and Turkey; a typical fare is US$700-800.

To Tibet

The ongoing Chinese occupation of Tibet complicates travel to this remote and fascinating region. Periodic political upheavals may close the Nepal-Tibet border or limit travel opportunities within Tibet. As of early 1995, access from Nepal to Tibet was supposed to be limited to tour groups with a registered company, though a "group" could consist of just one person. Independent travelers who arrive in Nepal with a Chinese visa in their passport are sometimes allowed to cross the border alone, but the Chinese embassy in Kathmandu was not issuing visas to solo travelers (the Delhi embassy was, however).

If and when the independent travel scene opens up, it's a piecemeal route on public buses or private trucks from Kathmandu to the border and from there to Lhasa. Nepal and China are discussing starting a weekly public bus service with overnight stops at Khasa, Shigatse, and Lhasa.

Several Kathmandu companies operate regularly scheduled departures for Tibet in season (March-Nov.), so it's easy to sign up on the spot. Prices run around US$100 a day. Try **Arniko Travel** in Baluwatar across from the Chinese Embassy, tel. (1) 414-594; **Tibet Travels,** tel. (1) 231-130, on Tridevi Marg; **Marco Polo Travels,** tel. (1) 414-192, in Gyaneshwar; or **Shiva Travels,** tel. (1) 212-256, near the Potala Guesthouse.

Most companies do a drive-in, fly-out trip. Traveling overland one-way is rigorous but worthwhile; otherwise you'll just see Lhasa, and the Kathmandu-Lhasa airfare is steep at US$190. Restrictions loosen once you're in Lhasa, where you're free to wander about rather than go with the official program. Travelers who entered Tibet with a group are able to stay independently and to continue traveling on their own. Talk to recently returned Tibet-trippers in Thamel to get the latest story.

A second point of access is from Simikot in far western Nepal up the Karnali River and into the border town of Purang. The pilgrimage site of Mt. Kailas lies a half-day's drive from Purang. Currently this route is open only to travelers who contract through a registered trekking company. Arniko Travel in Kathmandu is a good start.

To Bhutan

Bhutanese tours are even more structured than Tibetan ones; basically a guide escorts you around the country according to a strict itinerary. **Shambhala Travels & Tours** in Kamaladi, tel. (1) 227-229, is the official representative of the Bhutan Tourism Agency, or try the companies listed above under "To Tibet." Packages run 4-12 days, and rates depend on the season, with April and October considerably more expensive than Dec.-Feb. or June. Figure US$200-260 per day for individuals; group rates (four or more people) may be lower.

GETTING AROUND

For years Nepal held the title of country with the least amount of roads per area. Though a thin network of roads now covers the southern Terai, the mountainous interior north of Kathmandu and Pokhara is accessible only on foot. Some 20,000 km of footpaths web the country. Often these are too rugged even for pack animals, making manpower, rather than petrol, the force that drives the economy.

Distances here are measured not in kilometers but in the time it takes to walk them—more relevant than a simple measurement, since steep ascents and descents, rapid streams, landslides, rough trails, and a dozen other things combine to slow progress. Distances can also be measured in the number of cigarettes it takes to get a man from one town to the next, the quantity of rice a porter must eat to reach the top of a pass, or *kos,* a vague measurement roughly equal to two miles. Measures of distance are as maddeningly flexible as Nepali time. Ask how far away the next village is, and one man will tell you, *"pugihaalcha,"* "you've already arrived." The next passerby might well say *"aaja pugdaaina,"* "You won't reach it today."

Highways

In 1952 Nepal's transport network consisted of less than 100 km of railway track connecting Nepal to India, and a few short roads in the Kathmandu Valley and Terai totaling 376 km. The fastest way to cross Nepal was to go to India, ride the railway to a point vaguely south of one's destination, then walk back up north. Even the wheel was largely unknown except for the temple carts of the Kathmandu Valley. Pokhara got its first bullock cart in 1953; fittingly, it arrived by air.

Most of Nepal's roads have been built with foreign assistance. India and China in particular have competed in this politically sensitive area. The network now totals some 7,000 km, concentrated in the flatter Terai region and in central Nepal.

Constructed with Indian aid in the '50s, the **Tribhuvan Rajpath** linking Kathmandu to India was the Valley's main supply route until new roads made its twisting, winding curves obsolete. Meaning "highway," this *rajpath* has little traffic coming down its mountainous 200-km length, making it an ideal route for bike riders and motorcyclists.

The 114-km **Arniko Rajmarg** links Kathmandu with the Tibetan border. The commotion raised by its construction by China in the '60s inspired King Mahendra's famous retort: "I pity those who believe Communism arrives in a taxi-cab." China also built the **Prithvi Rajpath,** the 200-km highway between Kathmandu and Pokhara. The first half of this road connects with the **Siddhartha Rajmarg,** leading to Bhairawa, Sunauli, and the Indian border. This route is now the main highway for goods and travelers to and from Kathmandu.

The most ambitious project is the 1,000-km **East-West Highway** or Mahendra Rajpath crossing the length of southern Nepal. Started under the reign of King Mahendra during the '50s, the project is just now finishing up. A few unpaved stretches remain west of Nepalgunj, but all the bridges are in place. For the first time, it's now possible to drive across the entire length of Nepal.

LONG-DISTANCE BUS TRAVEL

Bus rides in Nepal can be as adventurous, and as punishing, as the hardest trek. Your fellow passengers may include chickens, goats, and 80 passengers squashed into a space designed for 40, with more riding atop the bus. Buying a ticket in advance guarantees you a seat, or a portion thereof, but the aisles crammed with short-term riders and the painfully slow progress make bus rides a test of endurance. Still, they can be perversely enjoyable if you can get in the right frame of mind to totally stop thinking about time and just be where you are.

Distances may seem short on paper, but the rickety vehicles plying the treacherous curved mountain roads travel no faster than 25 km per hour, and a simple 200-km journey that would take one and a half hours on a modern freeway

ROADS AND RAILHEADS

LHASA

SHIGATSE

LHATSE

TINGRI

NYALAM

CHINA (TIBET)

DHUNCHE

KODARI

CHARIKOT

JIRI

KATHMANDU

CHAUTARA

TRISULI

GORKHA

BESISAHAR

CHANKUTA

DHANKUTA

TERHATHUM

TAPLEJUNG

PHIDIM

ILAM

DARJEELING

KAKARBHITTA

SILIGURI (RAILHEAD)

DHARAN

BHADRAPUR

JOGBANI (RAILHEAD)

SIRAHA

JANAKPUR

JAYANAGAR (RAILHEAD)

BIRATNAGAR

RAJBIRAJ

HETAUDA

BIRGUNJ

RAXAUL (RAILHEAD)

POKHARA

BHARATPUR

TANSEN

BAGLUNG

PYUTHAN

BUTWAL

PARASI

SUNAULI

BHAIRAWA

JOMOSOM

LIBANG

TAULIHAWA

KOILABAS

TULSIPUR

SALYAN

JUMLA

NEPALGUNJ

NANPARA (RAILHEAD)

INDIA

BAITADI

DANDELDHURA

DIPAYAL

SILGADHI

MAHENDRANAGAR

DHANGADHI

0   100km

THE BORDERS SHOWN ON THIS MAP
ARE NEITHER CORRECT NOR AUTHENTIC

© MOON PUBLICATIONS, INC.

ends up taking all day. Journeys are further slowed by frequent police checks, local tolls, and regular breakdowns. Rarely will a bus complete a journey without at least one puncture; often two or three tires blow out in rapid succession. There's nothing to do in these situations but resign yourself to the inevitable wait. Drink another glass of tea, smoke another cigarette—the hassles of Asian travel seem to demand it—and make sure you've got a good book to read.

Bus Services

Dozens of private companies operate a chaotic network of routes to every possible roadhead, and for about US$30 you can travel the entire country that is accessible by bus. Most routes have "regular" and "express" buses, the former being even slower than the latter and making more stops. Night buses, some of them deluxe coaches with roomier seating, run to more distant destinations and are a good choice if the weather is hot or you want to cut down travel time. They're less crowded than the day buses, and short-legged passengers might even manage to doze on them.

The blue Japanese buses of the government-affiliated **Sajha Yatayat** have a reputation for being cleaner, more reliable, and faster than private ones, though the differences may be only marginal. They operate a limited network across central Nepal.

"Tourist buses" to Pokhara and Tadi Bazaar (the access point for Sauruha and Chitwan) are better-maintained private vehicles which supposedly don't stop to pick up passengers. They're less crowded, more comfortable, and somewhat faster than regular buses; passengers are almost exclusively foreign tourists. Travel companies advertise them all over Thamel; tickets are double the usual rate but still quite cheap. Most tourist buses leave from Kanti Path, the main northbound street in Kathmandu, near the Sarah Restaurant—more convenient than the Gongabu bus park north of Thamel.

BUS SERVICE FROM KATHMANDU

The times are only an approximation; similarly, prices change and are bound to rise.

DESTINATION	TIME	FARE (DAY/NIGHT)
Barhabise	6 hours	Rs33
Bhairawa	10 hours	Rs94/117
Bharatpur, Narayanghat	5 hours	Rs53
Biratnagar	16 hours	Rs180/225
Birganj	10 hours	Rs90/113
Dhankuta	21 hours	Rs247 (night only)
Dharan	18 hours	Rs180/225
Dhunche	8 hours	Rs65
Gorkha	6 hours	Rs50
Janakpur	12 hours	Rs125/156
Jiri	10 hours	Rs107
Kakarbhitta	20 hours	Rs203/254
Mahendranagar	24 hours	Rs290 (night only)
Nepalgunj	15 hours	Rs177/222
Pokhara	7 hours	Rs73/84
Tansen	12 hours	Rs103/128
Trisuli	5 hours	Rs31

Buying Tickets

Kathmandu's new long-distance bus park, a spacious edifice constructed with Japanese aid, is located at Gongabu on the Ring Road north of Thamel. Everyone knows it as the "Nayaa Bus Park." Destination signs on the ticket windows are exclusively in Nepali, so either ask, or stand about looking helpless until someone offers to shepherd you through. For an extra Rs20 you can purchase your ticket through a Thamel travel agent, possibly worth it to avoid the dusty trip out to Gongabu.

Note that all ticket prices are fixed, except those for tourist buses. It's good to book a day or two in advance, even further beforehand if you're traveling during the autumn festival season, when many Nepalis return home.

Tickets to Jiri (for the Everest trek) are sold from the municipal bus park east of the Tundikhel. Tickets for Sajha buses are available from an unmarked blue booth at Sundhara, near the General Post Office. Con-

Depending on fellow travelers, sitting atop a long-distance bus is often more comfortable than inside.

sult the accompanying chart for sample one way fares and travel times from Kathmandu. The times in particular are only an approximation: anything can happen on the road.

Travel Tips

Your ticket includes a seat number (written in Nepali) guaranteeing you a seat. Some ticket sellers will let you pick out a seat on a chart. To maximize leg room, minimize jolting, and make the best of frequent stops, get a seat as close to the door as possible. Seats over the rear wheels and in the back are the worst, but ticket-sellers often stick foreigners in back, because they seldom object. Buses are scaled to Nepali size and can be torture for anyone taller than the national norm. Special cases, like solo women travelers, can sometimes sit up front in the glassed-in cab with the driver, a bit roomier but crowded with his friends.

Some local hazards: Nepalis smoke like crazy on buses, and when one person lights up everyone else does too. Many villagers are poor trav-elers, losing their lunch at the slightest provocation. Hard to say whether you should sit near the window, or let your sick neighbor have the seat.

Big pieces of luggage generally go on top, except on the Sajha buses, which don't have roof racks. Either haul it up there yourself, or pay a rupee or so to have someone else do it. A tarp may be tied over the mound to protect against rain and possible pilferage. Theft of trekkers' luggage is increasing, especially on the Jiri bus, where ticket sellers may recommend you buy an extra seat to keep your bag inside with you. Night buses are another place to be extra-careful. On any bus, it's a good idea to secure your bag's opening with a padlock and tie or lock it to a friend's bag or the frame of the roof rack, if possible.

There are no formal bus stops; travelers wait by the side of the road and you may ask the bus driver to let you off at any given point.

Bring a small daypack or bag for vital travel goods (water, camera, maybe some food, and a good thick book) to be carried on your lap, or possibly wedged in an overhead shelf, but never let out of your sight. Passengers often ride on the roof of the bus once it's pulled out of town, though this is illegal and you'll have to climb back inside at police checkposts. Riding on top is a lot more fun and more comfortable than the inside, and can provide some great mountain views. A comfortable, sunny rooftop seat can make a bus ride downright idyllic. As for safety, well, one school of thought says you're better placed to jump should the bus roll down an embankment.

Bus drivers are usually admirably dedicated and stop only for a few short tea breaks and a quick meal break. If you're traveling to Pokhara or Bhairawa the food stop will be at Mugling, "Daal Bhaat Bazaar." You'll have 20 minutes to stuff down a plate of ready-made *daal bhaat,* wash up, and be back. Imminent departure is signaled by tremendous honking and revving of engines; try not to be late and make people wait, or worse yet, lose your bus.

RENTAL VEHICLES

Cars

Private vehicles give the maximum freedom to visit remote places at your own pace with a minimum of time and hassle. The main drawback is cost, aggravated by the high price of petrol, Rs29 per liter. Hertz and Avis are represented by American Express on Durbar Marg, tel. (1) 226-172. Cost is US$48 per day, which includes a driver and 50 km of travel within the Valley. Major hotels and travel agencies can also arrange car rentals, as can private rental concerns.

Taxis

Hiring a taxi for the day is much cheaper and usually easy to arrange. You'll need to discuss your itinerary with the driver and determine the price in advance. A full day's touring should be covered by Rs850, if you don't go too far out of the way. It's also possible to have the driver drop you off and pick you up several hours later at the end of a day hike (to guarantee he actually waits for you, don't pay till the end). Hotel staff may be able to help you arrange a taxi; you can call Kathmandu Yellow Cab at (1) 233-727, or just start asking drivers on the street. Look for the cars with the black plates and a meter.

Taxis can also be hired for long-distance destinations like Pokhara, Jiri, or Chitwan, though this may require a bit of a search for a willing driver. Sharing the cost with several others makes this kind of travel reasonable. Trekkers might consider taking a taxi to the trailhead rather than spending an exhausting day on a bus. Renting a taxi is definitely cheaper than a rental car; bargain hard, and ask Nepalis to help you calculate the price. Kathmandu Yellow Cab sends out cars for Rs 9 per kilometer. Often drivers will wait several days at Chitwan or Pokhara for a nominal charge and take you back too. As an example, roundtrip fare Kathmandu-Chitwan with two nights of waiting should be around Rs3300.

Motorcycles

Small motorcycles (100-250cc) can be rented for around Rs400 per day. Look for rental shops located on Dharma Path south of New Road, or in Thamel. You are responsible for returning the bike in the same condition you received it, so note down flaws carefully beforehand. Some shops may ask for your passport as a security deposit. A Nepali or International Driver's License is supposed to be required for motorcycle rental, but isn't always asked for. If you have a valid foreign license you can get a Nepali driver's license from the police station at Hanuman Dhoka—quite a souvenir.

Motorcycles can be fun, a great compromise between slow cars and buses and tiring bicycles. But you need to be extra-cautious in the crazy urban traffic, and watch out for wandering ducks, chickens, dogs, and children near villages. Don't overestimate how much territory you can cover in a day: Nepal's roads are rough, and long journeys are tiring. Go slowly and stop often.

DOMESTIC FLIGHTS

Domestic flights go to 42 locations inside Nepal, many of them remote grassy landing strips perched high in the mountains, served by 19-seat Twin Otter and even smaller Pilatus Porter

---

MOUNTAIN FLIGHTS

If trekking doesn't interest you and even Nagarkot and Dhulikhel seem too far away, the hour-long mountain flights offered by RNAC and other airlines provide brief but stunning views of an encyclopedic assortment of peaks. The US$99 flight has several departures daily 7-9:40 a.m. The earliest flight generally offers the best chances of clear views and crisp light.

The flight path curves over the south Valley, then flies east over Dhulikhel towards Jiri, offering panoramic views of peaks like Langtang, Shishapangma, the Jugal Himal, and Lapchi Kang. Heading up the Dudh Kosi Valley, it banks north to provide close-ups of Khumbu's four 8000-meter giants: Makalu, Lhotse, Everest, and Cho Oyu. It turns west at Namche Bazaar and glides back over Solu, passing close by Numbur and in front of the twin peaks of Gauri Shankar. Upon completion, passengers are awarded a certificate stating they've seen Everest; indeed, they can boast they've been within 25 km of it.

Where to sit? The right side of the plane is said to ultimately have the best view, including the possibility of sighting Kangchenjunga on Nepal's eastern border, and of glimpsing the Tibetan Plateau on the return flight (as the plane flies 20 km further north then). Different views can be had from Pokhara. Everest Air operates a Thursday and Sunday US$60 mountain flight from here which takes in the Annapurnas, Dhaulagiri, and Manaslu.

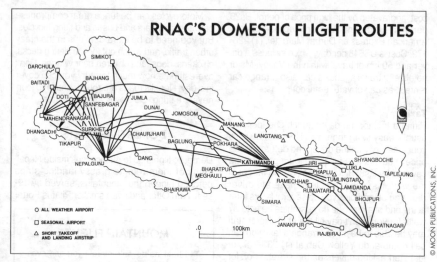

RNAC'S DOMESTIC FLIGHT ROUTES

SIMIKOT

DARCHULA

BAJHANG

BAITADI

DOTI BAJURA JUMLA
SANFEBAGAR
DUNAI JOMOSOM
MAHENDRANAGAR MANANG
SURKHET LANGTANG
DHANGADHI CHAURJHARI
TIKAPUR BAGLUNG POKHARA
DANG
SHYANGBOCHE
NEPALGUNJ KATHMANDU JIRI LUKLA
BHARATPUR PHAPLU TUMLINGTAR TAPLEJUNG
MEGHAULI RAMECHHAP LAMIDANDA
BHAIRAWA RUMJATAR BHOJPUR
SIMARA
BIRATNAGAR
JANAKPUR
RAJBIRAJ

O ALL WEATHER AIRPORT
☐ SEASONAL AIRPORT
△ SHORT TAKEOFF
    AND LANDING AIRSTRIP

.0   100km

© MOON PUBLICATIONS, INC.

aircraft. Flights to these STOL (Short Take Off and Landing) strips are exciting and sometimes hair-raising, though RNAC pilots have an excellent safety record. Onboard service is limited to a few pieces of hard candy and some cotton-wool to stick in your ears, but flights are brief. Sit directly behind the pilot for the expansive view from the cockpit. The baggage limit of 15 kg per passenger on these small aircraft is sometimes actually enforced.

Few STOL strips have radio communications, and the propeller-driven planes have no electronic navigational equipment on board, so pilots must resort to unorthodox methods like judging wind speed and direction from the smoke from chimneys below, and memorizing the shapes of mountain peaks as navigational aids. These small, light planes need good weather to land, and flights are frequently cancelled due to clouds or high winds, sometimes several days in a row. If this happens, you'll basically be starting all over again. Passengers on the next scheduled flight retain their seats, and you'll go onto a waiting list for vacant seats, whenever they may appear. Cancelled flights out of Kathmandu are an inconvenience rather than a problem, though they may lead to several successive mornings of waiting at the

airport; out in the mountains a flight cancellation can leave you stranded for days. The new private airlines and helicopter services have taken some of the pressure off trekking bottlenecks like Lukla. Still, if there's no seats, there's nothing to do but wait however long it takes, or walk out—not always an easy or quick alternative.

Airlines

The national carrier, **RNAC,** retains the most extensive network with 35 regular routes. RNAC's domestic office is on New Road, tel. (1) 213-772. Several new private airlines sprang up after the industry was deregulated in 1992. So far the deregulation appears to have done nothing but good: RNAC can no longer afford to be so complacent about its service, and the new airlines have taken the pressure off popular routes in peak seasons. Main new carriers include **Everest Air** on Durbar Marg, tel. (1) 224-188, **Nepal Airways** in Maharajgunj, tel. (1) 410-786, and **Necon Air** in Kamal Pokhari, tel. (1) 412-388. All these offer a 25% student discount to travelers age 26 and under.

Deregulation also generated a slew of private helicopter companies, including **Himalayan Helicopters** on Durbar Marg, tel. (1) 217-236, **Asian**

> *We don't fly into clouds, because in Nepal the clouds have rocks in them.*
> —RNAC PILOTS' MAXIM

Airlines in Bhatbhateni, tel. (1) 410-086, and **Dynasty Aviation** in Naya Baneshwar, tel. (1) 225-602. Fare for the regular helicopter service to Shyangboche, Lukla, Manang, and Phaplu is only slightly higher than an airplane ticket; companies also operate charter flights. Consider a sightseeing flight around the Valley and up into the mountains—a spectacular experience.

Buying Tickets

It may be simpler to make reservations through a travel agent, who gets his commission from the airline, not from you. An agent is well-positioned to handle the constant checking required to get a seat on a crowded flight.

Most destinations have two price lists: one for Nepalis and Indians, and another for tourists, the latter noticeably higher and payable only in foreign currency. Tickets for more obscure destinations can be purchased in rupees. Consult the chart for sample OW fares, which may vary slightly between airlines.

Flights are frequently booked in season. In fall and spring it's advisable to make reservations at least one week in advance. Return reservations to Kathmandu are especially problematic, as remote airstrips don't have phones and the reservation list is sent off from Kathmandu by plane several days before. Book far in advance, or do so immediately upon arrival at the airstrip.

Cancellations more than 24 hours in advance are charged a 20% fee; 33% for less than 24 hours. No-shows lose the entire price of the ticket. If you cancel, be sure to have it clearly marked on your ticket so you can get a refund in Kathmandu. Flight cancellations mean you can get your fare back, but only in rupees, and only in Kathmandu.

ONE-WAY AIRFARES

DESTINATION	LOCALE	FARE
Kathmandu-Bhairawa	Lumbini, Indian border	US$72
Kathmandu-Bharatpur	Chitwan	US$50
Kathmandu-Bhadrapur	East Nepal	US$99
Kathmandu-Biratnagar	East Nepal, Koshi Tappu	US$77
Kathmandu-Janakpur	Terai pilgrim city	US$55
Kathmandu-Jumla	West Nepal: Shey-Phoksumdo, Rara National Parks	US$122
Kathmandu-Lukla	Everest region	US$83
Kathmandu-Mahendranagar	Far West Nepal, Suklaphanta	US$150
Kathmandu Mountain Flight	sightseeing	US$99
Kathmandu-Meghauli	Chitwan National Park	US$72
Kathmandu-Nepalgunj	West Nepal: Bardiya, Rara National Parks	US$99
Kathmandu-Phaplu	Solu-Khumbu	US$77
Kathmandu-Pokhara	resort town, Annapurna region	US$61
Kathmandu-Taplejung	East Nepal: Kangchenjunga	US$110
Kathmandu-Tumlingtar	East Nepal: Makalu	US$44
Nepalgunj-Jumla	West Nepal	US$44
Nepalgunj-Mahendranagar	Suklaphanta, Khaptad National Parks	US$77
Nepalgunj-Simikot	Humla, Mt. Kailas	US$88
Pokhara-Dolpa	Dolpo trek	US$72
Pokhara-Jomosom	Annapurna region	US$50
Pokhara-Manang	Annapurna region	US$50
Pokhara Mountain Flight	sightseeing	US$60

BIKING, WALKING, AND CITY TRANSPORT

Bicycling and walking are ideal means of transport, especially in the Kathmandu Valley and in Pokhara, both of which are relatively small and flat.

Bicycles

Renting a cycle is the ideal way to get around town if you're adventurous and

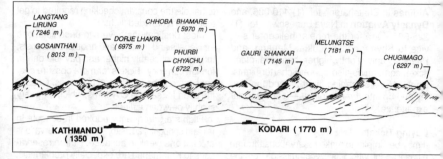

LANGTANG LIRUNG (7246 m)
GOSAINTHAN (8013 m)
DORJE LHAKPA (6975 m)
CHHOBA BHAMARE (5970 m)
PHURBI CHYACHU (6722 m)
GAURI SHANKAR (7145 m)
MELUNGTSE (7181 m)
CHUGIMAGO (6297 m)
KATHMANDU (1350 m)
KODARI (1770 m)

reasonably in shape. It's also a good way to train for a trek. Cycling's advantages are un-equaled by any other means of transport: it takes you through the countryside at a pace faster than walking, but still slow enough to enjoy.

Look for rows of cycles lined up on the pavement in Thamel, around Freak Street, and in Bhotahiti. Rental fees are around Rs40 for a regular bike, Rs90-150 for a mountain bike; during the off-season you can easily bargain this down. If you're renting for a full week you should get a substantial discount. No deposit is necessary—just give your hotel name and room number.

The basic choice is between mountain bike or the basic one-speed models of a kind you haven't ridden since you were a kid. A clunky old one-

MOUNTAIN BIKING

Short, fat-tired, and frisky mountain bikes are made for Nepal. They're not necessary for the city, but on the rugged dirt backroads of the Valley they come into their own, and they're a great option for highway travel. A mountain bike is half as fast as a bus, and about 10 times more pleasant. With one you can travel at your own speed, stopping to explore interesting places at whim, and enjoy-ing the endless downhill coasts of the foothills.

Serious bikers should bring their own cycles, since Kathmandu's rental cycles are low quality. Most airlines will take a bike as part of the baggage allowance. Pack a good selection of tools and spare parts; both are in short supply in Kathmandu and completely nonexistent on the road. Also remember a first-aid kit, a water treatment method, and a good dust mask for the city.

If you bring your own bike, be extremely careful about theft in Kathmandu. Keep it in your room at night, or ask your lodgekeeper to lock it in a down-stairs room. On the street, be sure to lock it se-curely, and don't leave it for too long. Even Kryp-tonite locks can be cut—one good reason to rent an old clunker for in-city touring. You can sell a bike for a good profit at the end of your trip, but beware of a potential buyer pedaling it off for a test ride, never to return.

Mountain bike rental shops in Thamel charge Rs50-160 per day, depending on the bike, the sea-son, and your bargaining skills. Most bikes are Tai-wanese; sturdier American-made ones are more expensive. Five gears is adequate for most Valley tours, but for ascents to mountain viewpoints or out of the Valley you really need 18 gears. For a long trip, search hard for a durable, well-maintained bike; you'll have to improvise panniers and a luggage rack. Renting by the week should garner a discount.

Day-Trips

The Schneider map of the Kathmandu Valley pro-vides great inspiration to solo cyclists. Start off with a fairly level trip to Godavari, Dashinkali, Sundarijaal, or Sankhu. The shady if bumpy 30-km dirt road looping through Nagarjun's forest is popular, while the trip up the surfaced road to Kakani gets raves. Local cyclists often porter their bikes from Kakani one km over onto Shivapuri, and return via Bud-hanilkantha. The Shivapuri road alone is excellent, except for the reserve's Rs250 admission fee. You can descend via Boudha, or, for an extra-long trip, continue around the mountain's back side.

The next step might be an overnighter to Na-garkot, a steep three-hour ride from Kathmandu via Bhaktapur. There are plenty of lodges at the top

MOUNTAIN FLIGHT SKYLINE

PIGFERAGO (6620 m)
KARYOLUNG (6683 m)
NUMBUR (6956 m)
CHO OYU (8153 m)
PUMORI (7145 m)
GYACHUNG KANG (7922 m)
NUPTSE (7906 m)
LHOTSE (8501 m)
SAGARMATHA (EVEREST) (8848 m)
CHAMLANG (7319 m)
MAKALU (8475 m)
AMA DABLAM (6863 m)
NAMCHE BAZAAR (3450 m)

speed bike may not be sleek, but it's perfectly adequate for city navigation and frees you from worrying about theft or damage when you lock it up to go exploring on foot. Get a Chinese-made bike (Flying Pigeon or Phoenix brands) if possible; they're better made and more comfortable than Indian models, and worth the higher rate. Mountain bikes are worth the higher price for day-trip-ping around the Valley, up hills or along dirt roads— though most are cheap and poorly maintained, either shoddy Indian imitations or slightly better Taiwanese and Korean ones. If you're planning a serious trip, bring your own mountain bike (see special topic "Mountain Biking").

Good bikes get snapped up fast in tourist season, so you might want to rent one the pre-

where you can catch views of the Himalaya. The following day, descend down the back side along the rough dirt road to Sankhu. Dhulikhel, 35 km east of Kathmandu, is another good choice: take the back road out of Bhaktapur through Nala to Banepa, then continue on to Dhulikhel for an overnight stay. Combined with visits to Namobuddha and Panauti, this makes an ideal two- to three-day tour.

Longer Trips

Don't view these as necessarily being roundtrips—it's easy to hop on a local bus and put the bike on the roof rack to return. The ride to Daman is the acknowledged classic, a hard ride up a steep untrafficked road, with an overnight at Daman for mountain views. It's easy to continue down to Chitwan from here. The Kathmandu-Pokhara route is not recommended; it's too busy, and has some dangerous curves. Out of Pokhara, the new Baglung Highway is paved, pretty, and untrafficked. The Pokhara-Tansen highway (the Siddhartha Rajmarg) is bumpy but again untraveled; cyclists can continue down to Lumbini and/or Chitwan.

The flat Terai can be a lot of fun in the cool winter months. Biking the length of the country across the East-West Highway would be an incredible trip, though you're likely to opt for either the eastern or western section. The former is prettier and lusher and offers interesting side trips into the Hills; the latter could be part of a Kathmandu-Delhi cycle

trip, via Mahendranagar. Cyclists to or from India usually pedal up the old Tribhuvan Rajpath via Daman. Tibet is an even more adventurous destination, though it's preferable to bike *down* the 800 km from Lhasa to Kathmandu, rather than make the journey up.

A few gung-ho bikers are pushing the envelope of the possible by bringing cycles onto trekking trails. This involves a considerable amount of carrying—a trail that's 50% cyclable is considered good—and is frequently dangerous to those on foot. Local people are understandably displeased with bikers zooming around corners, and bikes have been banned from Sagarmatha and Langtang National Parks.

Organized Tours

A handful of Kathmandu companies run organized mountain bike excursions, providing bike, helmet, gear, and guide, and on longer trips accommodations, food, and perhaps a support vehicle. Day-trips run US$20-30, longer trips US$40-50 a day.

The original, with the widest range of trips, is **Himalayan Mountain Bikes** with an office next to the Kathmandu Guesthouse in Thamel, tel. (1) 416-596. Write to P.O. Box 2236, Kathmandu, for more information, or fax (1) 416-870.

Equator Mountain Biking in Thamel, tel. (1) 416-596, does day-trips, overnights, and some custom trips. Write to P.O. Box 5282, Kathmandu, or fax (1) 417-190.

ceding evening. Check it over very carefully, looking for bald or leaky tires, wobbly wheels, bad brakes, loose or uncomfortable seats, loose chains. Good brakes and a bell are essential; a light is nice if you'll be riding at night. Getting a reasonable machine will save you the trouble of having repairs done out on the road.

If you do have a breakdown or flat tire, look for a streetside repair shop—sometimes no more than an orange crate, a strip of rubber, and a pump. Motorcycle mechanics might also take the time to help you out. Other shops may have an air pump leaning against the doorway. You can pump your own tires for a minimal charge.

Cycles come equipped with built-in locks on the back wheel. Better-quality mountain bikes should be locked with a chain to a post or another bike. In the countryside it's best to ask someone to keep an eye on your bike while you're out hiking. At places like Swayambunath and Changu Narayan, children swarm around new arrivals in a sort of blackmail, fighting for the privilege of "watching" the bike. If you decline, you may find your tires mysteriously deflated upon your return. Better to agree in advance, and suddenly discover you have no change upon return.

Personal equipment for bike-riding in Kathmandu includes a scarf or gauze mask (sold in local pharmacies) to screen out dust and exhaust, sunglasses to protect the eyes from dust, and maybe a chunk of cotton wool in the right ear to preserve it from shrieking truck horns. Nerves of steel are another prerequisite for dealing with chaotic city traffic. As you may have guessed, bike riding in Kathmandu is not exactly relaxing, but it can be a lot faster than a taxi in a traffic jam.

Walking

For most Nepalis, transport means neither bus nor road but walking, usually with a heavy load. On foot, the way most Nepalis travel, is the best way to explore Nepal, in conjunction with judicious amounts of motorized travel or bicycling to speed up the process. Walking is really the only way to pleasurably get through the crowded old bazaars; even pushing a bicycle is a hassle in the densely packed crowds. Only on foot can you journey slowly enough to appreciate the wealth of detail packed into Newar cities and villages, and travel through the surrounding countryside

a porter

on narrow paths through fields of green rice or yellow mustard. The outlying Hills and mountains are untouched by roads, and can *only* be explored on foot—a pursuit which is for some reason described by the old Boer term "trekking."

City Transport

Kathmandu, Pokhara, and the larger Terai towns have a wide if motley array of public transport. Public buses and minibuses are seldom worth considering as they're incredibly slow and crowded. Taxis (look for the black license plates) should go by the meter; they're most abundant in Kathmandu. *Tempo* are noisy, smoky little three-wheeled vehicles. Metered *tempo* are similar to taxis though slightly cheaper and hold three passengers, while the larger *bikram* hold six passengers and ply set routes around Kathmandu. Narrow city streets and Terai towns are served by fleets of cycle rickshaws; these also shuttle passengers out to Terai airports. Always negotiate the fare beforehand, and try hard to achieve a reasonable-sounding deal.

Occasionally political agitators may call a *bandh* or *chakrajam,* shutting down all shops and means of transport. Hotel Association of Nepal runs a bus from the airport to major hotels at these times, and cycle rickshaws operate at highly inflated rates. The ban is only on motorized transport (motorcycles excepted), so *bandh* are a lovely time to cycle about the Valley's empty roads, though it's wise to avoid downtown.

VISAS AND OFFICIALDOM

Everyone except Indian nationals needs a valid passport and visa to enter Nepal. Tourist visas can be obtained before arrival from any Royal Nepalese Embassy or Consulate; you'll need a valid passport and two passport-size photos. Single-entry visas run US$15 for 15 days, US$30 for 30 days. A double-entry 30-day visa is US$40, while a multiple-entry 60-day visa costs US$60. Children under 10 are exempted from visa fees.

It isn't necessary to get a visa before entry, as 15-day tourist visas are also issued at the airport and official border crossings. Bring two passport-size photos and US$15, or its equivalent in other foreign hard currency, to avoid having to change money on the spot, an often inconvenient process. Lines at the airport can be lengthy and confusing in tourist season, so make sure you're waiting in the right one.

Visa Extensions
Tourist visas can be extended up to a total of 120 days per calendar year by the Central Immigration Office in Thamel. An additional 30 days is possible with the consent of the Home Ministry, making the maximum 150 days. Extensions cost US$1 per day; late applications are fined double the regular fee. Bring your passport, a passport-size photo, and a filled-in visa application form.

Immigration Offices
The run-down **Central Immigration Office** on Tridevi Marg in Thamel is open Sun.-Thurs. 10 a.m.-5 p.m., Fridays 10 a.m.-3 p.m. Closing time in winter months is 4 p.m. A counter at the entrance dispenses application forms for visas and trekking permits. Note that applications for visa extensions and trekking permits are only accepted Sun.-Thurs. 10:30 a.m.-1 p.m. (12:30 p.m. in winter), Friday 10 a.m.-noon. Visas and trekking permits are normally issued the same day.

The restricted hours make for long lines in tourist season, especially around the Dasain festival, when the office closes for a few days. Get in line early to reduce waiting time. Be suspicious of Nepalis who offer to "help" fill out immigration or trekking permit forms: they are frontmen for local agencies, which charge double the fee, plus a commission of their own. The Pokhara Immigration Office near Damside will issue visa extensions and trekking permits for the Annapurna region.

Longer Stays
Four months in a calendar year is no problem; for the final fifth month, apply through the Immigration Office for an extension from the Home Ministry, which generally grants them for reasonable causes. Nontourist visas are legally available to anyone who will pay US$20,000 outright, to students and researchers at Tribhuvan University, to entrepreneurs who have made a sizeable investment in a business with a Nepali partner, and to employees of a handful of organizations.

Foreign Embassies
Your country's embassy may be able to help if you run into trouble, by arranging a helicopter rescue or emergency medical care, delivering an urgent message from home, or providing a limited amount of emergency cash. The registration service offered by the U.S. Embassy and a few others can expedite such efforts. It's a particularly good idea to register at the embassy before going out on a trek. Embassy registration forms are also available at the KEEP office in Kathmandu.

Lost or Stolen Passports
Getting your passport and visa replaced is a headache. Most embassies or consulates can issue a replacement within four working days *if*

all your papers are in order. An amazing number of people lose their passports (and sometimes their money) immediately upon entering Nepal—perhaps due to the confusion of jet lag. To replace a passport you first need a police report from the Interpol unit at the Hanuman Dhoka Police Station. Once the replacement is issued, visit Central Immigration to get your Nepali visa reissued. It expedites matters to keep a photocopy of your passport's front page and your Nepali visa in a separate safe place.

Customs

Customs checking of arrivals via the Tibet and Indian border crossings is usually minimal; it's heavier at Tribhuvan International Airport, where officials concentrate on suspicious-looking characters coming from Bangkok and Hong Kong,

prime smuggling centers. "Three Kilos of Gold Found in Jet Toilet" is a common headline in *The Rising Nepal*. Profits are high for the behind-the-scenes masterminds, but the "mules" who take the greatest risk get only a small part; not worth the risk of years in a Nepali prison. The same goes for bringing drugs into or out of the country. Kathmandu jails have a rotating clientele of several dozen foreigners of every nationality who have been busted for gold or drugs, mainly hashish.

Legally speaking, the duty-free allowance is 200 cigarettes or 50 cigars, one bottle of distilled liquor or 12 cans of beer. Bangkok's duty-free shop is a good place to stock up. Imported cigarettes and liquor are heavily taxed in Kathmandu, and duty-free items make good gifts. Johnnie Walker Red scotch and 555 cigarettes are the preferred brands.

NEPALI EMBASSIES AND CONSULATES ABROAD

Australia
377 Sussex St.
Sydney 2000
tel. (61) 2-264-7197

18-20 Bank Place
Melbourne 3000
tel. (61) 96-602-1271

Bangladesh
Road No. 2
Baridhara Diplomatic Enclave
Dhaka
tel. (880) 2-601-890

Canada
3/0 Duport St.
Toronto, ON M5R IV9
tel. (416) 968-7252

China
No. 1 Sanlitu Xilujie
Beijing
tel. (86) 1-532-1795

Norbulingka Rd. 13
Lhasa, Tibet
tel. (86) 891-36890

France
45, bis rue des Acacias
Paris 75017
tel. (33) 1-224-867

Germany
Im Hag 15
D-5300 Bonn 2
tel. (49) 228-343-097

India
Barakhamba Road
New Delhi 110001
tel. (91) 11-332-9969

19 Woodlands
Sterndale Road
Alipore, Calcutta 700027
tel. (91) 33-452-024

Italy
Piazzale Medaglie d'Oro 20
Rome 00136
tel. (39) 6-345-1642

Japan
14-9 Tokoroki 7-Chome
Setagaya-ku, Tokyo 158
tel. (81) 3-3705-5558

Pakistan
84 Attaturk Ave.
House No. 506
Ramna G-6/4, Islamabad
tel. (92) 5-210-642

Thailand
189 Sukhumvit Soi 71
Bangkok 10110
tel. (66) 2-391-7240

U.K.
12A Kensington Palace
Gardens
London W8 4QU
tel. (44) 71-229-1594

U.S.A.
2131 Leroy Place NW
Washington, D.C. 20008
tel. (202) 370-4188

247 West 87th St., Apt. 12G
New York, NY 10024
tel. (212) 874-2306

Bringing in a camera, video camera, bicycle, or tape recorder for personal use is usually no problem as long as you don't have a ridiculous amount of stuff. Customs officials may write the item in your passport upon entry. Theoretically you'll have to pay duty if you can't produce it upon departure; however, customs inspection upon departure is so relaxed it's rarely an issue.

Export Restrictions

The Department of Archaeology requires antique carpets, statues, and *thangka* be checked for historic value before they're taken out of the country. There is a ban on exporting items over 100 years old. Other restrictions involve gold, silver, precious stones, and wild animal skins.

If you're shipping or mailing obviously old items you need to show the customs desk a certificate of approval from the Department of Archaeology. The office is located in the National Archive building south of Singha Durbar, tel. (1) 215-358; hours are Sun.-Fri. 10 a.m.-3 p.m. A cargo shipping company can help obtain the certificate.

EMBASSIES AND CONSULATES IN KATHMANDU

Australia	Bansbari	tel. (1) 411-578
Austria	Naxal	tel. (1) 410-891
Bangladesh	Naxal	tel. (1) 414-943
Belgium	Lazimpat	tel. (1) 413-129
Britain	Lainchaur	tel. (1) 411-590
Canada	Lazimpat	tel. (1) 415-193
China	Baluwatar	tel. (1) 411-740
Denmark	Baluwatar	tel. (1) 413-010
Finland	Lazimpat	tel. (1) 417-221
France	Lazimpat	tel. (1) 412-332
Germany	Gyaneshwar	tel. (1) 416-832
India	Lainchaur	tel. (1) 410-900
Israel	Lazimpat	tel. (1) 411-811
Italy	Baluwatar	tel. (1) 412-280
Japan	Panipokhari	tel. (1) 231-397
Myanmar	Chakupat, Patan Dhoka	tel. (1) 524-788
Netherlands	Kumaripati	tel. (1) 522-915
New Zealand	Dilli Bazaar	tel. (1) 412-436
Pakistan	Panipokhari	tel. (1) 411-421
Russia	Baluwatar	tel. (1) 412-155
South Korea	Tahachal	tel. (1) 270-172
Sri Lanka	Baluwatar	tel. (1) 412-835
Switzerland	Jawalakhel	tel. (1) 523-468
Thailand	Thapathali	tel. (1) 213-910
U.S.A.	Panipokhari	tel. (1) 411-179

MONEY

The Nepali *rupiyaa* or rupee is issued in notes of Rs1, Rs2, Rs5, Rs10, Rs20, Rs100, Rs500, and Rs1000. Different colors make them easy to distinguish, and amounts are written in English on the back side. The smallest bills are being replaced by new gold-tone coins. Small change or *paisaa,* which come in 5-, 10-, 25-, and 50-paisa coins and larger one-rupee coins, is more confusing. The 25-paisa coin is called a *sukaa;* the 50-paisa coin is a *mohar.* Only Nepali numbers are written on them and many are so worn as to be indecipherable, so you need to learn them by size. Coins are worth very little, and are handiest as donations for beggars. Larger bills may be difficult to change with taxi drivers or while trekking.

Nepalis have an aversion to worn or slightly torn bills. Shopkeepers often pass them over to unwary tourists as change, but may refuse to accept them, though the note is still valid. If you get stuck with one, turn it in at the old-bill window of the Rastriya Banijiya Bank exchange counter in Bishal Bazaar on New Road in Kathmandu.

Value

In fall 1995, the exchange rate was Rs54 to US$1 (Rs160 to 100 Indian rupees). Inflation in the Kathmandu Valley averages 8-10% a year. The rupee is periodically devalued to keep it in line with the Indian rupee, to which it's loosely tied. Like Indian rupees, Nepali rupees are a nonconvertible currency, so spend or convert all your money before departure—but remember the Rs700 airport tax. The airport bank will convert rupees into foreign currency upon presentation of bank exchange receipts. Nepal is gradually moving towards full convertibility of currency in line with India's program. In the meantime, tourists are required to pay for hotels, travel or trekking agency services, and air tickets in foreign currency, though the cheapest guesthouses ignore this regulation.

With one rupee equalling about US$0.02, it may not seem like a lot of money, but in Nepal, a rupee is a rupee—that is, it's the standard. Try not to think of it as "funny money." When judging prices, keep in mind that the average laborer in Kathmandu earns Rs70 a day, while an industrial worker earns maybe Rs1300 a month. Another way to get your financial bearings is to look at prices of vital necessities: a kg of rice or sugar, a *maanaa* of cooking oil, a plate of *daal bhaat,* a glass of tea. Prices will vary according to the isolation of an area and its distance from a roadhead, with imported goods becoming increasingly more expensive the farther one goes. Knowing local prices gives you the background knowledge necessary for bargaining, and puts the cost of luxury goods into glaring perspective.

Planning Expenses

Nepal can be remarkably cheap even by Asian standards, but there's no limit on what you could spend if you put your mind to it. Out in the boon-docks, it's sometimes hard to find *anything* to spend money on. At the high end of the scale, Kathmandu's luxury hotels charge over US$150 a night, and there are plenty of high-priced antiques to splurge on. Restaurants, though they may be excellent, are never really expensive. As long as you don't drink it's difficult to get a dinner bill much over Rs500 per person even in the most expensive restaurants.

On the budget traveler's circuit you can live for as little as US$5 per day, though US$20-40 would be more comfortable. Transportation costs are ridiculously low if you take buses, but domestic flights up the bill quite a bit. It's only reasonable to allot some extra funds for things you can't find anywhere else—a Tibetan carpet, a porter on a trek, a ticket for the mountain flight, or an overnight in a Valley resort.

Expenses for independent trekkers depend on the region. Things are cheaper in the low-lands, more expensive in the mountains where supplies are carried in by porter. Figure on a minimum of Rs150 per day, more for premium regions like Everest, then take double that as a cushion. Bring a good assortment of lower denomination bills to avoid hassles with change.

BARGAINING

Modern price-tag cultures have bred a certain laziness in Westerners, who enjoy the comfort and ease of set exchanges where there's no need to talk. In Nepal, bargaining is not just a way to settle a price: it's a social interaction, a national sport, and a favorite time-passer. Visitors from fixed-price societies may take a while to appreciate the subtleties of bargaining, and even longer to hone their skills. Some people are naturals, while others loathe it.

There should be no need to bargain for general household and food items, medicines, restaurant meals, bus tickets, and trekking gear rentals. Guest-house rates are fairly firm in season but it never hurts to ask for a discount. If business is slow, this could be up to 50%.

Things to bargain for include produce from the bazaars (fruit vendors in particular raise their rates when they see you coming). Some vendors will quote the right price, others an inflated one. Ask several to get a feel for the range, and don't be surprised if they come down as you're walking away. A shortcut is to eavesdrop on a Nepali transaction, then insist on the same price.

It's possible to take the spirit of bargaining too far. Some independent travelers insist on haggling for every item, ignoring the fact that they paid more for their air ticket to Nepal than most Nepalis earn in a lifetime. *Paisa*-squeezers like these make life miserable for everyone. It's important to treat bargaining as a game, rather than a cutthroat competition.

The most stupendous markups are on items sold exclusively to tourists: souvenirs, jewelry, clothing, art. Bargaining is essential here, especially with street sellers who routinely ask incredible prices from tourists, and get them. First go around looking and asking prices. Once you know what you're interested in, go back to the reasonable places and commence bargaining. It's difficult to estimate the percentage the original price should be reduced, because a shopkeeper might quote a price 300% higher than his or her neighbor for an identical product. It pays to shop around.

Some bargaining techniques: first off, ask for the seller's "best price." Armed with the research you've done, you'll be able to tell if it's reasonable. Often a merchant will ask *you* what you're willing to pay, hoping you'll state some ridiculously high sum.

Be patient and good-humored in bargaining. You can't bully a good deal out of anybody. Decide in advance the maximum you're willing to pay for something, than make an initial offer three or four increments below that. Inch your way up slowly; once you reach your last price stick to it. If you've gotten stuck at a point close to agreement, it might work to pull out the money, saying, "Look, it's all I've got right now."

Don't give away the fact you've got your heart set on something; act cool. Walking away with feigned disinterest has saved many a deal. If you've gotten close to agreement, 80% of the time the seller will call you back and take your last offer. If he doesn't—well, you can always come back the next day and get it for *his* last price.

Add more for a porter and luxuries like beer and soft drinks. Avoid bottled water, which can eat a huge hole in your budget and is often contaminated; it's far cheaper and safer to treat it yourself. Trekkers should carry money in rupees—the only reason to bring dollars or traveler's checks would be to purchase an air ticket out. While there are banks in towns like Namche Bazaar and Jomosom, their hours are unpredictable.

Trekking companies vary wildly in price: local companies may charge as little as US$30 per person per day, while the foreign-based operations running through them will charge US$80-140 for essentially the same thing. Group trekkers need little cash on the trail, since food and lodging are taken care of and there's seldom much to buy. Don't forget to bring enough to tip staff and porters at the end of the trek.

Tipping

While it's not a Nepali tradition, tourism is making it one. Be wary of handing out lavish tips and accelerating the present trend. Money for nothing is disorienting, and that's what tips can seem like in a place where it's not customary. More expensive restaurants add a 10% service charge, which doesn't necessarily go to the employees. In smaller establishments a small gratuity (Rs5-50, depending on the bill) may be appropriate. Apart from tour guides and trekking employees, there's seldom reason to tip anyone unless they've given you exceptional service. Porters at the airport should get Rs5-10 per bag, although they would much prefer US$5-10. It's worse than useless to tip them in foreign coins, as these can't be changed into rupees.

Tipping has become institutionalized in the trekking business, and because most workers are miserably paid, the end-of-trek bonus is a necessity. Some group members will hand out their flashlights, frisbees, clothes, and boots at the end of a trip, but it's hard to distribute these equitably. The recommended method is for every member to pitch in around US$1.50 per trekking day, to be divided up among the trekking staff, with the *sirdar* and cook getting proportionately more. The company should be able to provide guidelines on tipping etiquette. It's best to hand over tips directly to the staff, preferably on the last night of the trek, when the group is all together. Often members are short of cash, though.

In such a case, hand the money over to a reliable person—the company manager or your trek leader—to distribute to the staff in Kathmandu. Porters should be tipped the last day of the trek and might get two days' extra salary for a two-week trek, less for those who joined up later. Ask your *sirdar* for advice on this one.

CHANGING MONEY

The Nepali black market is the economy's way of leveling things out. The rupee can't be used outside the country, but hard currency can; thus it's worth more. The black market in Kathmandu is widespread and remarkably accommodating, accepting cash, traveler's checks, even personal checks if the big man knows you. U.S. dollars are preferred. The rate is about 10% higher than the bank rate, with better rates given for large-denomination bills, easier for smugglers to carry out in bulk. Freak Street and Thamel are full of shady characters hissing, "Change money? Good rate, better than bank." They are the small fish who bring clients to the big bosses, who often work in tourist-related businesses—carpet and souvenir shops, hotels, travel agencies. You'll get a better rate dealing directly with these people, but needless to say, changing money on the black market is illegal. Police periodically sweep through and close down all the moneychangers, arresting a few as examples. Tourists themselves are never touched.

The government used to try to increase the inflow of hard currency by requiring tourists to show

OFFICIAL EXCHANGE RATES FOR THE NEPALI RUPEE
As of July 1995:

Australian Dollar	Rs36
Canadian Dollar	Rs36
French Franc	Rs10
German Mark	Rs36
Italian Lira (100)	Rs3
Japanese Yen	Rs5.96
Pound Sterling	Rs80
Swiss Franc	Rs43
U.S. Dollar	Rs50

bank exchange receipts in order to receive visa extensions and trekking permits. At one point, travelers were required to change US$20 per day, far more than many budget travelers needed. These regulations have been revoked, hopefully for good. Bank exchange receipts remain useful for converting rupees into hard currency, which can be done at the airport upon departure.

Banks

Modern computer banking has arrived in Kathmandu, even if power outages do occasionally disrupt the system. The government **Nepal Bank** and **Rastriya Banijya Bank** have outlets in all major cities. Private banks like **Grindlays** and **Nabil** on Kanti Path and **Indosuez** on Durbar Marg offer similar rates and more modern facilities; they may charge a one percent commission. Major hotels will also change money for guests. Licensed private moneychangers offer fair rates but charge a commission of Rs100 per US$100.

Standard bank hours are Sun.-Thurs. 10 a.m.-2:30 p.m., Friday 10 a.m.-12:30 p.m. Private banks tend to be more generous with their hours, while licensed moneychangers operate 12 hours a day. Nepal Bank on New Road is open seven days a week 7 a.m.-7 p.m.; Himalayan Bank in Thamel is open daily except Saturdays 8 a.m.-7:30 p.m.

If you need money transferred from abroad, contact one of the major banks above for a list of their international correspondent banks and account numbers. Have your bank telex transfer the money to their account, with your name and passport number on the order. If all goes well, the transfer can be completed in two working days—but don't count on it coming that fast. Money will be issued in traveler's checks or Nepali rupees.

Outside of major cities, money-changing facilities are scarce and sometimes uncooperative. If you're going trekking you should bring all the cash you think you'll need with you, and then some. Make sure a good portion is in notes of Rs500 and less; it can be hard to break larger bills on the trail. Always bring more than you calculate you'll need; 50% is a good cushion. If you're trekking in a region with regular STOL service, you might want to carry the return airfare in hard currency or traveler's checks in case you decide to fly out.

Cash, Traveler's Checks, and Cards

For safety's sake take the bulk of your money in traveler's checks, with a little cash for small deals and emergency changing. U.S. dollars are the preferred currency. Only American Express offers replacement checks in Kathmandu. Credit cards can generally only be used at expensive hotels and travel agencies, though Thamel shops are rapidly expanding their capabilities. An American Express card can also be used with a personal check to get up to US$1000 in traveler's checks.

The **American Express office** just off Durbar Marg in the Hotel Mayalu, tel. (1) 226-172, can replace lost cards and checks within three days, give emergency cash up to US$1000, and provide free mail service for clients. Grindlays Bank can provide cash off a MasterCard or Visa card, while Nabil Bank handles Visa. Alpine Travel Service on Durbar Marg is the local service center for Visa and MasterCard.

HEALTH

Nepal's health situation is among the world's worst. Nearly 130 of every 1,000 children die before the age of five, victims of diarrhea, disease, or respiratory infections, compounded by widespread malnutrition. The high infant mortality rate pushes national life expectancy down to 54 years—far better than 40 years ago, but still among the lowest in the world.

Providing even the most basic health care services is a daunting task in rugged Nepal. The government health care system is heavily centered in Kathmandu and urban areas, and even then is poor. Rural health posts are usually understaffed, ill-equipped, or unsympathetic to the problems of villagers. Most Nepalis turn to *jhankri* or shamanistic healers when they fall sick (see the special topic *"Jhankri"* under "Religion" in the general Introduction). A *jhankri's* treatment might include exorcism, animal sacrifice, herbal medicine, or physical manipulation. As often as not the cure is successful, due mainly to the strength of their patients' faith. *Jhankri* may not be trained in modern medical techniques, but they make excellent psychotherapists.

The dire health situation is less threatening to travelers, who are better nourished than Nepalis, are more likely to be immunized, and in any case don't stay very long. The most common traveler's complaint is gastrointestinal illnesses, transmitted through food or water contaminated with infected feces. You need to be careful about what you eat and drink, but constantly worrying about the purity of everything can spoil your trip. Some kind of gastrointestinal illness becomes more inevitable the longer you stay in Nepal.

The intestinal state of siege makes health a favorite topic among travelers, and reports of last night's bout of diarrhea are cheerfully given even to strangers. A favorite topic of speculation is where somebody contracted an infection. It's pretty much impossible to blame one restaurant or another, since infections like giardia and amoebas take at least 10 days to appear. Food poisoning is more immediate and dramatic and does occur in Kathmandu restaurants; fortunately it generally runs its course in 24-48 dramatic hours.

Even worse than contracting an illness in Nepal is to return home with some exotic bug unfamiliar to your doctor. The identification and treatment of giardia or amoebas can result in a spectacular bill in the West. Try to clear up lingering illnesses in Kathmandu, where doctors are accustomed to these problems and medicine is readily available.

PREVENTING ILLNESS

Drinks
Regard *all* water as contaminated. This includes the tap water in your hotel and crystal-clear mountain streams. Bacteriological contamination of the Valley's water supply is 10 times higher than the international World Health Organization standard. Water treatment facilities exist, but are poorly operated; the big problem is leaky pipes which suck in sewage, contaminating water in the delivery process.

The only way to be certain water is pure is to treat it yourself, as outlined below. Commercial bottled water is *not* safe and frequently tests impure. Local journalists visiting a water bottling plant once found workers filling bottles from a stream! The same goes for the drinking water and ice cubes in hotels and restaurants. Optimists can assume it to be safe, but there are no guarantees. Bottled soft drinks, beer, and hard liquor are all safe. Club soda is sometimes available, but often all you can find are soft drinks and beer—not much good for real thirst. Get in the habit of taking a bottle of treated water when you go out for the day.

Homemade liquor is usually dubious, and alcohol in general irritates gastrointestinal problems. *Raksi* is purified during distillation but it may be contaminated afterwards. The wonderful homemade beer called *jand* or *chang* is risky, since it's made with unboiled water squeezed through the mash with usually unwashed hands. *Tongba,* a hot toddy made from boiling water poured over fermented mash, is an in-between case—the water is probably okay, but the mash may not be. Sometimes you just have to live dangerously.

RECOMMENDED IMMUNIZATIONS

No immunizations are required for you to enter Nepal, but there is an intimidatingly long list of recommended immunizations. Exactly which ones you need depend on your plans and the season. A monsoon trekker will need more protection than a visitor to the Kathmandu Valley in the dry autumn. Without insurance or a national health plan, the pre-departure medical bill can run quite high. In the U.S., local public health departments often give cheap vaccinations. Or you can wait and get injections in Kathmandu, though it's a poor way to spend your vacation, and some shots don't provide immediate protection. CIWEC Clinic and Nepal International Clinic both charge US $20-35 per shot. The Kalimati Clinic, tel. (1) 271-873, is the cheapest place to go, depending on the injection about US$15; it's on the main road near the turnoff for the Soaltee Holiday Inn and is open Monday and Friday 12:30-2:30, Wednesday 11-2.

Tetanus-diptheria should have been updated within the last 10 years. A one-time **polio booster** is recommended for adults who received oral immunizations as children. **Measles and mumps** should be up-to-date for all travelers.

Gamma gobulin injections are effective against hepatitis A, one of the three varieties of hepatitis prevalent in Nepal. For a one-month visit get a two cc injection, for two months, three cc; for three months, four cc. Frequent travelers might consider the three-shot series of vaccinations, which provides 10 years of protection against hep.

Typhoid shots are recommended for trekkers and long-term visitors. These are usually given as a series of two injections, 30 days apart, and are 75-95% effective.

A **meningococcal A and C** injection is recommended for trekkers. Meningitis is a potentially lethal disease only recently recognized in Nepal. Effectiveness is 95%, beginning one to two weeks after the shot.

The **Japanese B encephalitis** vaccination is recommended for those who will be traveling in India and/or the Nepali Terai for more than one month.

Pre-exposure rabies prophylaxis: Rabies is prevalent in Nepal, particularly Kathmandu. You might want to consider this series of three injections, which is good for three years and reduces the number of required shots from five to two if you are bitten. The post-exposure series is not as painful as it once was, but it's quite expensive in Kathmandu.

Note that smallpox and cholera vaccinations and the BCG vaccine for tuberculosis are unnecessary.

Treating Water

Water treatment methods have undergone refinements over the past few years: what follows is the most recent advice. Boiling, the traditional method of purifying water, will kill organisms if you do it long and hot enough, but travelers are rarely in a position to boil their own water, or even supervise the process. Ideally water should be filtered first, then boiled three minutes to ensure the destruction of the hepatitis A virus. One minute is enough to wipe out cysts and bacteria. Note that freezing does *not* kill germs, so ice cubes must be made with boiled water to be safe.

Iodine or chlorine bleach is the simplest, cheapest, most portable way to purify water, guaranteed to wipe out every organism. The latter has a less objectionable flavor and doesn't stain the fingers. A small dropper bottle makes dispensing less messy; get a tough, tiny plastic bottle with a dropper spout.

Bleach should be five percent concentration, so either bring some Clorox or buy Kathmandu's Polar brand. Dosage is one tablespoon per one gallon water (slightly less than one teaspoon per liter); shake and let stand 20-30 minutes. Iodine is available in the West in tablet or crystal form, less messy than liquid. In Kathmandu look for Lugol's Solution. The recommended dose of the latter is two to three drops per liter, shaken and left for 30 minutes. Carry two bottles and shift between them so you don't run out of water. If you're using powdered drink mix to mask the iodine's flavor, wait the recommended time before adding it, as the ascorbic acid slows the purification process. Adding a pinch of vitamin C (ascorbic acid) after disinfection also helps eliminate the iodine taste.

Other purification methods are less than 100% effective against Nepal's wide range of bugs. Filtering devices don't destroy viruses like hepatitis, which rules out portable pumps equipped with Katadyn ceramic filters.

Food

Dining out in Kathmandu is a form of Russian roulette. No particular type of restaurant or food can be said to be safe or unsafe; it all depends on circumstances. Tourist and hotel restaurants are not necessarily any cleaner or better than local ones.

Generally anything that's been thoroughly and recently cooked is safe, but avoid cooked food that's displayed unprotected on counters. A slice of a precooked lasagne that's been touched by a single fly may be a hotbed of germs, while the next one is okay. Vegetables and fruits should be soaked 20-30 minutes in iodized or bleached water before eating raw. Okay, so you can risk an unwashed banana or orange, but be careful about how you handle the peel.

Milk should be boiled before drinking; this includes the pasteurized dairy milk sold in small plastic bags. Ice cream is risky if the scoop is rinsed off with tap water, as is usually the case. Yoghurt, made from boiled milk, is fairly safe if you scrape off and discard the top layer. Cheese is okay too; just wipe the piece off and discard the rind.

GASTROINTESTINAL ILLNESSES

Sooner or later virtually every visitor to Nepal gets some kind of gastrointestinal illness. The rate of infection among Nepalis has been estimated at 75-90% at any given time. There's a huge seasonal rise in diarrheal diseases, which quintuple April-July, due perhaps to the increase in the fly population.

CIWEC Clinic, which has the dubious distinction of having treated more cases of traveler's diarrhea than any other facility in the world, has found that 85% of its cases are bacterial in origin. Fourteen percent are caused by giardia, while viruses and worms cause some five percent each. Amoebas cause only one percent of diarrhea cases, but local labs frequently misdiagnose them.

The most common cause by far is bacteria, for which the recommended treatment is rehydration by consuming plenty of electrolyte solu-

tion. Such upsets should end within five days without medication. Treatment for any diarrhea begins with a mild diet of food like plain rice, bananas, toast, and soup, with plenty of fluids and no caffeine or alcohol. Try to avoid remedies like Lomotil which simply paralyze your bowels, though it could come in handy on a bus trip. Pepto-Bismol is very useful for quelling temporary stomach upsets; bring some tablets from home.

Longer cases or specific symptoms may indicate one of the gastrointestinal illnesses described below. Diagnosing these on your own is confusing, as the symptoms can be similar. If you're in Kathmandu or Pokhara, get a stool test and advice on medication from a local clinic. Trekkers must be prepared to treat themselves. Most viral and bacterial upsets will eventually go away without medication, but organisms like giardia are more persistent.

Giardia organisms inhabit the upper intestine, causing stomach pain and bloating, nausea, frequent diarrhea, and "rotten-egg" burps. Symptoms may come and go, and frequently the organism won't show up on stool tests. Recommended treatment is usually remarkably effective: two grams of metronidazole (Flagyl) or tinidazole (Tiniba) taken at one time, preferably after dinner to minimize potential side effects, for one to three days. Don't drink alcohol during the course of the treatment.

Amoebic dysentery is caused by a protozoan inhabiting the large intestine. Symptoms include abdominal pain, diarrhea, and possibly fever and bloody stools. A stool exam is useful in diagnosing amoebas. The treatment is again two grams of metronidazole or tinidazole as a single dose, this time taken three nights in a row.

Bacillary dysentery has symptoms similar to those of amoebic dysentery, but is more severe and rapid, with the addition of fever and chills, intense stomach cramps, and stools with mucus or occasionally blood. It is treated with an antibiotic like Norflex or Bactrim, 500 mg twice daily for two-three days.

Worms rarely cause symptoms beyond mild abdominal discomfort, but they're not something you want to bring home. Ask a pharmacist for worm medicine if you suspect you might have them.

The latest addition to this list is cyclospora, a protozoan discovered by CIWEC Clinic which causes diarrhea, weight loss, and severe lethargy. Cyclospora occurs almost exclusively in the monsoon and generally affects residents rather than tourists. It is impervious to iodine or chlorine, but is easily killed by boiling the water. Treatment is with the antibiotic Bactrim.

OTHER DISEASES

Respiratory Infections
Kathmandu's dust and pollution can prove particularly irritating in the dry spring season, when hacking coughs and sinus infections may linger for weeks. Seek treatment rather than toughing it out. Tuberculosis is common among Nepalis but is seldom a threat to travelers, who usually have strong immune systems.

Malaria
Malaria, once rampant in the Terai and lower hills, is under control in touristed destinations, although serious outbreaks have occurred in more remote areas. It rarely occurs above 1200 meters, so the Kathmandu Valley is safe; in fact, it's seldom contracted by visitors. Malaria prophylaxis is recommended for visitors to the Terai, especially during peak transmission season, mid-July through mid-September. A few days in Chitwan doesn't present a serious threat, and the best treatment may be simply preventative—using mosquito repellent and sleeping under a net. If you choose to err on the safe side, take weekly 500-mg doses of chloroquine phosphate (available in Kathmandu), starting one week before arrival in the malarial zone and continuing four to six weeks after departure.

Other Diseases
Typhoid fever is a debilitating illness that can last for several weeks. Since there are several varieties of typhoid and since immunization provides only partial immunity against one, avoiding it is a good reason to be careful about what you eat and drink. Typhoid and hepatitis cases both peak in May-June.

Hepatitis, a viral infection of the liver, is marked by lassitude, nausea at the sight of food, dark urine and whitish stools, possibly fever, and mild liver pains on the right side. By the time the skin and eyes turn the telltale jaundiced yellow, you know you've got hep. Western medicine offers no treatment beyond rest and a good diet. Victims should avoid anything that taxes the liver, like drugs, liquor, and greasy food. Dr. Mana's ayurvedic treatment for hepatitis (see "Medical Treatment" below) includes herbal pills and a special diet. Like most ayurvedic remedies it is scientifically unproven, but many people swear it has speeded their recovery.

AIDS exists in Nepal, like it does everywhere else in the world. Around 250 cases of HIV have been officially reported, but experts believe there are many, many more unreported cases, and the number is growing. Prostitution is the main means of transmission, principally infected Nepali women returning from India.

Animal Bites
Rabies is prevalent in Nepal, and any bite by a dog, monkey, cat, or whatever should be regarded as serious, especially if the attack was unprovoked or the animal was acting strangely or sick. Be careful of village dogs, especially in mountain areas where they can be vicious. Any bite or scratch should be immediately flooded with water for 15 minutes, then swabbed with a topical antiseptic to minimize the amount of germs introduced. Incubation time for rabies is 10-90 days. If the animal exhibits no signs of rabies 10 days later, you don't have to worry, but it's not always possible to follow up like this. If you can't confirm the absence of symptoms in the animal, you should get the full series of shots, expensive but quite possibly life-saving. You might want to put **pre-exposure rabies vaccinations** on your immunization list. While it doesn't give 100% protection, it reduces the number of shots needed after a bite.

MEDICAL TREATMENT

Kathmandu has the country's best medical facilities, but that's not saying much. While there are some excellent doctors, Nepali hospitals are crowded and very basic. Families are expected to provide for the patients, right down to bringing them food and supplies, and family members camped out in the wards make overnighting in a hospital a noisy and sleepless affair. For anything serious you'll need to fly to Bangkok or back home.

CIWEC Clinic, tel. (1) 228-531, on the Yak & Yeti road off Durbar Marg is staffed by Western physicians and nurses. It's the best place in town for medical care, and is a world expert in diagnosing diarrhea cases. A visit is US$35 (payable in rupees) plus lab fees. **Nepal International Clinic,** tel. (1) 419-743, across from the Royal Palace is run by a Canadian-trained Nepali doctor who charges US$30 a consultation. Both CIWEC and NIC have a 24-hour call service for emergencies.

The best all-round facility, which isn't saying a whole lot, is **Patan Hospital** in Lagankhel, tel. (1) 522-266. Also known as Shanta Bhawan, it was founded and is still partially supported by the United Mission to Nepal. Next choice is **Tribhuvan Teaching Hospital** in Maharajgunj, tel. (1) 412-808. Avoid the government-run **Bir Hospital** near the Tundhikhel: donors have equipped it with expensive high-tech equipment, but there's a chronic shortage of drugs and basic supplies, not to mention running water. The best facility for trauma is the **Military Hospital** in Chhauni behind Swayambhunath.

Plenty of pharmacies *(pharma)* are scattered about town, the largest on New Road and near various hospitals. No prescriptions are necessary and you can get a wide range of inexpensive medication, most of it made in India. Pharmacists will make recommendations for medications and dosages, but they're not always accurate.

In Pokhara, travelers should visit the **Western Regional Hospital,** tel. (61) 20-066, which does stool tests and provides treatment. The larger Terai towns and district centers may have a government hospital, but out trekking, medical care

is basically up to you—which is why you must carry medical essentials and be familiar with them. See special topic "Trekker's Medical Kit."

Alternative Health Treatments

Ayurveda is the ancient Indian science of health, evolved from 5,000 years of tradition and research. It's rooted in the concept of three humors which regulate health, disease, and body type: *pitta* or "fire," which controls bile and the circulatory system; *vata* or "wind," the nerve humor; and *kapha* or "water," regulating the digestive system. Imbalances in these aspects are believed to be the cause of all diseases: ayurveda treats these with a wide range of herbal remedies. Popular ayurvedic pracitioner Dr. Mana Bajracharya, tel. (1) 223-960, has an office in Mahabaudha behind Bir Hospital, while Nardevi Tol is lined with local ayurvedic pharmacies and doctors. **Himalayan Herbs,** tel. (1) 410-053, in Tangal Durbar compounds and prescribes ayurvedic treatments and runs classes in traditional medical treatments.

Tibetan medicine is rooted in ancient Buddhist texts and blends Indian and Chinese influences with indigenous herbal traditions. As in ayurveda, illnesses are said to result from an imbalance in one of the three major body humors. Doctors diagnose these through a subtle reading of pulses, and prescribe traditional herbal medicines perhaps compounded with a touch of ground minerals, powdered gemstones, or holy relics. There are many Tibetan doctors in Boudhanath, including **Dr. Kelsang Dolma** whose office is next to the Dharma Book Center. **Kunphen Tibetan Medical Center,** tel. (1) 213-820, has its main office north of Chetrapati Chowk, while a branch in Thamel's Hotel Star is open 5:30-8:30 p.m.

SAFETY

Until 20 years ago Nepal was virtually free of theft and violence. Though this is changing, Nepal remains far safer than most Western countries, especially regarding violent crime. A handful of foreigners have been attacked over the years, usually with robbery as a motive, but the odds of it happening to you are extremely low. Petty theft is a problem, however.

In general all you need is a little common sense: keep valuables out of sight, money and passport safely on your person, and an eye on your possessions. Try to keep valuables to a minimum. Watches, camera, and jewelry are all statements of wealth, whether subtle or blatant. The lighter you travel, the less hassles there are.

Much of the theft in the Valley and Pokhara is blamed on junkies. Nepal's population of heroin addicts is estimated at 15,000-20,000, which may not seem like much but is significant in a country with a low urban population. The rest can be attributed to the crumbling of a once-cohesive social system which guaranteed a thief would be quickly noticed, and a gradual change in attitudes spurred by increasingly materialistic values.

Sporadic political demonstrations in Kathmandu are not usually dangerous, but it's wise to avoid crowds and stay away from central locations like the Tundikhel and New Road at these times.

Precautions

Carry valuables in a moneybelt or pouch close to your body, preferably under your clothes. Keep traveler's check receipts and a photocopy of your passport's front page in a separate safe place to facilitate replacement if these are stolen. Be especially careful after changing money, when you've got a lot of cash on your person. Take as little cash as possible out with you on excursions; unless you're shopping you really don't need to carry much.

Hotel rooms are usually safe as long as there's a sturdy lock on the door and the windows are barred or inaccessible. You might want to bring a combination lock from home (it saves the hassle of sharing and losing keys) or buy a padlock manufactured in China if the hotel lock looks flimsy. In many hotels, fellow travelers present as big a threat as locals.

The biggest danger is from pickpockets, often deft-fingered kids who dip into your bag or pocket in the midst of a crowd. Festivals, bazaars, the packed public buses, and the General Post Office are all popular locales for thieves. Don't keep valuables in the back or side pocket of a backpack, where they're ridiculously easy to steal. Be wary if someone bumps into you or strikes up a particularly inane conversation: one member of a team may be distracting you, while the other picks your pocket. If you do catch the thief and haul him over to the police, they may vigorously beat him to your presumed satisfaction.

Bus Travel

On bus rides, keep an eye on your pack, which will be placed on top of the bus along with other luggage, riders, and possibly a few goats. Small articles may be pilfered from front and side pockets; more rarely the entire pack will disappear. The ride to Jiri is supposed to be especially bad. Bury valuables deep inside the pack and stuff the side pockets with undesirable items like old smelly socks. It helps to lock zippers with a small padlock. Carry a smaller bag on the bus for travel necessities and fragile valuables like cameras, and never let it out of your sight.

SPECIAL INTERESTS

NEPAL WITH KIDS

A trip to Nepal is a memorable experience for kids of any age, and it's also guaranteed to enhance your own experience. The mere presence of children bridges cultures. Nepalis have seen travelers galore, but meeting entire families is a rarity, and it reinforces the fact that you're just like them. Nepal is an extremely child-friendly place; men and women both are experts at cuddling and playing with kids, and you'll never receive an icy glare upon bringing children into a restaurant—on the contrary, the staff will be delighted.

As with travel anywhere with children, pacing is important. So is patience. The first big challenge is the long-distance flight. Request bulkhead seats for the extra leg room (bassinets can be provided for infants). Bring a child's backpack full of interesting peaceful diversions, and stash a few small surprises and snacks in your own bag to bring out at low points.

Veteran parents recommend ignoring healthy food rules for the duration of a trip. Snacks make great pacifiers and are needed more often than adults might realize. Local Wai Wai and Cheez-balls are popular local forms of junk food, readily available almost anywhere. Finicky eaters may find local food strange, but chips (french fries), fresh fruit, noodle soup, and omelets can be had almost anywhere. Traveling with a breast-feeding infant is surprisingly easy (and completely socially acceptable), but bottles are problematic, given the unsanitary water.

Sightseeing with kids requires frequent rest and snack stops, and a supply of toys and activities to get them through boring things *you* happen to be interested in. Try to intersperse such occasions with strategically timed, fun concessions. In Kathmandu, kids will enjoy Boudhanath and Swayambhunath; the monkeys at Pashupatinath (be wary of getting too close to them, though, due to potential bitings); exploring Hanuman Dhoka and the Basantapur Tower; and wandering through the bazaar. Concentrating on Patan and Bhaktapur will give them more freedom to run around, and make less worries about traffic for you. Mountain views will impress: go out to Dhulikhel or Nagarkot, take a long day hike (guaranteed to ensure a peaceful night), or catch the Mountain Flight. A helicopter flight is unforgettable, if expensive.

Involving kids in the trip from the beginning will help maintain their interest. Study up on Nepal beforehand together, and let them take part in the planning. Older children can keep a journal, complete with photos, and learn a few Nepali phrases. Give them Rs100 and let them shop in the bazaar for hair tassels, bead necklaces, *khukri,* or bananas.

Trekking is eminently do-able with children, as long as the schedule and route are appropriate. Don't expect kids to walk too fast or far, and allow some nonhiking playtime in the daily schedule. Younger children can be carried in a specially designed *dokko* which allows them to nap comfortably; an attached umbrella will provide shade. Many families prefer trekking through a company in order to get the relative privacy of tents. Others are happy with teahouse trekking on the more comfortable trails. North of Pokhara is a great choice for a short trip; try Dhampus-Chomrong-Ghandruk-Birethanti.

Altitude is a major consideration in trekking with children, particularly with infants, who can't tell you when they're feeling bad. General advice is to stay below 3050 meters with infants; with older children don't count on going above 4000 meters unless they appear to be doing exceptionally well.

Rafting on more moderate rivers avoids the walking and altitude issues altogether and is fine for kids age seven and up. You may want to insist they walk around the more difficult rapids. (For more information see special topic "River Rafting.")

Health concerns with children focus around gastrointestinal illnesses from contaminated water and food. Be careful about what they consume, and insist on frequent hand-washings. The most important treatment for diarrhea is replacing the lost fluid, as young children can become rapidly dehydrated.

WOMEN TRAVELERS

Nepal is a relatively easy Asian country for female travelers, even solo ones. However, many Nepalis find anyone traveling alone, male or female, basically incomprehensible and rather pitiable. A solo woman traveler is *really* strange, since Nepali women rarely travel, and if they do they're accompanied by hordes of relatives. This doesn't mean a foreign woman can't travel

underclad tourists, Thamel

alone, just that she should be prepared to deal with a certain amount of misunderstanding and suspicion. You may want to create a fictitious husband and family to mention at appropriate moments. This applies especially to trekking. Fortunately the major routes are so crowded with foreign trekkers it's easy to find casual companions. When people ask you if you're *eklaai* (alone) in a tone of disbelief, you can cheerfully assure them, "No, my friends are just behind," and be almost certain someone will turn up to fill the bill within an hour. Or you may want to hire a porter to provide a semblance of respectability. It's best to find an older man who will offer an element of fatherly concern, or a woman porter (possible in Sherpa regions).

The situation in Kathmandu is degenerating, as stories circulate of the sexual exploits performed by Western women in "blue movie" videos, coupled with the easy conquests Nepali lads find in Thamel. With the post-revolution "anything goes" mentality, Nepali women are targets for harassment as well. This charming custom goes by the quaint Indian misnomer of "Eve-teasing." You may be verbally hassled or very rarely furtively groped, but offenders are easily intimidated. Righteous indignation or an attitude of motherly amusement seem to work equally well. To avoid problems, dress modestly and studiously ignore loitering groups of young men. If things ever get out of hand, shout and scream and point. An insulted Nepali woman will slap the offender's face with her shoe—a gesture of supreme contempt.

There's no shortage of Nepali men looking for Western girlfriends, but they should be scrutinized carefully. The Thamel crowd almost universally looks for sexual favors, status points among their buddies, and optimally a green card and a ticket out of Nepal. Many foreign women fall for their trekking or rafting guides; Sherpas in particular seem to appeal to Western women.

WORK AND STUDY OPPORTUNITIES

Working in Nepal
The big hitch in long-term plans is a visa. It's illegal to work on a tourist visa, and obtaining a nontourist visa is extraordinarily difficult. Local language institutes often need English teach-ers (and sometimes teachers of other European languages) but they can't provide visas and don't pay much. Even more meager opportunities are offered by privately owned "English-medium boarding schools," which have become a major growth industry. Middle-class parents send their children to these schools to get ahead, but with no accreditation or regulations they are mainly money-making mills—for the owners, that is. The only really professional place is the American Language Center in Dhobidhara, which sometimes has openings for American teachers with ESL/EFL degrees.

The seemingly enviable position of trekking or rafting guide is not as ideal as it appears: there's seldom enough work, and it takes time and chutzpah to break into the adventure travel business. Some people export jewelry, clothing, or carpets, but this is not something to be done without checking the home market out first. Entering the lucrative foreign-aid circuit is likewise difficult, as foreign-aid missions are staffed by members of the foreign service, and generally hire consultants from their home countries. Doctors, nurses, and dentists can sometimes find opportunities in local clinics serving foreigners, while teachers might be able to work in the handful of schools for expat children.

Volunteer Opportunities
It's impossible to join programs like Peace Corps and VSO on the spot: these select applicants in their home countries and assign countries according to need rather than the volunteer's desire. Doctors can apply to staff the Himalayan Rescue Association's **Trekkers' Aid Posts** in Manang and Pheriche, though the waiting list is long. The **Sisters of Charity** in Chabahil sometimes take volunteers, as does the NGO **Child Workers of Nepal** in Tripureshwar. **Kopan Monastery** behind Boudhanath will take any extra medicine and clothing you might have.

Lonely and bored foreign prisoners in Kathmandu's four **jails** always appreciate visitors. There's a rotating supply of 15-20 prisoners of various nationalities, most arrested for trying to smuggle gold or drugs. Notices posted in popular restaurants list their names, nationalities, and which jail they're in (take notes, as you must ask for prisoners by name). Bring food, books, magazines, clothing, or cash—prisoners are expected to provide for all their own needs beyond a daily allotment of rice and *daal,* and without family members to help them out, foreigners are in a pretty grim situation. Most of all, though, they welcome a chance for conversation and human contact.

College Programs

Several programs offer college students the chance to spend a semester or a year in Nepal for college credit. Students may study Nepali or Tibetan, research special projects, go trekking, or live with Nepali families. The **Experiment in International Living** has its school in Naxal, tel. (1) 414-516; make arrangements with the main office at Kipling Road, Brattleboro, VT 05301, U.S.A. The University of Wisconsin-Madison's **School of South Asian Studies** offers a "College Year in Nepal" program; for information write to 750 University Ave., Madison, WI 53706, U.S.A. The three-month cross-cultural programs for college students offered by **Sojourn Nepal** feature homestays with Nepali or Tibetan families and opportunities for apprenticeships with local

artists or for social service work, all concluding with a month-long trek. Contact Jen Warren, 2436 North 56th St., Phoenix, AZ 85008, U.S.A.

Serious independent scholars can arrange a research visa with Tribhuvan University to study anthropological or sociological issues. The only widely accessible program is Tribhuvan University's **Campus of International Languages** across from the Exhibition Ground, tel. (1) 226-713, which offers courses in Nepali, Sanskrit, Newari, and Tibetan, beginning every August. Students are issued a visa and must attend class (two hours daily) and pass their exams. The quality of instruction depends largely on the teacher; you may end up doing rote work instead of learning to speak. For information on private language lessons and cultural study programs, see "Languages" in the general Introduction.

Yoga and Buddhism

Kathmandu is a great place to investigate a number of spiritual pursuits and holistic therapies. See "Recreation and Study" in the Kathmandu chapter for details.

COMMUNICATIONS

MAIL

The Postal System

Domestic and international mail are slow and unreliable in Nepal. Airmail letters take 10 days to three weeks coming or going to the U.S., a little less for Europe. Sea mail takes three or four months, and airmail sometimes equals that, as Christmas cards arrive in May after some mysterious detour. In addition, the mail is afflicted with a 10-20% disappearance rate. Packages are particularly vulnerable to pilferage. Sometimes they are delivered with only a fraction of the original contents; on other occasions worthless local items may be substituted for valuable originals in an effort to cover up the theft. The moral: avoid sending or receiving valuables and important documents by post. Either wait until you leave Nepal, or pass them over to a departing traveler to mail from another country. The Indian postal system is excellent compared to Nepal's. Important documents can be sent via DHL in Ka-

maladi, tel. (1) 222-358, or UPS, tel. (1) 225-392, in Thamel, but courier service is expensive.

Receiving Mail

As in all of Asia, letters should be addressed with the surname in capital letters and underlined. Poste restante is located in Kathmandu's **General Post Office** at Sundhara, near the Dharahara. Letters are filed according to last name in open boxes which you sort through yourself; it's good to check under your first name as well. The scene is chaotic in tourist season, but it's as reliable a place as any. Poste restante hours are Sun.-Thurs. 10:15 a.m.-4 p.m., closing at 3 p.m. in winter and 2 p.m. on Friday. If a package arrives you'll get a slip directing you to the **Foreign Post Office** just north of the GPO, which is open Sun.-Thurs. 10 a.m.-1 p.m. and Friday 10 a.m.-noon. Bring your passport for identification purposes and go early, as there are several lines to wait in and fees to pay.

The **American Express office** in Hotel Maya-

(top left) cycle rickshaw, Freak Street (Christopher Gamm);
(top right) prayer flags at Boudhanath, Losar during the Tibetan New Year (Kerry Moran);
(bottom) Thamel street scene (Kerry Moran)

(top) family watching festival in Bhaktapur (Kerry Moran);
(bottom) merchant's stall at Pashupatinath, Shiva Ratri (Kerry Moran)

lu just off Durbar Marg provides an efficient free mail service for clients who can produce an American Express card or traveler's checks. Pick-up time is Sun.-Fri. 10 a.m.-1 p.m. and 2-5 p.m. The address is c/o American Express, P.O. Box 76, Kathmandu, Nepal.

Some embassies (including the U.S., French, and British) will receive mail for their citizens, usually only letters and printed matter. You can also have mail sent care of your hotel or trekking company.

Sending Mail

While there are post offices across Nepal, domestic mail is unreliable and slow and it's really best to send everything from Kathmandu—though it *is* fun to mail off postcards from remote Namche Bazaar. GPO hours are Sun.-Fri. 10:15 a.m.-4 p.m. (3 p.m. in winter); stamps are sold from an outside counter Sun.-Fri. 8 a.m.-7 p.m., Saturday 11 a.m.-3 p.m. Mailing a letter involves waiting in several lines, so first, a lesson in line etiquette. Formerly, as in many Asian countries, mobs clustered about the windows thrusting money and letters at harried clerks. Now everyone is supposed to *linemaa basney*, and iron railings have been installed to channel the crowd. People may shove in front of you because they think you won't protest, but you have every right to reassert your place.

Postage rates for different countries are displayed on a board in the lobby; currently Rs20 for letters and Rs15 for postcards to the U.S. and Canada; Rs18/Rs12 for Europe. It's more efficient to buy stamps all at once and use them over the course of your visit. There are different windows for stamp-selling, registration, and insurance. Registering letters costs Rs10 extra and provides a measure of reassurance, but registered letters still do occasionally disappear.

Aerogrammes are a rupee cheaper than regular letters; buy them at stamp-selling windows. Postcards and envelopes are sold by street vendors outside the GPO gate, but it's cheaper to buy them in town. Local envelopes are short on glue, so seal with extra glue or tape.

Having assimilated all this information, you may decide to avoid the GPO altogether. Major hotels, Thamel communications offices, and Pilgrims Bookhouse all sell stamps for a slight markup, and will mail letters as well.

Shipping Goods

You can mail packages yourself from the Foreign Post Office just up the street from the GPO, but allow several hours for the chore. Bring your passport and packing materials, and don't bother to seal the box until it's been inspected by customs and you've paid the appropriate duty. Airmail packets have a 10-kg limit and take around two weeks; sea mail, which has a 20-kg limit, takes up to three months.

Anything over 20 kg must be shipped air cargo, which takes 7-10 days and is very reasonably priced considering it's more reliable than the mail. Packages in the range of 5-45 kg cost US$4.60 per kg to Europe, US$6.70 per kg to the United States. Sea cargo is cheaper but takes three to six months, and it's slightly less reliable as the goods must go through India.

It's easiest to pay a shipping company to do the dirty work for you. Companies will provide packing materials, help you pack your goods and make a customs list, obtain clearance certificates if necessary, and get your package through customs. Try **Sharmasons** at Satya Kunja, tel. (1) 222-709, **Overseas Cargo Service** in Thamel, tel. (1) 416-017, or **Atlas Cargo Service** in Thamel, tel. (1) 412-335.

TELEPHONE, TELEGRAM, FAX, AND THE INTERNET

Local Calls

There are no phone booths: public phones are located in city shops, where they're advertised by a tiny blue sign. Local calls are Rs2; many other shops allow the use of their private phones for a slightly higher fee. Finding an establishment's telephone number can be difficult, given the lack of a standard telephone book. Privately published directories are sometimes creative with the numbers they publish. For local directory assistance dial 197. Phone numbers in the Valley are six-digit; in other areas they are five-digit. There is also a multitude of area codes. Please refer to the adjacent chart for those of the largest cities.

Long-distance Dialing in Nepal

It is necessary when dialing within Nepal, from one area code to another, to preceed the area code by zero.

CITY CODES OF NEPAL

Nepal's country code is 977. When dialing from one area code to another within the country of Nepal, a zero must preceed the area code.

Bhairawa	71
Biratnagar	21
Birgunj	51
Butwal	73
Gorkha	64
Janakpur	41
Kathmandu	1
Narayanghat	56
Nepalgunj	81
Pokhara	61
Tansen	75

International Calls

Nepal has direct-dial service to 47 countries; dial 186 to place an international call to other destinations. Service has improved markedly in recent years, and direct-dial facilities are all over Kathmandu, Pokhara, and Terai towns. Look for signs advertising "ISTD"—an unfortunate connotation given the standard meaning of "STD" as "sexually transmitted disease," but here it means "international subscriber trunk dialing."

It's easiest to make international calls from your guesthouse or one of the many private **international communications centers** about town—there are at least a dozen in Thamel.

USEFUL TELEPHONE NUMBERS

Directory assistance	197
Long-distance domestic	180
International calls	186
Calls to India	187
Police Emergency	100
Police Service	(1) 226-998
Immigration Office	(1) 418-573
Night Taxi Service	(1) 224-374
Kathmandu Yellow Cab	(1) 414-565
CIWEC Clinic	(1) 228-531
24-hour emergency	
medical service	

These offer telephone, fax, telex, and mail services, and are efficient and reasonably priced, far more pleasant than the chaotic old **Central Telegraph Office** across from the National Stadium, which is just down the road from the GPO. The latter remains open 24 hours a day, however, and charges 20% less than private places. Phone/fax fees are Rs120-150 per minute for most Western countries, with an extra "report fee" tacked onto the first minute. Frequently there's a three-minute minimum. Collect calls can only be made to Japan, Canada, and the U.K., but most places will allow your party to call you back on the spot. Since it's much cheaper to call *to* Nepal than to call *from* it, this makes a lot of sense. If you dial from abroad, Nepal's country code is 977; the Kathmandu city code is 1.

Telegrams, Faxes, and the Internet

Telegrams are expensive and becoming obsolete with the advent of fax machines; to send one, go to the Central Telegraph Office across from the National Stadium. International communications centers and major hotels will send and receive telexes and faxes, as will travel agencies on Durbar Marg. Nepal is edging its way onto the Internet, and should be firmly in place in a year or two. Right now it's possible to send and receive e-mail through Mercantile Communications on Durbar Marg, postmaster@mos.com.np; full Internet access.

MEDIA

Newspapers and Magazines

Post-democracy, the number of small Nepali-language independent papers has mushroomed to over 650 publications—pretty amazing for a country with a 40% literacy rate. The local standard is the English-language daily *The Rising Nepal*, a semi-autonomous government offshoot combining oddly edited wire-service stories, vignettes of Nepali life (minor crime and bus accidents), and ads from development organizations. *The Kathmandu Post* is similar and slightly less stodgy. Local weeklies like *The Independent* and the newsmagazine *Spotlight* provide more insights into local political culture.

The International Herald Tribune, USA Today, Time, and *Newsweek* are available in larger

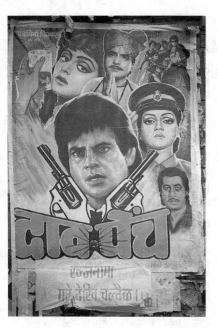

Indian movie poster

upcoming festivals. The more sober *Kailash—A Journal of Himalayan Studies* presents a scholarly cross-section of Himalayan life, anything from the spatial implications of a Bhaktapur procession to the development of modern art in Nepal.

Most provocative and interesting of the lot is the local magazine *Himal,* published every two months. It casts an incisive look at issues like foreign aid, tourism, and hydropower politics, and is essential reading for anyone interested in the deeper issues of the Himalayan region.

Radio and Television

Government-run **Radio Nepal,** the country's sole radio station, brings music and news to thousands of remote villages and has been a major force in the creation of a common "Nepali" identity. Programming includes Nepali folk music, radio dramas, and development-oriented skits, interspersed with commercial jingles for soft drinks and laundry soap. English-language news is broadcast daily at 8 a.m. and 8 p.m.; the BBC World Service is relayed 11 p.m.-12:15 a.m.

Check the papers for the program schedule of **Nepal TV,** a homegrown enterprise which broadcasts 7:30-8:30 a.m. and 6:30-10 p.m. and airs English news nightly at 9:40 p.m. Satellite TV service in major hotels includes Hong Kong's **Star TV,** broadcasting BBC World Service TV, MTV, sports events, and old American programs.

A television set and a VCR have become the new status symbols in Kathmandu, not least because of the heavy import duties slapped on them. Now it's not uncommon to see an aerial sprouting from the tiled roof of a traditional house. Video rental shops in Kathmandu stock all sorts of films: most popular are "Bollywood" epics (that's Bombay + Hollywood), kung-fu flicks, and the "sexy" films shown in dark local video dens.

bookstores and hotels. Other magazines are hard to come by, and are a good thing to pack if you've got some extra room—they become much more fascinating in Nepal, and people are always interested in the photos and glossy advertisements. If you've got a hankering for periodicals, browse through the reading room of the **American Library** in Gyaneshwar or the **British Library** on Kanti Path.

The locally published *Travellers' Nepal* is a tourist magazine distributed free through hotels and at the airport. The restaurant reviews are pure puffery, but it contains useful information and articles, including a monthly rundown of

INFORMATION

Tourist Offices

Nepal's Department of Tourism operates several Tourist Information Centers. The main one is on Ganga Path in Kathmandu, next to Basantapur Tower, just down from Durbar Square; there are also offices in Pokhara, Birgunj, Bhairawa, Kakarbhitta, Janakpur, and Jomosom. The Kathmandu office is open Sun.-Thurs. 9 a.m.-5 p.m (Friday 4 p.m.) and is the best by far, which isn't saying much. Staff can answer questions and help you find places on maps, but they have pathetically little in the way of handouts: currently a brochure on trekking, one on Pokhara, and one outlining Nepal's attractions. The tourist information counter near Patan Dhoka hands out free color posters to tourists. A massive **Kathmandu Tourism Service Center** under construction in the Exhibition Park east of the Tundikhel is slated to open in 1996, but its usefulness remains in doubt given the lack of information to stock it with.

The **Kathmandu Environmental Education Project** (KEEP) and the neighboring **Himalayan Rescue Association** (HRA) office in Thamel, near Immigration, are excellent sources of information for trekking and can also answer questions on other aspects of Nepali life. See the Trekking chapter for more details.

MAPS

Good maps of Nepal are hard to find, and Kathmandu is the best place to look. Try the big tourist bookstores like Pilgrims Bookhouse, or visit **Maps of Nepal** in Baneshwar, about a half-km before the Everest Hotel on the main road. See the Trekking chapter for a rundown of trekking maps and information.

Country Maps

All-Nepal maps are good for an overview and an idea of the road network, but the detail is generally too large to be useful in specific regions. Mandala puts out a basic 1:800,000 Nepal map showing main roads and trails; not terribly accurate, but cheap. Nelles's more expensive color Nepal map is even less accurate, and chops off the entire country west of Dhaulagiri. The ITMB/Estate Nepal map is great, except for the fault of depicting most trails as jeep roads.

The Survey Department's giant contour map of Nepal (1:500,000) makes an impressive souvenir, and it's amazingly cheap at Rs60 for the three-sheet set. The Suspension Bridge Division's six-sheet *Main Trail Map* series is useful for secondary trails and roads in the Hills. The *Planimetric Map of Satellite Images* (1:250,000) consists of a 19-sheet set of photographic maps which make beautiful souvenirs.

City Maps

The advertising-larded free city map handed out at the airport and at tourist venues makes a good start, though the thumbnail-sized inset of Bhaktapur is a travesty. For basic urban navigation pick up a copy of the yellow Kathmandu-Patan map for around Rs25 from Thamel streetstands or bookshops. This nameless series of tourist maps extends to Patan and Pokhara.

The Schneider map series reveals the convoluted backstreets and many temples of old Kathmandu and Patan. While they're over 20 years old, the essential points of interest remain unchanged. The Schneider *Kathmandu Valley* map is indispensable for delving into the Valley. Published in Austria, these color maps run around Rs700 apiece. Nepa Maps has published a cheap bootleg edition of the Schneider Valley map. Berndtson & Berndtson puts out a good 1:70,000 road map of the Valley, with details of the three main cities on the reverse.

TIME

Time Zone

Nepal is 15 minutes ahead of Indian standard time, more as a symbol of political independence than any actual time difference. Nepal time is two hours and 15 minutes behind Chinese/Tibet time (three hours and 15 minutes April-Sept.), and five hours and 45 minutes ahead of Greenwich mean time. Thus, 8 p.m. in Kathmandu is 2:15 p.m. in London, 9:15 a.m. in New York, and 6:15 a.m. in Los Angeles.

Like most of Asia, Nepal operates on flexible time; "rubber time," some call it. Scheduled events typically start 30 minutes or an hour late, bus rides are always longer than you imagined they could be, and *bholi-parsi* is the common phrase for when something will get done, i.e., "mañana." It's advisable to keep checking up on your travel agent or whoever, and to keep a sense of humor about it all.

Business Hours and Holidays

Government office hours are 10 a.m.-5 p.m., closing at 4 p.m. Dec.-Feb. and at 3 p.m. on Friday year-round. Private businesses are usually open till 5 p.m. regardless of the day or time of year, while shops are open 10 a.m. to dusk or 8 p.m., later in summer. Bank hours are Sun.-Thurs. 10 a.m.-2:30 p.m., closing Friday at noon or 12:30 p.m. Government offices have no official lunch break (the late start is meant to let office workers eat their main meal before they go to work), but some business offices close for lunch around noon. Given the late opening hours, long lunches, and constant tea breaks, trying to find someone at their desk can be a frustrating exercise. The best times seem to be 11 a.m. and 3 p.m.; otherwise, people are in and out.

Saturday has been the weekly holiday since Chandra Shamsher Rana proclaimed it so in the 1920s. Being an inauspicious day, it's considered better to stay at home and do *puja* than go to work. Most stores and businesses are closed on Saturday, leaving little to do in town, and picnickers descend on the few parks. Sunday is not an official holiday, but it runs on a distinctly slower schedule.

Possibly as a direct result of this six-day work week, the pace of business is leisurely throughout, and holidays are seized upon as an excuse to do nothing. The year's biggest holiday is the period from Dasain to Tihar, a month during which things more or less stop—though, as it's the busiest tourist season, restaurants, shops, and hotels all function.

ELECTRICITY

Electricity is 220 volts/50 cycles, with occasional tremendous surges that can fry the insides of delicate equipment. You'll need a surge suppressor or "spike" to operate a computer. Kathmandu just got 24-hour-a-day power in 1984, and demand is already exceeding supply. Power cuts have been instituted on a rotating schedule among neighborhoods, 5:30-7:30 p.m. two nights a week. Larger hotels have generators, while smaller ones provide their guests with candles. Sockets come in a variety of shapes and sizes, but normally take plugs of the three-round-pin variety, though sometimes the two-square-pin type are found. Plug adaptors may be found in department stores and supermarkets.

Only some 10% of Nepali households have electricity, and these are concentrated in the Valley, the Hetauda-Birgunj area, and the Terai. A few mountain villages are lit by mini-hydro-electric plants, but most villagers rely on oil lamps and firelight and go to bed early. Conservation-minded foreign donors who have helped install electricity in some remote villages have found to their dismay that people only stayed up later and burned *more* firewood in order to keep themselves warm.

Spectacular star shows and brilliant moonlight compensate for the lack of electricity. The sky is amazingly clear even in Kathmandu, and on moonless nights in the mountains it's possible to see by starlight alone. A flashlight is essential, as good streetlighting is rare even in Kathmandu. Bring a pocket-size one for convenience. Spare batteries are easily come by.

FILM AND PHOTOGRAPHY

Equipment

Unless you're a serious photographer, leave your clunky single-lens reflex and multiple lenses at home and take a light, portable, auto-focusing subcompact. Condensing your equipment down to one small piece will lessen the worry of theft and the amount of stuff you need to lug about. A thousand dollars of camera equipment about your neck is more than many Nepalis earn in their entire lifetime.

For those who opt for an SLR, a telephoto lens (135mm or higher) or zoom is great for unobtrusive close-ups of people, while a wide-angle lens packs in architectural details—28mm is a good choice. A flash will allow you to shoot all kinds of otherwise dim places, but use it sensitively. Also bring extra camera batteries, lens-cleaning paper and fluid, and an air brush. Nepali children love to touch exposed lenses.

Video cameras are increasingly popular among tourists. They're one of the few items customs officials still look for and write in your passport; you may be liable for duty if you can't show it upon departure. Videocam owners are also hit with an Rs3000 fee when entering a national park. Finally, Nepal's 220V electricity means that American videocams will need a transformer to recharge battery packs.

Film Processing

Many Kathmandu shops now have automatic developing machines for print film and offer same-day service. Try **Das Color Lab** on Kanti Path, **Photo Concern** on New Road (with a Thamel branch), or **Nepal Color Lab** in Thamel. For black-and white-prints, try Photo Concern or **Ganesh Photo Lab** in Bhimsenthan.

Slide film is a more difficult matter. Don't get slides mounted in Kathmandu; inevitably they come back scratched. Ask for developing only—even these are sometimes scratched—or, better yet, get it developed at home. Note that Kodachrome can't be processed in Nepal; the nearest place is Australia, and mailing it from Kathmandu is a risky proposition.

There are no instant do-it-yourself photo booths, but many local photo shops can provide inexpensive passport photos. It's a good idea to get a dozen or so made up at a time for trekking permits and visa extensions.

Repairs and Supplies

Photo Concern on New Road is the best place for camera repairs and for a wider than usual (though still scanty) range of supplies. Other camera shops in the neighborhood rent cameras, lenses, lights, and flashes, even video cameras—a popular item during wedding season.

Various brands of slide, print, and black-and-white film are available in Kathmandu and Pokhara at prices only slightly higher than in the West, though the selection isn't as wide. Check the expiration date on the box before purchasing. Outside of tourist destinations film is rarely available, so bring more than you think you'll need.

Photo Etiquette

In general, be sensitive of people's privacy; remember it's their celebration, their country, their life. Rituals and festivals are almost always sacred in some way or another, with a whole world of inner meaning beyond "getting a good shot." The masked dancers who appear at certain festivals shouldn't be photographed: the moment they don their masks they embody the gods and are treated as such by people. Avoid using intrusive flashes in temples where people are doing *puja,* and ask permission before shooting the interior of any shrine (it's almost always okay to photograph the exterior).

It's polite to ask permission to take photos of people or their homes, possessions, or children, but Nepalis have gotten used to foreigners marching up and snapping away without even acknowledging them. Ask for a portrait, and many people will get all dressed up and sit there stiffly without cracking a smile. It may be the opposite of the spontaneous shot you had in mind, but to them photography is a serious business, a legacy to posterity. Don't be surprised if they expect an immediate photo—everyone has heard of Polaroids. Many will ask for a copy of the photo; don't promise to send one unless you're sure you will. If they want money for posing, just forget about it entirely.

Above all, try not to spend too much of your trip behind a camera lens. It's too easy to be mentally looking through the viewfinder even when the camera is not in front of your face. Photography should be an enhancement, not an obsession.

WHAT TO TAKE

Clothing

Bring comfortable, casual clothes easy to wash and dry. Exactly what kind depends on the season and where you're headed; consult the Temperature Chart in the general Introduction. Medium-weight cottons are a good choice year-round. Short or long-sleeved shirts are good for spring and fall; add a pile jacket or sweater for chilly evenings. From Nov.-Feb. in the Valley you'll need a warm sweater, jacket or down vest, and warm sleepwear, as only the most expensive hotels have heating. Comfortable, durable walking shoes are a must; add another lighter pair to wear around your hotel. Velcro-strap rafting sandals are great for the monsoon.

If in doubt, pack too little rather than too much. It's easy to expand your wardrobe in Kathmandu, either by buying ready-made cotton clothing or by visiting a tailor. Better to travel light and leave room for purchases than to haul over massive amounts of clothing you don't really need.

More important is that clothes be comfortable and sufficiently modest. This last applies mainly to women. Though Thamel is full of Western women in skimpy shorts and tops, such dress is not acceptable. Long, baggy walking shorts are better, but best are loose trousers, a below-the-knee skirt, or a local outfit like a Punjabi or *chuba*. Men shouldn't wear shorts or go bare-chested in the city; bare chests are also inappropriate while trekking.

The virtues of a full mid-calf length skirt can't be stressed enough. They're useful even in the Valley, but for women on a trek they're essential. A skirt minimizes the difficulty of finding an absolutely private place to pee. In cool weather you can wear tights or long underwear beneath it for extra warmth, then slip them off as the day warms up.

Packs and Duffels

If you're only visiting the Valley, any kind of luggage will do, but for travel outside the Valley, especially on buses, a backpack or duffel bag is easiest. Most travelers prefer internal frame packs, which have fewer exposed parts to be damaged. Bring a small selection of vital spare parts like screws, nuts, and bolts—losing just one can be a disaster if your pack falls apart.

Cold, dust, and frequent use can lead to brittle, easily snagged or broken zippers on packs and sleeping bags. To avoid problems, look for wide-toothed plastic zippers or get a top-loading pack—less convenient, but trouble-free. Rubbing softened candle wax on a zipper will temporarily cure a sticky one. Sometimes broken zippers can be repaired by straightening the bent teeth with a pair of pliers, but you're not likely to find pliers outside of Kathmandu.

Group trekkers must pack gear in duffel bags, which are easy for porters to carry. If you're hiring a porter on your own, he may carry your pack on his back or simply stow it in his *dokko*. If it's the former, you'll probably have to show him all the adjustments.

All travelers should bring a small padlock with which to secure packs or duffels on bus trips. You'll also need a daypack or comfortable shoulder bag for brief excursions. Cheap duffels and daypacks are available in Kathmandu. These bear brand-name labels but are local knockoffs. Quality is low, but they'll last through a trek. Shops also rent packs for around Rs25 a day. See the Trekking chapter for advice on packing for a trek.

> *For my part I travel not to go anywhere, but to go. I travel for travel's sake. The great affair is to move; to feel the needs and hitches of our life more nearly; to come down off this feather-bed of civilisation, and find the globe granite underfoot and strewn with cutting flints.*
>
> —ROBERT LOUIS STEVENSON

PACKING CHECKLIST

Useful Items for Everyone

- [ ] lightweight towel (a handtowel will save space)
- [ ] good durable sunglasses with cord attached
- [ ] sunscreen and lip balm
- [ ] Swiss Army knife
- [ ] lightweight nylon cord (available in trekking shops) and clothespins (bring from home)
- [ ] flashlight, useful in Kathmandu at night, vital outside of Kathmandu
- [ ] small pack or shoulder bag for day-trips
- [ ] water purification method
- [ ] toiletries, including tampons and razor blades (unavailable outside major cities). Good toothpaste, shampoo, and dental floss are available but expensive. Pack them in a big durable Ziploc bag so you can see what's inside.
- [ ] sewing kit: at minimum light and dark thread, a few feet of ripstop duct tape for repairs of all sorts of things
- [ ] an inexpensive, inconspicuous, waterproof watch—or quit wearing one altogether
- [ ] money belt or neck pouch
- [ ] leakproof, durable plastic water bottle; one per person (these are hard to find in Kathmandu)
- [ ] journal or small pocket notebook for recording immediate impressions
- [ ] entertainment: novels, cards, small portable backgammon or chess set, crossword puzzles, soap bubbles to blow for kids, harmonica or small flute. A Walkman, maybe with a microphone and a blank tape for recording Nepali sounds—a great accompaniment to a slide show
- [ ] photos of your home and family, postcards of your country

Additional Useful Items for Trekkers

- [ ] glacier glasses with lenses and sidepieces for the high-UV light at altitudes
- [ ] spare eyeglasses if you wear them, plus a copy of your prescription
- [ ] dry-skin lotion for high altitudes
- [ ] flashlight and extra batteries and bulbs
- [ ] thread strong enough to repair packs and boots (dental floss can be used in an emergency). Throw in a few big safety pins in case a zipper breaks.
- [ ] sleeping bag (easily rented in Kathmandu or Pokhara)
- [ ] sleeping pad, if not provided by trekking company or if you plan on going off the beaten track
- [ ] medical kit (see "Health")
- [ ] a few candles thick enough to stand alone, or a headlamp or reading light
- [ ] butane lighters or good (non-Nepali) matches
- [ ] *khatak* (prayer scarves) if you plan on visiting lamas in Buddhist monasteries
- [ ] trekking permit
- [ ] maps and/or photocopies of route descriptions from a guidebook
- [ ] plastic bags for litter, wet clothes, dirty shoes
- [ ] emergency snack food to ease long days on the trail; local peanut butter packed in plastic containers is an excellent choice. Also nuts, dried fruit, biscuits, hard candies—heavy on the sugar for quick energy when you need it. Consider luxury items like Tang, Ovaltine, chocolate, muesli, spices.

THE KATHMANDU VALLEY

Cresting a low range of hills, which runs along the valley, we at length came in sight of Kathmandoo. This is another most remarkable view, and a very beautiful one. A picturesque and quaint-looking temple and a cluster of red wide-eaved houses, profusely adorned with carved wood-work, form a pretty foreground. In the plain below is a broad river, on the opposite bank of which stands the town, with its numberless Chinese-looking temples, the brasswork with which they are ornamented glittering in the sun . . .

—FRANCIS EGERTON,
*JOURNAL OF A WINTER'S TOUR IN INDIA,
WITH A VISIT TO NEPAL*

BOB RACE

INTRODUCTION

The Kathmandu Valley dominates Nepal, politically, economically, spiritually, and culturally. The Valley *is* Nepal, in name as well as fact. Traditionally it's known as Nepal Khalto or simply Nepal: ask a villager on a mountain trail where he or she is going, and the answer may well be a cheerfully called-out "Nepal!"

With its superb mix of man-made treasures and natural beauty, the Valley is often called an "open-air museum." Actually it's far better than a dry and stuffy exhibition—it's a living, breathing entity, a vital traditional culture that has, miraculously, survived to the end of the 20th century.

Increasingly, it's facing the stresses typical of third world urban centers: pollution, overcrowding, poverty, traffic jams. But the backstreets of the cities and the quiet country roads are still peaceful and remarkably unchanged, offering a sanctuary that's important to remember. Whenever Thamel's aggressive hawkers, the Immigration Office, the smoke-belching vehicles, or the mounds of garbage get you down, get beyond modern Kathmandu, still only a small percentage of the whole, and take refuge in the old town, or in the outlying Valley destinations described in the next chapter.

The old town, focused around the old Royal Palace or **Durbar Square,** is the first must-see; be sure also to visit the outlying holy sites of **Swayambhunath, Boudhanath,** and **Pashupatinath,** a trio which conveniently serves to highlight Newar Buddhism, Tibetan Buddhism, and Hinduism. With the erosion in quality of Kathmandu life it's wise to concentrate more on the Valley's other two cities: **Patan,** to the south and just across the river from Kathmandu, and to the east timeless **Bhaktapur,** a bit further out in the countryside. Don't ignore the outlying villages and still-lush countryside of the Kathmandu Valley. A day out will give a totally different perspective on the Valley, one still in tune with its cultural traditions and historic roots.

THE LAND

The flight into Kathmandu gives a perfect overview of the Valley's unique geographical position. A flat oasis set amid the rugged Himalayan foothills, the Valley is a roughly oval bowl measuring 24 km east-west and 19 km north-south, its flat bottomland patterned with

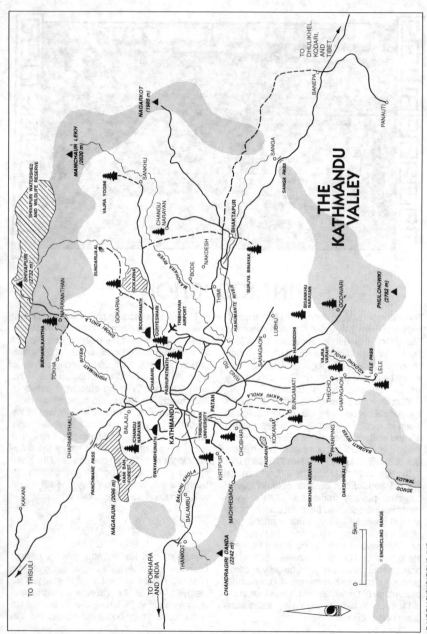

THE KATHMANDU VALLEY

TO DHULIKHEL, KODARI, AND TIBET

PANAUTI

BANEPA

SANGA

SANGA PASS

NAGARKOT (1988 m)

MANICHAUR LEKH (2030 m)

SHIVAPURI WATERSHED AND WILDLIFE RESERVE

SHIVAPURI (2732 m)

SANKHU

VAJRA YOGINI

CHANGU NARAYAN

BHAKTAPUR

NAKDESH

BODE

THIMI

SURYA BINAYAK

BISANKHU NARAYAN

GODAVARI

PHULCHOWKI (2762 m)

SUNDARIJAL

GOKARNA

BOUDHANATH

GUHYESWARI

TRIBHUVAN AIRPORT

HANUMANTE RIVER

MANOHARA RIVER

DHOBI KHOLA

NARAYANTHAN

BUDHANILKANTHA

TOKHA

VISHNUMATI RIVER

CHABAHIL

PASHUPATINATH

KATHMANDU

LUBHU

SANAGAON

HARISIDDHI

BAGMATI RIVER

VAJRA VARAHI

LELE PASS

KOKHU KHOLA

LELE

DHARMASTHALI

BALAJU

ICHANGU NARAYAN

SWAYAMBHUNATH

PATAN

TRIBHUVAN UNIVERSITY

NAKHU KHOLA

BUNGAMATI

THECHO

CHAPAGAON

PANCHMANE PASS

NAGARJUN (2096 m)

RANI BAN FOREST

CHOBHAR

KOKANA

TAUDAHA

SHIKHAR NARAYAN

PHARPING

DAKSHINKALI

BAGMATI RIVER

KOTWAL GORGE

KAKANI

BALKHU KHOLA

BALAMBU

KIRTIPUR

MACHHEGAON

TO TRISULI

THANKOT

CHANDRAGIRI DANDA (2242 m)

TO POKHARA AND INDIA

5 km

0

= ENCIRCLING RANGE

© MOON PUBLICATIONS, INC.

the textures of plowed, planted, and ripening fields. Cities appear at intervals, compact clusters of red-brick buildings crowned by the golden spires of temples and the stacked roofs of pagodas. Tiered terraces rise up the hillsides, meeting patches of forest. Beyond, mountains recede into the hazy distance, culminating in the stark frozen peaks of the Himalaya, the closest less than 50 km north.

After you've been in the Valley a while, head up to a hillside viewpoint to study the now-familiar scene at leisure. It's easy to pick out the three main cities: Kathmandu, Patan, and Bhaktapur, each once a kingdom in its own right. Smaller settlements dot the countryside, the houses huddled together to maximize precious farmland. The Newars, the original inhabitants, tend to live in the fertile bottomland near the Valley's center, while later arrivals such as Tamangs, Brahmans, and Chhetris settled on surrounding slopes. The luxuriant forests of oak, bamboo, and rhododendron that once covered these hillsides are vanishing as the demands for fuelwood and farmland grow. A century ago the woods swept all the way down to the Valley floor; now most hillsides have been carved into terraced fields.

The flat alluvial plain is ribboned by the shimmering tracks of sacred rivers: the Vishnumati, the Manohara, the Hanumante—a total of six, all flowing into the most sacred of all streams, the Bagmati. From its source high on the slopes of Shivapuri, the Bagmati bisects the Valley and exits to the south, eventually joining India's sacred Ganges.

The Climate

The Valley's subtropical latitude and 1300-meter altitude create a near-perfect climate: sunny days, cool nights, abundant monsoon rain, and snow only once in a generation (the last snowfall was in 1944). Average daily temperatures range 10-30° C, usually settling in the middle of this scale. Seasons are marked by the changing colors of crops rather than distinct shifts in weather. The rice paddies begin as floating mirrors in early monsoon, turning to vivid green, then gold. The autumn harvest gives way to the textured browns of fallow fields, followed by the green of spring wheat and the gold of flowering mustard. The year-round growing season allows two or even three crops a year to be coaxed from the fertile soil, enriched by the sedimentary deposits of the long-ago lake which once covered the Valley. The traditional fertilizer is *ko*, crumbly phosphatic black clay mined from riverside deposits. In fallow times the earth itself is harvested: farmers lease their fields to brickmakers, who carve the earth into blocks which they bake in kilns to feed the modern building boom.

HISTORY AND CULTURE

Ancient past and modern present blend in a valley which faces an increasingly uncertain future. On one hand are the political and economic realities of urban Kathmandu, the only real metropolis in a rapidly growing country of some 19 million. On the other are the Valley's rural roots (over half of it is still farmland) and its ancient status as a sacred space: the Valley itself is considered a mandala, its four quarters guarded by sacred groupings of deities.

Increasingly, the old traditions are being eroded by new social, economic, and cultural mores. Change is inevitable; what's amazing is that the Valley's culture preserves customs and beliefs long vanished from the rest of the world—Indian Buddhism, medieval Hinduism, Tantrism, and unique folk traditions. How much longer these will endure is questionable: probably a few decades at the most. The culture's extreme vulnerability makes the situation all the more poignant. The Valley's rich heritage represents an irreplaceable treasure, not just for Nepal, but for the entire world.

Early Times

The Valley was once covered by a lake, until, legend says, the bodhisattva Manjushri raised his sword of wisdom and sliced a passage through the mountain walls, draining the water to allow the first settlements. Certainly the Valley has been inhabited since prehistoric times. By the 4th century A.D. it was a flourishing center of trade; by the 7th century it was a highly advanced civilization, producing exquisite stone sculptures under the Licchavi dynasty.

Valley culture reached its peak under the Malla Dynasty (1220-1768), which saw the creation of splendid art and architecture that remains today. The Valley's cultural riches were funded by its rich soil, and by its strategic location on the India-Tibet trade route. Described as "the turntable of Asian culture," the Valley acted as a cultural bridge between India and Central Asia. Here Gangetic and Himalayan cultures meet, resulting in a rich cross-cultural tapestry.

> *... This comparatively small area [is] a veritable art museum of a particularly interesting character, with all the drawbacks to such an institution removed but with many an added charm.*
>
> —PERCY BROWN,
> *PICTURESQUE NEPAL*

The Newars

The underlying threads of this tapestry are the Newars, the Valley's indigenous inhabitants and the creators of its civilization. Less than five percent of Nepal's total population, they are a steadily decreasing minority even in their homeland, forming perhaps a third of the Valley's population.

Their influence remains disproportionately high. Although the Newars were conquered over two centuries ago with the Gorkhali unification of Nepal, they have managed to retain their identity and traditions. Their rich culture is distinctly nonmilitary, which perhaps explains their conquest by those consummate soldiers, the Gorkhalis. The Newars choose to turn their energy and talents to trade, farming, religion, and above all, art.

The Valley's magnificent heritage is all the more astounding for its relatively small size: nearly 3,000 monuments are packed into 570 square km. Seven of them (the three Durbar Squares, Swayambhunath, Boudhanath, Pashupatinath, and Changu Narayan) have been placed on UNESCO's World Heritage List, the densest concentration of such sites anywhere, and the entire Valley has been proclaimed a UNESCO World Heritage Site, "a refuge of beauty and spiritual repose."

Living Art

Far more than a well-preserved art collection, the Valley is a living, breathing creation, imbued with life by its people, who follow ancient customs and beliefs. Its traditional villages and cities blend harmoniously with the natural setting, miraculous when you consider that Valley villages have an average population density greater than those of most modern skyscraping capitals. In urban neighborhoods this figure can exceed 74,000 per square km, making places like Asan Tol among the most densely populated regions on earth. City-dwellers live in a vertical dimension, people piled atop people, crammed into tiny rooms. The crowded bazaar lanes are only a half-hour away from the open fields and sleepy peace of village life. The contrast between the two is what creates the Valley's inexhaustible charm.

THE OLD CITIES

Superbly arranged and skillfully built, the cities, temples, and palaces of the Kathmandu Valley are the Newars' finest artistic achievement. From the ordinary house to the multitiered temple, their buildings are masterfully designed and exquisitely decorated.

Urban Design

Warrens of narrow streets lined by densely packed buildings, regularly the old cities are punctuated by courtyards, water taps, plazas, and of course, temples. The masterful distribution of public space controls any feeling of crowdedness, though Kathmandu's backstreets are now jammed with an unplanned influx of motor vehicles. Patan and especially Bhaktapur better preserve the original atmosphere of Newar cities, where courtyards, streets, and squares serve as stage sets for the spectacle of daily life.

Newar towns are harmonic masterpieces of man-made and natural environments. The red brick and dark wood blend into the landscape, complementing rather than dominating it. The Newars excelled at urban design, and their

HIGHLIGHTS OF VALLEY ART AND ARCHITECTURE

Stonework

Ancient, classic stone sculptures litter the Valley, just waiting to be discovered. The quadrangle surrounding **Changu Narayan** shelters some of the finest pieces: Vishnu revealing himself in his divine glory before an awed Arjuna (a scene inspired by the Bhagavad Gita), another Vishnu taking a massive world-spanning stride, a curious stone Garuda with the features of a long-dead king, and the Valley's first piece of recorded history, an inscribed stone victory column dating back to A.D. 464. The Patan Durbar's sunken royal bath, the **Tulsi Hiti**, holds dozens of precisely executed stone sculptures set in a curved, sunken bath, as well as an exquisite metalwork spout. The **Sleeping Vishnu** at Budhanilkantha is a marvellously serene sculpture from the 6th century. Finally, everywhere about the old city are *chaitya*, lingas, and worn, shapeless ancient stones worshipped for millennia as embodiments of natural forces.

Bronzes

Visit the National Museum for close-up views, and admire the bronze images of Malla kings mounted on pillars in the three Durbar Squares. Bhaktapur's famed **Golden Gate** needs no introduction, but the "Golden Temple" of Patan outdoes it with an abundance of images and gilt repoussé work. Nearby, in a courtyard of the old Patan palace, graceful lifesized images of the goddesses **Ganga** and **Jamuna** guard a locked temple door, and the entrance to the northernmost palace courtyard bears a magnificent gilt window. Pay your respects to the two **Taras** at Swayambunath, and the lush leafy trellis overrunning the *torana* of the **Seto Machhendranath Temple** in Kathmandu. As a sad sidelight, note the many carefully wrought metal *torana* bearing gaping holes where thieves have wrenched out small images of deities.

Paintings

Examples in Nepal are more limited, but the **National Gallery** in Bhaktapur has some stunning *thangka* and *paubha,* plus restored frescoes from the old palace. Inside Bhaktapur's Woodcarving Museum, a room of painted frescoes is being painstakingly restored. The Tibetan monasteries of **Boudhanath** are overflowing with *thankga* and striking wall murals of the Vajrayana pantheon. Some of the finest and oldest Buddhist wall murals are in the small Sherpa monasteries of Solu, especially the *gompa* of **Thupten Choling, Junbesi,** and **Tragsindhu.**

Woodcarvings

The finest temple struts are the oldest: the 14th-century struts at Kathmandu's **Chusya Bahal, Musya Bahal,** and **Itum Bahal,** the *yaksha* of **Uku Bahal** in Patan, and above all the exquisite carvings of Panauti's **Indreshvara Mahadeva** temple. To marvel at lavish Newar woodwork you need go no farther than Kathmandu's old palace, especially **Basantapur Tower.** Bhaktapur's old **Pujari Math,** a former Hindu priest's house, has been transformed into the **Woodcarving Museum;** the building itself is a superb example of the art, with its intricate decorations, including the famed **Peacock Window.**

Temples

The hilltop Vishnu shrine of **Changu Narayan** is arguably *the* classic multiroofed temple, a richly decorated example dating back to the 17th century. Bhaktapur's five-story **Nyatapola** is the tallest, gracefully balanced on a towering stepped plinth. The mysterious, aloof **Taleju Temple** rising above Kathmandu's old palace is the most imposing, perfectly executed and richly adorned. You can only admire it from the outside, however: the exceedingly sacred temple is closed to all but its high priests, the royal family, and the Kumari.

---

generous use of public space makes the cities a joy for wanderers as well as residents. House interiors may be cramped and chilly, but courtyards and plazas are at everyone's disposal, and especially in the winter months people are outside all day, working, chatting, napping in the warm sunlight. There's no separation imposed here between life, work, and religion. All intermingle in a single setting, exemplified by the temple courtyard where women thresh wheat and children play.

Kathmandu, Patan, Bhaktapur, and to a lesser extent smaller ancient towns like Kirtipur and Thimi, share similar characteristics, as all were once medieval fortresses surrounded by thick walls and pierced by multiple gates. After the Gorkhali conquest the walls lost their protective function and gradually crumbled or were

THE *GUTHI* SYSTEM

The Valley's ancient traditions and temples have for centuries been preserved by *guthi*, communal associations bound by caste, kinship, or neighborhood links. These informal but very important Newar institutions acted as unofficial yet highly effective social regulators.

The *guthi* system dates back to Licchavi times. Its present form dates to the Malla era, when it was a vital part of the social fabric. A *guthi*'s authority was backed by the temple endowments it administered. Wealthy patrons would donate elaborate ornaments to a temple deity, or more commonly, plots of farmland for the support of temples. These were rented to tenant farmers, and revenues were used to maintain buildings or to sponsor the performance of an important ritual or festival.

As an integral part of an intensely communal society, *guthi* were extremely effective in supporting traditions and codes of behavior. Their duties were taken seriously, as shown by old inscriptions invoking curses on those who tamper with temple endowments. At Changu Narayan, the miscreant is threatened with rebirth as an insect in human excrement, or with being cooked in a pot, while the giver of land is promised 60,000 years of bliss. Another inscription threatens "he who defaces this wall" with a quantity of sin equivalent to the crime of slaughtering 10 million cows, 10 million Brahmans, 10 million women, and 10 million children. Too bad the vandals who deface temples with graffiti can't read the old Newari inscriptions.

Beyond preserving temples, *guthi* served as a sort of social glue, preserving shared values and beliefs and transmitting them through the centuries. But the institution has declined in recent years. Government land reforms instituted in the early '60s nationalized *guthi* endowments, stripping local institutions of revenues and prestige. The *guthi* remain active, but fewer young men are joining them, and with their authority diminishing, they're slowly turning into social clubs.

So far, no other agency has stepped in to replace the *guthi* in its vital role. The Department of Archaeology has proven a poor substitute in protecting and preserving buildings, and the poorly administered national Guthi Sansthan manages to collect only a fraction of its potentially vast revenues. In cases where private *guthi* retain control of property, the situation is little better, as in a 14th-century building recently pulled down in Patan by its *guthi* to make way for income-producing modern shops.

---

cleared away. The cities were designed in the form of a mandala, with the sacred center occupied by the royal palace and its temple-studded plaza (now known as the Durbar Square). From here neighborhoods fanned out, arranged by caste into *tol,* groups of 100 or so houses clustered around smaller temple-studded squares. Occupations cluster together, with potters living in one quarter, silversmiths in another, and so on. Low-caste and untouchable communities dwelt outside city walls; here also were the fearsome cremation grounds, haunted by terrible ghosts. Cities were protected against these evil influences by strategically placed shrines, often oriented to the four directions.

Social Structure

Though the Valley's cities may seem dirty and dilapidated today, they were once maintained by a well-organized social system. Royalty and the wealthy classes built monuments, water taps, and temples, and donated land and funds to the *guthi* organizations charged with maintaining them in perpetuity. Even simple farming villages boasted bricked gutters, sewers, and water systems. Low-ranking Newar castes cleaned the streets, hauling away garbage and waste to be used as fertilizer in nearby fields. The old cities were hardly spotless—a 19th-century Englishman wrote, "From a sanitary point of view, Kathmandu may be said to be built on a dunghill in the middle of latrines"—but the breakdown of the old social system and the rapid increase in population have not improved matters.

Houses

Traditional Newar houses are clustered closely together to conserve valuable space. The long rectangular buildings set end-to-end turn the already narrow city streets into canyons where the sun seldom penetrates. More houses are joined at right angles to these streetside ones to form courtyards which serve as peaceful refuges from the busy streets.

Old houses are built of sunburnt or kiln-baked clay bricks plastered together with a mud-mortar mix. The exceptionally thick walls make the interiors cool and dark. The front of the building may be covered with a more impressive facade of slipglazed or oiled brick. Wooden doors and window frames are decorated with lavish carvings, the varied patterns helping to distinguish each home. Traditionally there was no window glass, so windows were few and small to keep out the cold. Buildings were roofed with thatch or with *jhingati* clay tiles.

Due to the high water level in Valley subsoil, the damp ground floor is seldom used for living quarters. In rural areas the bottom rooms are used to stable animals, while in the cities they serve as shops or workshops. In some houses the ground floor is sealed off and used as a trash dump, cleaned out only when it becomes absolutely necessary, perhaps once in a generation.

On the upper stories are living quarters: sleeping rooms on the middle floors, and a general workroom/sitting room on the top floor where family members spend much of their time seated on straw mats, weaving, preparing food, chatting, or gazing through the latticed windows onto the street below. A large projecting bay of three or five beautifully carved windows admits light into the main living area. The kitchen and the family shrine are always on the topmost story, for both are ritually sacred and it would be disrespectful to walk over them. The rooftop terrace is used for drying items and warming oneself in the sun.

By modern standards living quarters are unenviable: cramped, dim, unheated, often without running water or toilet facilities, and maddeningly low-ceilinged. Garbage and wastewater are flung out the window onto the street, and woe to whoever happens to be below. In the winter the thick-walled buildings retain the cold, and life moves outside into sunny squares and courtyards.

Though houses are well-built, clay and wood cannot stand forever, especially in the earthquake-prone Valley. The old cities are filled with crooked, leaning, and downright tottering houses, some propped up by wooden beams and looking as though they might collapse at any moment—which they sometimes do. Most are still inhabited despite their precarious state. In 1975 an entire Kathmandu neighborhood dropped down 10 meters overnight, its hardened base of garbage having softened in the monsoon rains, and over two dozen houses crumbled into rubble.

As old buildings buckle, they are replaced by new ones, too often vertical boxes raised without any aesthetic consideration, often plastered with cement to give a "modern" look. Ugly and modern, like quaint and inconvenient, are simply two sides of the same coin. To the people who live in these structures, new buildings are easier to maintain: why have a thatch or tile roof when tin is cheaper and doesn't leak? As well, the new fashion is considered aesthetically preferable. Like people everywhere, they are not inclined to admire the commonplace reality they have grown up with.

Palaces

Royal palace compounds are designed like ordinary houses, with thick mud walls, massive carved pillars, and shaded porticoes embracing central courtyards. The resemblance ends there, however, as palaces are decorated to an extent equalled only by temples, and together with temples, represent the pinnacle of Newar architectural achievement.

BOB RACE

a Newar village

The old palaces of the Three Kingdoms were huge, sprawling affairs of linked courtyards: the Bhaktapur palace is supposed to have encompassed 99 courtyards, the Kathmandu palace 55, though only a few of these remain today. These were used as staging grounds for rituals and entertainment, as halls for public receptions, as quarters for courtiers, servants, and the ever-extensive royal harem, or as elephant stables. What remains today is only a fragment of the glories of the past, though thanks to painstaking restoration efforts they are in remarkably good condition.

The broad plazas across from the three main palaces became the focus of competition among rival kings, who sought to raise ever-more fantastic temples, shrines, and monuments. Only royalty could afford to finance such magnificent buildings, roofed and ornamented with tremendous quantities of gilded copper. Today we have the vanity and pride of these long-ago kings to thank for the architectural splendor of the three Durbar Squares.

TEMPLES

As dwelling places of the gods, temples inspired the very finest talents Newar artists had to give. They were built with a special type of oiled brick burnished with a glaze of red clay, inset with lavish woodcarvings, and decorated with "jewelry" of finely wrought metal ornaments. The classic Hindu temple or *mandir* is built on the geometric plan of a mandala, with the four directions symmetrically balanced and the deity residing in the exact center. The equivalent Buddhist shrine is the stupa, a solid hemispherical dome which is not a place of worship but a symbol of perfection and enlightenment. Worshippers walk around both temples and stupas clockwise, in an ancient ritual that replicates the sun's journey across the sky.

Like Newar art, temple architecture is infused with symbolic meaning and crammed with detail. One visit to a temple is seldom enough, and the greatest are inexhaustible treasuries you can never see too many times: each return visit reveals more unnoticed details hidden away in corners.

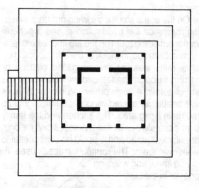

BOB RACE

side view and mandala floor plan of a Nepali pagoda

Multiroofed Temples

The classic Newar temple is a masterpiece of majesty and balance, reaching up to the heavens like a mountain peak linking earth and sky. The origins of the pagoda-type temple now found across Asia are disputed, but at least one school believes the Newars developed the design, which spread from Nepal into China and beyond. Whether or not they originated the idea, they undeniably perfected its execution, building structures of rich red clay bricks and dark sal wood, accented with shining gilded ornaments.

Symbolically the pagoda is a mandala in three-dimensional form, its square base sheltering the *garbha griha* or "womb house" of the deity inside. Every inch is a vehicle for art, myth, and religion lavished in an all-out display of talent.

Temples may be large or small, set on streets, within rows of buildings, or centered in courtyards. They can have anywhere from two to nine roofs (most have three) topped by a gilded finial or *gajur* symbolizing their sanctity. Most of the time the roofs are square, but temples dedicated to Bhairab are always rectangular, and a few rare examples of round and octagonal pagodas have also been built.

> *The temple is as much a part of life in Nepal as the supermarket in American life, more. People sleep beneath the temple eaves, light fires on its porch, hang their clothes on its rafters, store their grain in its inner shrine, tie their goats to it, dry their onions on it . . . in short, they live with it.*
>
> —RONALD BERNIER,
> *THE NEPALESE PAGODA*

Builders ingeniously combined structural needs with artistic display. The heavy slanted roofs are supported by massive struts locked into transverse beams above. These cunningly conceal the projecting roof beams and provide a surface on which deities manifest themselves in the form of woodcarvings. The design of squares within squares evenly distributes the tremendous weight of the tiled roofs. The structures are set atop stepped pedestals to increase their imposing grandeur, the steps echoing the lines of the stacked roofs.

Craftspeople adorned the brick facade with intricate woodcarvings and delicate metalwork. Semi-circular wooden tympanum or *torana* are mounted above doorways, windows, and sometimes even pillars, serving as message boards advertising the deity residing inside. Most important is the *dyo torana* mounted above the main entry, which identifies the god to worshippers. Usually the design is surmounted with the *kirtimukha*, the fearsome "Face of Glory," flanked by another character from Indian mythology, the sea-serpent or *makara* spouting strings of pearls and gems from its opened mouth. On the richest temples the *torana* might be rendered in fine metalwork. But public temples are open to thieves as well as worshippers, and many shrines now

bear gaping holes where ancient images once stood. Other figures have been secured with ugly metal bands or hidden behind metal grilles to protect them from a similar fate.

Malla kings lavished so much gold on temples that shallow trenches were dug in the ground beneath to capture particles washed off in monsoon downpours. The gilt of temple roofs is a symbol of purity, and delicate fringes of metalwork and bells decorate the edges, accenting them against the skyline. One peculiar feature is the *pataka,* a banner of hammered metal which descends from the pinnacle to the lowest story and drapes halfway to the ground. It serves as a sort of runway for the gods, a divine lightning rod upon which a deity descends to listen to, and hopefully act upon, prayers.

Shikara

Shikara means "mountain peak," and this soaring stone or brick temple replicates the towering peaks of the Himalaya. This architectural form was introduced into Nepal from Northern India in the 14th century. The square base symbolizes the mountain cave used for religious retreat. It is topped by a cigar-shaped tower faceted into multiple planes and surmounted by a gilded finial. Symmetrical porticoes and arcades are arrayed about the edges, supported by graceful columns. In the center is a small shrine housing the deity. *Shikara* may be of brick or stone (rare and expensive in Nepal, and thus sponsored only by royalty), or even faced with terra-cotta tiles, as in Patan's Mahaboudha Temple. The finest example is without a doubt the delicately carved **Krishna Mandir** of Patan's Durbar Square.

Stupas and *Chaitya*

Exclusively Buddhist monuments, stupas are hemispherical half-domes, sanctified by sacred relics enshrined inside. The whitewashed dome of major stupas is topped with a 13-step gilded spire culminating in a filigreed pinnacle, symbolizing the stages to enlightenment. The different parts of the stupa are associated with the five elements: the square base represents earth, the round dome water, the spire fire, the pinnacle air, and the surmounting ornament the invisible ether. Painted upon the square base, the all-seeing eyes of the Buddha stare out over the four directions, a uniquely Nepali addition to these originally Indian monuments.

Chaitya are small stupas, often elegantly detailed monuments of carved stone set up as memorials to a deceased family member. Some in the Valley date back to the 5th century. Historians believe they preceded the stupa and served as inspiration for the later, larger monument.

There are many distinct styles of stupa and *chaitya*, all derived from the original Indian model, which was based on burial mounds. Nepal's northern border regions have many Tibetan-influenced stupas, here called *chorten*, "supports for worship." Tibetans revere them as a tangible symbol of the Buddha's enlightened mind, enshrine sacred texts and images inside, and circumambulate them in worship. Some *chorten* guard the entry and exit points to town and have a passageway cut through them so they can be walked through; in such cases the ceiling is often decorated with elaborate frescoes.

chaitya, *Kathmandu Valley*

BOB RACE

Bahal

These sprawling, multistoried residential buildings set around a central courtyard structure the main cities of the Valley, lending their names to many neighborhoods—Thamel itself is a contraction of Tham Bahal. The *bahal,* or *vihara,* began in the 7th century as a monastery for Buddhist monks and a center of religious learning and art. As Newar Buddhism evolved, monks dropped their vows of celibacy to became householder priests, and the *bahal* were transformed into housing for Buddhist lay communities. Families live in separate apartments or houses in the compound, sharing the public space of the courtyard.

Every *bahal* has its own shrine set in the center, either free-standing or directly opposite the main entrance. The ground floor is for public worship, while the second storey houses the *bahal's agama* or family deity. Sculptures and *chaitya* dot the courtyard, offerings from past generations that now provide local children with an ultimate playground.

The greatest concentration of *bahal* is in the thoroughly Buddhist city of Patan: here the linked courtyards form an invisible world behind the streets. From the outside you may see only the main entrance, often guarded by stone lions. Inside is a peaceful, shady sanctuary, its quiet punctuated by the cooing of pigeons.

Resthouses and Water Taps

The crumbling resthouses dotting the rural and urban landscape once provided shady resting places and overnight shelter for travelers and pilgrims. They range from the *pati,* a simple raised and covered platform used by wayfarers, to more substantial *sattal* offering longer-term shelter, and the even larger *mandapa,* open pavilions used as community meeting halls. All these were built and maintained by wealthy patrons as a community service.

The wealthy also sponsored the construction of sunken water taps *(dhara),* still used today for drinking water, laundry, and bathing. The only difference is now the rich have indoor taps, while the poor line up at the ancient outdoor ones. The finest examples channel water from underground springs through an ingenious filtering system of sand, stone, and charcoal, to bring clear water gushing out of the mouths of stone taps carved in the form of *makara.* The walls may be ornamented with sculptures of deities,

Garuda, and the *naga* associated with water sources, and a handful of water is customarily offered before and after bathing. Some of the old *dhara* are drying up due to new construction which has blocked their sources; others are buried or choked with filth; but many others are still in use, some of them dating back to Licchavi times.

The old stone water tanks *(tutedhara)* which once dispensed drinking water to thirsty passers-by have fallen out of use, but can still be found. Look for a freestanding stone quadrangle or a smooth stone slab set into a wall, with a round spigot drilled in the middle.

CHANGING TIMES

It's easy to romanticize the Valley's cultural and artistic treasures. It's also easy to be shocked by one's first sight of life in a third world country. Reality lies somewhere between the extremes of fairy-tale kingdom and squalid slum. The Valley is a traditional society in transition to a modern one, buffeted by forces which are at work over the globe: development, motorized transport, popular culture, even tourism. In this sense the Valley is a cultural laboratory where the effects of so-called modernization may be observed.

Behavior and values are rapidly changing, as traditional religious values are pushed aside by the new gods: VCRs, motorcycles, and Hong Kong/Bangkok fashions. Michael Jackson and Madonna have replaced Rama and Sita as folk heroes, and entertainment is increasingly from Hindi films and violent or "sexy" videos rather than *bhajan* and festivals. The Valley's ancient traditional culture is still alive, but just barely.

Part of the problem is the population boom. The Valley's population has grown from 400,000 in 1951 to 1.45 million today and is increasing at around six percent annually. Add 330,000 tourists each year, and you begin to strain both the society and its infrastructure. Motor vehicles clog narrow streets that were built centuries before the invention of the combustion engine. Gridlock has become a daily event on the city's main roads. Smog veils the Himalayan views, and the sacred rivers carry raw sewage and chemical wastes. Herewith is a primer on Kathmandu's urban woes, to be read, perhaps, on a

day when you have spent a little too long pedalling a bike behind a smoke-belching *tempo* and are disgusted with it all.

Garbage

Solid waste is a highly visible problem in Kathmandu, especially since Germany pulled out of the waste management project it had supported for over a decade and turned it over to the municipal government. The latter appears determined to make a travesty of its slogan "A Clean, Green, Healthy Kathmandu." Mountains of rubbish fester for days on roadsides before the concerned authorities finally manage to send out a truck. Kathmandu's dump site has been closed since 1993, and authorities have been searching ever since for a permanent site for the 500 cubic tons of garbage generated daily. In the meantime, the refuse is being dumped in the Vishnumati River, an appalling solution.

Compared to the sanitary giant landfills of the West, there's something to be said for traditional waste disposal methods. The repulsive heaps of garbage are part of an unusually thorough waste recycling system. Cows, dogs, and crows are the first wave of attack, devouring anything edible. Then the ragpickers arrive to sort through the trash and cart away cardboard, paper, plastic bags, plastic containers, bottles, and tins—anything of conceivable value. Residential neighborhoods are patrolled by men calling out, *"Khaali sisi, purano kagaaj"* ("Empty bottles, old paper"), who buy leftovers from householders and cart them down to informal recycling agencies. A purely private sector system, it is efficient even if unsightly.

Water Woes

Water pollution isn't hard to miss—just glance at the black sludge of the Bagmati, a.k.a. the "Sewer of the Valley." The Bagmati's burden is particularly horrific given its sacred status: it's a toxic cocktail of solid waste, sewage and sludge, industrial effluents, cremation ashes, and animal carcasses, mixed with some water. The water flowing through city pipelines is clearer, but not much cleaner.

Look closely and you'll notice another water problem, in the buckets and jugs and plastic jerrycans lined up in front of bone-dry city water taps. The water supply in the dry season is half of demand. People must wait in queues for hours, and water is rationed in certain neighborhoods just like electricity. The worst-off areas get it only on alterate days. Richer people call in tankers to fill up their ground tanks; poorer ones must visit relatives to do the laundry, or do without. The supply shortage is exacerbated by enormous leakage and wastage rates of some 40%. Groundwater supplies have already been tapped, and urban planners are now eyeing alternate sources, the grandest project involving rerouting Helambu's Melamchi Khola through a 30-km tunnel into the Valley.

Air Pollution

Kathmandu's air quality has taken a beating lately, and it's not been totally justified. It started when visiting American researchers took sample measurements of vehicle emissions and announced Kathmandu had the worst ratings of five Asian cities they had studied. This was exaggerated by the press into "the worst air quality in all of Asia," but the study was only of vehicle emissions, not overall air pollution.

In all truth it probably *is* difficult to exceed the amount of black smoke belched from the buses, trucks, and *tempo* which clog Kathmandu roads. About a third of the Valley's fleet of vehicles are *tempo* and motorcycles with polluting two-stroke engines; the lack of good mechanics doesn't help either. A good deal of the problem is simply dust kicked up on unmaintained roads. Particles per cubic meter of air at busy intersections have been found to be 6-11 times U.S. standards. Away from the main roads, however, the air remains remarkably clear, especially considering that the bowl-shaped Valley is a prime site for a thermal inversion à la Mexico City.

Urban Sprawl

The traditional landscape of the Valley is radically and rapidly transforming. The lovely old red-brick buildings have become obsolete, replaced by modern concrete boxes. The general rule seems to be the bigger and uglier the better: some houses exceed even the bad taste of the Ranas, which at least was confined to walled compounds. The very concept of private housing is a break with the past. Previously several generations of a family shared a building; now the trend is towards single-family dwellings isolated from the web of caste and kin, set out in neighborhoods which until recently were farmland.

Urban sprawl is gobbling up the Valley's rich fields at a frightening rate. About half of the Valley is still agricultural land, but many former fields are disappearing. The cementing over of some of the country's richest farmland is accompanied by the destruction of farming villages and their traditions. In exchange for incredible prices, farmers give up not just their land, but a way of life.

Within Kathmandu, the skyrocketing value of city land drives landowners to erect high-rise concrete boxes, maximizing the rental value of their tiny plots. One *ropani* (a standard 74- by 74-foot plot) on Durbar Marg costs an incredible Rs150,000,000, about US$5 million. The city

sacred cows on Kathmandu city street

skyline is changing from a harmonious sea of red-tile roofs to a jumble of concrete boxes festooned with power lines. The old neighborhoods remain, but they're changing fast.

Though urban planning has existed for decades, it often works in the city's worst interests, as in the case of the official "concretization" drive accompanying Queen Elizabeth's 1961 visit. Similar efforts to modernize the city occur before major events or state visits, as authorities frantically renovate monuments, plant flowers, and widen roads, frequently demolishing all the houses in the way, with meager compensation to the owners. Countless teams of advisors have devised countless urban "master plans," but little has been implemented. As things stand now, Kathmandu has pretty much lost its charm. One can only hope the plague will not spread to the rest of the Valley, but Patan appears to be next on the list.

Vanishing Art

In light of the above concerns, the ancient temples crumbling from neglect and the art treasures snatched up by thieves seem a quaint concern. International aid is already spread thin, and the government, besieged with its own problems, has little to offer. How can it justify the tremendous expense of preserving ancient monuments when people need piped water, sewers, and paved roads? Restoring temples has traditionally been the duty of the wealthy, but increasingly they are abandoning the old gods for VCRs and shiny new Land Rover vehicles. Exceptions to this trend are Boudhanath, Pashupatinath, and Patan's Kwa Bahal, all well-tended by wealthy devotees. Organizations like UNESCO and aid missions from various European governments have stepped in to restore masterpieces like Hanuman Dhoka, Swayambhunath, and many important buildings in Bhaktapur, but these constitute only a tiny fraction of the Valley's priceless heritage.

Meanwhile, precious portable pieces of heritage are exiting Nepal due to organized art trafficking. Nepali artist Lain Singh Bangdel documents the losses in his book *The Stolen Images of Nepal,* which displays page after page of stone sculptures accompanied by photos of their now-vacant settings. Some have since materialized in Western museums; most are in private collections. Remaining images in the Valley are now frequently encaged, trussed, or set in cement to prevent thievery. Several decades ago these were left confidently out in the open, but nothing is sacred any more. Even a fragment of the Buddha's bone donated by Sri Lanka was recently dug up and stolen from Swayambhunath.

Cultural Pollution

Development, or whatever you want to call it, threatens not only artifacts but the fabric of society itself, as demonstrated by the increasing alienation and frustration of Kathmandu's youth, evident in rising drug abuse and suicide rates. The tightly knit social network which preserved traditions for centuries is unravelling, giving way to a new, as-yet-indistinct culture. You can view the process in different stages in the Valley's three cities: Kathmandu is gone, Patan is going, Bhaktapur is just sensing the first tremors of change.

As in societies around the globe, it seems impossible to control the process. Social dislocation is merely a reflection of larger social and economic changes. The process is accelerated by the development of links to the outside world. Forty years ago Kathmandu hadn't even a road; now there are highways, satellite dishes, telephone lines, newspapers, and tourists. The ongoing process involves the death of a traditional world and the birth of a new one. While some of the implications are sad, even heartbreaking, it's patronizing to bemoan it for too long. Modern life is what people are choosing worldwide, even if they are unaware of the full implications of their choice.

Having said all this, it's necessary to restate that the problems are relative. The capital is by far the most pressured part of the Valley. Much of Patan remains virtually untouched, and Bhaktapur is still a world apart. Travelers tend to base themselves in Kathmandu, which has facilities to suit every taste and wallet. But spending all of your time here can be disappointing, not to mention exhausting. To glimpse what the city was like even 20 years ago you need to venture beyond, to Patan, and Bhaktapur, and into the surrounding countryside, where village life continues much as it has for centuries. Exploring the Valley reveals treasures beyond those outlined in guidebooks, even more rewarding for their element of surprise.

CHRISTOPHER GAMM

KATHMANDU

The city still awakens with prayer, the tinkle of morning *puja* bells, and chanting, followed by the first taxi horn, raucous throat-clearing spitting, and 6 a.m. Radio Nepal reveille. Dawn and dusk are the best times to explore the backstreets of Kathmandu, as the slanting light gives a magical, timeless quality to the narrow lanes. These are also the preferred hours for *puja,* especially early morning, when women head out to take care of the day's religious obligations.

By late morning, the bazaar is in full swing, and the stream of shoppers picks you up and sweeps you along past small shops brimming with goods, their colorful contents most intriguing when quickly glimpsed: stacks of brass pots, bolts of cloth, mountains of nails, red-and-gold wedding saris, porcelain cups, a dozen kinds of dried lentils, sacks of saffron-colored turmeric, freshly severed goat heads, flower garlands, brown cannonballs of soap. Taxi horns merge with the solemn clang of temple bells; the scent of fresh oranges and flowers mingles with the blood of butcher shops and the filth of an open sewer. Crowds eddy and swirl around the little golden island of a temple,

where people pause to fold hands and recite a brief prayer, or simply touch their foreheads in respect as they pass by.

A little farther along the ambience changes in the tourist quarters of Freak Street or Thamel. Signs shout "Good News! Inquire here for trekking, bus to Pokhara, river rafting, jungle safari" . . . "We have Set Breakfast" . . . "Mousaka, French Onion Soup, Crassant." Music from the '60s blares from restaurants, as hustlers whisper their incantations: "Change money . . . good rate, better than bank"; "Buy hashish, cocaine, marijuana"; "Massage, madam?"; and the all-purpose "Anything?" Salespeople fling themselves in front of you to point out "Caaarpet," "Baaag," "Cheap price"—anything to get your attention.

Contrast is Kathmandu's single common denominator, and centuries are compressed into a few blocks. Herds of sheep are driven past Durbar Marg's luxury hotels, and cows amble amid traffic jams. Around the corner from a group of blue-jeaned *punk-haru* ("punk" having entered the Nepali lexicon) you stumble onto a threshing scene straight out of a Breughel painting. Traffic roars around ancient temples, sweating porters compete for the right-of-way with sleek black Hyundai autos, TV antennas sprout from tiled roofs. Everywhere, the ancient past and busy present rub elbows.

ORIENTATION

Legend has it the Valley's three cities were laid out in the form of sacred symbols: Patan in the shape of a wheel, Bhaktapur as a conch shell, and Kathmandu as Manjushri's sword, with the handle at the confluence of the Bagmati and Vishnumati Rivers and the apex in the outlying village of Timmale. Today "Timmale" is Thamel, no longer a village but a busy tourist district, and Patan and Kathmandu have merged into a single sprawling mass. The legend of deliberate design is most certainly a legend: Valley cities were not planned, but evolved over time as villages grew and merged.

Upper and Lower Kathmandu
The old city is located on a bluff at the confluence of the Bagmati and Vishnumati Rivers, an easily defended site with rich soil and plentiful water. This core is traditionally divided into two sections: "lower" (southern) Kathmandu and "upper" (northern) Kathmandu. The traditional rivalry between the two was vividly demonstrated in the annual stone fight between inhabitants of each side, held on Kumar Sasti, the festival of the warrior god. This was serious stuff—wounded participants were dragged away by members of the opposing side and sacrificed in temples. The custom was finally abolished in the 1870s when the British Resident, an innocent bystander, was hit by a stone.

The division point between the two sections is Makhan Tol, at the northern end of Durbar Square. North of here are Asan Tol, Indra Chowk, Chhetrapati, and Thamel, busy commercial areas well known to travelers. Few venture down the quieter streets south of Durbar Square, still mainly inhabited by Newar Jyapu peasants.

Even in its present relatively enormous state Kathmandu's urban area is easily covered on foot. The most interesting part of old Kathmandu covers only about five square km. It is bounded

by the Vishnumati River on the west, Kanti Path and the Tundikhel on the east, Thahiti in the north, and the Bagmati River to the south. Finding your way around this small area can be wonderfully confusing. With few exceptions, streets are not named. Location is expressed by *tol* or neighborhood, their precise boundaries a mystery known only to local residents. You navigate by periodically taking bearings on a nearby stupa, shrine, or prominent garbage dump. Giving or getting directions in Kathmandu is a maddeningly complicated yet entertaining endeavor.

Neighborhoods
The names of city neighborhoods deserve a chapter in themselves: Sorha Khuttapati ("Sixteen-Legged Resthouse"), Kalimati ("Black Dirt"), Battis Putali ("32 Butterflies"). Baneshwar ("Forest Lord") and Gyaneshwar ("Wise Lord") now watch over new suburban neighborhoods bearing their names, and the old "Kingdom of the Naga," Nag Sala, has become Naxal. The plethora of names combines with a lack of street numbers and a shortage of telephones to make finding a particular shop or home a real challenge. On the other hand, simply wandering becomes a delight. The old city is a mass of fascinating little nooks and crannies, courtyards and shrines, packed together as tightly as its populace. For intensive explorations, get a copy of the old Schneider map of Kathmandu, which details *chaitya* and stupas and shrines. Even without a good map, though, the relatively small area guarantees you'll never get *really* lost; a major street or landmark is always nearby.

New Kathmandu
Durbar Marg is the kingdom's premier street, lined with airline and travel agency offices and ritzy hotels. Kanti Path, one block west, is the other major artery, extending north into the embassyland of Maharajgunj and Lazimpat, and south to the Patan bridge. Squeezed between Durbar Marg and Kanti Path is the Tundikhel, a parade ground in the finest Raj tradition. The local city bus park is off to one side of this; opposite is the General Post Office, and a little further up, New Road, a busy shopping area which leads straight into Durbar Square.

East of Durbar Marg extend suburban neighborhoods, many of which were until quite re-

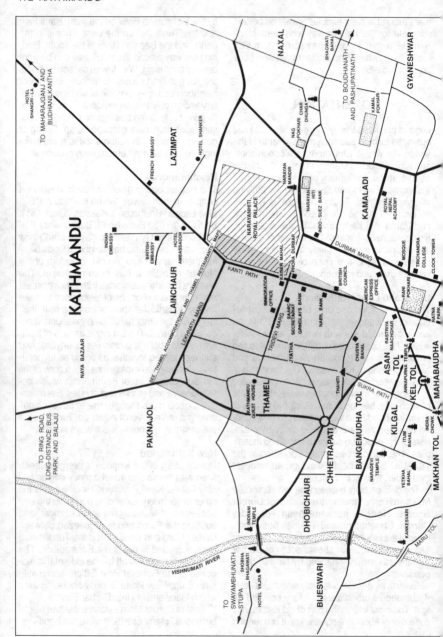

KATHMANDU

MAITI DEVI

BANESHWAR

TO PASHUPATINATH

TO EVEREST HOTEL

TO AIRPORT, BHAKTAPUR, AND ARNIKO RAJMARG

DHOBI KHOLA

DILLI BAZAR

RAM SHAH PATH

SINGHA DURBAR

LAW COURTS

NATIONAL ARCHIVES

BABAR MAHAL

THAPATHALI

PADMA KANYA COLLEGE

BAGH BAZAAR

MUNICIPAL BUS PARK

BHRIKRUTI MANDAP MARG

EXHIBITION GROUND

PRITHVI PATH

RNAC OFFICE (DOMESTIC)

SINGHA MAHAL

THAI EMBASSY

MAHAKALA

TUNDIKHEL

ARMY HEADQUARTERS

SWIMMING POOL / MINISTRY OF TOURISM

BLUEBIRD SUPERMARKET

BIR HOSPITAL

RNAC BUILDING

MARTYRS' GATE

BHADRAKALI

NATIONAL STADIUM

BHAKTAPUR TROLLEY BUS

TRIPURESHWAR MAHADEVA

GHATS

PATAN BRIDGE

TO PATAN

KANTI PATH

SUPERMARKET

NEW ROAD

NEPAL BANK

GENERAL POST OFFICE

BHIMSEN'S TOWER (DHARAHARA)

KHICHA POKHARI

CENTRAL JAIL

INTERNATIONAL TELEGRAPH OFFICE

BAGMATI RIVER

DHARMA PATH

VEGETABLE MARKET

LAGAN TOL

BHOTE BAHAL

HANUMAN DHOKA PALACE

KUMARI BAHAL

DURBAR SQUARE

KASTHAMANDAP

JHOCHEN

CHIKHANMUGHAL

BRAHMA TOL

TRIPURESHWAR MARG

TEKU

PACHALI BHAIRAB

TINDEVAL

GHATS

GHATS

RAJ GHAT

FOOTBRIDGE

250m

0

TAHACHAL

TO NATIONAL MUSEUM

KALIMATI

TO SOALTEE HOLIDAY INN AND POKHARA

TO DAKSHINKALI

© MOON PUBLICATIONS, INC.

cently fields. With the exception of ancient and relatively unchanged settlements like Deopatan and Hadigaon, they don't deserve intensive exploration. Instead, hop from point to point by taxi or by bicycle, an ideal means of transport in the surprisingly flat Valley.

DURBAR SQUARE: A WALKING TOUR

Kathmandu's old Durbar Square (Hanuman Dhoka) is the Valley's number-one tourist attraction. Patan's Durbar Square is lovelier, and Bhaktapur's is more peaceful, but Kathmandu's sprawling complex seethes with life. On warm summer nights people linger on temple steps, and vegetable sellers display their wares by candlelight near the Kasthamandap. Early on a winter morning the square is even more evocative, with the pagoda roofs barely visible through the fog. Temple bells clang in the mist, and women hurry past wrapped in shawls, bearing trays of *puja* offerings.

The oldest of Durbar Square's more than 50 monuments dates back to the 12th century, when the area was already an important center at the junction of two major trade routes. Most of the temples you see today are a mere three or four centuries old, the bequest of Malla kings. Greatest of all was the 17th-century Pratapa Malla, the self-described "Pearl in the Diadem of Kings." Amorous (it's said he had over 3,000 concubines) and quarrelsome, he was also a talented artist, poet, and performer. Most importantly he was a generous patron, endowing the palace and the facing square with some of

their finest features. The Shah kings moved into the palace after their 1786 conquest, but being more interested in warfare than art, they continued to patronize Newar artisans, thus ensuring a continuity of style.

THE SOUTH SQUARE

Start at the west end of New Road, where a statue of former Prime Minister Juddha Shamsher Rana stands majestically amid swirling traffic. He presided over the rebuilding of Kathmandu after the 1934 earthquake, pushing through New Road atop the ruins. Continue straight ahead until the pavement ends and ancient flagstones begin.

Basantapur

On the right is the red brick and dark wood of the old Royal Palace. This wing is dominated by the nine-storied, four-roofed **Basantapur Tower,** which lends the neighborhood its name. Tradition says Malla kings were born on the first floor of the tower, held audiences on the second, viewed their dancing girls on the third, and

flute sellers in Bansantapur Square

CHRISTOPHER GAMM

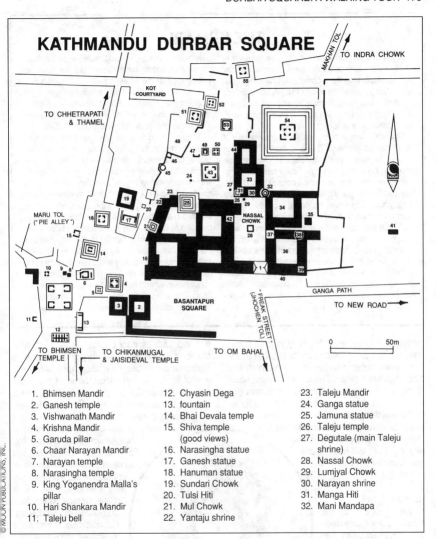

KATHMANDU DURBAR SQUARE

1. Bhimsen Mandir
2. Ganesh temple
3. Vishwanath Mandir
4. Krishna Mandir
5. Garuda pillar
6. Chaar Narayan Mandir
7. Narayan temple
8. Narasingha temple
9. King Yoganendra Malla's pillar
10. Hari Shankara Mandir
11. Taleju bell
12. Chyasin Dega
13. fountain
14. Bhai Devala temple
15. Shiva temple (good views)
16. Narasingha statue
17. Ganesh statue
18. Hanuman statue
19. Sundari Chowk
20. Tulsi Hiti
21. Mul Chowk
22. Yantaju shrine
23. Taleju Mandir
24. Ganga statue
25. Jamuna statue
26. Taleju temple
27. Degutale (main Taleju shrine)
28. Nassal Chowk
29. Lumjyal Chowk
30. Narayan shrine
31. Manga Hiti
32. Mani Mandapa

climbed to the fourth floor every evening to survey the smoke from the city's cooking fires and make sure none of their subjects were going hungry—a dubious story, as the tower was much shorter in Malla times. The structure's variegated brick reveals many different eras. It's inset with superb woodcarvings, some of the best in the Valley. The struts depict tranquil gods with frantic erotic scenes beneath.

Before the earthquake, the palace sprawled far beyond its present boundaries. The tower looks down on red-bricked **Basantapur Square,** which once held stables for royal elephants. Now it's filled with souvenir vendors who dis-

THE KUMARI

Nepal's religious syncretism is epitomized in the tradition of the Kumari, a Buddhist Newar girl worshipped as the incarnation of the Hindu goddess Durga. Even the King of Nepal bows before Kathmandu's Royal Kumari, for she has the power to confirm his rule for the coming year. Kumari worship dates back at least to the 16th century, when Malla kings worshipped her as an incarnation of their patron goddess Taleju, a manifestation of Durga. Legend says the goddess used to pass the day playing dice with one particular ruler, but withdrew in anger after he made a pass at her. The repentant king begged forgiveness, and the goddess finally agreed to return, no longer in person, but incarnated in the body of a Newar virgin.

There are nearly a dozen different Kumaris worshipped in various settlements of the Valley, but most are informal positions where the girl attends a few festivals and otherwise leads a normal life. This is not so in the case of Kathmandu's Royal or State Kumari, who resides in a richly decorated house on Durbar Square. Her regimented life is a throwback to the 15th century.

It begins with her investiture. Five high priests conduct the search for likely candidates among the young girls of the Shakya caste. The perfection they seek is symbolized by the *battis lakshin* or "32 Perfections." A partial excerpt: "thighs like a deer, chest like a lion, neck like a conch shell, eyelashes like a cow, and body like a banyan."

The final candidate, usually two to four years of age, is tested by being left in a dark room filled with bloody buffalo heads, remnants of the Dasain ritual sacrifices. The girl who endures this frightening ordeal with equanimity has proven she embodies the fierce goddess Durga. In a last step, her horoscope is compared with the king's to avoid conflict. She is then installed in a secret ritual held at the Taleju temple, as the spirit of Taleju slowly possesses her body.

The new Kumari is settled in the 18th-century Kumari Bahal, where she lives a sheltered life, cared for by attendants who daily bathe her, dress her in a red robe and ritual jewelry, and paint black kohl about her eyes and the ritual third eye on her forehead. The high priest of the Taleju temple worships her daily, and she spends several hours receiving

---

play acres of wares. The area is also home base for hordes of roving vendors selling everything from flutes and jewelry to hashish and black-market rupees. The street running south alongside it is the notorious **Freak Street** (the local name is Jhochen Tol), once a hippie haven in the anything-goes '60s. Traces of its exotic past remain in shops selling Indian brocades and silver jewelry, but the hash houses are gone, as are most of the flower children.

Kumari Bahal

At the west end of the square is the richly decorated Kumari Bahal, the home of the young girl chosen to serve as Royal Kumari. Inside and out, it's decorated with beautiful woodcarvings; check out the gilded window directly over the entrance. The building was raised in

the mid-18th century by Jaya Prakash, Kathmandu's last Malla king. Its style is that of a Buddhist *bahal,* but the iconography is a weird mix of Buddhist and Hindu. Most of the doorway *torana* depict Durga slaying the buffalo demon; the Kumari, though a Buddhist herself, is considered an emanation of this fierce Hindu goddess. The lower temple enshrines images of the Five Tathagatas behind a wooden screen. The main shrine is upstairs in the Kumari's living quarters, where she grants worshippers a daily audience; non-Hindus are not admitted. If you want to glimpse the Kumari, for a few rupees donation she'll make a brief appearance in the upper window across from the entrance. You'll see a little girl dressed in red, her eyes lined with black kohl and her hair pulled up in a topknot.

BOB RACE

devotees who come to do Kumari *puja*, said to bring wealth and good fortune. She is favored by women with menstrual and child problems, and by government servants. The Kumari is also used to divine Nepal's future: if she behaves restlessly or erratically during a *puja*, it's a bad omen for the country.

Apart from the rituals she leads a fairly normal life, playing with the children of her attendants, eating specially prepared meals, occasionally making a perfunctory appearance at a carved wooden window. The Kumari doesn't attend school, and is not allowed to play outside because her feet shouldn't touch the ground. On the rare occasions she leaves her house for a festival appearance, she is carried by attendants. She has her own special festival, Kumari Jatra, three days set within the longer celebration of Indra Jatra. Men drag her chariot through the streets of the old city, and crowds gather to receive the blessing of the regal little girl enthroned on her wheeled shrine.

The Kumari leads a charmed life until she reaches puberty or sheds blood, at which point Taleju is believed to leave her body and another girl is appointed to take her place. The transfer of power is not always smooth. A former Patan Kumari held onto her position from her investiture in the '50s until a few years ago by maintaining she had never reached menarche. Greatly disturbed by this turn of events—by this time she was into her forties and far too big for her palanquin—the temple priests examined her and found traces of a small scratch, evidence of having bled at one time. Following further drama a new, young Kumari was installed, but the old Kumari continues to receive worshippers at her family home near Haka Bahal, and many believe she retains the spiritual power of Taleju.

Upon losing her divine status, the ex-Kumari is free to lead a normal life—however "normal" a mortal life can be for an ex-goddess. Former Kumaris get no extra respect or honors beyond a small stipend from the state. The belief that the husband of an ex-Kumari will die young makes marriage unlikely, and many find mundane life difficult after their deified childhood. Partly because of this, it's becoming harder to find candidates for the position. The position of Kathmandu's Mu Bahal Kumari, considered the most powerful of all from a spiritual point of view, has remained empty for want of takers. Parents nowadays don't want an uneducated and unweddable daughter on their hands.

No photographs allowed; for this you'll have to wait for one of her official appearances at festivals.

As you leave Kumari Bahal, there is a large and impressive **Vishnu temple** to your left. On its western side, a massive and finely sculpted **stone Garuda** kneels, waiting to serve its divine master. The main portion of Durbar Square lies to your right, but continue further west a few steps, past a row of moneychangers and flower-sellers operating out of an ancient building which over the centuries has been converted from resthouse to Vishnu temple to shops.

Around Kasthamandap

Just beyond is the broad-roofed Kasthamandap, a large, multistoried, open hall ringed by a picket fence, with a new shrine to the master yogi Goraknath on the ground floor. Although it's not much to look at, historically it's quite important, one of the oldest buildings in Kathmandu. It once lay at the start of the Tibet trade route, serving as a resthouse for travelers and pilgrims. Later a king donated it to *sadhu* of the Kanphatta sect, and their descendants lived here until the mid-'60s. Records trace the building back to the 12th century and the site may easily be twice as old, but the current structure dates back no more than 500 years and has been restored many times. Legend says the structure was built from the wood of a single magical tree, thus its name, Kasthamandap or "Pavilion of Wood," which eventually became the source of the name "Kathmandu."

The old **"Pie Alley"** (Maru Tol) of hippie days runs downhill along the north side of Kasthamandap; its once-renowned pastry shops have relocated in Thamel, and the only site of interest here is the 8th-century sunken tap of **Maru Hiti,** a busy laundry site. At the top of the street is **Ashok Binayak,** a small but extremely popular shrine to the elephantine god of fortune, Ganesh. Decked with metal pennants and a gilded roof, the tiny temple would be easy to miss were it not for the steady stream of people circumambulating it. Travelers come here before their journey (some even maneuver their motorcycles about it) and the number of worshippers doubles on the unlucky days of Tuesday and Saturday, sacred to Ganesh. Inside, a stone image of the elephant-headed god rests beneath a gilt replica of the *ashoka* tree said to have once shaded this shrine. Across the road is a wonderful gilded image of Ganesh's mount, the faithful shrew. The square to the south, surrounded by minor temples, is filled with farmers selling produce, illuminated at night by small oil lamps.

The Main Square

Head back to the main square and climb the steps of the tall triple-roofed **Maju Deval temple** consecrated to Shiva to survey the scene below. Tour groups are tailed by souvenir vendors and sellers brandishing flutes; porters and rickshaws jostle for space, and a few brightly dressed pseudo-*sadhu* wander about, earning a living posing for photos.

Across the way, brightly painted doll-like mannequins of **Shiva and Parvati** lean from a top window of a large rectangular temple. Actually the Navadurga goddesses are enshrined below, but the whimsical figures above dominate the shrine, looking more like a pair of happy householders than like the great Lord of Yogis and his consort. The temple is set atop a low raised platform where costumed dances were performed in Malla times. Just behind it is a massive **bell** dedicated to Taleju, cast in 1786.

Directly ahead is a rather startling intrusion: the neoclassical white facade of **Gaddi Baitak,** a Rana addition to the royal palace which served as an official hall of state in the early part of the century. Modeled after the National Gallery in London, it once included tiers of grandly sweeping steps, now removed to make room for traffic.

Continue northeast up a flagstoned lane between the Shiva-Parvati temple and a beautifully decorated wing of the old palace, crowned with a small pagoda and housing a row of *thangka* shops on the ground floor. The second-storey windows are classical masterpieces; monkeys occasionally scramble over the tiled roof. Glance at the last set of windows on the corner, where kings once sat and watched their subjects. Their insets of carved ivory and gilded metal were hidden under layers of dirt until the palace underwent a thorough cleaning in 1975.

Around Hanuman Dhoka

Here the street opens onto a second forest of temples, more peaceful than the first and a favorite haunt of pigeons. This area is called Hanuman Dhoka, after the entrance to the old Royal Palace. On the right is a large latticed screen of painted wood: peer between the slats to see the fierce, painted metal mask of **Seto Bhairab,** one of the 64 terrifying manifestations of Shiva, erected to drive evil spirits away from the palace. The gilded image, four meters tall, is unveiled only once a year during the week-long festival of Indra Jatra, when it's garlanded with flowers and paper streamers. In the evenings, rice beer flows from a spout projecting from Bhairab's mouth, and crowds of young men jostle beneath to catch a mouthful.

Across the way, seated atop a lotus-capped column, is a beautiful memorial statue of **King Pratapa Malla,** who financed many of Durbar Square's monuments. Surrounded by smaller images of four sons and two favorite wives, his statue kneels facing his former private prayer room on the third floor of the **Degu Taleju temple.** The Malla kings of all three cities chose to immortalize themselves kneeling in prayer, gaining eternal blessings—as opposed to the martial poses of monuments to Shah and Rana rulers.

Continuing past an open arcade, you arrive at the actual **Hanuman Dhoka.** The doorway's namesake and guardian stands nearby, robed in red and shaded by a royal umbrella. This is Hanuman, the Monkey King of the Ramayana, his features completely obscured by layers of *sindhur* mixed with mustard oil, three centuries' worth of offerings. Hanuman was a favorite patron of the Mallas, protecting them and bringing victory on the battlefield. It's said the image is endowed with the evil eye to keep smallpox, witches, and demons away from the palace; the thick coating of *sindhur* prevents innocent worshippers from getting zapped.

The frame of the golden *dhoka* is brightly painted, flanked by lions bearing images of Shiva and Shakti. Above the lintel are more painted figures, including Pratapa Malla and his queen on the right. Admission tickets are sold here at Rs10 for the palace complex; hours are daily except Tuesday, 10:30 a.m.-4:15 p.m. closing an hour earlier in winter and two hours earlier on Fridays.

THE OLD ROYAL PALACE

This complex was once far more extensive, with 40-50 courtyards reported in 1880. Today fewer than a dozen remain; much has fallen into ruin or been destroyed by the 1934 earthquake, while other portions have been recklessly demolished. The remainder still covers more than five acres. Though none of the buildings predate the Malla era (the Hanuman Dhoka area is a mere 300 years old), there may have been a palace here as far back as A.D. 500. Sections from many different rulers and eras are cobbled together in a maze of buildings, temples, towers, courtyards, and passages.

This is really a Malla dynasty dwelling. The Shah kings occupied it for little more than a century before moving in 1896 to the more modern Narayanhiti Palace, the site of the present palace. They left the old Durbar for ceremonies, storage purposes, and offices. The ancient palace still retains great ceremonial importance, perhaps explaining why so much of it is closed to the public.

Nassal Chowk

The first courtyard is Nassal Chowk, named after the dancing form of Shiva. During Malla times, dance dramas were performed on the low raised platform in the center. The Shah kings have turned this into the coronation courtyard; all have been crowned from atop the platform.

Immediately after the entrance to the left is a spectacular silver-trimmed black sculpture of the man-lion **Narasingha** disembowelling a demon with his bare hands. Narasingha is one of the 10 incarnations of Vishnu, who took this form in order to kill the demon, who could not be killed by human, beast, or weapon, on earth, water, or land. Taking the demon on his lap and rending it with his bare hands, Vishnu broke the charm. The installation of the statue is another interesting story: Pratapa Malla once impersonated Narasingha in a masked dance, and was afflicted with the deity's restless spirit afterwards. On the advice of his priests, he commissioned this image to absorb the troublesome god.

In the open gallery on the left are portraits of the entire Shah dynasty, each king wearing the fantastic plumed Sri Pech which serves as the royal crown. Once this served as the audience hall of Malla kings. A superb multiarmed gilt image of **Vishnu** is enshrined in a glass case along the eastern wall. The courtyard's northeast corner is crowned by the unique five-storied round pagoda of **Panch Mukhi Hanuman,** "Five-Faced Hanuman," the five-times powerful protector. Atop the northwest corner is a small pagoda marking the site of the **agam chen** housing the family deity of Malla kings. Both these temples are still kept secret, though their ruling dynasty is long gone.

In terms of pure lavishness, Nassal Chowk has some of the finest woodcarvings you'll ever see. Windows are framed by a riot of complex patterns; protective *naga* run the length of the brick walls, their heads emerging at doorways; the doorway to Lohan Chowk is ribboned by nearly two dozen different designs.

Basantapur Tower

This tall rectangular tower in the southeast corner has more magnificent carvings, including some vigorous erotic scenes at the bases of struts which require a telephoto lens to decipher the tangle of limbs. Prithvi Narayan Shah added additional stories onto an existing tower, building it up to its present height of 30 meters. His goal was to create a pleasure pavilion; thus its name, "Pavilion of Spring." Climb the tower's series of narrow, steep staircases for a dizzying overview of the Valley, Basantapur Square, and the palace's many roofs, especially the dramatic pagoda of Taleju to the north, built in the form of Taleju's yantra (magical diagram) atop a 12-story plinth. Each successive floor yields interesting views, but the top room, with its latticed walls and chiming wind bells, is well worth the climb.

Mahendra Memorial Museum

This numbingly large collection of memorabilia focused on the late father of the present king is accessed through the third floor of the Basantapur Tower. It's a recent addition to the palace, inspired by the Tribhuvan Memorial Museum collection described below and sharing a similarly breathless tone of homage. It's a toss-up as to which of the two you should visit, if either, but you may not have the patience for both.

WOODCARVING

Wood is abundant in Nepal, and Newar craftspeople long ago perfected their skill at manipulating it with chisels, scrapers, shavers, hammers, files, and drills. Their favorite medium was the dark, strong timber of the sal tree, said to be capable of enduring 1,000 years of immersion in water. They transformed this solid substance into fantastic carvings, geometric designs, and graceful figures of deities. In temples and palaces, wood was treated like the pages of a book, a blank surface on which to inscribe a story, usually the standard religious themes of the gods and mythical beings. Houses too were decorated with delicate traceries of wooden lace adorning door and window frames.

The Newari language has a technical term for each part of a carved pillar, window, or screen. Complex carvings were made from separate pieces of wood skillfully fitted together to create a single seamless piece. The windows of a house often displayed virtuoso woodcarving, particularly the third-floor *sa jhya,* often a bay window flanked by smaller ones. Window lattices let in light and air yet retain privacy. They are formed by fitting together precisely cut strips in an interlocking pattern that is both structural and decorative, requiring no nails or adhesive. The technique can be used to produce an endless variety of patterns: squares, diamonds, circles, sunbursts, lotuses, geometric forms.

Door jambs, lintels, brackets, frames, and entablatures were treated equally lavishly. A temple pillar might be carved with 14 different motifs. The most dramatic carvings are displayed on the slanted wooden struts supporting the sloping roofs of temples—tilted at just the right angle to convey a message to a viewer standing below. Carvers used these strategically placed surfaces to tell more about the god enshrined inside. Temple struts might display dozens of different incarnations of the main

erotic carving at the base of a temple strut

Lohan Chowk

At the southeast corner of Nassal Chowk an elegantly carved doorway surmounted by Ganesh leads into Lohan Chowk, the living quarters of Malla and early Shah kings. Later it housed the government loan office. The four corners of the courtyard support different towers, said to have been donated by the former city-states of the Valley after their unification by Prithvi Narayan Shah: the copper-domed **Kirtipur Tower,** the octagonal **Bhaktapur Tower,** the square **Lalitpur (Patan) Tower,** and the tall rectangular **Basantapur Tower,** Kathmandu's own. Between the latter two stretches the finely carved facade of the three-storied **Vilas Mandir,** "Temple of Luxury," with a riot of patterns spilling across its window grilles.

The beauty of this portion of the palace owes as much to the skill of its renovators as to the original artists. By the early '70s, between rotten timbers and structural damage from the 1934 quake, the palace was on the verge of collapse. UNESCO and its sister agency, UNDP, funded an extensive four-year restoration project, combining the skills of local craftspeople with modern techniques. Entire structures, like the copper-roofed Kirtipur Tower, were dismantled and reconstructed with new timbers. The elaborate woodwork, totalling over 20,000 pieces, was dismantled, carefully numbered, cleaned

deity, or other members of the pantheon and minor deities and spirits.

The oldest existing examples date from the 14th century and depict *yaksha,* ancient nature spirits converted to Buddhist demi-goddesses. Shown clinging to a cluster of foilage, these graceful nymphs' tall slender bodies extend in sinuous curves beneath. A temple's corner struts are the largest, carved always in the form of winged griffons *(vyala),* with horned heads, clawed feet, and giant phalluses. Originally woodcarvings were left in their natural state, but as time eroded their features they were brightly painted in an effort to disguise the wear. Over the last few hundred years colorfully painted woodwork eventually became the norm. One of the most time-consuming tasks facing restoration projects is patiently chipping away the layers of gaudy paint.

The space below the main figures holds minor scenes where the artist's imagination could run free, unfettered by standard iconography. Here are mythical beings like *yaksha* and *naga,* minor deities, dwarfs, ascetics, even scenes from daily life. Most notorious are the erotic carvings featured mainly on Hindu temples, displaying multiple participants (including animals and helpful servants) contorted in impossible postures. Many theories have been developed to explain these apparently "obscene" vignettes: they were meant to train the population in resisting temptation, or conversely to increase the reproductive rate; to attract people to temples, or to serve as a sort of tantric manual for ritual sex. The standard cliché delivered by tour guides maintains the explicit scenes are meant to frighten away the virginal goddess of lightning; this old chestnut was quoted as early as 1870. In reality, all these attempted explanations are superfluous. Erotica needs little justification in Nepal, where cults of fertility, the Mother Goddess, and tantra combine to make it natural.

Modern woodworking is a fading craft, though it's received a boost from foreign-sponsored restorations of old temples and palaces, which hire woodcarvers to reproduce the exquisite old carvings. There is little contemporary demand for quality carving: wealthy Newars now build cement houses instead of the traditional wood-adorned brick structures, and few people sponsor the construction of new temples. Competent woodworkers exist, creating carved wooden doors and windows for new upper-class homes, but the quality and delicacy of their work fall short of the originals, partly because patrons are less perfectionistic than the Malla kings of old. The best place to shop for woodcarvings is Bhaktapur, particularly Tachapal Tol, which appropriately also holds the National Gallery's Woodworking Museum.

---

of layers of paint and grime, and replaced in its original unpainted condition, letting the beauty of the carving speak for itself.

Mul Chowk

Behind Lohan Chowk lies Mul Chowk, the palace's oldest remaining portion, built in 1564 and used by the Mallas for coronations and weddings. Much of it is dedicated to Taleju: the southern wing shelters a shrine to her, roof struts depict her destroying demons, and animals are still sacrificed to the goddess here during Dasain. It's closed to all but the Royal Family, though Hindus are admitted during the ninth day of Dasain to watch the animal sacrifices. You can, however, stand in the doorway and admire the splendid carvings, or peek down upon it from the lower levels of Basantapur Tower.

Sleeping Vishnu

Beyond Lohan Chowk's eastern wall, in the royal gardens or **Bhandarkhal,** is the Valley's third great *Sleeping Vishnu* sculpture. The gardens are closed to visitors, but you can get a bird's-eye view from the roof garden of the Hotel Classic behind. Pratapa Malla discovered the statue in a pond in Gyaneshwar and ordered a tank built for it, to be filled with water from the original *Sleeping Vishnu* in Budhanilkantha. Workers labored for a year to build a canal linking the two tanks, in the process unearthing the Kaalo Bhairab which now stands outside the Durbar. The day the water arrived, Pratapa Malla worshipped Vishnu. That night he had a dream warning him if he or his successors visited Budhanilkantha, they would surely die. From that time on no king has gone to the site.

Tribhuvan Memorial Museum

This exhibition, installed in a wing of the old palace near the exit, highlights the life of King Tribhuvan, grandfather of the current king, who reestablished the Shah dynasty's leadership in 1951. The combination of drowsing guards and reverent exhibits makes for a weird experience. Exhibits begin with "The Royal Babyhood" (tiny royal baby clothes, even then encrusted with gold braid) and progress through the king's coronation at five years old in 1911, and his marriage to a pair of Rana sisters at the age of 13. Newspaper accounts document his break to the Indian Embassy and his historic return as Nepal's ruling monarch on 15 February 1951. Don't miss the display of personal effects, including the royal gun, the royal punching bag, the royal monogrammed bicycle, the royal aquarium (drained), and the royal parakeet (stuffed).

THE NORTH SQUARE

Exiting the palace, admire the erotic carvings on the base of the struts of the 14th-century **Jagannath temple,** the oldest temple in this area. The steps are carved with inscriptions in many

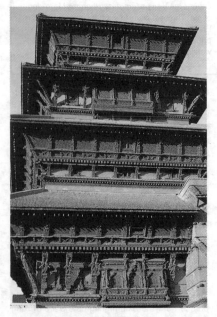

Detailed woodwork adorns the Basantapur Tower inside the old Royal Palace.

languages. A duplicate of this strange conglomoration lies across the way, where a low picket fence protects a *tutedhara,* a stone drinking tank inset into the palace wall. In a fit of grandeur, Pratap Malla had the slab inscribed with a potpourri of verses praising the goddess Kali, written in 15 different languages and alphabets. Supposedly great pandits who decipher the entire inscription will receive milk, not just water, from the *tutedhara,* while the inscription proclaims those dummies who fail to be "worthless." Some say the inscription contains coded directions to a treasure Pratapa Malla buried beneath Mohan Chowk. The words *l'hiver, l'otomne,* and *winter* can be distinguished, possibly obtained from Capuchin missionaries who visited the Valley in the 17th century.

Retrace your steps past the Seto Bhairab and head north. On the left is the unusual octagonal **Krishna temple** which Pratapa Malla built in memory of two of his favorite queens; the images inside are said to resemble the king and his wives. Just after the temple is a pair of **giant drums,** consecrated to the goddess Taleju and installed in 1800. They are reputed to have great power: according to one account, a goat and a buffalo must be sacrificed before they can be beaten. Like the giant bell used to ring away evil spirits, the drums were once used in daily worship, but today remain silent.

On the right is the luridly painted *Kaalo Bhairab,* a huge bas-relief adorned with six arms and a garland of human heads. The sculpture is said to have been discovered several centuries ago in a field by workers digging a water pipe from Budhanilkantha to Kathmandu. The image was installed in Durbar Square and quickly gained a reputation as an infallible lie detector. It was said that anyone telling a lie in its presence would vomit blood and instantly die. Civil servants were sworn into office in front of it, and criminals were dragged before the image and forced to swear their innocence while touching its feet. Conveniently, the city's main police station is right across the street.

Taleju Mandir

One of the largest and finest temples in the Valley rises behind a locked gate on the right, dedicated to the royal family's patron deity Taleju Bhawani. Access to the temple is restricted to its

Taleju Mandir, Durbar Square

high priests, the Royal Family, and the Kumari, who is invested here in a secret ceremony. Once a year, on the ninth day of the Dasain festival, Hindus are admitted.

Even from the outside this potent, powerful temple projects a remarkable presence. On a moonlit night it towers against the sky, aloof and forbidding. Taleju is a bloodthirsty form of Durga, and well-founded legend says human sacrifices were once performed here. The temple towers 40 meters above the street, surrounded by 16 smaller symmetrical pagodas. The embossed golden gates and woodwork are masterpieces, though they're difficult to examine without a telephoto lens or binoculars.

The building was erected in the mid-16th century by King Mahendra Malla, who poured an incredible amount of effort and money into outdoing the Taleju temples of Bhaktapur and Patan. To make it the highest of all he had it set atop a 12-tiered plinth, and issued a royal edict banning the construction of any building taller than it. For centuries this served as an effective housing code, preserving the skyline of Kathmandu. The Taleju temple also saw the fall of the Malla dynasty. King Jayaprakash Malla hid here as the invading Gorkhalis breached the city walls, and made a desperate last-ditch attempt to blow up the shrine and its attackers with gunpowder. Fortunately his efforts fizzled, and the temple remains today. Another bit of history can be glimpsed on the left as the road turns: green metal gates mark the entry to the old courtyard called the **Kot,** scene of the bloody massacre which brought Jung Bahadur Rana to power in 1846.

OLD KATHMANDU

THE OLD BAZAAR

The old trade route to Tibet began at the Kasthamandap resthouse and ran through Durbar Square to Indra Chowk and through the heart of what's now Kathmandu's main bazaar. If you have only a single day in Kathmandu, make it a point to wander through this perennially crowded and fascinating area, which always has something to watch, and occasionally even something to buy. Most of the goods on sale are necessities of daily life.

Indra Chowk

Makhan Tol, running north from Durbar Square, leads past shops displaying Chinese sneakers, spectacular golden wedding saris, and a rainbow selection of colored cotton. It is one of six streets leading into busy Indra Chowk, a crossroads dominated by the rectangular shrine to **Akash Bhairab,** guarded by four leaping griffons and inset with whimsical ceramic tiles. The temple's ground floor houses small shops; their steps are a good refuge from the crowd. The second story (open only to Hindus) enshrines the blue mask of this particular Bhairab, miraculously fallen from the sky. Old men gather in the evening here to sing *bhajan,* accompanied by the soft tap of hand drums and the gentle wheeze of a harmonium. The *chowk* itself is crammed with fruit and flute sellers, and porters and laborers looking for work.

Tucked behind a row of buildings in a narrow passageway opposite the temple is the bead bazaar or **Potey Pasaal,** especially lovely at night with its strands of glittering glass beads. Nepali women shop here for red or green *potey,* multistrand necklaces which married women wear set with a golden *tilhari.* Most of the traders are Muslims, descendants of 18th-century merchants invited to the city to sell their wares.

The **Shiva temple** on the north side of the square overflows with displays of carpets and shawls which hide the ancient sculptures set in the base. This is a big neighborhood for *pashmina* shawls, but make sure you get the real

thing instead of acrylic. Real *pashmina* is silky soft and most often undyed.

Jana Bahal

This classic Newar temple honors Seto Machhendrenath, a form of the compassionate Bodhisattva Padmapani Lokeswara. This "White" *(Seto)* Machhendranath is the patron deity of Kathmandu's Buddhist Newars; his red counterpart Raato Machhendranath looks after Patan. The temple is set in a courtyard on the left. Look for a tall stone pillar topped by back-to-back Buddhas standing by a white plaster archway. The front of the big courtyard is filled with *chaitya* and a diverse array of offerings, among them a Greek nymph used as an oil lamp, and adopted by Nepalis as an *apsara.*

The magnificently proportioned main temple is caged in lotus-patterned iron grilles to protect its fine metal images from theft; too many have already disappeared. Over the main door is a richly worked leafy trellis of bronze, set with a triple *torana* and images of Buddhas and bodhisattvas. In the sanctum is the doll-like image of Seto Machhendranath, bejeweled and robed in royal garments, richly ornamented and tended by lay priests. The lower struts depict the bodhisattva Avalokitesvara, and the first story is ringed by framed paintings of the deity's 108 manifestations.

Jana Bahal's charm lies in its fantastic metalwork, its great importance with local people, and its huge courtyard which offers a different scene every time you visit. Children play, women bathe near the well, pigeons coo, shopkeepers tend small stores selling nails, cloth, and grain. In the evenings people come to offer lamps, sometimes passing their hands over the flame and then over their eyes in a ritual believed to keep eyes healthy. Sometimes at night there's *bhajan*-singing in the entrance portico, and elaborate *puja* are often performed in the courtyard, with offerings of red powder, incense, flowers, and rice. Even local Tibetans stop in to prostrate themselves before the statue, for Avalokitesvara, or Chenrezig as he is called there, is the patron deity of Tibet.

KATHMANDU
BACKSTREETS
AND THE
OLD BAZAAR

Kel Tol

Exit through the low passageway in the courtyard's rear wall into Kel Tol and a temple stacked with all sizes and shapes of red clay pottery. More spills out the doorways of surrounding shops: ashtrays, chillums, hookah bowls, clay molds for festival cakes, flowerpots embossed with Vishnu or shaped like rhinos and griffons. The largest urns are used to store grain and water. On the corner, streetside barbers give haircuts and shaves to squatting clients.

This area specializes in printed Indian cottons. Terai men loiter on the street with strange stringed instruments they use to fluff the cotton filling of pillows and quilts. Head back east down Kel Tol to the main road. At the crossroads is a small temple to the terrible **Chamunda,** its twin doors embossed with the symbol of the Mother Goddess—an eye over a full water pot. Disarmingly, it's been turned into an outdoor shop selling makeup, mirrors, and the red cotton strands used to lengthen women's braids.

shop set up
under the eaves
of the Kel Tol temple

Tilang Ghar

Continuing up the main street, on the left is the 19th-century Tilang Ghar, with green shutters and a stucco frieze of marching soldiers. Beside it is an old octagonal-roofed pavilion. Inhabited by ginger-sellers, it looks like a resthouse but is actually a **Krishna temple,** its back side long vanished into surrounding buildings. Its lovely carved pillars and windows are worth examining if you can find a firm foothold against the crowds.

The bazaar is a living river of people endlessly flowing past tiny shops, each with its own specialty: dried fruits and nuts, toys and tinseled holiday decorations, plastic housewares, brass pots. The oldest are so small the shopkeeper can reach every item without shifting from his cross-legged position. Merchants sit thus from morning to night, watching the changing street scene as their friends stop by to share a glass of milk tea, play a round of chess, or puff meditatively on a waterpipe.

Asan Tol

This crossroads is the heart of Kathmandu. Six streets meet in a crowded bazaar filled with sellers of turmeric, ginger, garlic, fruit, oil, spices, and wandering cows on the prowl for a mouthful. The old open-air vegetable bazaar here was shut down by city authorities a few years ago on the pretext of cleaning up the city. All it's done is open Asan to further traffic, while the produce sellers now line the side streets.

Asan is a nonstop uproar of bicycle bells, vendors advertising their wares, porters shouting to clear the way for rattling pushcarts, and the occasional blare of an auto horn trying to get through the dense crowd. Don't even *try* to bring a motor vehicle through Asan except late at night; even a bicycle is difficult. The rush of activity is overwhelming at first, so find an out-of-the-way corner from which to absorb the scene. The second-story Annapurna Seed House is a good place for photographs.

Three small temples are nearly hidden in the blur of activity. The beautiful little **Annapurna Mandir** is dedicated to a form of Lakshmi, the goddess of wealth. Annapurna means "Full of Grain," and she's represented by a silver *purna kalasha* or overflowing vessel, a symbol of abundance. People visit here all day long to toss in a coin and whisper a brief prayer with folded hands, for this is the Valley's most popular Lakshmi shrine—and Lakshmi, the giver of wealth, is a very popular goddess. The old grain market, now moved southeast to Mahabuddha, used to stand in front of the temple, and a few vendors remain nearby with their scales suspended from a tripod.

Nearby is a small **Ganesh temple,** its steps a good vantage point on the surrounding bustle. The third and smallest shrine belongs to **Vishnu** and contains some ancient stone sculptures. Families visit here to divine the sex of an expected child by pouring mustard oil over the statue. If the substance flows down the right side, it's a boy; if the left side, a girl. A bit further north is a big, bathtublike stone basin with the relief of a fish which supposedly fell from the sky one miraculous day. Normally it's completely covered over by vegetable sellers and is difficult to spot except late at night.

From Asan, streets radiate out in every direction: northwest to Thamel, south to Indra Chowk and Mahabaudha (an interesting walk) and a pair running east to Rani Pokhari. The lower one passes through Bhotahiti, a name which means "Tibetan water tap." In the old days Tibetan traders congregated here at the site of a spring-fed public bath. The tap was eventually buried and forgotten, and the name became just another one of Kathmandu's mysteries until it was recently unearthed, its water still running, during excavations for a pedestrian subway.

KATHMANDU BACKSTREETS

This route proceeds from Durbar Square to Kanti Path, traversing old Newar neighborhoods full of little-known temples and *bahal.* Take it as a launching point for similar explorations down interesting side streets.

Yetkha Bahal

Head west from the **Shiva-Parvati temple** on Durbar Square and turn right on the first street into **Pyaphal,** a less-trafficked back route to Chhetrapati and Thamel. Shops along the southern portion feature lurid posters of Hindi film stars, while farther up the specialty is traditional musical instruments: sitars, *tabla,* and the local *madaal* or hand drums. A green metal gate on the right marks an entrance to the infamous **Kot,** the scene of the 1846 massacre which brought the Ranas to power. The original buildings have been demolished, but the courtyard once ran red with the blood of Nepal's ruling class.

Next is a **Kankeshwari temple** to a bloodthirsty mother goddess, set into a larger building and marked by two doors. The first is of gilded metal embossed with eyes and a dancing skeleton, and the second is of carved wood with a six-pointed star carved in the window above—a very old Hindu symbol, used among other things to represent the goddess Kali.

Just past the second door is a crumbling **16th-century resthouse** with beautiful, weath-

BAZAAR ODDITIES

Some of the mysterious items encountered in the Kathmandu bazaar:

Sticky brown cakes: This is *gur,* an unrefined molasses fed to recently calved cows and nursing mothers to build up their strength. It's sometimes mixed with tobacco and smoked in a hookah.

Matte-brown "cannonballs": Cheap laundry soap made from the oil of the neem tree, mixed with a special kind of clay and sold by weight.

Flower garlands: Used for worship or to honor a person—someone leaving on or returning from a journey, for example.

Sacks of golden powder: Turmeric, a spice produced from a rhizome similar to ginger, is an essential ingredient in Nepali and Indian cuisine. Called "poor man's saffron," it's also used as an antiseptic and skin softener.

Stacks of green leaves: Stitched together with bamboo fibers, the glossy leaves of the sal tree are used as 100% biodegradable plates for ceremonial feasts and offerings. Great quantities are imported from outside the Valley to fill the demand for a ritually pure material for use in religious rites.

Bins of dried fish: These are used as a salty flavoring for *achaar.*

Brown bricks: Pressed blocks of tea made from poor-quality leaves and preferred by Tibetans, each is shaped like a brick, and about as tasty as one.

Orange-tinted goat heads: Seen nailed to posts at butcher shops, which also sell bright orange goat meat (the color comes from turmeric). After slaughtering, the skin is rubbed with a mixture of mustard oil, lemon juice, ashes, and turmeric, said to keep the meat fresh and repel flies. Newar cooking utilizes every bit of the animal: head, eyes, lungs, even the blood, cooked into a coagulated jelly.

Animals: Kathmandu's sacred cows generally have owners who milk them daily and set them loose to feed for free off the streets. Bulls are usually ownerless. According to Hindu custom, 11 days after a man's death his son chooses a bull calf, brands it with the trident of Shiva, and sets it free as a living memorial. Another member of the streetside menagerie is the huge and stinking male goat dedicated to a temple and set free. A pendant tied around the neck identifies it as a sacred animal.

metal plaques depicting Guru Mapa devouring a child (left), and munching on buffalo meat provided by residents of Itum Bahal (right)

ered *yaksha* carved on the wooden struts. The small side street running off from here is inhabited by sign painters (look for the license plates drying in front of their shops), and some of the few **stonecarvers** still working in Kathmandu.

Opposite, a narrow passageway leads to the spacious open courtyard of Yetkha Bahal, built around a stupa with slightly startled-looking painted eyes. The 14th-century wooden struts on the temple behind were taken down for safekeeping a few years ago, but may be reinstalled. Continuing north, the road passes a crumbling but beautiful three-roofed pagoda with a big electrical tranformer right next to it.

Naradevi Temple

At the next intersection is the richly decorated temple of Naradevi, a fierce tantric goddess who is a form of Kali. Painted struts display the Ashta Matrika, while the goddess herself, skeletal and terrifying, appears as the central figure in the golden *torana*. Naradevi is said to have appeared to a king in a dream to request the temple and a platform for dances, and the masked Naradevi dance troupe still performs in the small open square opposite the temple during the spring festival of Pisaach Chautardasi. The fact that the temple survived the 1934 earthquake

unscathed was considered proof of the goddess's power, but the quake's high death toll was attributed to her appetite for human flesh. She is still actively worshipped by neighborhood residents, as reflected in the excellent condition of her imposing shrine.

Itum Bahal

Turn right here onto **Kilgal Tol.** About 75 meters down on the right a sign for "Krishna Printers" points into a vast open courtyard dotted with *chaitya* and shrines. This is Itum Bahal, one of the city's oldest. The main temple is in another courtyard midway down on the right. Over the entrance is a 16th-century wooden *torana* depicting the temptation of Buddha, a superb if dusty example of the storytelling function in Nepali art. Demons and the seductive daughters of Mara surround the main figure of the Buddha, seeking to distract him from his meditation. In response he simply touches his right hand to the earth, calling it to witness his many lifetimes of sincere effort.

The inner courtyard is said to have once been the abode of Guru Mapa, an ogre with a taste for young children. When his appetite became too excessive and local children began disappearing in great numbers, residents coaxed him to move to the Tundikhel and leave their offspring alone in exchange for the yearly sacrifice of a buffalo. The deal is kept to this day, as courtyard residents deliver the feast to the Tundikhel. Two embossed copper plaques on the north wall depict Guru Mapa: in one he's devouring a child; in the second he's munching on his buffalo-meat substitute. Apart from this diversion into folk religion the shrine is properly Buddhist, with Licchavi-era *chaitya* and an unusual 9th-century *chaitya* composed of a quartet of standing Buddhas. Itum Bahal has some very ancient (14th century) and beautiful wooden struts—not the painted ones over the main temple, but the slender *yaksha* on the rear wall over the entrance, both inside and out. They are exquisite, but so worn they seem to be vanishing before your eyes. A few have already disappeared, to be replaced by plain wooden planks.

Bangemudha Tol

Returning to the road, continue east through a busy and interesting Newar neighborhood to the next intersection, where the **Kel Tol temple** sits with its stacks of pottery. Turn left here and proceed to the next corner, where **Washya Deo,** the Newar "toothache god," dwells in a chunk of wood mounted on the side of a building. Toothache sufferers seeking a cure have driven hundreds of nails into the slab. If this folk remedy doesn't work, several dentists' offices up the street display false teeth in their dusty shop windows. This neighborhood is called Bangemudha or "Crooked Stick" after an immense and legendary piece of wood of which the toothache god's abode is only a fragment. It's a busy corner, as yet untouched by many modernities. Porters frequent the small teastalls here, some no more than a kerosene stove and a few glasses set into a niche.

Continue north past a square ringed with many shrines, including the small **Ikhu Narayan temple** with recently restored struts and a 10th-century Vishnu image. On the north side of the square, set into the wall, is a small standing Buddha image which is perhaps 1,500 years old. Next come the aforementioned dentists' offices, and a little farther up on the right, a beautiful 9th-century **Uma-Mahesvara** or **Shiva-Par-**

vati sculpture set in a cemented niche. Shops around here specialize in exotic cloth—Bhutanese striped cotton, colorful Chinese brocades and silks, and bolts of printed gauze prayer flags. On the left, its doorway flanked by two tubas, is a shop which provides the uniforms and musical instruments for raucous Nepali wedding bands.

Kathesimbhu

A little further is a courtyard housing the gilt-topped stupa of Kathesimbhu, literally the "Swayambhu of Kathmandu." For the aged and infirm a pilgrimage to this stupa is said to earn as much merit as the 365-step ascent to Swayambhu. Every detail of the original is replicated, down to the five "mansions" of the elements and the temple to the smallpox goddess Sitala in the rear right-hand corner. Supposedly this stupa was constructed with earth and stones remaining from Swayambhu. According to another legend, it was built in 5th-century Buddhist India. A Nepali sage happened to pass by, and the builders challenged him to breathe life into the monument. The sage muttered a mantra and strolled over the hills back to Kathmandu, with the stupa following obediently behind. While the stupa itself is probably not nearly as old as these tales imply (the present one was built in the 17th century), the site is very ancient, as proven by some magnificent Licchavi stone sculptures, including a Padmapani Lokesvara embedded in a wall near the Sitala temple.

Thahiti and Beyond

The next intersection is Thahiti, the site of a miraculous fountain said to have once spouted forth gold, until it was covered over in the 15th century by a Tibetan-style stupa ringed with prayer wheels. Behind it is a small shrine to Nasadyo, the dancing form of Shiva who is the Newar patron of music. The doorway is decorated with embossed metal images of divine musicians; the central image is merely a hole, the only representation of this invisible god.

This street continues into Thamel, but for now turn east down the narrow street beyond, passing many garment shops. About 200 meters down, a pair of stone lions mark the entrance to the ancient and beautiful **Musya Bahal.** A little further down on the same side is the larger free-standing **Chusya Bahal,** which dates back to 1649. It has superb carved struts and a beautiful entrance *torana* depicting the Buddhist goddess Prajnaparamita. Continue east on this road past Jyatha Tol, and you'll soon reach Kanti Path.

> *For here and there, through carved and corrugated old archways, are glimpses of courtyards and shrines, containing idols smeared with vermilion and ghee, festooned with flowers, and framed with burnished brass ornament. . . . delightful conglomerations of bright colour, rich shadows, flickering sunlight, religious devotion and unmitigated dirt, the last not the least striking of them all."*
>
> —PERCY BROWN,
> *PICTURESQUE NEPAL*

NEW KATHMANDU

Kanti Path and the area immediately east of it is all busy roads and concrete buildings. It lacks the character of the old town but contains most of the modern offices and shops, and encompasses quite a bit of history which is not readily apparent. Knowing the landmarks makes getting around easier and a lot more interesting. This is one tour you probably won't walk all at once, but you're bound to do bits and pieces over the course of your visit.

ALONG DURBAR MARG

Durbar Marg is the elite street of Kathmandu, lined by top airline offices, travel agencies, restaurants, shops, and hotels. Property here is the most expensive in the country, and prices of goods and services are correspondingly high.

Narayanhiti Palace

At the north end of the street is Narayanhiti Royal Palace, the official residence of Shri Panch Maharajdhiraj Birendra Bir Bikram Shah Dev, otherwise known as King Birendra. The Shah kings moved to this compound from the old palace in the late 18th century. The new edifice was inaugurated in 1970 on the occasion of the wedding of then Crown Prince Birendra. The compound is immense, surrounded by high walls and guarded by grim-looking soldiers.

The main rooms of the palace's state wing are open to the public one day a week—for tourists, Thursday 10 a.m.-noon and 1-4 p.m. Admission is Rs250, no cameras or children under 12 allowed. Visitors are accompanied by an attentive tour guide who points out the sights. The decor is tacky but beautifully executed; a welter of auspicious symbols scattered with overstuffed sofas and stuffed tigers. Rooms that are open include the reception hall and the throne room, with its 60-foot-high ceilings and an uncomfortable-looking throne.

The palace takes its name from the **Narayan Hiti**, a recently restored water tap opposite and a little east of the main entrance. Most *makara* spouts have downward curving snouts, but this pair curves upwards—in disgust, it's said, at a royal parricide they once witnessed. Across the road hidden behind high whitewashed walls is the *shikara*-style **Narayan temple** built in 1793, its shady courtyard a peaceful, parklike haven.

South Durbar Marg

A statue of the late King Mahendra, the father of the present king, presides over a traffic roundabout, periodically placated by the sacrifice of a goat. A block further is the city's main **Muslim mosque** or Jame Masjid. Some three percent of Nepalis are Muslim, and white-capped worshippers crowd the streets on Friday afternoons. Past it is the campus and distinctive white clock tower of **Trichandra College,** built in the Rana era. Turn left at the next intersection to tour **Bagh Bazaar** and **Dilli Bazaar,** major shopping areas for construction supplies and furnishings.

The Tundikhel

On the right is **Ratna Park,** an unmaintained patch of grass that hosts political rallies and serves as a public urinal—the fate of any "park" in Kathmandu. Behind it stretches the huge grassy swath of the Tundikhel, the local parade grounds. It's used for official functions and displays of military might, which the king occasionally observes from the reviewing stand on the north end. The city's largest open space, it's a favorite practice ground for soccer and cricket. During the monsoon it's maintained by peasant women, who cut huge mounds of grass and haul them away to feed livestock. Marking the four corners are massive **bronze statues** of noble mustachioed Ranas majestically mounted on horseback, cast in Europe and carried in over the mountains by porters. At 4,000 pounds apiece these are said to be the heaviest objects ever hauled into the Valley.

Midway down, the municipal **Central Bus Park** on the left provides local services around the Valley. The exhibition ground further south houses a popular **open-air market,** and is the site of the new **Kathmandu Tourism Service Center,** supposed to be completed by spring 1996, which will have display facilities and an information center.

SINGHA DURBAR

This immense building was at one time the most magnificent of all Rana palaces and the largest private residence in Asia, with 17 courtyards and up to 1,700 rooms. It was built in 1901 by the order of Prime Minister Chandra Shamsher Rana. Teams of laborers worked round the clock for nearly a year to complete it in record time at a cost of Rs2.5 million. The exterior facade, with its acres of colonnaded white stucco porticoes, was the last word in Rana baroque. The interior was equally magnificent, overflowing with mirrors in gilded frames, Carrera marble, and Belgian crystal chandeliers. Every bit of this splendor was imported from Europe and carried over the mountains by porters.

Chandra made the building large enough to accommodate his extensive family, but soon his sons were agitating for palaces of their own. So he sold Singha Durbar to the state to be used as the prime minister's official residence (in those days the prime minister *was* the state) and with the proceeds built palaces for all his sons.

The giant palace must have been something of a white elephant: the last Rana prime minister is said to have employed 1,500 servants to maintain it. After 1951 Singha Durbar became headquarters of the new government, its rooms filled with hundreds of cross-legged scribes wielding brushes and pens. The great reception halls were maintained for official functions. They were adorned with "as many stuffed animals as a natural history museum," according to one visitor, and include a famous side audience hall with distorting mirrors brought back by Jung Bahadur Rana from London.

Singha Durbar endured until July 1974, when a disastrous two-day fire fanned by monsoon winds consumed its overstuffed furniture and official government documents. Much of the complex had burned to the ground by the time the center section was finally dynamited in order to save the palace's majestic front facade and the reception halls. A lengthy inquiry never determined the cause, but popular suspicion was arson.

BOB RACF

At the lower end of the Tundikhel the large **Bhadrakali Temple** provides a convenient roundabout for one-way traffic. Branching off to the left is **Prithvi Path,** among the widest, smoothest, and best-paved roads in Kathmandu, leading, naturally, to the Parliament at **Singha Durbar.**

The road curves round the Bhadrakali temple and swings west, bisecting the Tundikhel. Midway down in the marble arch of **Martyrs' Gate** (Shahid Gate), commemorating a group of revolutionaries who plotted to overthrow the Ranas and restore King Tribhuvan to power. Five ringleaders caught in 1940 were tried and convicted of attempting to contact the king. Four were promptly executed; the fifth was thrown in prison, his life spared only because he was a Brahman and thus not subject to capital punishment. Bronze busts of the quintet flank an image of King Tribhuvan in the monument.

ALONG KANTI PATH

Around the GPO

The road soon meets Kanti Path, the main northbound street. The **General Post Office** is at this intersection. A little behind is the whiteplastered spire of the **Dharahara,** frequently mistaken for a Muslim minaret. Actually it was built as a watchtower by Prime Minister Bhimsen Thapa in 1830 to "amaze the populace." Originally it had 11 sections, but the two topmost ones toppled in earthquakes. Popular belief has it that the Jung Bahadur Rana once leapt from the tower astride his horse, holding an unfurled umbrella as a parachute. The horse died, but he survived.

The plaza around the Dharahara has been transformed into a park of sorts, where people can sit on the scanty grass and munch on peanuts and oranges. Nearby is the giant **Sundhara,** a popular bathing and laundry spot for old-town residents still without indoor water. Opposite and hidden from the road are the crumbling remains of **Bagh Durbar,** the "Tiger Palace," its gates once guarded by two live caged tigers. It was built by Bhimsen in 1805; he eventually met a bloody end here.

New Road

Heading north up Kanti Path, the **RNAC Office** is at the next intersection, identified by a metal sculpture of a carafe-bearing yeti. The road branching west here is New Road, straddled by a painted white plaster gate. The road's official name is Juddha Saddak, but everyone calls it New Road, the "New" referring to 1934, when Prime Minister Juddha Shamsher Rana ordered the the wide boulevard be built over the earthquake's rubble. Wealthy Nepalis and Indian tourists shop here for electronic goods, watches, modern clothes and shoes, jewelry, cameras, toys, perfume, all brought in from Hong Kong and Bangkok on the "gray market," and expensive compared to items in the West.

Midway down New Road on the left is the **Pipal Bot,** a very old and sacred tree presiding over a few small idols and numerous news and shoeshine stands. This is a hotbed for political gossip: if you can't track down a rumor here, it hasn't even started yet. At the end of New Road is the **Supermarket** (Bishal Bazaar), a shopping center crammed with small perfume and clothing shops, boasting the country's first escalator. With the growth of the local upper class, many other modern shops, including a few small department stores, have sprung up in this area over the last few years.

The side streets leading off New Road deserve some exploration. To the north is a network of narrow lanes lined by goldsmiths, Indian sweet shops, and a big and popular cinema hall. In a compound to the south is the **Subji Bazaar,** the city's largest fruit and vegetable market. Avoid the street in front, lined with tables of fly-ridden meat and fish.

Mahakala Temple

Back on Kanti Path and heading north, you'll see the small Mahakala temple on the right, one of the city's most popular shrines. The black stone image with silver eyes is laden with jewelry offered by devotees. To Hindus, Mahakala is "The Great Black One," a form of Shiva as Bhairab. To Buddhists, Mahakala is a protective deity, created by the great Indian sage Nagarjuna as the protector of the Swayambhunath Stupa. A tantric Buddhist priest is said to have once glimpsed Mahakala flying over the Valley, and impressed with his size and power, decided to lure him to Kathmandu. Fashioning an image, he forced Mahakala to enter it by the power of mantra. Unhappy, the god offered to visit voluntarily on Saturday evenings if he would be released, and the priest agreed. You'll notice larger crowds here on Saturdays. The image is said to be exceptionally powerful and is worshipped to relieve pain and injury; conveniently, it's located close to **Bir Hospital.**

Rani Pokhari

Further up Kanti Path on the same side is Rani Pokhari, the "Queen's Pond," an enormous artificial tank created in 1670 by King Pratapa Malla to console one of his wives after the death of their son. Water from 51 sacred pilgrimage sites was poured in to sanctify the pond. Despite this, Rani Pokhari quickly acquired an unsavory reputation. First it was ghosts (Pratapa Malla met his *kichkinni* lover here); later it became a popular suicide spot, necessitating the high fence now surrounding it.

At the north end is **Jamal,** which links Kanti Path to Durbar Marg; from here public *tempo* ply regular routes to northern Kathmandu. Continue up the street, past the **British Council Library.** Opposite it is the Election Commission, housed in the renovated palace of **Bahadur Bhawan,** the former site of Boris Lissanevitch's famed Royal Hotel. This neighborhood, now filled with offices, is dotted with fragments of old Rana palaces. The American Recreational Center compound on the corner is for residents only; it's housed on the grounds of the old Phora Durbar palace. Before it was fragmented by fire and the demands of modern life, this palace stretched all the way to the Yak and Yeti's Lal Durbar, over one km away. You can still glimpse bits of the facade behind the buildings of Durbar Marg.

The Kaiser Library

Yet another palace is across the street on the opposite corner: Kaiser Mahal, now housing the Ministry of Education and Culture. A por-

tion is occupied by the Kaiser Library, a fabulous collection of 35,000 old volumes open to the public on a nonborrowing basis. Stroll inside to inspect the decadent decor: a stuffed Bengal tiger, suits of armor, mounted buffalo heads, and marble nymphs, plus oil paintings of Shiva, King George V, and the library's founder, Kaiser J.B. Rana. A sweeping formal staircase leads to the second floor, where you'll find more books and old photos of Ranas wearing their spectacular plumed helmets. Window seats overlooking the overgrown garden make the perfect hideaway for an afternoon spent browsing through volumes like *Topee and Turban* and *We Ended in Bali*. The library is open daily except Saturday 10 a.m.-5 p.m.

SOUTH KATHMANDU

South of Durbar Square and New Road is a sleepy neighborhood seldom visited by tourists. South Kathmandu is still largely inhabited by Jyapu or Newar peasants and basically unchanged by modernization, which means it's poor and crowded as well as quaint. The two streets leading south from Kasthamandap, **Chikhanmughal** and **Bhimsenthan,** link up into a good 20-minute circuit, passsing the towering **Jaisideval Mandir** dedicated to Shiva, and the brightly painted **Bhimsen Mandir** to the god of merchants. Streets stretch south past here all the way down to busy **Tripureshwar Marg,** a main artery usually jammed with traffic.

ALONG THE BAGMATI

Most travelers know this busy neighborhood near the Patan Bridge as the home of the Bluebird Supermarket. Behind the streetside shops, the ghats along the banks of the sacred Bagmati River are lined with a peaceful array of crumbling old temples and stone sculptures. Exploring this little-known area takes an interesting few hours, during which you'll see few if any foreigners, but plenty of Nepali life. Be forewarned that this trip is not for the fainthearted. Sacred as it is, the Bagmati also serves as the sewer of Kathmandu, and its tributary streams are pungent. This tour is best done on foot—you can easily catch

a taxi at the end—but if you've got a bicycle you can manage by pushing it along.

Kalmochan Ghat

Start by descending the staircase beside the Patan bridge on the east bank of the Bagmati. In winter pilgrims pitch their ragged tents on the grassy riverbank here. The buildings to the right enclose various resthouses for sadhus and pilgrims. In one of them is the unusual Moghul-inspired temple of **Hem Narayan,** its bulbous white dome topped by a cupola of gilded serpents. Construction was started under Prime Minister Bhimsen Thapa in the early 19th century and completed by Jung Bahadur, who is said to have hidden the ashes of the victims of the Kot Massacre in the foundations. Perhaps this explains the brooding air of this massive structure. Giant gilded griffons salvaged from a long-ago temple on the Tundikhel leap from the four corners. The gilded figure in court dress atop a pillar was also transferred from the Tundikhel and is of King Surendra Bahadur Shah. Though his hands are folded in prayer, he's armed with a rifle and a wicked-looking sword.

Tripureshwar Mahadeva

Exiting the compound, cross over the evil-smelling black Tukucha Khola, which has the misfortune to run through the middle of Kathmandu before joining the Bagmati at this point.

The next shrine is an impressive large pagoda set a little back from the river in another courtyard; unlike Kalmochan, it can be accessed from the main road. This is Tripureshwar Mahadeva, built in 1818 by a wife of the ill-fated King Rana Bahadur Shah (assassinated in 1806) and dedicated to the repose of his soul. A gilded image of the queen kneels atop a stone pillar carved with *naga*, while a gilded bull and a giant trident identify this as a Shiva temple. The lower struts display characters from the Mahabharata. The temple is impressive mainly because of its size, but the crumbling, grassy courtyard has a charm lost in the impeccably restored and varnished temples of Durbar Square. Squatter families who have taken over the surrounding buildings give this entire area a rural feeling.

Along the River
In front of the temple on the riverbank is a small cluster of stone sculptures called **Hanumansthan;** the stone lingas and the Shiva-Parvati stela here are extremely ancient, dating perhaps to Licchavi times. From here it's a 10-minute stroll to the next cluster of temples, across an open field and past people bathing and washing clothes in the filthy black river. In the winter, vegetables are planted right up to the water's edge, making use of every available scrap of land. The wooden shanties lining the banks are home to the lowest of the low castes, mainly butchers and ragpickers, who practice their trades along the riverbank. Juxtaposed with the squalor is the dignity of people getting on with their daily lives: knitting, drying vegetables, massaging babies in the sun.

Around Teku
The clustered buildings and shrines resume again along the stone steps of Hanumanghat, where a red-faced Monkey King guards the entrance to a **Ramchandra temple** featuring Indian-influenced images of **Sita and Rama,** where a resident *sadhu* does *puja* all day long in a tiny side room. The row of 50 crumbling brick niches on the ghat's eastern edge was built to hold the clothing of bathers in the sacred river.

Next is the striking temple of **Tindeval,** a unique triple-domed *shikara* set in a courtyard. Terra-cotta *naga* and *nagini* encircle the building, partly as decoration and partly to protect against

evil spirits. Further down at **Pachali Ghat,** brick niches contain an unusually large collection of sculptures of various deities, not particularly old but very well-executed. The 80-odd sculptures in the area were donated by various devotees and span the religious spectrum from Buddhist to Shaivite and Vaishnavite. More temples and resthouses crowd this area, including the crumbling **Lakshmishwar Mahadev Mandir** near the bridge, with fine woodcarvings and some mildly erotic struts.

The faintly swaying middle of the big old **Kaalo Pul** footbridge offers good overviews of local activity: sand being mined from the river to feed Kathmandu's hunger for cement, buffalo enjoying a last wallow before their impending slaughter, perhaps a cremation on Teku's active *masan*. These temples once constituted a miniature holy city, separated from the city by rich fields. Only over the last decade or two has it become a built-up extension of Kathmandu. The new Japanese-built bridge and road paralleling the footbridge are part of an "inner ring road" being built along the Vishnumati that will further urbanize Kathmandu's ancient interior.

Teku Dhovan
Temples and resthouses continue west of the bridge up to Teku Dhovan at the confluence of the Vishnumati and Bagmati Rivers, like all river junctions an auspicious and sacred place. This particular spot is said to be joined in spirit by the Ganga, Jamuna, and Saraswati, the three most sacred rivers of Hinduism. Residents of south Kathmandu, both Hindu and Buddhist, use it as a cremation site, and stone sculptures and memorial *chaitya* dot the area. The *shikara*-style **Jagganath Mandir** on the road behind here is dedicated to Vishnu and is surrounded by beautifully carved buildings and stone images. Look for the window on the compound's west side, depicting Krishna astride a beautiful young woman.

Pachali Bhairab
When you've finished the riverbank, aim towards the huge pipal tree visible in a courtyard just behind Pachali Ghat. With its twisted roots, it provides an appropriately mysterious setting for the elemental shrine of Pachali Bhairab, a fearsome manifestation of Shiva. This simple open-air shrine is among the Valley's most important

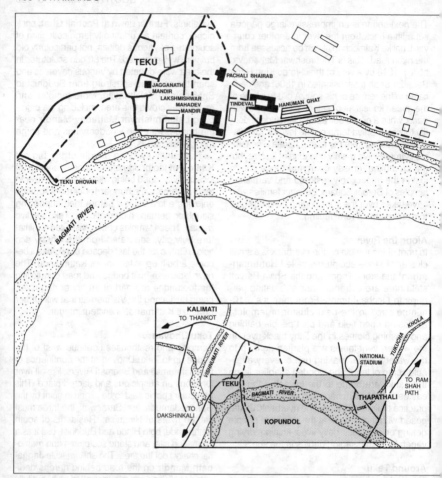

for Newars. The deity is actually embodied in a small boulder set along the edge of the pit, but the small gilded figure in front has become the focus of worship, honored with flower garlands and red powder. Nearby is a brass image of **Betal,** a goblinlike being depicted as a supine, naked corpse with a ghastly grin. As Bhairab's companion and vehicle, he receives blood sacrifices on the god's behalf. Tuesday and Saturday are the most popular days for worship

here, but local people constantly pass by. The multicolored thread wrapped around the tree's trunk is a ritual remedy advised by astrologers for unlucky people whose horoscopes are misaspected by Saturn.

From here two roads lead to the main road in Kalimati, a short walk. At the junction is a small temple to the **Navadurga,** its ancient woodwork set into a more recent facade. Goat tails are stuck on the wall as tokens of sacrifices.

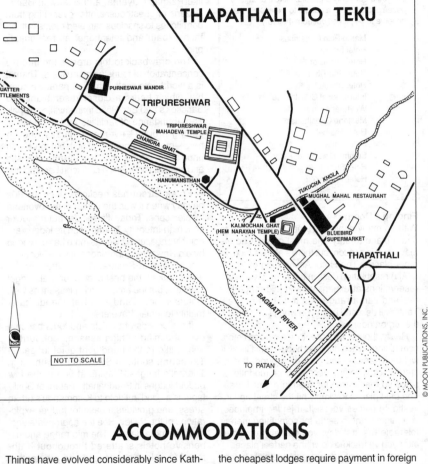

TO DOWNTOWN KATHMANDU

THAPATHALI TO TEKU

SQUATTER SETTLEMENTS

PURNESWAR MANDIR

TRIPURESHWAR

TRIPURESHWAR MAHADEVA TEMPLE

CHANDRA GHAT

HANUMANSTHAN

TUKUCHA KHOLA

MUGHAL MAHAL RESTAURANT

KALMOCHAN GHAT (HEM NARAYAN TEMPLE)

BLUEBIRD SUPERMARKET

THAPATHALI

BAGMATI RIVER

NOT TO SCALE

TO PATAN

© MOON PUBLICATIONS, INC.

ACCOMMODATIONS

Things have evolved considerably since Kathmandu's first tourist-class hotel opened in 1954. Today hundreds of lodges, guesthouses, and hotels cater almost exclusively to foreign tourists. Nepalis themselves generally stay with family or friends when traveling. Rates listed here are for high season (Oct.-Nov.), but are always negotiable, especially for lengthy stays. In the monsoon, expect discounts of up to 50%. All except

the cheapest lodges require payment in foreign currency and state their prices in U.S. dollars. You may have to show a bank exchange receipt to pay in rupees. Medium- and upper-range establishments add 10-15% government tax to the bill, depending on the number of stars in their ratings. When two prices are shown in the listings below, the difference is common bath/attached bath.

RECOMMENDED HOTELS

With no shortage of good places to stay in Kathmandu, any attempt at a definitive list would be highly arguable. Here's a baker's dozen of places, from budget to expensive, that deserve to be picked out from the crowd:

Marco Polo Guesthouse
Hotel Shakti
Hotel Excelsior
Hotel Shri Tibet
Hotel Utse
International Guesthouse
Wayfarer's Inn
Mustang Guesthouse
Hotel Thamel
Hotel Vajra
Summit Hotel (see "Patan")
Hotel Shangri-la
Hotel Yak & Yeti

Finding a Room

With so many choices it's never a problem to find a place to stay: the most popular hotels may fill up in season, but there's always room at other places. The Hotel Association of Nepal (HAN) reservation desk in the airport will make reservations at expensive and mid-range hotels and can arrange free transport as well. Touts will descend upon you when you step out the airport doorway.

Really, though, it's better to see a place before committing. Pick a neighborhood—most likely it will be Thamel—and go look around. It's incredibly easy to find decent accommodations, since so many are clustered in a small area. The best plan is to simply hit the street and investigate places yourself. If jet lag impinges, you might want to settle for something merely tolerable the first day: you can always move after you've tracked down the perfect place.

It may be wise to stay at least one night before striking a deal, in order to check out nighttime noise levels (barking dogs are a real problem). Rooms on upper stories are marginally quieter and may offer a view. Rooms can be cold and damp in winter months, so look for a south-facing room and a hotel with a sunny garden or rooftop patio, and bring warm pajamas.

Lodgings by Neighborhood

The budget travelers' scene focuses on **Thamel** (Ta-MEL), yuppie successor to the notorious Freak Street. The name has been extended by lodgekeepers to cover smaller neighborhoods like Paknajol, Jyatha, and Bhagwan Bahal. Dozens of guesthouses offer everything from dormitories to spacious carpeted rooms with attached bath and telephone, all reasonably priced.

The drawback to this area is the intense concentration of tourists and hustlers. Thamel is a world unto itself, a budget paradise-cum-hell which bears a closer resemblance to Bangkok's Kao San Road than anything Nepali. The abundance of facilities and the ease of getting around—everyone speaks English here—make it appealing at first, but there's an unpleasant edge in the air, a mixture of hustle and self-delusion, which can soon become distasteful.

Freak Street has declined since its '60s heyday when it was the center of the overland hippie scene. Today it's seedier but mellower than high-intensity Thamel, and its lodges are notably cheaper, as well as more basic. Ringed by old Newar neighborhoods, it's well-located, just off Durbar Square. Rock-bottom prices alone make it the best choice for real budget travelers, but the ambience is pleasant as well. Hotels in south and east Kathmandu cater mainly to Indian travelers.

If the crowds of tourists and touts become overwhelming in high season, look further afield, like to the handful of quiet lodges in **Tahachal,** south of Swayambhunath, or in Thamel's fringes. Staying at one of the few budget lodges in Boudhanath, Patan, or Bhaktapur is a good antidote to Kathmandu's urban stress, and provides a base for further explorations of the Valley. See the appropriate sections for more details. The mid-range and expensive hotels scattered throughout Kathmandu are less ghetto-ized and are another way to avoid the tourist trap syndrome.

BUDGET

These are the cheapest rooms you can find, as low as Rs40 single up to Rs250 for a double.

Freak Street
Now well past its '60s heyday, Freak Street is reverting back to its original identity as the Newar neighborhood of Jhochen Tol. The tourist shops are intermixed with old silver shops, *momo pasaal,* and motorcycle repair stalls, and only a few hardy budget tourists are to be seen. Being the real thing rather than a tourist ghetto has something to recommend it, though accommodations here are mostly spartan.

Typically tiny, dim rooms for Rs40 s, Rs80-120 d are found in the **Monumental Lodge,** tel. (1) 214-864. Up the street in a courtyard redolent of hashish is the old **Century Lodge,** tel. (1) 214-241, with rooms for Rs100-130. If they're full, try the adjoining **Pagoda Lodge.**

Annapurna Lodge, tel. (1) 213-684, is bigger and busier than most places, with 19 rooms. Rates are Rs125 s, Rs150 d, add Rs50 for a room with bath. The **Paradise Vegetarian Restaurant** here is quite good.

Down an interesting side street is **Himalaya's Guesthouse,** tel. (1) 215-416, a tidy new building set well back from the fray with rooftop views and rooms for Rs80-120 s, Rs150-200 d.

The **Buddha Guesthouse** above the Lost Horizon restaurant is a quiet place with rooms for Rs60 s, Rs100-150 d. Further down the main street is the neighborhood of Om Bahal. **Hotel Eden,** tel. (1) 213-863, is more upscale than most places around here, a two-star hotel with a lobby, an elevator, and rooms with bath for Rs320-480 s, Rs480-640 d.

Friendly Home, tel. (1) 220-171, down a nearby side street has been operating since 1968. It's a popular and basic classic, with a pleasant proprietor and clean if tiny rooms for Rs50-60 s, Rs80-100 d, Rs120 t; Rs140 for attached bath. There are a few more quiet, cheap lodges down the main road, including the newish **Mustang Cottage.**

Around Durbar Square
This is a great location, untouristy and thoroughly Nepali, if a bit noisy. **Kathmandu Lodge,** tel. (1) 214-893, is a popular old standby just off Durbar Square on Pyaphal Tol. Rooms are Rs150 s, Rs300 d for common bath, add Rs25-50 for attached bath. **Kumari Lodge,** tel. (1) 222-498, in a tall, narrow building facing Durbar Square has clean rooms with separate bath for

Rs100 s, Rs200 d, Rs270 t; the front rooms have great views and there's a tiny rooftop balcony. A few minutes' walk south in the interesting neighborhood of Chikhamughal is the **Golden Bird Lodge,** tel. (1) 220-133, a quiet, fairly new building with simple rooms for Rs60 s, Rs120 d.

Thamel
Central Thamel: Hotel Star, tel. (1) 411-000, is nothing special except for the location and the low price: Rs100-200 s, Rs150-250 d. **Cosy Corner,** tel. (1) 417-799, next to it is similarly nondescript, with rooms with common bath for Rs80 s, Rs150 d. Around the corner and behind it is **Lodge Pheasant,** tel. (1) 417-415, quieter, and because it's partly housed in an old Rana palace, with more ambience than most places. Rooms are Rs100 s, Rs150 d, again with only common bath. The dingy **Friendly Guesthouse** in front of it is similarly priced and not so nice.

Pilgrims Hotel, tel. (1) 416-910, run by the same folks as the bookstore, has rooms and dorm beds for Rs85 per person. Tiny cheap rooms for around Rs200 s, Rs300 d can be found at **Bali Guesthouse** or the adjoining **Deutsche Guesthouse,** both of which are decent and clean enough. **Om Guesthouse** is a good deal, charging Rs100 s, Rs120 d with attached bath.

Marco Polo Guesthouse, tel. (1) 227-914, is at the top end of this category, with rooms for US$4/6-8 d; nice, clean, new, with a friendly staff, its a very good deal for the price. **Sagarmatha Guesthouse,** tel. (1) 410-214, is more run-down but cheerful, with some nice balconies overlooking the street. It has an unusually wide range of rooms, including a five-bed room for Rs500. Singles are Rs150-300; doubles Rs200-500. **Kunal's Guesthouse,** tel. (1) 411-050, is more of a flophouse, though rooms are all outfitted with fans, a plus for the cheap price of Rs100-200. **Gorkha Guesthouse,** tel. (1) 214-243, towards Chhetrapati is popular for its large sunny garden courtyard and balcony. Rooms with common bath are Rs150 s, Rs250 d.

Kwa Bahal: Tara Guesthouse, tel. (1) 220-634, is much larger than its exterior would indicate, built around a central courtyard. Adequate rooms are Rs100 s, Rs150-300 d. The nearby **Tibet Home,** tel. (1) 224-986, is Tibetan in name only, with steep dim stairways, but surprisingly large rooms for Rs150 with bath—insist on a

THAMEL ACCOMMODATIONS

© MOON PUBLICATIONS, INC.

heavy discount over their published rates, though. **Downtown Guesthouse,** tel. (1) 224-189, is a bit of a dump, with cheap rooms with attached bath for Rs150 s, Rs250 d.

Paknajol: Down a dirt road in extreme northwest Paknajol are a few remote budget guesthouses, quiet and out of the way, with views extending out over fields, backed by Nagarjun. **Tibet Peace Guesthouse,** tel. (1) 415-026, and **Kathmandu Peace Guesthouse,** tel. (1) 414-

623, are similar, though the latter is more basic and gets more sun on its terrace. Rooms are quite cheap at both: US$5-8, easily knocked down.

Chhetrapati: This is a more authentic neighborhood, away from Thamel's clutter but still close to its shops and restaurants. **Dolpo Guesthouse** is more promising than its gloomy entryway indicates, a small new building with a tiny sunny courtyard and rooms for Rs150-300.

1. Kathmandu Peace Guesthouse	21. Kathmandu Guest House	40. Hotel Pisang
2. Tibet Peace Guesthouse	22. Pilgrims Hotel/Narayan's Restaurant	41. Imperial Guesthouse
3. Hotel Manang	23. Deutsche/Bali Guesthouse	42. New Shangrila Guesthouse
4. Hotel Marshyangdi	24. Hotel Earth House	43. Mustang Holiday Inn
5. Buddha Guesthouse	25. Hotel Star	44. Gorkha Guesthouse
6. Hotel Malla	26. Cosy Corner	45. Tara Guesthouse
7. Hotel Iceland	27. Lodge Pheasant	46. Hotel Blue Diamond
8. Pilgrims Inn	28. Friendly Guesthouse	47. Trans-Himalayan Guest House
9. Hotel Mandap	29. Sagarmatha Guesthouse	48. Tibet Guest House
10. Yeti Home	30. Hotel Excelsior	49. Dolpo Guesthouse
11. Hotel Shri Tibet	31. Kunal's Guesthouse	50. Hotel Tayoma
12. Hotel Karma	32. Newa Guesthouse	51. Potala Guest House
13. Hotel Thamel	33. Downtown Guesthouse	52. Hotel Utse
14. Thamel House	33. Downtown Guesthouse	53. Hotel Norling
15. Wayfarer's Inn	34. Hotel Tashi Dhele	54. Lhasa Guesthouse
16. Hotel Shakti	35. Thorong Peak Guesthouse	55. Tibet Resthouse
17. Capital Guesthouse	36. Om Guesthouse	56. Tibet Home
18. Holy Lodge	37. Marco Polo Guesthouse	57. Hotel Siddhartha
19. Hotel Garuda	38. Hotel Tilicho	58. Hotel New Gajur
20. Prince Guesthouse	39. Hotel My Home	59. Thahity Guesthouse

Around the Chhetrapati bandstand and down the hill is **Dhalko Chhetrapati,** a thoroughly local street with a few lodges: **Dikey Guesthouse,** tel. (1) 215-996, has rooms for Rs100 s, Rs150 d, Rs100 more for a room with bath. **Sita Guesthouse,** tel. (1) 215-927, is similarly priced, a tall, narrow building with a few balconies on its front rooms. Down the hill and tucked down a side lane, **Nepal Peace Cottage** is really just an ordinary house with a few rooms in the Rs100-200 range.

Alternatives

If you're looking for budgetary peace, try across the Vishnumati River and south of Swayambhu. **Peace Guesthouse,** tel. (1) 271-093, in Tahachal on the road to the National Museum is exceptionally cheap: Rs40 s, Rs65 d for fairly decent rooms, a little more for rooms with bath. In the same neighborhood, **Hotel Shrestha,** tel. (1) 270-528, behind the Holiday Inn has rooms for Rs100-250 s, Rs200-350 d.

Near Thamel but away from the fray in an authentic but noisy local area is **Thahity Guesthouse,** tel. (1) 217-509. Adequate rooms with bath are US$5-6 s, US$8-10 d; it's a little gloomy, but there's a small rooftop garden and a decent restaurant attached. **Hotel K.T.** at Makhan, Indra Chowk, tel. (1) 222-981, is a run-

down but well-located place with rooms for Rs150 s, Rs280 d, all with common bath.

LOW TO MODERATE

Hotels in the US$8-20 range may have three price categories: rooms with common bath, rooms with attached bath, and "deluxe" rooms with extras like wall-to-wall carpeting, telephone, and balcony. They're bargains considering the comfort-to-price ratio.

Central Thamel

The **Kathmandu Guest House,** tel. (1) 413-632, fax (1) 417-133, started the Thamel boom in the early '70s, and it remains popular despite the increased competition. It's now US$17 s, US$20 d for rooms in the new wing, or US$25 s, US$30 d for a garden view. The smaller old wing, housed in a remnant of a Rana palace, has simpler rooms for US$10 s, US$12 d, and a few with common bath for US$6 s, US$8 d. Nice rooms, big sunny garden, interesting ambience, located in the heart of Thamel but set off the main road. It's usually full in season, so try to reserve in advance.

Hotel Excelsior, tel. (1) 411-566, behind the Pumpernickel Bakery is unusually spacious and elegant for this price category, with a rooftop garden and even an elevator. Rates are US$18-25 s, US$22-36 d; the more expensive rooms have balconies, a/c, and bathtubs.

The big new **Hotel Pisang,** tel. (1) 220-097, has a range of rooms, all with bath, from US$8 s, US$10-12 d, all the way up to deluxe rooms with a/c for US$30 s, US$40 d. **Hotel My Home,** tel. (1) 231-788, in the next arcade has small, dim, quiet rooms for US$5-7 s, US$8-10 d.

Thorong Peak Guesthouse, tel. (1) 224-656, is a big, stylish place, well maintained, and set back from the main road in a sunny courtyard. Adequate rooms are US$8-14 s, US$12-18 d. Next door, **Hotel Tashi Dhele,** tel. (1) 217-446, has larger and nicer rooms for US$18 s, US$25 d; the hotel boasts some big sunny balconies as well.

Newa Guesthouse, tel. (1) 420-151, has good newly decorated rooms for US$10-12 with bath; those facing the street are noisy, though. **Hotel Tilicho,** tel. (1) 410-132, near Immigration is a big, clean, usually empty place with rooms for US$15 s, US$20 d.

Hotel Shri Tibet, tel. (1) 419-902, tucked down a side street north of the Kathmandu Guesthouse, is a great, friendly place with a Tibetan ambience. It's clean and quiet, with a small sunny garden and scrupulously kept new rooms. The single rooms facing the back are a bit cramped but reasonable at US$10; south-facing sunny doubles are US$15. The **Hotel Karma,** tel. (1) 417-897, nearby charges slightly more (US$15 s, US$20 d) and is not quite up to the same standard, though it's still good. It has a rooftop terrace and some rooms with balconies.

Sat Ghumti

The name of this twisting street west of Thamel means "Seven Turns." It's quiet and peaceful except for the beeping motorcyles racing around the blind curves. The new facade of **Holy Lodge,** tel. (1) 416-265, hides an older building, where rooms are US$3-10 s, US$10-15 d. Across the street, **Prince Guesthouse,** tel. (1) 414-456, is a sparkling new place with a rooftop garden and nice rooms with bath for US$8-12 s, US$12-15 d. **Capital Guesthouse,** tel. (1) 414-150, is similar, with the addition of some sunny front rooms and a small courtyard: US$5/8 s, US$7/15 d.

International Guesthouse, tel. (1) 410-533, in Kaldhara is *way* back down a narrow lane, removed from the tourist clutter. It's a very nice

place, a house, really, with flower-laden balconies and a sunny, quiet courtyard. Clean rooms, all with bathrooms and some with bathtubs, are US$16 s, US$19 d.

Paknajol

Take a right at that intersection and you're in Paknajol. There are plenty of moderately cheap places here, including **Mustang Guesthouse, Yeti Home,** and **Valentine Guesthouse,** all with rooms for around US$4-6 s, US$9-12 d. **Hotel Iceland,** an unpleasant name for the winter months, is larger and slightly more expensive at US$6-12 s, US$10-18 d.

Bhagwan Bahal

The street east of Thamel proper is coming up with new lodges. It's quieter and more Nepali than central Thamel, though just a short stroll away—a good location, all in all. **Hotel Earth House,** tel. (1) 418-197, is at the low end of this category, with adequate rooms for US$6 s, US$10 d. Those facing the street are slightly noisy. **Hotel Shakti,** tel. (1) 410-121, behind the Hotel Malla at the north end of this neighborhood, is a good choice, quiet, with character and a nice garden, and a range of rooms as cheap as US$4-6 without bath to US$6-16 with bath. Next door is the excellent peaceful **Wayfarer's Inn,** tel. (1) 413-471, surrounded by a sunny spacious garden, with very nice rooms for US$7-10 s, US$10-15 d.

One block west of Bhagwan Bahal is a nameless street; tourist goods now cram the old storefronts, but the neighborhood retains a traditional feel. **Pilgrims Inn,** tel. (1) 416-910, run by the people who own Pilgrims Bookstore, has 21 rooms and is popular for its full-service approach: garden restaurant, bike rentals, travel service, massage, and an ayurvedic and yoga clinic. The rooms themselves are nothing special, and run US$8-15 s, US$10-20 d.

Jyatha

Southeast of central Thamel, this street is lined with smart new guesthouses. Turn left at a garbage pile and walk down to a quiet enclave behind Bahadur Bhawan, the old Royal Hotel, now the Election Commission. The best place here is **Mustang Holiday Inn,** tel. (1) 226-538, fax (1) 228-216, with a friendly atmosphere and competent service. Rooms with attached bath are US$8/15-20 s, US$10/20-30 d, depending on size and decor. Next-best is the **Imperial Guesthouse,** tel. (1) 229-339, a new, quiet, clean place with rooms for US$12 s, US$15 d. The **New Shangrila Guesthouse** next door has slightly cheaper rooms, including some with common bath for US$5 a bed.

Back on the main street, **Hotel Blue Diamond,** tel. (1) 226-392, is a moderately smart place with a range of rooms, all with bath, from US$6-18 s and US$8-22 d; the top two prices include a/c, a bargain at this price. Across the street are two exceptional Tibetan-run hotels. **Hotel Utse,** tel. (1) 228-952, is an expansion of Thamel's famous old Utse Restaurant, which has also moved here. It's big enough to provide a hotel-like atmosphere but remains personal, friendly, and well-maintained; there's a nice rooftop garden too. Clean rooms with bath and fan are US$13-17-22 s, US$20-24-29 d; the more expensive rooms are carpeted and have TV and bathtub. **Hotel Norling,** tel. (1) 230-734, right next door is similarly good, with another rooftop garden and even a small fountain in the lobby. Rooms are US$10-16 s, US$16-25 d.

This stretch of Jyatha is a little Tibet; the air is fragrant with juniper incense in the morning. Down from the Utse is **Tibet Resthouse,** tel. (1) 225-319, a less spiffy place with rooms for US$6-8 s, US$9-11 d. The adjoining **Lhasa Guesthouse,** tel. (1) 226-147, is similar. The Nepali-run **Hotel Siddhartha,** tel. (1) 227-119, has basic rooms for US$7 s, US$10 d with bath; a quiet back garden adds some atmosphere. **Hotel New Gajur,** tel. (1) 226-623, has a number of very plain rooms with bath for US$12 s, US$16 d.

Near Chhetrapati

This busy neighborhood southwest of Thamel manages to retain a scrap of Nepali character and is on the fringes of the scene. The street between Thamel and Chhetrapati proper is one long line of tourist businesses. **Potala Guest House,** tel. (1) 220-467, is a busy, friendly place with a small courtyard garden: rooms are painted an unattractive shade of green and cost US$8-10 s, US$15 d. Next door, **Hotel Tayoma,** tel. (1) 211-149, has a few tiny single rooms for as low as US$15, but the general scale is pricier: US$25-35 s, US$30-40 d, the more expensive rooms having a/c and TV. **Tibet Guest House,** tel. (1) 214-383, is favored by

mountaineers and for good reason: friendly staff, nice basic rooms, and a rooftop garden with views; rates are US$9-14 s; US$9-15 d. **Trans-Himalayan Guest House** next door offers similar prices and accommodations. Further down towards town, **Shambala Guest House,** tel. (1) 225-986, has carpeted rooms with phones, a quiet courtyard and balcony garden, and rooftop views; rooms are US$6-8 s, US$10-18 d.

Paknajol

Hotel Garuda, tel. (1) 416-776, is a well-maintained place with a very friendly and helpful staff and a small rooftop garden. The 34 rooms are small but immaculate and run US$11 s, US$15 d for a basic room; add US$3 for one with a balcony, and US$5 for a larger "deluxe" room. The semi-fancy **Hotel Mandap,** tel. (1) 413-321, doesn't really make the grade. Rooms are US$24 s, US$28 d; the best deal is US$35 for a big corner room that sleeps three.

Lazimpat

These are real hotels rather than guesthouses. Only a 10-minute walk north of Thamel, **Hotel Ambassador,** tel. (1) 410-432, in Lazimpat is well-located at a main intersection . The rooms are a little seedy, and rats have been spotted scurrying about the lobby, but the price is reasonable at a negotiable US$25 s, US$30 d. A little further up the road is **Hotel Manaslu,** tel. (1) 410-071, a well-maintained place set back from the fray, with a big sunny garden and rooms for US$24 s, US$28 d.

Other Areas

These hotels cater mainly to Indians and Nepalis. **Hotel Evergreen,** Bagh Bazaar, tel. (1) 220-740, charges Rs285 s with bath, Rs385 d, while the nearby **Tivoli Hotel,** tel. (1) 221-961, has rooms for US$10-15 s, US$15-25 d. **Hotel Mayalu,** tel. (1) 220-820, boasts a great location at the foot of Durbar Marg, if a rather dubious reputation ("any service, 24 hours"). Rooms are Rs383 s, Rs553 d.

MID-RANGE

Around US$40 a night will bring a hotel that offers not only conveniences and modernity, but an exceptional dose of ambience. Since these are not locked into providing the sterile five-star atmosphere of the top hotels, they can risk some creativity. This category includes three of the nicest hotels for the price in the city. They tend to be booked in season, so reserve in advance, preferably via phone or fax.

Thamel

Hotel Thamel, tel. (1) 417-643, is a quiet new place, with no garden but a rooftop terrace and south-facing balconies on some rooms. Very clean rooms are US$30 s, US$45 d; add US$10 for a deluxe room with a/c, TV, and a bathtub.

Hotel Marshyangdi, tel. (1) 414-105, fax (1) 410-008, is an anomaly in this budget neighborhood, a towering and frankly ugly building with a surprisingly attractive interior. Elegantly decorated a/c rooms with cable television are US$50 s, US$65 d; larger deluxe rooms are an additional US$10. Some of the upper rooms have fantastic views of Swayambhu and Nagarjun.

Hotel Manang, tel. (1) 410-993, fax (1) 415-821, east of the Marshyangdi is a similarly high-class operation with nicely decorated large rooms with a/c and TV for US$35 s, US$50 d; deluxe rooms are US$55 s, US$66 d.

Chhetrapati

Down in south Chhetrapati towards the old town, **Hotel Harati** has a big sunny backyard garden offering views of Swayambhunath Stupa, and surprisingly elegant rooms with molded gilt ceilings and teak furniture. How well it will be maintained is a different question. Standard rates are US$40 s, US$50 d, add US$15 for a/c.

Down the hill in Dhalko Chhetrapati, **Hotel Dipankar,** tel. (1) 217-194, is unusually smart for such a run-down neighborhood, with a small marble-floored lobby, a well-trained staff, and a range of rooms, all with bathtubs and heaters in the winter; US$35-60 s, US$45-70 d. The pricier category includes television and minibar.

Bijeswari

Across the Vishnumati River is **Hotel Vajra,** tel. (1) 271-545, fax (1) 271-695, a 20-minute walk from both Thamel and Swayambhunath. Quiet surroundings and well-executed traditional design more than compensate for the out-of-the-way location. The rooftop terrace offers stunning views, and there's a full schedule of cultural programs, including ritual Newar dance and modern dramas, plus an eclectic library tended by a

swami. The only drawback is it's hard to get a taxi around here. The Vajra has a huge range of room categories: US$14 s/16 d for a room with common bath, US$33 s/38 d with bath; US$41 s/44 d for a super room; US$53 s/61 d for a deluxe room; and US$85s/90 d for a suite.

New Baneshwar

Hotel Sunset View, tel. (1) 229-172, fax (1) 220-049, is in Baneshwar, down the road across from the Everest Hotel. It's a remote location, a 10-minute walk up from the main road and taxis. Apart from that it's an impressive place, different from the run of the mill and really nice, run by a Thakali family. The 30 rooms are enormous, bright, airy, and well-kept; a Japanese garden offers views of the city and fields, and there's a good restaurant. Rooms are US$45 s, US$60 d.

Naya Bazaar

Thamel's crush is pushing new hotels northwards across Lekhnath Marg and into Naya Bazaar. This ugly, noisy, dusty road leading to

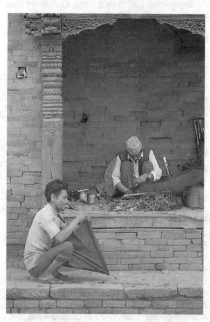

umbrella repair shop set up on the porch of a resthouse

the bus park is best avoided; trudging down it just once can be a discouraging experience. **Garden Hotel,** tel. (1) 411-951, is an exceptionally nice place, however, with a/c rooms with TV and minibar and even a small swimming pool; US$60 s, US$80 d.

EXPENSIVE

Many hotels in the US$60-100 range offer facilities and services nearly equal to those of the most expensive lodgings. Remember government tax will be added to the bill, 11-14%, depending on the hotel's rating.

Durbar Marg
Hotel Sherpa, tel. (1) 227-102, fax (1) 222-026, is quite good, rated just a hair below the big-name hotels; good service and a swimming pool. Rooms are US$100 s, US$110 d. **Hotel Woodlands,** tel. (1) 222-683, on Durbar Marg caters mainly to Indian tourists and charges US$97 s, US$108 d.

Kanti Path
This is a very central and convenient location. **Hotel Mountain,** tel. (1) 224-086, fax (1) 227-736, is a new place with spiffy rooms for US$70 s, US$80 d. The older **Hotel Yellow Pagoda,** tel. (1) 220-337, fax (1) 228-914, has rooms for US$60 s, US$70 d.

Lazimpat and Maharajgunj
Hotel Malla, tel. (1) 410-320, fax (1) 418-382, in Lainchaur has been newly remodelled with a glass elevator in the lobby. It's conveniently close to Thamel; rooms are US$100 s, US$118-130 d. **Hotel Shanker,** tel. (1) 410-151, fax (1) 412-691, is housed in an old Rana palace; rooms are small and gloomy, especially for US$90 s, US$105 d, but the sweeping Raj-era lawns compensate somewhat. **Hotel Shangri-La,** tel. (1) 410-108, fax (1) 414-184, is recommended: beautiful decor and gardens with a small swimming pool and some better-than-average restaurants. It's a 20-minute walk from Thamel, with rooms for US$95 s, US$110 d. Further north, too far north in fact, is **Hotel Kathmandu,** tel. (1) 418-494, fax (1) 414-091, in Maharajgunj, with rooms for US$96 s, US$108 d.

Other Locations
Dwarika's Kathmandu Village Hotel, tel. (1) 470-770, in Battisputali is far from the city center and not close to anything but Pashupatinath, but the skillful use of traditional architecture and old woodcarvings make it someplace special. Rooms are US$69 s, US$89 d.

TOP HOTELS

These international-standard luxury hotels have restaurants, shopping arcades, business and communications services, even 24-hour casinos. For location and ambience, the best hotel in town is the **Hotel Yak & Yeti,** tel. (1) 222-635, fax (1) 227-782, on Durbar Marg, built around a wing of an old Rana palace. The lavishly decorated old ballrooms are used as meeting halls and restaurants; there are extensive gardens, a swimming pool, lighted tennis courts, a sauna, a casino, and several top-class restaurants. Rooms are US$140 s, US$150 d, US$10 more for rooms in the new wing. Suites are US$200-500, culminating in the Tibetan-decorated "Presidential Suite."

Hotel de l'Annapurna, tel. (1) 221-711, fax (1) 225-236, across the street is somewhat less appealing, but boasts the best swimming pool in town. Remodelled rooms are US$125 s, US$135 d; older, plainer rooms are US$110 s, US$120 d.

The **Soaltee Holiday Inn Crowne Plaza,** tel. (1) 272-550, fax (1) 272-205, in Tahachhal is inconveniently located but totally modern, if blandly generic; on clear days mountain views from here are stunning. Rooms are US$150 s, US$160 d; suites run US$350-575.

The **Everest Hotel** in Baneshwar, tel. (1) 220-567, fax (1) 226-088, formerly the Everest Sheraton, is similarly isolated out on the Ring Road, but it's high-class, with bar, restaurants, sports facilities, disco, casino, and mountain views from upper floors; US$130 s, US$140 d.

OTHER OPTIONS

Camping
It's really not advisable, or comfortable, in Kathmandu, though camping in Rani Ban at Nagarjun would be a quiet retreat.

CENTRAL KATHMANDU
RESTAURANTS
AND HOTELS

MAHARAJGUNJ

U.S. EMBASSY

BLUEBIRD SUPERMARKET

LAZIMPAT

LAINCHAUR

THAMEL

TO HOTEL VAJRA

CENTRAL
IMMIGRATION
OFFICE

ROYAL PALACE

POLICE
HEADQUARTERS

JYATHA

NAG POKHARI

NARAYAN HITI

NAXAL

ASAN TOL

TO BOUDHANATH

RANI POKHARI

DURBAR
SQUARE

BAGH
BAZAAR

TO DWARIKA'S
KATHMANDU
VILLAGE HOTEL

NEW ROAD

TUNDIKHEL

CITY BUS PARK

DILLI BAZAAR

DHARAHARA
GENERAL POST OFFICE

PRITHVI PATH

SINGHA
DURBAR

TO SOALTEE HOLIDAY INN

TRIPURESHWAR MARG

TRIPURESHWAR

BAGMATI RIVER

0   500 m

BLUEBIRD
SUPERMARKET

THAPATHALI

EVEREST
HOTEL

TO PATAN

TO HOTEL SUNSET VIEW

TO BHAKTAPUR
AND ARNIKO
RAJMARG

© MOON PUBLICATIONS, INC.

1. Hotel Kathmandu
2. Garden Hotel
3. Hotel Shangri-La
4. Him-Tai
5. Hotel Manaslu
6. Hotel Ambassador
7. Hotel Shanker
8. Hotel Malla
9. Fire and Ice
10. Mike's Breakfast
11. Kushi Fugi
12. Saino
13. Hotel Mountain
14. Hotel de l'Annapurna
15. Hotel Yak & Yeti
16. New Kebab Corner
17. Hotel Yellow Pagoda
18. Nanglo's Pub
19. Nirula's
20. Hotel Sherpa
21. Cafe Lungta
22. Hotel Woodlands
23. Delicatessen Corner
24. Hotel Mayalu
25. Mangalore Coffee House
26. Amber/Moti Mahal
27. Mei Hua
28. Aroma
29. Bakery Cafe
30. Bhanchha Ghar
31. Tripti
32. Hotel Evergreen
33. Moghul Mahal
34. Bluestar Hotel
35. Tamura

Long-term Accommodations

If you're staying in the Valley a month or more you might want to rent a room from a Nepali family. Meals can be included in the deal and you're guaranteed intimacy: in fact, it may be overwhelming. Some of the language schools listed in "Work and Study Opportunities" under "Languages" in the general Introduction will help organize a homestay.

Available accommodations range from tiny low-ceilinged rooms in the old city, sans plumbing, for a few hundred rupees per month, to deluxe flats and houses with beautiful gardens and mountain views in Kathmandu's residential neighborhoods, up to Rs50,000 monthly for a real palace. Gairidhara, Lazimpat, Sanepa, and Boudha are popular areas with foreigners. A decent flat big enough for two is Rs3000-6000 a month, and a deposit or advance is seldom necessary unless you request special work. Do check the noise level before settling on a place—screeching radios and barking dogs can drive you mad faster than anything.

Furnished flats or houses rented by foreigners are frequently up for sublet during the monsoon. Check the bulletin boards at the Kathmandu Guest House, Pumpernickel Bakery, two Bluebird Supermarkets, Peace Corps office, British Council, and Phora Durbar. Or just start asking—most things happen here by word of mouth. If you're looking for a pricier long-term place, contact one of the real estate agents advertising in the *Rising Nepal.* Their fee is paid by the landlord, so you've got nothing to lose.

FOOD

Kathmandu is a paradise for hungry trekkers and overland travelers, offering everything from borscht to brownies, quiche to kebabs. Thamel's tourist restaurants are a deal, dishing up a huge plate for less than US$2, and a reasonable breakfast or monster slab of cake for half that. Don't stick solely to steaks and lasagna, though. Kathmandu is a great place to try Indian food, one of the world's richest and most varied cuisines, and there's something to be said for Nepali and Tibetan food as well. Travelers usually assume that Western-style restaurants are more sanitary than local ones, perhaps because the dining rooms are more upscale, but the type of food served is no guarantee as to what goes on in the kitchen.

More expensive restaurants add 10-15% government tax to the bill; a few places add a service charge as well. Tipping is not mandatory, but if you're patronizing a place regularly the staff will appreciate a small tip of maybe five percent. Dinner reservations are only necessary in the most expensive restaurants in the height of the tourist season; telephone numbers are included where necessary.

WESTERN RESTAURANTS

Thamel Eateries

Dozens of restaurants serve a kaleidoscopic variety of foreign dishes, from spaghetti to tacos to apple pie. The best all-rounders are noted here, while specialty restaurants are classified by cuisine below. See the "Thamel Restaurants" map for exact locations.

Le Bistro, near the Kathmandu Guest House, is an old standby with a wide range of vegetarian and meat dishes. People start lining up at 10 a.m. for the incredibly rich chocolate cake; the lemon cheese pie is excellent as well. **K.C.'s Restaurant** is famed for its sizzling steaks, cheese-laden pizza, and good desserts; prices are slightly higher than at other places.

Helena's Restaurant serves all the basics plus some excellent desserts; the interior is more spacious than the dim front room indicates. Upscale **The Third Eye** serves Western and Indian food, while the **Rum Doodle** has a pleasant garden courtyard out back and **Narayan's,** next to the Kathmandu Guesthouse, has an even better one. All these have wideranging menus featuring international dishes prepared with a fair amount of conviction.

Old Vienna Inn serves Austrian food: bratwurst, sauerkraut, Wiener schnitzel, goulash, and

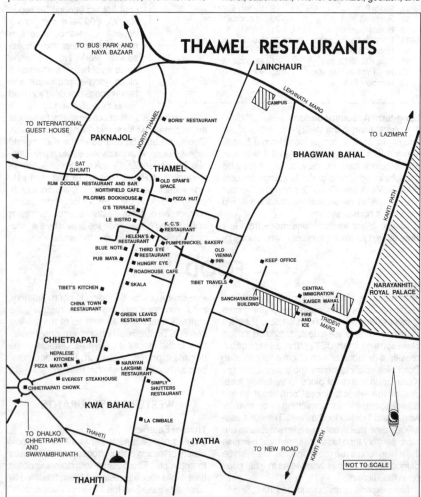

THAMEL RESTAURANTS

LAINCHAUR

TO BUS PARK AND
NAYA BAZAAR

LEKHNATH MARG

CAMPUS

TO INTERNATIONAL
GUEST HOUSE

BORIS' RESTAURANT

TO LAZIMPAT

PAKNAJOL

BHAGWAN BAHAL

SAT
GHUMTI

THAMEL

RUM DOODLE RESTAURANT AND BAR
NORTHFIELD CAFE
PILGRIMS BOOKHOUSE
G'S TERRACE
LE BISTRO

OLD SPAM'S
SPACE

PIZZA HUT

K. C.'S
RESTAURANT

HELENA'S
RESTAURANT
BLUE NOTE
PUB MAYA

THIRD EYE
RESTAURANT
HUNGRY EYE
ROADHOUSE CAFE

PUMPERNICKEL BAKERY

OLD
VIENNA
INN

KEEP OFFICE

NARAYANHITI
ROYAL PALACE

TIBET'S KITCHEN

CHINA TOWN
RESTAURANT

SKALA

GREEN LEAVES
RESTAURANT

TIBET TRAVELS

SANCHAYAKOSH
BUILDING

CENTRAL
IMMIGRATION
KAISER MAHAL

FIRE
AND
ICE

TRIDEVI
MARG

CHHETRAPATI

NEPALESE
KITCHEN
PIZZA MAYA

NARAYAN
LAKSHMI
RESTAURANT

EVEREST STEAKHOUSE

SIMPLY
SHUTTERS
RESTAURANT

CHHETRAPATI CHOWK

KWA BAHAL

TO DHALKO
CHHETRAPATI
AND
SWAYAMBHUNATH

THAHITI

LA CIMBALE

JYATHA

TO NEW ROAD

THAHITI

NOT TO SCALE

© MOON PUBLICATIONS, INC.

apple strudel. The deli counter does sandwiches and is a good source of picnic supplies. **G's Terrace** is another German-themed place with a livelier atmosphere. **Skala** is a quiet vegetarian place with bland food but a nice garden. The nearby **Green Leaves Restaurant** has excellent food, including organically grown salads, served indoors or in a pleasant courtyard; there's Nepali music in the evenings here. Down towards Chhetrapati there's **Pizza Maya,** with pizza and veggie food, and the popular **Narayan Lakshmi Restaurant,** with great baked goods (excellent cinammon rolls). **Everest Steakhouse** is poorly ventilated—diners emerge reeking of french fries—but carnivores love the big slabs of beef.

The **Northfield Cafe** is a spacious place run by Mike of Mike's Breakfast fame (see "Central Kathmandu," below.) It serves all the original's regular specialties, plus the best Mexican food in Kathmandu. **Simply Shutters** is a tiny, beautifully decorated little retreat modeled on a French bistro, down to the daily menu displayed on a chalk board. The food is good, if not superb, and it's a great place to spend a quiet afternoon or evening.

Up in north Thamel is the upscale **Boris' Restaurant,** run by the son of the late Boris Lissanevitch. It's in a spacious house with several dining rooms and a lovely garden; the food is expensive for Thamel, but unusually good, with both vegetarian and meat dishes.

Few of Thamel's Italian restaurants manage to produce convincing food, though **La Cimbali** serves good coffee. **Pizza Hut** (no relation to the chain) in Thamel does adequate pizzas, but it's outdone by **Fire and Ice** in the Sanchayakosh Building across from Immigration. This nicely decorated little place serves superb thin-crust pizzas and soft ice cream and has a take-out service too.

For dessert, try **Hungry Eye, Le Bistro, Helena's,** or anywhere else with a mouthwatering window display. **Dairy House** in Jyatha has excellent cakes and pies for half the price of many other places.

Freak Street

Everything here is budget by definition. **Cosmopolitan Cafe** overlooking Basantapur Square is a great place for tea and views. **Paradise Restaurant** specializes in vegetarian food, with excellent fried potatoes. **The Lunchbox** does unbeatable breakfast specials complete with Nescafé cappuccino. **Kumari Restaurant** has a simple basic menu, while **The Oasis** boasts a small garden courtyard, a rarity for this neighborhood. **Jasmine's** serves Chinese food. The famed dessert shops of Pie Alley (Maru Tol) have all vanished, but the dark little **Snowman** near the Lunchbox may still produce magic brownies.

Right in Durbar Square, **Big Bell Cafe** has a peaceful rooftop terrace with nice views. The rooftop garden of the **Hotel Classic**—covered with turf!—serves Western and Indian dishes. Better than the food are the fabulous views of the city skyline and the adjoining royal palace; climb up for tea.

street vendor selling pineapple, Kathmandu

Central Kathmandu

Cafe Lungta off Kanti Path is a quiet refuge from traffic, with an outdoor garden and a typical all-purpose menu. The giant **Delicatessen Center** on Kanti Path is a glittering ultramodern monstrosity, the biggest of its kind in Kathmandu.

Don't miss **Mike's Breakfast** in Naxal, past the Royal Palace and around the corner from Nag Pokhari. It's a local institution, set in an old house with a lovely sprawling garden and, for once, really good music. Breakfasts feature homemade bread, muffins, and preserves and limitless brewed coffee; lunch is soup-salad-sandwiches and daily specials. Tuesday and Friday nights are pizza nights. It's more expensive than most places (up to Rs200 for breakfast) but worth it.

Local Restaurants

While these cater to tourists, they're popular with locals as well, unlike Thamel eateries. **Nanglo's Pub** on Durbar Marg serves good fried chicken and *daal bhaat* indoors or on the rooftop terrace. **Saino Restaurant** up the street is a bit

THE LEGENDARY BORIS

H is name was Boris Lissanevitch, but everyone knew him simply as Boris, a larger-than-life character possessed of superhuman charm. He seemed to have lived 10 lives in the space of one: White Russian émigré, ballet dancer, raconteur, master chef, big-game hunter. It was only natural that he would end up running Kathmandu's first hotel.

The Royal Hotel, opened in 1954, was not only the first hotel; it was the *only* hotel for 450 miles, all the way to Calcutta. One guest characterized it as "a sort of stranded Ritz." It was situated in a wing of Bahadur Bhawan, a huge, white-colonnaded Rana palace, a remodeled fragment of which now houses the Election Commission.

The Royal was decorated in "Kathmandu Baroque," all tigerskin rugs and overstuffed furniture. Its Yak and Yeti Bar was the social center of Kathmandu's foreign community, a meeting place for mountaineers, diplomats, journalists, tourists, and Boris's international coterie of friends. The liquor supply was equally eclectic—it generally had either Scotch or soda, but never both at the same time.

Boris is often portrayed as the father of tourism in Nepal. The first official tourists entered the country in 1955, and naturally stayed at the Royal Hotel. Boris arranged a reception, which was attended by the king and his ministers. The king is said to have been visibly surprised at the sight of tourists fighting one another to buy out a display of handicrafts. From the very next day, visas were issued to all who requested them.

Kathmandu in the '50s had many things to offer tourists, but facilities were not among them. Linen, soap, silverware, toilet fixtures, glassware—all the little things that make a hotel had to be imported from Europe and hauled into the Valley by porters. Cooking was done over wood fires, and water was heated in small boilers attached to the fireplaces that were an essential feature of every room in the Royal.

Food was another problem, as the only items locally available in abundance were rice and buffalo meat. Boris arranged for fish and fruit to be flown in from Calcutta; everything else was ordered from Europe and arrived via India. Constant battles with Indian customs meant that crates of food often arrived well past their prime. Boris planted vegetables on the grounds of his palatial hotel, introducing many to the Valley for the first time. He raised ducks and pigs to supplement the menu, adding to the hotel's bizarre atmosphere. It already housed a zoo with Himalayan black bears, deer, mountain goats, panthers, and an anteater.

Boris served as master chef for Kathmandu's official banquets, serving crepes à la Boris, sole à la Boris, and wild boar à la Boris. He catered the banquet for King Mahendra's coronation, and for the state visit of Queen Elizabeth II in 1961. For this the largest hunt in history was organized in the Terai. A tented camp was erected, with an 11-room tent for the royal couple. Boris had 48 tons of goods shipped in and requisitioned a herd of "bar elephants," outfitted with waitresses serving drinks from their broad backs. The queen was said to have been delighted.

The Royal Hotel closed in 1970; Boris died in 1985. The Hotel Yak & Yeti preserves vestiges of his reign over Kathmandu's social scene, like the original copper-chimneyed fireplace from Boris's Yak and Yeti Bar which is now installed in the Chimney Room Restaurant. The biggest memorial is perhaps the tourist trade which Boris helped start, now exceeding 300,000 visitors per year.

more elegant and still quite reasonably priced, with Indian, Chinese, and Tibetan food and indoor or outdoor dining.

The **Aroma Restaurant** near Rani Pokhari is a more basic place with a rooftop garden and the usual Western/Chinese/Indian menu. The **Bakery Cafe** in Kamaladi serves fast food in a sitdown setting—good fried chicken and *momo,* bad pizza and hamburgers. There are others on New Road and in Jawalakhel.

For ice cream it's **Nirula's,** an Indian chain serving 24 flavors, plus a coffeeshop-style menu. The original shop on Durbar Marg is a popular hangout with teenagers, and there's a smaller branch on New Road. **Kwality** is the second choice (limited flavors), with branches scattered around the city.

Coffeeshops

Hotel coffeeshops serve conventional Western and Asian food in a mercifully quiet, air-conditioned setting. Try the Yak & Yeti's spacious **Sunrise Restaurant,** or the **Annapurna Coffeeshop** across the street. The food at the Hotel Shangri-La's **Shambala Garden Cafe** is merely adequate, but the big lovely garden is worth the trip, and the Rs450 breakfast buffet is wonderful on a sunny morning. It's also the only 24-hour restaurant in town.

Buffets

A buffet makes a nice splurge if you're returning from a trek with an amplified appetite. **Sunrise Restaurant** overlooking the Yak & Yeti's garden has breakfast, lunch, and dinner buffets (around Rs400) as well as an a la carte menu. **The Cafe** at the Everest Hotel puts on an international brunch buffet every Saturday 11 a.m.-3 p.m.; the price includes swimming in season. **Hotel Himalaya** does a Saturday poolside brunch 10:30 a.m.-3 p.m. The **Summit Hotel** in Kopundol hosts a popular Friday-night outdoor barbecue buffet, with beautiful views of city lights from the garden.

During tourist season many hotels offer weekly Indian/Nepali buffets with performances of Nepali music and dance—inauthentic, but still entertaining. Nightly entertainment is featured at the elaborate **Naachghar** in the Yak & Yeti as well as at the Holiday Inn's **Himalchuli Room** and at the Sherpa Hotel's **Sherpa Grill.** The **Ghar-e-Kebab** and the Everest Hotel's **Far Pavilions** feature performances of Indian ghazal music. The Hotel Shangri-La's dramatic **Bhaktapur Night,** held Friday evenings in the wonderful garden, combines a barbecue buffet with traditional masked dances.

Top Restaurants

Kathmandu's best restaurants are found in expensive hotels, but they're not necessarily expensive. As long as you don't indulge in the high-priced imported liquor, the tab should be less than US$15 per person for a multicourse splurge without drinks.

The Gurkha Grill at the Soaltee Holiday Inn and the **Kokonor Room** at the Hotel Shangri-La both serve Continental food. The Holiday Inn's **Al Fresco** is an excellent Italian restaurant, well worth a splash. At the Yak & Yeti, the **Chimney Restaurant** continues the late Boris Lissanevitch's culinary traditions with a European/Russian menu that includes borscht, chicken Kiev, and baked Alaska. The food is rich and a bit bland, but it's a great place to sit around the fire in winter. Top Indian restaurants like the Naachghar, the Himalchuli Room, and Ghar-e-Kebab, all listed below under "Specialty Restaurants," also deserve mention in this section.

SPECIALTY RESTAURANTS

Nepali Food

The "Special Nepali Meal" offered by some Thamel restaurants ends up being *daal bhaat* at a highly inflated price. Instead, try the fare in a *bhojnalaya*—there are several good ones around Chhetrapati, like **Tribeni Bhojnalaya**—or get invited to someone's house, where you'll get the *daal bhaat* of your life.

Nepalese Kitchen in Thamel/Chhetrapati goes beyond the standard *daal bhaat* and has a nice outdoor garden. **Thamel House,** elegantly situated in a restored old Newar house in north Thamel, is modelled on the successful Bhanchha Ghar described below. It has Rs400 set meals and a pricey menu, a nice place for a splurge.

Bhanchha Ghar in an old house in Kamaladi, tel. (1) 225-172, serves exquisite Nepali food, delicious even if you've been eating *daal bhat* for a solid month on the trail. It's relatively expensive, but worth it.

Tibetan

Tibetan cuisine in general is fairly limited. None of these places serve the staple *tsampa* and butter tea you'll find in Tibet—which is perhaps just as well. In Thamel, the newly revamped **Hotel Utse** serves cheap, good Tibetan and Chinese food. **Lhasa Kitchen** near Old Spam's Space has good food and a nicer setting than many places, *and* it serves *tongba* in the winter. **Tibet's Kitchen** does more stylized Tibetan dishes. Or, explore the authentic *momo*-and-*thukpa* joints around Boudha.

Indian

Most of Kathmandu's Indian restaurants specialize in Mughlai food, a Persian-influenced cuisine from northern India which gets its complex flavors from dozens of spices enriched with cream. It's as sophisticated as French cooking, and as taxing on the digestive system. Order plenty of oven-roasted breads *(naan)* to balance the rich vegetable and meat dishes, and spiced yoghurt *(raita)* for cooling relief. Tandoori meats roasted in a special clay oven are flavorful and juicy without a lot of added spices.

Starting at the budget end of things, the **Tripti** just north of New Road serves superb, cheap southern Indian vegetarian food. **Mangalore Coffee House** at the foot of Durbar Marg is a clean, spacious place with a similarly good if more limited menu: try the special *masala dosa* or a massive Rs50 *thali*.

New Kebab Corner in the Hotel Gautam off Jyatha has a wide menu of Mughlai and tandoori food, and powerful air-conditioning for the hot months. An authentic local place, ferociously popular in the evenings when loud ghazal music is performed, is **Moghul Mahal** next to the Bluebird Supermarket in Thapathali.

On Durbar Marg, the **Amber Restaurant** and the **Moti Mahal** both serve good Indian food in semi-deluxe settings. **Tansen** is a bit too precious and crowded, with overly rich food served in specially designed brassware.

Ghar-e-Kebab at the Hotel de l'Annapurna is an elegant, dimly lit place with live classical Indian music and the opportunity to watch chefs skewering food for the tandoori oven and stretching *naan* in the glassed-in kitchen. It's considered among the best restaurants in town,

though many others put out equally good food in less swanky settings. Reservations are suggested in season, tel. (1) 221-711. The Soaltee Holiday Inn's **Himalchuli Room** and **Far Pavilions** at the Everest Hotel feature excellent Mughlai food and nightly entertainment. The Yak & Yeti's **Naachghar** offers classical Indian dishes in the rococo setting of an old Rana theater—mirrors, crystal chandeliers, stuccoed pillars, and dancing and music nightly.

Finally, a growing number of "fast-food" takeout places around town serve tandoori chicken, *naan,* and spicy vegetable dishes, if you're looking for picnic fare or an in-room feast (look for signs advertising "home-pack system"). There are several near the Hotel Shangri-La and around the Patan bridge. For a dazzling selection of incredibly sweet Indian desserts, visit one of the big emporiums along New Road.

Chinese and Thai

The hard part is finding food that hasn't been Westernized into chop suey. The best choice is the **Mei Hua** on Kanti Path, a classic, reasonably priced place that's very popular with locals. Try the hot-and-sour soup and the *jiaotse*. **China Town Restaurant** above the Lazimpat Bluebird has a big menu, a Chinese chef, and fast service; **Chinatown Restaurant** (big difference) in Thamel is also good, though no relation. **New Mandarin** on Freak Street is a cheap place with good vegie food, mostly Chinese and Tibetan dishes. Moving upscale, there's **Tian Shan** at the Shangri-La Hotel, and—a favorite with local Chinese expats—**Mountain City** at the Hotel Malla.

Currently there's only one place for spicy Thai food: the **Him-Thai Restaurant** in Lazimpat. The setting is pleasant and the food reasonably authentic, though many dishes end up tasting more or less Chinese.

Japanese

Kathmandu has some of the world's cheapest Japanese food. **Kushi Fuji** on Durbar Marg has a pleasant dining area, while **Koto's** down the street has slightly better food. Best values are the set-menu *bento* or lacquered lunchboxes and the one-bowl *tenburi don*. Over on Kanti Path, the **Fuji Restaurant** dishes out meager portions of mediocre food, but the setting is wonderful: an old Rana concubine's cottage ringed by a fishpond (take the island table).

Few tourists hear about **Tamura Restaurant** in Thapathali Heights, but it's among the best restaurants in town, exquisitely decorated and serving a range of Japanese dishes, including fresh sushi flown in from Bangkok. It's hidden down a winding road past the United Mission to Nepal headquarters and is very difficult to find—there's not even a sign. Call for directions, tel. (1) 526-732; when you see the Hotel Kido, you're at the right place.

FOOD SHOPPING

Bakeries, Sandwiches, and Picnic Fare
Gourmet Deli in Thamel and the related huge **Delicatessen Center** on Kanti Path sell sandwiches and salads and stock a wide range of sausages, cheeses, and breads. **Prasuma Deli** at the foot of Durbar Marg is also good; there's a smaller branch in Thamel. Thamel's **Pumpernickel Bakery** is a classic old-time hangout, always crowded with travelers looking for a cheap breakfast or lunch. **Hot Breads** on Durbar Marg is part of an Indian chain producing all kinds of pastries—delicious, but they all taste the same. The bakery at the Shangri-La Hotel makes excellent pastries, cakes, and crusty Italian bread. Get cheese and yoghurt in little clay pots at cold stores, or at the well-stocked

Nepal Dairy outlet in Thamel near Les Yeux Restaurant.

Groceries
The **Sabji Bazaar** behind New Road, and the street market around **Asan Tol,** have the widest produce selections, selling mushrooms, tofu, lettuce, and other delicacies favored by foreigners—even asparagus and strawberries in season. In the spring, papayas and many varieties of mangoes are cheap and delicious. Make sure you're getting the right price, though, as the fruit sellers are known to inflate prices for tourists. **Organic produce** is sold at the Summit Hotel in Kopundol on Sunday and Wednesday mornings, along with wild honey, morels, fresh pasta, and Italian bread.

Small mom-and-pop stores scattered throughout town sell butter, cold beer, and other perishable items. They're nicknamed "cold stores" or "fresh houses" because they possess refrigerators. If they're in areas where foreigners live, they will stock imported chocolate, ice cream, California wine, even beef.

Easiest one-stop shopping is done at supermarkets like **Nanglo Bazaar** on Ram Shah Path or the two big **Bluebird Supermarkets,** one in Lazimpat and the other in Thapathali near the Patan bridge. Prices may be higher than elsewhere, but it's convenient to find everything in one place. Bluebird also sells expensive imported goods and liquor.

ENTERTAINMENT

Beyond restaurants and hotel bars, there's little nightlife in Kathmandu—perhaps a relic of Rana times, when a nightly curfew kept people inside after 10 p.m. Browsing through Thamel bookstores can keep you entertained till 9 p.m. or so; after that it's bedtime with a good book. Everything shuts by 8 p. m. in the winter, but in warm weather people stay out on the street later, making a stroll through the old town pleasant, with the chance of catching a *bhajan* performance—listen for the cymbals and drums. A nighttime visit to Boudha or Swayambhu is also worth considering, especially on a full-moon night in the warmer months, when butter lamps are lit and worshippers are out in full force.

Dance Performances
Many of the larger hotels offer entertainment and dining packages, usually a Nepali-style buffet with a cultural show featuring stagey and inauthentic, but still entertaining, dancing. See the "Buffets" section under "Western Restaurants" in "Food," above, for listings, or check the latest issue of *Travellers' Nepal.*

Performances without the dining are put on by the **New Himalchuli Culture Group,** tel. (1) 410-151, at the Hotel Shanker, and the **Everest Cultural Society,** tel. (1) 220-676, at the Hotel de l'Annapurna. Featuring heavily made-up performers in hokey costumes, these shows are primarily tourist oriented. All the more reason to catch the classical Newar dance performances of **Kala Mandapa,** held weekly at the Hotel Vajra. On a good night, these sacred temple dances can be a powerful experience. Call the hotel, tel. (1) 271-545, for performance dates and times.

Bars and Pubs

Cocktail lounges in the expensive hotels are plush, quiet, and all more or less the same; try the bar at the Yak & Yeti or the Annapurna. **Old Spam's Space** (say it the Nepali way: "EEspam's EE-space") in Thamel has draught beer, darts, and British pub food, with occasional live music on weekends. **Silk Road** is the other Thamel venue for live music. **Pub Kathmandu,** on the same road as the Yak & Yeti behind the Hotel Sherpa, has live music Friday and Saturday 6:30-9:30 p.m.

The bar scene in Thamel is limited and fairly unconvincing, but most of its clients seem happy—after all, there's nothing else to do. Most everywhere shuts down by 10:30 p.m., so start early. **Pub Maya** usually draws a crowd with its loud music; the nearby **Blue Note** and the quieter **Roadhouse Cafe** make this street an island of nightlife. Also here, **Rustic Mountain Jack's,** an American-themed bar with a CD menu and a long drink list. Around the corner, **The Maya Pub** near the Pumpernickel is noisily popular. The **Rum Doodle Bar** in Thamel is where expedition members hang out to swap tall tales. Or drink with the locals in the many small *raksi* and *chang* shops, which serve brews of dubious purity but proven potency.

Discos

Discos appear and disappear regularly in Kathmandu. They suffer from a chronic shortage of women, and are usually shut down after a brawl generated by some innocent asking the wrong girl to dance. **Galaxy Discotheque** in the Hotel Everest is the best choice, though admission is sometimes limited to members and guests. The flashiest disco, at **Casino Royale** in the

the lotus flower, pema, symbolizing purity and perfection

Yak & Yeti, has a light show, video wall, and occasional live band.

Casinos

Nepal has the only casinos on the Indian subcontinent, catering mainly to Indian tourists. Nepalis themselves are not supposed to enter, though many do, unofficially. Affiliated with Kathmandu's four main hotels, the casinos are part of the local gambling empire of an expat American and are more or less all the same. Games include baccarat, blackjack, pontoon, roulette, paplu, and flush; the atmosphere has been described as "third world kitsch."

You might not want to play, but a stroll through one is among the few nightlife options in town, and they're open 24 hours a day, every day of the year. **Casino Nepal** is at the Soaltee Holiday Inn, **Casino Everest** at the Everest, **Casino Anna** at Hotel de l'Annapurna, and **Casino Royale** in the Yak & Yeti. The last has the most interesting ambience, housed in the ballroom of a 150-year-old Rana palace.

Films and Videos

Kathmandu's five movie theaters specialize in Hindi movies bursting with exaggerated action, song, and dance. These are musical comedies in the true sense of the word, and you don't need to understand what's being said to figure out the plot. Hindi is close enough to Nepali to keep the audience riveted. Occasionally a Nepali film of the same genre draws big home crowds. Check out the cinema hall across from the Royal Palace, or in Jamal across from Rani Pokhari. The other three theaters can be difficult to locate.

Local rental shops offer a full range of Western and Hindi videos, which increasingly keep people home at night. A few Thamel guesthouses and restaurants, like **Cinderella,** offer daily and nightly video shows; check local bulletin boards for titles and times. Small, dark local dens show films with an emphasis on sex and violence. The French, German, and British cultural centers occasionally screen films from their countries (see "Libraries" under "Information," below).

RECREATION AND STUDY

Sports

The Olympic-size public **swimming pools** at Balaju and behind the National Stadium in Tripureshwar are permanently crowded—better to visit a hotel pool, most of which sell day passes for around Rs200 to nonguests. The largest is the Hotel de l'Annapurna's, 35 meters long. Hotel Shangri-La, the Everest Hotel, the Summit Hotel, and the Yak & Yeti are other possibilities, more for paddlers than serious swimmers.

Tennis courts are found at Hotel de l'Annapurna, Everest Hotel, Soaltee Holiday Inn, and the Yak & Yeti, along with exercise facilities and good beauty/massage parlors. Golf may be played at the **Royal Nepal Golf Club**, tel. (1) 472-836, near the airport, or at Gokarna Safari Resort, tel. (1) 226-144; the latter also offers elephant rides.

Banu's Total Fitness in Kamal Pokhari, tel. (1) 413-024, has regular aerobics classes and a well-equipped gym with exercise and weight equipment. **Kathmandu Physical Fitness Centre** in Lazimpat has Universal weight-training equipment, a sauna, and a daily aerobics class; a day pass for the weight room is Rs100.

Runners should avoid the daytime traffic and its attendant pollution, which does more harm than good. Either get up early to jog about the Tundikhel as Nepalis do, or head out to a remote location—and be prepared to be stared at.

Yoga, Ashrams, and Massage

The well-equipped **Yoga Studio** in Tangal, east of Narayanhiti Royal Palace, offers 90-minute morning and evening classes in hatha yoga; call (1) 417-900 for information. **Patanjali Yoga Center** near the National Museum in Chhauni conducts residential courses and daily classes 7-9 a.m. and 4-6 p.m. Call (1) 270-508 or (1) 272-321 for details.

More isolated and intensive is the **Ananda Yoga Center** in Matatirtha, a peaceful setting some 12 km east of Kathmandu. Hatha yoga, meditation, and *pranayama* (breathing exercises) are taught here, and a naturopathic doctor performs treatments based on the elements—water therapy, sun and steam baths, do-it-yourself mud baths. Facilities are basic, but it's a very relaxing and beautiful place. The center also conducts eight-day courses at Rs400 per day for room/board and instruction. The center has no telephone, so contact Travellers' Service in Jamal, Rani Pokhari (beneath the Aroma Restaurant), tel. (1) 225-184 or (1) 222-875. To get to Matatirtha, go eight km down the Tribhuvan Rajpath to Satungal. Turn left and follow the signs—it's a 20-minute walk.

Most of the massage places in Thamel are disreputable, or at the very least not very good. More wholesome is the **Natural Health Center** in Gaushala, tel. (1) 470-776, which offers meditation instruction and massage. **Holistic Yoga Ashram**, tel. (1) 419-334, in front of Lodge Pheasant in Thamel offers yoga, massage, and various natural therapies. Thamel's **Pilgrims Hotel** also has a yoga and ayurvedic clinic.The **Oriental Massage Clinic** in Dilli Bazaar, supervised by a Japanese woman, does wonderful shiatsu massages.

Kathmandu beauty parlors have bargain-priced luxuries like pedicures, massages, and facials; try the big hotels, especially the Shangri-La. Or pamper yourself after a trek with a sauna at the Yak & Yeti or Hotel Vajra.

Buddhism

Ironically for a country that bills itself "the world's only Hindu kingdom," Buddhism is the preferred focus of many visitors. The scene focuses around Vajrayana Buddhism, fueled by the great number of Tibetan refugees who have settled in the Valley. For more details, see special topic "The Buddhist Scene."

The **Himalayan Yogic Institute** in Maharajgunj introduces Westerners to Mahayana Buddhism through workshops, lectures, and courses. It's very accessible, operated by Western Buddhists who are happy to answer questions. Look for posters of the month's program around Thamel, or call (1) 413-094. HYI is located in a white building down the first right past the Kathmandu Hotel; there's a small library and bookstore on the premises.

HYI is affiliated with **Kopan Monastery,** a hilltop *gompa* housing about 100 Nepali and Tibetan monks that's a 45-minute walk or a bumpy taxi ride north of Boudhanath. Kopan operates residential courses of varying lengths for Westerners interested in Buddhism. A seven-day course is Rs2660, including dorm accommodations and food; private rooms are also available. The month-long meditation seminar in the fall is very popular; another, shorter course is held each spring. Kopan also welcomes drop-in visitors with questions. Contact HYI for more information.

Kathmandu Buddhist Center conducts afternoon talks on Buddhism in tourist season, and hosts occasional meditation retreats and courses. Look for flyers in Thamel; currently the talks are held at the Nepalese Kitchen.

In a Hinayana mode, the **Nepal Vipassana Center,** tel. (1) 290-655, offers monthly meditation retreats on the 1st-12th and 14th-25th of each month at its compound north of Budhanilkantha. These courses, based on the teachings of S.N. Goenka, require discipline and strict silence and are very popular with Nepalis. For information contact the center's office behind Nabil Bank on Kanti Path, tel. (1) 225-490.

Finally, it's possible to study individually with various lamas at Boudhanath; see that section in the Kathmandu Vicinity chapter for more details. Several lamas here give extended annual teachings to Westerners. Two of the most popular sessions are Thrangu Rinpoche's annual January course, and Chokyi Nyima Rinpoche's two-week seminar over the Dasain holidays. Write to the **Rangjung Yeshe Institute,** P.O. Box 1200, for details on the latter.

Fortune-telling

Itinerant Indian palm-readers seated along the sidewalk across from the General Post Office will entertain you for a small fee—be sure to determine the price in advance. The ancient palm-reader **Babu Singh** served customers from his stand on the driveway of the Kathmandu Guest House until his recent demise; his son **Iqbal Singh** has now taken over his position.

In a different category altogether is **Lalji,** who treats palm-reading as psychological analysis. He's expensive at Rs400 per hour, but many people find him uncannily accurate. His office is in Thamel south of the Kathmandu Guest House; show up 9 a.m.-noon to make an appointment. Many Newars rely heavily on astrology to reveal auspicious moments and situational undercurrents. **M.R. Joshi** of Patan is a renowned local astrologer, visited by a steady stream of supplicants.

INFORMATION

Forget the government tourist information offices in Basantapur; your innkeeper is likely to be a more helpful source of information about the practicalities of Kathmandu. The **Kathmandu Environmental Education Project** office in the Potala Tourist Home in Thamel (down a side street near Immigration) provides mainly trekking advice but can also answer questions on local culture, festivals, and so on.

Libraries

English readers should try browsing the **British Cultural Center** on Kanti Path or the American Library in Gyaneswar. These have periodical sections and good reference sections on Nepal and Tibet. Other possibilities are the **Alliance Francaise** in Dilli Bazaar, and the **Goethe Institute** in Ganabahal, behind the Dharahara. In order to check out books visitors must have a local sponsor. All of these institutions also offer concerts and film shows.

The **Tribhuvan University Library** in Kirtipur has a huge room filled with books on Nepal, India, and Tibet. Finally, the **Kaiser Library,** in an old Rana palace at the corner of Kanti Path and Tridevi Marg, is worth a visit for the decor alone; see the description in "New Kathmandu," above.

Bookstores

Kathmandu is an international center for books on Himalayan regions, especially those of Nepal and Tibet. Other regional specialties include mountaineering, the Himalaya, Tantrism, Hinduism, Asian travel accounts, and lavish photographic books on the Himalaya.

A tremendous number of bookstores in Kathmandu offer bargains on new as well as used books. Some are sold at Asian edition prices, 35-50% less than in the West. Locally published books are remarkably cheap, while Indian editions are reasonable. You can find specialty books long out of print or unavailable in the West. Best of all are the many discounted books sold on remainder, often of popular titles pushed off the market by new arrivals. Many texts are printed in English with a few available in French and German.

A good place to start browsing is **Pilgrims Bookhouse** in Thamel, an ever-expanding warren of rooms with New Age stock. With over 70,000 titles, Pilgrims has spilled over into a second operation, **Kailash Book Distributors** near the entrance to the Yak & Yeti. Here the emphasis is more general interest; there's also a rare book branch upstairs. **Mandala Book Point** on Kanti Path has an excellent selection of regional and scholarly books as well as general-interest volumes. Other good shops are **Himalayan Booksellers** and **Ratna Book Distributors** in Bagh Bazaar, and **Educational Booksellers** on the Tundikhel, which has a wide selection of Penguins and modern fiction. **Tibet Bookstore** in Thamel stocks all sorts of titles on Buddhism and Tibet.

The used bookshops of Thamel and Freak Street are like a perennially rotating library, buying books back for 50% of the purchase price. Shelves are stocked with an eclectic cross-section of travelers' reading, with quantity predominating over quality—thick historical novels seem to be popular buys for long treks. In Thamel, check out **Tantric Booksellers** and **Walden Book House.**

GETTING AROUND

The vast majority of Nepal's vehicles are crammed into the Kathmandu Valley, onto narrow roads that not long ago served as footpaths. Venturing out in rush hour is a harrowing experience for drivers, cyclists, and pedestrians alike. Right-of-way is better termed might-of-way, as it's claimed by the largest vehicle. Trucks and buses thunder past at a terrifying rate, air horns blasting. Taxis screech to a halt so the drivers can chat in the middle of the road; buses stop anywhere to deposit their passengers; motorcyclists pass on blind curves going uphill. Sometimes a vehicle will try to pull around another vehicle that's *already* passing, in a mad race to see who can get ahead before being obliterated by a head-on collision.

Motorized traffic is a recent addition to Kathmandu's urban environment. Roadways are still considered public domain, the proper place to dry grain and stand and chat. People may look before they cross the street—usually in the *opposite* direction as they step into a lane of speeding traffic. Drivers and cyclists must make allowances for dazed pedestrians, as well as dogs, chickens, sheep, goats, kids racing along rolling wobbly hoops, and sacred cows sleeping in the middle of the road. The constant repair of water and sewage pipes means roads are frequently dug up, but the open manholes and trenches are seldom marked with more than a sprig of bamboo. For this reason if no other you should never go fast at night. Cows slumbering in the middle of the Ring Road have occasioned more than one nasty after-dark accident, as a biker barreling downhill crashes into their bulk.

Taxis, *Tempo,* and Rickshaws
Taxis are an easy, reasonably priced way to get around the city. Flagfall is presently Rs5, with a charge of Rs1.60 for every 200 meters thereafter. Trips around the city are usually under Rs50. Taxis have black license plates with white lettering, while private vehicles have red. The easiest way to find one is to look for the meter in front, and expect the driver to use it for all daytime in-town fares. If he doesn't agree, find another taxi. *Tempo* drivers are usually more amenable to using the meter. A small private fleet, **Kathmandu Yellow Cab,** operates cars with electronic meters.

Meters are still only vague markers, as fares are frequently raised without corresponding adjustments. The present rate is 115% over the metered price; check with a local for the latest situation. Accurate, new, electronic meters are being slowly introduced.

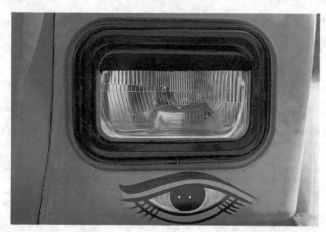

a protective eye painted below a truck headlight

If you're going to a remote corner of the Valley, you'll have to bargain the fare in advance. After dark taxis become scarce, though you can usually find one in Thamel, on Durbar Marg, and on New Road. Drivers are reluctant to go just about anywhere at night, and you'll have to pay extra. The going rate after dark is supposed to be *dedhi,* one and one-half times the metered fare, but if your destination is a remote neighborhood you may have to pay double or more. A **Night Taxi Service** near the Nepal Bank office at Dharmapath, just off New Road, operates 8 p.m.-midnight; call (1) 224-374 for pickup.

Tempo are roaring little black three-wheeled scooters that can seat three passengers in a pinch. They're noiser, bumpier, and slower than taxis, but their drivers seldom argue about destinations, and they're about 25% cheaper. They are also less refined vehicles. Drivers grasp the handlebars of the contraption like cowboys mounting a bucking bull, and wrestling with the steering leaves their heads ringing and shoulders aching. You may have the same feeling after a ride.

Cycle rickshaws are convenient for getting around the crowded streets of the old city. They can be found in Thamel, Durbar Square, Durbar Marg, and other tourist areas, even late at night. They're supposed to be cheaper than motorized transportation, and they are, for Nepalis, but they won't be for you unless you bargain hard. Always negotiate the fare before you climb

in. A few blocks should be Rs10; a journey of several kilometers should cost less than Rs50.

City Buses

Public *tempo,* buses, and minibuses run regular routes around the city and Valley, but they're not a recommended means of transportation. They're crowded and slow; service ends early in the evening; and destination signs are written only in Nepali. However, they're cheap—Rs1.75-2.50 or so for fares inside town, up to Rs9 for fares to the edges of the Valley.

Public buses ply regular city routes 5:30 a.m.-7:30 p.m. daily, leaving from Kathmandu municipal bus park on the east side of the Tundikhel. Main routes include Jorpati (passing Pashupatinath and Boudhanath), the Tribhuvan University campus near Kirtipur, Thankot on the Valley's western rim, Tribhuvan International Airport, Patan Dhoka, and Lagenkhel in Patan (near Jawalakhel). From this last stop, minibuses run to south Valley destinations like Godavari and Dakshinkali, but these can take two hours to travel 15 km; better to bike or hire a taxi. Six-seater public *tempo* and minibuses to north Kathmandu (Lazimpat-Maharajgunj-Balaju-Budhanilkantha) operate from Jamal, across from Rani Pokhari; fares for these are around Rs4.

The 10-km Chinese-built trolley bus line from Tripureshwar to Bhaktapur is an exception among city buses. Efficient and seldom crowded, it's a convenient, cheap way to reach or return from that city. The route ends south of Bhaktapur, about a 15-minute walk from Durbar Square.

Rentals

Rental car companies are overpriced at US$50 per day, but it's easy to arrange for a taxi driver to take you about for a flat fee instead, say Rs1000 for a full day of touring in the Valley. See "Getting Around" in the general Introduction for more details.

Bicycling

With its flat terrain, gentle climate, and spectacular views, the Valley was made for cycling. Downtown traffic can be intimidating at first, but it diminishes outside the city center. Both mountain bikes and single-speed cycles can be rented in Kathmandu; see "Getting Around" in the general Introduction for details.

Walking

On foot is really the best way to explore the Valley. Within the old cities, it's practical because of the dense crowds; beyond them, walking through fields and villages provides an intimate look at the countryside. The Schneider map suggests endless possibilities for day hikes. Especially if you're not going trekking, getting out into the countryside will give you a feel for the rural life that characterizes 80% of Nepal.

Organized Tours

Packaged tours to Valley sites are an easy way to cram several places into a single morning or afternoon. Dozens of travel agencies offer custom tours as well as regularly scheduled guided departures for around Rs300. Popular itineraries include Pashupatinath and Boudhanath stupa; Patan and Kathmandu Durbar Squares; Patan and Swayambhunath; Bhaktapur; and excursions to Himalayan viewpoints like Nagarkot or Dhulikhel for sunrise and sunset mountain views. **Yeti Travels** on Durbar Marg, tel. (1) 222-285, is among the largest local companies.

   International Community Services (ICS) is an independent nonprofit organization which puts on tours, day hikes, and lectures for Valley visitors and residents. Call or visit the ICS office near the British Council, (1) 220-598, for the monthly program; it's open Mon.-Fri. 12-3 p.m. Events require advance registration and a membership fee of Rs275.

the conch shell, dunkar, *symbolizing the calling to prayer*

KATHMANDU VICINITY
SWAYAMBHUNATH

The most ancient and enigmatic of all the Valley's holy shrines lies northeast across the Vishnumati River from urban Kathmandu. The golden spire of Swayambhunath Stupa crowns a wooded hillock that has been a holy site since at least the 5th century. Visitors trying to avoid its tongue-twisting name often call it the "Monkey Temple," after the simian bands roaming the surrounding forest.

Swayambhunath's origins are an integral part of the legend of the emergence of the Kathmandu Valley, described in the Introduction. The *Swayambhu Purana* tells of a miraculous lotus which blossomed from the lake that once covered the Kathmandu Valley. It radiated a dazzling light called "Swayambhu," the Self-Created or Self-Existent. Gods and men came from afar to worship this miracle, until the wise monk Shantikar Acharya, sensing the coming of the present dark age, buried the magical light beneath a stone slab and atop it built the stupa. In another version, after the bodhisattva Manjushri

drained the waters of the lake to reveal the Kathmandu Valley, the lotus was transformed into the hillock, and the blazing light became the stupa.

Swayambhunath, or Swayambhu, is the Valley's most sacred Buddhist shrine, the equivalent of the Hindu Pashupatinath. Its most fervent devotees are the Newar Buddhists of Kathmandu, who crowd here for festivals like Buddha Jayanti and more personal rituals conducted by the family priest. During the sacred summer month of Gunla, hundreds come daily to worship, assembling before dawn in Kathmandu to make the journey together. Vajrayana Buddhists are equally devout, and the sizeable Tibetan community here is outdone only by Boudhanath's.

Getting There
Swayambhu is a short taxi ride from Kathmandu, but it's easy to bike or walk, leaving the city's hustle for the quieter neighborhoods on the grungy banks of the Vishnumati River. The old

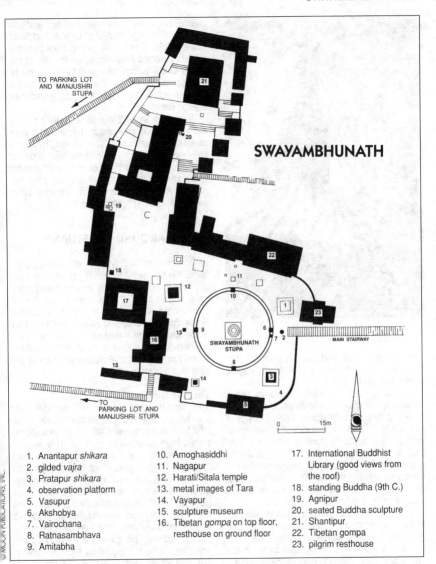

TO PARKING LOT
AND MANJUSHRI
STUPA

SWAYAMBHUNATH

C

SWAYAMBHUNATH
STUPA

MAIN STAIRWAY

← TO
PARKING LOT AND
MANJUSHRI STUPA

0   15m

1. Anantapur *shikara*
2. gilded *vajra*
3. Pratapur *shikara*
4. observation platform
5. Vasupur
6. Akshobya
7. Vairochana
8. Ratnasambhava
9. Amitabha
10. Amoghasiddhi
11. Nagapur
12. Harati/Sitala temple
13. metal images of Tara
14. Vayapur
15. sculpture museum
16. Tibetan *gompa* on top floor, resthouse on ground floor
17. International Buddhist Library (good views from the roof)
18. standing Buddha (9th C.)
19. Agnipur
20. seated Buddha sculpture
21. Shantipur
22. Tibetan gompa
23. pilgrim resthouse

pilgrim path from the city branches off from Chhetrapati and passes some interesting temples. Beside the Vishnumati bridge is an **Indreni Temple** dedicated to a fierce goddess the Newars call Luti Ajima, who once demanded human sacrifices. Across the river is the shrine of **Shobha Bhagwati,** the most famous of Kathmandu's many temples to the great goddess Durga, as well as a reported haunt of witches. On both sides of the river are ancient and pow-

Swayambhunath

erful cremation sites, and you may pass a Newar funeral ceremony being enacted with wailing relatives and clanging cymbals.

Continue past the Hotel Vajra to reach Swayambhu's **main entrance gate,** a Tibetan-style brightly painted plaster confection. Gangs of kids extort protection money to "watch" visitors' bicycles—"so that the Tibetans don't break it," they say. A direct refusal to pay risks a flat tire on your return. Either leave your bike before the entrance, or promise them anything and then suddenly discover you have no change. If you give in, a couple of rupees is sufficient *baksheesh.*

Taxis ascend the hill to a small parking lot just below the stupa. Tour buses use this route avoiding the steep stairway, but the latter is the traditional pilgrim route, imbued with atmosphere and guaranteed to earn religious merit.

The Climb Up
A giant prayer wheel is enshrined in a small room past the main gate, and Tibetans perform prostrations on the flat stone slabs beside the

staircase, in front of three giant orange-and-yellow Buddhas constructed of carved and fitted stone blocks. The oldest, dating back to 1750, depicts **Buddha Akshobya,** the Buddha of the Mirror-Like Wisdom, seated in the earth-touching gesture. Further up the hill is a more recent trio of Buddhas donated by the great-grandfather of King Birendra.

Worn stone steps, 365 in all, lead straight to the top, where Swayambhunath's painted eyes peer down at an impressively steep angle. There are plenty of shady places along the way to pause and admire the clusters of delicately carved *chaitya* and watch the monkeys sliding down the railings. A few Tibetans have set up shop along the steps, carving *mani* stones for sale.

AROUND THE STUPA

When you breathlessly arrive at the stupa platform, the first sight to catch your eye is a gigantic **gilt *vajra*** resting on an embossed mandala, set on a stone base carved with the 12 animals of the Tibetan calendar. King Pratapa Malla donated this, and raised the imposing white *shikara* on either side. These temples are dedicated to secret tantric deities and christened Anantapur and Pratapur in honor of the king and a favorite wife.

The Five Buddhas
The stupa has evolved in ever-richer form over the centuries, rebuilt after its destruction in the brief Muslim invasion of 1349 and periodically repaired from earthquake damage. This was no small task: a typical 17th-century repair session required 39 kg of gold. Centuries of royal gifts have made it the most magnificently decorated of all Nepal's stupas. Much of the wealth has gone to the elaborate little gilded shrines of the five directional Buddhas—the Pancha Buddhas or Dhyani Buddhas—attached directly to the stupa's dome. The quintet are symbolic expressions of the five elements, earth, air, water, fire, and ether. Each is associated with a particular gesture, consort, color, and wisdom. More tangible than the formless light of Swayambhu, they serve as intermediaries in worship, receiving the stupa's offerings. Their combined wisdom is said to be embodied in the stupa's dome, and

their infinite compassion is represented by a diamond set atop the spire.

The first shrine encountered is that of **Buddha Akshobya,** the Buddha of the East; close beside it is that of **Vairochana,** which in a true mandala would be envisioned in the center. Look for the animal vehicles or *vahana* of each Buddha set in niches below the shrines, and for their consorts in smaller shrines beside them. Above the stupa's painted eyes, gilded plaques depicting the Pancha Buddha continue the theme.

The Swayambhu hilltop offers a commanding view of Kathmandu city; at one time the site was also used as a military fort. The bricked **observation platform** on the southwest side was created in 1979 as a byproduct of reinforcement work after a landslip threatened the entire hill. From here you can see the red brick silhouette of the old city rapidly being swallowed by cement buildings, and on clear days, a jagged line of Himalayan peaks. The view is splendid at dusk, as city lights flicker on one by one, and even better when there's a full moon hanging in the sky.

Vasupur and Amitabha

As at all temples, visitors should move around Swayambhu clockwise in the gesture of respect, keeping it on their right. To the left, as you enter from the main staircase, sits the small copper-roofed shrine of Vasupur, sacred to the Buddhist earth goddess Vasundhara. Inside, her graceful seated figure appears on the left of a row of sculptures. This is the first of Swayambhu's five ancient shrines or "mansions" *(pura)* dedicated to the five elements—a relic of ancient folk beliefs that blends nicely with the worship of the Five Buddhas. A little further west the marble-faced shrine of **Vayapur,** the "Sanctuary of the Wind," is worshipped in the form of a boulder. Behind this is a small **museum** with a fine collection of stone sculptures discovered around Swayambhu—certainly one of the few museums in the world where the exhibits are actively worshipped. It's open daily except Saturday 10 a.m.-5 p.m.; admission is free.

The stupa's western side is the major focus of activity. It houses the shrine of Amitabha, Buddha of Boundless Light and most beloved of the Pancha Buddhas. Facing him are two lovely statues of **Tara,** now encased in a metal cage

to protect them from theft. Between them, Amitabha's mount, the peacock, is perched on a pillar. Behind it is an open **resthouse** often crowded with families preparing offerings and feasts. The top floor of this structure is occupied by a small Tibetan *gompa;* it's usually possible to visit the colorful shrine.

Sitala Temple

The small, richly gilded shrine just beyond the resthouse is among the busiest in the Valley: families reserve the space in front of the temple for their priests to perform *puja,* and a nearby chalkboard outlines the daily schedule. It's dedicated to the terrible goddess of smallpox, who plagued the Valley with fearsome epidemics well into this century. Hindus call her Sitala; to Buddhists she's Harati or simply Ajima, one of the ancient Newar grandmother-goddesses. The story goes that Harati was in the habit of kidnapping and eating one child a day, until finally the Buddha appointed her the protector of Valley children, promising that she could dine on the first of his offerings. Harati is still placated before any other deity at Swayambhunath. Devotees bring her duck eggs, grain, yoghurt, and incense, lighting the oil lamps around the temple and carrying their children inside for a blessing. The black stone image of the goddess is depicted surrounded by a half-dozen children, and has a silver skullcup around her neck for offerings. This replacement is a mere two centuries old; the original was smashed by order of King Rana Bahadur Shah in a fit of fury after his beloved queen died of smallpox.

Climb up on the roof of the building indicated by signs for the **International Buddhist Library** for a superb overview of the temple compound. The cluster of whitewashed memorial *chaitya* below have been built over the centuries to honor the dead; monkeys scamper amid them, playing hide-and-seek. In the southwest corner of this compound is a fine 9th-century sculpture of a **standing Buddha;** the northwest corner holds **Agnipur,** the "Mansion of Fire," embodied in a white-painted rock guarded by a pair of stone lions.

Nagapur

Back on the stupa's north side is the shrine of **Buddha Amoghasiddhi.** In front of it is an oblong stone set in a simple open pit, usually the repository of a filthy puddle. This is Nagapur, the "Mansion of Water," ruled by the serpent kings; worshippers light lamps and burn incense here in supplication for rain. The yellow-walled **Tibetan** *gompa* behind here houses an enormous image of Shakyamuni and an equally large statue of the 16th Gyalwa Karmapa, a contemporary master who died in 1981. Monks perform *puja* here early in the morning and again around 4 p.m.

Shantipur

Shantipur, the "Mansion of Peace," representing the mystic element of ether, lies within an unremarkable cream-colored building down the steps north of the stupa, just beyond a large seated **stone Buddha.** The entrance chamber holds an ancient locked door guarded by two fierce tantric deities and a pair of strange painted eyes. Inside, in a secret underground chamber, the 8th-century tantric master Shantikar Acharya is said to live still, seated in a meditative trance which has preserved his life for centuries. Shantikar Acharya was a great magician, so skilled in mantra he could control even the gods. It's said he once drew a magical mandala to invoke the monsoon, using the heartblood of the Eight Great Naga as ink and a snakeskin as parchment. Sealing the scroll in a copper tube, he placed it by his side in the underground chamber. When the Valley is threatened by drought, the king of Nepal is to retrieve the mandala and rain will fall.

Pratapa Malla did just that in 1658. Purified by rituals and prayer, he braved guardian ghosts and serpents to enter the sealed room and take the copper tube. The moment the magical parchment was unrolled in the light of day, rain began to fall. All this is detailed in an account written by the king, inscribed on a stone slab beside Shantipur's locked door. Frescoes painted on the walls depict the story, complete with slithering *naga,* but this powerful and mysterious shrine is largely neglected, and the walls have been defaced with graffiti.

Other Sites

Swayambhu's quiet wooded hill is a popular picnic site, but watch out for aggressive thieving monkeys, who will steal the food right out of your hand. The slightly lower summit to the west

holds a small stupa dedicated to **Manjushri,** the bodhisattva who drained the lake to reveal the Kathmandu Valley. Hindus worship Saraswati here, and images of the pair guard the top of the stairway. These deities are considered the embodiments of knowledge, and students visit here on the festival of Basant Panchami seeking a blessing in their studies.

Museum of Natural History

Located off the road leading up to Swayambhunath, this collection resembles a giant science classroom, with specimens of animals, birds, reptiles, fish, insects, plants, and minerals crammed inside a single large room. Notable exhibits include jars of pickled marijuana and an impressive collection of Kathmandu's native rats, the largest nearly a half-meter in length. Amid the stuffed cats, goats, and guinea pigs are more exotic creatures typical of Nepal, including the *danphe* pheasant, the *gharial,* the Himalayan black bear, and the barking deer. The museum is open daily 10 a.m.-5 p.m. except Saturdays; admission is Rs10.

Practicalities

There's not much in the way of food available around Swayambhu apart from a few basic local places around the stupa serving tea, soft drinks, and noodles. **Even Point Restaurant** across the Ring Road serves basic food, and its outdoor tables provide the opportunity to observe the auto repair shop sharing the compound. **Tavern Zorba's,** a Rajneeshi enterprise, dishes up Greek food and homemade ice cream; it's open daily noon-3 p.m. and 6-10 p.m., with weekend brunches 10:30 a.m.-3 p.m. It's on the road to the National Museum, just beside a Buddhist monastery.

The other choice is **Hotel Vajra** in Bijeswari near the river, worth a stop anyway to admire the architecture and explore the library and art gallery. Order tea and *momo* on the rooftop and bask in the view of the city.

AROUND SWAYAMBHUNATH

Swayambhu is the launching point for the easy, pleasant hike to Ichangu Narayan described in "Exploring the Valley." The boxy building atop the hill west of the stupa is **Ngedön Ösel Ling,** a Tibetan *gompa* that's the residence of Tsokni Rinpoche, a younger brother of Boudhanath's well-known Chokyi Nyima Rinpoche.

The National Museum

With the entire Valley serving as a vast open-air art museum, indoor exhibits may seem redundant. They're not. Nepal has only a few small museums, but they include ancient art of a quality you won't find anywhere else. It's a good idea to visit them before you shop for *thangka* or bronzes.

The National Museum in Chhauni, a 15-minute walk south of Swayambhunath, has the country's oldest and largest collection of art and historical material, housed in what was once a Rana arsenal. The museum is divided into separate collections you could well categorize as "Newar" and "Gorkhali"—one devoted to art, the other to the art of warfare. The art section is housed in a tiered white wedding cake of a building. Its stone sculpture section is probably the least significant, as there are so many masterpieces scattered around the Valley, but classics include a famous depiction of the Buddha's birth, and three monumental 13th-century sculptures from the Terai district of Bara. Most images are displayed in the open rather than behind glass, giving a sense of perspective.

There are small terra-cotta and woodworking exhibits as well, but the museum's high point is **metal sculpture.** Nowhere else in Nepal will you find such a collection of medieval treasures with a delicacy of detail that is unequaled today. The figures are perfectly proportioned and resting at ease; they seem almost to be breathing. Most of the images are Buddhist, like the Patan metalworkers who created them. There are some beautiful smaller images of Shakyamuni, Tara, and Vajrasattva which you can study for shopping pointers. Most spectacular is the massive 14th-century **Sukhavarna Samvara,** a

tantric deity with five heads, 16 legs, and 32 arms, each hand holding a different implement, each fingernail perfectly proportioned. His consort wraps her legs around his massive body, head lolling back with tongue touching nose—every inch depicting power and sex combined. Equally elaborate is a man-sized mandala of Lokesvara made of filigreed metal inset with crystal, ivory, and semiprecious stones.

The painting section has some beautiful old *thangka, paubha,* and sequences of small meditation paintings, though it's rivalled by the National Art Gallery in Bhaktapur. Upstairs is a random assortment of artifacts, jewelry and inlay work, illuminated manuscripts, and Tibetan ritual objects.

Opposite the art museum is the **Historical Museum,** blending politics, history, and trivia. The ground floor features a rather motley natural history display, including the mandibular bones of a blue whale, a stuffed baby rhino, and a Nepali rock taken to the moon aboard Apollo XI. The second floor holds a vast collection of weapons, medals, and uniforms. Displays include the personal arms of Jung Bahadur and other Ranas (an average of six swords per person), a leather cannon captured during the Nepal-Tibet War, and full-length oil paintings of Nepal's rulers. The ornately decorated red building resembling a temple is a memorial dedicated to the life of King Mahendra; his favorite hunting jeep is enshrined in a small pavilion beside it. The buiding also houses the **National Numismatic Museum,** a collection of Nepali coins from the 2nd century.

Museum hours are daily 10:30 a.m.-4:30 p.m. except Tuesday and holidays, closing an hour earlier in the winter and two hours earlier on Friday. Admission is Rs5. You can picnic in the overgrown gardens, and there's a teashop outside the gate.

PASHUPATINATH

Pashupatinath is Nepal's most sacred Hindu shrine, a sprawling collection of temples, rest-houses, images, and inscriptions raised over the centuries along the banks of the Bagmati River. The essence of Hinduism is condensed into a rich brew, as pilgrims, yogis, priests, and devotees worship Shiva in his form of Pashupati, "Lord of the Beasts" and divine protector of Nepal.

Despite the For Hindus Only signs posted at the entrance to its major temples (or perhaps because of them), Pashupatinath is a magical place. The largest temple complex in Nepal, it retains its integrity as a living place of worship. There is *so much:* rows of lingas, long lines of stone *nandi,* crumbling stone shrines, and Licchavi-era sculpture fragments jumbled together in careless heaps. Even without access to the main temple, the wooded grounds deserve several hours of exploration. Early morning or evening, the prime *puja* hours, are the best times to visit.

Visits to Pashupatinath begin and end the pilgrim circuit of the Valley's holy places. Thousands of Indians flock here as well: Pashupatinath is one of the great Shiva sites of the Indian subcontinent. Homage peaks on full-moon days and during festivals like Magh Sankranti, Teej, and Bala Chaturdasi. The greatest of all occasions is Shiva Ratri, which usually falls in February, a boisterous 24-hour celebration of the sacred and bizarre.

Pashupatinath's supreme holiness stems from two things: the hallowed linga enshrined in its main temple, and its location on the banks of the sacred, if slimy, Bagmati River. Little more than a trickle in the dry winter months, the blackened waters flow past stone ghats where worshippers and mourners mingle with pilgrims intent on mundane tasks like laundry and dishwashing. Daily, devout Hindus plunge into the murky waters, immersing themselves three times and reciting verses from the ancient Vedas. The spiritual equivalent of bathing in India's sacred Ganges, a dip in the Bagmati assures release from the cycle of rebirth. Given its exceedingly polluted state, it may also expedite one's progress out of the present life.

The Bagmati's sanctity makes Pashupatinath Nepal's most sacred Hindu cremation site. Wrapped in cloth and placed on a bamboo litter, the bodies are delivered by barefoot pallbearers accompanied by male relatives and mourners (women stay at home to weep). At the cremation ghat, the eldest son performs rites to assure the soul a smooth transition into the next world. The body is placed on a log pyre, and the white-clad mourners retreat to a nearby porch to observe its slow destruction. A few hours later the ashes are swept into the river, where they are carried south to join the Ganges. These open-air ceremonies are conducted with apparent disregard to gaping tourists filming the scene with video cameras. A sense of propriety applies, vultures with 1,000-mm zoom lenses notwithstanding.

The Cult of Pashupati

Of all the gods of the Hindu pantheon, it's Shiva with his 1,008 names and forms who dominates the Kathmandu Valley. His name is a sort of triple pun: Pashupati is the Lord *(pati)* and man his creature *(pashu),* bound by the fetters *(pasha)* of the world. The cult of Pashupati began in India around the 2nd century B.C., but soon became closely associated with Nepal, to the point where he has become the patron deity. Lord Pashupati is invoked in official treaties, pledges, and speeches, and appears on coins and the royal coat of arms. Official government proclamations end with "May the Lord Pashupati protect us all!"—a tradition the recently installed Communist government has continued.

The temple's origins are obscure. The oldest inscription is dated A.D. 477, but a shrine may have stood here 1,000 years before that. Legend says that Shiva, weary of throngs of worshipping demigods, once took the form of an antelope for an anonymous frolic in the forest of Mrigasthali on the Bagmati's eastern bank. The gods caught up with him and, grabbing him by the horn, forced him to resume his divine form. The broken horn was worshipped as a linga, and over time was buried and lost. Centuries later an astonished herdsman found one

woman doing laundry next to 6th-century Buddha image, Rajarajesvari Ghat, Pashupati

of his cows showering the earth with milk. Digging deep at the site, he uncovered the divine linga of Pashupati.

The linga is an ancient symbol which is Shiva's self-proclaimed "double self," and temple grounds are littered with hundreds of these cylindrical stone shafts. They are generally set in a *jalhari,* an oval, spouted base which represents the feminine counterpart of the phallic linga and has a practical function in draining off the liquid poured in offering. Apart from these, Pashupatinath is an open-air museum containing ancient sculptures dating back to the 2nd and 3rd centuries A.D., though many of the finest have been stolen in recent years.

Getting There

Taxi, bike, or take the bus to the **Gaushala** intersection; the airport bus passes by here also. Cyclists can navigate quieter back roads to emerge a little further north at a large temple to **Jaya Bagesvari,** identified by the colorful mural painted on one wall. The image of the goddess inside is bedecked with ornaments, the final offerings of widows going to Pashupati's ghats to be burned on their husbands' funeral pyres, a custom outlawed only in 1920. The sunken fountain across the way dates back to Licchavi times.

The neighborhood extending east from here down to the temple is among the Valley's most ancient settlements. Known as **Deopatan,** "City of the Gods," it's riddled with sculptures, *chaitya,*

inscriptions, and fragments from ancient temples incorporated into the structure of slightly less ancient ones. Just about every piece of stonework you see here is likely to be 1,500 years old.

THE MAIN TEMPLE

Entrance to Pashupatinath's main temple is restricted to Hindus, a definition which stretches to encompass Buddhists, Sikhs, and Jains, but excludes Western converts to Hinduism. Ancient Vedic regulations mean the shrine would have to undergo extensive purification if the ritually impure were to enter, and police are permanently posted inside to prevent this. It's perfectly all right to peer through the doorways, though, and you can get a good overall view of the eastern facade from several vantage points across the river.

The Main Gate

The area around the temple is crowded with shops selling Indian sweetmeats and vegetarian food, rosaries of furrowed *rudraksha* seeds, and *tika* powder in a rainbow of colors. The temple's main gate is on the western side. It's topped by a giant plaster image of Shiva as Yogesvara, Lord of Yogis, seated atop Mt. Kailas; below this appear his sons Ganesh and Kumar. You can't miss the backside of the massive kneeling bull **Nandi,** which is the vehicle of

TO CHABAHIL

TO BOUDANATH

PASHUPATINATH

GAURI GHAT

SUNKEN FOUNTAIN

GANESH TEMPLE

SHANTIKAR ACHARYA TEMPLE

DEOPATAN

PASHUPATINATH TEMPLE

GUHYESWARI TEMPLE

JAYA BAGESVARI TEMPLE

KUMAR TEMPLE

GORAKHNATH SHIKARA

GODDESS STATUES

TERRACE, MONUMENTS

RAM GHATS

RAJA-RAJESVARI GHAT

RAM/VISHNU TEMPLES

6th-C. BUDDHA

GIANT LINGA

VISHWARUPA TEMPLE

BAGMATI RIVER

MRIGASTHALI FOREST

GAUSHALA

RING ROAD

0   100m

TO AIRPORT

TO DILLI BAZAAR AND CENTRAL KATHMANDU

1   MAIN GATE
2   NANDI
3   SOUTH GATE
4   EAST GATE
5   ARYA GHAT
6   STANDING VISHNU
7   PARVATI TEMPLE

© MOON PUBLICATIONS, INC.

Shiva, with its hooves of silver and tail and horns of gold. Jagat Jung Rana had the ancient figure regilded to atone for the sin of having accidently shot a cow on a Terai hunt.

The temple complex has been ceaselessly renovated and improved over the centuries, one result being that the main building little resembles typical Newar architecture. Most of the present gilt-roofed edifice dates from the reign of King Pratapa Malla, but every king and prime minister since has added to it, sheathing the temple doors in embossed gold and silver and contributing to Pashupatinath's fabulous treasury. Rumors of its tremendous endowments

have inspired many thieves, among them Kathmandu's last Malla king, Jaya Prakash, who ransacked the treasury to pay his troops in the doomed war against Prithvi Narayan Shah.

The Sacred Linga

The temple's famous linga is a meter-high cylinder of black stone carved with four faces, each depicting a different aspect of Shiva. On top is the featureless and omnipotent fifth face, said to be infused with the power of the sun and hot enough to instantly evaporate water. It's tended by a retinue of Brahman priests imported from Karnataka in Southern India and chosen on the basis of their ritual knowledge. Their emphasis on orthodoxy partly accounts for the "no-for-eigners" policy so atypical of Nepali shrines.

Clad in red robes and rosaries of *rudraksha* seeds, they conduct an elaborate daily round of worship, beginning at 4 a.m. The linga is undressed and bathed in the "five nectars," a mix-

ture of yoghurt, ghee, honey, sugar, and milk, then bathed again in sacred water collected from holy pilgrimage sites. (In winter months, it even gets a hot bath.) Wrapped again in brocade robes, it's adorned with *tika;* a Sri Yantra is drawn on its topmost face with sandalwood paste imported from India, and it's shown its re-

SADHU, SAINTS, AND SINNERS

Around February they start to appear on Kathmandu's dusty streets: lean, fierce-eyed men who prowl the lanes with brass begging bowls, summoning householders to attention with the rattle of small double-headed drums. They belong to a millennia-old Hindu tradition of vagabond ascetics who renounce family and caste to follow Shiva. *Sadhu* may be naked and dusted with ashes or wrapped in brilliant orange robes. Some spend their lives performing austerities, refusing to lie down for years on end or surviving on a diet of milk. Others are skilled musicians, while still others, red-eyed, smoke staggering quantities of Shiva's favorite herb, ganja, consecrating each hit with the invocation "Bom Shankar."

Sadhu wander the Indian subcontinent, following an unwritten itinerary that brings them each February to Pashupatinath for the festival of Shiva Ratri. "Shiva's Night" is the quintessential Hindu *mela,* a religious carnival blending equal parts of the bizarre and the divine. Encampments of ash-smeared, dreadlocked *sadhu* settle into temple courtyards, drawing crowds of gaping young Nepali men fascinated by their prodigious consumption of hashish *(charas)* and ganja. *Sadhu* renounce most sensual pleasures and intoxicants, but *charas* is among the 16 essentials of Shiva worship, said to increase spiritual insight and help transform consciousness. Shiva himself is known to smoke up a storm, and eye-popping inhalations from small clay chillums fuel many of Shiva Ratri's marathon musical sessions. The government-affiliated Guthi Sansthan supplies *sadhu* with a stipend of *charas* along with a supply of firewood and food for the duration of the festival.

Though *sadhu* have rejected social conventions like the Hindu caste system, their own subculture is demarcated by a complex network of sects and traditions extending far beyond the main division between Shaivaite yogi and Vaishnavite *bairaagi.* A *sadhu's* affiliation is shown by his garments, or lack thereof, as well as the implements he carries and the colored designs painted on his forehead. The naked

Nagas dust their bodies with ashes from cremation fires and wield a trident and skull cup, while Kanphatta yogis wear giant earrings of gold, rhino horn or leather, up to seven inches in circumference. (The splitting of the ear is said to cut a nadi or vital channel, accelerating the attainment of mystical powers.) The *sadhu's* wild dreadlocks symbolize the matted chaos of the world. Other essential implements of a *sadhu* are a begging bowl, made of brass or from a smoothed coconut shell or gourd; a bag of red cloth; fire tongs; and a staff or trident, the three-pronged symbol of Shiva.

Shiva Ratri is a carnival of the bizarre and sometimes grotesque austerities performed in the quest for enlightenment. Here you can see *sadhu* who have pierced their tongues or penises with tridents, or who have stood upright for years on end on shapeless and swollen feet. These efforts are meant to conquer passions and liberate the soul—but the proud, erect posture and fierce eyes of many indicate the fires have been banked, but not extinguished. The *sadhu* spectrum ranges from brooding, intense individuals who are often a little crazy (and sometimes a lot), to mild-mannered gentlemen in orange robes who retire from the world after completing their careers and raising their families to complete the final stage of the Hindu life cycle as *sannyasi* or spiritual seekers.

Like any other slice of humanity, the *sadhu* community spans a full assortment of saints, sinners, and rogues. Having taken a vow not to trade or work, they beg for a living. Yogis may make charms, cast spells, tell fortunes, or cure illnesses as sidelines; mostly, though, they are wanderers on an eternal barefoot pilgrimage, journeying into the Himalayas as far north as Muktinath, and beyond that to Mt. Kailas in Tibet. Ancient Indian texts portray Shiva seated atop the mountain dressed as a mendicant yogi, his body "shining like an evening cloud," the crescent moon caught in his matted locks—all depicted in the luridly colored pop posters displayed in homage in Pashupatinath's teastalls.

flection in a mirror. Later in the afternoon it's offered a selection of sweetmeats, fruit, and *daal bhaat*. All day long worshippers circumambulate it—the recommended minimum is five circuits—happy with the ritual *darshan* or viewing of this supremely sacred object. Only the priests may touch the linga: they serve as intermediaries for worshippers, delivering offerings and dispensing *prasad* like *tika* and flower petals.

THE TEMPLE GROUNDS

Arya and Ram Ghats
Continue around the temple's south side, past more *tika* stands and teastalls, until you reach the Bagmati. The pair of **small bridges** spanning the river here are the perfect vantage point from which to observe Pashupatinath's constant round of bathing and cremation, death and laundry. Upstream, marked by another For Hindus Only sign, is Arya Ghat, reserved for cremations of the royal family and important persons. Interspersed amid the cremation platforms are slanted stone slabs upon which the dying are placed, feet in the water, and given a last drink from the sacred Bagmati—a ritual which brings great blessings. Ram Ghat downstream constitutes four square platforms used for general public cremations (again, high castes only) and is usually busy with one or more examples of the dramatically grisly ceremony. The flat roof of the building behind them affords a discreet bird's-eye view of the process.

Between the two bridges stands a small pagoda-roofed **Parvati temple** with beautiful woodwork, including some vivid erotic struts and *torana* depicting Durga slaying the buffalo demon. Beside it, sheltered in a brick niche, is a massive terra-cotta image of **Vishnu,** said to have been built in a single night. In a little brick enclosure near the lower bridge are two ancient

five-faced linga of Pashupati

BOB RACE

sculptures of goddesses—the eight-armed mother goddess **Bachhlesvari** and **Lakshmi** standing on a tortoise—both embodiments of the word "statuesque."

Raja-Rajesvari Ghat
The ghat extending south from here has a museum's worth of ancient sculptures scattered along its length, including a serene 6th-century **Buddha.** Nearby, enclosed by a circular wall, is the biggest **linga** ever, over 1,500 years old and listing to one side. The various compounds on the western side house cows, dogs, and every imaginable variety of temple and shrine; **Raja-Rajeswari Temple** across from the giant linga is dedicated to the Navadurga. The courtyards also house a large population of pilgrims and squatters. Daily life gives the scene a rural flavor: women cook, spin wool, and comb their hair; men wash clothes and chat; children play and old people doze in the sun.

The Eastern Bank
At the end of the ghat, cross the Bagmati via a modern footbridge and walk back up along the eastern bank, passing a small graveyard where are interred the few categories of Hindus who are not cremated: *sadhu* and infants. A stairway ascends into a series of interlinked temple compounds dedicated to Ram and Vishnu; the shrines are modern and nothing special to look at, but during Shiva Ratri these courtyards house an amazing variety of austerity-performing *sadhu.*

Beyond the temples is a raised terrace holding a row of identical, elaborately decorated stone monuments, each housing a polished linga. These are variously said to be dedicated to deceased *sadhu* or to loyal wives who committed sati on their husbands' funeral pyres, a tradition continued into the present century. Look upriver into an almost-bucolic river gorge, where retreat dwellings have been gouged into the sheer stone cliffs.

Gorakhnath and Guhyeswari

The main stairway ascends steeply past past the forest of **Mrigasthali,** where Shiva once roamed as an antelope. Now it shelters several hundred scowling, red-bottomed rhesus monkeys; guard your camera. At the top is a shady, quiet wooded glen, a timeless, evocative place where white-clad pilgrims drift amid crumbling stone shrines and statues. Shiva appears everywhere, embodied in the abstract linga or as a four-armed deity displaying a yogi's possessions: rosary, water pot, trident, and shaman's drum. Off to the east rises the bulbous white dome of **Vishwarupa Mandir,** another "For Hindus Only" site, this one enshrining a form of Vishnu.

The main path leads north past a large whiteplastered *shikara* temple dedicated to the 12th-century yogi and wonderworker **Gorakhnath.** His footprints, enshrined in silver atop a lotus pedestal, are the only symbol of this mysterious magician who serves as a special patron of *sadhu.*

Follow the steps down to **Guhyeshwari Mandir,** sacred to Shiva's consort Durga or Sati, who is said to have immolated herself from shame after her father insulted her husband.

Mad with grief, Shiva wandered the skies with her corpse; pieces of her body dropped off and fell to earth, creating sacred sites or *pitha,* 51 in all dotting the Indian subcontinent. Sati's "secret" parts *(guhya)* fell near Pashupatinath, thus the name Guhyeshwari, "Secret" or "Hidden" Goddess. An extremely holy site, it's closed to non-Hindus as well.

From here you can walk the paved road back along the complex's northern outskirts, passing **Gauri Ghat,** where Parvati is said to have bathed, and eventually reaching the Gausala-Chabahil road. Or, cross the Bagmati on a narrow plank and continue up the dirt road for about 20 minutes to **Boudhanath,** passing some reeking garbage dumps en route.

Practicalities

The neighborhood around Pashupatinath offers a multitude of tea and sweet stalls, the largest of them dishing up *daal bhaat* and Indian vegetarian food. Hotels in the Gausala area cater almost exclusively to Indian pilgrims. **Dwarika's Village Hotel** not far south in Battisputali is a tourist-oriented establishment incorporating lovingly restored old woodcarvings in its architecture—a nice place for tea in the garden.

BOUDHANATH

Simple, massive, and powerful, the Great Stupa of Boudhanath rises above a huddle of buildings some seven km east of Kathmandu, its painted eyes gazing solemnly into the distance. Among the most important Buddhist sites in Nepal, Boudha draws a cross-section of Himalayan pilgrims: tall Khampas from east Tibet with big knives and red tassels woven in their hair; Ladakhi women with seed-pearl earrings and winged hats; Bhutanese in knee-length robes and argyle socks; and wide-eyed Bhotias from remote Nepali regions like Dolpo and Mugu, wrapped in striped woolen blankets.

Boudha is a magnet for Kathmandu's Tibetan community, as well as pilgrims. Their faith transforms it into a showcase of Buddhist practices— prayer beads, mantras, prayer wheels, prostrations. All day long, people walk clockwise about the stupa in ritual circumambulation. Crowds

are greatest in early morning and at dusk, and on full- and new-moon days, when virtuous actions are believed to earn extra merit, and beggars line up to profit from the maxim.

Boudha has developed dramatically from the '60s, when it was set in the midst of open fields, encircled by a single row of traditional tile-roof houses. The influx of Tibetan laypeople and the monastery construction boom began in the '70s, and the rapid expansion was fueled by the success of the carpet industry centered in this area. Boomtown Boudha is a squalid mix of muddy roads, heaps of garbage, and side-by-side shanties. But the stupa itself remains magic, especially at dusk, when the long horns blown from monastery roofs fill the air with deep, booming tones, and the crowds circle beneath the stupa in a steady stream of murmured prayers and creaking prayer wheels.

Stupa Symbolism

Stupas are as essential to Buddhism as the cross is to Christianity, a tangible symbol of the Buddha's enlightened mind. Boudha has been formed by centuries of additions and improvements, until its multiple layers resemble a giant onion. Its core shelters ancient relics: Boudha is said to hold the remains of Kasyapa, the Buddha of a previous age. A cross-section bore of the great stupa would be most instructive for archaeologists, but will never be permitted as long as there are people to worship it.

With a diameter exceeding 100 meters and a wall-to-wall length roughly equaling a football field, Boudha is among the largest stupas in the world—certainly the biggest in Nepal. Set atop a triple-terraced plinth, it rises 36 meters above the street. Its form, alternated squares and circles, replicates a mandala. In fact, it *is* a three-dimensional mandala, a perfectly proportioned embodiment of abstract religious concepts; this becomes apparent when the stupa is viewed from above.

Every portion of the structure is imbued with symbolic significance. The base, dome, square *harmika*, spire, and pinnacle represent the five elements of earth, water, air, fire, and ether. The spire's 13 tiers stand for the stages to enlightenment, while the umbrella atop is the symbol of royalty. Most striking are the bow-shaped eyes painted onto the square *harmika*, a stroke of genius unique to Nepali stupas. They are said to represent the eyes of the primordial Adi Buddha, or the guardians of the four directions; or perhaps they symbolize the omniscience of enlightenment. Whichever, they add an uncanny presence to the stupa, endowing it with a curious intelligence.

History

Although some historians believe King Manadeva I built the original stupa in the 5th century, its origins remain obscure. The Tibetan version of its creation centers around Jadzimo, a poultrywoman (some say a prostitute) with four sons who somehow managed to amass a fortune. Wishing to build a stupa she asked the king for a piece of land—nothing much, just big enough to be covered by a buffalo skin. He granted this seemingly modest request, and the shrewd woman then cut the hide into thin strips and gir-

dled off a considerable plot. The king had to concede this was all according to their agreement, but his rueful words *"Jarung kashor"* gave the stupa its Tibetan name. With typical Tibetan pithiness, it means something like, "Saying it was okay to do this was a slip of the tongue."

A second legend tells of a terrible drought at the time of construction which forced brickmakers to spread out sheets to catch the morning dew—thus another name, the "Dewdrop Stupa." A Tibetan religious text states that the essence of 100 million Buddhas dissolved into the stupa's dome at the time of its consecration, imbuing it with immense spiritual power. Tales of the miraculous materialization of relics (tiny white pellets called *ringsel*) are common even today.

The old Tibetan trade route passed near Boudha, and Tibetans early on adopted the stupa as their own, taking responsibility for its upkeep. Local people still scrupulously maintain it with donations dedicated to the memory of deceased family members. Several times a month painters

Tibetan woman giving a donation to a monk, Boudhanath

CHRISTOPHER GAMM

BOUDHA'S BUDDHIST SCENE

Boudhanath (Boudha) is among the world's premiere centers for studying Buddhism. Many Westerners consider it better even than Dharamsala, the seat of the exiled Dalai Lama. Dharamsala focuses on the Gelukpa sect, while Boudha offers a broad cross-section of all four main schools of Tibetan Buddhism, with a special emphasis on the Nyingma and Kagyü sects; in addition, it has a remarkably intense concentration of teachers and monasteries. Teachings are frequent, as are *wang* or empowerment ceremonies meant to pass on the essential blessings embodied by a particular teaching or text.

Boudha displays the diversity of a living Buddhist community, drawing not just Tibetans but Newars, Sherpas, Tamangs, Bhutanese, and Ladakhis. The ethnic richness of the local community is often not perceived by visitors, who see everyone as "Tibetan." In fact, some two-thirds of its monks are not.

Another confusing matter involves the terms "monk" and "lama," which contrary to popular English usage are not synonymous. Most monks aren't lamas, and a lama is not necessarily a monk—some are married and have children. A lama is simply a spiritual teacher who is able to transmit realization and guide others on the path to enlightenment. Personal guidance from a lama is an essential element in Tibetan Buddhism. No amount of individual study can substitute for a teacher's insight or his power to directly transmit spiritual wisdom.

Developing a close relationship with a lama can be difficult, though, as they are often surrounded by older students who act as sometimes ferocious guardians. The most accessible teacher is Chokyi

Nyima Rinpoche, an English-speaking lama who is abbot of the white monastery north of the stupa. He has regular visiting hours and gives informal teachings every Saturday at 10:30 a.m. Other teachers include Thrangu Rinpoche, who generally teaches a month-long course sometime around January; Rabjam Rinpoche; and Khenpo Tsultrim Gyatso. Another main point of access is Kopan Monastery atop a hill behind Boudha, which was developed specifically to teach Western students.

Pick up a white *khatak* or prayer scarf from a Boudha shop and bring it to your meeting with a lama. This traditional Tibetan greeting serves as a formal gesture of respect and symbolizes one's pure intention. Fold it in seven sections (a monk can show you how) and present it fully extended in both hands. The lama will return it, draping it around your neck as a symbol of acceptance.

The ongoing meeting of West and East as demonstrated in the spread of Tibetan Buddhism is a fascinating process. Historically, Buddhism has changed its form each time as it was successively transmitted from the original Sanskrit into Chinese, Japanese, and Tibetan. The modern transition into English is lending it a distinctly psychological caste. Some fear it's becoming diluted into a pop self-help mechanism and is in danger of losing its religious essence. Others perceive a remarkable ability to adapt to circumstances and cultures. More philosophical Tibetans perceive the machinations of karma in the process. "We held onto the Dharma too tightly in Tibet; we didn't want to let the outside world in," commented one lama. "And so the Chinese came in and scattered it into the outside world, just like shaking the apples off a tree."

will whitewash the dome and touch up the eyes, topping off their work by flinging buckets of saffron-tinted water to create a golden lotus pattern—quite a scene if you happen to catch it.

Festivals

Boudha has a busy festival schedule, beginning with the full-moon night of Magh (Jan.-Feb.), when the silver Ajima idol is paraded in a palanquin, and hundreds of butter lamps illuminate the stupa. Tibetan New Year or Losar in Feb.-March is a cheerful community celebration which often includes ritual *cham* dances

(see "Music and Dance" in the Introduction) in local monasteries. The full moon of March-April, **Tamang Jatra,** draws gambling, drinking, and flirting crowds; the following month brings the more sedate **Buddha Jayanti.**

Getting There

Boudha is a 20-minute bike ride from Durbar Marg; not difficult but unpleasant, especially around Chabahil, which with the dust, horns, and traffic jams can resemble Central Beirut. If you care to risk a bus to Boudha, they depart regularly from the Kathmandu municipal bus park. Transport is the biggest drawback to staying in Boudha: midmorning competition for taxis, which congregate in front of the main gate, can be fierce, and drivers don't like to go there after dark.

AROUND THE STUPA

The Main Kora

Kora is the Tibetan word for circumambulation, an act of devotion which earns religious merit and provides the pretext for a pleasant stroll. Everyone proceeds clockwise around the stupa; try always to follow the flow.

The elaborate plaster gate on the main road is technically speaking only a side entrance to the stupa. The proper entry is on the north side, where, set into the wall girdling the stupa, is a small shrine with a silver image of **Ajima,** one of the terrible Newar mother-goddesses who must be placated to prevent disaster. *Puja* is held here on auspicious days, with chanting, music, and offerings—mountains of puffed rice decorated with oranges, packets of biscuits, and white bread, all soon snatched by children and beggars. Opposite the temple in a dingy white-washed building is an old **Nyingma shrine** with good but soot-covered frescoes and an image of Guru Rinpoche flanked by his consorts Mandarava and Yeshe Tsogyal. Butter lamps are offered here on auspicious occasions; for Rs5 or so you can light a set number of lamps.

The Ajima shrine is flanked by the entrance and exit to the stupa's upper levels. The small courtyard behind is set with Hindu and Buddhist images and bells to be clanged as loudly as possible. Itinerant holy men often establish themselves here for marathon prayer sessions. Give a spin to the giant prayer wheel housed in a side room here, then climb up onto the three terraces, each of which yields a different view. During your *kora,* look for devout practitioners performing prostrations in the enclosed courtyard on the stupa's east side. The topmost terrace circles the actual dome, inset with 108 niches holding figures of tantric deities.

Consumer Opportunities

The shops ringing the stupa used to house Newar gold and silversmiths who manufactured Tibetan jewelry and ritual objects. Now the em-

phasis is on Tibetan-esque tourist souvenirs of varying quality. Much of it is the usual junk manufactured in Valley workshops, but good antiques do exist: jewelry and ritual items, metal and wood crafts, Bhutanese textiles, and a large selection of old carpets. Everything good is expensive, and prices are guaranteed high in the plate-glass antique showrooms which have been appearing of late. Comparison shop and bargain *very* hard, remembering that Tibetans are notoriously good traders.

Inexpensive purchases include incense, prayer flags, and small brightly painted wooden tables and chests. Explore Boudha's backstreets to observe skilled metalworkers hammering out silver altar bowls, carpenters carving wooden tables, and women knotting woolen carpets. The success of the carpet industry has attracted thousands of rural people to Boudha and has contributed greatly to the area's over-development; the present drop in sales is not likely to cause the number of new buildings to disappear.

The second-floor **Dharma Book Center** on the stupa sells photos of lamas, posters, Tibetan and English texts, *khataks,* and "Free Tibet" T-shirts. Local tailor shops display lengths of cloth to be made into women's *bakkhu,* worn over an elegant silk blouse. Other items are furry brocade hats; massive silver, turquoise, and coral jewelry; ornate trinkets; and ritual paraphernalia for Buddhist practitioners. Boudha is also headquarters for many Tibetan herbal doctors *(amchi)* and acupuncturists.

TIBETAN MONASTERIES

With a half-dozen major *gompa* or monasteries and three or four times as many smaller ones, Boudha serves as headquarters for a vigorous revival of Tibetan Buddhism, a hopeful indicator that this ancient religion may survive Chinese attempts to eradicate it in its homeland. About 10,000 Tibetans fled to Nepal in the wake of the 1959 Chinese annexation; the community has since grown to over 90,000. Many of the original refugees settled around the stupa in a comfortingly familiar Buddhist environment. The local community's religious and cultural centers are the elaborately decorated *gompa,* constructed with contributions from the now-prosperous local

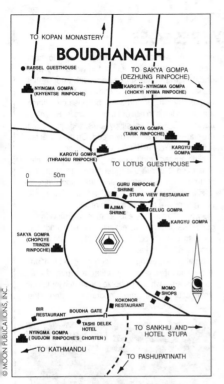

BOUDHANATH

TO KOPAN MONASTERY

RABSEL GUESTHOUSE

NYINGMA GOMPA
(KHYENTSE RINPOCHE)

TO SAKYA GOMPA
(DEZHUNG RINPOCHE)

KARGYU - NYINGMA GOMPA
(CHOKYI NYIMA RINPOCHE)

SAKYA GOMPA
(TARIK RINPOCHE)

KARGYU
GOMPA

KARGYU GOMPA
(THRANGU RINPOCHE)

TO LOTUS GUESTHOUSE

0   50m

GURU RINPOCHE
SHRINE
STUPA VIEW RESTAURANT

AJIMA
SHRINE
GELUG GOMPA

KARGYU GOMPA

SAKYA GOMPA
(CHOPGYE
TRINZIN
RINPOCHE)

MOMO
SHOPS

KOKONOR
RESTAURANT

BIR
RESTAURANT
BOUDHA GATE

TASHI DELEK
HOTEL

TO SANKHU AND
HOTEL STUPA

NYINGMA GOMPA
(DUDJOM RINPOCHE'S CHORTEN)

TO KATHMANDU

TO PASHUPATINATH

© MOON PUBLICATIONS, INC.

community and from Buddhists abroad, especially overseas Chinese communities in Taiwan, Malaysia, and Singapore.

A monastery's main hall serves as a public shrine; its monks conduct ceremonies, its lamas give spiritual advice. It's a treasure house of art, filled with statues, *thankga,* woodcarvings, embroidered banners, and murals, all rendered in typically vivid Tibetan colors. Some visitors are disturbed by the *gompas*' lavish displays of wealth, but Tibetans perceive little tension between money and religion: the *gompa* in old Tibet were tremendously wealthy and powerful establishments. The rich displays are intended to "turn the mind," inspiring it to rise above mundane concerns.

Notable *Gompa*

Boudha's *gompa* represent all four of the major sects, with a particular emphasis on the older Nyingma and Kagyü schools. The monks may

be Newar, Manangi, Tamang, Mustangi, locally born Tibetans, or recent Tibetan immigrants. Boudha's monasteries are relatively new: the oldest, the "Mongolian *gompa*" on the stupa's northeast corner, was built only in 1959.

The colorful main shrines of the older, larger monasteries near the stupa are generally open to visitors: consult the Boudhanath map for their location. Highlights to look for include the exquisite paintings of **Tarik Rinpoche's** *gompa;* the richly decorated main hall of **Ka-Nying Shedrup Ling,** and the 10-meter-tall figure of Maitreya, the Buddha of the Coming Age, enshrined in **Jamchen Yiggha Choling** on the main *kora* route. Inside the new-ish **Urgyen Dongak Chökorling,** a jewelled reliquary stupa holds the remains of Dudjom Rinpoche, the head of the Nyingmapa sect who died in 1989; his reincarnation was recently discovered as a young Bhutanese boy living at Boudhanath.

Most exquisite is **Shechen Tennyi Targye Ling,** constructed in the early '80s with support from the king of Bhutan, who sent the best of everything, including 200 master craftspeople. This monastery was the seat of H.H. Dilgo Khyentse Rinpoche, tutor to the Bhutanese royal family and a great master of the Nyingma sect who died in 1991. It is now possible to meet with the current rinpoche, Rabjam Rinpoche. The main shrine houses three Buddha images; panels on either side depict the 16 Arhats, and the wall frescoes illustrate masters of the four major Tibetan Buddhist sects.

Gompa Etiquette

Don't let the maroon-robed monks racing about on motorcycles fool you—monasteries are conservative communities, and visitors should dress accordingly, especially women. Take off your shoes in the sheltered porch before you enter the main shrine, and ask permission if a ceremony is being held inside, as you may have to take a sip of consecrated water before entering. If the door is locked, the key can often be found nearby—ask. A young English-speaking monk may even appear to show you around.

Walk clockwise about the shrine room. Photos are usually okay but it's best to ask permission. A small donation left on the altar or placed in the offering box will go to maintain the temple and support the monks.

MONASTERY FRESCOES

The Tibetan Buddhist pantheon embraces a bewildering array of beings, not deities in the conventional sense, but expressions of different aspects of the enlightened mind. They appear in painted form on the interior walls of temples, protecting the shrine against evil influences and reminding all who see them of the existence of realms beyond the senses.

Buddhas are fully enlightened beings, there being countless numbers in addition to Buddha Shakyamuni, whose birth 2,500 years ago is a matter of historical record. Bodhisattvas are Buddhas-in-training, compassionate emanations on the way to full enlightenment. *Dharmapala* serve as ferocious protectors of the faith: often they are local deities converted to Buddhism. Their terrifying forms usually appear on the back walls nearest the entrance in order to guard the temple. *Yidam* are tutelary deities visualized in meditation, appearing in both peaceful and wrathful forms. The fiercer versions, multiheaded, many-armed, and wreathed in flames, may be difficult to reconcile with Buddhism's peaceful reputation, but they embody the energy necessary to banish anger, desire, and ignorance from the mind. In addition to these fantastic beings, historical figures like great lamas and lineage founders are often depicted, surrounded by disciples or scenes from their life.

The *gompa*'s entrance porch is dominated by the Guardians of the Four Directions. These gigantic figures, colored yellow, white, green, and red, each display a different symbol—Kubera, the Southern God of Wealth, clutches a mongoose spewing jewels from its mouth, and so on. On one side is a cosmological diagram of Mt. Meru, the center of the universe according to traditional Tibetan cosmology, surrounded by the various continents and worlds.

Opposite it is the Wheel of Life, a complex figure depicting the manifold but ultimately limited possibilities of samsaric existence. The fanged and clawed monster is Mahakala, "Great Time." Within his grasp the wheel revolves in an endless circle of suffering, driven by hatred, desire, and ignorance—symbolized by the snake, cock, and pig set in the hub. Surrounding it is a narrow ring with a chain of human bodies ascending to enlightenment or descending into suffering, driven by their karma.

From here extend the six realms of samsaric existence. At the bottom are the hells—eight varieties each of hot and cold hells, where demons torment sinners. On the lower right is the world of hungry ghosts, strange-looking beings with needle-thin throats and huge bellies. They are eternally tormented by hunger and thirst, because everything they touch turns to filth or burning flames. Rebirth in this realm is the fate of stingy souls, and symbolizes the state of mind driven by greed. On the lower left is the animal realm, dominated by ignorance. Above it is the human world, showing scenes of daily life. This is considered the most fortunate of the six realms, as only humans have the opportunity to practice the Dharma and gain liberation. The upper two realms are divided by a miraculous tree: here the warlike *asura* battle for its magical fruit with the gods. The *asura* are celestial beings who lead long and blessed lives, but they too will die and be reborn according to their karma.

Small panels along the outer rim depict the 12 interdependent links of origination, a series of allegorical scenes which symbolize the search for the ultimate cause of samsara—ignorance, rooted in the belief in the individual ego.

the Wheel of Life

Inside the Shrine

Tibetan temples are rich in both color and symbolism. There are butter lamps, from tiny cups to huge standing chalices, their flames symbolically dispelling the darkness of ignorance. In Tibet these would be fueled with pungent yak butter, but Nepali monasteries substitute vegetable ghee. Offerings like incense, food, and flowers symbolize the dedication of sensory pleasures to enlightenment, while the small silver bowls of water lined up on every altar represent one's essential pure nature.

Torma, conical offering cakes molded of barley flour mixed with water, play a role in many ceremonies. Decorated with red-dyed dough and knobs of butter, they are made in different shapes and sizes, according to the rite and deity—at least 108 different kinds, ranging in height from 30 cm to three meters. In historical terms they're substitutes for the animal sacrifices of the ancient Bön religion.

Larger monasteries perform daily *puja* in the early morning and again at dusk. Longer ceremonies are periodically held, lasting several weeks. The dim light, the seated red-robed monks, the musky incense, and the sonorous ritual music combine to make a powerful experience. Droning chants alternate with the groaning of the long horns, the clanging of cymbals, the scream of shrill bone trumpets, the steady bass thump of the hanging drum. The object is not to produce a melody—indeed, the "music" is distinctly cacophonous—but to accompany the chanting of texts and prayers. The deep, roaring din creates an ocean of sound that is said to be an exaggerated rendition of the sounds the human body would be heard to make if all external sounds were blocked. "The sound of the mind at work," one Western scholar called it, pointing out that the purpose is not to soothe the listener, but to wake him or her up.

PRACTICALITIES

Food

Boudha's old, dark *momo*-and-*chang* caves have almost all disappeared, replaced by modern "coffeeshops" and more souvenir stores. Many small local restaurants serve tasty and cheap *thukpa*, fried rice, and noodles; look for the signs advertising "Tibetan Restaurant,"

though the proprietor might equally well be Tamang. **Amdo Restaurant** on the main road makes good *thukpa*.

The local Westerners' hangout is the old **Bir Restaurant,** a few hundred meters before the gate; the notice board here tells what's going on around Boudha, and the food is good and cheap. The **Stupa View Restaurant** on the main *kora* is more upscale, a pleasant place with safe if bland food. The specialty is "Austrian vegetarian," but the menu stretches to include sheep's cheese, pasta, and espresso. Best of all are the stunning views of the stupa from the rooftop terrace.

Accommodations

A few days spent in Boudha is not a bad alternative to Kathmandu: lodging prices are fair, the atmosphere off the main road is peaceful, if grotty; and the culture is distinctly different. A stay here is especially interesting around festival time, though the few guesthouses tend to fill up around Losar and during major teachings.

Best value is the **Lotus Guesthouse,** tel. (1) 472-320, a big, peaceful place surrounded by *gompa* and built around a garden. Large moldering rooms are Rs180 s, Rs250 d; add Rs30 for attached bath. **Rabsel Guesthouse** behind Dilgo Khyentse Rinpoche's *gompa* is a spiffy new place with clean rooms for US$7.

Hotel Tashi Delek, tel. (1) 471-380, on the main road across from the stupa entrance is a big, cavernous building with large, sparsely furnished rooms for Rs220 s or d (common bath only). The back rooms overlook a panorama of fields, with the airport and Pashupatinath in the background: try to ignore the garbage in the foreground. The nearby **Hotel Tibet** is supposed to open sometime in 1995 and will probably be a similar standard; all that's open now is a fancy, dimly lit restaurant. Down the road in the opposite direction is **Snow Lion Lodge,** a small place with simple rooms for Rs150 common bath, Rs300 with bath. Cheap rooms are also available through the **Bir Restaurant** and the **Kokonor Restaurant.** It's easy to find a room to rent from a Tibetan or Sherpa family if you plan a longer stay; just ask around in local shops and restaurants.

Moving upscale, **Hotel Stupa,** tel. (1) 470-385, is the yuppies' choice in Boudha, a trim, efficient place with reasonable rooms in several categories for US$15-25 s, US$20-30 d; it is a

10-minute walk east of the stupa, though. The government-run **Taragaon Hotel** on the road to Boudha is due to be replaced by a US$38 million, 271-room spin-off of the Hyatt Regency chain, which is supposed to open in 1997. It's hard to believe that Nepal's first five-star hotel will be located here, of all places.

AROUND BOUDHA

Walks

The network of dirt roads north of Boudha leads through fields and small villages; very scenic, if you can tolerate the kids shouting, "Hello, monkey!" A favorite destination is **Kopan Monastery,** founded by the charismatic Lama Yeshe, whose reincarnation was discovered in the son of a Spanish couple who were his students. Lama Yeshe's successor, Lama Zopa, occasionally teaches here, and the monastery holds popular annual meditation seminars (see special topic "Boudha's Buddhist Scene" for more details). Kopan is about a 45-minute walk from the stupa; head north towards a few small buildings set atop a hillock. It's receptive to drop-in visitors; it attracts so many, in fact, that villagers will autuomatically point the way, even if you're *not* planning on going there.

Atop the next hill to the east is the new shrine of **Phulhari,** with a reliquary containing the remains of Jamgon Kongtrul Rinpoche. Khenpo Tsultrim Gyatso teaches here occasionally; he's affiliated with the Marpa Institute, a translation project headquartered on the Mahankal road behind Boudha. The next hill to the east from *here* is a peaceful pine plantation that makes a good picnic site; it often serves as a "countryside" set for Nepali films. A trail continues north beyond it through another pine plantation and along a peaceful ridge, eventually entering the **Shivapuri Watershed Reserve** and reaching **Nagi Gompa,** a two and a half hour hike from Boudha.

Beyond Boudha

It's hard to spend more than a leisurely half-day at Boudha: a visit is easily combined with a trip to Pashupatinath, 20 minutes' walk south down the dirt road opposite the main gate. The path skirts heaps of garbage; hardly pleasant, but more peaceful than the main road through Chabahil. Further afield you could continue east past the stupa to Gokharna and perhaps Sundarijaal, or on to Changu Narayan or Sankhu. All these destinations are described in the chapter on Exploring the Valley.

Chabahil

The road to Boudha runs past the Chabahil stupa, said to have been built with the bricks and earth left over from the construction of Boudhanath. The stupa is smaller and more dilapidated than its cousin, and as such is probably much closer in appearance to its Licchavi-era original, apart from the lightbulb dangling above the stupa's third eye.

Not so long ago Chabahil lay on the farthest outskirts of Kathmandu. Families of Newar traders bound for Tibet would travel this far to send them off; thus its name, "Monastery of the Overnight Stop." Chabahil was an early Licchavi settlement, and the stupa's grounds are littered with ancient *chaitya,* sculptures, and architectural fragments, many now badly worn. The dome is adorned with unusual relief plaques dating from the 7th century, their details nearly obscured by time and whitewash. Peer into the small brick building in the compound's southwest corner to glimpse a beautiful standing image of the bodhisattva **Padmapani Lokesvara** sculpted in black stone.

The old and remarkably unchanged Newar bazaar of Chabahil is 100 meters north of the stupa, Turn left at the main intersection and stroll past the huddle of shops to the attractive old temple of **Chandra Binayak,** the "Moon Ganesh." One of the Valley's quartet of sacred Ganesh shrines, it lies on the Tibet route and was once visited by Newar traders seeking blessings for their business. It is still said to cure disease and grant fame and riches. The temple is lavishly decorated and actively worshipped, and the courtyard is filled with sculptures, giant lingas, and natural stones.

PATAN

Patan (PA-tan) is a world away from Kathmandu in terms of ambience, and frequent visits are prescribed for anyone stressed out by Kathmandu's noise, dust, and traffic. This ancient city, once a kingdom in itself, is set atop a high plateau across the Bagmati River from Kathmandu. Until recently the two cities were separated by an expanse of fields; today new construction has merged them into a single urban mass.

Despite its proximity, Patan retains, at least for the moment, the tranquillity and charm Kathmandu has irrevocably lost. The city's core is distinctly urban, but in a peaceful way; 10 minutes' walk in any direction reveals the rural vignettes so typical of the Valley, with ducks and pigs wandering the streets, and grain being threshed in the open brick-paved squares.

Walking down the quiet, narrow streets still lined mainly by traditional buildings, it's hard to believe Patan is Nepal's third-largest city. The Malla-era population of 15,000 has increased tenfold, but most of its inhabitants are Newars, who resolutely maintain their distinct identity. Many of them remain Buddhist, holdouts in an increasingly Hindu-ized Nepal. Even in political terms Patan is independent: during the 1990 democracy movement, local people dug trenches to block the entrance of police vehicles and declared the area a "liberated" zone, raising the then-banned Congress Party flag over the city gate.

About a third of Patan's residents are Jyapu or Newar farmers, most living on the edges of the city near their fields. Many of the inner city residents are craftspeople who work in tiny shops, clustered in different quarters according to occupational caste—stonecarvers in one neighborhood, metalworkers in another, and so on. The fine images and delicate jewelry produced by Patan's Newar metalworkers have been renowned for over 1,000 years, and they continue to dominate the market today. Shopping for metalwork here is far more interesting than in the tourist shops of Kathmandu.

History

Patan retains the most ancient air of all the Valley's three main cities, beginning with its un-proven reputation as the capital of the near-mythic Kiranti dynasty. Another mystery are the "Ashoka" stupas, four primitive-looking grassy mounds set around the outskirts of Patan, said to have been built by the Indian Buddhist emperor Ashoka. This story is pure fiction—Ashoka never visited the Valley—but the strange mounds may predate even the 2nd-century B.C. emperor. We will likely never know: archaeological tunnelling on such sacred monuments would be unthinkable.

During the Licchavi era Patan dominated the Valley: by the 7th century it was one of Asia's major Buddhist cities. Pilgrims, scholars, and monks from India, Tibet, and China traveled here, often staying in the city's characteristic *bahal,* monastic complexes built around open courtyards. At one point it was said that half of Patan's population was monks; the other half were artists.

As Hindu influence grew, Newar Buddhism slipped into decline: the Buddhist priesthood became a hereditary caste affair, and the population of Patan's *bahal* shifted from celibate monks to families sharing the same caste and profession. The *bahal* sent out offshoots as their population swelled, until today they number over 175. These interlocking residential courtyards still structure the interior of the old city: peaceful, monument-studded spaces with a distinctly medieval feel. Along with Patan's 50-odd major temples and countless smaller monuments and shrines, they give the town its classical name, Lalitpur, "The Beautiful City."

Medieval Patan was the largest of the Three Kingdoms, encompassing all of the prosperous south Valley and beyond. Most of its architectural glory dates to the late Malla era, beginning with the reign of Siddhi Narsingh Malla, who ascended the throne in 1619. Following Gorkha's conquest of the Valley, Patan was ignored in favor of the capital of Kathmandu. A British visitor of the late 19th century noted its forlorn and gloomy air: "Ruined buildings and deserted shrines, broken archways, and mutilated sculptures meet the eye at every turn . . . the city looks much too large for its inhabitants."

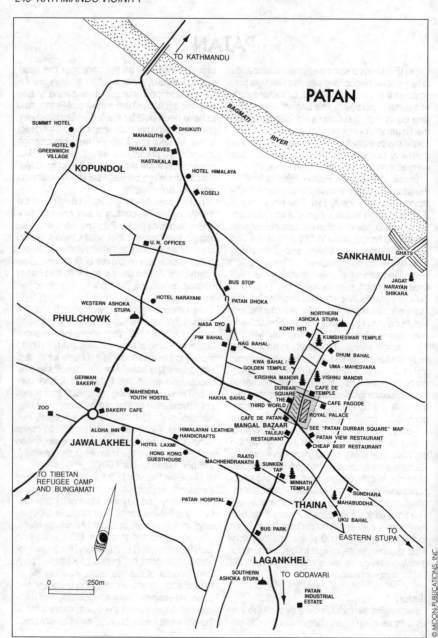

PATAN

TO KATHMANDU

BAGMATI RIVER

SUMMIT HOTEL

MAHAGUTHI · DHUKUTI

DHAKA WEAVES

HOTEL GREENWICH VILLAGE

KOPUNDOL

HASTAKALA

HOTEL HIMALAYA

KOSELI

SANKHAMUL

GHATS

U. N. OFFICES

JAGAT NARAYAN SHIKARA

BUS STOP

WESTERN ASHOKA STUPA

HOTEL NARAYANI

PATAN DHOKA

PHULCHOWK

NASA DYO

NORTHERN ASHOKA STUPA

KONTI HITI

KUMBHESWAR TEMPLE

PIM BAHAL

NAG BAHAL

DHUM BAHAL

KWA BAHAL / GOLDEN TEMPLE

UMA - MAHESVARA

GERMAN BAKERY

KRISHNA MANDIR

VISHNU MANDIR

CAFE DE TEMPLE

MAHENDRA YOUTH HOSTEL

DURBAR SQUARE

THE THIRD WORLD

CAFE PAGODE

ZOO

BAKERY CAFE

HAKHA BAHAL

ROYAL PALACE

ALOHA INN

CAFE DE PATAN

SEE "PATAN DURBAR SQUARE" MAP

JAWALAKHEL

HOTEL LAXMI

HIMALAYAN LEATHER HANDICRAFTS

MANGAL BAZAAR

TALEJU RESTAURANT

PATAN VIEW RESTAURANT

CHEAP BEST RESTAURANT

HONG KONG GUESTHOUSE

RAATO MACHHENDRANATH

SUNKEN TAP

TO TIBETAN REFUGEE CAMP AND BUNGAMATI

MINNATH TEMPLE

SUNDHARA

PATAN HOSPITAL

THAINA

MAHABUDDHA

UKU BAHAL

BUS PARK

TO EASTERN STUPA

LAGANKHEL

SOUTHERN ASHOKA STUPA

TO GODAVARI

PATAN INDUSTRIAL ESTATE

0   250m

MOON

MOON PUBLICATIONS, INC.

Patan became a quiet provincial backwater—a hidden stroke of fortune which has helped preserve its treasures to the present day.

Modern Patan
In terms of atmosphere, Patan today lies somewhere between harried Kathmandu and still-medieval Bhaktapur. Exploring its streets remains pure pleasure, but the initial signs of change can be seen: the advent of traffic jams in Mangal Bazaar, a growing network of tourist shops and restaurants, and an ever-expanding suburban sprawl eating up the rice fields which once ringed the city.

Patan's lovely old buildings are slowly crumbling, to be replaced by new ones. Municipal restrictions limit height and try to control style, but the new buildings lack the harmonious patina of age. Where to get the artisans, the sal wood, the special bricks to build an old-style house—and who would want to live in it anyway? In terms of interior comfort the new cement structures are a big improvement on the dank, dim old homes; it's only from the outside they seem jarring.

A similar process of distintegration is occurring in the ancient public buildings, Patan's wealth of resthouses and *bahal* and temples. Traditionally these were created and maintained

PATAN DURBAR SQUARE

1. Bhimsen Mandir
2. Ganesh temple
3. Vishwanath Mandir
4. Krishna Mandir
5. Garuda pillar
6. Chaar Narayan Mandir
7. Narayan temple
8. Narasingha temple
9. King Yoganendra Malla's pillar
10. Hari Shankara Mandir
11. Taleju bell
12. Chyasin Dega
13. fountain
14. Bhai Devala temple
15. Shiva temple (good views)
16. Narasingha statue
17. Ganesh statue
18. Hanuman statue
19. Sundari Chowk
20. Tulsi Hiti
21. Mul Chowk
22. Yantaju shrine
23. Taleju Mandir
24. Ganga statue
25. Jamuna statue
26. Taleju temple
27. Degutale (main Taleju shrine)
28. Nassal Chowk
29. Lumjyal Chowk
30. Narayan shrine
31. Manga Hiti
32. Mani Mandapa

Patan Durbar Square with statue of King Yoganendra Malla

Getting There and Around

Patan is 20 minutes by bike from Thamel, a straightforward if dusty and noisy ride. Automotive traffic over the two-lane Bagmati bridge can be horrendous, but cyclists and pedestrians can bypass the snarls. Another plus is the freedom to explore the handicraft shops of **Kopundol** on the way into town, or to visit the carpet-oriented Tibetan settlement of **Jawalakhel** on the southwest fringes of Patan.

Buses from the municipal bus park run to the Patan city bus park at **Lagankhel** on the south end of town; Lagankhel is the departure point for minibuses to many south Valley destinations. A few buses stop at **Patan Dhoka,** the old city gate on the north-west side. This is a good place to leave a taxi, as it allows a leisurely 15-minute wander through town and into Durbar Square. Most visitors head straight for **Durbar Square** in the center of town: the most direct route is the road from the western Ashoka Stupa into Mangal Bazaar. Patan itself is easily managed on foot. Taxis back to Kathmandu can be found in Mangal Bazaar and at Patan Dhoka.

PATAN DURBAR SQUARE

The plaza fronting the old Royal Palace holds the finest collection of Newar urban architecture in all Nepal. An extraordinary variety of monuments built over the course of centuries blends into a magical whole, each perfectly placed and balanced. Frenchman Sylvain Levi described its dreamlike beauty in 1901 as "a world of almost luminous white stone, of pillars crowned by bronze statues, of light-filtering colonnades, and of fragile dream temples—guarded all by a company of fantastic beasts, chimeras, and griffins." Early morning in winter is particularly evocative, as shawled figures drift beneath temple roofs shrouded in mist.

Patan's Durbar Square, like Kathmandu's, is set in the heart of the city at the junction of two ancient trade routes. Originally it was the site of a pre-Licchavi palace; later it became the favored neighborhood of the wealthy nobles who ruled Patan. Durbar Square and the palace emerged in its full glory after the Mallas took control of Patan. Much of its splendor is due to Siddhi Narsingh Malla and his son Shrinivasa

by local people through the collective instrument of the *guthi* (for more on this institution, see "The Old Cities" under "History and Culture" in the Kathmandu Valley section). It is no coincidence that Patan's best- preserved *bahal,* like the "Golden Temple" and Uku Bahal, have managed to stay out of the government-operated Guthi Sansthan and are still supported by wealthy community members.

In most of Patan, however, it seems that people are waiting for someone else to step in and restore the town—and someone else *does* regularly step in, in the form of German, Austrian, and Japanese projects, and the U.S.-based Kathmandu Valley Preservation Trust. Meanwhile, the local resources that formerly supported temples and monuments are being channelled into new shops and elaborate multistory single-family homes. There is no shortage of wealth in Patan, as the growing number of upscale shops here shows—there are simply new ways to spend it.

(top left) image of Ganesh, Bhaktapur (Kerry Moran);
(top right) gilt repoussé images of bodhisattvas, Swayambhunath (Kerry Moran);
(bottom) masks for sale, Kathmandu (Kerry Moran)

(top) fresco of Bhairab painted on wall of Chandesvari Mandir (Kerry Moran);
(bottom left) Newari boy next to Buddha displayed during Gunla, Golden Temple, Patan (Kerry Moran);
(bottom right) brightly painted facade of Minnath Mandir, Patan (Kerry Moran)

Malla, whose combined rules spanned 1619-84. They renovated and rebuilt the small existing palace and added a number of the great monuments in the facing square.

A Walking Tour

Begin at the north end of the square, at the richly decorated three-story **Bhimsen Mandir,** dedicated to the legendary strongman of the Mahabharata. Bhimsen is the patron of merchants, and wealthy traders have endowed his temple with a faux-marble facade and silvered wooden struts. Older gilt-wood struts above these depict deities with their consorts.

> *As an ensemble, the Durbar Square in Patan probably remains the most picturesque collection of buildings that has been set up in so small a place by the piety and pride of Oriental man.*
> —PERCIVAL LANDON, 1928

Look for the pots, pans, and brooms nailed up under the eaves, customary offerings to assure the comfort of the dead in the afterworld. From the rooftop a long golden *pataka* streams down, a pathway for the gods to descend.

Beside it is **Vishwanath Mandir,** a classic Newar-style pagoda dedicated to Shiva and built in 1627. The building collapsed without warning in the 1990 monsoon, killing several people. It's since been reconstructed with much of its beautiful old carved sal wood intact, though the stone elephants flanking the steps are worse for the experience.

The adjoining **Krishna Mandir** is an exquisite example of stone architecture, a delicate, airy creation that defies its heavy material. Its form is an improbable yet inspired combination of a solid Indian *shikara* and airy Moghul-influenced colonnades. Scenes from the Mahabharata with explanations etched in Newari encircle the entire first story; the second-story pavilions are banded by friezes from the Ramayana. In front of the temple, a brilliantly executed large metal **Garuda** kneels in homage facing it. The shrine was built at the command of Siddhi Narsingh Malla following a dream he had of Krishna and Radha in union on this spot. A black stone image of Krishna with consorts Radha and Rukmini is installed on the second floor, which is closed to non-Hindus. Unlike most Durbar Square temples, which tend towards white elephant-hood, this is a very active shrine and the sound of devotional singing and bells often drifts down from the open gallery. During the August festival of Krishna Jayanti the entire temple is trimmed with glowing oil lamps, a pretty sight at night.

The rather stodgy **Chaar Narayan Mandir** beside it is the oldest surviving temple in the entire ensemble, completed in 1566. The main image, largely ignored today, is a four-faced Vishnu, each side depicting a different emanation. The bases of the struts are carved with imaginative couplings of women, men, and mythic beasts.

Beside it is a small fenced-in **park** with laundry drying atop its clipped hedges and two small cement shrines dating to 1972. The first encloses a black stone image of **Radha** with a flute-playing **Krishna,** unearthed by workers digging the foundations for the second shrine, which holds a large bronze **Buddha.**

A stone pillar supports a gilded image of **King Yoganendra Malla,** shaded by the spread hood of a royal cobra. Hands folded in prayer, he faces the impressive triple roofs of the palace's main **Taleju temple.** This 17th-century king is said to have renounced his throne in grief after the death of his son and wandered off to become an ascetic. Before he left he told his people that as long as the face of the statue was bright and untarnished and the small bird atop the cobra's head remained, they would know he was still alive. The bird is still there, and historians recount that for more than a century a mattress was laid out nightly in a palace room, with the window left open for the king's return.

The next large temple is the **Hari Shankara Mandir** jointly dedicated to Vishnu and Shiva, and similar in form to the Vishwanath Mandir. The large cast bronze **bell** beside it was erected in 1737, for use in Taleju's worship and also, state the *Chronicles,* "in order to terrify the king's enemies."

At the south end of the square is **Chyasin Dega,** an unusual eight-sided stone *shikara* built in the 18th century by the daughter of a king, in memory of the eight wives who followed her father's body onto the funeral pyre. *Shikara* generally have an odd number of facets, but this one is dedicated to Krishna, who favors octagonal temples. The stone steps are a favorite resting spot for porters waiting for work.

The area bordering the southern end of the square is **Mangal Bazaar,** an important and ancient trading center where gold brocade, rope, tea, and rayon dresses are sold in a hectic jumble forming the heart of Patan commerce. Cross the road and climb onto the rooftop of the corner building for an impressive overview of Durbar Square's stacked temple roofs, fringed with delicate bells, backed by the white massif of Langtang Himal.

The Old Royal Palace
Double back to explore the old Royal Palace along the eastern side of the square. It's much smaller than its Kathmandu counterpart, a simple row of quadrangles, but unlike the Kathmandu Durbar all of the courtyards are open to the public. After the fall of the Mallas, the Patan palace was ignored by the Shah rulers, and thus retains much of the exquisite detail of the 17th-century original.

The entrance to the southernmost compound, **Sundari Chowk,** is flanked by a trio of stone guardians: **Ganesh, Narasingha** disemboweling the helpless demon, and a red-smeared effigy representing **Hanuman** the Monkey King. A dignified-looking Indian *sadhu* has recently taken up residence alongside the Ganesh image, and makes a handsome living posing for tourist photographs. Over the entrance, which once held golden doors, is a dilapidated **gilt window** flanked by two of carved ivory.

Sundari Chowk is finely decorated with columned arcades, delicately ornamented windows, and screened galleries. In the middle is a sunken oval basin, the **Tulsi Hiti** or royal bath, circa 1646. Its walls are inset with niches holding finely sculpted images of deities, over 70 in all, a miniature museum. (More than a dozen more have been stolen, despite the presence of District Police Headquarters in a wing of this very courtyard.) Most of the statues are of stone, a few of gilt metal; all are multiarmed and tantric in their complexity, including the eight Ashta Matrika, the eight fierce Bhairab, and the eight Great Naga. A pair of sinuous stone *naga* embrace the rim, an unusual example of the *nag bandh* meant to avert evil influences.

The gilded conch-shaped water spout is another work of art, topped with gilt repoussé figures of Vishnu and Lakshmi atop Garuda. Directly above is a small stone replica of the Krishna Mandir standing in Durbar Square. An image of Hanuman kneels humbly between the bath and a huge stone slab said to have been the bed of the ascetic King Siddhi Narsingh Malla, who spent his nights in meditation and worship.

The next and central courtyard, **Mul Chowk,** is the palace's oldest section, dedicated almost entirely to the Malla patron goddess Taleju. In the center is a small gilded **shrine** to Yantaju, a sister-goddess of Taleju, a formerly important but now-forgotten patron of the Mallas. On the southern side is the **Taleju Mandir,** marked by a small and rather clumsy triple-roofed pagoda perched atop the main roof. The temple's lovely repoussé door is topped with a 1715 *torana,* now bearing nothing but gaping holes—the images were stolen in 1970. The door is flanked by two life-sized metal images of **Jamuna** atop a crocodile and **Ganga** on a tortoise. The graceful goddesses are deified representations of India's two holiest rivers; similar pairs guard the Taleju shrines of the palaces of Kathmandu and Bhaktapur, but they stand in courtyards which are closed to the public.

Two more **Taleju shrines** are visible from Mul Chowk: a triple octagonal pagoda with a gilt *shikara* as its spire, and a bit further back, the main temple, built in 1736 and reconstructed in 1934. Similar to the Kathmandu Durbar's main Taleju temple, the shrine is open to Hindus once a year, during the ninth day of Dasain. Behind this courtyard are the palace gardens or **Bandarkhal.** They are usually closed to the public, but try to peek over the rear wall; you may be able to inspect the interesting stone sculptures here on request.

The northern courtyard is called **Lumjyal Chowk** in Newari, after the magnificent golden window crowning the entrance, the local equivalent of Bhaktapur's famed Golden Gate. According to its inscription, this 19th-century addition was financed by the sale of old gilt images from the palace treasury. The glitttering door is framed by a braided band of *naga,* fanning out into a royal crown at the top; a multitude of deities appear in the golden windows above. The courtyard holds a small white plaster shrine dedicated to Narayan. The quadrangle was completely dismantled and reassembled during an Austrian-sponsored restoration program in the early '90s. When work is completed sometime in 1996, this wing is expected to again house the **Patan Museum** and its collection of some 850 bronze images, which includes a gilt-copper Malla throne, ritual masks of copper, and exquisite Buddhist bronzes. Step back a few paces and look upwards to glimpse one of the collection's pieces that has been placed on the palace roof to avert bad luck and lightning: a rare 17th-century gilt image of **Sanischar,** one of the nine planetary deities, wielding a trident.

On the north side of the palace is the ancient sunken water tap of **Manga Hiti.** Water spouts from three stone *makara,* while little girls struggle with water jugs nearly as big as themselves, as they have done for some 1,500 years.

NORTH OF DURBAR SQUARE

Old Patan is even smaller than old Kathmandu—about three square km, a 20-minute walk end to end. Taking Durbar Square as your starting point, you can wander in every direction, strolling through neighborhoods dedicated to metalworking or stonecarving, past ancient *bahal* and temples. Highlights are described below, but there are many more possibilities to discover on your own.

"Golden Temple"
Stay any longer than two minutes in Durbar Square and an eight-year-old tour guide is certain to volunteer to lead you to the "Golden Temple." With or without him, you should visit this lavish *bahal,* called **Hiranyavarna Mahavihara** in Sanskrit or **Kwa Bahal** in Newari. From Bhimsen Mandir, it's a five-minute walk west and then north down the main street. Duck through a lion-guarded stone archway (there's a big sign) and into the courtyard, which is a glittering example of extravagant metalwork.

A small gilt-roofed shrine stands in front of the gilt and silver-covered facade of the main temple, the whole surrounded by images of strange animals, donors, and mythic beasts. The detail work deserves several visits; there's simply too much to take in during a single outing.

Leather items like shoes and belts are prohibited in the courtyard; enter in stockinged feet if necessary to examine the facade and the sacred Buddha image close up. Look for a tiny three-cm-high frieze at eye level, showing scenes from the Buddha's life, beginning with his mother's auspicious dream of a white elephant and continuing on through his birth, his four fateful excursions in a chariot, and so on.

Unlike many of Patan's crumbling *bahal,* Kwa Bahal is still actively supported and is a good place to observe Newar Buddhist festivals and rituals like the symbolic initiation of young boys into the monkhood. The temple's wealth has accumulated since its founding in 1409, when merchants involved in the Tibet trade would donate a portion of their earnings to temples. The courtyard is ringed by balconies and shrines, including a lovely gilt image of the female bodhisattva **Tara.** Climb up the wooden staircase to inspect the **Tibetan Buddhist shrine** on the second floor, which has vivid wall frescoes, rafters painted with sacred mantras, and an immense prayer wheel.

Kumbheswar Mahadev
Just a few hundred meters further is the slender five-storied pagoda of Kumbheswar, Patan's oldest temple. This is the abode of the "Lord of the Water Pot," one of the many names of Shiva, who is said to dwell here during the six winter months (in the summer he migrates to Mt. Kailas in western Tibet). It is one of two five-storied temples in the Valley, the other being Bhaktapur's Nyatapola. Kumbheswar's graceful proportions are remarkable when you consider it was originally constructed in 1392 as a two-storied shrine; the upper three tiers were added in the 17th century. The stone sculptures scattered about the compound, some dating back to Licchavi times (and many of them, oddly, honoring Vishnu) mark this as an exceedingly ancient holy site. Look for the little shrine on the temple's north side, where mossy ancient images stand alongside a rivulet of clear water.

The big open tank behind is fed by a sacred spring said to be mystically linked by underground channel to the lake of Gosainkund, a pilgrimage site in the mountains north of Kathmandu. During the annual festival of Janaai Purnima (usually the August full moon), dancing white-clad *jhankri* perform at Kumbheswar, and worshippers wait in long lines to reverence an embossed silver sheath which has been placed over the temple's linga, then set in a special pavilion in the middle of the tank. Boys frolic in the suddenly sacred waters, splashing worshippers, while the temple attendents wear rain slickers.

In the opposite corner is a much-visited rectangular shrine with an entryway laden with bells. Inside, the goddess **Bagalamukhi** is embodied in a tiny image beneath an elaborate silver canopy of snakes. A manifestation of Durga, Bagalamukhi is placated as the sender of cholera, which still plagues the Valley in the rainy season. Outside the temple's main entrance is the old **Konti Hiti,** a busy neighborhood water tap set with some lovely sculptures.

Northern Stupa
Patan's northern Ashoka stupa is a few minutes past Kumbheswar. Go out the back gate by

the ancient pipal tree and follow the road for a few hundred meters to a quiet courtyard. The hemispherical stupa is the most impressive of the quartet, completely plastered over and painted a shining white. The compound provides good views of the rich fields surrounding Patan and the mountains behind.

Sankhamul Ghat
The road continues down through fields to the banks of the Bagmati. Its junction with the Manohara is the site of the ancient Sankhamul ghats, stone steps lined with peacefully crumbling courtyards, shrines, and temples. It's a lovely, unusual, and timeless site that's surprisingly clean compared to the Kathmandu or Bhaktapur ghats. The only monument of note is the brick *shikara* of **Jagat Narayan,** with some finely executed stonecarvings and terra-cotta *naga.* A new Japanese-built footbridge spans the river; the road continues up to the Everest Hotel in Baneshwar.

SOUTH PATAN

Mahabuddha
From the southern end of Durbar Square, walk east five minutes to a sunken water tap with four gilt spouts, the locally renowned **Sundhara.** Turn right here, passing many shops specializing in bronze images. Just before the end of the street a narrow passage leads through a plaster archway into a small courtyard, nearly filled by the unusual *shikara*-style temple of Mahabuddha. It's said to have been built by a 17th-century Nepali pilgrim who visited the great temple of Bodhgaya in India and returned home determined to reproduce it. His memory perhaps failed over the ensuing 36 years it took to complete it, because the resemblance is vague at best, but it's pleasing in its own right. The facade is decorated with terra-cotta relief plaques of tiny Buddhas and floral designs, creating an ornate monument whose overwhelming amount of dense detail can hardly be absorbed at such close range. Follow the signs up to the second floor of a courtyard building to get a better view of the soaring tower, crowned by a small gilded stupa. The edifice crumbled in the '34 quake and was reconstructed in less-than-accurate fashion: the leftover

Janaai Purnima being celebrated at Kumbheswar Mahadev Mandir, Patan

pieces were used to make a smaller shrine dedicated to the Buddha's mother, Maya Devi.

Mahabuddha is a fertile hunting ground for statues of Buddhist deities. Tibetans as well as tourists prowl the neighborhood's shops, looking for the perfect image. Ratna Jyoti Shakya's shop in the courtyard's southeast corner displays examples of the different casting stages, which he's happy to explain.

Uku Bahal

Continue to the end of the road and turn left into this ancient and rich complex dating back perhaps to Licchavi times. The *bahal's* written records go back to A.D. 1117, making it the oldest in Patan. Its supporters, the quarter's metalworkers, continue the traditional daily offerings of the "fivefold puja" in the morning and a lighted lamp in the evening. The large red-faced Buddha image inside is submerged beneath elaborate clothing and ornaments. Above the door are 10 images of Buddha's disciples and parents, and of various bodhisattvas. The stone *chaitya* in front of the shrine is in the Licchavi style, undated but built before the 11th century.

The courtyard houses a bizarre menagerie of mythic beasts wrought in metal. The sight of them leering from the evening gloom caused a British historian to call the temple "one of the weirdest sights in the whole of Nepal." Pause to admire the superb 13th-century wooden struts on the courtyard's rear wall, depicting graceful nymphs standing atop crouched dwarves.

Head west down the street in front of Uku Bahal, through the busy old metalworkers' quarter of **Thaina,** where the air rings with the constant tapping of hammers on metal. In less than 10 minutes you'll reach the main bazaar road and **Ibaha Bahi,** described below. Turn left and continue to the first large clearing on the right, where the Minnath temple stands behind a large sunken water tap.

The Bazaar

The road running south from Durbar Square is a crowded and interesting bazaar lane selling daily necessities and a variety of brassware: telescoping Tibetan horns, water pots, temple *gajur,* hanging oil lamps, shiny flowerpots, and embossed *puja* baskets. Head down a narrow lane on the right to explore the artisan's quarter of Jombahal where these items are made. The

resident deity is **Bishwakarma,** god of craftspeople, and the facade of his narrow little temple is plated entirely in hammered metal.

Back on the main road, stop at **Ibaha Bahi,** a 15th-century *bahal* that was on the verge of collapse before a Japanese organization stepped in. The courtyard is being reconstructed in its original form, incorporating as much as possible of the original materials.

Minnath Temple

Behind a sunken water tap on the left is a fenced-in temple compound containing a shrine dedicated to Minnath, an ancient local deity associated with the bodhisattva Padmapani Lokesvara. The woodwork of his richly decorated small pagoda is painted in bright candy-colored hues. The old buildings of the compound are being replaced by modern cement boxes. Behind the temple are two gigantic wooden shafts once used for Machhendra's chariot.

In appearance the red-faced Minnath image is nearly identical with the more famous Machhendranath who resides across the street. Minnath is usually described as Machhendranath's "son" or "daughter," or sometimes as "little" *(saano)* Machhendranath; actually his cult is even older. In the 7th century he and many other local deities were honored with yearly chariot processions. After the arrival of Machhendranath these celebrations were terminated in favor of the new god. But various omens indicated Minnath was displeased at losing his annual outing, and his smaller chariot now accompanies Machhendranath's every spring.

Raato Machhendranath

A footpath opposite the Minnath temple weaves between buildings into a large grassy compound. The 17th-century temple here is the abode of Patan's most beloved deity. Nepalis call him Raato or "Red" Machhendranath; to Newars he's Bunga Dyo, "God of Bungamati." A menagerie of bronze animals stands on pillars in front of the temple, while the carved struts depict different forms of Padmapani Lokesvara, the bodhisattva associated with Machhendranath. On the bottom portion are miniature scenes of sinners being tortured in hell—boiled in oil, beaten in a pestle, all rather appalling for a temple dedicated to a compassionate bodhisattva.

Machhendranath is really more a folk deity, as is immediately seen by his strange flat-faced idol, which is painted red, with staring eyes and large gilded ears, and draped with jewels, gold, and flower garlands. Some say the image is made of wood, others say it's clay-covered gold or even ground bone mixed with clay. From Dec.-June the deity dwells here; the other six months he's enshrined in his temple in Bunga-mati, a Newar village six km south of Patan.

Machhendranath's history is a lengthy and convoluted blend of Buddhism and folk beliefs. The local deity Bunga Dyo existed by the early 7th century. He eventually became associated with the bodhisattva Padmapani Lokesvara, whom Budhist legend describes as the creator of the world and the guru of all the Hindu gods. By the 18th century he had assumed another title: Machhendranath, "Lord of the Fishes," or "Master of the Senses," according to the mystic terminology of tantra.

Machhendranath has long been Patan's favorite deity: coins were struck in his name, and a royal edict proclaimed no building could top the towering spire of his chariot. His annual chariot procession, dating back at least to the 13th century, is the city's biggest festival and one of the most memorable displays in Nepal. It begins with a public bathing ceremony, usually in late April. The spirit of the god then retires to a sacred water pot, as members of a special caste refurbish and paint the image. Then the deity is loaded into his great wooden chariot and slowly pulled through the city, spending a night in each neighborhood, according to ancient schedule, so residents can worship him.

The chariot is laden with other deities as well: five Bhairabs are said to inhabit it, one in each wheel and one in the gilded image at the prow. Naga occupy the ropes and streamers hanging from the mast, and the king of the naga resides in the shaft. Usually the parts are reassembled yearly for the festival, but every 12 years the entire chariot is built anew. The great curved wooden shaft is carted off by a guthi to serve as a bench, and many from past years can still be seen in bahal and resthouses.

By late May the chariot reaches Jawalakhel, where it may wait several days for the astrologically perfect moment required for the Bhoto Jatra, the climax of the whole celebration. The

Patan Kumari and the king of Nepal attend this ceremony, usually held around the first week of June. Machhendranath's magical jeweled vest (bhoto), a doll-sized black shirt, is held up to the adoring crowd, and if all goes well rain begins to fall at this exact moment, signaling the beginning of the rice-planting season. As a sort of Newar rain god, Machhendranath is closely associated with the arrival of the monsoon, explaining his importance with Newar farmers. After this grand finale, the deity is hauled off to Bungamati on a palanquin for a six-month stay at his "family home."

Around Lagankhel
Back on the main road, the quaintness of the bazaar tapers off as you approach the crowded Lagankhel bus park. Continue south and visit the shaded temple of **Machhendrako Aamaa** or "Machhendra's Mother," followed by the **southern Ashoka stupa,** a spacious grassy mound from which boys fly kites.

A little further is the unappealing-sounding **Patan Industrial Estate,** where the manufacturing focus is on handicraft shops oriented to group tours. The biggest is **Cottage Crafts Exposition** located towards the back: an impressive array of goods arranged in spotless showrooms, with a workshop where you can observe weavers, woodcarvers, thangka painters, and other craftspeople.

WEST AND SOUTH PATAN

West of Durbar Square
A short walk west through Mangal Bazaar is **Hakha Bahal,** where some families still follow the old and peculiarly hard profession of retrieving precious metal from the sweepings of metal-working shops. Hakha Bahal once stood on Durbar Square, where Sundari Chowk is now located. When the palace expanded southward in the 17th century the entire building was dismantled and relocated in its present location.

Haka Bahal is the seat of Patan's main Kumari. She is chosen from the daughters of the Vajracharya or priestly caste affiliated with the complex, but unlike Kathmandu's Royal Kumari continues to live with her family, coming to Hakha Bahal for ritual ceremonies. Intrigue surrounds the Patan Kumari: the girl installed in the late '50s, who is now well into her 40s, has refused to relinquish the title despite being replaced a few years ago with a new four-year-old Kumari. She insists that the goddess Taleju remains within her, and continues to receive offerings and devotees at her family home in the neighborhood. Some local people believe she has more power than the young Kumari who is paraded outside during festivals.

Back at Durbar Square, the narrow little alley behind Krishna Mandir leads past a line of locally popular sweet shops, their timbers blackened with centuries of smoke, and into Patan's **vegetable market,** where vendors hawk their wares in an open courtyard. The road ends at **Pim Bahal,** a dilapidated ancient compound dominated by a mysterious-looking stupa. Its squinting eyes overlook a large algae-covered pond. On the northern bank is a temple to **Nasa Dyo,** the Newar patron deity of music and dance. Shiva dancing in the form of Nataraja appears on the *torana* above the entrance, but this is a later association: Nasa Dyo is a much older indigenous deity, represented by three series of holes in the shrine's facade, as he, like music, is formless. Chicken feathers are stuck on the temple walls as tokens of past sacrifices—blood offerings precede the major musical performances which local men carry out in the resthouse facing the temple.

The Zoo

Across from Jawalakhel Chowk, Nepal's one and only "Jew" (as it's locally pronounced) is essentially an animal prison. Frantic tigers and leopards pace their tiny cages, tormented by gawking villagers who bombard them with peanuts and poke them with umbrellas to make them "dance." Rhinos and monkeys live in slightly better conditions; it might be worth a stop on a slow day, if only to view the manually operated Ferris wheel. Admission is Rs10 for foreigners; the zoo is open daily 10 a.m.-5 p.m., 4 p.m. in winter.

Jawalakhel

South of the zoo is the neighborhood of Jawalakhel, known principally as the site of a Tibetan transit camp established in the early '60s to deal with the influx of refugees fleeing the Chinese. With Swiss assistance the Tibetans founded the carpet-weaving industry, and today handwoven woolen carpets rank among Nepal's main exports. The Tibetans are refugees no longer, but have become prosperous and well-integrated members of society, though they cling to the hope that one day they will be able to return to Tibet.

Jawalakhel's Tibetan atmosphere is minor compared to Boudhanath's. The only real reason to visit is carpet shopping. Start at the **Tibetan Handicraft Center,** where you can observe the entire process from wool carding through spinning, dyeing, and weaving in the cavernous main hall. Here the fixed-price sales showroom gives an indication of prices; for better deals explore the dozens of shops lining the road. See "Crafts" in the On the Road chapter for more details on buying carpets.

PRACTICALITIES

Accommodations

Facilities in the very few inexpensive lodges in central Patan are nothing special, but the chance to stay in the old town is worth some inconvenience. Mid-range to expensive places are clustered in the newer, blander western suburbs. The following accommodations are in order of increasing cost.

The seldom-used **Mahendra Youth Hostel,** tel. (1) 521-023, is just south of Jawalakhel Chowk. A bunk bed in a bleak crowded dormitory is Rs25; beds in an equally gloomy four-bed room are Rs50. The number of staff in this IYHF affiliate usually exceeds the number of guests.

Lodges in the old town open and close; if the places listed below are full or unappealing you might find a room by enquiring at the tourist cafes around Durbar Square. **Cafe de Patan** maintains six guest rooms with common bath above the restaurant; rates are Rs300 s or d. Next door, the **Pizza Palace Restaurant** has a few noisy rooms with sink for Rs200 s, Rs300 d. In Man Bhawan, on the road between Lagankhel and Jawalakhel Chowk, is the gloomy **Hotel Laxmi,** tel. (1) 523-968; dilapidated rooms are Rs200 s, Rs260 d. The **Hong Kong Guesthouse,** tel. (1) 523-537, next door is a better bet, with rooms for Rs125 s, Rs250 d.

Aloha Inn, tel. (1) 522-796, near Jawalakhel Chowk is a decent two-star hotel with rooms for US$26 s, US$36 d.

For more character, try **Bakena Batika,** tel. (1) 523-998, in far southern Jawalakhel on the Ring Road. It's isolated but peaceful, with a beautiful garden and traditional Nepali decor in its rooms, which are US$30 s, US$35 d.

Summit Hotel, tel. (1) 521-810, fax (1) 523-737, is set atop a hill in Kopundol Heights, with stunning views of Kathmandu city and the mountains. Despite its out-of-the-way location it's very popular for its traditional brick-and-wood architecture and lovely gardens (including a small swimming pool). Rooms in the garden wing are US$55 s, US$70 d; those in the new wing, facing the Himalaya, are US$10 more. Its budget wing, **Holland House,** has nine rooms with common bath at US$20 s, US$25 d. Next door is **Hotel Greenwich Village,** tel. (1) 521-780, a small and very personal place with unique architecture and similarly good views. Rooms are US$60 s, US$70 d.

Hotel Narayani, tel. (1) 521-711, in Pulchowk is a conveniently located four-star place, but lacks the ambience of the Summit. Rooms are US$70 s, US$85 d; there's also a swimming pool.

Top of the line is the Japanese-run **Hotel Himalaya,** tel. (1) 523-900, fax (1) 523-909, in Kopundol. This Japanese-managed place has 100 spotless a/c rooms (some featuring stunning Himalayan views), a big garden with a swimming pool, and tennis courts. Rates are US$105 s, US$115 d.

Food

With Kathmandu so close by, Patan has developed few restaurants of its own. Tourist cafes around Durbar Square serve the usual mediocre Indian/Chinese/pseudo-Continental fare, though they tend to fill up at lunchtime. **Cafe Pagode** abuts a wall of the old palace; its pretty little courtyard features old woodwork and a miniature shrine, while the rooftop patio facing the Bhimsen Temple is perennially full. **Cafe de Temple** nearby is slightly less charming but also has rooftop seating. Great head-on views of Durbar Square can be had from **The Third World,** where the Western food is above average. There's a glassed-in dining room and a rooftop patio from where you can admire the pigeons flitting about Krishna Mandir a stone's throw away.

A classic view of the stacked-roof temples lined up in front of the Himalaya can be had from the tall **Taleju Restaurant** south of Durbar Square. A little west of Mangal Bazaar in a quiet garden courtyard is the old **Cafe de Patan,** which plays tranquilizing New Age music. Down the road in the opposite direction is the basic **Patan View Restaurant** with yet another rooftop patio, and the definitively named **Cheap Best Restaurant.**

Local eateries include *momo* shops around Patan Dhoka and any number of places along the Kopundol-Phulchowk road. The **Downtown Restaurant** in Phulchowk has a good selection of cheap Chinese and Indian food. The **German Bakery** at Jawalakhel Chowk serves brewed coffee, cakes, and sandwiches; across the street is the **Bakery Cafe,** an upscale fastfood offshoot of Nanglo's, serving bad pizza, and good *momo* and fried chicken.

For classier dining try the **Base Camp Coffeeshop** in the Hotel Himalaya, which is very proper and still reasonably priced, and has wonderful mountain views. **Bakena Batika** at the extreme south end of Jawalakhel is an upscale tourist place with jazzed-up Nepali food served in a pretty garden. A very unusual find is **Three Sisters Italian Restaurant,** across from the Hotel Narayani, with innovative appetizers, authentic pizza and pasta, and wine by the glass. Finally, if you're on your way back to Kathmandu you might stop at the excellent Indian **Mughal Mahal,** near the Bluebird Supermarket in Thapathali.

Shopping

Patan is a good place to look for metalwork. There's still a lot of schlok, and the best Kathmandu shops buy direct from Patan artists and thus deplete the local market of its finest pieces, but Patan's narrow streets have their own brand of charm. Visit the row of shops on the street north of Durbar Square, and walk over to Mahabuddha. See "Art" in the On the Road chapter for tips on statue buying.

The old Tibetan Camp described above in Jawalakhel has the city's largest and most reasonably priced selection of new Tibetan carpets and is also a good place to hunt for rare old ones. For naive paintings of the Valley, visit the **B.B. Thapa Gallery** in Ekantakuna, Jawalakhel.

Visit the handicraft outlets at **Patan Industrial Estate** (described above) for *thangka,* woodcarvings, metalwork, and embroideries.

The Kopundol neighborhood is the place to shop for housewares; many shops here cater to the large local community of foreign-aid workers. Most interesting are the not-for-profit shops selling reasonably priced handicrafts made by low-income women and the handicapped. A single visit could take care of all your souvenir and gift needs. Items include handmade paper, Maithili paintings, block-printed and handwoven material, quilted cushion covers, clothing, pottery, wooden toys, and excellent woolen sweaters. The best shops are **Dhukuti** and **Hastakala;**

Mahaguthi runs a close third. Other recommended shops (though these are not nonprofit outlets) include **Koseli,** with an exceptionally large selection, including colorful Tharu baskets; and **Dhaka Weaves,** which stocks traditional cloth in an array of modern colors. **Himalayan Leather Handicrafts** east of Jawalakhel Chowk sells leather goods and batiks made through the Nepal Leprosy Trust. Finally, **Patan Handicraft Cooperative Center** is hidden away in a courtyard down the side street immediately west of Cafe de Patan. Craftspeople work in the open courtyard, and the showroom stocks some unusual items not duplicated in other handicrafts stores.

BHAKTAPUR

Once the capital of the entire Valley, Bhaktapur is now the most isolated and unchanged of the three former kingdoms. Its peaceful yet busy streets preserve nearly intact the medieval atmosphere of bygone days. Bhaktapur is one of Nepal's greatest treasures, but few tourists spend more than an afternoon touring its main squares. This is a pity, because more than any other place it embodies the serene essence of a Newar city. A stay here will reassure you of the possibility of a sane urban life, and provide a better picture of how the rural 80% of Nepal lives. Apart from the art galleries and restored temples and shopping there's the attraction of any number of walks through the peaceful surrounding countryside. Not many visitors choose to overnight here, partly because accommodations are simple and limited, but a few days in Bhaktapur offers the chance to immerse yourself in traditional life.

Tradition and the Newars
Stretched along a ridge above the sacred Hanumante River 14 km east of Kathmandu, Bhaktapur grew from a collection of villages strung along the old Tibet trade route. The overview of town from the Arniko Rajmarg is worth seeking out: huddled red-tiled roofs are punctuated by the soaring spire of the five-story Nyatapola, set against the movie-set backdrop of the Himalaya and surrounded by lush fields.

Bhaktapur is adamantly rural at heart, an agri-

cultural city. Over half of its residents are farmers, among the country's best. From the rich black soil they coax forth giant cauliflowers and rice yields which are the highest in Nepal. Bhaktapur's deep roots in the land are apparent in its people: Jyapu women in red-bordered black saris pleated in front and raised high in back to reveal blue-tatooed calves; farmers with double baskets of giant radishes suspended from their shoulder poles; work crews of laughing girls heading out to the fields with hoes for a day of backbreaking labor.

Until 1966, when the Chinese-built road linked Bhaktapur to Kathmandu, it was a dusty 14-km walk to the capital. Bhaktapur has remained a world apart, economically self-sufficient and strongly independent. A village in many ways, it maintains a rich cultural and religious life rooted in Newar traditions. A 1974 survey found only 50 non-Newars in the entire town. Bhaktapurians speak a dialect of Newari distinct from Kathmandu's, and even today many older people don't understand Nepali—living in a pure Newar society, they don't need to. Bhaktapur has always been a more Hindu city than mixed Kathmandu or Buddhist Patan; its name translates as "City of Devotees," and its resolutely Hindu character reinforces its conservatism.

Jubilant festival days are celebrated by groups of Jyapu men banging *dhimey,* the cylindrical drums played with cymbals in a local tradition. Major celebrations include Gai Jatra, at its

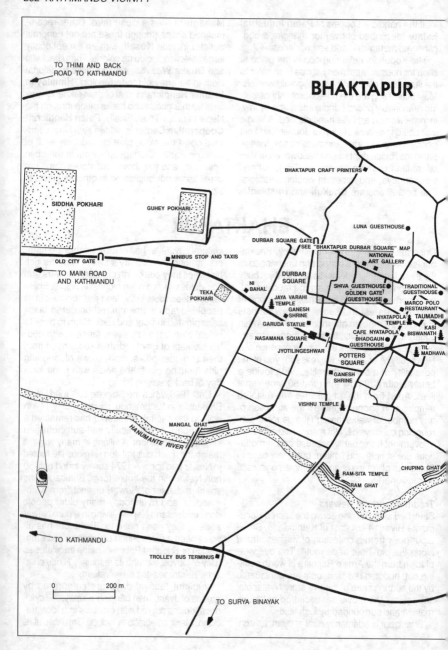

BHAKTAPUR

TO THIMI AND BACK ROAD TO KATHMANDU

SIDDHA POKHARI

GUHEY POKHARI

BHAKTAPUR CRAFT PRINTERS

LUNA GUESTHOUSE

DURBAR SQUARE GATE

SEE "BHAKTAPUR DURBAR SQUARE" MAP

OLD CITY GATE

TO MAIN ROAD AND KATHMANDU

MINIBUS STOP AND TAXIS

NATIONAL ART GALLERY

DURBAR SQUARE

TEKA POKHARI

NI BAHAL

TRADITIONAL GUESTHOUSE

SHIVA GUESTHOUSE
GOLDEN GATE GUESTHOUSE

MARCO POLO RESTAURANT

JAYA VARAHI TEMPLE
GANESH SHRINE

NYATAPOLA TEMPLE

TAUMADHI

GARUDA STATUE

KASI BISWANATH

CAFE NYATAPOLA

NASAMANA SQUARE

BHADGAUN GUESTHOUSE

TIL MADHAVA

JYOTILINGESHWAR

POTTERS SQUARE

GANESH SHRINE

VISHNU TEMPLE

HANUMANTE RIVER

MANGAL GHAT

RAM-SITA TEMPLE

CHUPING GHAT

RAM GHAT

TO KATHMANDU

TROLLEY BUS TERMINUS

0   200 m

TO SURYA BINAYAK

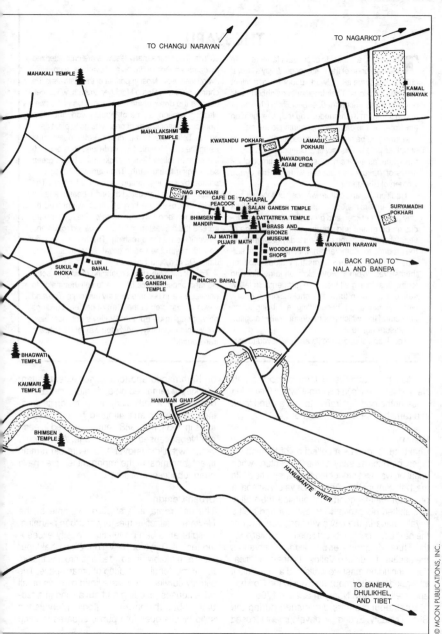

THE JYAPU

The Jyapu, a subcaste of peasant farmers, form the backbone of the Kathmandu Valley's Newar culture and serve as stalwart supporters of ancient religious traditions. Their traditional neighborhoods remain largely unchanged, especially in Bhaktapur and in southern Kathmandu. You may see them on the streets in the early dawn, heading to the market with swinging baskets of produce suspended from shoulder poles. This *nol* is a distinctive feature of the Jyapu, as are the homespun red-trimmed black skirts or *hakuwa patasi* still worn by the Jyapu women of Bhaktapur.

Traditional Jyapu culture was completely self-sufficient. Farmers mined deposits of phosphatic black clay *(ko)* for fertilizer, and grew all their own food, focusing on grains and an unusually wide range of vegetables (the Jyapu of Thimi today grow much of the produce for Kathmandu). Families sold the surplus to obtain the few items they didn't produce themselves. Women wove cloth on large clacking looms, fashioning all their own garments. In fallow seasons the men turned to brickmaking, pottery, woodcarving, and homebuilding, exhibiting an architectural flair which has made the Valley a cultural treasure-house.

The Jyapu support a festival cycle keyed to agri-culture. The year's many festivals are characterized by *dhimey* bands of drums and cymbals, a uniquely Jyapu institution. Most important of the festivals is the chariot-pulling of Raato Machhendranath, which celebrates the onset of the monsoon. This is the rice-planting season, a time of intense work and play. Collective associations of peasants go to plant each other's fields, the men turning over the heavy mud using the short-handled *ko,* while long lines of bending women follow behind sticking the bright green seedlings into the earth. The hard work is accompanied by singing, flirting, and mud-flinging. The ripened grain is harvested by hand, beaten against rocks to loosen the kernels, then winnowed on woven bamboo trays or *nanglo.* Clever farmers spread the harvested grain along paved roads and let vehicles do the threshing. The harvest season concides with the year's greatest festivals: Indra Jatra, Dasain, and Tihar.

Traditional Jyapu life is changing rapidly, as soaring land prices induce farmers to sell their fields to developers and become wealthy overnight. The land yields its last crop in the form of cement buildings now springing up from the Valley's rich ricefields. Slowly but inevitably, the Jyapu way of life is being transformed.

rowdiest here, and Bisket Jatra, coinciding with Nepali New Year's in mid-April, when the gilded mask of the god Bhairab is towed around town in a ramshackle wooden chariot.

History

Bhaktapur began as a collection of farming villages, perhaps as early as the 3rd century, when irrigation was first brought to the Valley's fields. In the 12th century King Ananda Deva of Banepa, a powerful mini-kingdom just outside the Valley rim, shifted his capital to Bhaktapur and built a royal palace in the city's western quarter. For the next three centuries, until the fragmentation of the Three Kingdoms era, Bhaktapur served as the capital of a unified Valley. Its heavy fortifications, including massive walls and a moat, did it little good after its troops sold out to the Gorkhas and it fell to Prithvi Narayan Shah in 1768.

Bhaktapur's status diminished during the Shah Dynasty. Economic development focused on Kathmandu and to a lesser extent Patan: Bhaktapur remained an agricultural city. Earthquakes took a particularly heavy toll on its buildings, destroying an estimated 70% of its structures in 1934; the 1988 tremor centered in eastern Nepal caused more damage. As a result, very few buildings over 170 years old remain intact, and most of the important temples have been rebuilt several times.

Urban Design

The city remains a superb example of the Newars' instinctive mastery of urban planning. Despite an urban population density exceeding that of Tokyo or New York City, Bhaktapur feels remarkably uncrowded and orderly, thanks to the masterful structuring of urban space. The slightly curving streets are lined by rows of tall brick houses receding and advancing in a regular, subtle rhythm. At strategic intervals the solid blocks open into public squares forming the center of each *tol* or neighborhood. Here are the local temples (usually to Ganesh and Vishnu), resthouses where men sit and talk, and wells or sunken taps where women fetch water and wash clothes. Old Bhaktapur boasted an elaborate drainage system to funnel rainwater into outlying fields, as well as a nine-km canal dug in the 17th century to supply fresh water to its tanks and ponds. This Raj Kulo collapsed in the 1934 quake, thus the present repulsive state of the large *pokhari,* formerly used for washing, swimming, watering livestock, and emergency firefighting.

The public squares are the focus of Bhaktapur life. Here people dry and thresh grain, pound pungent chili peppers in wooden pestles, shape clay pots, spin thread and weave cloth, draw water, bathe, massage their babies, and sit in the sun to chat with their family and neighbors. Living quarters are dark and cramped, but townsfolk are rich in public space. Different squares are decorated with unexpected touches: skeins of indigo yarn hung up to dry; acres of black pottery laid out in geometric patterns; or mountains of shiny red chili peppers spread out in the warm sun, filling the air with their spicy fragrance.

Bhaktapur Development Project

Much credit for the city's relatively pristine condition goes to the Bhaktapur Development Project (BDP), a 15-year German-sponsored effort which attempted to preserve Bhaktapur's unique atmosphere while improving the local quality of life. Roads were paved with red brick instead of asphalt; water and sewer lines were laid; storm gutters and a sewage treatment plant built; schools and crafts cooperatives created. Most visible are the dozens of crumbling temples and valuable old buildings renovated, in many cases saved from complete destruction. It's difficult to appreciate the magnitude of BDP's efforts until you view old photos of the decrepit old temples, *patis,* and *maths* that were given a new lease on life—often to the bafflement of residents, who saw nothing special in their old-fashioned town. Restoration efforts are especially apparent in the older, eastern portion of the city around Tachapal Tol where the BDP was headquartered. The project culminated in a detailed plan for future development, hopefully ensuring the city will retain its unique character.

GETTING THERE

Bhaktapur lies 14 km from Kathmandu, just north of the Chinese-built Arniko Rajmarg, the highway to Tibet. It's a 45-minute bike ride from Thamel along the Ring Road and down the truck-clogged, factory-lined highway. The road is in especially sad shape after over-enthusiastic lopping crews killed many of the tall poplar trees that once shaded it. If the traffic is intolerable, which it usually is on weekdays, turn left after the airport and take the back road through Thimi, which passes by rich farmland and some very active brick factories.

Busing here is, for once, a viable option: the **electric trolley bus** to Bhaktapur is seldom crowded and fairly efficient. Buses depart Tripureshwar regularly on the 45-minute trip. From the terminus south of Bhaktapur it's a 15-minute walk across the Hanumante River at Ram Ghat and through Potters' Square into Taumadhi Tol. Regular buses from the Kathmandu city bus park (not recommended) end at the minibus park, across from Guhey Pokhari on Bhaktapur's western fringes. Otherwise, negotiate for a taxi from Kathmandu; one-way to Bhaktapur shouldn't be more than Rs200. Taxis for the return trip can be found at the entrance to Durbar Square and around the minibus park.

Entering Town

Coming by cycle, the Bhaktapur turnoff is just after the Hanumante Bridge. At the crossroads, take the right-hand fork up the pine-forested hill of **Sallaghari,** a lovely picnic site with two old shrines to Saraswati and Ganesh which are visited by newlyweds. Past the army barracks, where you just might hear a soldier practicing the bagpipes, is the big open field of the local **Tundikhel,** and beyond it, **Siddha Pokhari,** an enormous walled-in 12th-century pond, now filthy and neglected. The legend that a giant serpent dwells in its depths may explain a general reluctance to clean it. Look in the distance for a glimpse of the hilltop temple of Changu Narayan, a lovely day walk from Bhaktapur.

Past Siddha Pokhari the road forks. If you're in a hurry, the left-hand road leads past **Guhey Pokhari,** where the minibuses stop, and continues east into Durbar Square. For a more

*Bhaktapur
Durbar Square*

leisurely introduction to the town, take the right-hand lane, which passes through an old plaster gate that's the last remnant of the city walls. This is the old commercial route, and it meanders past elaborately decorated houses and a few impressive temples, including a beautifully decorated **Jaya Varahi Temple** to the boar-headed goddess Varahi. The road continues further (Potters' Square is only a short detour south of it) into Taumadhi Tol; from here it's easy to double back into Durbar Square.

Bhaktapur municipality currently charges non-Indian tourists Rs50 to enter the city; the money is supposed to go into a monument maintenance and renovation fund. Collection stands are set up at the entrance to Durbar Square and at Babarcho Tol behind the minibus park at the old city gate.

DURBAR SQUARE

Once, visitors described Bhaktapur's Durbar Square as "the most entrancingly picturesque city scene in Nepal." The 1934 earthquake shattered its glory, leaving gaping holes in the architectural composition. Though some structures have been rebuilt, over a quarter of the original total is gone, and the square seems curiously vacant compared to the bustling plazas of Patan and Kathmandu. Partly due to the fact the palace was moved here from the center of town only in the 15th century, the rela-

tively new location has never quite been incorporated into daily or ritual life. Still, its bricked expanses are evocative on a foggy morning, when shawl-shrouded locals drift past and a distant temple pinnacle glints out of the mist. Try to imagine it holding the elaborate set built for Bernardo Bertolucci's film *The Little Buddha,* filmed here in 1992. The square held a replica of Buddha Keanu Reeves's royal palace, providing the most excitement, and hard cash, the town has had in centuries.

The Palace and Art Gallery

The cluster of **minor temples** to the right immediately upon entering Durbar Square are substitute shrines for four great Indian pilgrimage sites, conveniently provided by a thoughtful king for the spiritual benefit of his subjects. The most notable is the largest, the finely carved **Bansi Narayan Mandir** dedicated to Vishnu.

The square's northern side is dominated by the **old royal palace,** most of which dates back 300-400 years. It was said to have 99 courtyards; today there are only six, most of them closed to the public. On the left, fearsome stone sculptures of **Durga** and **Bhairab** flank the gates of what was once a pleasure pavilion for Malla queens, now no more than a grassy lot. The next courtyard is occupied by a police station.

Then comes the **National Art Gallery,** housed in a renovated wing of the old palace. This museum has over 200 paintings from the 14th-20th centuries, allowing you to compare styles and colors. Interesting exhibits include a *Yoga Purusha* depicting the chakras of the human body (now widely copied in Thamel *thangka* shops), a 15th-century painted leather handbag, and a few old *thankga,* worn nearly to shreds but with superb, muted colors. Recently restored rare frescoes are displayed in what used to be Bhupatindra Malla's private quarters. The museum is open daily 10:30 a.m.-4:30 p.m. except Tuesday, closing an hour earlier on Friday. Admission is Rs5, and it's another Rs10 to bring in a camera.

Further down a golden image of **King Bhupatindra Malla** kneels atop a pillar, dressed in the turban and court dress of the Malla kings, sword and shield by his side. Dignified and grave, his is perhaps the most beautiful of the Valley's three royal portraits. Bhupatindra's statue was made in imitation of the others, and he was forced to ask the Kathmandu ruler for help in raising the pillar. The king obligingly sent a team of workers along, with secret instructions to break the pillar. They obeyed, but then quickly repaired their mistake, pleasing both kings and earning a handsome reward from each.

Golden Gate and Mul Chowk
The statue faces the Golden Gate of Bhaktapur, perhaps the most famous piece of art in all Nepal. Much of the credit for this goes to Percy Brown, who in his 1912 book raved on for pages about it. Percival Landon called it "perhaps the

BHAKTAPUR DURBAR SQUARE

TO LUNA GUESTHOUSE

TO TRADITIONAL GUESTHOUSE AND MAIN BAZAAR

DURBAR SQUARE GATE

POLICE OFFICE

NATIONAL ART GALLERY

PUBLIC TOILET

SHIVA GUESTHOUSE

GOLDEN GATE GUESTHOUSE

TO POTTERS SQUARE

TO TAUMADHI TOL

0   25m

1. Jagannath temple
2. Rameshwar temple
3. Kedernath temple
4. Bansi Narayan Mandir (Badrinath)
5. Bhairab statue
6. Durga statue
7. sunken fountain
8. Shiva *shikara*
9. Kumari Chowk
10. Mul Chowk
11. Taleju temples
12. Bhairab Chowk
13. sunken royal bath
14. Shiva temple
15. Vatasaladevi temple
16. stone lions
17. Siddhi Lakshmi *shikara*
18. Chyasalin Mandap
19. Taleju bell
20. "Golden Gate"
21. Palace of 55 Windows
22. King Bhupatindra Malla's pillar
23. Vatasaladevi *shikara*
24. water tap
25. Pashupatinath temple

most exquisitely designed and finished piece of gilded metalwork in all of Asia." It is an incredibly extravagant monument, set up in 1753 by Jaya Ranjit Malla to honor the goddess Taleju, whose richly decorated temple lies in the palace's central courtyard. Repoussé sculptures of deities are set in the doorjambs, and sea serpents swirl about an image of Taleju set in the middle of the *torana*. The workmanship is superb, but what astounds is the sheer quantity of gold lavished on the gate—just one example of the wealth of the Valley's kings.

Go through the Golden Gate and around the corner to the entrance of Mul Chowk, the palace's central and oldest courtyard, dedicated to Taleju. Here the three last Malla rulers huddled together during the siege of Bhaktapur, until Gorkhali soldiers broke down the golden doors and found them, finally united in defeat. Mul Chowk and the smaller **Kumari Chowk** behind are said to be the most beautiful structures in the Valley, but both are closed to non-Hindus. From the doorway you can glimpse golden lizards, elephants, dragons, and snakes swarming over the temple roof ahead. The main temple to the left is hidden from view, but if you stretch you can glimpse one of the statues of Ganga and Jamuna, even finer than those in the Patan Durbar. Beside the outer door are two huge copper drums dedicated to the goddess, formerly beaten daily in worship.

In the northeast corner of the outer yard a small wooden door leads to a courtyard enclosing the **bathing pool** of Malla kings. Once it was surrounded by elegant buildings; statues filled the empty niches, and oil lamps illuminated the gilded metalwork. The surrounding buildings have crumbled and the fine statues have disappeared; about all that remains is the beautifully worked water spout, bursting with sea serpents and *naga*. A golden *naga* is coiled above the tap, and another rises from a column in the middle of the pool. The water is said to be piped in from the hills 15 km away.

Palace of 55 Windows

Back out in the square, the famed Palace of 55 Windows stretches off to the east, built in 1697 by Bhupatindra Malla. In one window he enshrined a single pane of glass brought from India as "an object of wonder for the people."

The wing was completely rebuilt after the 1934 earthquake, with some readjustments: only 53 windows remain today. Nothing is left of the extensive palace or the great square to the east except a vast open plaza marked by a few sad reminders—a pair of stone lions standing guard over nothing, and the massive platform of a once-great Shiva temple, now crowned by a dumpy white plaster shrine.

The balance and harmony of this part of the square was greatly improved in 1990 by the resurrection of **Chyasalin Mandap,** an 18th-century octagonal pavilion that had collapsed in the earthquake. It was rebuilt by local craftspeople with support from Germany. Restoration was no easy feat. The original carved columns had to be retrieved from resthouses where they'd been installed. Everything else, including the entire upper story, was reconstructed from scratch, using a set of old etchings as guidelines. Some carvings are a startling match of old and new, but if close up the building jars (the steel reinforcements used to make it earthquake-proof were deliberately left exposed, a technique known as "dynamic restoration"), from a distance it adds a vital element to the square. The top floor makes a great people-watching viewpoint, just as it was for 18th-century nobles—only the modern loiterers are now likely to be long-haired, leather-jacketed youths.

Pashupati Temple

This heavy-roofed pagoda was built by King Yaksha Malla in the 15th century as a convenient substitute for the original Pashupatinath he was in the habit of visiting daily—a 12-km roundtrip. The struts depict manifestations of Shiva and characters from the Ramayana, with smaller erotic scenes below. Inside is a large black stone linga carved with four faces of Shiva, said to be a replica of Pashupati's.

The narrow street behind here funnels tourists down to the next great square, Taumadhi. Predictably, it's crammed solid with souvenir shops and street vendors: from the balcony of the nearby Marco Polo Restaurant, you can watch sales attacks being perpetrated on the tourists herded down through here by their guides. A more interesting detour would be to first visit Potters' Square, described below, then walk over to Taumadhi Tol. Head down the narrow street behind the prominently labeled "Tourist Toilet" on the south side of Durbar Square. Note the carved stone lotuses set in the ground in front of the entrance to every house, a symbol of the god Kumar which is worshipped every morning.

TAUMADHI TOL

This plaza is more important than Durbar Square to local people, more closely woven into daily life and festivals. It marks the center of the "new" town, the western portion of Bhaktapur which has developed since the 12th century.

Nyatapola Temple

Taumadhi is dominated by the five-roofed Nyatapola, at 30 meters the tallest temple in Nepal, so perfectly balanced it has survived numerous quakes since its construction in 1702. Set atop a stepped five-story plinth mirroring its receding roofs, it's decorated with beautiful carvings beneath layers of bright paint. The 108 struts depict various deities, including Durga in her different forms. The main stairway is guarded by protective images: first the beefy wrestlers Jai and Patta Malla, said to possess the strength of 10 men; then pairs of elephants, lions, griffons, and minor goddesses, each 10 times stronger than the preceding pair. These guardians protect a hidden tantric goddess—exactly which one is open to dispute, as the temple is closed to all but its high priests, who worship there at night. Some call her Siddhi Lakshmi, others Bhairabi or Durga, while some say there is no image at all inside, only the goddess in spirit form.

Kasi Biswanath

This powerful goddess has an intimate relationship with the ferocious Bhairab inhabiting the large temple to the east. The Kasi Biswanath is a finely proportioned rectangular pagoda, with three roofs (the topmost one gilded), elaborately carved struts, and a rich gilt-inlaid facade. Bhupatindra Malla had this deity brought from Benares and installed for the protection of the kingdom. The Bhairab proved so troublesome priests suggested placing the tantric goddess of the Nyatapola nearby to counterbalance him—and indeed the unruly deity was said to calm down after the secret goddess arrived on the scene.

The Bhairab mask inside is worshipped unseen; offerings are shoved through a small niche cut in the temple facade. Every spring his gilded mask is paraded about town in the rowdy, joyous chariot procession of Bisket Jatra. The front facade of the temple is actually the rear wall: the proper entrance is behind, via a small shrine to **Betal,** Bhairab's companion and *vahana* or vehicle. This malignant godling accompanies Bhairab on his yearly jaunt, mounted on the prow of the great chariot. Betal is worshipped for a brief half-hour period during the festival, then is strapped face-down to the rafters of his temple for the remainder of the year, for he's said to be a pesky spirit overly fond of causing trouble.

Cafe Nyatapola

This tourist restaurant in the middle of the square was renovated by the Bhaktapur Development Project in 1978 from a crumbling old resthouse formerly used to store the dismantled pieces of the Bisket Jatra chariot. The menu is limited and relatively expensive, but the chance to eat french fries in a pagoda is too good to pass up, and views from the upper story are fascinating. Periodically a tour group sweeps in with video cameras whirring, surrounded by vendors thrusting forth necklaces, peacock-feather fans, and Tiger Balm. Bhaktapur's salespeople are the most tenacious of all the three cities, but they concentrate on tour groups—one good reason to visit the town on your own.

Til Madhava Narayan

Taumadhi is flanked by some lovely old houses, their ground floors occupied by souvenir shops. Behind the south side facade is the compound of Til Madhava Narayan, a very important Vishnu temple founded in 1080. Vishnu's implements stand atop ancient stone pillars in the courtyard. The metal *torana* depicts a dancing Shiva atop his bull, but inside is enshrined an ancient and worn image of a standing Vishnu, adorned with a silver necklace. Its name refers to a legend that it was discovered buried in a merchant's heap of sesame seeds *(til),* which remained miraculously undiminished despite brisk sales. Once a year the idol is massaged with ghee and worshipped with offerings of sesame sweets in memory of this event. On certain auspicious dates the quiet courtyard is the center of great pageantry, as local girls dressed in dazzling finery take part in the *ihi* ceremony wedding them to the deity, a unique Newar custom.

POTTERS' SQUARE

Bolachha Tol is the neighborhood of the potter caste, called simply "Potters' Square," after the hundreds of vessels of all shapes and sizes set out to dry here. It is located west of Taumadhi on the main road. In winter months local farmers turn to pottery making, and entire families work in the open, producing tiny disposable saucers for *raksi,* enormous rice and water urns, yoghurt bowls, flowerpots, and water jugs, plus more whimsical items for tourists—small animals, candlesticks, ashtrays, and the like. Men and boys sit amid a sea of pots, skillfully sculpting the cones of wet black clay into vessels of all sizes. Many have abandoned their heavy wooden wheels for old truck tires fitted with a crossbar, lighter and easier to spin.

The items are set out in the sun to dry, and women thump the bottoms of vessels flat with blunt sticks or polish dried pots with a smooth stone, etching them with designs and dipping them in liquid clay to give them a red finish. The final step is firing in ingenious temporary kilns of heaped straw where temperatures can reach 700°C. German foreign aid (Bhaktapur is distinctly German territory) has financed a Ceramics Promotion Project which is teaching new techniques, including glazing, and is trying to expand the market for this traditional craft.

Bolachha Tol has its own assortment of deities, including a little 17th-century temple to **Ganesh** donated by a long-ago potter, its small gilt image brightly polished from constant worship. Five minutes' walk south is **Ram Ghat** on the Hanumante River, and an interesting temple to **Rama-Sita.** Returning, take the same road up to join a main lane that soon enters Taumadhi.

THE MAIN BAZAAR

The 10-minute stroll from Taumadhi to Tachapal runs through the city's main bazaar, following the path of the old trade route. It showcases Bhaktapur's thriving local economy, with shops selling daily necessities, tea, and sweets, interspersed with temples and water taps. Look for the small **Golmadhi Ganesh temple** halfway along its length, a typical example of Bhaktapur's many tiny Ganesh shrines, one in each *tol,* which are worshipped daily for good fortune.

This brick-paved winding street and the interesting side lanes and courtyards branching off it reveal the heart of Bhaktapur. Life spills out onto the street in a public display, as women pound laundry, children play, and old men share a hookah in a shop doorway, squatting in the sunlight for a morning chat. Even a short walk gives the sense of Bhaktapur's continued vitality. Society here is still strongly integrated, re-

woodcarvers working on a restoration

sisting the dislocative forces of change that are ripping apart Kathmandu.

Bhairab's Tongue

The only traffic is an occasional tractor, and deities still reside in the middle of the road in the form of sacred rocks embedded in the ground at Tekhacho, Taumadhi, and Inacho. These are known as the *svanghu lohan,* and mark the places where a certain Bhairab lost parts of his tongue. Masana Bhairab was a particularly fearsome being who used to devour mourners returning from the cremation ghats. On one particularly terrifying occasion he entered the city: tantric priests tried to subdue him by chopping off his long, slobbering tongue, but it kept growing back more quickly. A milkman, who through the habit of making Bhairab a daily offering of milk had gained power over him, eventually pacified the demon, and the three flat stones of **Inacho** represent where he cut Bhairab's tongue into three pieces once and for all.

TACHAPAL TOL

The street debouches into Tachapal Tol, the old, old, original center of town, dating back perhaps to the 8th century when Bhaktapur was no more than a village. Tachapal is still the heart of "upper" or eastern Bhaktapur (as opposed to "lower" Bhaktapur centered around Taumadhi), and its day begins at dawn as farmers come to sell fresh vegetables and milk straight from the water buffalo. The square is lined with ornate Hindu *math,* nine in all, the densest concentration of these Hindu monasteries anywhere in the Valley. These houses once sheltered communities of male ascetics gathered around a religious leader. Like the Buddhist *bahal,* the *math* have long since been taken over by secular families and turned into private dwellings. Many of Tachapal's old *math* now house crafts shops, like the splendid **Taj Math** on the right, with a five-opening window edged with delicate carvings. The carving involved in restoring this building alone took the Bhaktapur Development Project some 18 years in man-days, a record for the project. Step inside one of the building's courtyards to observe woodcarvers at work, this time producing tourist souvenirs.

Dattatreya Temple

These *math* and the fine **Bhimsen Mandir** on the square's western end once fed and housed pilgrims who came to worship at the stately Dattatreya temple at the eastern side of the square. This ancient building began itself as a resthouse for pilgrims and yogis; in the 14th century it was expanded into a full-fledged temple. Like the Kasthamandap in Kathmandu, it is said to have been constructed from the wood of a single tree. *Sadhu* occasionally stay in the temple's screened gallery, and on the day after the great festival of Shiva Ratri hundreds come here to worship.

Dattatreya is a three-headed combination of Brahma, Vishnu, and Shiva, with Vishnu dominating the trinity; thus his symbols the conch, the wheel, and the Garuda, mounted on stone pillars in front. The painted doll-like image peering out of an upper window is not Dattatreya but Indra, hoisted up decades ago by tipsy revelers during Indra Jatra. Guarding the temple's door are images of the two legendary strongmen, Jai and Patta Malla, who also guard the Nyatapola. Malla rulers adopted them as protectors because of their names, but actually they were historical figures, Indian warriors who died defending a Rajput fort. Their images still stand guard at Rajasthani palaces.

Pujari Math and Museums

Just behind Dattatreya is the famed Pujari Math, its intricate woodwork restored with German assistance as a wedding present to Crown Prince Birendra in the early '70s. The exterior is decorated with fantastic carvings of cavorting wild boars, monkeys, and sea serpents, and the famous if overrated **Peacock Window** can be found on its eastern side. While its design is undeniably brilliant, too many copies rob one of the delight of seeing it unexpectedly.

Appropriately, Pujari Math houses the National Art Gallery's **Woodworking Museum,** a small but fine collection of one of the premier Newar arts. The building's lavishly carved little interior courtyard is a miniature jewelbox of woodcarvings on all four sides. Dislays include some rare freestanding images and weathered struts salvaged from Bhaktapur and Patan temples, a unique opportunity to view this typical element at close range. The museum is open daily 10 a.m.-5 p.m.

except Tuesday, closing at 4 p.m. Friday. Admission is Rs5, Rs10 extra for a camera.

Across the street, the **National Brass and Bronze Museum** is housed in Chikampa Math; hours and admission are the same as those of

the Woodcarving Museum. Its collection of ritual and household vessels can be skipped unless you have a particular interest; the fine statues one might expect here are the specialty of the Patan Museum instead.

BHAKTAPUR'S MASKED DANCERS

The ritual dance-dramas performed during the autumn festivals of Dasain and Indra Jatra blend mysticism, drama, and entertainment. Just as artists provide painted or sculpted forms for deities to manifest themselves in, masked dancers offer their bodies and minds to the god, entering a trance the moment they don their heavy masks. The tradition dates to Malla times, when kings sponsored ceremonial dances in palace courtyards, offerings meant to please the gods and edify their subjects.

Perhaps a half-dozen troupes today preserve the Valley's once-widespread tradition of ritual dancing. Most famous are the Nava Durga dancers of Bhaktapur, representing the nine sister goddesses who protect the city. Dancers are chosen every year from the young men of a Jyapu subcaste, and train for several months under the direction of priests. Eventually the high priest of the Taleju temple invests the dancers with mantras so they can control and bear the tremendous power of the massive painted masks, which have been consecrated with tantric rituals. Unlike most ritual dance masks, considered sacred only during the performance, the Nava Durga masks are worshipped year-round in their own temple.

Bhaktapur's Nava Durga tradition began two centuries ago; the masks are carefully modeled anew every year by members of the same family. A special black clay called "god-soil" is kneaded together for hours with cotton and flour paste. The mixture is plastered over a low relief mold, dried and sanded, then painted with a white clay base. Then the features are painted on in brilliant colors, exactly the same as the year before. Each goddess has a symbolic third eye, an elaborate headress, and gi-

gantic earrings; different facial features and colors distinguish skull-faced Kali, serene Maheshvari, bright-red Kumari. There are also attendant deities: Shiva, Ganesh, various Bhairabs, and the fanged and fierce lion and tiger goddesses Sima and Duma. The miniature masks sold as souvenirs in tourist shops are often modeled after these.

For performances the masks are topped with heavy gilded copper crowns; some have wild manes of yak tails attached. Dancers dress in full skirts and tight blouses, with gold bracelets, silver chain necklaces, and silver bells strapped on their calves. The story they tell through steps and gestures is of Durga's conquest of the buffalo-demon, commemorated by the festival of Dasain.

Unlike the controlled and refined movements of other city troupes, the movements of Bhaktapur's dancers are vigorous sweeping gestures and whirling steps. Instead of sophisticated study, they rely on devotion. Those with sufficient faith become a vehicle for the gods the moment they don the masks. Their role falls somewhere between that of a transformed shaman and a mere actor. Sometimes the presence of the god is felt within them as a "coolness in the heart," sometimes not. Then the dancer may resort to drink to stimulate the power.

When the Nava Durga cycle is completed in June, dancers bring the masks to the priest of Taleju, who divests them of power in a ritual known as "cutting their life." Now the dancers cannot dance even if they try. The masks are burned in a funeral ritual near the Hanumante cremation ghats. The ashes are preserved in a sacred vessel immersed in the river until September, when they're mixed with clay to make new masks, and the cycle begins again.

BOB RACE

Navadurga *Agam Chen*

The main road continues past Tachapal Tol, passing more temples and houses before it abruptly ends in full countryside, with sweeping views of fields backed by the ridge of Nagarkot, and behind it, the Himalaya. This neighborhood turns to pottery-making in full force during the dry winter months, when the smooth black forms are laid out in every available open space.

One of Bhaktapur's three **Kumari** is worshipped in a simple three-story house near here: the system is much less elaborate than Kathmandu's, and the selected girls lead largely normal lives apart from being worshipped during the Dasain festival with chariot processions.

Just before the paved crossroads, turn left up a narrow street and head uphill. Almost at the top is the long rectangular building dedicated to the famed Navadurga, the fierce Nine Durgas who are depicted on the shrine's many carved *torana*. The painted masks used in the goddesses' dances are kept on the first floor and worshipped with blood sacrifices. From here you can make a short loop back to Tachapal, or continue westward to explore more of Bhaktapur's back streets. The city was made for aimless wandering; it's big enough to be interesting but small enough that you never get lost for long.

THE GHATS

A final concentration of sacred sites and temples is the series of ghats along the Hanumante River on the southern border of town. Clusters of shrines dot the riverbank at periodic intervals, running from **Hanuman Ghat** south of Tachapal Tol to **Chuping Ghat** south of Taumadhi and **Ram Ghat** down from Potters' Square, and **Mangal Ghat** on the town's western border, where the cremation grounds are located. Here too live the untouchable Newar castes, in small, tightly packed homes that were traditionally restricted in terms of their height and construction material. The shrines and sculptures found along here are fully as interesting as those of the Bagmati ghats of Kathmandu, but the Hanumante is, if possible, even more polluted than the Bagmati, a stinking open sewer, and it's hard to recommend any kind of visit within 100 meters of it.

PRACTICALITIES

Accommodations

Overnighting in Bhaktapur is a good idea in order to capture the flavor of the city, or to simply enjoy the Nepali countryside without embarking on a trek. It's a quiet getaway, a dramatic and pleasant contrast to urban Kathmandu. With few exceptions, the local tourist lodges have tiny dim rooms with nothing but a bed, a common bath, and sporadic hot water.

The best of the cheapies is **Golden Gate Guesthouse**, tel. (1) 610-534, its location between Durbar Square and Taumadhi Tol yielding good views of both from the upper floors. The staff is friendly and there's a good restaurant; small clean rooms are Rs200 s or d, and there's one huge, sunny upstairs room with bath for Rs500. Next choice is **Shiva Guesthouse**, tel. (1) 610-740, off Durbar Square, where spartan, dark rooms are Rs125 s, Rs250 d. **Traditional Guesthouse**, tel. (1) 611-057, slightly east of Durbar Square has even smaller rooms for Rs125 s, Rs165 d; the "attached bath" here consists of a shower pointed directly over the squat toilet. **Panas Guesthouse** down the lane has a spiffy exterior but the rooms are poorly maintained. Finally, **Luna Guesthouse** a few minutes north of the square is the oldest and most primitive of the lot (no hot water), with rooms for Rs100-150.

Moving upscale, **Bhadgaun Guesthouse**, tel. (1) 610-488, off Taumadhi Tol is a sparkling new place with a rooftop terrace and nice rooms with marble-tiled bath—at last, rooms of a decent size in Bhaktapur!—for US$12 s or d. Some overlook the Til Madhava temple directly across the road.

The place to head for if you're looking for a retreat is **Bhaktapur Guesthouse**, tel. (1) 610-670, which bills itself as a "countryside resort." Facilities are simple, but the peaceful hilltop location and spacious grounds make for something special. Rooms with bath are US$6-16; a big dining room serves Nepali and Chinese food. Continue past the Bhaktapur turnoff and look for a sign pointing up a dirt road: the guesthouse is atop a hill past the Chundevi temple, a leisurely half-hour walk into town and an easy connection from the trolley bus.

Food

Food is another Bhaktapur shortcoming: meals are generally more expensive and less varied than Kathmandu's. Quaint tourist traps include the **Cafe Nyatapola** in Taumadhi Tol, located in a former resthouse that once was used to store the parts of the Bisket chariot. Food is so-so, and service slow if it's filled with tour groups, but the ambience and views are unparalleled. The **Marco Polo** nearby has a slightly more varied menu and a small balcony overlooking the square. The other popular choice is **Cafe de Peacock,** located in a restored *math* overlooking Tachapal Tol: again, great location, mediocre food. In addition, all the guesthouses have their own restaurants; the best is the **Bhaktapur Gate Restaurant** (try the *momo*) at the Golden Gate.

Local teashops and sweet stalls in the bazaar provide a sugar-ridden breakfast, and little shops sell clay cups of Bhaktapur's renowned *juju dahi,* "King of Yoghurt." Bring munchies, bread, and cheese if you plan on doing day hikes out of here, as Western-style picnic fare is unavailable.

Shopping

Bhaktapur has become quite a souvenir capital overflowing with the same items you'll find in Kathmandu—brass masks, tacky jewelry, wooden puppets, Indian print bedspreads, and the like. There are a few reasonable *thangka* shops around Durbar Square and along the street between here to Taumadhi. Gyankar Vajracharya's shop in the easternmost section specializes in small *paubha*-style animal paintings, a change from the usual.

Thanks to the support of the German Development Project, which provided traditional craftspeople with steady employment for many years, Bhaktapur is a center for **woodcarving.** Shops are particularly thick around Tachapal Tol, where you can buy elaborately carved four-poster beds, picture frames, statues, miniature and full-sized windows, or carved rocking horses. **Himalayan Wood Carving Masterpieces** in Taj Math has an especially wide selection, or explore the lane down from the Peacock Window.

Bhaktapur Craft Printers north of Durbar Square produces handmade paper and block-printed stationery, including clever locally themed cards. While it's not set up for tourists, they will show you around the factory, and the sales outlet here is cheaper than Kathmandu's crafts stores. Plenty of simple **pottery** is sold around Potters' Square: wall planters, flowerpots, ashtrays, little animal figurines. Again, bargain hard. Puppets of Bhaktapur's masked dancers—a purely tourist invention—and **papier-mâché masks** of deities are all over, but the latter are better in nearby Thimi.

Bhaktapur is also a good place to hunt for old **brass:** polished plates, vessels, hanging oil lamps, *sukunda,* and embossed *puja* baskets. Several shops specializing in old and new brass are at the beginning of the bazaar just below Taumadhi Tol. Compare prices, bargain hard,

Potters' Square

and be aware that many items, like the charming little wire-mesh animal figurines, are new and Indian-made.

AROUND BHAKTAPUR

Bhaktapur offers many possibilities besides the city itself, all the more reason to spend several days out here. Stroll in the surrounding fields, where peasants may laughingly try to recruit you to help with planting or harvesting. Go down to the highway past the trolley bus stop to photograph the unbelievable sunset view of the city backed by Himalayan peaks.

Further afield, the ancient temple of **Changu Narayan** is an easy two-hour walk north, while the mountaintop viewpoint of **Nagarkot** is a longer hike (very slow buses run from Bhaktapur). The main road past the Dattatreya temple continues through countryside and villages to the ancient Newar town of **Nala** and from there to **Banepa** on the Chinese highway—a wonderful mountain bike ride or a longish hike.

Kamal Binayak

Northeast of town on the Nagarkot road, just beyond the city, is Kamal Binayak, a large pond which is as close as Bhaktapur gets to a park. This is a favorite site for picnics and feasts as well as buffalo bathing and laundry. There's a small **Ganesh shrine** in the northeast corner.

Surya Binayak

One of the four most sacred Ganesh temples in the Valley, this "Sun Ganesh" is a 20-minute walk up the paved road south of the trolley bus terminus. People come here to pray for a happy marriage, strong and clever children, success in business—just about anything involving luck. The temple is set amid a cluster of shops and houses; just below are good views of Bhaktapur, ringed by fields. A steep flight of steps leads to the shrine, set in a shady forest on the eastern side of a wooded hill and angled to catch the first rays of the sun. Ganesh dwells beneath a golden *torana* and a big white *shikara*. Mounted on a pillar in front is a large and very realistic rendition of his vehicle, the shrew. At the top of the hill there's a shrine to Ganesh's mother and good mountain views. The peaceful surrounding

forest is a popular picnic ground for Nepali families. It's particularly busy on Tuesday and Saturday, when worshippers bring Ganesh's favorite offerings: radishes, *laddu* (a sweetmeat), and sesame-seed balls.

Thimi

This old Newar town is three km west of Bhaktapur, set in the exact center of the Valley. Thimi is surprisingly big—in fact it's the fourth-largest settlement in the Valley—but its form is long and narrow, strung out along a raised plateau. A typically crowded Valley town surrounded by a sea of fields, it's rather dirty and unfriendly compared to other villages.

The paved back road linking Thimi and Bhaktapur makes a good alternative route for cyclists endangered by thundering trucks. The town's main road, which runs north from the highway bus stop, intersects this, first leading up a very steep hill and through the heart of town, linking a series of temple-studded squares.

a Thimi family

The first is Thimi's most important shrine, a pagoda with three gilded roofs dedicated to **Balkumari,** "Child Kumari." This is the most important of the Valley's many shrines dedicated to this tantric mother-goddess, whose mount, a gilded peacock, perches atop a pillar in front of the temple. She's worshipped by farmers for rain, by women hoping for children, and by parents for the cure of ill offspring. Dozens of coconuts, a fertility symbol and an offering peculiar to her, are nailed up on the temple facade. Every April for Nepali New Year, the goddess is paraded about in a palanquin in Thimi's biggest festival.

In the next square is a temple to the bodhisattva **Karunamaya** (Avalokitesvara), ringed by paintings of his 108 manifestations. The walk continues thus, alternating Buddhist and Hindu shrines strung along the constant thread of Newar village life. The road eventually joins the paved backroad to Bhaktapur, then continues on to the village of **Bode** described below, and the riverside shrine and picnic site of **Nilvarahi.** Few tourists visit here; the same goes for the village of **Nagdesh** slightly northeast of Thimi.

Whimsical clay planters and **papier-mâché** masks are sold in the village of **Nikosera** on the eastern outskirts of Thimi. It seems Bhaktapur has taken the lead in producing portable pottery for tourists, but the intricately painted masks here are still good buys, though bargaining is necessary. Look (or ask) for the wickedly clever salt-and-pepper shakers painted to resemble Nepal's king and queen, right down to the dark glasses. Kanchha Chitrakar's shop, the last one on the right as you're heading to Bhaktapur, is particularly good.

Bode

This small village a 20-minute walk north of Thimi centers around a famous temple dedicated to the tantric goddess Mahalakshmi, site of a bizarre tongue-boring festival each Nepali New Year's Day (mid-April). A village man purified by days of fasting has a thin metal spike thrust through his tongue by the temple's priest. The penitent parades around town bearing a bamboo rack of lit oil lamps. When he returns to the temple, the needle is removed and the wound packed with mud scraped from the temple floor. If no bleeding occurs, it's a sign that he's earned great religious merit with this offering of his body.

EXPLORING THE VALLEY
INTRODUCTION

Beyond the three old kingdoms lies an inexhaustible storehouse of fascinating destinations, limited only by your time, energy, and imagination. The Valley's small size and relative accessibility makes it ideal for explorers. A day-trip is far simpler to arrange than a trek, yet it can be equally satisfying. You can take in temples, forests, countryside, and mountain views and be back in your hotel by evening. What many people find most eye-opening is not the classic architecture or picturesque landscape, but the opportunity to see a traditional way of life that has vanished from the West, and is in the process of disappearing around the world.

Every shrine and temple in the Valley has its own special days when worshippers flock to it. A bit of planning can pay off in this respect. Time your exploration right and you can catch temple fairs, elaborate festivals, or full-moon *puja*. Above all, don't hesitate to get off roads and into fields and villages, striking out at random— you can't go wrong. In many ways these are the best part of the Valley: crops and colors

change with each season, and the rhythms of harvest and planting still control the pace of life.

The countryside also displays the ethnic diversity so typical of Nepal. Newar villages are clustered in the central and south Valley, with settlements of Hill people (mainly Brahman-Chhetri and Tamang) scattered about the fringes. It's easy to identify the different types of villages: Hill people generally live in thatched-roof, mud-walled houses painted two-tone ochre and white. Their homes are separated by fields and gardens, in contrast to the densely packed Newar farming villages, with their tall brick buildings set in rows.

PRACTICALITIES

Navigating the outer reaches of the Valley is best accomplished on a bicycle or a taxi hired for the day. Local buses running to outlying destinations are typically slow and crowded. With a little searching, day hikers can find a taxi driver willing to drop you off at your starting point and meet you at your destination. Drivers generally enjoy the break from routine, and you're spared the hassle of looking for transport at the end of the day.

What to Bring

Water is scarce along Valley ridgetops, so bring plenty, plus sunscreen, sun hat, and possibly some food, as little is available beyond tea and biscuits. It's nice but not absolutely necessary to have a good map (the Schneider map of the Valley is a must for serious walkers) and a few direction-finding phrases in Nepali. Don't worry about getting lost for long. There are people everywhere you look, and many will go out of their way to guide you to the major local attraction—even if it's *not* your destination.

> *The identification of very distant peaks is a harmless and fascinating amusement so long as the results are not taken seriously.*
>
> —H.W. TILMAN,
> NEPAL HIMALAYA

Mountain Views

Many of the mountains ringing the Valley offer superb views of the Himalaya. Choosing the best among them depends more on the type of trip you'd like than the views, which don't vary that much. It's hard to be disappointed with Nagarkot, Phulchowki, or Dhulikhel on a clear day; perspective differs slightly, but all are more or less spectacular.

Some of these sites can be driven to, while others require a day walk, no more than four hours. All can be combined with visits to nearby temples and villages. For hikers they provide a perfect warm-up for a trek, while for nontrekkers they encapsulate the experience in a single day, with the comforts of Kathmandu close by. Shivapuri, Nagarjun, and Phulchowki are among the most pleasant all-around hikes because of their comparatively lush forests.

Timing is crucial for mountain views. Sunrise and sunset are the most stunning, as the mountains reflect the golden light. Even on foggy winter mornings, mountaintops rise above the mist to reveal a panorama stretching above the cloud-covered bowl of the Valley. Midday, even if clear, is often hazy. Wait for a windy day to magically blow away the dust, leaving hillsides 20 km distant distinctly visible.

Overnighting or camping at a viewpoint makes it easy to catch sunset and sunrise, and offers the chance of a moonlight Himalayan panorama or a spectacular star show on moonless nights. Nagarkot and Dhulikhel are the best-known resort areas, but it's also possible to overnight at Kakani and Champadevi; for more adventure, pitch a tent atop a remote summit.

Most visitors to Nepal desperately want to see Everest, but the tiny nub glimpsed from Nagarkot and other viewpoints is not a very satisfying experience. RNAC's daily mountain flight brings you as close to the mountains as you can get without trekking—closer, in a way, since the plane flies at eye level along a stretch of the range and back. See special topic "Mountain Flights" under "Getting Around" in the On the Road chapter for details.

Another luxurious method of mountain viewing is driving out to Nagarkot or Dhulikhel for a meal

---

BAGH CHAAL

You'll see this game played all over the country, by adults and children both. Souvenir vendors sell elaborately embossed brass versions, but most players rely on a crude diagram scratched in the dirt and a handful of pebbles. The board involves four times four squares, each sliced by a diagonal. One player assumes the offensive role of tiger *(bagh)*, the other the defensive role of goat. Four tigers are placed on the four corners, then 20 goats are added, one at a time. Tigers and goats alternate moves. Tigers can move from one point to the next, or jump over a goat and capture it. But they can jump over only straight lines rather than diagonals, so the goats must huddle together to defend themselves. Tigers win after accumulating five goats; goats win if they can encircle the tigers so they can't move at all. It's an engrossing game that involves more strategy than you might first suspect, and it, along with the game of caroom board, absorbs a good deal of energy nationwide.

in a resort restaurant (the food is better at Dhulikhel). Sunset views of the Himalaya followed by fine cuisine, even a bottle of wine if you're prepared to splurge, are an unbeatable combination. Finally, practically the entire Valley south of the Ring Road offers surprisingly good Himalayan views without you having to climb a bit.

Mini-treks

Overnight hikes and mini-treks in the Valley are largely ignored in favor of treks in more remote and exotic regions, but they are definitely worth exploring. One interesting possibility would be to trace the old pilgrimage routes linking shrines. The 44-mile circuit of the four main Narayan temples is traditionally made in one day, but you could take several. It's possible to do entirely on your own, finding lodging in people's homes, although it's necessary to speak Nepali and/or have a guide.

A trek along the Valley rim is a favorite for those short on time; it can take anywhere from 2-10 days and blends fields, forests, occasional mountain views, and small villages. One possible seven-day route is Kakani-Bisankhu-Panauti-Dhulikhel-Nagarkot-Chisapani-Shivapuri-Kakani. The two- to three-day walk from Nagarkot to Shivapuri via Sundarijaal is popular. You can bunk in local teahouses, or trek through a local company, which will provide tents, food, guide, and perhaps porters. **Himalayan Eco-Trekking** in Gyaneshwar, tel. (1) 411-790, runs regular departures for Valley treks Oct.-May. **Guiding and Trekking Expedition Service** in Naxal, tel. (1) 413-645, also specializes in Valley treks.

NORTH OF KATHMANDU

ICHANGU NARAYAN

One of four sacred Vishnu shrines in the Valley, this "Vishnu of the East" is hidden in a secret little valley in the hills behind Swayambhunath. For being so close to urban Kathmandu, it's amazingly peaceful and rural.

Follow the gravel road across the Ring Road from the Swayambhu bus stop, soon passing above a limestone quarry. The road eventually crests a hill and turns into a trail, leading through beautiful scattered settlements dotted with Narayan shrines. This is an old pilgrimage route: Ichangu was supposedly founded around the 5th century, though the present shrine and image, set in a bricked courtyard at the end of a little village, are much more recent. While the art and architecture are unimpressive compared to those of its sister shrine of Changu Narayan, it's a pleasant, mostly level one-hour walk that can be easily done on the spur of the moment or with small children.

If you'd like something more strenuous, take the right fork at the village and continue a little over an hour uphill into the forest preserve of **Rani Ban**, and all the way up to the summit of **Nagarjun**, described below. Another easier trail links Ichangu with **Balaju**, about an hour's walk away across flat fields, passing below the impressive new Bönpo monastery set at the foot of Nagarjun.

BALAJU

Once a pleasure garden for Malla queens, Balaju is now open to the public as a combination pilgrimage site and picnic ground. The small Newar settlement of Balaju has been absorbed into Kathmandu's urban sprawl, and the dusty potholed road leading here is lined with small industrial enterprises and wicker furniture factories. Many more are headquartered in the Balaju Industrial Estate immediately before the park, which is about three km northwest of Thamel.

Balaju Water Gardens centers around the **Baais Dhara,** 22 carved stone water spouts set in a long line. The taps are used for daily bathing and laundry as well as for ritual bathing by pilgrims who flock here for festivals. The largest crowds congregate for Balaju Jatra, usually the April full moon, when the water is said to be magically linked with the Trisuli River.

The *dhara* are set in a well-maintained park filled with bamboo groves, flowers, trees, and fountains. Off to one side is a Sleeping Vishnu set in a pond, a smaller replica of the famous image in Budhanilkantha. This is **Bala Nilkan-**

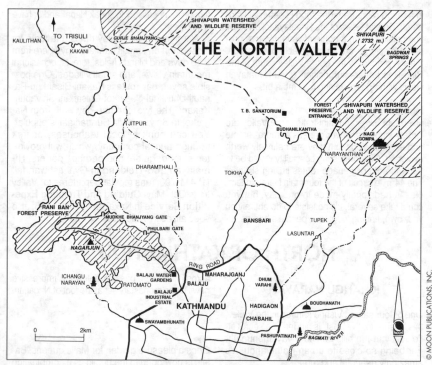

THE NORTH VALLEY

© MOON PUBLICATIONS, INC.

tha, "Young Blue Throat," as opposed to Budhanilkantha's "Old Blue Throat." For a long time it was thought to be a 17th-century reproduction of the better-known 7th-century Budhanilkantha sculpture; historians have now determined it's a contemporary. There's also a 14th-century image of the smallpox goddess Sitala enshrined in a small pagoda, and various other Hindu and Buddhist deities. Look for the 16th-century sculpture of Harihara, a rare composite of Vishnu and Shiva, holding the former's wheel and conch shell and the latter's trident.

Balaju serves as a nearby picnic ground for city dwellers, and on Saturday it's crowded with families and groups of merry-making young people. Come here to see Kathmandu at play: feasting, playing cards, sleeping in the sun, bathing at the taps, strolling about admiring the flowers. Admission is Rs1.50.

Up the next road to the west of Balaju (follow the green and yellow signs) is an exceptional restaurant: **K.C.'s Consequence,** tel. (1) 272-274, the pet project of Thamel's well-known K.C. Located in a beautifully renovated old farmhouse surrounded by spacious gardens, it's a lovely place to while away a sunny afternoon; the food is pricey but original. Call in advance to make sure it's open, as it's a long trip up a bumpy dirt road.

NAGARJUN

Not to be confused with Nagarkot, this humpbacked mountain northwest of Swayambhunath is closer to Kathmandu than any other of the Valley's surrounding peaks. It's a fairly easy two-hour hike along a wide ridge trail to the grassy, open summit. The Sherpas and Tibetans who flock here for weekend picnics usually drive up the winding unpaved road, rutted but doable in a taxi.

Newars call the mountaintop Jamacho, after the wooded ridges which cascade down its flanks like the pleated folds of the *jamma* or long skirt worn by ritual dancers. The mountain is included in the **Rani Ban** or Queen's Forest, an old Rana hunting preserve that's now a government-protected forest. Dense stands of rhododendron, bamboo, oak, and pine shelter pheasants, deer, and a few small leopards. The population of fierce, ugly wild boar has increased to problematic levels under the protection of the preserve, as villagers are forbidden to hunt them. Ingeniously, they now hook up bare wires to power lines each evening in crop-raiding season to electrocute the pigs while they are foraging in the darkness.

History
The peak is named after Nagarjuna, a 2nd-century Indian Buddhist sage and sorcerer who is said to have meditated and died in a limestone cave on the mountain's eastern slopes (an image enshrined here marks the supposed spot). A remarkably subtle metaphysician who

view tower strung with prayer flags, Nagarjun

developed the Madhyamika school of Buddhist philosophy, Nagarjuna is said to have had the gift of communicating with the serpent deities or *naga* who had been entrusted with the Buddha's most profound esoteric teachings. The *naga* transmitted these teachings to Nagarjuna in the form of 16 massive volumes of scriptures written in golden ink on paper of lapis lazuli; these texts, encapsulating the *Prajnaparamita* or "Perfection of Wisdom," are enshrined today in Tham Bahal in Thamel.

Getting There
The reserve's entrance is a half-hour bike ride from Thamel. Continue north on the Trisuli Road past the Balaju Water Gardens to the reserve's entrance gate at Phulbhari, about nine km from the city. Here you can leave your bike and pay a small admission fee: Rs5 for pedestrians and cyclists, Rs15 for motorcycles, Rs50 for vehicles or elephants. If you're camping in the preserve, register here and obtain a permit (Rs90 a week).

To the Summit
The dirt road up is far too long to walk, though it makes a good mountain bike ride. A footpath begins just past the gate on the right, starting off steeply but leveling out on a ridgeline after 30 minutes. From here it's a relatively easy walk along the forested ridge up to the 2096-meter summit, which is topped by a white stupa and a viewtower strung with colorful Tibetan prayer flags. The slightly higher summits to the west offer similar views.

Nagarjun is a popular Buddhist pilgrimage spot. Some believe the Buddha once preached here; others say this is the summit from which the bodhisattva tossed the lotus seed that was to blossom into Swayambhunath. The summit is littered with tiny colored slips of paper printed with Tibetan prayers. Tossed from the viewtower, they flutter slowly down to earth, a pretty sight. There's a cooking shelter at the summit and a few small tin-roofed pavilions scattered about. Many families combine worship with a picnic and spend all day up here, the men whiling the hours away with card games or vigorous dice sessions.

Mountain views stretch from Annapurna to Sikkim on a clear day, though they are partly obscured by Shivapuri to the east. To the left is the icy pyramid of Manaslu, and beside it Peak 29 and Himalchuli. Directly north is Ganesh Himal, only vaguely resembling an elephant's head; to the east are Langtang Lirung, Dorje Lhakpa, and the serrated peaks of the Jugal Himal. The best panorama is that of the Kathmandu Valley below.

Other Descents

The 30-km motor road leading up the mountain loops around the backside to exit at another gate at **Mudkha Bhanjyang** further north. Don't make the mistake of *walking* the road; with its many switchbacks it takes three times as long as the trail. A different trail, difficult to find, starts southeast of the observation tower and descends south down a spur running towards Balaju, passing a big limestone cave with images of **Nagarjun** and **Akshobhya Buddha.** Further down, the trail joins the road, which you can follow for three km to the gate, or from where you can exit the preserve and cut across fields to Swayambhunath or Balaju.

There's little in the way of facilities around Nagarjun. **Zorba the Buddha Osho Restaurant** is a Rajneesh-inspired vegetarian enterprise set on the ridge behind Nagarjun, a few kilometers past the second gate. The Osho Forest Retreat Center, tel. (1) 271-385, here offers rooms and a meditation program.

KAKANI

Perched on the Valley rim 29 km northwest of Kathmandu on the Trisuli road, Kakani offers views of Langtang, Himalchuli, the Annapurnas, and a superb closeup of Ganesh Himal. You can catch the Trisuli bus to a point just below here and walk up, or mountain-bike the untrafficked road—great on a full-moon night. The well-maintained road passes Balaju and Nagarjun, heading uphill to the small settlement of **Kaulithan,** "Cauliflower Place." Leave the bus here and walk four km uphill to Kakani (2073 meters), essentially a few huts strung along a ridge.

The government-run **Taragaon Resort,** tel. (1) 228-222, here has rooms for overnighters who want to catch morning views, though they're pretty shabby for US$16 s, US$21 d. Sit on the back lawn and admire the mountain views over a pot of tea; the drop-off is straight down into the valley of the Likhu Khola. From the front lawn you can look down at the impressive Police Training Center and perhaps watch stick-brandishing officers practicing *lathi* charges, the subcontinent's preferred method of crowd control. Next to the Taragaon is a small yellow plaster bungalow, which serves as a weekend retreat for the British Embassy. A landscaped memorial to the 114 victims of the 1992 Thai Airways crash north of Kakani is a short walk distant.

It's an easy descent back into the Valley, starting along the dirt road leading east from Kakani. A dirt road drops down to the south, meandering through oak and rhodie forests with occasional good Valley views. Stay near the ridgetop and avoid the trails descending to the highway, a boring plod. Turn east through the village of **Jitpur** and continue south to **Dharamthali,** where a dirt road leads down into Balaju, for a roundtrip of five or six hours in all.

BUDHANILKANTHA

The Hindu creation myth centers around Vishnu in the form of Jalasayana Narayana, "Narayana Lying-on-the-Waters." For aeons the god slumbered in the primordial ocean, floating on the coils of the serpent Ananta. Finally, the creative force issued from his navel in the form of Brahma, bringing forth the universe and all its beings. A trio of unknown Licchavi-era sculptors masterfully interpreted this timeless theme in three huge statues of the "Sleeping Vishnu," as Jalasayana Narayana is commonly called. One is set in the Balaju Gardens; another is hidden in a locked courtyard in Kathmandu's Hanuman Dhoka palace; and the third, reputedly the original, lies in the walled temple compound of Budhanilkantha, set in the small village of **Narayanthan** nine km north of Kathmandu. To reach here, you can hike, bike, take a taxi to Narayanthan, or catch a Bikram from Rani Pokhari. The new houses lining the road exemplify the rapid suburbanization of the Valley's countryside.

Consecrated in A.D. 641, the Budhanilkantha image is the largest (six meters long), most important, and finest of the trio. Carved from a single block of black stone of a type not found in the Valley, the statue was most likely dragged here from afar by forced labor. Despite its massive bulk it seems to float in the placid waters. Vishnu slumbers with a half-smile, relaxing in the coils of the nine-headed serpent, whose hoods form a crown. The temple's builders chose one of the most beautiful sites in the Valley for this masterpiece, though much of its harmony has been destroyed by the monstrous concrete fence raised around the pool.

Devotees come all day long, bringing offerings which they hand over to the white-clad Brahman priests who are the only ones allowed to walk upon Vishnu's body. Morning and evening they perform an elaborate daily worship routine, bathing, anointing, and adorning the sculpture as carefully as if it were human. The 11th days *(ekadasi)* of both the light and dark fortnight are good times to visit, as these dates are sacred to Vishnu. Three times a year a big *mela* fills the temple grounds with pilgrims, and the surrounding village with tipsy revelers.

Newar and Tibetan Buddhists come here as well, for they've adopted the image as a form of Lokeswar, the buddha of compassion. The temple's name, however, has nothing to do with Buddha; "Budha" (or "Burha"—the Nepali letter in question is somewhere between "r" and "d") means "Old," and "Nilkantha" is "Blue Throat." The name refers to the legend of Shiva, who drank down the poison produced in the epic Churning of the Ocean (a legend in itself) and had his throat burned blue as a result. What this has to do with a Vishnu temple is unclear, but the waters of the tank are believed to be mystically connected with the Himalayan pilgrimage lake of Gosainkund, where Shiva immersed himself to cool off.

A prophetic dream of Pratapa Malla's generated the belief the king of Nepal should never visit this site on threat of death. But the explanation that the king, as an emanation of Vishnu, should not view his own image doesn't hold water—he's allowed to visit hundreds of other Vishnu shrines, including the Sleeping Vishnu of Balaju. Pratapa Malla even installed a Sleeping Vishnu on his palace grounds, where it remains today, hidden away in a back garden.

Around Budhanilkantha

The road west of the temple makes for good wandering, ascending past the elite Budhanilkantha School and into a scanty pine forest with Valley views. Past the old tuberculosis sanatorium another road curves south to the village of **Tokha,** an ancient Newar town with its own Kumari and several interesting temples, including the shrine of Swapratirtha, visited once a year to exorcise the evil effects of bad dreams. The main road continues up past a guard post onto the flanks of Shivapuri and up to **Gurje Bhanjyang,** a mountain-bikeable route yielding some amazing mountain views. Guards may demand to see an Rs250 entry ticket for the Shivapuri Watershed Reserve, which must be purchased at the reserve office north of Narayanthan.

The paved road heading north from Narayanthan is another nice walk, leading through rural territory with a real village feeling, plus a few roadside teashops to nourish you on your "trek." It ends at the guard post for the Shivapuri forest preserve, described below.

Finally, you could hike back several hours across fields to the Ring Road or beyond, over uncommonly (some would say mercifully) flat territory. This is best done in the winter months when the fields are dry and open. From Narayanthan, head east and then south to the village of Tupek and cross the Dhobi Khola to **Lasuntar;** from here take another footpath southwest, crossing the Dhobi Khola again to reach the Ring Road. Across it is the shrine of **Dhum Varahi,** with a powerful 6th-century sculpture of Vishnu's incarnation as a boar. From here you can continue along back roads through the ancient and decrepit settlement of **Hadigaon** and into Kathmandu. Or, if you take the left fork at Lasuntar and veer slightly to the east, you'll soon meet a dirt road leading to Boudhanath.

SHIVAPURI

This bulky mountain directly north of Kathmandu is the Valley's most important source of water. Shivapuri's views are not as complete as, say, Nagarkot's (Langtang is blocked), but its upper reaches are covered by a magnificent virgin oak forest, and a dirt road traversing its slopes makes a superb mountain-biking track.

Shivapuri's forests were heavily cut for firewood, to the point where far-sighted urban planners lobbied to have the mountain set aside in the Shivapuri Watershed and Wildlife Reserve. Managed by the FAO and guarded, like Nepal's national parks, by the Army, the reserve is bounded by a 111-km wall, now broken at many points. Though local villagers still make illicit incursions to collect firewood and fodder, the forest is coming back with abundant new growth. Shivapuri harbors tremendous natural diversity: some 300 butterfly species and 150 bird species have been spotted here, as well as an insect, an evolutionary link between damselflies and dragonflies, that is one of two such subspecies in the world. Such biological wealth may not be unusual for the ecologically diverse hills of central Nepal, but Shivapuri is one of the few areas to have been studied in depth.

The Road Up

From Budhanilkantha, continue up the well-paved road to the gate of the Shivapuri Watershed and Wildlife Reserve, guarded by soldiers. Here you must register your vehicle—impossible on Saturday when the office is closed—and pay a stiff fee to enter: Rs250 for foreigners (Rs10 for Nepalis), plus an extra Rs40 for a taxi. Note there's an Rs3000 fee for bringing in a video camera. The fees go not to the Shivapuri project but to the Ministry of Forestry.

A map board beyond the gate outlines the main trails threading across the reserve's 150-km area, and the 95-km dirt road which loops around the mountain. Mountain bikers can take the road up along the ridge to the point where it meets the Sundarijaal trail. The road continues all the way around the backside of the mountain, a shady and unpopulated locale that's a peaceful hike. Most of it is bikeable if you're willing to lug your cycle over a few gullies.

If you're on foot, a trail starting behind here is the steepest and most direct route to the summit. Or head up the rutted gravel road one hour to a point just below **Nagi Gompa**, a Buddhist nunnery housing an active community of Newar, Tamang, and Sherpa nuns. The *gompa*'s grassy lawn is a favorite picnic ground for trekking groups.

The Trail

A steep trail behind Nagi Gompa's boxy yellow main shrine leads up along a ridge set with flap-ping prayer flags. After a tough half-hour it levels out through dense forest, passing through several clearings with mountain views. There are good campsites, but make sure there's water nearby. The woods from here on are superb: Shivapuri is protected from woodcutters and harbors an abundance of birds, langur monkeys, and game, including leopards. The nuns at Nagi Gompa frequently report sightings of a tiger.

A bit over an hour from Nagi is **Bagdwar**, literally "Bagmati's Door," a quiet, shady hideaway seldom visited by anyone but pilgrims. Look for a flight of stone steps leading down to a shady clearing with a few *chaitya* and fragments of old sculptures. Prayer flags and white prayer scarves mark the spot where water pours from a tiger-headed spout, the fabled source of the Valley's sacred river.

Legend says that aeons ago a buddha came to the Valley to worship Swayambhunath. Later he preached on Shivapuri, at that time waterless. To obtain the water needed to initiate his hundreds of disciples, he created a stream with the power of his voice—thus the name Vak-mati, "Stream of Mantra"—endowing the water with the power to purify sins. From here the river flows east through Sundarijaal, then drops into the Valley, lined its entire length by sacred bathing sites and shrines.

The Summit

Above Bagdwar the forest is old growth, degraded but original, a rarity in Nepal. Shivapuri's summit, at 2732 meters the second highest of the Valley's peaks, is a large flat open area about an hour's walk past Bagdwar. It's a good campsite if you want to catch early-morning views; water is available nearby, and there's a military post with a few lonely soldiers. The famous **Shivapuri Baba** lived here till his death in 1963.

Descending via Nagi Gompa, you can walk all the way to Boudhanath along the prominent ridge dropping south towards the stupa. Alternatively, from the road below the *gompa* a steep, small trail leads down in about 45 minutes to Budhanilkantha and buses or taxis.

Newar girl and temple guardian, Bhaktapur (Kerry Moran)

worshippers in Kwa Bahal, Patan's "Golden Temple" (Kerry Moran)

SOUTH OF KATHMANDU

This prosperous region is thickly dotted with ancient villages, some well over a thousand years old and filled with fine old houses, temples, and sculptures. More than any other area, the south Valley is a Newar stronghold; virtually all its villages are dominated by this ethnic group. The road to Dakshinkali is particularly interesting as it passes through Chobhar and Pharping, but the green tranquillity of Godavari and the perfect little towns of Bungamati and Kokana, only an hour's walk from Patan, are hard to pass up. Because the south Valley is slightly elevated, many of its open fields offer stunning Himalayan views without any climbing at all. For more impressive overviews, hike up lushly forested Phulchowki in the southeast of the Valley, or the high bare ridge of Champadevi in the southwest. Buses for many south Valley sites depart from Patan's Lagankhel bus park, while buses to Kirtipur go from Kathmandu's municipal bus park.

GODAVARI AND PHULCHOWKI

Well-paved and not too steep, the 20-km road to the Royal Botanical Gardens at Godavari makes a good cycling excursion. The first sight is the **National Potato Improvement Center** just past the Ring Road. Next is **Harisiddhi** or Jala, a compact Newar village housing the notorious **Bhavani Trishakti temple** honoring Durga. It is said to have been the site of human sacrifices until this century, and is still served by tantric priests who dress in the old fashion, with long white pleated skirts and long hair in buns. Harisiddhi is also the home of a famous ritual dance troupe which occasionally performs here.

Godavari is a collection of sights scattered at the foot of massive Phulchowki. Minibuses from Lagankhel stop in front of **St. Xavier's**, a Jesuit-run boys' school partly housed in an old Rana summerhouse.

Royal Botanical Gardens

Just east of the school are the 24-hectare Royal Botanical Gardens, a peaceful green sanctuary far removed from city dust and noise. This area receives the highest rainfall in the Valley, with a correspondingly high leech count in monsoon. The well-maintained grounds include orchids, cacti, ferns, succulents, a lotus pond, and a small Japanese garden. Picnicking is technically not allowed here, but Nepali families crowd in on Saturday with hampers of food, so you could certainly risk sneaking a sandwich. On clear days you can catch Himalayan views, including Manaslu and Annapurna to the west.

Godavari Kunda

Down the road past the Botanical Gardens is a government-run fish farm, and beside it the sacred spring of Godavari Kunda. The water emerges from a natural cave and flows through nine carved stone taps into a stepped pool. This spring is the mythical source of the the sacred Godavari River in Madras. This legend began with the tale of an Indian *sadhu* who had once lost his ritual paraphernalia—rosary, club, bag, gourd, and tiger skin—while bathing in Madras, and miraculously rediscovered them in Godavari Kunda. Once every 12 years, when Jupiter is in Leo, a *mela* held here attracts thousands of Hindu pilgrims.

Phulchowki Mai

Behind St. Xavier's School a controversial marble quarry business has gouged out a considerable hole in the hillside and is chewing away at the lush forests carpeting Phulchowki's flanks. Across from it is a triple-roofed pagoda dedicated to Phulchowki Mai, the ancient mother goddess of the forest. The deserted, tranquil temple has carved struts depicting the Ashta Matrika; nearby is a 17th-century sunken water tap.

Phulchowki

This massive triple-peaked mountain at 2762 meters is the highest of the summits ringing the Valley. Snow occasionally dusts the top on winter mornings, and groups of curious locals hike up to frolic in the seldom-seen substance. Woodcutters and the marble quarry have depleted its once-virgin forest, but the subtropical climate, high rainfall, and varied altitude still support a rich variety of butterflies, birds—260 species have

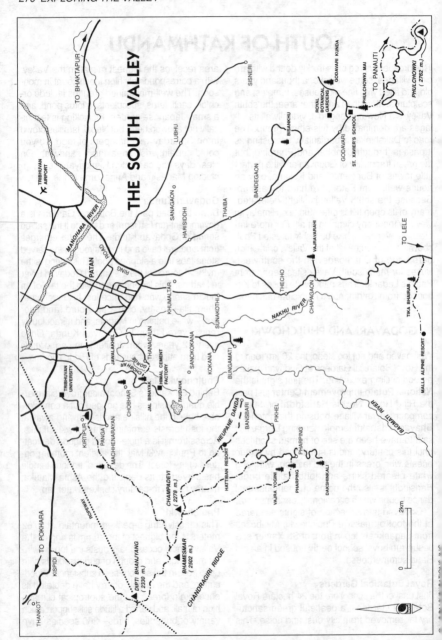

THE SOUTH VALLEY

BOB RACE

been sighted, an enormous quantity—and vegetation, including some species of plants unique to this part of the world. In the spring the slopes are covered with pink, white, and red rhododendrons and dozens of kinds of orchids: thus the name Phulchowki, "Place of Flowers."

The winding, bumpy jeep road leading from St. Xavier's to the summit is barely manageable on a mountain bike, but makes a leisurely walk. Taxi drivers may grumble about the rough ride, though it's usually possible to take a car up. The road is long but with lots of switchbacks so it's not very steep. A more direct foot trail starting behind St. Xavier's School takes about four hours to the top.

Atop the summit is another shrine to Phulchowki Mai, a simple open altar that's quite unlike her elaborate pagoda below. The top offers spectacular views of the Valley, the ranges leading down to the Terai, and a 320-km panorama of the Himalaya from Annapurna to Everest and even beyond. The area is thickly littered with picnic debris, so it's probably better to come enjoy the views first, then picnic in a nice patch of forest below.

KIRTIPUR

Spread along the top of a long ridge in the southwest Valley, the old Newar village of Kirtipur is a natural fortress, founded around the 12th century A.D. as an offshoot of Patan. Prithvi Narayan Shah and his Gorkhali troops targeted the town for conquest early in their 18th-century campaign for the Valley. They besieged Kirtipur three times, finally succeeding in 1766. In revenge for the death of his brother, killed in an earlier siege, the conquerer ordered the noses cut off every Kirtipur male over 12 years, exempting only the players of wind instruments. According to historical chronicles, 865 people were mutiliated, and their detached noses weighed 80 pounds. Another account noted the conqueror ordered the town's name be changed to Naskatipur, "City of Cut Noses."

After this bloody episode Kirtipur drifted into decline. Though its ridgetop location affords protection from earthquakes, many of its buildings are crumbling, and there's a general atmosphere of seediness about the town. In the early '70s the Tribhuvan University Campus was built on land belonging to Kirtipur's farmers; many have since turned to day work in the city or crafts like weaving. Both hand-loomed cloth and Tibetan-style carpets are made in Kirtipur homes.

Perhaps because of its proximity—only 10 km southwest of Kathmandu—Kirtipur is frequently visited by tourists. It's not among the Valley's best Newar villages, though; the streets are filthy and the people could stand to be a little friendlier. A pity, because there are interesting sculptures and shrines everywhere. The hilltop is dumbbell-shaped, with higher summits at either end, each marked by a distinctive shrine. The western portion of town clusters around a stupa and is Buddhist; the upper town near the hilltop pagoda is Hindu. In between, set in a lower saddle, is the famous temple to Bagh Bhairab, honored in an annual procession each August.

Naya Bazaar

The road to Kirtipur leads through the **Tribhuvan University** campus and curves left. Buses from Kathmandu's municipal bus park stop here,

from where it's a short walk up the road to the western side of Kirtipur's hill and "New Bazaar," a wide, shop-lined street with a number of good teashops. Look for anise-flavored fried bread, *malpuwa,* made from rice flour and served with spicy chickpeas. At the end of the road is an odd intrusion: **Nagara Mandapa Sri Kirti Vihar,** blending Thai and Newar architectural styles. This Theravadan temple complex was built in 1990 with contributions from Thai and Nepali Buddhists. In the main shrine is a big Thai-style image of a standing Buddha, flanked by his disciples. Gaudy plaster images set in an arcade depict scenes from the Buddha's life: his birth at Lumbini, his enlightenment at Bodhgaya, his first teaching at Sarnath, and his death at Kushinagar.

Chilamchu Stupa

Vehicles can be driven up to the Bagh Bhairab temple but it's more interesting to walk, taking one of several stone staircases set into the hill. At the top is the old town: typically close-packed

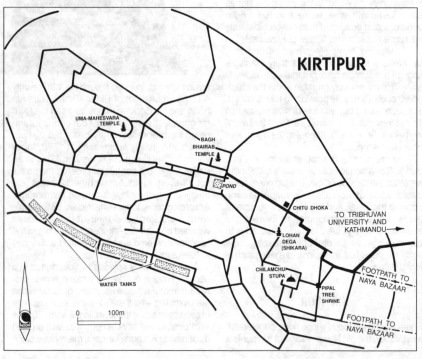

KIRTIPUR

© MOON PUBLICATIONS, INC.

houses lining flagstoned streets, and people everywhere. Look for the Chilamchu Stupa, the oldest monument in town, rumored to have been built by Ashoka. An inscription on its base indicates it was renovated in A.D. 816. It's set on a stepped pedestal and surrounded by four smaller stupas, all built in the early 16th century. A few beautifully decorated facades of old *bahal* remain in the surrounding square. Near the entrance a giant pipal tree has nearly burst through an ancient shrine, leaving fragments of carved stone entangled in the roots.

Bagh Bhairab

Continue east to the saddle in between the two hillocks. A large fenced-in pond is lined by houses; the one on the western side has a beautifully carved facade. At the north end of the square is the important and impressive temple of Bagh Bhairab, a large rectangular pagoda with Bhairab in the form of a tiger *(bagh).* It's said that one day a group of Kirtipur children out tending their sheep fashioned a toy tiger out of clay, and carelessly left it for a moment. Returning, they discovered Bhairab had possessed their toy and devoured their flock.

The temple is imposingly large and well-proportioned, capped with a row of gilt pinnacles and decorated all around with unusual frescoes that are on the verge of completely fading away. Under the third-story eaves are nailed old weapons—daggers and wicked-looking curved swords—said to have been surrendered by the town's Newar defenders. There's also a number of cooking pots and utensils given as offerings.

The compound contains a collection of ancient stone sculptures set in small shrines. Immediately to the right at the entrance, a series of five buxom **mother goddesses** from around the 4th century are embedded in concrete, the boar-headed goddess Varahi on the right. The standing **Shiva-Parvati** set in a niche is equally ancient. To the rear a graphic image of a naked **Kirtimata** lies on her back giving birth to an unidentifiable object. Behind the temple are fine views of fields, a large brick factory, and the temple of Swayambhunath backed by the green hill of Nagarjun. On the left-hand side is a gallery papered with posters of Hindu deities, where village men gather to sing *bhajan.*

Uma-Mahesvara Temple

Leave the compound and continue west, past a house decorated with painted stucco plaques, including one of the tiger-god Bhairab. The upper portion of town is better maintained, with many resthouses sheltering images of Ganesh. Kirtipur's old palace was located around here at Layaku Tol, but there's nothing left to see. Five minutes from Bagh Bhairab atop a windy hilltop is a tall but plain pagoda dedicated to Uma-Mahesvara (Shiva and Parvati), recently rebuilt and not particularly notable. The stone elephants guarding the steps are perhaps the most interesting thing: they wear spiked saddles to fend off local children, and one crushes the image of a helpless man underfoot. Set on the edge of town, the shrine offers good views of Phulchowki, Kirtipur, and to the southeast the smaller villages of **Panga** and **Nagaon.**

On Foot to Chobhar

The nearby village of **Chobhar** is set on another ridge to the southeast. To reach it from Kirtipur, return to the Chilamchu stupa and continue along the ridge to the next hill, passing a small **Vishnu temple** with many sculptures. Chobhar's Adinath temple is visible from afar, easily reached by a combination of roads and trails. From Chobhar it's an easy walk across the river to Jawalakhel in Patan.

CHOBHAR

Chobhar Village

A little past the Tribhuvan University entrance is a pine-forested hill. A flight of stone steps leads up it and through an archway into the old Newar village of Chobhar, accessible only on foot. The path leads directly to the temple of **Adinath Lokeswar,** dating back to 1640. Inside the pagoda is the image of Adinath Avalokitesvara, an apparent replica of Patan's Raato Machhendranath. To Buddhists, the deity is the embodiment of compassion; Hindus worship him as Surya, the Sun God.

Most amazing are the hundreds of pots, pans, and kitchen utensils nailed onto the exquisitely carved roof struts and under the eaves of surrounding buildings. These appear frequently on Valley temples, but nowhere else in such profusion. There are many different explanations for the practice. Sometimes they're offered in gratitude to the deity for a granted wish or as a sign of devotion. Newlyweds may offer them for a happy married life, or children will offer them after the death of a parent, placing them in the keeping of the gods so that these things will be provided in the next life. Every 10 years or so the temple keepers take down the old contributions and bury them in a pit in order to make room for new ones. Facing the shrine is an old stone *shikara,* said to be built over a tunnel leading directly to the semi-legendary cave of Chobhar below the hill (see below). Inside it is enshrined a Shiva linga, a most unusual choice for a Buddhist temple compound.

Chobhar Gorge

Below the village and a little further down the road, the Bagmati flows through a narrow gash in the hills. Chobhar Gorge is nowadays firmly associated with the fabled sword cult of Manjushri, but traditionally that site was considered the Kotwal Gorge further south on the Valley rim. This gorge is spanned by a beautiful old iron suspension bridge made to order for the Ranas by a Scottish foundry and erected in 1907. All the parts were manufactured in Glasgow, shipped to India, and carried in over the Hills by lines of porters. The trail beyond it leads back to the Ring Road and Jawalakhel.

On the west side of the gorge are several meditation caves cut into the rock. Tunnels behind them are said to lead to an underground lake; one, now bricked up, is said to emerge at the Adinath Lokeswar temple. Supposedly this passage was dug by Ganesh after he was left out of a gathering of the gods at the temple. Furious, he tunneled straight up from his riverside shrine to demand an explanation.

a naga

Jal Binayak

Ganesh's home is visible just below the gorge, the 17th-century temple of Jal Binayak, set in a courtyard. On the riverbank behind are old cremation ghats and stone steps where women do laundry. The temple is one of the Valley's four most important Ganesh sites, and is a favorite pilgrimage site for worshippers seeking the boon of wisdom. The brightly painted struts depict the Ashta Matrikas, with clever erotic scenes at the bases. On the front facade is a plaster portrait of the happy divine family: Shiva, Parvati, and young Ganesh seated on his daddy's lap.

The main image is a huge rock, vaguely resembling an elephant's head, ringed by a collar of gold. Besides granting wisdom, this Ganesh bestows fertility and is visited by women hoping to bear a son. If they come 21 Tuesdays in succession, bringing a total of 1,000 red *mula* (a kind of radish) and 1,000 *laddu* (Ganesh's favorite sweet), their wish is supposed to be granted. Ganesh's mount, a meter-long shrew, is ensconced in front, offering a *laddu* in his right paw. He's flanked by two bells; an inscription on their supports announces they were made from the very first bag of cement produced by the nearby **Himal Cement Factory**. This dust-belching factory a little further down the road is among the Valley's main polluters; on otherwise clear days its emissions cast a gray pall over the entire south Valley.

Taudaha

Past the grim cement factory, the scenery begins to improve. One km further is Taudaha, "Great Lake" (more like a big pond), the fabled residence of the king of the *naga,* the snakelike beings said to protect the Valley's underground wealth. Legend has it that Manjushri asked the *naga* king to remain as guardian of the Valley's fertility and prosperity, and provided an elegant underwater home in Taudaha, a golden palace with diamond windows and jewelled pillars. Here the *naga* dwell, dispelling the underwater gloom with the light of large jewels set in their foreheads. Though small, the lake is said to be immeasurably deep, or at least deep enough to defeat attempts by the Valley's rulers to drag it for the fabled treasure.

CHAMPADEVI

This relatively short hike offers good views with a minimum of walking, plus the chance to visit several of the Dakshinkali road's interesting sites along the way. It's about a two-hour walk to the first summit, with the option of continuing on for several more hours.

Champadevi is a minor hilltop pilgrimage site that's part of the larger Chandragiri Ridge. Several trails lead up here from small villages between Chobhar and Pharping; begin at **Bansbari** or at **Pikhel,** or look for the poorly marked, steep dirt road leading up to **Hattiban Resort.** The resort is set in a peaceful pine forest overlooking the Valley and the Himalayas and has 17 well-appointed double rooms in four separate cottages, a spacious restaurant, and gardens. Rooms are US$55 s, US$65 d; as usual, rates are negotiable. The resort's Kathmandu office is in Naxal, tel. (1) 221-181; the local number is (1) 290-622.

From Hattiban, the trail ascends steeply to the ridgeline through a pine plantation. In about 45 minutes it begins to level out and the Himalaya appears. It's a moderate walk to the base of the summit, then another stiff climb to the top (2278 meters), where there's a small Buddhist stupa and a Hindu shrine honoring the goddess Champadevi Mai. Between the litter and the sacrificial remnants, it's a fairly grotty location. The pine forest below is a more appetizing and shady picnic site.

Hikers can continue 45 minutes west to **Bhamesmar,** a higher summit at 2502 meters, then drop down to meet a trail which eventually becomes a dirt road leading to Kirtipur. The most energetic can continue northwest to **Dipti Bhanjyang,** 2330 meters, where a cable ropeway hauling freight over the hills intersects the trail. Follow a trail descending to **Kispidi** on the Kathmandu-Pokhara highway.

PHARPING

Eighteen km south of Kathmandu is the small fortress town of Pharping, once an independent kingdom sited atop a hill for defensive purposes. With its sacred shrines to Vishnu, Vajra Yogini, Gorakhanath, and Guru Rinpoche, the site draws both Hindus and Buddhists. The entire hill is loaded with shrines, temples, and monasteries, skillfully integrated into a beautiful natural setting.

Shikar Narayan Temple
For Hindus the main attraction is the Shikar Narayan temple (also called Sekha Narayan or Shesha Narayan), one of the Valley's four main Vishnu shrines. At the roadside one km before Pharping village is a series of clear pools filled by a sacred spring. A stone stairway leads up past the **monastery** of the Tibetan lama Chatrul Rinpoche to the small Vishnu temple, a cunning combination of cave and shrine set beneath a weird overhanging cliff naturally colored in orange, white, and black stripes. The shrine's main Vishnu image, carved in the 15th century, was stolen several years ago and has been replaced by a glossy black stone sculpture. To the left is a natural stone representing Chamunda or Kali, here considered the *shakti* or source of Vishnu's energy. Bhajan singers come here to worship her with offerings of songs. To the right is another Vishnu sculpture, then a series of Buddhist deities set behind a metal grille. Monkey-faced Hanumans kneel in front of Vishnu's shrine, and a marble plaque of the sacred cow, Khamdhenu, is set in the pavement.

The cave to the right, meanwhile, is a Guru Rinpoche meditation spot, its roof marked with indentations said to be his hand and head prints. As he meditated here a jealous *naga* sent poisonous snakes to disturb him, but the great master froze them into stone with a blow from his ritual dagger *(phurbu),* transforming them into the stalactites hanging from the crag overhanging the temple.

Vajra Yogini
Work your way around the east side of the hill, passing above a former royal summerhouse now turned into a boarding school, to the gilt-roofed temple of Vajra Yogini enclosed in a walled compound. The tantric goddess appears as the central figure in the 17th-century *torana* above the gate, her left hand bearing a skull cup, her right wielding a chopper to cut away delusion. Instead of being horrifying as ancient texts describe, here she's rather pretty. The temple's side courtyards or the open hillside make a nice place for a picnic lunch; or head up the steep prayer-flag-hung hillside behind the *gompa.*

Asura Cave
A stone pathway leads from the pagoda to the village of Pharping, passing by a cluster of Ti-

betan monasteries on the south side of the hill. Above the buildings, marked by strings of faded prayer flags, is a natural and very sacred cave, actually little more than a cleft in the rock. Hindus worship it as a Gorakhnath shrine; his footprints, carved in 1390, are set in a platform in front. To Tibetans, this is the main meditation cave of Guru Rinpoche, where he did a *mahamudra* retreat and achieved the level of knowledge-holder. This area was once a favorite stopover point for pilgrims on the walk from India to Kathmandu. Tibetans will point out to you the head and handprints of Guru Rinpoche left in the rock. After Boudha, this is the holiest site in the Valley for Tibetan Buddhists, and many come here on pilgrimage.

Most of the recently built Tibetan **monasteries** clustered below belong to the Nyingmapa sect, and their temples display images of Guru Rinpoche. The lowest shrine is built about an image of Tara said to be miraculously appearing from the rock. In 1978 a Tibetan lama built the "Saraswati-Ganesh Temple" here, a good example of Nepali religious diversity. Village Hindus come here to worship Saraswati, while Tibetans revere the image as Tara.

From here a flagstoned path leads to and through the old village of **Pharping,** a miniature replica of what Kathmandu was like a generation or two ago. Spend a pleasant 20 minutes weaving through town, then follow the path to Dakshinkali two km further south.

DAKSHINKALI

Set in a shaded grotto beside the confluence of two streams, this is the Valley's most significant shrine to Kali, "The Black One." Scowling and emaciated, with protruding tongue and red eyes, decked with a necklace of skulls, Kali is an aspect of Shiva's consort Durga, appearing in fearsome form to battle with evil. Kali is said to be extremely powerful and accomplished, as well as the most easily pleased of all Hindu deities. Placated with a sacrificial offering, she will readily bestow gifts and blessings and absolve sins.

Kali serves as family lineage deity *(kuldevata)* or personal deity *(ishtadevata)* for thousands of high-caste Hindus. Those with a family linkage must worship at her temple at least once a year,

while *ishtadevata* devotees come as often as they like to beseech a boon. Before the road was built, Dakshinkali was a four-hour walk from Kathmandu, and the site was still popular. Today it draws some 400,000 pilgrims a year, most visiting on Tuesday and Saturday, the preferred days for sacrifices.

The road ends here at a parking lot, the scene of major Saturday-morning traffic jams. Busy days are like a cheerful temple fair, with crowds of worshippers dressed in their best clothes tugging along goats or chickens for sacrifice. A shaded stone pathway leads past small stands selling offerings—flower garlands, eggs, chickens, and pumpkins (a satisfyingly substantial substitute for blood offerings), as well as snacks like *phuwa,* a creamy, slightly sweet condensed milk, and buffalo-milk yoghurt dished out of black wooden pots. Souvenir stands display tourist trinkets and Hindu devotional postcards; in the springtime women sell red rhododendron blossoms, considered a sovereign antidote for bones stuck in the throat.

Down a flight of steps and across a bridge is the shrine, open to the sky as Kali is said to prefer, decorated with a canopy of gilded snakes. The black stone image of Kali shows her squatting on a corpse, symbolizing victory over time. Grinning and hideous, she holds among other terrifying emblems a skull cup, a severed head, and a sword. Along the sides

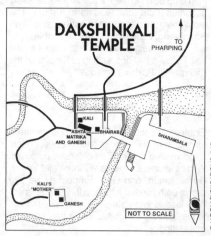

DAKSHINKALI TEMPLE

TO PHARPING

KALI

ASHTA MATRIKA AND GANESH

BHAIRAB

DHARAMSALA

KALI'S "MOTHER"

GANESH

NOT TO SCALE

© MOON PUBLICATIONS, INC.

are enshrined images of Ganesh, the Ashta Matrika, and a plain stone Bhairab. Tourists may
photograph these but are not allowed inside the
sanctum; you may have to remove your shoes in
order to approach.

The surprising dearth of legends about this
place indicates it was probably a natural power
spot to the mother goddesses taken over by Kali
relatively recently—say, a mere 500 years ago.
This is the most important site in the Valley for
animal sacrifices, and Saturday here is exceed-
ed only by the Dasain festival for bloodiness.
Only uncastrated male animals are offered, first
sprinkled with water to make them shrug and
signify their "assent." Caste butchers perform
the sacrifice for a small fee or the reward of the
animal's head. The carcasses are hauled off,
eviscerated, cleaned in a nearby stream, and
collected by the donor, often to be immediately
cooked and served at a family picnic on a nearby hillside.

At the top of the steep hill behind Dakshinkali
a shrine dedicated to Kali's mother offers an
overview of the precincts. Teashops lining the
road above the glade offer fried breads, *pakora,
chana,* and other spicy Indian treats. The **Dakshinkali Resort** being constructed up a side
road about two km before the temple entrance
will provide upscale lodging and food.

Getting There

The 22-km road from Kathmandu is in need of
repaving and is uphill most of the way; take a
mountain bike if you're cycling out (about 90
minutes). Dakshinkali is a 45-minute taxi ride
from Kathmandu; negotiate a half-day or full-
day price to allow you to explore other sites
along the road. Travel agents offer coach tours
of Dakshinkali on Tuesday and Saturday, stopping at other points along the way; cost is around
Rs350. Last choice is the incredibly crowded
public buses that leave from the Kathmandu
city bus park.

BUNGAMATI AND KOKANA

These two beautiful little Newar villages are on
the opposite side of the Bagmati from the Dakshinkali road, about an hour's walk from the Ring
Road. Buses run to Bungamati from Patan's Lagankhel bus park, but it's a pleasant cycle or
hike along a flat gravel road. Head straight south
from Jawalakhel, crossing the Ring Road and
descending to the village of **Nakhu** on the river of
the same name. The ominous-looking square
building on the right is a prison, housed in an
old Rana arsenal. An old iron suspension bridge
imported from Scotland spans the shallow river,
and there's a modern bridge as well. Continue
straight south about three km, passing lush fields
and a huge tract of land set aside for new housing for Members of Parliament (Communist and
Congress MPs joined together in voting themselves this privilege). The Himalayan views from
this area are superb.

Bungamati village

Shortly after the pavement ends the rooftops of Bungamati appear on the right, looking like a medieval European village but for the white plaster *shikara* in the center of town. The smaller town of Kokana is a little northwest of here. Both epitomize the word "quaint," with their timeless untrafficked streets and friendly people.

Bungamati

Bungamati is the winter residence of Raato Machhendranath, the beloved red-faced patron of Buddhist Newars, who divides his time between Patan and here. His association with the town goes back to the 7th century; he's also called Bunga Dyo, "God of Bunga." An 18th-century Capuchin missionary described the shrine's marble-tiled courtyard set with blue flowers as "magnificent . . . I do not believe there is another equal to it in Europe." The marble tiles and much of the magnificence have disappeared; today the shrine is a big open square centered around a 10-meter-high *shikara,* ringed by smaller crumbling shrines and interspersed with scenes from village life. As in Bhaktapur, life is a public affair spilling out onto the streets, and it seems you meet most of Bungamati's 3,000 residents in the course of walking through town. Spinning wool for the carpet industry is a common occupation in winter, when women sit out on the streets with their spindles and wheels. Bungamati is also known for its fine local woodcarvers.

Kokana

About 10-15 minutes' walk northwest of Bungamati is this slightly smaller village, focused around an exceptionally wide main street built after the 1934 earthquake wiped out much of the old town. It's always lined with women sitting in the sun to spin wool, chat, and massage their babies. At the end of the square is a multistoried temple to the local mother-goddess or Ajima **Shekali Mai.** Kokana is famous as an oil-pressing center. Mustard seed is crushed with heavy wooden beams to produce an oil used for cooking and massage. The path continues through town and down a flight of flagstoned steps into fields. Eventually it reaches the Bagmati River, crossed by several footbridges in the vicinity. The road to Hattiban is just around the bend; the more adventurous can hike up to Pharping.

CHAPAGAON

The next road south from the Ring Road goes to Chapagaon, an old Newar village with a big temple to Vajravarahi set in a sacred grove. En route it passes through the smaller village of **Sunakothi,** with an old temple to Nasya Dyo, or Shiva as the patron of dancers. Niches in the compound once held a collection of beautiful ancient stone sculptures, now stolen.

In the next village, **Thecho,** you might see a traditional Newar *bhoj,* with women ladling food onto leaf plates for cross-legged diners. Chapagaon itself is a larger town with many of the amenities typical of well-designed Newar villages, all now crumbling: stone water tanks *(tutedhara)* for thirsty passersby; ponds for bathing, laundry, and protection from fire; brick-lined gutters to channel waste water. There's also the classical art—old carved wood windows and a small pagoda in the center of town with elegant erotic carvings and an old *torana.* The turnoff to the Vajravarahi temple is on the left, the narrow dirt road just past a Krishna sculpture. Ten minutes down is an eerily quiet forest of large, evenly spaced trees, harboring birds and an occasional leopard, and a favorite picnic ground. Tradition says it's ringed by eight cremation grounds. Parents with children who are slow to talk bring them here and leave them in the forest—guaranteed to make the kid talk, if not scream.

Vajravarahi Temple

The forest surrounds the temple of Vajravarahi, the boar-headed goddess who is the protector of livestock. People from all over the Valley come here to offer the first milk from their cows, pouring it over the large stone bull kneeling in front of the temple. The same ritual is used to seek a cure for sick cattle.

Built in 1665, the temple still lacks a pinnacle—supposedly the goddess herself insisted she didn't want one and kept disrupting its construction until builders gave up. On Saturday people from all over the Valley bring offerings. Vajravarahi accepts animal sacrifices, and the floor in front of her image is a sea of blood and flower petals. It's an undeniably powerful place, an impression reinforced by the *bhajan* singing emanating from the corner room, wilder and more macabre than the usual lilting melodies.

LELE VALLEY

Seven km further down the Chapagaon road, up and over the Valley rim, is the small and isolated Lele Valley, a world apart from Kathmandu. Very few visitors make it this far, and the bumpy, dusty road makes it an adventurous mountain bike ride.

Lele is the valley time forgot. Aside from the road and the power lines, the rest of it is straight from the 14th century. Lele village has little of note aside from a few very old temples on the edge of town, set by a sparkling stream, and

the wide-eyed people. The area's main attraction lies before it, in **Tika Bhairab,** a little settlement set along a river. Along the opposite bank is a sacred boulder fronted by a brick wall, upon which is painted a huge multicolored fresco of Bhairab. His ferocious mouth is sunken into the ground, and the composition focuses on his staring eyes, a strikingly abstract representation that's unusual for Nepali art.

The road continues up from here to Kalitaar and **Malla Alpine Resort,** 15 minutes' drive from Tika Bhairab. This out-of-the-way setting is the site of an unusually smart place, complete with terrace restaurant, sauna, even a small swimming pool. Rooms are US$61 s, US$72 d; book at Kathmandu's Malla Hotel, tel. (1) 410-320.

EAST OF KATHMANDU

The road through Chabahil is none too pleasant, but past Boudhanath things get even worse. The suburb of **Jorpati** is a mess: a huddle of shanties and carpet-dyeing factories, crowded with minibuses and tractors chugging up the hill. No wonder the carpet-weaving industry is getting a bad name.

Persist past the bridge over the Bagmati River (a favorite car-washing spot) and things improve. Beyond Gokarna the road winds through classically peaceful and lush countryside. The ancient temples at Sankhu and Changu Narayan are exceptionally interesting and tranquil sites.

THE SUNDARIJAAL ROAD

From **Jorpati,** about one km east of Boudhanath, a wide dirt road runs north all the way to the Valley's rim at Sundarijaal.

Gokarneswar Mahadev
This 14th-century Shiva temple is a few kilometers north of Jorpati, near the confluence of three rivers, at a point where the Bagmati River passes through a wooded gorge. An old cremation site, the temple retains its association with funeral rites. Here Hindus, and Newar Buddhists as well, celebrate special festivals in honor of their dead, in particular the Babuko

Mukh Herne, when people make *shraddha* offerings to their deceased fathers.

The compound was originally much larger but has diminished over time. What remains is beautifully preserved, thanks to a UNESCO-sponsored restoration project in the early '80s. Aside from fine woodcarvings there's a remarkable sculpture collection of various gods on the temple grounds, most not particularly old, but impressive en masse. The 8th-century **Parvati** placed in a small shrine in the northwest corner is exceptionally old and beautiful. Past the temple is the small Newar village of **Gokarna,** and further down, the waterfall of Sundarijaal. Across the river is a walled-in old game preserve, sublet to a private enterprise which operates it as Gokarna Jungle Resort, described below.

Sundarijaal
The road improves past Gokarna Mahadev, and ends five km further at this tiny village set on the edge of the Valley. Climb about 30 minutes up the stone stairway alongside the stream to Sundarijaal, literally "Beautiful Water," a series of waterfalls. Don't bother looking for them in the dry season; by April the flow is reduced to a trickle. This stream is one of the main sources of the sacred Bagmati. There are good picnic sites around here, especially near the old reservoir, or you can continue up to the small village of

THE EAST VALLEY

MANICHAUR DANDA
(2403 m.)

TO HELAMBU AND
GOSAINKUND TREKS

SUNDARIJAAL

BAGMATI RIVER

VAJRA YOGINI

GOKARNESWAR
MAHADEV

GOKARNA

SANKHU

ARUBARI

BRAHMAKHEL

JORPATI

GOKARNA
FOREST

TO BOUDHANATH
AND KATHMANDU

MANOHARA RIVER

CHANGU NARAYAN

CHANGU

PIKHEL

NAGARKOT PHEDI

NAGARKOT
(1985 m.)

NILVARAHI

BORE

VIEWTOWER (2164 m.)

NAKDESH

THIMI

BHAKTAPUR

HANUMANTE RIVER

BRAMHAYANI

TAIKABU

TATHALI

NALA

SURJYA BINAYAK

SANGA

CHANDESVARI

BANEPA

TO TIBET

DHANESWAR

0   2km

PANAUTI

PUNYAMATI KHOLA

TO GODAVARI

INDRESVAR
MAHADEV

© MOON PUBLICATIONS, INC.

Mulkharka. If you *like* steep uphill hikes, you can even continue on to the 2400-meter pass of **Burang Banjyang.** Sundarijaal is a starting point for the Helambu and Gosainkund treks described under "Treks North of Kathmandu" in the Trekking chapter.

The best way to get here is to bike or take a one-way taxi and walk back to Boudhanath. The quiet road passes by fields and villages, a nice country stroll. Local minibuses from the hideous Jorpati intersection are crowded.

GOKARNA JUNGLE RESORT

Three km east of Boudha is the Gokarna Jungle Resort, located in one of Jung Bahadur's old hunting preserves, the Gokarna Forest. Walled-in to protect it from local woodcutters, the lush vegetation shelters spotted and barking deer, wild boars, monkeys, and an occasional leopard. There is a variety of birds (267 counted species), not to mention leeches in the rainy season. It's a great place for a peaceful walk: for once you will not run into people on the trail. Day admission is Rs50.

For entertainment, Gokarna offers a nine-hole **golf course** and the only **elephant rides** in the Kathmandu Valley (Rs550 for foreigners, Rs325 for Nepalis). As of early 1995 the over-priced restaurant and small lodge were closed, but double rooms here used to go for US$30 per night. The resort's city office is on Kanti Path, tel. (1) 226-144.

CHANGU NARAYAN

This superb pagoda temple has been called "a building that could stand alone to represent the very best in Nepalese art and architecture." The Valley's oldest proven existing temple and its holiest Vishnu shrine, Changu Narayan is endowed with glorious woodcarvings and metalwork; its courtyard is a veritable museum of fine ancient stone sculptures. Despite its status few tourists come this way—in fact, few have even heard of it.

Getting There
The temple is set atop a hillock at the end of a long ridge descending from Nagarkot, 13 km east of Kathmandu and four km north of Bhaktapur. On foggy winter mornings its gilded roofs and square form loom up like a floating ship anchored in a sea of mist.

Changu Narayan makes a fine walking destination from either Boudha or Bhaktapur. From Boudha, cycle or take a taxi down the road east through increasingly lush and peaceful countryside. About six km down you'll sight the hilltop temple on the right. Continue to the village of Brahmakhel, where you can entrust the bicycle to the care of a local family, or push it up the hill (a bit rough) if you're cycling down into Bhaktapur.

Strike out across the fields, wading across the shallow Manohara River if there's no foot-bridge, and ascend the hill on a trail which later becomes an ancient stone staircase. Young boys will offer to "guide" you, but really you can't get lost—the temple is easily visible at the top. The climb ascends past scattered settlements, passing some fine private picnic sites on abandoned rice terraces overlooking the fertile countryside.

It's also possible to hike from Bhaktapur to Changu in two and a half hours, a countryside ramble through villages and fields that's a wonderful introduction to rural Nepal. Or, you can walk down from Nagarkot to Changu in around three hours, and continue on to Bhaktapur that same day. Failing all this hiking, a well-maintained paved road runs north from Bhaktapur, stopping just below the little village of **Changu.** Take the Nagarkot road and veer left on a fork after the Mahakali temple.

Temple Architecture
Changu Narayan's main image was installed at about the same time as the Shiva linga of Pashupatinath, in approximately the 4th century. Though the temple has been destroyed many times since by fire and earthquake, most recently in 1702, it's always reappeared, richer and more elaborate each time.

The classically proportioned triple-roofed pagoda is a masterpiece of form and decoration. The lower struts depict Vishnu's 10 incarnations. Sometime during this century the woodwork was brightly painted, masking the fine detail but creating a riot of color. The main entrance is a stunning amassment of gilded repoussé copper,

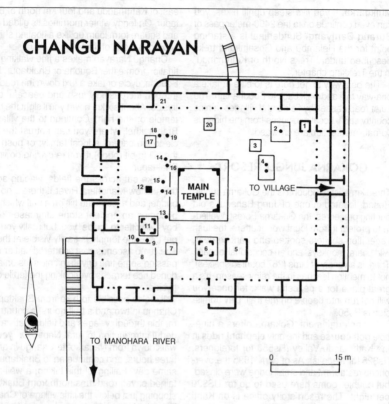

CHANGU NARAYAN

TO VILLAGE

MAIN TEMPLE

TO MANOHARA RIVER

0   15 m

© MOON PUBLICATIONS, INC.

1. Shiva linga
2. Lakshmi-Narayan image
3. Vishnu image
4. Vishnu and Avalokitesvara images
5. Dashamavidya (Durga) shrine
6. Shiva linga
7. Vishnu Vishvarupa ("Universal Form")
8. Lakshmi-Narayan temple
9. Vishnu Vikranta sculpture
10. Narasingha sculpture
11. substitute shrine for Pashupatinath
12. Malla king and queen
13. pillar with conch shell
14. Manadeva's pillar inscription
15. Garuda statue
16. pillar with wheel
17. Krishna shrine
18. Vishnu atop Garuda sculpture
19. Vishnu sculpture
20. Uma-Mahesvara (Shiva-Parvati)
21. dharamsala (resthouse)

topped with a *torana* depicting Narayan. Inside is enshrined the sacred image, hidden from the eyes of nonbelievers, though even believers don't come around much nowadays. A century ago Westerners were not allowed to set foot in the temple compound. French historian Sylvain Levi conducted his 1901 investigation by standing in the doorway and listening to a Nepali assistant describe interesting objects.

Sculptures

The spacious brick-paved temple compound contains smaller shrines dedicated to Krishna, Shiva, and the Ashta Matrika, and scattered all about are images of Buddhas, folk gods, lingas, inscriptions, and above all, images of Vishnu in his many forms, many of them priceless masterpieces. There are several renditions of Vishnu astride Garuda (one on the north side appears on the Nepali 10-rupee note), and a gruesome Narasingha disemboweling a demon with his bare hands. **Vishnu Vikranta** strides across the universe with mighty steps, a rendition of the old legend of Vishnu the Wide-Strider. Finest of all is the 8th-century **Vishnu Vishvarupa** sculpture on the southern side, inspired by the chapter of the Mahabharata in which Vishnu displays his Universal Form to Arjuna. With 10 heads and multiple arms displaying different emblems, the god stands atop Garuda, surrounded by multitudes of adoring deities. A Sleeping Vishnu appears below, resting on the cosmic ocean in the coils of a serpent. The detail and expressions of the figures are hauntingly beautiful.

There's more: the Valley's earliest **inscription,** dated the Nepali equivalent of A.D. 464, is engraved on a stone column behind the Garuda image on the east side. It records the victory of King Manadeva over "barbarians" from the north and east. Nearby and encased in a wrought-iron cage are gilded images of Kathmandu's King Bhupalendra Malla and his mother the queen regent, players in Kathmandu's bloody 17th-century politics who, between plots and intrigues, found time to make generous donations to the gods. Rice grains and flower petals littering their enclosure indicate the elegantly wrought statues have become objects of worship in themselves.

The massive kneeling **Garuda** image beside them once crowned King Manadeva's inscribed victory column, until an earthquake toppled it off its perch. Some historians believe the figure is a portrait of Manadeva himself. Mustachioed, with pudgy cheeks and curly locks, it resembles a well-fed archangel.

Inside the shrine is an even more sacred gilt image of Garuda, said to be self-manifested from a gigantic ruby. Once a year, on the festival of Nag Pachami, this image is said to sweat, commemorating the anniversary of Garuda's wrestling match with the great serpent Taksaka. Temple priests and local people collect the miraculous moisture as a remedy against *naga*-induced diseases like leprosy and ulcers.

Changu Town
Out the compound's eastern door, a looming tower bearing an airport directional light has been anchored in an exercise in bad taste. Directly below is the ancient, typically compact Newar settlement of Changu. A single flag-stoned lane, full of rambunctious sheep and wide-eyed children, leads past brick houses festooned with corn. Exit out the compound's western door and descend a bit into a scrubby forest and a hillside with sweeping views of fields, mountains, and the Manohara River, and the chance, if local children don't discover you, of a quiet picnic overlooking the Valley.

Food and Accommodations
There's a little restaurant/teashop shop in the temple courtyard and a few similarly dinky ones in town. Spiffiest is the **Valley View Restaurant** at the very end, perched at the edge of the hill overlooking the countryside around Bhaktapur. No recommendations on the food, but the views are superb. The gravelled parking lot is a good place to look for a stray taxi for the ride back down, though finding one would be a stroke of luck.

The only place to stay up here lies 10 minutes' walk before town, set above the road from Bhaktapur. The grandly titled **Changu Narayan Hill Resort** is a rather run-down lodge with rooms that can be had after some negotiation for Rs200 d, and a rooftop restaurant. Great views, but no hot water; very few travelers stay here, which may actually be a plus.

SANKHU

Past Changu, the Boudhanath road continues through an increasingly peaceful and prosperous countryside ending at the large old Newar village of Sankhu. Once an important stop on the old Tibet trade route, Sankhu has been virtually forgotten. Except for a few radios and motorcycles, it seems almost untouched by the modern world. The ride out here, past prosperous ochre farmhouses and people snoozing in the sun, is enjoyably peaceful.

The Town
Sankhu is a treasury of Newar architecture. Remaining dignified, many of its richly decorated old houses now sit at crooked angles or are crumbling; the plaster pillars and pediments ornamenting the facades of some demonstrate the Rana-era fascination with European opulence.

An ornate plaster arch marks the entry to town from the bus park. Essentially there are two main roads: take the easternmost, which runs down a flagstoned path through the old bazaar. The two routes meet on the northern outskirts of town, en route to the Vajra Yogini temple.

Being a traditional town, Sankhu is still noted for its religious devotion, and is a prime site for the Swasthani rites performed in the chilly month of Magh (generally January). This month-long purification involves fasting, the reading of sacred texts, and morning baths in the Salinadi River, along with bizarre penances: white-clad men rolling down the main street, or prostrating, or balancing earthen jugs of water on their heads.

To Vajra Yogini

Set on a hillside a few kilometers north of town is an ancient shrine to Vajra Yogini, who began as a nature goddess, was adopted by Buddhists, and is now revered by Hindus as a form of Durga. It's a leisurely half-hour climb up from town which gets quite steep towards the end. A motor road leads to just below the temple, but driving up spoils the approach. If possible, take the old flagstoned pilgrim path, which is lined by finely carved stone water taps, *chaitya,* and small *pati* or resthouses, appropriated by local farmers in the autumn as shelters for harvested grain. If the bridge is out, as it was at the time of writing, you'll have to walk up the road, but keep an eye out for the point where you can cut over to the pilgrim path.

The staircase up to the temple passes a blood-spattered triangular stone embodying Bhairab, who symbolically receives the blood sacrifices intended by Hindus for Vajra Yogini. This is a neat way of getting around the Buddhist aversion to sacrifices, and of avoiding any conflict between Hindu worshippers and the many Tibetan Buddhists who visit here.

The Temple

At the top of the steps is a 17th-century temple, set in a monkey-infested pine forest. Its gilt repoussé *torana* depicts the unusually lovely goddess Vajra Yogini, who is the wisdom deity Ugratara. Defined in texts as a ferocious protector of the Buddhist doctrine, here she's been tamed into a beauty, albeit a fierce one. She and her companion *dakini* Baghini and Simhini, "Tigress" and "Lioness," are all depicted trampling corpses.

Inside the shrine Vajra Yogini is embodied in an elaborately clothed and ornamented image, usually kept hidden from sightseers. She's said to be the eldest sister of the Valley's four main Vajra Yoginis, another way of underscoring her power. A painted mural on the temple's rear wall depicts her in Tibetan form: red-skinned and naked but for a bone girdle, holding a skull cup.

The smaller shrine beside the main temple with a sword-wielding Manjushri on its *torana* encloses a replica of Swayambhunath stupa. Vajra Yogini is said to have persuaded Manjushri to cut the Valley and release the waters of the lake, making it possible for Swayambhu, and the Valley's civilization, to emerge. There's no doubt this is one of the most ancient sites in the Valley. During the Licchavi era it was a Buddhist holy site, later taken over by the tantric goddess Vajra Yogini—and even she is an ancient presence.

Behind her temple, a path leads up to her *dyochhen,* an unremarkable stuccoed quadrangle that conceals ancient sculptures like a 7th-century head of the Buddha, seldom revealed, and a cold-drinks shop with a jarringly modern illuminated sign for San Miguel beer. The portico shelters the three *khat* which bear the godesses during their annual springtime procession. In the middle of the courtyard is a finely carved sunken tap from the 10th century. The pine forest behind, strung with prayer flags, makes a fine if steep picnic site.

Manichaur Danda

The Vajra Yogini temple is set midway up the forested hill of Manichaur ("Heap of Jewels"), said to be dotted with the meditation caves of Tibetan and Indian *siddha.* Further up is a medicinal herb farm, and at the summit a grassy meadow with an image of Ganesh. A *mela* is held every August at the nearby spring. From the temple you can walk to Nagarkot along an old trading route, an uphill journey of about six hours.

Practicalities

Public buses from the Kathmandu municipal bus park take a long, long time to reach Sankhu. It's much better to cycle out, perhaps visiting Boudha or Gokharna en route, or to mountain bike down the steep back road from Nagarkot (described below). There is no food in Sankhu except for a few basic teastalls and cold-drink stands.

NAGARKOT

This small hilltop resort on the Valley's northeast rim overlooks a big chunk of the Central and Eastern Himalaya, including five of the world's 10 highest peaks—Everest, Lhotse, Cho Oyu, Makalu, and Manaslu. While the mountains are distant compared to the views trekkers experience, the panorama is impressively expansive. Nagarkot is a popular destination with overnighters who come for sunrise or sunset

mountain views and to enjoy a quiet retreat from the city.

Don't expect a lot of action. Nagarkot is a pseudo-resort rather than an indigenous village, little more than a few huts and shops, a bus stop, and a dozen or so guesthouses and hotels. Those along the ridgeline offer equally spectacular views, stretching from Manaslu and Ganesh Himal in the west, through Langtang and Gauri Shanker, to Numbur and Karyolung in Solu. Everest appears, but just barely, as an unimpressive nub amid much larger-looking and closer summits.

The vaunted mountain views are not always to be had: the best time is early morning or late

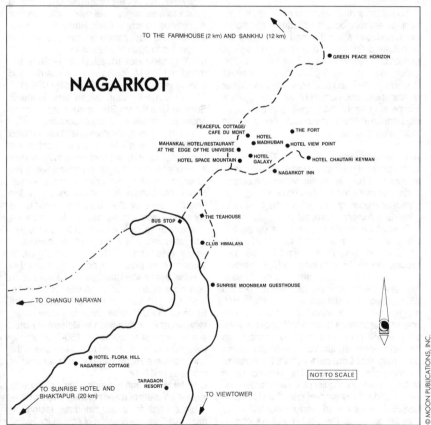

NAGARKOT

TO THE FARMHOUSE (2 km) AND SANKHU (12 km)

● GREEN PEACE HORIZON

PEACEFUL COTTAGE/
CAFE DU MONT ●   ● THE FORT
                    HOTEL
MAHANKAL HOTEL/RESTAURANT ● ● MADHUBAN
AT THE EDGE OF THE UNIVERSE ● ● HOTEL VIEW POINT
HOTEL SPACE MOUNTAIN ● HOTEL   ● HOTEL CHAUTARI KEYMAN
                     ● GALAXY
                        ● NAGARKOT INN

● THE TEAHOUSE
BUS STOP ●

● CLUB HIMALAYA

● SUNRISE MOONBEAM GUESTHOUSE

TO CHANGU NARAYAN

● HOTEL FLORA HILL
● NAGARKOT COTTAGE
        TARAGAON
        RESORT ●
TO SUNRISE HOTEL AND
BHAKTAPUR (20 km)   TO VIEWTOWER

NOT TO SCALE

© MOON PUBLICATIONS, INC.

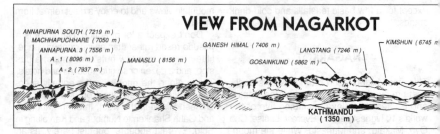

VIEW FROM NAGARKOT

ANNAPURNA SOUTH (7219 m)
MACHHAPUCHHARE (7050 m)
ANNAPURNA 3 (7556 m)
A - 1 (8096 m)
A - 2 (7937 m)
MANASLU (8156 m)
GANESH HIMAL (7406 m)
GOSAINKUND (5862 m)
LANGTANG (7246 m)
KIMSHUN (6745 m)
KATHMANDU (1350 m)

afternoon. Sometimes a cloudy day will segue into a flawlessly clear moonlit night. It's also nice to head up very early to catch morning light on the mountains, have breakfast, and then walk downhill.

To tell the truth there's not much to do here besides eat mediocre food, admire the mountains, and stroll along the road. Most foot trails drop down precipitously, making hiking a serious endeavor. Unlike forested Phulchowki or Shivapuri, the surrounding hillsides are heavily farmed and denuded of forests. The **view tower** on Nagarkot's true summit (2164 meters), a few kilometers east of the lodges, makes a good destination if the Army checkpost is letting tourists up the road.

Accommodations

Lodge prices drop in the summer off-season by as much as half. Mountain views are scarce during the monsoon but they do occur, and Nagarkot is a good getaway from the heat, with green and flowers all around.

The road from Bhaktapur winds up the hill, first passing **Sunrise Hotel,** tel. (1) 290-873, about four km below the summit. Rooms in its upscale new red-brick building are US$40; mountain views are partial but present, and the hotel has well-maintained grounds. Next up, but still 2.5 km below the summit, is **Hotel Flora Hill,** tel. (1) 226-893, Kathmandu tel. (1) 223-311, a resort with garden and (a rarity for Nagarkot) electricity. At US$45 d, it's rather pricey, especially as the rooms are musty and poorly maintained. Next door, **Nagarkot Cottage,** tel. (1) 290-876, caters mainly to group tours but will take individuals as well. It's a very nice, quiet place with local architecture and a pretty garden; rooms are US$20 s, US$26 d, and there are partial mountain views from the top rooms. The problem with this location

is it's still a 20-minute hike up to the ridge for complete mountain views.

At the top of the hill is the dusty little Nagarkot bazaar, basically a few teastalls and a bus stop. Every morning, porters haul in big jugs of milk to pour into a stainless steel milk truck. Past the monstrous concrete **Club Himalaya,** an offshoot of the Kathmandu guesthouse which is scheduled to open in 1996, is the government-run **Taragaon Resort,** tel. (1) 211-008, Kathmandu tel. (1) 470-409, with a nice garden and relatively large if run-down rooms for US$21 d. There are a few cheap lodges here, including **Sunrise Moonbeam Guesthouse** in a Tamang house just before the Army checkpost.

The main group of lodgings is clustered atop a subsidiary hill, a 10-minute walk north of the bus stop. This area has something to be said for it: the ridge towers straight up above a sea of terraces, overlooking the valley of the Indrawati Khola. The simple accommodations here are being replaced by more elaborate resorts, and prices have risen dramatically of late. If money is a factor, arrive early enough in the day to bargain; after dark they *know* you're not going anywhere. Also leave time to look around a bit, as some of these places are poorly maintained.

Hotel Space Mountain, tel. (1) 290-871, is an ugly big edifice with so-so rooms for US$34 s, US$44 d. The lodge at the **Restaurant at the Edge of the Universe** changes names regularly—most recently it was the **Mahankal Hotel,** with a range of rooms for Rs150-500, among the cheaper places around here. Next door is the unremarkable **Hotel Galaxy,** with a range of rooms at US$8-18.

Hotel Madhuban has innovative ambience, at least. It consists of a few bamboo shacks barely big enough for a bed (windows facing the mountains provide a sense of space) for Rs250

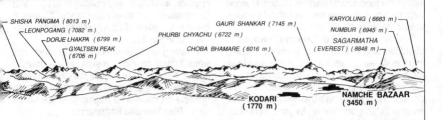

SHISHA PANGMA (8013 m)
LEONPOGANG (7082 m)
DORJE LHAKPA (6799 m)
GYALTSEN PEAK (6705 m)
PHURBI CHYACHU (6722 m)
GAURI SHANKAR (7145 m)
CHOBA BHAMARE (6016 m)
KARYOLUNG (6683 m)
NUMBUR (6945 m)
SAGARMATHA (EVEREST) (8848 m)
KODARI (1770 m)
NAMCHE BAZAAR (3450 m)

s, Rs300 d. A single big room with bath and kitchen goes for US$15. **Peaceful Cottage,** tel. (1) 290-887, further up has shabby rooms for US$8, and shabby "deluxe" rooms for US$20. Its nicest feature is the glassed-in **Cafe du Mont** restaurant.

Down the road is **Green Peace Horizon,** a row of bamboo bungalows precipitously perched at the edge of a terrace facing a spectacular panorama. The tin-roofed huts are hot in summer, and overpriced at Rs600 for a tiny three-bed room, but it's among the better budget places here. **Nagarkot Inn,** behind the View Point, consists of two A-frame bamboo huts and a restaurant; it's simple and relatively cheap at Rs350 a room.

Probably the best deal is **Hotel View Point,** tel. (1) 290-870, Kathmandu tel. (1) 417-414. The brick cottages are well maintained and there's a spacious dining room and terrace, though the looming Fort directly north of them has partially blocked views. Rooms range from US$5 for a basic single to US$15 for a double with bath and a big terrace. There's even electricity, a rarity for Nagarkot.

The aforementioned **The Fort,** tel. (1) 290-869, can't be missed—it's the tall, narrow brick building blocking the View Point's views. The interior is nicely decorated in local style. Rooms with mountain views are excellent, and there are a few separate two-room guest cottages below. Rates are US$57 s, US$63 d. Off to the side is the gaudily decorated **Hotel Chautari Keyman,** tel. (1) 290-875, with rooms for US$40 s, US$50 d, and again a few separate guest cottages.

The Farmhouse, about two km past the main cluster of resorts down the road to Sankhu, is something special. It's set in a renovated old Newar house with raised ceilings, tiled floors, fireplace, even a small library and a Monopoly

game. Rates are US$47 d, which includes set meals; it's peaceful and isolated, a great weekend getaway. Call Kathmandu's Hotel Vajra, tel. (1) 272-719, for reservations and transport arrangements.

Food

Food served in lodges usually involves poorly rendered dishes from impressive-sounding menus. The focus is on the views rather than quality. The glassed-in **Cafe du Mont** at Peaceful Cottage has great ones, while the **Restaurant at the End of the Universe** takes the prize for best name. The best place for a meal is blue-roofed **The Teahouse** atop the ridge, which does good Indian dishes and Western food too.

Getting There

Nagarkot is some 30 km east of Kathmandu and 20 km northeast of Bhaktapur. Public buses running between Bhaktapur and Nagarkot three times daily take about two hours: it's better to hike, bike, or taxi up. On foot from Bhaktapur, take the trail rather than the winding road. Or pedal up the paved road on a mountain bike, and fly back down at top speed (returning via Sankhu is a bumpier option). Several Nagarkot lodges operate daily tourist minibuses for Rs70 one-way, departing Thamel at 1:30 p.m. and returning around 10 a.m. the following morning. Check with the Lodge Pheasant or Hotel View Point, or book through a Thamel travel agent.

Hikes

One of the best reasons to visit Nagarkot is the array of interesting downhill return walks. The old town of **Sankhu** is about four hours' walk away, following the rutted road past The Farmhouse, winding north, then west—a very rough ride for cyclists. Hikers can take the old trail that leaves the road shortly past the lodges. Nearing Sankhu, you can circle around behind the town to visit the Vajra Yogini temple.

The hilltop temple of **Changu Narayan** is about two hours down a prominent ridge jutting into the Valley, as easy a trek as you could ask for in Nepal. The trail passes through fields and scattered Tamang and Chhetri settlements. The odds of finding a taxi in either village are small; arrange to have one waiting for you, or count on

sporadic minibuses and walking to get you into Boudhanath and then Kathmandu. There's a lodge just outside of Changu Narayan if you arrive late in the day.

Heading south from Nagarkot, a steep trail leads through scrubby forest all the way down to the old Newar village of **Nala,** described below. From here it's a few level kilometers on to Banepa on the Arniko Rajmarg, where buses run to Dhulikhel and Kathmandu.

OVER THE RIM

The following destinations lie just east of the Valley rim, but they are so easy to reach—and so worthwhile to visit—they should really be considered part of the Valley. An overnight visit to the old village of Dhulikhel on the road to Tibet is highly recommended. Dhulikhel has magnificent Himalayan views, lodges ranging from basic to deluxe, a pastoral setting, and plenty of good day walks. It combines villages, farmland, mountain views, and cultural sites, and is a wonderfully peaceful retreat from Kathmandu. Especially if you're not trekking, a visit here will provide a glimpse of rural Nepal, with the added bonus of Newar culture.

BANEPA

Beyond the Valley rim extends the territory of the ancient kingdom of Banepa, once the most powerful in Nepal. Settlement in this region began in the Licchavi era, as documented by fragments of ancient stone carvings. By the 14th century Banepa dominated the entire Valley and extended all the way to the banks of the Sun Kosi River. Its power and wealth derived from the flow of trade passing through here to Tibet. When China sent envoys to the Nepali court in Bhaktapur, the shrewd Banepans, their first hosts, passed themselves off as the rightful rulers of the Valley, and appropriated the rich gifts intended for the Valley's rulers. It is also believed to be the birthplace of Arniko, the skilled artisan who was summoned to Beijing by Kublai Khan in the 13th century to teach metalwork and architecture.

At first glance, modern Banepa, 26 km east of Kathmandu, is unimpressive, a modern, dusty,

noisy sprawl of buildings. Much of it was razed by fire in 1961, accounting for the modern look, but turn left at the statue to find the remainder of the interesting old bazaar, one km north. Old houses and temples blend here and it's hard to believe this is the same town as the one on the main road. There are several restaurant-guesthouse combinations on the main road, like **Banepa Guesthouse** and **Chandika Guesthouse,** the latter with a rooftop restaurant. There's no reason to stay here, but the restaurants might come in handy.

Chandesvari Temple

Take the right-hand fork at Banepa's first main intersection, marked by several shrines and a water tap, and head one km northeast to this ancient and impressive shrine, set in a wooded grove on the bank of a river gorge. The beautiful, seductive, and angry young goddess Chandesvari, a manifestation of Durga, appears in a modern plaster relief set over the compound's gate. Her name derives from the demon Chand whom she slew in a fierce battle; local people call her Chandesvari Mai, identifying her as one of the Newar mother goddesses.

The temple's main image, laden with silver jewelry, is honored with an annual chariot procession. The fine temple struts, recently restored by local woodcarvers, depict the Ashta Matrikas and the eight Bhairabs. Most striking is the colorful stylized **fresco** painted on the western wall, depicting a great blue-faced Bhairab, fangs bared and hands displaying tantric mudras. A gateway in the temple compound leads down the hillside to a cremation site on the banks of the Punyamati River.

© MOON PUBLICATIONS, INC.

Map labels:
TO CHANGU NARAYAN
TO NAGARKOT
TO NAGARKOT
TO THIMI
BHAKTAPUR
TROLLEY BUS STOP
TO KATHMANDU
SURYA BINAYAK
TAIKABU
TATHALI
BHAGWATI TEMPLE
NALA
LOKESWAR TEMPLE
SANGA
CHANDESVARI TEMPLE
BANEPA
TO TIBET
ARNIKO RAJMARG
TO DHULIKHEL
NOT TO SCALE
DHULIKHEL
KALI TEMPLE
BATASE
PUNYAMATI KHOLA
INDRESVAR MAHADEV
PANAUTI
SHANKHU
ROSI KHOLA
NAMOBUDDHA

NALA

Up a dirt road four km northwest of Banepa is the medieval-feeling Newar village of Nala, seldom visited by foreigners. The children here have yet to learn to beg, though you can hear them giggling and whispering "give-me-one-rupees" in preparation for the day. In the center of town is a beautifully proportioned four-storied temple to **Bhagwati** built in 1647, one of two such four-storied temples in or near the Valley, and one of the sacred quartet of shrines to the great goddess. The image inside, dating from the 12th century, is so old it's weathered down to a nearly featureless stela.

On the western outskirts of town is another important shrine, this one to **Lokeswar** or Karunamaya, a white-faced image dressed in robes and crown and framed by a gilt and silver *torana*. His appearance recalls the Seto Machhendranath of Kathmandu, and indeed this is another Buddhist deity, this one said to be the guru of the nearby goddess Chandesvari. Nala

is a rather odd setting for this Buddhist shrine, as it's a 100% Hindu village. The ancient shrine was abandoned long ago and recently revived by Kathmandu Buddhists, who funded the temple's restoration and have instituted an annual chariot procession.

Nala is linked by a 10-km dirt road to Bhaktapur, a great mountain bike route, and by a steep trail to Nagarkot, five hours up or three hours down.

PANAUTI

This ancient Newar settlement 32 km from Kathmandu is a fascinating relic of bygone days. Once it was a tiny kingdom, with a palace where the main square stands today. It was also an important trading center, but Banepa has replaced it with the advent of the road.

Panauti today is a charming, as yet unspoiled village, larger and better maintained than most Newar towns, exhibiting a seamless blend of Buddhism and Hinduism. Its backstreets meander past stone *hiti,* stupas, *bahal,* elaborately carved resthouses, and some exceptional temples. In dark little shops, gold- and silversmiths hammer out an array of ornaments. Just like the Germans in Bhaktapur, the French have adopted Panauti with an elaborate project to restore crumbling old buildings and develop a sewage system. The fruits of this labor are already visible, in the finely carved *pati* scattered about this pilgrim town.

Indresvar Mahadev

This ancient temple dates back to 1294, which makes it Nepal's oldest existing shrine, albeit many times restored. The temple enshrines the linga of Indresvara, "Lord of Indra," a reference to Shiva. The woodcarvings are not particularly elaborate, but the carved wooden struts, believed to date to the 14th or 15th century, are exceptionally fine: slender, rounded figures endowed with a grace and harmony that speak across the centuries. Concentrate on the lovely restrained couples carved on the bases of the struts—erotic in the finest sense of the word. The 1988 earthquake centered in eastern Nepal left a gaping hole in the temple's roof and smashed several of the struts; happily the French restoration project has saved it from collapse and is repairing other monuments in the courtyard.

The Ghats

Panauti's other focus is a cluster of temples set at the auspicious confluence of two streams, the Rosi and Punyamati. The streams are said to be joined here by a third and mystic stream, the Lilamati, visible only to sages, which issues from the **Gorakhnath shrine** on the forested hilltop across the river. The confluence is a famous bathing and pilgrimage site; the first day of Magh in mid-January is marked with a big festival here, and every 12 years a month-long *mela* is held, the next being in 1998.

The ghats here are lined with shrines, including a big old plaster-walled temple painted with charming scenes of blue-skinned Krishna with the Gopinis. It's an enchanting place, with ducks paddling in the stream (fairly clean for once) and temples all around. The stone steps include several slanted slabs where the dying are laid with their feet in the holy water. An old

suspension bridge leads across the river to a 17th-century **Brahmayani temple,** dedicated to the patron goddess of Panauti.

Practicalities

Panauti is seldom visited by tourists and has only the most basic facilities: several fly-ridden tea and sweet shops around the bus park, and the **Tribeni Guesthouse** nearby. It's best to day-trip here out of Kathmandu or Dhulikhel, or even Banepa. Minibuses run down the bumpy seven-km paved road from the Banepa roundabout (a wonderful bike ride), or it's a two-hour hike from Dhulikhel.

Start early and walk fast and you can visit Panauti in a single day from Dhulikhel and Namobuddha, following the trail descending from the northwest corner of the stupa. To return, catch a local minibus from Panauti to Banepa, and another to either Dhulikhel or Kathmandu. Panauti can also be reached in five or six hours from Godavari in the south Valley, a moderately difficult walk beginning behind St. Xavier's school and descending a scenic ridgetop along the lovely valley of the Rosi Khola. It's a beautiful walk but it's easy to get lost, as there are many small trails branching off and there only the occasional woodcutter to give directions.

DHULIKHEL

Increasing numbers of tourists are fleeing urban Kathmandu for a few days to seek peace, quiet, and fresh air. The most popular place is Dhulikhel, a sleepy little Newar town four km east of Banepa and 32 km beyond Kathmandu. Dhulikhel boasts an extraordinarily large number of resorts—there's even one with a revolving tower restaurant planned. Compared to Nagarkot's the mountain views here are less expansive, but it's lower (1440 meters) and therefore warmer in winter, and is less touristy and more authentic. The surrounding countryside offers interesting walks to the Buddhist stupa of **Namobuddha** and the beautiful old village of **Panauti;** mountain biking here is another possibility. Dhulikhel is best explored with an overnight stay, but if time is limited it's still lovely to drive out for a meal and mountain views at one of the upscale resorts.

The Town

Once Dhulikhel was an important stop on the main trade route between Kathmandu and Tibet, and the wealth amassed through trade funded the construction of handsome buildings inlaid with intricate woodcarvings, many now alarmingly swaybacked and buckling. Dhulikhel is fertile ground for collectors of classic woodcarvings, though prices have skyrocketed as people realize the value of their old windows with their detailed hand-carved frames. The money earned from their sale allows them to build an entire modern house.

About 5,000 people live in this densely packed town, around half of them Newar, the remainder Tamang and Brahman-Chhetri. The main road begins a block up from the typically nasty little bus park, and curves westward from a murky water tank and a roundabout enshrining a royal bust. It's a pleasantly rural and low-key place, larger than the normal village but still peaceful. Goats wander the streets, tiny shops sell vegetables and cloth, and tinsmiths hammer out metal pots. The old town square holds a **Narayan temple** and a rare shrine to the deity **Harisiddhi**—depicted in the central *torana* as a goddess, but generally considered to be a god. The western outskirts of town hold a small hill topped with temples to Krishna and Bhagwati, their steep steps offering a panorama of the lush countryside.

The road heading east from the water tank meanders slowly uphill, lined with official buildings like the high school, post office, and jail. The large grassy field of the **Tundikhel** is the best place in town for unobstructed Himalayan views; as the litter evidences, it's a popular picnic site.

Kali Temple

Continue southeast up the dirt road (footpaths through gullies provide shortcuts) to ascend the long ridge southeast of town, about a half-hour walk to a small red-washed open-air Kali shrine. Views from here are superb, not least because they include the huddled town below. The done thing is to rise before dawn and walk up with a flashlight and catch the sunrise over the mountains, but sunset is equally stunning and a lot

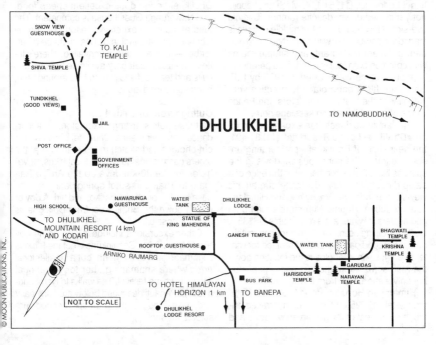

easier to arrange. There are plenty of good picnic sites with spacious views further along this ridge. This road is the beginning of the walk to Namobuddha, described below.

Accommodations

Inexpensive lodges located in the village include the well-kept but noisy **Rooftop Guesthouse** overlooking the bus park and the quaintly decrepit **Nawarunga Guesthouse** 10 minutes' walk up the road to the east. Rooms at both of these places are about Rs150. Still further up the road in a peaceful location is the new but already elderly-looking **Snow View Guesthouse,** tel. (11) 61-229, where uninspiringly decorated rooms with mountain view and bath go for Rs500-700. You can avoid the predawn trek up to the Kali temple by staying at the simple **Panorama View Lodge,** which is *way* up on top of the ridge near the shrine and offers spectacular dawn mountain views right out the door. Rooms are around Rs150, and they serve simple food; the problem is the hike into town.

The best budget choice remains the **Dhulikhel Lodge,** tel. (11) 61-114, which has happily not yet closed down, despite rumors. This old five-story Newar house in the middle of town is loaded with ambience, with a courtyard and garden, a decent restaurant, and simple rooms with common bath for Rs180 d. This perennially popular place was started in 1969 by B.P. Shrestha. It's a good place to practice your Nepali with the friendly proprietors: the Peace Corps often holds training sessions here.

The family business has expanded to the new **Dhulikhel Lodge Resort,** tel. (11) 61-494, the best-sited of Dhulikhel's proliferating upscale resorts. The enormous windows in the spotless Nepali-style rooms, set at the edge of a steep dropoff, take full advantage of dramatic views of the Indrawati Valley and the Himalaya floating above. Rooms with marble-tiled bath and heaters in winter are a reasonable US$35 s, US$40 d; dining options include a rooftop restaurant, a terraced garden, and a fireplace for winter evenings. Another plus is the location down the road across from the bus park—peaceful, but only a short walk from town.

Himalayan Horizon, tel. (11) 61-260, Kathmandu tel. (1) 225-092, is set on a terraced hilltop one km west of town. Carved windows and woodwork salvaged from old Dhulikhel houses have been lovingly restored and set into new buildings designed in the old style. There are 30 rooms at US$49 s, US$53 d. A garden patio offers full-on mountain views; more secluded dining spots are set on terraces lower down. The restaurant serves Chinese, Indian, and Continental food. Ignore **Hotel Arniko** across the road, which charges nearly as much for prosaic rooms and mountain views fronted by the highway.

Dhulikhel Mountain Resort, tel. (11) 61-466, Kathmandu tel. (1) 226-799/220-031, is in an isolated but striking setting some four km past Dhulikhel. The red-brick architecture harmonizes with landscaped garden terraces, and the dining room and thatched guest cottages take in sweeping mountain views. Rooms are US$72 s, US$74 d; three meals a day will add an additional US$40 per person.

Food

The only restaurants are those attached to resorts and guesthouses: in the budget category Dhulikhel Lodge does excellent cheap food, and Nawarunga Guesthouse is competent. The food at the more expensive resorts is stodgily Continental—the Indian dishes might be a better bet—but the setting is unrivalled. There's little in the snack category available beyond biscuits and tea, so if you plan to hike around here, bring some food along.

Outings from Dhulikhel

All these hotels arrange excursions in accordance with their means: Dhulikhel Lodge hands out photocopied sketch maps of the area; the others can provide guides for local hikes, or vehicles for the 80-km drive up the Arniko Rajmarg to Taatopani's hot springs and the Chinese border, or off to Charikot and Jiri. A day of rafting down the Bhote Kosi from Dolalghat is another possibility.

Other excursions include hiking up nearby "Red Mountain" to Gosainkund—not the famous pilgrimage spot to the north, but a smaller local *tirtha* where shamans gather for the annual Janaai Purnima festival. The walks to Namobuddha and Panauti described below are fairly easy and make good pre-trek warmups, or good substitutes for one.

Getting There

Buses leave every 30 minutes from Kathmandu's municipal bus park and take an agonizing 90 minutes to travel the 30 km; a taxi or motorcycle is much faster. Dhulikhel's major resorts will arrange transport from Kathmandu, though it's likely to be pricey, around US$40. Mountain biking is a good idea, as the highway past Bhaktapur is not heavily trafficked. Even better, take the Thimi road into Bhaktapur and another dirt road from here through Nala and Banepa, through fields wearing the colors of the season.

NAMOBUDDHA

Namobuddha means "Homage to the Buddha!" This site is one of the southernmost pilgrimage spots for Tibetan Buddhists, who flock here in especially large numbers in the spring. To them Namobuddha is the most important stupa around the Valley, after Boudhanath and Swayambhunath. Somehow the Southeast Asian Jataka tale of the Buddha and the starving tiger has come to be associated with this remote place. In the Nepali version, the son of Panauti's king was hunting with companions when the group discovered a starving tigress too weak to even feed her newborn cubs. Moved by compassion, the prince offered the tigress his own body as food. Some say he went so far as to feed himself to her, piece by piece.

Namobuddha is about a two and a half hour walk from Dhulikhel, a wonderful nine-km mini-trek through fields, pine plantations, and small villages. Start from Dhulikhel's Kali shrine and continue south along the ridge, dipping up and down along a rutted, seldom-trafficked dirt road. **Dhulikhel Lodge** provides simple sketch maps of the route for Rs2, and there are plenty of opportunities to ask for directions along the way. Namobuddha's prayer-flag-bedecked stupa and Tibetan monastery remain hidden by hills until you top the final ridge.

Namobuddha consists of two sites, the first being a whitewashed stupa said to enshrine the prince's remains, encircled by houses and teashops and a small, decrepit Buddhist shrine. Newar and Tibetan worshippers light butter lamps here, circumambulate the stupa, and vigorously clang the bells surrounding it. A 15-minute climb above on the ridgetop is a Kagyü *gompa* and retreat center associated with Thrangu Rinpoche's monastery in Boudhanath, and another smaller stupa, said to mark the site where the sacrifice occurred. A carved black stone slab below depicts the gory tiger-feeding legend. It may be possible to overnight in the monastery for a small donation, though it's not really equipped to handle tourists. In fact, most of Namobuddha's charm comes from its authenticity as a Tibetan and Nepali pilgrimage site rather than a tourist destination.

The teashops around the lower stupa are a good place to sit in the sun and watch pilgrims

threshing wheat near Dhulikhel

MORE VALLEY WALKS

Roundtrip travel time is not included for destinations where transport back is available.

DESTINATION	WALKING TIME	COMMENTS
Shivapuri	6-8 hours RT	Superb forest preserve, Buddhist *gompa,* mountain views from summit; Rs250 entrance fee.
Nagarjun	4-5 hours RT	Fairly easy walk through private forest preserve; summit is a Buddhist holy site with mountain views.
Ichangu Narayan	2 hours RT	Easy walk up secluded valley to ancient temple.
Sundarijaal-Sankhu	2-3 hours	Moderate hike through fields and a few villages, ending at sleepy old Newar town.
Sankhu-Changu Narayan	3 hours	From the Vajra Yogini temple outside Sankhu, through fields to the hilltop shrine of Changu Narayan.
Budhanilkantha-Balaju	3-4 hours	An easy walk linking the two sleeping Vishnus through mostly flat fields.
Kakani-Budhanilkantha	4-5 hours	Starting at the mountain viewpoint, down through forests and fields to the Newar village of Tokha, and on to the Sleeping Vishnu of Budhanilkantha.
Champadevi	3-9 hours RT	Steep uphill walk into pine forest, then along an open ridge with several summits—continue as far as you like.
Godavari-Phulchowki	4-6 hours	Exceptionally lush forest full of rhodies and orchids in spring; expansive mountain views from the top.
Jawalakhel-Bungamati	3 hours RT	Easy and flat; take the gravel road or cut through fields. Good mountain views along the way, and an interesting Newar village at the end.
Pharping-Kirtipur	6-8 hours	Moderate walk from Buddhist/Hindu holy site through forest, fields, and villages to the old fortress town of Kirtipur; mountain views along the way.
Lele-Chapagaon	6-8 hours	From Tika Bhairab, over the Valley rim, and down to the Vajravarahi temple.
Chapagaon-Godavari	2-3 hours	From the ancient Vajravarahi temple, up onto a ridge to peer into the Lele Valley, then down through fields into Godavari.
Chapagaon-Jal Binayak	3 hours	Mostly flat hike through fields and Newar villages, crossing a few roads; some good mountain views.
Sanga-Godavari	8 hours	Lengthy walk from Valley rim to the Botanical Gardens, weaving up and down hills and through villages. Bring a good map and be prepared to ask directions.
Surya Binayak-Lubhu	3 hours	Starting at a sacred Ganesh shrine, a ramble through fields to a small Newar village.

DESTINATION	WALKING TIME	COMMENTS
Godavari-Panauti	6-8 hours	Lovely secluded hike uphill through forest, then down along the Rosi Khola Valley into Panauti. Hard to find the trail at times, and there are few people to ask for directions.
Nala-Bhaktapur	3-4 hours	Mostly flat along dirt roads, from ancient secluded Newar village through fields to the Hanumante ghats on Bhaktapur's eastern edge.
Nagarkot-Nala	4-6 hours	Mostly downhill along a trail overlooking the Valley, concluding at peaceful Newar town (for transport, walk four km further into Banepa).
Nagarkot-Changu Narayan	3-4 hours	Largely downhill but some ups, through Tamang and Chetri villages and past small shrines to ancient hilltop temple.
Changu Narayan-Bhaktapur	3 hours	Superb easy walk through fields and villages linking two interesting sites.
Thankot-Sitapaila	5-7 hours	An excellent, fairly easy walk through fields, offering good mountain views and ending near Swayambhunath.

spinning prayer wheels and reciting mantras. Colorful prayer flags flutter in the breeze, and there's an inspiring 360-degree panorama of the surrounding countryside, including Panauti in the distance. To return, descend through forests and villages to wind back in a loop to Dhulikhel, or if it's early enough in the day, continue seven km along a rough dirt road to Panauti, about two hours away. After exploring the town (described above) you can catch a minibus to Banepa and return to either Dhulikhel or Kathmandu.

PALANCHOWK

The small ridgetop village of Palanchowk is 15 km down the highway past Dhulikhel and up a dirt road. It shelters a famous and beautiful image of **Bhagwati,** one of the Valley's quartet of important Bhagwati images all supposedly carved by the same sculptor. The story goes the Palanchowk Bhagwati was carved first, and was so fine the king who commissioned it ordered two of the sculptor's fingers chopped off to prevent him from making its equal. Undeterred, the sculptor produced the Bhagwati image of Nala, and promptly lost his right hand. He managed to carve the Shobha Bhagwati image with his left hand, and losing that too, produced Kathmandu's Naxal Bhagwati using only his feet. Carved of shining black stone and decked with silver jewelry, the Palanchowk image is indeed the most beautiful of the group, and it attracts devotees from a long way off.

The hilltop **Sunkosi Adventure Retreat** located here offers river rafting, horseback riding, and cultural tours of local villages. Nicely appointed bungalows are US$60 d, US$75-80 for big deluxe rooms. The Kathmandu office phone number is (1) 223-019.

BEYOND THE VALLEY

A whole country can never be reduced to a single concept, and perhaps the name of Nepal evades concise definition more than any other.
—DAVID SNELLGROVE,
HIMALAYAN PILGRIMAGE

INTRODUCTION

Most of Nepal's visitors never get past the Kathmandu Valley. With its unequaled blend of luxuries and attractions, the Valley inspires inertia in its residents as well. Nepalis seldom travel unless they have to. Rough roads make bus travel punishing even by Asian standards, and food and accommodations are generally very basic. Apart from a few pockets like Pokhara, Chitwan National Park, and the main trekking regions, most of Nepal remains unvisited.

· Nepalis are fond of pointing out the Valley isn't Nepal any more than New York is the United States, or Paris is France—a standard cliché, but true. A related tourist mantra might run something along the lines of: "Thamel is not Kathmandu; Kathmandu is not the Valley; the Valley is not Nepal." Over the last 20 years the realm of possibilities has widened to embrace Pokhara, now the Number Two destination in Nepal, and Chitwan National Park, which has undergone a phenomenal increase in popularity. The list is bound to expand further as adventurous travelers investigate new places, bringing them into the main circuit.

Some of the destinations described in this chapter are teetering on the brink of discovery:

Lumbini, the peaceful birthplace of the Buddha; the hill station of Tansen; the vibrant Hindu city of Janakpur; the scenic roads to Tibet and India. For now, most of the nontrekking destinations outside the Valley are little-known, but exploring them brings great rewards, not least the satisfaction of being among the first.

Getting Around

For mountain bikers, Nepal is one giant unexplored paradise, rugged and demanding but immensely gratifying. See the special topic on "Mountain Biking" for details and ideas. Hiring a taxi with driver for several days is an ideal way to get around at a still-reasonable cost. Domestic air flights are another option: while tickets aren't cheap, flying is the easiest way to travel. But even the notorious bus rides are perversely enjoyable in the way they thrust you into local reality—especially if you break the journey into manageable chunks.

Nepal's expanding road network is centered in the Terai, which is largely ignored by travelers intent on crossing the Indian border in one direction or another. It's true that most Nepali border towns are little more than grimy and depressing bazaars, but some places, like Janakpur, have all the magic of India without the hassle, and the national parks and wildlife reserves here are among Southeast Asia's finest. If nothing else, the Terai deserves attention as home to nearly half of Nepal's population. The **East-West Highway** spanning the region is nearing completion, and it is now possible to drive the length of the country—a tremendous psychological shift for fragmented Nepal.

The balance of roads radiate from Kathmandu to penetrate the central Hills, with their rich and varied traditional cultures, steep terraced hillsides, and mountain views. Mini-treks from roadside Hill destinations provide a taste of rural Nepal without the exertion of a full-out trek, and are an easy way to access seldom-visited regions.

Exploring Nepal by road can be an arduous mission: even travel by car is rough. Mountain bikers have the luxury of going slowly and enjoying every bit of the way. Frequent stops break up the arduous journeys, and provide a kaleidoscope of Nepal's tremendous diversity. The classic trip is Kathmandu-Gorkha-Pokhara-Tansen-Lumbini-Chitwan National Park-Daman-Kathmandu, which with extra days at Pokhara and Chitwan would take about two weeks by car or three weeks by bicycle. Pieces can be deleted or added along the way, of course; Gorkha slots well into any trip to Pokhara, and Tansen is a logical break if you're heading down to Lumbini or Bhairawa.

TO TIBET: THE ARNIKO RAJMARG

The 115-km Arniko Rajmarg follows the ancient trade route linking Kathmandu to Lhasa. This sounds more exotic than it actually is, but as Nepali highways go it's quite a pretty one. The road's construction by China in the mid-'60s was a big deal, especially for India: rumors darkly hinted it was "wide enough for one tank." The highway was intended to serve as a trade link with Tibet and China, but the road's chronically miserable state, combined with the fact Tibet itself is an awfully long way from China, have limited the economic benefits. Each monsoon the highway threatens to crumble; each fall it's salvaged to last another year. Late summer is not the time to drive down it—but summer is the main season for travel to Tibet, and tour groups often end up walking across landslides to reach the border. As of early 1995, independent travelers to Tibet were being allowed to cross the border in the winter months; summertime travel was restricted to groups. See "Leaving Nepal" under "Getting There" in the On the Road chapter for more on traveling to Tibet.

Kathmandu to Dolalghat
As a day drive north-east out of Kathmandu the Arniko Rajmarg offers pretty scenery, following the gorge of the Sun Kosi and Bhote Kosi Rivers the entire way. Motorcyclists can overnight at the small village of Taatopani. Mountain bikers

should allow four days for the trip, with overnights at Dhulikhel or Barhabise and Taatopani. The truly spectacular part begins *across* the border, as the road climbs up to the Tibetan Plateau, a wide-open realm of stones and sheep and mountain plains.

Past Bhaktapur, traffic on the road is dramatically reduced, making it a much more pleasant ride. The highway winds past Dhulikhel, then drops into the red-tinted, severely deforested **Panchkhal Valley,** crossing the braided strands of the **Indrawati Khola** at Dolalghat. The lowest point on the entire road at 634 meters, Dolalghat can be downright steamy in springtime. Rafting groups put in here for the 10-day trip down the Sun Kosi River. From the road you'll see small factories producing handmade paper from the boiled bark of the daphne shrub.

The Jiri Road
Eighteen km beyond is the turnoff to Jiri, the starting point for the classic trek to Everest. The hilly 65-km road was built by the Swiss as part of a foreign aid package of projects focused on Jiri and its surrounding hills. The district headquarters of Charikot lies on a short spur about halfway down this road; an hour's walk from it is the Newar trade entrepôt of **Dolakha.**

It takes a painfully long time to reach the busy little roadhead town of Jiri, with its single long street lined with shops and lodges vaguely remi-

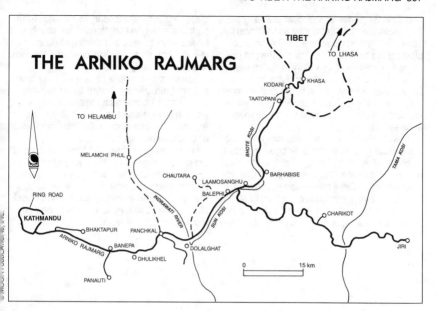

THE ARNIKO RAJMARG

niscent of the Wild West. Once here, the best place to stay is the **Mt. Everest Lodge,** which has a top-floor restaurant overlooking the street.

Laamosanghu to Barhabise
Back on the Arniko Rajmarg, the rickety teashops of Laamosanghu ("Long Bridge") are a few km past the Jiri turnoff; 13 km further is the bazaar town of Barhabise. From here on it's dicey: each year laborers clear off monsoon landslides and cut a new road through the hillsides. Things are okay for a while, then the rains come again, sending huge sections tumbling down.

If the road is out, regular bus service from Kathmandu ends at Barhabise. Minibuses, jeeps, taxis, and trucks ply the driveable sections of the road—the situation changes annually. Towards the end of the monsoon you may have to cross over landslides on foot, but passenger buses or trucks resume after a few kilometers at most. As always in Nepal, porters are available to help with luggage over the rough parts—bargain.

Taatopani and Kodari
As the road climbs, the river gorge deepens. The sheer rock walls are hung with waterfalls

and festooned with greenery, a spectacular sight in the monsoon. Twenty-three km past Barhabise is Taatopani (literally "Hot Water"), a string of roadside shops, basic lodges, and teashops. The hot springs at the north end of town aren't exactly soaking tubs, just boiling hot water gushing out of five spouts—wonderful if you've just made the cold and dusty descent from Tibet. This is the last village of note in Nepal, and is certainly a better place to stay than the border town of Kodari three km further, which is little more than a collection of huts.

From Kodari you can gaze across the river into Tibet. The landscape remains pure Nepali, a narrow river gorge cloaked in green forest and low-hanging clouds. At 1640 meters, Kodari is the lowest point along the entire Nepal-Tibet border; this, combined with easy access to the Kathmandu Valley, made it the preferred trade route to Lhasa.

Khasa
The Tibetan town of Khasa appears high up on the opposite hillside. The name translates as "Mouth Place," referring to the yawning hole the Bhote Kosi has breached in the mountain wall

(the Chinese name for the town is Zhangmu). This profitable trade entrepôt was snatched by Tibet after besting Nepal in a 1792 miniwar, explaining the border's unusual southward protrusion—generally it runs along the Himalayan crest. Since China runs its far-flung empire on Beijing time, Khasa is two hours and 45 minutes ahead of Nepal; plan accordingly if you're crossing the border and hope to change money at Khasa's bank.

Travelers with Chinese visas can cross the self-proclaimed "Friendship Bridge," guarded at one end by Nepali troops, at the other by poker-faced young Chinese soldiers in baggy green uniforms. Once there was a paved road to Khasa, but as this section is exceptionally steep and landslide-prone, it will probably never be rebuilt. It takes about an hour to hike the 600-

meter ascent from Kodari to Khasa. Again, porters are easy to find. Nepalis can travel up to Khasa without a visa, and many go to load up on cheap Chinese goods like blankets, thermos flasks, and brandy.

Khasa is a busy little bazaar town, its multinational mix demonstrated by its teashops, which serve Tibetan butter tea, Nepali milk tea, and Chinese green tea. Lodgings include an expensive cement-block tourist hotel and several decent cheaper places.

Buses run from here to Lhasa, climbing up the sheer-walled Bhote Kosi gorge through increasingly spectacular scenery. It takes the better part of a day to ascend to a nameless 5050-meter pass and emerge onto the vast open plains of the Tibetan Plateau—one of the world's most dramatic transitions.

DAMAN AND THE TRIBHUVAN RAJPATH

The tiny ridgetop village of Daman, 75 km southwest of Kathmandu, offers some of the finest Himalayan views in Nepal. The route there, the Tribhuvan Rajpath, is the most exciting—indeed, hair-raising—of the country's mountain roads. Before its completion in 1956, the Kathmandu Valley was isolated from India and the outside world. Teams of porters lugged supplies, dignitaries on palanquins, even automobiles over the rugged mountains. It took India more than three years to build the stretch from Bhainse to Kathmandu: drive down it and you'll see why. Nepal's Hills simply were not made for roads, and this particularly rugged stretch was an enormous challenge.

Today most vehicles on the Kathmandu-India route use the Butwal-Narayanghat-Mugling road, longer in distance but wider and less nerve-racking. This leaves the Tribhuvan Rajpath nearly empty, perfect for mountain bikers, motorcyclists, and private cars.

Daman is about a three-hour drive from Kathmandu, four or five hours by bus. You might pass through here en route to Birganj and India, or as an alternate route to Chitwan National Park—it's only an hour longer than the usual road. Day-trippers to Daman risk missing mountain views lost in afternoon haze, but overnighters are virtually guaranteed clear morning views. There's a limited selection of rough and soft lodging available.

Reaching Daman by bus is problematic as there's only one Sajha bus a day each way between Kathmandu and Hetauda, departing at 7 a.m. Night buses are more common, but the thought of making those hairpin curves in the dark is terrifying. Mountain bikers proclaim this the best ride in Nepal. By cycle it's a tough one-day haul from Kathmandu to Daman; the trip could be extended to Chitwan National Park or down into India. If you're cycling up from India, the Tribhuvan Rajpath is undoubtedly the best way in, as the main Pokhara-Kathmandu road is too crowded to be fun, or even safe.

THE TRIBHUVAN RAJPATH

The Road There
For the first hour the road to Daman parallels the Prithvi Rajpath to Pokhara, an important trade route that's crowded with wheezing Tata trucks and overloaded buses. Beyond the Ring Road, the countryside gradually emerges from the recently built industrial overlay. Smells, sounds, and sights are thoroughly rural by the time you reach **Thankot,** an unattractive little town perched on the Valley rim 10 km from Kathmandu. Highlights include a police station and a **King Tribhuvan Memorial Park** enshrining an ill-proportioned statue.

Cross the prayer flag-strung pass behind Thankot and you're out of the Valley. The road abruptly drops—and drops and drops; the hairpin curves twisting far below give a taste of what's to come. Guardrails are practically nonexistent; this route is not for the squeamish. The road twists and turns a total of 52 times before arriving in the village of **Naubise,** 29 km from

Kathmandu. The teashops here are among the few places to eat before Daman.

Here the road forks: the Prithvi Rajpath follows the Trisuli River to Mugling, while the Tribhuvan Rajpath branches off to the left. It's narrow and twisting, and far less trafficked than the busy stretch up to Naubise would suggest. There are no villages along the way, just some scattered homes of Buddhist Tamangs marked by prayer flags. The road climbs slowly to **Tistung Deorali** (2030 meters), 34 km from the turnoff, and descends into the broad **Palung Valley,** an intensively farmed Newar settlement since Licchavi times. Cross the Palung Khola on a suspension bridge and pass through several pleasant bazaar villages. There are a few hotels here if you conk out before the final ascent; signs are in Nepali, so ask.

The road climbs a final 10 km through pine forest. About three km below Daman is a strange clearing with gigantic concrete benches lined up facing the Himalaya—an abandoned campsite for giant tourists? Then comes Daman (2322 meters), a handful of houses strung along a ridge and several dozen people carrying on their daily lives in front of one of the most incredible views in the world.

Daman

Daman's pride is the **Everest Viewtower and Lodge,** an ugly cement structure built and run by the government. The observation deck (admission Rs5) gives an expansive 386-km panorama from Dhaulagiri all the way east to Kangchenjunga. The view is incredibly comprehensive: all the five Annapurna peaks, the impressive form of Himalchuli, Ganesh Himal, the rarely seen Shishapangma (Gosainthan) in Tibet, Langtang, the Jugal Himal, and the many peaks of Khumbu Himal, including an excellent view of Everest. The eastern Himalaya is partly obscured by a forested ridge, but climbing up past the schoolyard gives a completely unobstructed view. The pivoting telescope, if it's working, is a marvellous idea that lets you zoom in on selected peaks.

The viewtower is crowned by a glassed-in, circular room with four beds at Rs50 each. The setting is unique, but flaws include outdoor toilets, cramped quarters, and shattered windowpanes which make it freezing in winter. The battered guestbook makes good reading—evidently the windows have been broken since 1984. There's no electricity in the tower, but the moonlit mountain views are incredible, and turning the telescope upwards yields the advertised "Whole Mountains and Space View from Bed." A few teastalls near the viewtower dish out *daal bhaat* and will put up travelers in a pinch. The small hilltop **gompa** about a half-hour walk up the road makes an interesting excursion.

The new **Everest Panorama Resort** is three km beyond town, just below Sim Bhanjyang. At the moment it features deluxe safari tents, but bungalows should be under construction soon; the site has excellent mountain views. Rates are US$56 per person, meals included (possibly negotiable for walk-ins). The restaurant, with its outdoor garden, is a much better place to eat than Daman's *daal bhaat* diners. The resort's Kathmandu office is in Lazimpat, tel. (1) 415-372; the Daman telephone number is (57) 21-346.

Daman to Hetauda

Continuing south, the Rajpath crests at the pass of **Sim Bhanjyang** (2487 meters), three km past Daman, then rolls down the gently sloping Lami Danda all the way to **Bhainse.** The succession of altitudes is laid out as clearly as in a botany textbook, as pines give way to rhododendron forest, jungle, and terraced fields.

The industrial town of Hetauda (466 meters), about 50 km from the pass, is the usual overnight stop for cyclists from India. **Motel Avocado,** tel. (57) 20-429, set in a shady grove north of the bazaar, is a pleasant surprise in this nondescript town, with rooms for Rs250-550 and the only guacamole in Nepal. Travelers to Chitwan National Park should catch a bus to Narayanghat/Bharatpur and get off at Tadi Bazaar, a quick 60 km from Hetauda. The bus park is in the southwest corner of town.

Hetauda itself is a dull roadside town noted only for its location at a major highway intersection. Its main claim to fame is as the starting point for a cableway to haul goods over the mountains into Kathmandu (visible from the highway, and again in the Kathmandu Valley from the Ring Road, near Kirtipur). A ropeway has been in use since the 1920s; the current version was installed in 1958, and is still used to carry cement from the Hetauda factory.

Hetauda to Birganj

The Rajpath ploughs south over the Churia Hills, the final range of foothills separating the Himalaya and the Terai. A few km past **Amlekhganj** is the entrance to Parsa Wildlife Reserve, an adjunct of Chitwan National Park providing extra territory for its wide-ranging tigers. Parsa is not equipped to deal with individual tourists, though you can enter on foot, with a guide, after paying an entry fee of Rs650.

Beyond here the countryside becomes increasingly built up as you approach the outskirts of Birganj, home to some 80,000 people, many of them recent immigrants from across the open border with India. The highway is lined with dilapidated "factories": this is Nepal's most industrialized city. Birganj is a popular access point to and from India, mostly used by travelers from Patna and Calcutta. It's frankly squalid, a disappointing introduction to, or send-off from, Nepal. Trucks and buses jam the main road, though a new bypass has diverted the worst of the traffic from the center of town.

Birganj has two bus parks: a new one on the east side of town for long-distance buses, and a more central old one a block west of the main road for night and local buses. Buses to Kathmandu and Pokhara take around 10 hours and go through Narayanghat, passing Tadi Bazaar en route (there are direct buses to Tadi as well). If you'd like to travel via Daman, catch a bus to Hetauda and wait for the once-a-day bus to Kathmandu. It's easy to reach any Terai city from Birganj; Janakpur is only a five-hour ride away.

There are plenty of cheap hotels and Indian restaurants around the old bus park in the center of town. **Hotel Diyalo** overlooking the bus park or the slightly cheaper **Hotel Kailas** behind it have decent rooms for Rs200-250, a/c rooms for Rs500-600.

The Indian border lies four km south of town, a half-hour ride in a cycle rickshaw (Rs40). Customs and immigration offices are open 7 a.m.-7 p.m. The Indian town of Raxaul is just across the border; catch another rickshaw to get to the Raxaul bus station. From here it's a five-hour bus ride to the Patna railway station.

GORKHA

The ancestral home of Nepal's ruling family, the hill town of Gorkha lies in the very heart of Nepal, midway between Kathmandu and Pokhara. Though it's easy to reach, only 21 km up a paved road off the Pokhara-Kathmandu Highway, few travelers stop here—and therein lies much of its charm. A brief visit on the way to or from Pokhara will provide more insights into Nepal than you're likely to get at either Lakeside or Kathmandu.

Gorkha's main attraction is its medieval **palace,** fantastically perched on a steep ridge above the huddled town. While small by Kathmandu standards, it's among the most historically significant sites in Nepal. Gorkha proper offers only quiet charm: its cobbled streets are traversed by pedestrians, not vehicles, mostly Hill people come to the bazaar for serious shopping. Gorkha is the launching point for several treks in the Central Hills, including the Manaslu Circuit. It's also the midpoint of the untrekked Pokhara-Trisuli trail, and can be used as an alternate starting point for the Annapurna Circuit or Manang treks. Finally,

it's a great place to break the Pokhara-Kathmandu journey, especially for cyclists.

History

Gorkha's small-town air belies its tremendous historical importance. From its hilltop fortress King Prithvi Narayan Shah launched his drive to unify the independent states of Nepal, a wildly ambitious project which succeeded due to his brilliance, and to the fierceness of his locally recruited troops. The British term "Gurkha" initially referred to the famed fighting men of the region and evolved from the name Gorkha.

Originally controlled by tribal chieftains, Gorkha was one of many petty hill states taken over in the mid-16th century by Hindu warriors from western Nepal. The Shah princes traced their lineage back to Rajasthani royalty displaced by the Muslim invasion. The claim was dubious, but they did replicate the Rajputs' concern with warfare and the purity of Hindu rituals.

The eighth in his line, Prithvi Narayan Shah was born in 1722, following a dream of his moth-

© MOON PUBLICATIONS, INC.

er's that she had swallowed the sun. He assumed the throne at 20, and soon demonstrated he was more than the run-of-the-mill local ruler. His burning ambition to conquer the Kathmandu Valley inspired his people to support a long and costly war. He was shrewd enough to exploit the differences between the Valley's warring kingdoms, and preferred to persuade rather than fight his opponents, a tactic which had increasing success as his power grew.

Prithvi Narayan Shah and the Gorkhalis devoted 26 years to the siege and conquest of the Valley, then turned to conquering new territory. By the beginning of the 19th century, Nepal had been welded into a nation, and Prithvi Narayan Shah had earned a place in its history as its founding father.

GORKHA BAZAAR

Gorkha is basically a one-street town, but the lack of traffic makes it quite a pleasant one. The road leading from the outskirts of town up to the bus park is lined with newish shops displaying anything a Hill consumer could want—clothes, backpacks, pots and pans, stick-on *tika,* and bangles. The noisy, dusty bus park itself is redeemed by an enormous pipal tree, beneath which porters sit and watch the passing parade.

From the bus park a dirt road leads uphill past the local **Tundikhel** or parade ground and an army camp. Near the small pond called **Rani Pokhari** are a cluster of temples and a statue of

Prithvi Pati Shah, an ancestor of Prithvi Narayan who visited Kathmandu and brought back Newar traders and builders. He's credited with sponsoring most of Gorkha's monuments, all clearly Newar in their style. The Gorkhalis were happy to call in expert Newar architects and artists to improve their city, while they devoted themselves to warfare.

The cobbled main street curves east from here to run through Gorkha's quaint old bazaar. It's packed with small shops and teastalls where men gather to argue politics. The women's meeting place is the public water tap, **Tin Dhara,** on the eastern end of town.

Roughly in the middle of town is **Tallo Durbar** ("Lower Palace"), a big mid-18th-century quadrangular building used as administrative headquarters, in contrast to the royal abode up on the ridge. It's said to be built on the site of Gorkha's original, pre-Shah palace. Supposedly several attempts to shift the building higher ended with the stones returning by themselves at night, until people finally gave up. Tallo Durbar was recently renovated and its impressive woodwork is in fine condition; there's talk of establishing a history museum here.

GORKHA DURBAR

The old Shah palace, **Upallo Durbar,** or Gorkha Durbar, looms over the town, perched atop a ridge like an eagle's eyrie. It was sited there for defensive reasons, but the intent was no doubt to impress as well. Gorkha's palace is the holiest and most impressive of all central Nepal's hilltop forts or *kot.* Unlike many of its ruder cousins, it's a real little palace, with handcut stones set in battlements. First built by Ram Shah (1606-36), the palace was expanded and improved by succeeding kings who, even before they conquered Kathmandu, brought in Newar woodcarvers to decorate their abode. More recently the Nepali government has poured large sums of money into restoring this historically significant site. One of the most elaborate and best-maintained monuments outside the Kathmandu Valley, it's doubly impressive in tiny Gorkha.

The Trail Up
Multiple trails lead up the steep hillside from the bazaar; start from the Tin Dhara water tap or

the stone staircase across from Tallo Durbar. The stiff half-hour climb will leave you breathless and can be sizzling in springtime, though a few shady pipal trees and water taps along the way offer relief. Tour groups are routed around the front of the palace to enter its western side; it's more pleasant to follow the stone staircase up to its end, a shady *chautaara* on the palace's eastern side.

This is Hanuman Bhanjyang or Hanuman Pass, named after the Monkey King of the Ramayana, depicted as an axe-wielding figure in a stone sculpture along with Ganesh and Shiva-Parvati. A tea seller is usually set up here, and it's pleasant to sit and watch the foot traffic from Gorkha into the surrounding hills—porters, villagers, schoolchildren. The central Nepal Himalaya form a stunning backdrop, with mountain views from Dhaulagiri to Ganesh Himal, 8156-meter Manaslu rearing up straight ahead. To the south the lower Mahabharat Range is visible, separating the Hills from the Terai.

The Palace Compound

When you've recovered from the climb, enter the palace compound. The lower level holds a rest hall for pilgrims built by Rudra Shah, featuring some explicit erotic woodcarvings, nicely restored. The upper level contains the actual palace, which is divided into two sections: **Kalika Durbar** and **Raj Durbar.**

A small **Pashupati shrine** was installed here by Prithvi Narayan Shah as a sacred substitute for Kathmandu's temple. A four-faced Shiva linga stands beside a resthouse occupied by four *sadhu* of the Kanphata or "split-ear" sect—one look at their enormous earrings explains the name. The *sadhu* perform *puja* complete with horns and drums daily around 10 a.m. and 6 p.m.

A narrow flight of steps between two bells leads down to the sacred **cave-temple of Gorakhnath,** hewn out of solid rock. Fraught with ritual significance, this is among the most important sites in Nepal for mainstream Brahman-Chhetris. The powerful 12th-century yogi Gorakhnath has been semi-deified into a mysterious figure some say is an emanation of Shiva. As patron of the Shah kings (his footprints appear on the royal coat of arms), he's credited with assisting Prithvi Narayan Shah's stunning victories. It's said Gorakhnath made a promise to appear on battlefields wherever Gurkhas fight. You can peer into the cave's dim interior, which features a forest of tridents, a symbol of both Shiva and Gorakhnath. There is supposed to be a lotus pedestal bearing silver footprints representing Gorakhnath.

Turn to the right to enter the main palace complex, which has achieved the status of a shrine as the birthplace of the revered Prithvi Narayan Shah. Leather shoes, bags, and belts are prohibited inside this compound; so are cameras, and there are plenty of unsmiling soldiers to enforce these rules. Tourists are not admitted inside the palace, but you can peer though a wood-latticed window to see the throne

palace window

room with a tiny seat said to belong to Prithvi Narayan Shah.

The east wing, **Dhuni Pati,** was once the royal living quarters, though what impresses now is the less-than-palatial scale of Gorkha's royal abode. The westernmost portion enshrines a **Kali temple,** served by a special subcaste of Brahman priests. They and the king are the only ones allowed to proceed beyond the courtyard; it's said ordinary people would die if they gazed upon the goddess's image. Worshippers perform animal sacrifices at the entrance on the eighth day of the lunar month, reaching a bloody crescendo during the autumn festival of Dasain and the smaller Chaitra Dasain in the spring, when hundreds of goats, chickens, and buffalo meet their doom.

the eight-spoked wheel, the Khorlo, symbolizing the supremacy of religious law

Around the Palace

Twenty minutes' walk up the ridge east of Hanuman Bhanjyang is **Upallokot,** "Upper Fort," little more than an enclosed pen, now flanked by a microwave tower. Comprehensive mountain views include an impressive angle on the palace below.

On the western side of the palace is the royal **helipad,** occasionally used by the king for ceremonial visits. A trail leads from here to **Tallokot,** another lookout point. It has less impressive views than Upallokot, but it's an easier walk. A trail leads back down from here to town.

AROUND GORKHA

Gorkha's attractions are easily viewed in a single day, but consider allotting more time to explore the quintessentially Nepali countryside, with its Hindu villages, spreading pipal trees, and traditional teashops. This lowland area is particularly nice to visit in wintertime (Dec.-Feb.); by April it's steaming hot. Seldom visited by trekkers, the rolling hills are laced with trails considered easy when compared to many of Nepal's steeper routes.

Manakamana Temple

The "wish-fulfilling" temple of Manakamana on a ridgetop south of Gorkha is renowned as one of the most effective shrines in the country. Suppliants sacrifice animals to the goddess Bhagwati here, and a few teashops put up overnight visitors. It's 18 km from Gorkha, a full day's walk. Several more hours downhill, the trail emerges at **Abu Khaireni,** at the intersection of the main highway and the Gorkha turnoff. If you're starting from here, the temple is a four-hour walk uphill from Abu Khaireni.

Gorkha to Trisuli

The region's main trail is the old Trisuli-Pokhara trade route, still a good choice for an unspoiled and relatively easy trek. From the Hanuman Bhanjyang *chautaara* beside the Gorkha palace a trail leads to **Ali Bhanjyang,** climbs up an open ridge with good views to the Brahman village of **Tapli,** then drops down to **Khanchok Bhanjyang,** four hours from Gorkha. The trail continues to **Arughat Bazaar** on the banks of the Burhi Gandaki 20 km from Gorkha, and eventually joins the road at Trisuli, a three-day walk total.

Gorkha to Pokhara

West of town past the Tundikhel, a trail drops 800 meters to the **Darundi Khola** and the route to Pokhara. The river is good for swimming, but remember it's one hour going down, and nearly twice as long to get back up. Continuing to the west, a long day's walk away the trail meets Tarkughat, a village on the Dumre-Besisahar road. Besisahar is the usual launching point for the Manang/Annapurna Circuit treks, but walking in from Gorkha might be a better choice than the agonizingly bumpy truck ride from Dumre to Besisahar. Pokhara is two or three days further west, an easy, satisfying walk through remarkably unspoiled countryside.

North of Gorkha

The three-day walk up the Darundi Khola to the big Gurung village of **Barpak** is best attempted with a guide, tents, food, and porters, unless you're prepared for very basic accommodations. That said, it's an interesting walk, and with a guide and tents you could loop back via the hilltop viewpoint of **Darche** (3247 meters), returning via Khanchok Bhanjyang to Gorkha.

PRACTICALITIES

Accommodations
A number of basic lodges are clustered around the noisy bus park. **Hotel Thakali** and **Hotel Meenu** have decent rooms for around Rs50, but you're better off avoiding the earsplitting predawn departure racket and staying further down the road. Try the **New Thakali Lodge** down the dirt road west of the bus park, or one of several small lodges **(Hotel Pamper, Hotel Park, Hotel Yatri)** along the main road east of the bus park.

The best place in town, though it likes to rest on its laurels, is **Hotel Gorkha Bisauni,** tel. (64) 20-107, set above the road about one-half km east of the bus park. Big, if bare rooms with attached bath are Rs300-400, dorm beds are Rs50; there's a pleasant garden and an adequate restaurant.

The upscale choice, **Gorkha Hill Resort,** Kathmandu tel. (1) 271-329, is inconveniently located four km before town on a ridge off the highway. You'll need your own vehicle to be able to access Gorkha at your leisure, but the site is spectacular: rooms have views of the Himalaya and Gorkha Durbar, and there's a nice garden. Rooms with attached bath and hot water are US$30 s, US$40 d.

Food
The situation is not very inspiring. Look around the bus park for restaurants serving *daal bhaat* and *momo*. **Hotel Gorkha Bisauni**'s restaurant is the only place in town to serve even pseudo-Western food, though the Chinese/Nepali dishes are better, and service can be painfully slow. **Gorkha Hill Resort** serves tolerable food to its guests at steep prices—US$8 for lunch or dinner.

Getting There
Gorkha is a five- or six-hour bus ride from Kathmandu (140 km), four hours from Pokhara (109 km), and only about two hours (78 km) from Tadi Bazaar and Chitwan National Park. Daily buses also link Gorkha to Birganj and Bhairawa. Direct buses from Kathmandu are few, but you can get off at **Abu Khaireni** eight km west of Mugling and catch a minibus or truck running up the paved 21-km road to Gorkha. Cyclists should note the road is well-maintained but steep.

POKHARA

Soon after Nepal opened to the outside world, rumors began to trickle out of a remote valley a week's walk (200 km) west of Kathmandu, where tropical flowers grew on the shores of a tranquil lake and Himalayan peaks filled the skyline. The Pokhara Valley's idyllic reputation was fueled by praise from veteran travelers like the Japanese monk Ekai Kawaguchi, who found it the most enchanting place of his five-year travels through the Himalaya. The Swiss geologist Toni Hagen, who has walked over 14,000 km in Nepal, called it "one of the most extraordinary and beautiful places in the whole world."

In just a few decades, Pokhara has gone from secluded Shangri-La to major tourist destination, but its stunning natural beauty remains largely unspoiled, enhanced by an air of decided relaxation. Most of the 124-square-km Pokhara Valley remains farmland, unbelievably lush in the monsoon rice-growing season. Soft-eyed water buffalo wander the back lanes of Lakeside, where rice fields still stand amid the proliferating guesthouses, and huge old pipal trees fill the air with the sound of their rustling leaves.

The tourist area of Lakeside, stretched out along the southeast shore of the valley's largest lake, is a little Never-Never Land centered around sun, fun, and the next meal. Restaurants playing Simon and Garfunkel and Elton John only add to the feeling of a '60s time warp. In the height of tourist season the scene borders on the absurd, as preening couples prowl the street in search of the trendiest restaurants.

water buffalo
swimming hole
near Pokhara

Despite its tourist-trap aura and high-season claustrophobia, Lakeside has its own charm, especially in the evening, when darkness hides the clutter and the shops are lit up like Christmas trees. Shopkeepers sit in front of their stores along the strip, chatting and playing with their kids. It's easier to meet Nepalis here than in Kathmandu, perhaps because both they and you have more time.

Trekkers know Pokhara as the starting point for classic routes like the Jomosom trail, and as the ideal site for lazy recuperation after the three-week Annapurna Circuit. For nontrekkers the valley offers mountain views and glimpses of rural Nepali life going far beyond those of the Kathmandu Valley. For everyone, Pokhara is a wonderfully relaxing place, the closest Nepal has to a resort.

THE LAND

The Pokhara Valley is a lusher, lowland version of the Kathmandu Valley, a blend of rich farmland and forests rimmed by hills. With an average altitude of 900 meters, the climate is mild, averaging 15-26° C: steamy in the summer months, but downright balmy in the winter, a relaxing antidote to the chilly Kathmandu Valley. Pokhara's average annual rainfall exceeds 4,100 mm, making it one of the wettest places in Nepal. Most falls during the monsoon, but afternoon thunderstorms may occur even in dry winter months.

Greenery thrives in the gentle climate: orchids, bougainvillea, banana trees, poinsettias, big spiky cactuses, and of course rice—Pokhreli rice is famous for its flavor. The flower displays are magnificent year-round, and lush gardens turn even simple guesthouses into exotic hideaways.

Juxtaposed against this subtropical paradise are 7000- and 8000-meter-high Himalayan peaks, some a mere 30 km north and separated only by low foothills. Pokhara's mountain views span a choice 140-km section of Nepal's central Himalaya, including Dhaulagiri, the 56-km long Annapurna Range (which has 16 summits over 6000 meters), Manaslu, Himalchuli, and at center stage the unforgettable **Machhapuchhare,** a single soaring white spire.

The 124-square-km valley is dotted with a half-dozen lakes, the only ones of any note in Nepal beyond Rara Lake. The largest, three-km long **Phewa Tal,** is a major tourist attraction—for many people, the *only* attraction. The valley is cut by the **Seti Gandaki River,** part of the Gandaki river system that drains the central Hills and meets in the Terai. It's called Seti or "White" Gandaki because of the limestone sediment which gives the water a milky tint. The river appears and disappears throughout its course, in some places carving dramatically deep and narrow canyons in the valley's soft subsoil.

HISTORY

Pokhara is the meeting point for two peoples: the Hindu caste groups now inhabiting the valley and its encircling low hills, and the Gurungs of the surrounding highlands. For centuries power ebbed and flowed between them, with the caste groups gaining the upper hand as they gradually moved eastwards across Nepal.

By the 17th century Pokhara was part of the Kingdom of Kaski, one of the most powerful of central Nepal's Chaubise Rajaya or 24 Kingdoms. Kaski was ruled by a sub-branch of the Shah royal family, who situated their court atop a windy, waterless ridge for reasons of defense. The hilltops surrounding Pokhara are dotted with the ruins of medieval stone forts *(kot)*. Kaski and the rest of the Chaubise Rajaya were annexed by Prithvi Narayan Shah in 1786 and absorbed into the growing kingdom of Nepal.

Around this time Pokhara developed into an important trade entrepôt, lying as it does on major trails between both Jumla-Kathmandu and India-Tibet. Each winter, mule caravans arrived from the north, laden with bags of salt and wool from the Tibetan Plateau. These were exchanged in Pokhara for grain and goods carried in from Butwal by porter. Naturally, a considerable portion of profits went into local pockets. Modern roads have largely wiped out this traditional trading system, but on trails and roads around Pokhara you may still encounter jingling, clopping caravans of dusty brown mules.

As a major government center in central Nepal, Pokhara has naturally became a focus of development. Progress has perhaps been accelerated because it's such a pleasant place for foreign-aid workers to visit and live. Development has proceeded backwards in the isolated valley: the first airplane landed in 1952 and the first oxcart arrived the following year—by air. Tourism began in the early '70s, with the opening of the Kathmandu and India roads and the start of the trekking boom. Pokhara is now the biggest tourist destination in Nepal outside of the Kathmandu Valley, drawing 25% of all visitors to Nepal.

the vase, bumpa, *symbolizing longevity when holding life-giving water*

ORIENTATION

Little more than a village in many ways, Pokhara manages to sprawl in every direction, making getting about both time-consuming and confusing. The town is best described as three distinct areas, separated not just by distance but by character—it's hard to believe Lakeside and Bhimsen Tol (the old bazaar) belong to the same town.

Home base for travelers is **Lakeside,** also called **Baidam,** on the eastern shore of Phewa Tal, and its sidekick, **Damside,** or **Pardi,** one km further south. Lakeside's main road is a seemingly endless strip of lodges, restaurants, and shops. You have to scratch hard to find its Nepali roots, but the old Chhetri village it once was lingers on Lakeside's back lanes, with their ricefields, thatched-roof cottages, and ambling water buffalo.

A good hour's walk northeast is Pokhara's new bazaar, another long strip taking its name from the nearby **Mahendra Phul** (Mahendra Bridge). It's like a dusty, flashy, noisy Terai town, crammed with new shops selling modern goods. The city's old, original bazaar, called **Bagar,** is a few kilometers northwest. Its small shops with a sleepy old-time feel form yet another world. Scattered between these three areas are offices, banks, hospitals, development agencies, a college campus, and the bus park and airport, which are not very close to anything at all. It's all chaotically unorganized, not to mention a very long haul between sections. Local bookstores sell yellow city maps, and there are plenty of You Are Here signs posted about town.

SIGHTS

Pokhara's sights are admittedly minor: there are no "must-sees" and most serve as excuses to wander about the lovely valley. Most visitors never make it past hypnotically seductive Lakeside—the rest of town seems impossibly distant. It's definitely worth rallying one's forces and getting out, though, if only for the pleasantly righteous glow felt upon return.

TO TASHI PAKHEL

BAGLUNG HWY

TO BATULECHAUR
AND MAHENDRA CAVE

KALI KHOLA

POKHARA

BHALAM KHOLA

TO SIKLIS

SETI KHOLA

GURKHA
CAMP

K. I. SINGH
BRIDGE

SHINING HOSPITAL

BAGH
BAZAAR

BHIM BAZAAR

PRITHVI
NARAYAN
CAMPUS

TO SARANGKOT

BINDYABASINI
TEMPLE

KAHUN DANDA
(1443 m)

THUPTEN NYINGJE LING

KHAHARE

PUSKAR GUESTHOUSE

POKHARA-BAGLUNG HWY.

NALAMUKH

CHIPLEDHUNGA

POST
OFFICE

NAYA BAZAAR

ARMY
CAMP

MAHENDRA PHUL BRIDGE

RANIPAUWA

MANANGI
GOMPA

CAMPGROUND

GRINDLAY'S BANK

PHEWA TAL

HOTEL FEWA

MANSWARA

LAKESIDE (BAIDAM)

POKHARA
MUSEUM

WESTERN
REGIONAL
HOSPITAL

VARAHI TEMPLE

BARAHI
TOL

ROYAL PALACE

GHAORI GHAT

FISH TAIL LODGE

IMMIGRATION
OFFICE

NEPAL
RASTRA
BANK

DAMSIDE
(PARDI)

HOTEL
DRAGON

TIBETAN
HANDICRAFTS
CENTER

NEW HOTEL
CRYSTAL

PRITHVI
CHOWK

NAGDHUNGA

BUS
PARK

RNAC OFFICE

RAM GHAT

POKHARA GATE

PRITHVI RAJMARG

PARDI DAM

HOTEL
MONA LISA

AIRPORT

TO SISUWA, GHORKA,
AND KATHMANDU

TO TANSEN,
LUMBINI AND INDIA

DEVI FALLS

SIDDHARTHA RAJMARG

SETI GANDAKI RIVER

0   1km

TASHI LING
TIBETAN VILLAGE

TO NUWAKOT

© MOON PUBLICATIONS, INC.

BOB RACE

TAIL OF THE FISH

The epitome of what a mountain should look like, Machhapuchhare dominates Pokhara, serving as the centerpiece of its splendid views. The tongue-twisting name can be avoided by using the English translation: *machha* is "fish," *puchhare* "tail." The mountain's twin summits, only one km apart and a few meters different in altitude, do indeed resemble a notched fishtail when viewed from the west, but you have to walk at least as far as Naudanda to see it.

From Pokhara only the austerely beautiful southern summit is visible, a perfect, single shining peak. Machhapuchhare is often compared to Switzerland's Matterhorn, a mere 4572 meters to Machhapuchhare's 6977 meters. Actually it far outshines the Alps. "Compared to that vision the Matterhorn would have looked crude, the peerless Weisshorn a flattened lump," wrote mountaineer Wilfred Noyce. He was a member of the 1957 British expedition to Machhapuchhare, the only one to ever attempt the mountain.

One of the first mountaineering expeditions in Nepal, it was led by British Army Col. J.M. Roberts. On reconnaissance the preceding year he found local Gurungs reluctant to help. Machhapuchhare stands guard over the Annapurna Sanctuary, a holy site to local Gurungs, but Roberts was the local Gurkha Army recruiter, and his clout eventually prevailed. The next year the expedition got within 60 meters of the summit, only to be turned back by a steep, ice-covered pitch. A few years later Roberts was asked by the Nepali government to recommend a peak to be set aside as forever inviolate. He

---

Apart from the lake, the main sight is mountain views: the Annapurna massif lies only 40 km north and dominates the horizon with its multiple peaks, 16 of them over 7000 meters. Taking center stage is unforgettable Machhapuchhare, the "Fishtail Peak." Everest Air's twice-weekly sightseeing Pokhara Mountain Flight (US$50) flies past Dhaulagiri and the Annapurnas, providing close-ups of the central Himalaya.

Phewa Tal

The single best thing to do in Pokhara is laze about in a boat on the placid waters of Phewa Tal. Bring drinking water, sunscreen, a picnic lunch, and a good book. Brightly painted wooden rowboats can be rented at several points along Lakeside for around Rs150 per day, Rs50 per hour—bargain. Hotel Fewa rents clunky wooden sailboats and a few modern ones, but there's seldom enough wind.

Mountain views are splendid here, especially when the still waters reflect the peaks, creating a double range. The lake is neither deep (45 meters at most) nor particularly clean, but the water is warm and swimming is pleasant if you don't think about the pollution. A few Lakeside shops rent fishing rods, if you'd like to try catching one of the half-dozen local varieties.

The first stop in a boating journey is usually the **Varahi Temple,** prettily located on a small island across from Lakeside. On Saturday, colorfully dressed boatloads of Nepali families paddle here to perform *puja* and sacrifice a goat or a chicken to the boar-headed goddess Varahi. It's a pretty site, marred only by litter.

Phewa Tal's opposite shore includes some lushly forested steep cliffs. Secluded coves make shady hideaways; they're not secluded enough for skinny-dipping, however. The little Gurung village of **Anadu** across from Lakeside makes a logical destination; aim for the white building on its outskirts, the **Typical Restaurant,** which serves simple food, including delicious peppery fried fish. The two red-brick buildings next to it are outposts of Hotel Fewa, which rents them for around US$20 a night.

More energetic types could take one of many trails from here to the ridgetop, which has superb views. Ambitious rowers could continue on to investigate the lake's northwest end, **Phewa Faant,** a vast flat expanse of ricefields planted on reclaimed land. The lake's southern end, **Damside,** is much closer, and rowing there is a pleasant way to explore this secondary tourist district. The Indian-built dam located here supplies water for irrigation and electricity. It's actually enlarged Phewa Tal slightly, while the valley's other lakes are shrinking, due mainly to increased siltation from deforestation and farming. Siltation also threatens Phewa Tal: according to one gloomy estimate, the lake will be entirely silted in within 50 years if nothing's done to remedy the situation.

Lakeside and Damside

These twin tourist districts prove hypnotic to most visitors, who find it easy to while away lazy days strolling the restaurant-studded strip, poking through bookstalls and crafts shops. The lake is prettier, and more visible, towards the southern end of Lakeside, around **Gauri Ghat,** where several little temples and shrines overlook its placid waters. It's always pleasant to sit at **Barahi Tol** beside the royal palace and watch Indian tourists get their photographs taken.

More inspirational might be a visit to **Thupten Nyingje Ling,** a Buddhist center affiliated with Kathmandu's Himalayan Yogic Institute and developed specifically for Westerners. The center has a library and sponsors teachings and talks on Buddhism. It's up in Khahare at the northern end of Lakeside; look for the white building up on a hillside.

Pokhara Bazaar

Yes, there actually is a Nepali town called Pokhara, a world away and quite a distance from the tourist version. The old town lies between Sarangkot and Kahun Danda ridges, where the Seti River has cut a narrow gorge. The best way to get here from Lakeside is by bike, preferably with gears, as it's uphill all the way, although it looks deceptively level. The old bazaar begins at **Ganesh Tol,** a good four km from Lakeside. With its ochre-tinted houses and broad quiet streets shaded by big pipal trees, it's retained its charm—you can almost imagine the mule caravans clopping through here.

Like many major Hill trading posts, Pokhara's old bazaar is essentially Newar. In 1752 the rulers of Kaski invited a group of Bhaktapur Newars to settle in their kingdom to improve local trade. Newars were even then renowned as astute traders with all the necessary connections. They've left their mark on local architecture in a modest way. Minor temples stand in the middle of the road, each lending its name to the surrounding neighborhood, and there are a few magnificent old thick-walled houses adorned with woodcarvings. Much of the old town was destroyed in a 1949 fire, which explains why the architecture is so bland. But even the rebuilt houses look old compared to Kathmandu's, and a stroll through here reveals a busy traditional bazaar, with saris, soap, rice, and gold jewelry all jumbled together.

The old quarter culminates at **Bindyabasini Mandir,** Pokhara's only temple of note. Its shady hilltop location is more interesting than its several shrines, none of notable design or antiquity. The original temple was destroyed in the 1949 fire, which started from a fire offering run amok. The main temple is of white plaster and is dedicated to a form of the goddess Bhagwati. Worshippers flock here to perform animal sacrifices, and on Saturday the parklike grounds take on a festive air. Look for the silver-painted kneeling images of Nepal's rulers set atop a pillar facing the main shrine—not the usual 17th-century Malla kings, but the current king and queen.

The New Bazaar

Past the temple the bazaar becomes more densely packed and modern. If you're cycling, loop around to the east and return via a parallel road which passes **Prithvi Narayan Campus** and heads through the new part of town. There's little of interest apart from a view of the Seti Gorge, but it's a fast, swooping cycle downhill. A few kilometers south is the new bazaar area around **Mahendra Phul,** with modern shops and small Indian restaurants serving Sikh truck drivers. Veer off onto the bridge to peer down at the narrow slit of a gorge carved by the Seti River, barely two meters wide and 45 meters deep. Shortly after, the road's intersection with the Prithvi Rajmarg is marked by a statue of Prithvi Narayan Shah; Pokhara's squalid bus park is nearby. The road continues past the airport to join Damside about one km further.

Museums

The **Annapurna Regional Museum** is located on Prithvi Narayan Campus east of the old bazaar. Its focus is natural history, primarily a butterfly collection, and the only reason for a visit would be to pick up some of the informative literature of the Annapurna Conservation Area Project. It's open daily 10 a.m.-5 p.m. except Saturday; admission is free.

More interesting is the **Pokhara Museum,** sited between the bus park and Mahendra Phul. The collection focuses on ethnic groups encountered in treks around Pokhara, with exhibits of jewelry, musical instruments, costumes, and photographs. A new exhibit highlights the ancient history of Upper Mustang. It's open daily 10 a.m.-5 p.m. except Tuesday; admission is Rs10.

AROUND POKHARA

The sprawling valley is a great training ground for would-be trekkers and offers many options for those fleeing the fleshpots of Lakeside. Cycling is the best way to get around, preferably mountain bike; there are also many day walks, easily extended into mini-treks—or maxi-treks: you just keep going.

Sarangkot

The slightly lopsided summit topping the long ridge to the north of Phewa Tal makes an excellent day walk. Satisfying but not *too* long, it rewards with incredible views.

The shortest but steepest route starts south of Lakeside. Pass Khahare and round the bend into the next indentation; multiple trails run up a

shepherdesses near Pokhara

subsidiary ridge, through terraced ricefields and past small farmhouses where you can get directions and tea.

An easier route leads off to the left from Bhairab Tol in the old bazaar. It's a two- or three-hour climb up, with progressively better mountain views as you ascend. Small teashops sell simple food en route. Alternatively, hire a taxi for around Rs600 and drive up the new dirt road behind Bindyabasini Temple to the huddle of teashops about 15 minutes' walk below Sarangkot's summit.

The 1592-meter summit is a bald knob, crowned by the ruins of a *kot,* a stone fortress of the old Kaski kingdom. A viewtower and temple are under construction here. The sight of shimmering Phewa Tal is stunning enough, but to the north the hillside drops straight down into the Suikhet Valley, with a breathtaking vista of Dhaulagiri, the Annapurna range, and Machhapuchhare filling the horizon. You have to get up here pretty early to be guaranteed a clear view, though. There are several simple lodges and restaurants just below the summit if you want to overnight. Return via one of the described routes, or walk towards Kaski about an hour and descend a long way down a stone staircase to the village of **Pame** along the Harpan Khola, one of the lake's main tributaries. Boats run from here to Phewa Tal.

Kaski and Naudanda

The ridge trail heading west from Sarangkot used to be the starting point for the Jomosom trek, but the new Baglung Road now funnels trekkers in further west, and the small touristy villages along the old trail are languishing for lack of attention. Day hikers will find it remarkably peaceful.

A half-hour from Sarangkot is Kaski, once the capital of the surrounding countryside, now a minor village. A stone staircase leads about 300 meters above the village to the ruins of the old **Kaski Kot** or fortress. The small Durga shrine here, little more than a rock pen, is a favorite site for Dasain animal sacrifices. Many of the summits along this ridge have old temples to the goddess Durga, who serves as bloodthirsty protectress of the villages below.

Ninety minutes further along the ridge is the village of Naudanda (1458 meters), where good mountain views include the first glimpse of Machhapuchhare's twin-peaked "fishtail." The village is not particularly pleasant but has lots of lodges and restaurants. A police checkpost will prevent you from continuing further without a trekking permit, and the Baglung Road cutting across the ridge has pretty much ruined the immediate vicinity for trekking—there's little joy to be had in plodding down a dusty road. (Things do improve after the road veers west down to Kusma, and the trail continues on to Chandrakot.) If you can't find a ride back to Pokhara from Naudanda, take the steep trail dropping down north, which reaches **Phedi** in about 90 minutes. From here, jeeps run back to town on a regular basis.

Pumdi

For quintessential views of Phewa Tal, Lakeside, *and* the mountains, hike up to this little ridgetop village, part of the wonderfully named district of **Pumdi-Bhumdi** on Phewa Tal's southern rim. Row to **Chisapani** on the southern corner of the lake and hike up about an hour to a

fork in the trail, passing several stunning viewpoints en route. The right-hand path leads to an elaborate ridgetop **Buddhist monastery** built with Japanese funding (its lights are visible from Lakeside at night). The left fork continues steeply uphill to Pumdi. Bring a picnic, as there's no food available.

Kahun Danda

This ridge on the east side of town is a bit lower than Sarangkot, with slightly less spectacular views. On the other hand it's closer, the walk to the top is shorter, and it's not at all crowded. Several trails lead to the 1443-meter summit, including one starting behind the university campus and another beginning just below the **Manangi Gompa,** a modern monastery funded by Buddhists of Manang, apparently hoping to recycle some of their trading profits into religious merit. Cross Mahendra Phul and continue two km east; past a dirt road to the left the monastery appears atop a small hill. There are good valley views from the steps, and monks do prayer ceremonies every morning and afternoon. On the opposite side of the main road atop a wooded hill is a **temple** to the goddess Bhadrakali.

From here it's about a 90-minute climb to the top of Kahun Danda (aim for the viewtower), through some minor strung-out settlements. The route is not at all commercialized—bring your own food. The summit offers mountain views and a bird's-eye panorama of the Pokhara Valley, split by the gorge of the Seti Gandaki River.

Devi Falls

The Pardi Khola flows from the south end of Phewa Tal for two km, then suddenly drops straight down into a dramatically deep sinkhole called Devi, David's, or Devin's Falls, scene of a dubious-sounding modern legend. Supposedly a Westerner named David (or alternatively a "Miss Devins") was skinny-dipping in the Pardi Khola when the floodgates of the dam were opened, sweeping him into the subterranean chasm, never to be seen again.

The falls are two km down the Siddhartha Rajmarg, a 15-minute bike ride from Pardi or an easy walk along a riverside trail: cross the dam and head south. Moderately impressive in autumn, the water flow dwindles to a disappointing trickle by January, and the litter and the metal railings do little for the natural beauty. A local high school has adopted the site and collects Rs5 admission from sightseers.

The entrance is lined by persuasive Tibetan trinket-sellers, many of them from **Tashi Ling Tibetan Settlement** just across the street. A trail beginning here leads 15 km south to the old fortress town of **Nuwakot,** the former headquarters of the chieftains who once ruled the area.

Begnas and Rupa Tal

These smaller sisters of Phewa Tal are lovely and largely unvisited, all the better for the few who do make it out here. The lakes are about 15 km east of town. Minibuses to Sisuwa leave hourly from Chipledhunga near Mahendra Pul, but they're slow and crowded. Better to cycle 10 km down the Prithvi Rajmarg, turn left at a sign onto a dirt road, and proceed a few kilometers to the village of **Sisuwa.** Begnas Tal is hidden just behind the village, past a fisheries project—fish farming is becoming big business here. Wooden rowboats, complete with boatmen if desired, are available for rent at the lakeshore.

The lakes are divided by the forested **Panchbhaiya Danda,** and an hour-long hike up here to the viewpoint of **Sundari Danda** yields sweeping views of mountains and both lakes. Follow the road north of Sisuwa, and turn off onto a trail on the left which heads up the ridge.

The area's main attraction is peace and quiet—few tourists make it out here—but a luxury resort being built along the ridge should soon take care of that. There are a few teastalls in Sisuwa, and very simple lodging is available should you stay late. Two more lakes, **Dipang Tal** and **Maidi Tal,** are nearby, but they're really just swampy ponds. The last bus to Pokhara leaves Sisuwa around 5 p.m.

Batulechaur

The village of Batulechaur is said to have once served as the winter court of Kaski's kings. Royalty introduced the delicious oranges the area was once famed for, but disease killed most of the trees in the '60s. Now the only remnant of the village's royal heyday is a community of *gainey,* minstrels who perform folk ballads to the plaintive accompaniment of the fiddlelike *sarangi.* They'll be more than happy to put on a show for you and your camera, tape recorder, or

videocam, but they expect to be well-paid in return—say, the price of a goat for a community feast. From the K.I. Singh Bridge at the north end of Pokhara's old bazaar, Batulechaur is less than an hour's walk north.

Mahendra Gufa

One km further north is Mahendra Gufa or Cave, locally known as Chamero Odhaar, "House of Bats," and once believed to be the abode of the red-eyed, long-haired demoness Nidhini. Another legend is related by the man selling Rs15 entry tickets: the cave is so immense that a team of Swiss spelunkers walked for two hours and still didn't reach the end. You can enter the first 135 meters, dimly lit by a fallible generator. It's best to bring a flashlight—local boys will vie to be your guide, but the candles they carry don't illuminate much. Most of the stalactites have been carted off by souvenir hunters and there's little to see unless you're a fan of caves and sleeping fruit bats.

Tibetan Settlements

The Dalai Lama's 1959 flight from Lhasa triggered a Tibetan exodus. Between 1959 and 1962 more than 30,000 Tibetan refugees flooded into Nepal, most settling around Jomosom. As their numbers swelled, Swiss aid workers helped transplant several thousand to refugee camps in the Pokhara Valley. In this subtropical land, so different from the high Tibetan plains, the Tibetans have built a miniature version of their old life, complete with whitewashed houses, prayer flags, *chorten,* and monasteries.

The names of Pokhara's three Tibetan settlements are all prefixed by *tashi*—"good luck." After years of hardship, life is turning lucky for the refugees. Many have become moderately prosperous through tourism, mainly by weaving carpets or selling trinkets. Charmingly aggressive Tibetan saleswomen ("Just looking, looking only!") are a Pokhara hallmark. A visit to a settlement involves a heavy dose of salesmanship, but it also provides insights into Tibetan life. People are more accessible than at Kathmandu, and are eager to talk, especially if you express some awareness of Tibet's plight. As for shopping—it's an interesting venue, and prices are better than the street sellers', but don't expect any bargains.

The largest and most interesting settlement is **Tashi Pakhel**, also called Hyangja, after a nearby Nepali village. It's four km west down the Baglung Highway, set atop a low cliff overlooking the Seti Gandaki. The settlement of small whitewashed houses, marked by more prayer flags, houses nearly 1,000 Tibetans, many of whom work in the settlement's large carpet factory. Other handicrafts include jackets, boots, and jewelry. There are several small shops near the entrance, and nearly every resident sells goods from home. There's also a monastery, some small restaurants, and a simple **guesthouse** should you decide to stay overnight.

To the south, the smaller settlement of **Tashi Ling** is only a few km from Damside—look for the bright-yellow monastery across the road from Devi Falls. The settlement has a carpet-weaving factory and the usual persuasive salespeople. Nearby is an orphanage for Tibetan children.

Paljor Ling, better known as the Tibetan Handicrafts Center, is little more than a carpet-making compound with families in residence, but it's conveniently located just west of Pokhara's bus station.

The Baglung Highway
This new 72-km road linking Pokhara with the zonal headquarters of Baglung has dramatically improved access to the territory immediately west of Pokhara, chopping off one or two days' walk for villagers and trekkers alike. The route has some steep stretches but very little traffic, making it a good choice for mountain bikers. Buses depart from Bagh Bazaar, north of Bindyabasini Temple; the trip takes around two hours. Taxis can be rented for Rs800-1000.

The paved road runs past lush ricefields, passes the Tibetan settlement of Tashi Pakhel, and climbs to Naudanda Bazaar. Views back towards Pokhara are incredible; from Kaare the road drops down, down, down. **Naya Phul,** a collection of teastalls on the side of the road about 40 km from Pokhara, is the jumping-off point for the Ghodepani trek. The lovely little riverside village of **Birethanti** with its riverside cafes is a 30-minute walk from here, a worthy destination even for day-trippers. From here you can walk to Poon Hill and on to Jomosom, or take a different route to Ghandruk and the Annapurna Sanctuary.

The highway continues on through Kusma to reach the bazaar town of **Baglung** on the bank of the Kali Gandaki. Eventually the road will go up the river gorge all the way to Jomosom—so much for that trek—but that's a long way in the future.

MINI-TREKS

The Hills north of Pokhara are rich in possibilities for short trips. If your time is limited or you doubt your enthusiasm for a full-out trek, consider spending just a few days exploring the comparatively low-altitude and gentle countryside. Permits are available from the local Immigration Office, and equipment can be rented in local shops. Ask your lodgekeeper or any of a number of local trekking companies for help in arranging guides and porters, though the major trails are easily done on your own.

"Pony trekking," a Pokhara specialty, is not as good as it sounds: the ponies are scruffy and poorly cared for. A trip to Jomosom runs around Rs2000 a day; day-trips to Sarangkot or Begnas Tal are around Rs500.

One option would be to walk the early days of a longer trip described in "Trekking"—for instance, the three-day walk to the lovely village of **Chomrong** at the entrance to the Annapurna Sanctuary, or the popular **Ghorepani loop** via Ghandruk, which could be squeezed into less than a week. The new Pokhara-Baglung Highway has opened up more possibilities. The hilltop village of **Chandrakot** and **Birethanti** are both worth visiting; Ghandruk is a half-day's walk from Birethanti.

Ghachowk
Seldom visited by foreigners, this Gurung village is one of the region's oldest settlements, an attractive mix of traditional houses and fields. As an added bonus it offers close-up views of Machhapuchhare. Start from Tashi Pakhel near Hyangja (it's possible to overnight here) or take a jeep to Suikhet on the Phedi Road. From here turn north to cross the Mardi Khola and continue through **Lhachowk** to Ghachowk, about five hours total. Farther upvalley, locally renowned **hot springs** bubble up at **Bharbhure.** You can return via an alternate route through Bhurjang

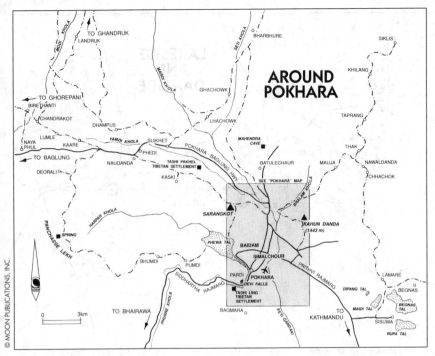

Khola to the *gainey* village of Batulechaur, described above.

Siklis and Ghandruk

Another seldom-visited Gurung village is Siklis, 24 km northeast of Pokhara up the Madi Khola. With over 500 neat slate-roofed houses huddled on a hillside, it's the biggest Gurung village in Nepal. Trekkers generally overnight in the village of **Thak,** then continue to Siklis. A more traveled route to the northwest, with better accommodations, is the three-day walk via Dhampus to **Ghandruk,** another impressive Gurung town.

Panchasse Lekh

This is the highest of the ridges encircling the Pokhara Valley, cresting at 2512 meters. The first and last day of this four-day trek passes through interesting Brahman-Chhetri and Gurung villages; in the middle is a two-day ridge walk with full-on mountain and lake views alternating with lush jungle. The ridge is uninhabited except for a few woodcutters and shepherds, and you'll have to camp for at least two nights. Bring a guide who knows where to find the dry ridge's few water sources.

The trek starts on the opposite side of Phewa Tal, and may be reached by boat across Phewa Tal or by a short drive along the Siddhartha Rajmarg to Tansen. There's a gradual climb to a high point of 2500 meters on the second day, when you'll be walking through forests of rhododendrons and oak. The trail winds northwest and then north around Phewa Tal, concluding at Naudanda.

ACCOMMODATIONS

Finding a good cheap room is never a problem in Pokhara: there are well over a hundred lodges, guesthouses, and hotels in Lakeside and Damside, with more opening every month. Simple

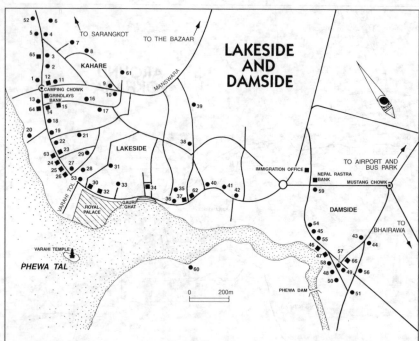

LAKESIDE AND DAMSIDE

1. Municipal Campground
2. Puskar Guesthouse
3. Hotel Sahana
4. New Pleasure Home
5. Shiva Guesthouse
6. Lonely View Guesthouse
7. Excellent Lake View Guesthouse
8. Tibet Home
9. Himalayan Country Lodge
10. Mountain Villa
11. Fairmount Hotel
12. Little Tibetan Tea Garden
13. Amrit Guesthouse
14. Pyramid Restaurant
15. Old Blues Night Pub
16. Tranquillity Lodge
17. Temple Villa
18. Hotel Monal
19. Yeti Guesthouse
20. Hotel Fewa
21. Keiko's Cottages
22. Hotel Mountain Top

23. Once Upon A Time
24. Everest Steakhouse
25. Boomerang
26. Ganesh Bakery
27. Hotel Meera
28. Sarowar
29. Iceland Guesthouse
30. Moondance
31. Hotel Barahi
32. Hungry Eye
33. Travelers' Guesthouse
34. Laxman
35. Tourist Lakeview Guesthouse
36. Lakeview Resort
37. Roadhouse
38. Gurkha Lodge
39. New Solitary Lodge
40. Base Camp Resort
41. New Baba Lodge
42. Trekkers' Retreat Lodge
43. Hotel Dragon
44. Hotel New Pagoda

45. City Annapurna Hotel
46. Rodee Lakeview Restaurant
47. K. C.'s
48. Hotel Monalisa
49. Hotel Garden
50. Ashok Guesthouse
51. Hotel Twin Peak
52. Venus Home
53. Hotel Snowland
54. Hotel Florida
55. Hotel Yad
56. Hotel Greenview
57. Hotel Peaceful
58. Hotel Jarna
59. Hotel Tragopan
60. Fishtail Lodge
61. Hotel Full Moon
62. Le Bistro
63. Beam Beam
64. Moti Manal
65. Guru Lotus
66. German Bakery

original lodgings have been replaced by elaborate multistoried cement buildings—frankly ugly on the outside, and not at all the sleepy country look Pokhara deserves, but these rooms with all the mod cons can be very nice. The latest trend is rooms with bathtubs, which may cost US$5-10 more than rooms with showers.

Room prices are often quoted in US$, a more stable currency than the Nepali rupee, but most places accept payment in rupees, and heavily discount their inflated published rates—a 50% reduction isn't uncommon. Even in season, the competition for guests is so intense there is room for bargaining in all but the most popular places. At the bottom end of things, figure on Rs100-200 for a simple, clean room without bath, Rs250-350 with. Moving upscale, US$10-20 will bring a more comfortable room with bath in any number of places. Look for a clean, sunny, quiet place set off the noisy main road, with rooftop views and/or a nice garden—Pokhara's flowers are splendid year-round.

Some more tips: electricity goes off in a twice-weekly load-shedding ritual, and brownouts are common; buy some good thick candles. Many lodges have solar-heated hot water, admirable in principle but limited in supply; it's best to shower in late afternoon. Thievery is on the increase in Pokhara hotels, so be sure to lock your doors and windows and hide or lock up valuables.

Finding a Room

There's no need to make advance reservations except for the upper-end hotels, which do fill up in season. Hotel touts pounce upon new arrivals at the bus park and airport; it's necessary to be firm and not betray any indecision. Best advice is to flee the scene quickly; if you accept a ride with them, they will take you where they want you to stay, regardless of any agreements you might have made. Don't feel obligated to stay in a place you don't like. Park your bags in a restaurant and check around till you find something suitable. Things change quickly in Pokhara: new lodges open each month, and older ones age, not always gracefully. Newer places are often the best choice, as poor maintenance hasn't had time to become an issue. And the staff is eager to please—and often willing to reduce room rates.

Most travelers stay near Phewa Tal, either in Lakeside or south in Damside. The latter offers better mountain views, but Lakeside is the heart of a real scene and is arguably more pleasant, with big pipal trees shading the strip and the lake making a guest appearance when the buildings thin out.

Most of the more expensive tourist-class hotels are located across from the airport, inconveniently far from the lake. Hotels in the bazaar area cater mainly to Nepali and Indian travelers. It's hard to imagine why you'd stay here unless you got stuck at night, in which case there are lots of cheap lodges around the bus park. **Hotel Sayapatri** and **Hotel Santosh** across the road are a little quieter and reasonably clean.

Lakeside (Baidam)

Lakeside is one long, highly developed strip of restaurants, fruit-juice stalls, travel agents, trekking goods shops, tour companies, and more guesthouses than you could ever imagine. The main road is often noisy. For peaceful lodgings explore the network of dirt lanes leading east from the strip. Here tourist lodges still alternate with fields and farmhouses; the cheapest of these are often family-run operations, relics of Pokhara's sleepier days.

The strip is surprisingly long, and you're unlikely to explore it thoroughly in a single day, at least not on foot. Places at the southern end have some glimpses of the lake, but there is only one hotel actually on the water here, and it's hard to recommend. Lakeside's mountain views are spotty at best, and they progressively vanish as you head north. The northernmost neighborhood, **Khahare,** compensates with some unobstructed lake views and a few untouched ricefields. Formerly a rural neighborhood, it's becoming filled with low-budget lodges, but the countryside atmosphere lingers in places.

It would be pointless to describe every single guesthouse in Lakeside: the following listings cover the current best choices. They are arranged in order from south to north. When two prices are listed, the difference is common bath/attached bath.

Budget: At the southern end of the strip **Trekkers' Retreat Lodge,** tel. (61) 21-458, has a decent garden and basic rooms for Rs150/250. **Tourist Lakeview Guesthouse,**

tel. (61) 21-497, is simple but quiet, with rooms for Rs150.

New Solitary Lodge, tel. (61) 21-804, is indeed solitary, 10 minutes' walk down a side road. Small and simple, it has a beautiful garden and rooftop patio; rooms are Rs250-350.

Hotel Barahi, tel. (61) 21-879, has an enormous sunny garden and somewhat shabby rooms with bath for Rs300-350. The next road up, **Sarowar** is similar, with a good garden, complete with traditional Gurung roundhouse in back, and adequate rooms with bath for Rs300-500 d (the upstairs rooms are best).

Keiko's Cottages consists of five stone cottages set too close together, but at least the architecture is different. Rooms are Rs300 s, Rs350 d, all with attached bath.

Yeti Guesthouse, tel. (61) 21-423, is an older but well-maintained place, set well back from the strip in a pleasant compound. Rooms are Rs150/350 s, Rs250/500 d.

Across the street is **Hotel Fewa,** tel. (61) 20-151, the only place near the lake. Despite being managed by the same family for 15 years, or perhaps because of it, it's drab and run-down, with musty rooms. The quiet waterfront location and big garden compensate somewhat. The stated tariff is US$10-12 s, US$15-18 d; actual prices are Rs300-400 with shower, Rs100 for small rooms with common bath.

At the top of the strip across from Grindlays Bank, **Amrit Guesthouse,** tel. (61) 21-239, is a new place popular for its location. The sunny courtyard is a bit cramped, but the higher-priced rooms, which run Rs200-400 d, offer lake views from the upper balcony.

The road running east from Camping Chowk is lined with nearly a dozen new mid-range hotels. The most interesting budget place here is **Himalayan Country Lodge,** a long building of mortared stone—even the bathrooms have this Flintstonesish decor. The small rooms are US$4 s, US$6 d; there's a verandah but no garden to mention.

Set down a side road, **Tibet Home** is worth seeking out. It bills itself as "quiet, friendly, and different" and so far at least, it is. The little house, complete with sitting room and sunny garden, is managed by a friendly Tibetan woman and offers lake views from the roof. Rooms are Rs150/300 d.

Behind it, the basic **Excellent Lake View Guesthouse** is set way off the road in the midst of ricefields, with rooms for around Rs100. The road leading past here runs into Kahare, a budget paradise, where cheap lodges mix with Nepali teastalls and there's still a rural atmosphere. The best budget place in this neighborhood is **Puskar Guesthouse,** run by three cheerful sisters, with rooms for Rs100 and good lake views from the roof. **New Pleasure Home** has a pleasant garden and rooms with lake views for Rs150. The nearby **Venus Home** and **Shiva Guesthouse** are smaller and simpler, with rooms for around Rs100 d. **Lonely View Guesthouse** a little further up is also cheap and simple, with still better views. Walk further around the ridge up to Sedi Danda and you'll find **Green Peace Guesthouse,** a very simple lodge with rooms projecting right over the lake.

Moderate: Since room rates are highly negotiable, many of these might well fit into the budget category. **Gurkha Lodge** consists of a few thatched-roof stone cottages set in a huge and gorgeous garden: simple but peaceful. It's usually full, so the US$11 rate is seldom discounted.

Lakeview Resort, tel. (61) 21-477, on the main road has okay rooms for US$16 s, US$22 d—better rooms with tub are US$28/40. The grounds are large, there's a restaurant with outdoor seating, and the lake is right across the street.

Hotel Hungry Eye, tel. (61) 20-908, centrally located behind the restaurant of the same name, is popular but overpriced at US$20 s, US$30 d for rooms that are nothing special. The same goes for **New Baba Lodge,** tel. (61) 20-981, where adequate if ugly rooms are listed at US$30 s, US$45 d.

Hotel Mountain Top, tel. (61) 20-779, should be boycotted for the way its hulking concrete form has ruined the Lakeside skyline, but the rooms are quite pleasant, especially the top-floor ones facing the lake. Big balconies and a rooftop restaurant are other pluses. Rates are US$12/16 s, US$18/25 d.

Hotel Meera, tel. (61) 21-031, is fairly ugly on the outside, but inside is a marble lobby and exceptionally nice rooms with big windows, some with balconies and views. It's run by a retired Gurkha soldier, who keeps everything in

"The Strip," Lakeside

mpeccable order. All in all it's one of the best places in Pokhara, and a relative bargain at US$10/25 s, US$15/30 d.

Two older hotels that can still be recommended are Hotel Snowland, tel. (61) 20-384, where top-floor rooms on the rear building have balconies with lake views and rooms are US$12/25 s, US$25/30 d. **Hotel Monal,** tel. (61) 21-459, is centrally located but back far enough from the strip to be peaceful. Bright, airy rooms are listed at US$25 s, US$30 d.

On the next side road down you'll find **Tranquillity Lodge,** tel. (61) 21-030, with a big sunny yard and rooms for US$10 s, US$15 d. Down a bit further is **Temple Villa,** tel. (61) 21-203, an upscale private house doing hotel duty for a few years. With only five rooms and a big garden, it's more of a house than a hotel; some rooms have mountain views. Rates are US$25 with bath, US$15 without.

Fairmount Hotel, tel. (61) 21-252, is a big new palace, clean and well-maintained, with large rooms and a generator to provide electricity during load-shedding: US$18 s, US$25 d. Down the road is the new and nice **Mountain Villa,** tel. (61) 21-954, with balconies to lounge on and lake views from the top rooms: US$16 s, US20 d.

North of here, the spectacularly sited **Hotel Full Moon,** tel. (61) 21-511, clings to a steep hillside. It's a stiff 10-minute ascent, but at the top is a new building with six big rooms and shared large balconies with spectacular lake views (no

mountains, though). The view from the roof terrace is absolutely dizzying. Rooms are US$25 s, US$40 d; doubles in a separate cottage with no views and common bath are US$7. Simple food is available if you don't want to hike down for a meal.

Up in Kahare, **Hotel Sahana,** tel. (61) 21-229, is a classier place than most around here, quiet, with a big garden and somewhat musty rooms for a bargainable US$25 s, US$30 d.

Finally, to *really* get away from it all you could boat across the lake to the little village of Anadu, where the two red-brick buildings next to the Typical Restaurant are rented out by Hotel Fewa (contact them in advance). Rooms are around US$30 a night; lake and mountain panoramas are right at your door. Hotel Monal is also building a resort near here.

Expensive: Base Camp Resort, tel. (61) 21-226, bills itself as the "finest lodge in Pokhara." Built around a handsome garden, it's certainly several cuts above most Lakeside accommodations; large rooms with a/c and heating are US$51 s, US$55 d.

Fish Tail Lodge, tel. (61) 20-071, is built on a promontory jutting into the lake. Visitors reach it by a rope-drawn raft, kept no doubt for drama—it would be simple enough to bridge the gap. The rooms are nothing special for US$75 s, US$85 d, but the grounds are beautifully landscaped and offer superb views over the lake out to the mountains. It's especially nice in the dry winter and spring, when other gardens look a bit scruffy. The round glassed-in restaurant offers more good views but indifferent food. The lodge is managed by the Hotel de l'Annapurna in Kathmandu, tel. (1) 221-711.

Camping: Pokhara's municipal campground is on the lake but treeless and guarded by police, altogether unpromising. With so many good lodges around one can only pity campers (usually group trekkers) broiling in their cramped tents at the Camping Chowk. There's another equally bare place, **International Tourist Camping Site**, up the road from here towards town. Both charge Rs40 to pitch a tent—you're better off spending it on a room.

Damside (Pardi)

Located at the south end of Phewa Tal, midway between the airport and Lakeside, this up-and-coming area is a less trendy alternative to Lakeside's scene. Mountain views are better from here, and a few hotels are right on the lake. It's quieter and less developed (which means fewer shops and restaurants to choose from), and it's also less scenic — downright hot in the spring, as there are few trees. Damside lacks the shady charm of Lakeside, but snatches of local life are still visible in between the bookstalls and guesthouses, whereas Lakeside is 100% touristed.

Budget rooms for around Rs150 are available at **Hotel Yad** and **Hotel Florida** right across from the lake; or try the string of lodges along the road leading up to Hotel Dragon. The nicely landscaped **Hotel Greenview**, tel. (61) 21-844, and the **Hotel New Pagoda,** tel. (61) 21-802, are a little more expensive: rooms are US$3-4 without bath, US$10-13 with. **Hotel Twin Peak,** tel. (61) 20-455, is a quiet place run by a Gurung ex-Gurkha soldier, with rooms for US$5/10 s, US$8/15 d.

Hotel Garden, tel. (61) 20-870, is central, popular, and clean, with large sunny rooms and big balconies—no garden, though. Prices range from US$3 s, US$4 d without bath to US$10-30 for a double with bath; the most expensive rooms have views. **Hotel Peaceful** next door is similar if slightly less spacious. The large **Ashok Guesthouse,** tel. (61) 20-374, one block behind on the lake, has a big sunny garden and basic rooms with bath for US$8 s, US$10 d. There are dam views from the back rooms and mountain views from the roof. The Ashok also operates the **Hotel Annapurna** next door, which has larger rooms, some with lake-facing balconies.

The balconied back rooms at **Hotel Mona Lisa,** tel. (61) 20-863, have the best lake and mountain views of any Pokhara hotel. It's scrupulously clean—Japanese foreign-aid workers are headquartered here, a good recommendation. Rooms are US$6/20 s, US$10/25 d. **Hotel Jharna,** tel. (61) 21-925, next door has similar views and prices.

Moving slightly further upscale, the quiet, Thakali-run **Hotel Dragon,** tel. (61) 20-052, is built around a big garden courtyard. Its Tibetan-themed a/c rooms are US$40 s, US$50 d; some have mountain views, though they're marred by power lines. **Hotel Tragopan,** tel. (61) 21-708, on the main road began promisingly but hasn't been maintained. Mildewed rooms with fans are US$35 s, US$45 d.

Around the Airport

The tourist-standard hotels across from the airport are inconveniently far from the lake or any other point of interest. They're generally used by group treks and prearranged tours; independent travelers may feel stranded here.

New Hotel Crystal, tel. (61) 20-035, is the largest and best of the lot, with a swimming pool and tennis court. Deluxe air-conditioned rooms (central heating in winter!) are US$56 s, US$68 d; smaller cottages are US$22 s, US30 d.

Next door is the virtually useless government **Tourist Office,** and beside it the government-run **Hotel Taragaon,** tel. (61) 20-255, wears a similarly forlorn air. Its rooms are clean and fairly cheap at US$18 s, US$20 d.

The big old **Hotel Himal** is popular with Sherpas and Tibetans. Basic rooms are around Rs80, though you may awake with fleabites. The restaurant here serves good *momos.*

Last in the line is **Hotel Mount Annapurna,** tel. (61) 20-037, decorated in Tibetan style. There's a big sunny garden with views, but the rooms are a bit cramped; US$26 s, US$37 d.

FOOD

Lazy Lakeside life revolves around the pursuit of food. Dining out is virtually the only thing to do after dark, and restaurants are good places to meet other travelers and compare notes. You choose a restaurant by its clientele and music as much as by its food; the season's favorites are easy to pick out by the crowds. Most have outdoor dining; some have rooftop views over the lake.

Pokhara's Western food doesn't meet Kathmandu standards, but it tastes pretty good after three weeks on the trail. Menus are typically ambitious lists of Italian, French, Mexican, American, and Chinese dishes, seldom authentic ("Chicken Cotton Blue," anyone?) but tasty enough. Highlights include fresh fish from the lake—or, increasingly, from fish farms. When you tire of the pasta and steak routine, seek out the little *momo* shacks and teastalls around Camping Chowk or Kahare, good places for cheap *daal bhaat* and *thukpa*. There are some good local Indian restaurants in Mahendra Pul.

Lakeside
The neighborhood is one long string of restaurants, from the well-regarded **New Baba Restaurant** on. **Le Bistro** is as popular as its Kathmandu counterpart, with a patio overlooking the lake. **The Roadhouse** is a cool place to hang out over tea and music, as is funky **Laxman** further up the strip.

Firmly established in mid-strip, **The Hungry Eye** serves decent if pricey entrees and exceptional desserts, though food quality had declined at last visit. The more casual **Moondance** next door does good pizza. Across the street is the big **Garlic Garden Bakery**, a pleasant place to sit, but the food and cake display looks better than it tastes. The cheap little **Ganesh Bakery** next door has great food and fresh breads daily.

Next up is a string of places set on supposedly public land along the lakeshore. Disregarding the legality of this arrangement, they're nice places to sit and admire the lake views, complete with swimming buffalo, at any time of day. The long sloping gardens feature outdoor tables shaded by thatched shelters and brightly colored umbrellas. Best food and service are provided by **Boomerang,** the original establishment, with a bakery takeout counter and good breakfasts. The neighboring **Fewa Park** and **Elegant View** are close rivals. There's also a spinoff here of Kathmandu's **Everest Steakhouse** for carnivores. **Beam Beam** has a narrow garden and a cosy interior with a fireplace for cold winter nights; it's a popular nightlife spot.

Across the street, **Once Upon a Time** is a charming ochre-walled place with airy verandahs and Christmas lights strung along the roof; the food, unfortunately, is poor. **Nirula's** in the ground floor of Hotel Mountain Top serves 21 flavors of ice cream; the fast-food menu is best avoided. Up the strip, **Pyramid Restaurant** has better-than-average pasta, and **Moti Mahal** puts out authentically spiced Indian dishes. **Little Tibetan Tea Garden** has a pleasant outdoor dining area and pays more attention than most places to the quality of its food, which is consistently good. Further west, the cheap tourist restaurants in Kahare are eager to please but have a less-than-firm grip on the fundamentals of Western cuisine. **Guru Lotus** is a quaintly funky place. The best bet around here are the little teashops and *momo* stalls.

Damside
The premiere restaurant here is **K.C.'s** (no relation to Kathmandu's eatery of the same name), with lake views and steaks. Across the street is an offshoot of the ubiquitous **German Bakery,** serving breakfast, sandwiches, and picnic ingredients—bread, rolls, lunchmeat. **Rodee Lakeview** is a pleasingly cheap cafe with a big menu including Indian food and ice cream, and open-air lakeside seating. Stop here for a sunset drink if nothing else. Next door, the **Momo Kitchen** also has lake views and prepares tolerable local food. **The Nest** in the Hotel Tragopan serves good Indian food, including tandoori chicken, in a moderately elegant settling.

Groceries and Street Food
Pokhara's trekking provisions are similar to Kathmandu's, if slightly less varied. Chocolate, bicuits, cheese, whole-wheat bread, peanut butter, and granola are all available, most conveniently in the big tourist-oriented "supermarkets" of Lakeside. Vendors sell fresh produce and Indian snacks from rolling carts, and at least a dozen fruit stalls supply seasonal juices (often heavily diluted).

ENTERTAINMENT

Nightlife
Nightlife focuses on dining; the other main highlight is strolling up and down the strip, seeing and being seen. A few bars are expanding the

possibilities: **Maya Pub** on the main strip and **Beam Beam** are both popular, with a variety of drinks and some loud music when things get going. **Old Blues Night** is generally deserted, but still manages to stay open late.

Beyond this there's not much—the bar at the Fish Tail Lodge, playing *caroom* boards in local teashops, drinking *chang* in *momo* shops. Stagey but enthusiastically delivered Nepali dance shows are put on nightly in the main tourist season at **Hotel Dragon** in Damside, tel. (61) 20-052, and **Fish Tail Lodge** at Lakeside, tel. (61) 20-071; showtimes are around 6 or 7 p.m. and tickets are Rs90. Some of the ritzier restaurants in Lakeside, like the Hungry Eye and Hotel Meera's restaurant, also present folk dance programs.

Shopping

Most things are better bought in Kathmandu. One exception is the batiks, perhaps because there are so many stores clustered together. There's a big huddle of **batik** shops past the airport in Nagdhunga. While it's not a native craft, some of the scenes of Nepali life come across surprisingly well.

A *dhaka topi* shop on the road into the old bazaar sells handwoven *dhaka* cloth and hats; a handicrafts store a little further north sells simple old brassware and the checked woolen blankets woven by Gurungs. Many shops are piled with *shaligram,* black stone fossils found in the Kali Gandaki Valley. Associated with Vishnu, they're regarded as sacred.

Persuasive, cheerful Tibetan hawkers are everywhere, presiding over the usual junky souvenirs imported from Kathmandu. Locally woven Tibetan **carpets** are sold in the Tibetan settlements and in Lakeside shops, but the best carpets are found in Kathmandu. The same goes for *thangka.* When it comes to authentic curios, though, it's best to buy if you find something you like—things like wooden vessels, old Tibetan carpets, and turquoise aren't necessarily rare, but each piece is unique.

SERVICES AND INFORMATION

Banks

The most convenient place for money-changing is **Grindlays Bank** in Lakeside, open Sun.-Fri.

10 a.m.-4 p.m. You can also get cash advances with Visa or MasterCard here. **Nepal Rastra Bank** located north of Damside has a foreign exchange counter across the street that's open daily. If you're considering the black market, know that Pokhara's is subdued, and you'll have to hunt for someone to change at a better-than-bank rate.

Visas and Trekking Permits

The **Immigration Office** just north of the Nepal Rastra Bank issues visa extensions and trekking permits for the Annapurna and Jumla regions. (Photo shops nearby do instant photos.) Application hours are daily 10:30 a.m.-1 p.m. (12:30 p.m. in winter) except Saturday; permits and visas are available the same afternoon. Trekkers to the Annapurna region pay an Rs650 fee for the Annapurna Conservation Area Project here.

Communications

The main **post office** near Mahendra Phul is open Sun.-Thurs. 10 a.m.-5 p.m., Friday 10 a.m.-3 p.m. Local **telephone calls** can be made from any number of shops and guesthouses; the classier hotels also have international dialing. "Communications centers" in Lakeside provide IDD services and fax capabilities. Calls to Kathmandu average Rs20 per minute; international calls are Rs200 a minute, depending on the country.

Health

Visit the **Western Regional Hospital,** tel. (61) 20-066, in Ram Ghat or the missionary-run **Shining Hospital,** tel. (61) 20-111, in Bagh Bazaar (it got its name from the way the original tin roofs glinted in the sun). Private medical clinics are found around Mahendra Pul. There are plenty of do-it-yourself pharmacies in Lakeside, Pardi, and the old bazaar; several of these provide stool tests.

Laundry

This is taken care of by local women who wallop the heck out of clothes on the Camping Chowk pier, bringing them back clean, if a little worse for wear. A few places near the campground and the road to Hotel Fewa advertise laundry services; machine washing is also available.

Information

The government **Tourist Office,** tel. (61) 20-028, across from the airport languishes in a big building with a pathetically small amount of literature to hand out—it's not worth a visit. Lakeside and Damside **bookstores** sell city and trekking maps and local publications about the Pokhara region; they also have a good selection of fat novels to read while boating. Keep up with world events, if you must, with the *International Herald Tribune, Time* and *Newsweek,* available a few days later than in Kathmandu.

GETTING THERE

By Air

All four domestic airlines fly to Pokhara; US$61 tickets are easily available in all but the busiest season. The half-hour flight passes by a 100-mile stretch of peaks, skimming over what used to be a seven-day trek. Sit on the right side for mountain views. Passengers are deposited at the **Nagdhunga Airfield,** which offers a great view of the five Annapurnas fronted by Machhapuchhare. Unfortunately, the voracious taxi drivers and hotel touts don't give you any time to admire it.

From the airport it's a half-hour walk to Lakeside and about 15 minutes to Damside. Pick a taxi driver immediately and with great firmness, or the touts will eat you alive. If you can get a taxi to Lakeside for Rs50 you're doing fine. There's a cycle rental stand outside the airport gate, and a few hotels, mostly expensive, across the way. If you just want a basic place to crash for a night, try the **Hotel Himal.**

By Road

Public buses are typically slow and crowded, taking seven or eight hours to make the 200-km journey from Kathmandu. Tourist buses charge more than double (Rs150) but are less crowded and marginally faster. **Student Travels and Tours** and **Swiss Travels and Tours** in Thamel are among several companies with tourist service to Pokhara. These depart daily around 7 a.m. from the upper end of Kanti Path, more convenient than the Gongabu bus park that public buses use.

All buses end at the Pokhara bus park at Prithvi Chowk, a vast dusty or muddy expanse,

depending upon the season, which is without a doubt the least pleasant place in town. The hotel touts here are even more aggressive than those at the airport and will eat the indecisive alive. Take a taxi to Lakeside for Rs50 or plod the three km; Damside is two km away. If you're coming in from the south on the Siddhartha Rajmarg ask to be let off at Pardi, the local name for Damside.

On Foot

Before the highway to India was built, this was the *only* way to reach Pokhara. From Kathmandu, it's a gentle six- or seven-day trek through lowland hills, perfect in the winter, hot in spring. The trail starts at **Trisuli,** 70 km north of Kathmandu. Three days away is the historic old capital of **Gorkha,** connected by road to the main highway should you decide to catch a ride. See the Trekking chapter for more details on this route.

Onward Travel

Pokhara is a convenient launching point for travel to Tansen, Lumbini and India or the Terai, and/or Chitwan National Park. Lakeside travel agents sell bus tickets for a small markup, sparing you a return visit to the bus park. Tourist buses to Kathmandu cost double the local rate but may be worth it as they're less crowded and they pick up passengers from Lakeside. Tourist "express" buses also run to Tadi Bazaar, the jumping-off point for Sauruha in Chitwan. Regular buses run to Bhairawa/Sunauli on the Indian border, Biratnagar, Birgunj, Butwal, Gorkha, Janakpur, Narayanghat, Nepalgunj, and Tansen. Longer runs depart at night, and there are several night buses to Kathmandu.

Be wary of package bus-train deals for travel to Indian cities; as in Kathmandu, agents may promise more than they deliver—first-class seats that turn out to be second-class, or nonexistent sleeper reservations.

Hiring a taxi to the next destination is a pricer but more comfortable alternative to buses, and is surprisingly easy to arrange—just ask drivers on the street.

Flights out of Pokhara operate daily to Kathmandu (US$61) and Jomosom (US$50). Air tickets can be purchased through an agent or directly through the airline: RNAC, tel. (61) 21-

THE KATHMANDU-POKHARA ROAD: THE PRITHVI RAJMARG

The 202-km Prithvi Rajmarg connecting Kathmandu to Pokhara was built in the early '70s by China. The road most frequently travelled by tourists, it's not just en route to Pokhara, but also the first leg of the journey to Chitwan, the Terai, or India. A drive down is frequently lengthened by road construction, repairing the annual havoc wreaked by the monsoon.

The road climbs up out of the Kathmandu Valley past Thankot and drops, twisting and turning in a frightening fashion, down to the teastalls of **Naubise.** From here to Mugling it follows the Trisuli River, favored by rafters for its easy accessibility. Note the narrow military bridges installed across several tributaries after the disastrous monsoon flooding of 1993 wiped out big stretches of the road.

Mugling, halfway between Kathmandu and Pokhara, is popularly known as *"Daal Bhaat Bazaar"* because everyone stops here for a meal. It's not really a village, just a giant truck stop. The wide main road is lined by dozens of wooden buildings purveying *daal bhaat* and tea. The bus pulls in, passengers pile out, and 20 minutes later—the time it takes to consume two plates of *daal bhaat*—it's time to go again. For a leg-stretcher, walk down to the suspension bridge over the Trisuli; the Marsyangdi River joins it nearby. There should be no reason to stay overnight here, but there are plenty of small local guesthouses if necessary. **Motel du Mugling,** across the bridge, is an upper-class operation with a reasonable restaurant, managed by Hotel de l'Annapurna, with rooms for US$25 s, US$35 d.

Mugling is the turnoff for the road to Narayanghat and the Terai, so the Pokhara highway is less crowded from here on. It first follows the course of the Marsyangdi Khola. Look for the sluiceways and turbines of the Marsyangdi Power Project, a recently completed $200 million venture intended to fill Kathmandu's insatiable need for electricity. Shiny new metal towers line the road, but the Valley's demand is increasing so fast that the project was outdated even before completion.

Himalayan peaks appear on this stretch, mainly Annapurna, Himalchuli, and Manaslu. Eight km beyond Mugling is the small village of **Abu Khaireni,** and the turnoff to the old historic hill town of Gorkha. It's a four-hour walk uphill to the wish-fulfilling temple of Manakamana. Ten km further is **Dumre,** a dusty, unlovely roadside stop which is the turnoff for the eastern side of the Annapurna Circuit. Local vehicles ply the bumpy dirt road up to Besisahar, a jolting trip. If you come too late to catch one or prefer to walk, you can climb for two hours to the old Newar town of **Bandipur,** once a major trading village on the route to Manang.

The Pokhara road continues through **Damauli,** a big bazaar town and district headquarters set at the juncture of the Madi and Seti Rivers (good swimming here if you happen to stop). Pokhara is 55 km further, through flatter and more open countryside, following the course of the Seti Gandaki River. The main bus stop is at the end of the highway, marked by a statue of Prithvi Narayan Shah; it's midway between the airport and the bazaar, a long walk from Lakeside.

021, and Everest, tel. (61) 21-883, have their offices near the airport; Nepal Airways, tel. (61) 21-178, is just across the street; and Necon Air, tel. (61) 20-256, is at Ratna Chowk, near the Immigration Office.

GETTING AROUND

Pokhara on foot is out of the question unless you're a real fiend for walking: the vast distances between places will grind down even the most dedicated trekker. Taxis are unmetered, so set the price before you start and look for people to share with. From Lakeside it should be about Rs50 up to the old and new bazaars or the bus park, Rs40 to the airport. Taxis are not always immediately available, so if you're catching a flight or bus have your lodgekeeper book one in advance.

Motorcycles can be rented at Lakeside for Rs350-500 a day. Car rentals are pricey at US$50 per day; better to arrange for a taxi driver to take you about. Local bus service is limited to a single slow loop around the bazaar, passing the bus park and airport en route. In Lakeside,

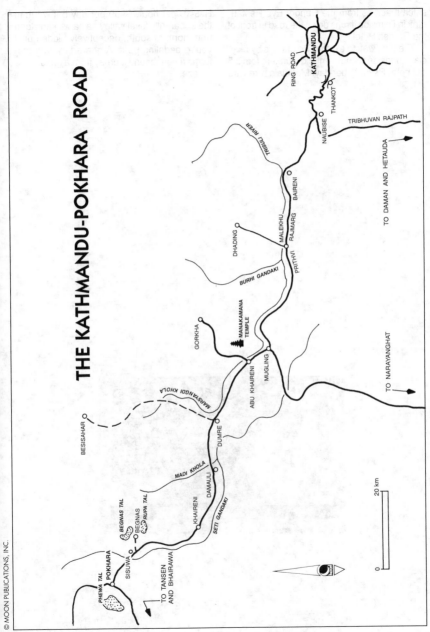

THE KATHMANDU-POKHARA ROAD

catch it across from the Hungry Eye Restaurant; in Damside it runs down the road in front of the Garden Hotel.

The best way to explore Pokhara is by bicycle. Roadside stands rent old clunkers for Rs5 per hour, Rs20-30 per day. Mountain bikes are Rs8-10 per hour, Rs50 per day but worth it: the apparently level valley has a wicked slope from north to south, deceptively hidden until you're pedaling up it. A geared cycle transforms a northbound journey from a grind into a breeze.

TANSEN

Tansen is that great rarity: a Nepali town big enough to be interesting, yet so far utterly unspoiled. Set at 1400 meters on the southern side of the Mahabharat Range in south-central Nepal, it's a sleepy little hill station with a marvellously fresh climate. Much of its charm comes from the fact it's *way* off the tourist circuit. In truth there's not much going on in Tansen, and it's probably best visited by genuine fans of Nepal.

A prosperous-looking collection of red-brick houses set on a steep hillside, Tansen is among the largest of the far-flung Newar trading posts scattered across the Hills. Some 60% of its 16,000 people are Newar, but the surrounding region is the homeland of the Magars, one of the most delightful of Nepal ethnic groups.

History

Tansen originally belonged to the Barha Magarat, a dozen small tribal states ruled by Magar chieftains. In the 15th century it became the capital of the powerful kingdom of Palpa, ruled by the Sen Dynasty, distant cousins of the royal Shahs. The semi-legendary king Mukunda Sen is said to have extended his rule all the way up to the Kosi River, launching an attack on the Kathmandu Valley and making off with a pair of gilded Bhairab masks he installed in two temples. Tansen was finally brought into Nepal in 1806, the last of the independent Hill kingdoms to be annexed. It became an important district headquarters and tax collection center, and a dumping ground for troublesome Rana relatives packed off into unofficial exile as regional governors.

The town has a confusing multiplicity of names: Tansing is the original Magar name, Tansen the modern Nepali version. It's frequently called Palpa, the name of both the ancient kingdom and the surrounding district of which Tansen is the administrative capital.

SIGHTS

Tansen's greatest attraction is itself. Narrow cobbled streets, some set at impossibly steep angles, are lined with old brick buildings and filled with the cheerful bustle of city life, minus the racket of Kathmandu. Tansen is a friendly, unspoiled, completely natural type of place seldom found without trekking into an unvisited part of the Hills. The kids haven't yet learned to beg, and people are remarkably blasé about the rare foreign traveler—a relief after the ogling encountered in the Terai and India. It's not that they're unfriendly; they just all seem to have something better to do.

Tansen Durbar and Bazaar

The center of town is dominated by the rambling pink Tansen Durbar, built in 1927. Once the Rana governor's residence, it now houses government offices. The north gate, **Baggi Dhoka,** is said to be the largest in Nepal, big enough for an elephant, or at least a carriage (*baggi* = "buggy"), to pass through. Behind the Durbar is an ugly renovated temple to Bhagwati, built in 1815 to commemorate a Nepali victory over the British at Butwal. The glee was shortlived, as the British won the war the following year, forcing Nepal to cede most of its Terai holdings.

The main bazaar street fronting the Durbar is full of Hill people buying supplies—grain, cooking oil, tiny dried fish from the nearby Barangdi Khola, all hauled back home in the region's distinctive narrow *dokko*. Magar women in velvet blouses pick through the displays of hair tassels and bangles. The people around here are exceptionally handsome: the women in particular have glowing complexions, probably something to do with the exquisite climate.

A variety of occupations are clustered down the narrow side streets, including a row of Newar goldsmiths who etch delicately designed earrings and necklaces. Inside the town's old brick houses, both men and women weave *dhaka* cloth on upright looms, using *pashmina* thread. Palpali *dhaka* is famous for its fine texture and intricate patterns. Finished pieces, *topi,* and shawls are sold in the main bazaar, or you could inquire of a weaver. The other speciality is metalwork, found in the Taksar area, but stick to simple metal vessels rather than the generally clumsy images.

TANSEN

Other Sights

On the east side of town is the **Amar Narayan Mandir,** one of the finest multiroofed temples outside the Kathmandu Valley, with clever erotic struts, a superb facade of beaten metal, and some exquisite gilt statues of Garuda and various donors kneeling in front. It's tended by a *sadhu* with 30 years' retreat experience living in a nearby cave. Drums, bells, and horns are sounded here twice daily in worship, adding to the town's timeless air.

Tansen's other temples are unnotable (the 1934 earthquake did a lot of damage); there are a few Buddhist *bahal* and *chaitya* as well. The big open **Tundikhel** near the bus park yields views of the green Madi Valley below, on winter mornings filled with billowing silver fog.

Tansen is headquarters for a surprisingly large number of foreign-aid projects, including a hospital run by the big United Mission to Nepal.

Tell people you're going to Tansen, and most will assume you're working for UMN. The idea of tourism hasn't caught on yet, despite some half-hearted government efforts.

Srinagar Danda

Behind Tansen rises the 1525-meter hill of Srinagar Danda. The crest is a half-hour climb from the **Siddhi Ganesh temple** on the hillside, or an easy ridge walk from the Hotel Srinagar. The ridge provides exceptionally panoramic Himalayan views, from Dhaulagiri in the west to Gauri Shankar in the east; to the south, the Churia and Mahabharat Ranges stretch into the Terai flatlands. There's an incongruous helipad up here, the ruins of a few old Rana summer homes, and a pine plantation, part of a recent effort to combat deforestation. One effect of the tree-cutting has been the gradual drying-up of the town's water supply; your hotel may only have water intermittently.

Around Tansen

Itself practically untouched, Tansen is a launching point for day walks and treks into virgin country. With its friendly Magar villages, the surrounding region provides a taste of what popular trekking trails were like 30 years ago. Trekking possibilities include the 10-day Pokhara-Dhorpatan-Tansen route, a four-day hike along the Kali Gandaki to Beni, or the leisurely week's trek along Panchasse Lekh to Pokhara.

Ask your lodgekeeper for advice and directions for day hikes in the vicinity. An easy destination is the Magar village of **Chilangdi** an hour's walk from town. Nearly every family here has a son or two in the British or Indian Gurkhas, so the local standard of living is relatively high. The potters' village of **Ghorbanda,** a few kilometers north off the Siddhartha Rajmarg, is inhabited by Kumals, the original inhabitants of the area, predating even the Magars. Traditionally they served as palanquin carriers; today they work as fishermen, porters, and potters throwing big earthen pots by hand on spinning wheels.

Among the most intriguing day hikes is the 14-km walk to the north over Srinagar Danda and along the Kali Gandaki to **Rani Ghat,** a vast abandoned Rana palace on the riverside. Built in 1896 in memory of a Rana governor's wife, the huge edifice was designed by British engineers and constructed by Nepali soldiers. For a few years it served as a Rana summerhouse, then its builder fell into disgrace and the building was abandoned. It's on the verge of collapse, but the sight of the huge pillared edifice looming out of the forested riverbank is worth the trip. Returning, you could take an alternate trail along the Kali Gandaki to **Ramdi Ghat** on the Siddhartha Rajmarg, and catch a bus back to town.

An unpaved road connects Tansen with the town of **Tamghas,** 40 km west. Minibuses to here depart the Tansen bus park several times daily, but it's a slow journey. Ten km down the road is **Ridi Bazaar,** a mainly Newar town of about 2,000 at the confluence of the Kali Gandaki and the Ridi Khola. The **Rikheswar Narayan temple** here is the local version of Kathmandu's Pashupatinath, featuring some similarly auspicious cremation ghats. The Vishnu image enshrined inside is said to have begun no larger than an infant and gradually grown to the size and appearance of an adult. You can walk here via a 13-km route that manages to stay off the road most of the way, and return to Tansen by bus.

The **Palpa Bhairab temple** is eight km west of Tansen, just off the Tamghas road. Marked with a huge gilded trident, it enshrines a replica of Kathmandu's Kaalo Bhairab, reportedly so terrifying it's frightened several viewers to death, which explains why it's now hidden from view. The temple draws animal-sacrificing supplicants on Tuesday and Saturday.

PRACTICALITIES

Accommodations

The cheap hotels around the bus park are subject to an awesome racket beginning at 5 a.m., so stay elsewhere unless you're leaving early. **Hotel Siddhartha,** tel. (75) 20-226, has rooms for Rs40 s, Rs70 d without bath, Rs200-250 with.

Just up from bus park, the new **Hotel Bajra,** tel. (75) 20-443, has a tolerable restaurant and decent rooms with attached bath for Rs200 s, Rs250-320 d, and dorm beds for Rs50. Next door is the slightly smaller **Hotel Lumbini,** tel. (75) 20-455, where rooms are Rs200.

Walk up the steep road to the right to reach **Hotel Sangam,** small, basic, and cheap (Rs60) but beyond the blare of bus horns. **Hotel Gautam Siddhartha,** tel. (75) 20-280, on Bishal Bazaar Road is run-down but peaceful, with rooms for Rs150 d. Better is the new **Hotel White Lake,** tel. (75) 20-291, a bit further down the road, where very nice rooms with bath are Rs400 d.

The only *pukka* place to stay is **Hotel Srinagar,** tel. (75) 20-045, perched atop Bataase Danda ("Windy Ridge") about two km northwest of the bus park. It's at least a 20-minute walk uphill, complicated by lack of directions. The motor road to Gulmi runs close by the hotel, if you have a vehicle at your command. The hotel manages to rise above its cement-block architecture: big rooms are reasonably outfitted considering the obscurity of the location, and cost US$20 s, US$28 d. One wing faces the Himalaya while the other overlooks Tansen and the Madi Valley—splendid breakfast views either way.

Food

The bus park area holds many small restaurants and snack shops. The basic little **Dokko Restaurant** behind the bus park is somewhat more peaceful. Traditional teashops scattered through town provide a more cheerful vantage point for people-watching, but they are seldom advertised by signs—look for the array of plates and glasses displayed inside. **Hotel Bajra**'s restaurant does decent Indian food, and **Hotel Srinagar** can produce a Western breakfast, best consumed in the garden.

Getting There

Located midway between Pokhara and Bhairawa, Tansen is best visited en route between the two. By bus it's six hours from Pokhara, two hours from Bhairawa, and six hours from Chitwan (via Butwal). From Kathmandu, there are a very few direct buses, or go to Butwal and catch a local bus to Tansen. From Pokhara, a taxi will drop you off in Tansen in five hours for about Rs1500.

Tansen is 117 km down the Siddhartha Rajmarg from Pokhara. The road is little-trafficked, though steep and constantly twisting—a great mountain-biking route. It winds through the gorge of the Anahi Khola, passing through small, sleepy Magar villages, past beautiful terraces and some great swimming spots. The road is currently in very bad condition, which means it may be repaired soon—then again, it may not be.

Lunch is invariably at **Waling,** a fairly squalid town two hours from Pokhara. More attractive is small, shady **Ramdi Ghat,** where a suspension bridge crosses the turbid, gray Kali Gandaki. You may see rafters camped on the sandbars downstream. Signs for Gurkha Welfare Centers indicate the strong hold soldiery has on local people—this is Magar country, and Magars constitute a high percentage of British and Indian Gurkhas. Most families here are partly supported by remittances from soldiers.

Tansen lies three km up a spur road from the small town of **Bartun.** If your bus is not direct to Tansen you'll be deposited here. Take a minibus up the hill or walk via a steep footpath to the local Tundikhel. Roads skirt the edges of town, but most of it is so steep vehicles seldom penetrate its roads—inconvenient, but a source of its great charm.

Onward Travel

From Tansen there are two or three buses daily to Pokhara-Kathmandu, and regular service to Butwal and Bhairawa-Sunauli. The ride to the latter is, for once, not murderously long; only around two hours.

BUTWAL, BHAIRAWA, AND SUNAULI

As a convenient and popular border crossing, Sunauli provides access to a big chunk of northern India, including Delhi, Varanasi, and Agra. There's little to say about Sunauli itself, though. It's so small it's not even a village, just a depressingly low-grade strip of restaurants and hotels. Bhairawa, four km north, is a real town, but it's flat, dusty, and charmless Terai. The surrounding countryside has its redeeming features, especially in the cooler winter months. Brilliantly colored birds flicker across green ricefields, and the small villages shaded by mango trees have a feel very much like rural India. Few travelers make the 20-km detour to Lumbini, the birthplace of the Buddha, but the trip is worth considering, if only because Lumbini is the most important historical site in Nepal.

Butwal

The unillustrious "gateway" to the central Terai is Butwal, a nondescript town huddled at the base of the hills where the Mahendra Rajmarg from Bharatpur and the Siddhartha Rajmarg from Pokhara meet. Through buses stop at **Traphik Chowk** on the east side of town, a modern bazaar area. Butwal's redeeming feature is streetside cappuccino vendors who will serve you aboard the bus—okay, so it's Nescafé, but it's a change from the usual *chiyaa*.

Local buses end up at the bus park on the western edge of town. There's no reason to stay in Butwal, but if you get stuck there are several cheap hotels near here and in the bazaar. **Hotel Sayapatri** near the bus park is run by an ex-Gurkha and is a clean and friendly place with good food and rooms with bath for Rs150. The best place in town is **Hotel Sindoor,** tel. (73) 20-189, near Traphik Chowk, charging a negotiable US$20 s, US$30 d; the dining room serves good Indian food. If you have some time to kill, explore old Butwal, across the river, much more interesting than the modern main town along the highway.

Bhairawa

Bhairawa, a half-hour south of Butwal, is another basic Terai town. Officially its name has been changed to Siddhartha Nagar, but nobody calls it that. Buses unload at the big traffic circle. The main bazaar lies just west of here, along Bank Road and Market Road.

Cheap, basic lodgings in this area charge Rs60-100 for a room without bath. **Sayapatri Guesthouse** near the bus park and **City Guest House** are as good as any. **Hotel Yeti,** tel. (75) 20-551, right on the central circle is the best place, charging US$15 s, US$20 d for a clean room with bath; US$25 for an a/c room. **Hotel Himalayan Inn,** tel. (75) 20-347, is second choice, a 10-minute walk north down the Siddhartha Rajmarg. It's not as well-maintained but remains tolerable; rooms are US$10 s, US$12 d.

Apart from the dining rooms of these two hotels, food is limited to *daal bhaat* diners, tea and sweet stalls, and a handful of Indian restaurants.

At the Border: Sunauli

Sunauli lies four km south of Bhairawa: reach it by cycle rickshaw (around Rs15), *tempo,* or jeep (Rs3). Sunauli is actually the name of the Indian town across the border—the Nepali side is called Belhiya—but few people distinguish between the two. It encompasses a half-dozen very basic hotels, a huddle of teastalls and grotty *bhojnalaya,* and a constant traffic jam of honking, exhaust-belching vehicles. On a hot afternoon, it can be a miniature realm of hell.

Prearranged bus-train packages from Kathmandu to India often include an overnight in Sunauli. If you have the choice, Bhairawa is marginally more interesting and has better facilities. Sunauli's half-dozen hotels are basically flophouses with little to distinguish between them. The best strategy may be to look for the newest place, which is bound to be the cleanest.

Package travelers are usually assigned to **Hotel Mamta,** tel. (75) 20-512, at the far end of the strip, where seedy rooms are Rs60, Rs90 with bath; Rs30 for dorm beds. There's a shady garden and it's relatively quiet. Across the street, **Nepal Guesthouse** has similarly cheap rooms and dorm beds. **Hotel Deep Jyoti** and **Hotel**

BHAIRAWA
AND
SUNAULI

TO BUTWAL

BUSES
TO LUMBINI

HOTEL
HIMALAYAN INN

TO LUMBINI

BUS STOP

BANK RD.   BANK

AIRPORT   SAYAPATRI   HOTEL YETI
               GUESTHOUSE

MARKET RD.

SIDDHARTHA HWY.

APPROXIMATELY 3 km

NARAYAN PATH   HOTEL MAMTA

NEPAL GUESTHOUSE

HOTEL DEEP JYOTI

HOTEL JAY VIJAY

HOTEL TANAHUN   BELHIYA

BUS PARK

BANK

HOTEL HOLIDAY

FOREIGN EXCHANGE COUNTER

HOTEL PARADISE

JANASEWA LODGE

NEPALI
CUSTOMS   NEPALI IMMIGRATION

NOT TO SCALE

TO GORAKHPUR

NEPAL   INDIAN CUSTOMS   SUNAULI
INDIA

© MOON PUBLICATIONS, INC.

Jay Vijay next door are newer and relatively decent; **Hotel Paradise** south of the bus park is also okay. It might be better to stay on the Indian side in the government-run **Hotel Niranjana,** which has dorm beds for IRs15 (that's Indian rupees, approximately twice the value of Nepali rupees) and private rooms with bath for IRs50 s, IRs75 d.

The Nepal Rastra Bank here is open daily 7:30 a.m.-6 p.m. (the bank on the Indian side doesn't open till 10 a.m.). Nepali customs inspection is generally mild; the Immigration Office at the border gate is open 6 a.m.-7 p.m. Just beyond is Indian customs and immigration, which is supposed to be open 24 hours. Formalities shouldn't take more than 30 minutes in all, and if the immigration official on either side happens to admire your pen, don't feel obliged to give it to him. From the Indian side, buses depart every half-hour up to 7 p.m. for the Gorakhpur railway station, a two and a half hour ride away. Look for the red state buses, rather than the slower private buses. Other direct buses go to Varanasi, Allahbad, and Lucknow.

Getting There
Kathmandu-Bhairawa airfare is US$72; flights are five times weekly. Cycle rickshaws ply the three km between the airport and town. By bus, Bhairawa is a nine- or 10-hour journey from Kathmandu or Pokhara, and five hours from Tadi Bazaar. There are regular buses from Birganj and Butwal, or again you could hire a taxi.

Onward Travel
Sunauli is so small it's no problem to find the buses—just follow the horns. Most buses start at Sunauli, but it's possible to reserve a seat from stalls near the traffic circle in Bhairawa

and board there. Sajha buses depart directly from the traffic circle. There are several day and night buses to Kathmandu and Pokhara; for Chitwan, take the Birganj bus and get off at Tadi Bazaar.

LUMBINI

Travelers rushing through Sunauli and Bhairawa invariably bypass Lumbini, the birthplace of the Buddha 22 km west of Bhairawa. A Buddhist pilgrimage site marooned in the midst of thoroughly Muslim and Hindu countryside, Lumbini is ignored by just about everyone except a few devout Japanese, Thai, and Tibetan pilgrims. At 250 km from Kathmandu it would be a long journey in itself, but it fits nicely into a Pokhara-Tansen-Chitwan loop, and if you're heading to India, an extra day is well spent at Lumbini.

HISTORY

Siddhartha Gautama, the man who became the Buddha—the title means "The Awakened One"—was born a prince of the Sakya clan ruling Kapilvastu, a small independent kingdom on the Indian plains. (Lumbini only became part of Nepal in 1856, and it's unlikely Buddha ever set foot in present-day Nepal.) Renouncing his pleasurable life with the realization of the inevitability of suffering, he left his father's palace at age 29 and tried various means of attaining spiritual enlightenment. Succeeding at the age of 34, he spent the remainder of his life wandering India's dusty Gangetic Plain, teaching the "Middle Way" that leads to spiritual enlightenment. He died at the age of 81. Today the sites of his birth, enlightenment, first teaching, and death—Lumbini, Bodh Gaya, Sarnath, and Kushinagar—are visited by Buddhist pilgrims from across Asia.

The Buddha was born around 543 B.C. (the actual date is disputed). According to legend, Queen Mayadevi was traveling to her parents' home for the birth of her first child when labor pains started in the shady grove of Lumbini where her party had stopped to rest. The child was born painlessly from her right side as Mayadevi clung to the overhanging branch of a flowering *ashoka* tree—a favorite scene for sculptors.

Upon his birth the infant Buddha is said to have taken seven steps in each of the four directions, proclaiming "This is my final rebirth." The earth quaked; flowers fell from the heavens; Indra, Brahma, and a host of other gods descended to worship the baby; and family priests quickly realized this infant with the 32 marks of perfection on his body was destined for greatness—either a world monarch, they decided, or an Enlightened One.

Lumbini's earliest patron was the Indian emperor Ashoka, who came here on pilgrimage in 249 B.C. and commemorated his visit with a stone column, an imperial trademark. A devout Buddhist, Ashoka raised these pillars to serve as memorials and to demarcate the boundaries of his vast kingdom—there are others at Niglihawa and Kotihawa, 33 km northwest and west of Lumbini. The Lumbini pillar is the best available evidence that Lumbini was indeed the Buddha's birthplace, though coming some 700 years after the fact, the proof is less than conclusive.

Chinese pilgrims visiting Lumbini a thousand years after the reign of Ashoka found temples, monasteries, and stupas, but the site was already declining as Indian Buddhism waned. Weakened by resurgent Hinduism, it received the final blow with the rise of Islam. By the 14th century, with Buddhism eradicated from the land of its birth, Lumbini slowly sank beneath the jungle. An ancient stone sculpture of the Buddha's nativity survived, worshipped by local women as a fertility symbol, but so completely forgotten was Lumbini that it took a German archaeologist to rediscover it in 1895 by stumbling upon the Ashokan Pillar in the jungle. A Rana archaeologist excavated further in the 1930s, damaging some of the ruins in the process.

Little was done in the ensuing years to preserve or protect Lumbini. By 1967 it was in such disrepair that U Thant, Secretary General of the U.N. and a devout Buddhist, is said to have

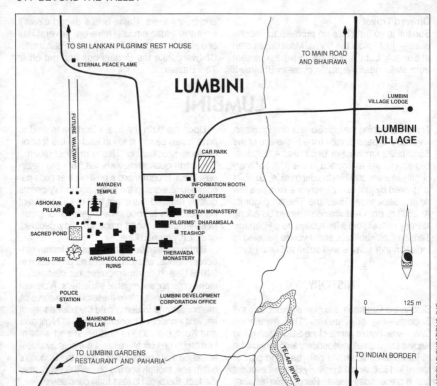

wept at the sight. An international development committee was formed shortly thereafter, and the wheels of development began to creak.

The Master Plan

Ten years later came a master plan, designed by Japanese architect Kenzo Tange for the United Nations Development Program. It envisions a five-square-km complex of gardens, monasteries, temples, and monuments to be established at Lumbini. The design is patterned on the mandala, with circles enclosing squares. The core area, the **Sacred Grove,** will encompass the Mayadevi temple, pools, stupa bases, and other excavated ruins. A **monastic complex** to the north will contain monasteries and retreats built by various countries in their national style, plus a meditation center. A third sector, **Lumbini village,** will form the entrance

and will include lodges, restaurants, library, and museum.

A 4.5-km central canal will divide the two zones and encircle the Sacred Grove, while pedestrian walkways will run along its banks. A large portion of the complex is to be forested, sure to provide welcome relief on the treeless plain, and appropriate in light of the fact that the main events of the Buddha's life—birth, enlightenment, first teaching, and death—all took place beneath trees. Some 600,000 saplings are said to have been planted so far, but none are in evidence.

While the master plan has its opponents among the mainly Muslim local people (many of whom were evicted when the zone's boundaries were established), 13 countries plus the U.N. have enlisted in the project. The Lumbini Development Trust has assembled a consider-

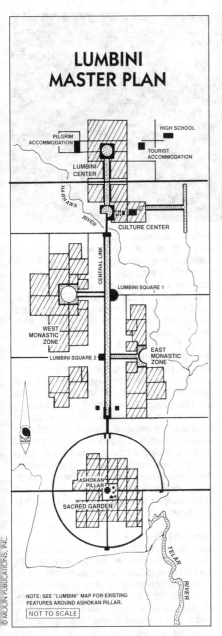

LUMBINI MASTER PLAN

HIGH SCHOOL

PILGRIM ACCOMMODATION

TOURIST ACCOMMODATION

LUMBINI CENTER

HARHAWA RIVER

CULTURE CENTER

CENTRAL LINK

LUMBINI SQUARE 1

WEST MONASTIC ZONE

EAST MONASTIC ZONE

LUMBINI SQUARE 2

ASHOKAN PILLAR

SACRED GARDEN

TELAR RIVER

NOTE: SEE "LUMBINI" MAP FOR EXISTING FEATURES AROUND ASHOKAN PILLAR.

NOT TO SCALE

© MOON PUBLICATIONS, INC.

able amount of funding and at least US$3 million has been spent, but present progress is limited to a few forlorn buildings far north of the main site. As of now, Lumbini is well-maintained but undeveloped—the ideal balance of attention and neglect. Given the tendency for development to uglify, it may be best to visit Lumbini now, rather than later.

SIGHTS

Ancient religious texts describe Lumbini as a marvelous pleasure garden dotted with mansions and fountains and wandered by peacocks and peaceful elephant herds. Today it's a thoroughly nondescript stretch of Terai plain. There's little to see beyond the Mayadevi Temple, the sacred pond, the Ashokan Pillar, and a pair of rather ordinary monasteries. But the place radiates a feeling of peace strong enough to soothe the most restless souls. Somehow it's enough to sit in the shade of the big pipal trees and gaze out over the flat green plains. A few pilgrims circumambulate the temple, and local people drift across the parklike grounds, stopping to peer curiously inside the Tibetan monastery.

Things liven up during the full moon of April (Chaitra Purnima), when thousands of Hindu pilgrims gather for a *mela*. Buddha Jayanti, the festival marking Buddha's birth, which falls on the May full moon (Baisakh Purnima), draws comparatively few Buddhists—it's too hot by then.

Mayadevi Temple
Tangible objects of interest are clustered near the Mayadevi Temple, a boxy whitewashed structure recently dismantled in an effort to preserve it from the strangling embrace of a giant pipal tree. The temple will be reassembled, sans tree, on the same site. Inside the temple is a 3rd-century stone relief of the Buddha's birth, worn smooth from centuries of worship. The features of the main figures were chiselled out by iconoclastic Muslim invaders. Beside it stands a modern marble copy, the details intact: Mayadevi grasping a tree branch, the newborn Buddha standing by her side being welcomed by the god Brahma.

The image is tended by Hindu priests and worshipped by local Hindus, who regard Mayadevi as Rupadevi, a goddess of abundance and

the sacred pool and
Mayadevi temple

fertility. Buddhism has vanished utterly from the region, and only the recently excavated and heavily restored foundations of ancient monasteries and stupas dotting the site show this was a sacred place from the 2nd century B.C. to the 9th century A.D. The corrugated surface of the level plain around the temple complex indicates that many more ruins remain underground. Some archaeologists believe it's best this way, as excavated monuments are subject to vandalism and theft. The two grassy mounds near the temple are not ruins, but piles of dirt from earlier excavations.

Ashokan Pillar

The cylindrical Ashokan Pillar west of the temple is fairly unimpressive for the oldest historical monument in Nepal and resembles nothing so much as a giant chimney. The metal bands about it are supposed to protect against lightning; a 7th-century Chinese traveler reported the pillar split in two by a demon who hurled thunderbolts down against it. The inscription, written in Brahmi script, reads: "The king, friend of the gods, he of the kindly countenance, came here in person 20 years after his coronation and rendered homage, because this was the birthplace of the Buddha, the saint of the Sakya." In an act of pure chutzpah, the father of the present king erected a marble **Mahendra Pillar** nearby. The stepped square pool is said to be the one Mayadevi bathed in before labor; the infant Buddha is said to have been washed here by two dragons, one spouting hot water, one cold.

Two Monasteries

Across the way are two monasteries, the first a **Tibetan *gompa*** constructed by Chogye Trinzin Rinpoche, a venerable Sakya lama who has a monastery at Boudhanath, and financed by the Raja of Mustang. Completed in 1975, it already has an air of timeless antiquity. The main image here is said to contain bone relics of the Buddha; detailed wall murals depict the Buddha's life story. Maroon-robed monks from the Boudhanath monastery stay here in winter, but the summer heat is too much for them.

The second monastery was built by the Nepali government in an odd melange of styles. Called the **Theravada Monastery** (Theravada being the Buddhism of Southeast Asia), it has a plaster *vajra* over the entrance; inside are Buddha images from Burma, Thailand, and Nepal, and wall murals including a Tibetan Wheel of Life and a scene of Hindu deities welcoming the Buddha. The Lumbini Development Plan dictates that both these monasteries be demolished and relocated in new quarters in the monastic complex north of the Mayadevi Temple.

Along the Canal

You can view this area by following the walkway north, past the **Eternal Peace Flame,** brought from U.N. Headquarters in 1986 to mark the International Year of Peace, and along a one-km-long canal. Work is underway on a Korean temple-monastery, a Vietnamese Buddhist center, and a Thai Buddhist temple, and agreements have been signed for 18 other projects. Further north, a new research library and museum are slated to open in 1995.

Around Lumbini

Across from the street from the main entrance is the small village of Lumbini, with a Hanuman temple and a weekly bazaar on Saturday. About 15 minutes' walk south down the road is **Paharia**, a slightly larger village relocated here after the zone was established. The open-air market held on Monday involves lively trading under mango trees, but buses are even more crowded than normal.

Kapilvastu

Ruins of the capital city of Kapilvastu, the Buddha's ancestral home, have been uncovered near **Tilaurikot**, 27 km west of Lumbini and three km north of the village of **Taulihawa**. The ruins of King Suddhodhana's palace and several giant stupas are slowly being excavated here. The eastern gate from which the Buddha is said to have departed on his search for enlightenment is of particular significance to Buddhists. A small museum nearby displays ancient coins, pottery, and ornaments and is open daily, except Tuesday, 10 a.m.-5 p.m.; entrance is Rs15.

To reach Taulihawa, either cycle down the dirt road that runs past the Lumbini Hokke Hotel; or catch a minibus from Bhairawa. Once you're in town, walk three km north along the paved road to the museum. The ruins are down the dirt road on the right.

PRACTICALITIES

Accommodations

Most people stay in Bhairawa and day-trip out to Lumbini, but there's much to be said for overnighting there. Bhairawa and its hotels are pretty dismal—better to stay in peaceful Lumbini and enjoy sunset, sunrise, and the birds. Minibuses run back to Bhairawa beginning at 6 a.m. and aren't crowded early in the morning. If you book your ongoing bus ticket in Bhairawa before you head to

Lumbini, you can depart directly on your return the next morning.

The pilgrim's *dharamsala* between the two monasteries provides simple rooms for the cost of a donation. It's undeniably well-situated, though you'll need your own bedding and the outdoor toilets are thoroughly disgusting. The **Lumbini Village Lodge** in the small village across from the main entrance has a few clean rooms with fan, Rs100 dorm, Rs150 s, Rs250 d. Simple food is available as well.

The **Sri Lankan Pilgrims' Rest House** is a modern brick building set in a shady grove a few km north of the temple area. Completed several years ago with funding from the Sri Lankan government, it stood empty until Butwal's Hotel Sindoor assumed management. The high-ceilinged brick rooms are equipped with fans and look fairly pleasant. Dorm beds are US$5; private rooms without bath are US$10, and moderately priced meals (Rs150-250) are served as well. The main problem is access: while the hotel is located within the precincts of the zone, it's a bit of a hike to the main attractions. If you plan to stay here, call the Hotel Sindoor in advance, tel. (73) 20-381, to arrange for transport from Bhairawa.

Top choice is the **Lumbini Hokke Hotel,** tel./fax (71) 20-236, a big Japanese-built edifice several kilometers north of the gardens. Room rates are US$79 s, US$120 d, US$144 t, though there's room for negotiation. This is arguably the best hotel in Nepal, with Western and Japanese-style rooms. The deluxe Japanese rooms sleep seven and are outfitted with tatami mats,

Lumbini

BOB RACE

sliding paper screens, and complimentary kimonos. The big Japanese-style public bath operates when there are 10 or more guests. The electronic bug-zapper on the grounds slaughters thousands of sentient beings nightly in a most un-Buddhistic way. Another expensive Japanese establishment, **Hotel Mikata**, is being built a few kilometers further down the road.

Food

Between the monasteries is an open-air teashop which does simple dishes like noodles and closes at dusk. The **Lumbini Gardens Restaurant** 10 minutes' walk south is pretty decent, especially given the lack of alternatives. There are a few dinky fly-ridden teashops in Paharia. Farther afield to the north, the restaurant at the Hokke Hotel serves excellent Japanese food, and the Sri Lankan Pilgrims' Rest House produces simple meals.

Getting There

See above for advice on getting to Bhairawa. From Bhairawa, jam-packed minibuses to Lumbini leave frequently from the intersection

one km north of the main traffic circle. The ride is actually enjoyable if you sit on top, but bring a brimmed hat and sunglasses to avoid scrambling your brains. It takes a little over an hour to cover the 22 km; fare is Rs10.

While minibuses are crowded, uncomfortable, and slow, hiring a *tempo* to Lumbini for Rs200-300 is merely uncomfortable and slow. It would be worthwhile to hire a taxi, especially if you're with several people. All day at Lumbini costs Rs700, but two hours is sufficient for most people, and simply being dropped off would cost much less. Taxis can be hard to find on short notice, however.

Bicycling to Lumbini is a wonderful option, but start in early morning before it gets too hot. Ask around enough and a cycle will materialize—try a cycle repair shop, or your hotel. It certainly won't be a mountain bike, but the road is well-paved and level and the surrounding countryside is lovely—lush green fields with little roadside villages reminiscent of India, white bullocks pulling creaking oxcarts, and graceful sari-clad women balancing impossible loads atop their heads.

CHITWAN NATIONAL PARK

Nepal's Terai possesses a beauty that's totally unexpected in a country known best for soaring snow-covered mountains. Nowhere is this beauty better displayed than in Chitwan National Park, a majestic, powerful, downright primeval place teeming with wildlife. A few days here yield unforgettable images: a rhino looms out of the early morning mist like some prehistoric prototype of the armored tank. Vast seas of elephant grass ripple beneath a blood-red sunset, the silvery flowering tassels swaying in the breeze like plumes. The noisy silence of the jungle is full of bird calls, and so lush you can almost hear the plants growing.

Chitwan is among Asia's finest national parks, renowned for its variety and abundance of wildlife and its top-class tourist lodges, which provide the opportunity to see animals in their natural environment without missing any creature comforts of one's own. Inexpensive lodges in the little village of Sauruha, at the park's eastern entrance, offer less luxurious but equally

comprehensive budget safaris.

The park's fame rocketed in the mid-'80s, and the number of visitors has jumped from less than 1,000 in 1981 to over 55,000 in 1992. This has altered the experience, and not necessarily for the better. Sauruha has become a little Terai Thamel, and the piece of jungle directly across from it is definitely overused. Still, few visitors stay more than two days, leaving the surrounding countryside, and the park interior, nearly untouched.

Don't expect the jungle to be lush tropical rainforest: in truth it's rather scrubby. Don't expect African-style herds swarming savannahs—Chitwan's wildlife is more discreet. Stalking the animals, whether by elephant, dugout canoe, jeep, or on foot, is the main activity here. Monkeys, rhinos, and birds are all over the place, but you'll have a better time if you don't expect too much. Chitwan's big appeal is the pervasive sense of relaxation, which soaks in deeper the longer you stay.

Arranging a Trip

It's dead easy to visit Chitwan on your own and stay in one of Sauruha's many lodges. Book in advance for the luxury lodges inside the park, but avoid the budget packages touted in Thamel, invariably more expensive than simply showing up at Sauruha and checking into the same lodge. By going down on your own you'll be able to check out several places and pick one you like, and you'll avoid getting tied down by inconvenient scheduling.

THE LAND

Chitwan is among the last surviving examples of a continuous band of forest and grassland which once extended from the Indus River in Pakistan to the Burmese border. Through the 1940s, a huge swath of this prehistoric landscape was preserved in Nepal's untouched Terai. Much has since succumbed to development, but remnants of the once-vast forests and grasslands are preserved in Chitwan and a few other parks.

The Chitwan or Rapti Valley is part of the Inner Terai. It's the largest of the broad, flat valleys *(dun)* which lie between the two outermost Himalayan foothills: the Siwalik and Mahabharat Ranges. The park's 932 square km (1,431 square km including the adjoining Parsa Wildlife Reserve) seems huge, until you realize 40 years ago practically *all* the Terai was like this.

About 70% of the park is sal-forested hills, an important wildlife habitat that's largely inac-cessible to visitors. The best-known areas are the flat floodplains of the three rivers which bound the park—the Reu, the Rapti, and the Narayani. Carpeted with grasslands, this region is criss-crossed by ever-changing streams and dotted with marshes, swamps, and lakes.

Climate

Only 150 meters above sea level, Chitwan is noticeably warmer than Kathmandu year-round. From March-June it can get steamy, with violent thunderstorms and peak temperatures of 36° C. The June-Sept. monsoon is intense, with pounding rains, swollen rivers, and luxuriant vegetation. While the rain isn't constant, the humidity is all-pervasive, as are the leeches. Several lodges in and outside the park remain open through the monsoon.

Winter (Oct.-Feb.) is the best time for a visit. Apart from morning fog, the sky is gorgeously clear, with the Himalaya visible to the north. Early morning can be damp and chilly (bring a jacket) but afternoons are pleasantly sunny and warm. February and March are considered peak game-viewing season because the grass has been cut and burned, leaving animal movement fairly well exposed.

Flora

About one-fifth of the park is savannah, carpeted with over 70 different species of grasses, known generically as "elephant grass," because elephants eat it and because only they can penetrate the tall, dense thickets. Every January tens of thousands of villagers are admitted into the

elephants crossing Rapti River, Chitwan

park to harvest grass, which is used as roof thatch and animal fodder, or in making local products, or is sold to paper mills. The cutting also has the side benefit of improving game viewing. Following the harvest, villagers set the grasslands on fire, an old custom which ensures the growth of new grass and prevents the transition to forest which might otherwise occur. By the end of the monsoon the new grases are as high as eight meters. They flower in the fall, carpeting the plains with feathery silver blossoms.

Along the water courses are riverine forests of quick-growing *shishoo* and *khair,* valuable timber trees. Further inland are simal trees, their seedpods bursting with fluffy white kapok, and "flame-of-the-forest" *(palash),* named for the bright red blossoms which appear in early spring.

The natural succession climaxes with forests of sal trees, which grow up to 40 meters high. The giant trees inside the park bear little resemblance to the unprotected and heavily lopped ones seen along Terai roadsides. Sal is a superb hardwood, used for railroad sleepers,

bridges, and Kathmandu's famous woodcarvings; its glossy green leaves are stitched into plates for feasts and offerings. Ridgetops are less densely forested, mainly with chir pine.

Tigers

At the top of Chitwan's food chain is the master predator, the elusive Royal Bengal tiger *(bagh).* Of the 3,000 or so left worldwide, about 140 live in or near Chitwan. The main cause of their demise has not been hunting, but habitat destruction, primarily the deforestation and road-building which opened the Terai to human settlement. More recently, Chitwan's tigers are facing a renewed threat from poachers seeking tiger bones for use in traditional Chinese medicines. The army battalion stationed in Chitwan appears to be unable to prevent poaching, though some 75% of the park's budget goes to it.

The tiger's striped camouflage works so well it's far more likely to see you than you it. Only about five percent of park visitors get daytime sightings of these mainly nocturnal beasts, but

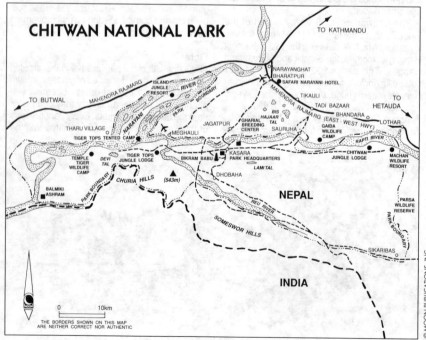

CHITWAN NATIONAL PARK

TO KATHMANDU

NARAYANGHAT
BHARATPUR
SAFARI NARAYANI HOTEL

TO BUTWAL

MAHENDRA RAJMARG

ISLAND JUNGLE RESORT

RIVER

PARK BOUNDARY

NARAYANI

MAHENDRA RAJMARG (EAST-WEST HWY)

TIKAULI

TADI BAZAAR

BHANDARA

TO HETAUDA

LOTHAR

BIS HAJAAR TAL

JAGATPUR

GHARIAL BREEDING CENTER

SAURUHA

GAIDA WILDLIFE CAMP

THARU VILLAGE

TIGER TOPS TENTED CAMP

MEGHAULI

RAPTI RIVER

TEMPLE TIGER WILDLIFE CAMP

DEVI TAL

TIGER TOPS JUNGLE LODGE

BIKRAM BABU

KASARA PARK HEADQUARTERS

LAMITAL

CHITWAN JUNGLE LODGE

MACHAN WILDLIFE RESORT

BALMIKI ASHRAM

PARK BOUNDARY

CHURIA HILLS

(543m)

DHOBAHA

NEPAL

REU RIVER

PARSA WILDLIFE RESERVE

SOMESWOR HILLS

PARK BOUNDARY

SIKARIBAS

INDIA

0   10km

THE BORDERS SHOWN ON THIS MAP
ARE NEITHER CORRECT NOR AUTHENTIC

© MOON PUBLICATIONS, INC.

TROUBLE IN PARADISE

At first glance Chitwan seems idyllic: neat villages and shining fields outside the park, thriving wildlife within. But the proximity of humans and nature creates stresses seldom encountered in the West, where natural lands are neatly segregated from populated areas—and where population pressures haven't reached the rolling boil of Nepal.

Nepal's rapid population increase has centered on the Terai, now home to nearly 50% of the country's population. Within a few decades, the Terai's natural balance has shifted from coexistence to conflict. Parks are islands of virgin territory preserved by force: some 850 troops stationed at Chitwan protect it against poachers and woodcutters.

Thousands of villagers living in or near the park are prevented from tapping its resources, and for good reason. The area surrounding Chitwan has one of the highest livestock populations on the Indian subcontinent; unprotected, the park would soon become like the surrounding land, nearly bare of trees.

And yet . . . wildlife sanctuaries created to fulfill the needs of animals give short shrift to human needs. People who have always depended on the land find themselves barred from their ancestral heritage, unable to use the jungle for fodder, food, cultivation, and grazing. Increasing wildlife populations (especially deer and rhino) destroy villagers'

crops. Unable to kill predators, farmers must sleep out in their fields and try to scare them away with stones, shouts, and fire. To them, tigers and rhinos are not part of natural heritage: they are a threat to their safety and their livelihood.

Understandably some local people feel cheated by the park, yet it provides tangible benefits as well. An example is the high-quality tall grass once harvested across the Terai, now found only in the park. Every January some 120,000 villagers harvest the grass, which plays an important role in traditional life and is used in dozens of different ways. Park tourism benefits hundreds of locals who are employed either by the park or by lodges, or who sell goods to tourists.

The vast majority of people, however, are excluded from its potentially valuable resources and land, for reasons they do not comprehend and would not agree with if they did. What kinds of rights *do* tigers have, compared to people?

These issues demonstrate what planners are slowly discovering—that national parks and wildlife preserves are not as isolated as their pristine ecology would suggest. Rather, they're tangled in a complex web of economic, political, and social forces. Ultimately the only sustainable method is to involve local people in the protection of park resources— for their own benefit, not just that of the animals.

---

finding a tiger's tracks or claw marks on a tree or hearing a warning cough from the bush can be enough of a thrill.

Rhinos

Chitwan's mascot is the greater Asian one-horned rhinoceros *(gaidaa),* a prehistoric prototype of the armored tank. Headed for extinction a few decades ago, rhinos are making a comeback in Chitwan: the park's current population estimate is 466, up from 100 in the early '70s, and second only to the rhino population of Kaziranga National Park in Assam, India. Rhino sightings are especially common around Sauruha, where they have become markedly tamer than normal rhinos and occasionally wander onto the grounds of lodges.

Local farmers are dismayed by the increasing rhino population, which has wrought havoc on

crops. Several dozen of the surplus animals have been transplanted to Bardia National Park in western Nepal in the hope of establishing a second viable population.

The vegetarian rhino is a solitary and bad-tempered creature. Its exceptionally small brain and poor vision may account for its unpredictable nature. Rhinos are unable to distinguish immobile objects beyond 30 meters, but they compensate with a highly developed sense of hearing and the ability to scent a human 800 meters distant. They are prone to blind charges on possible aggressors and are surprisingly agile for their bulk, capable of swivelling, turning, and charging again—though sometimes their poor vision leads them to charge a tree, or a Land Rover.

Because it has no sweat glands, the rhino spends much of its time basking in rivers, coating its hide in mud to protect itself from sun and insects. The rhino's apparently armor-plated skin is vulnerable to bullets and spears, but its weakest point is its horn, a mass of densely compressed dermal fibers. This appendage has no visible use—rhinos defend themselves with their tusks—but powdered rhino horn is a prized fever remedy in traditional Chinese medicine as well as an Indian aphrodisiac. A kg of rhino horn can fetch Rs500,000, which has led to poaching. Eleven rhinos were slaughtered in Chitwan in 1992, despite the presence of soldiers assigned to guard the park. Locals have their own uses for rhino products: a rhino-skin bracelet protects against evil spirits, rhino dung is a laxative, while rhino urine cures asthma and tuberculosis.

Other Mammals

Leopards *(chituwa)* are sometimes sighted as they tend to prowl in the daytime. The existence of the rare and elusive **clouded leopard** in Chitwan has not been conclusively proven, but there are plenty of smaller jungle cats, foxes, jackals, and hyenas. Other small carnivores include mongoose, marten, and civets.

All these animals feed on hoofed herbivores like deer, cattle, and pigs. Herds of graceful **spotted deer** *(chital)* are common, as are the clunkier **hog deer** *(laguna)* and the smaller **barking deer.** The big **sambar** deer are more impressive, standing almost 1.5 meters tall at the shoulder. Serow and antelope are rarer, as is the shy **gaur** *(gauri gai),* the largest type of wild cattle, standing up to 1.8 meters at the shoulder and weighing over 1,000 kg. Bristly, ferociously tusked **wild boar** *(bandel)* congregate in groups in the grasslands.

Monkeys *(bandar)* include the silvery gray langur and the red-bottomed rhesus. The most feared animal is the **sloth bear** *(bhalu),* a long-snouted, furry beast equipped with wickedly curved claws. While it's not a carnivore, its unpredictable nature makes it the most dangerous creature in Chitwan.

The Narayani River harbors a very few **Gangetic dolphins** *(sisu),* but sightings of these aquatic mammals are dwindling, partly due to the irrigation dam at Tribenighat which prevents their return after their monsoonal migration downriver.

Aquatic Fauna

The Rapti, Narayani, and Reu Rivers hold over 70 species of fish. Low-lying marshy areas and riverbanks support waterbirds and the aptly named **marsh mugger** *(magar-gohi),* a sinister-looking crocodile which drowns its victims, then devours them. There are only a few hundred of these creatures left in Chitwan.

Even rarer is the **gharial.** Rapid destruction of its riparian habitat left this slender-snouted crocodile nearly extinct by the 1970s. While it's harmless to humans, it's sometimes slaughtered for its skin and long bulbous snout, which is believed to have aphrodisiac properties. A Gharial Conservation Project launched in 1978 with German funding has boosted Nepal's gharial population from 50 to around 165. Gharial eggs are collected from riverbanks and allowed to hatch at the conservation center near Kasara Durbar in the park. Hatchlings are nurtured in pools for up to three years, then released. Those in the Narayani River have had a low survival rate, but gharial populations in remoter areas are doing well. Captive breeding of gharials has not been successful.

Birds

Of Nepal's more than 800 bird species, over half have been spotted in Chitwan: the park's multiple habitats make it a birdwatcher's paradise. Species include the colorful peacock, jungle fowl, quail, partridge, hornbills, woodpeckers, drongos, cuckoos, and chattering bright green parakeets, as well as birds of prey like kites, owls, and vultures. River birds include gulls, terns, ruddy shelduck, storks, ibis, egrets, herons, sandpipers, and brilliant blue kingfishers.

HISTORY

Two factors conspired to preserve the Terai's virgin environment well into the 1940s. One was a high rate of malaria, which frightened away everyone except the indigenous Tharus, who had developed a limited natural resistance. From the 19th century on, strategic Terai areas like Chitwan were deliberately protected by the Ranas, who banned poaching, woodcutting, and settlements. Part of their motivation was defense—no army could equal the deadly effect of malaria—and part was the fact they viewed portions of the Terai (especially Chitwan) as their private hunting reserve.

Hunting

Typical was the first Rana prime minister, Jung Bahadur, a tireless hunter who pursued his quarry day and night, impeccably clad in white gloves and patent leather boots. In a typical two-week hunt he shot enough animals to stock a Noah's Ark of endangered species: 31 tigers, 21 elephants, 20 deer, 11 wild buffalo, 10 boars, plus leopards, rhinos, a boa constrictor, and a crocodile. The ultimate record goes to Juddha Shamsher Rana, who over seven seasons shot 433 tigers, 53 rhinos, and 93 leopards.

India's governor-generals and viceroys and three generations of Britain's royal family took a similar toll on Chitwan wildlife. King George V and his court shot 39 tigers in a 12-day spree. Their Rana hosts did their utmost to make their stay comfortable: for King George's visit in 1911, a special jungle camp was built that included electricity and hot and cold running water, while for the Prince of Wales's visit 10 years later, 36 miles of motor road and telephone lines were laid. But they were careful to never invite the British into Kathmandu, lest India's rulers get any ideas about extending their domain.

Hunts were conducted on elephant back, both safe and comfortable for the shooter, or from game blinds *(machaan)* camouflaged in treetops. The biggest shoots used the ring hunt, a spectacular event demanding an enormous number of trained *shikar* elephants, expert drivers and beaters, and of course a plentiful supply of tigers. Preparations began months before, as roads were built in order to bring in vehicles and elephants. After the guests had gathered, several dozen buffalo calves were staked out overnight in different locations. As soon as one was killed the tiger's location was known. The elephants, up to 600 of them, were driven into a slowly converging circle. A white linen cloth stretched out at ground level helped close the circle further by frightening the tiger. The tiger might leap and charge in his attempt to escape, but he was an easy target for the hunters on elephant-back, for not even a tiger will charge an elephant. Given this method, success was practically guaranteed. Old photographs show hunters standing behind a row of tiger carcasses, lined up like so many rugs.

Rhino-hunting was a trickier matter, as elephants fear them more than tigers, and a rhino

rhinoceros

BOB RACE

charge could break the ring. Usually they were stalked through tall grass, using only three or four elephants. The rhino's virtually impenetrable hide meant the hunter had to kill the beast with an accurate shot between the eyes, or between an eye and an ear. A wounded rhino might charge even a fleeing elephant. Cleaned and cured, rhino hide made "capital water buckets," noted a British writer; "These are immensely strong, never break, and are impervious to water." The horns were transformed into carved cups and *khukri* handles.

Development

Despite the periodic massive slaughter of such hunts, the wildlife population remained relatively stable. It took development to destroy the Terai's virgin jungle. A malaria eradication drive launched in 1955 doused the region with DDT, virtually eliminating the disease in Chitwan by 1960. The Rapti Valley became the site of a model resettlement program sponsored by foreign aid, and hundreds of thousands of Hill people poured down to farm the flat, fertile fields of the Terai. By the early '60s two-thirds of the region's forest had been cut.

The ecological destruction and the accompanying threat to wildlife occurred so quickly it left officials gasping. Efforts had been made as early as 1962 to establish a rhino sanctuary in Chitwan, going so far as to relocate 22,000 villagers who had settled in prime rhino habitat. The World Wildlife Fund's Operation Tiger gave further impetus to the drive. In 1973 Chitwan was declared the country's first national park.

EXPLORING CHITWAN

A visit to Chitwan involves wildlife-tracking by a variety of means—foot, dugout canoe, jeep, elephant-back. Don't let the term "safari" fool you into imagining broad savannahs teeming with game. Chitwan's wildlife is hidden in the dense jungle, forcing you to get out and actively look for it, and the hunt is most of the fun.

How to do this depends on where you stay. Luxury lodges inside the park fill their guests' days with a well-planned schedule of activities interspersed with relaxation. Independent travelers can replicate everything on their own for far less cost, if slightly more hassle, either through Sauruha lodges or completely independently. Competition for elephants in particular is intense in the fall tourist season, so book in advance.

What to Bring

You don't need much for a few days. Start with comfortable shoes that can stand getting wet, plus a pair of plastic flip-flops for showering and river-wading. Choose clothing in neutral colors for jungle walks, as wildlife may be alarmed by shocking pink, red, or white. Afternoons are usually sunny and warm to hot, but winter mornings can be chilly, so bring a light jacket or sweatshirt from October through February. A *lungi* is handy for bathing, swimming, and treks to the bathroom.

Insect repellent is a must for evenings; you might also bring mosquito coils to ensure a good night's sleep. Binoculars and a telephoto camera lens make spotting game easier. Also bring sunscreen, sun hat, flashlight (there is no electricity in Sauruha), water bottle and water treatment method, and perhaps a big umbrella for shade. You might want to pick up a map of Chitwan National Park in Kathmandu, as Sauruha shops don't always have them in stock, but it's not a necessary item. Don't forget a book or two—there's little to do at night.

Park Basics

Park entry permits are sold for Rs650 at the ranger's office in Sauruha and are good for two days; you need one regardless of whether you enter the park on elephant, by jeep, or on foot. The park is closed from sunset to sunrise and no movement is allowed inside. The ranger's office also sells tickets for elephant and boat rides. Across the way from the office is a well-organized **visitor's center** with informative exhibits on local wildlife and ecology. It's open daily 8 a.m.-5 p.m.

Safety

Chitwan is one of the few wildlife parks to allow visitors to enter on foot, but you do so at your own risk. It's advisable to go with a guide. Tourists are occasionally injured or killed (usually by rhinos), because they foolishly assume the animals are tame. If you're prudent there should be no problem; the big thing is to avoid hanging around mother animals with offspring, who are especially sensitive to intruders.

Some emergency tips: if a rhino snuffles its signal to charge and lowers its head, climb a tree or run in big zig-zags, dropping a piece of clothing as a decoy—rhinos rely on scent rather than sight, and will hopefully stop to sniff it. (Their eyesight is so bad they've been known to charge trees and parked Land Rover vehicles.) It's highly unlikely you'll encounter a tiger, but if you do and it appears disturbed, back away slowly, and climb a tree quickly. Make sure the tree is too small for the tiger to climb up after you. Chitwan's most dangerous animal is the sloth bear, relatively small but with vicious claws and exceedingly poor eyesight. Again, climb a small tree. Guides will shepherd you through these safety measures if necessary, but you can't count on them to save your life in a true emergency.

Jungle Walks

Hikes through the jungle give opportunities to view animals as well as observe their tracks, signs, and sounds. Early morning and late afternoon are the best times to spot wildlife and avoid the midday heat. Birds, monkeys, and deer are the most likely sightings, though rhinos are not uncommon (see the warning above). In the overused strip of jungle directly across from Sauruha, the most frequently sighted creature is the tourist. The luxury lodges inside the park put you in virtually untouched territory.

Entering the park on your own is allowed but not recommended: it's too easy for a greenhorn to blunder unwittingly into a rhino, or something even more dangerous. Aside from safety considerations, without a guide you'll probably miss most of the details of the jungle. A local guide will enthusiastically share his intimate knowledge of the land, pointing out different kinds of plants, explaining animal tracks and scat, and recounting amusing anecdotes.

Sauruha has no shortage of guides, many of them with credentials from a training program with the Peace Corps. The going rate is about Rs50 for a two-hour walk, Rs100 for a half-day, Rs200 for a full day. Most lodges have their own guides, or you can hire one from private companies in Sauruha.

Two half-hour walks to *machaan* or treetop game blinds near Sauruha might be chanced alone. A map at the visitor's center gives directions; check to make sure the blinds are in operating condition. **Tal Machaan** overlooks an oxbow lake that's a favorite rhino bathing spot; cross the Rapti River and go up the main Kasara road, and the *machaan* is on the left. To reach **Isle Machaan,** a meadow wallow also favored by rhinos, walk south of Sauruhaalong Dhungreli Creek and cross the Dhungre River.

Elephant Rides

This is *everyone's* favorite thing to do in Chitwan. Luxury lodges maintain their own elephants, so it's seldom a problem to arrange a pachyderm jungle tour. They are equipped with howdah, wooden carriers with side railings, while beasts from the government stable in Sauruha are ridden more or less bareback—quite a stretch for the middle passenger who must straddle its girth.

Government elephants go out twice a day, at 8 a.m. and 4 p.m. Rides of 60-90 minutes cost Rs650, and competition in season is stiff—lines at the ticket office in Sauruha form long before opening. Your lodge will get tickets for an additional Rs100 or so, but be sure to give them advance notice. Only government elephants and those from concessionary lodges can enter the park. The handful of Sauruha lodges with their own elephants are restricted to touring the surrounding villages and forests. These rides are longer (one and a half to two hours) and cheaper (Rs450-550), but the chances of spotting wildlife are slim.

Boat Rides

Dugout canoe trips down the Rapti River offer a procession of waterbirds: osprey, brilliant blue Eurasian kingfishers, egrets, ospreys, and ruddy sheldrakes colored the same ochre-white-black scheme as Nepali houses. A marsh mugger may be spotted basking on the banks in winter, and there are year-round views of local life: Tharu fishermen with nets, women digging a freshwater well, children gleefully splashing in a swimming hole.

The standard routine is a 45-minute float downstream (ample time in the cramped boat) followed by a two-hour jungle walk back. The boat trip costs Rs50; tickets are sold near the visitor's center, and the boats are moored just behind. You'll also have to pay the guide's fee.

Jeep Safaris

A jeep ride into the park provides surprisingly good opportunities for game-spotting and gets you past the heavily trodden area surrounding Sauruha. The standard four-hour trip (Rs650) visits park headquarters at **Kasara Durbar,** 20 km southwest of Sauruha. Offices are in a former Rana hunting lodge that also holds a very small museum featuring mainly animal skulls. Nearby is the small jungle temple of **Bikram Babu,** a sort of local fertility shrine where villagers may sacrifice a goat after the long-awaited birth of a child.

The main attraction is the **Gharial Breeding Center** on the Rapti's banks near Kasara (admission Rs15). Here the slender-snouted crocodiles are hatched, raised, then released after two years. Operating since 1980, the project is showing signs of success—35% of the baby crocs are surviving, compared to two percent in the wild, and over 400 have been released.

Try to persuade your driver to stop at **Lami Tal** a little east of Kasara Durbar. This oxbow lake is home to a colony of marsh muggers and is a birdwatcher's paradise. There's a *machaan* here if you get a chance to stay and wait for wildlife to come.

Jungle Treks

Though most visitors don't stay long enough to do one, overnight hikes into the park take you deep into the jungle. The standard two-day route follows the dirt road from Sauruha to Kasara

ELEPHANTS

The best part of an elephant ride is the chance to view one of these contradictory beasts close-up and in action. Bulky yet graceful, with an absurd appearance and a wise expression, the elephant shuffles along, its leathery skin a baggy gray suit two sizes too big for its body. Riding an elephant is somewhat akin to being aboard a ship, rolling through a sea of grass instead of water. The creatures are remarkably surefooted, but from atop one the landscape pitches and heaves to a surprising degree.

The Asian elephant is slightly smaller than its African cousin, averaging five tons and 2.7 meters tall at the shoulder. A few odd facts: its ears act as heat regulators, with huge quantities of blood vessels on the posterior surface for cooling. Like rhinos, elephants need frequent baths (in water, dust, or mud) to cool their vast bulk. Elephants are simply too big to lay down—any more than an hour might damage their internal organs. They sleep only three hours a night, standing up. Elephants' lives closely parallel those of humans: work from ages 15-55, followed by 10 years or so of retirement. As they age, their heads turn paler, with mottled pink setting in, just like a human going gray. They are believed to communicate by subsonic frequencies below the hearing threshold of humans.

Most amazing is the trunk, composed of over 40,000 muscles. It's used to eat, shower, drink, signal, and attack, and it has a very good sense of smell. As elephants grow up they learn more uses for it, scratching themselves with a stick or using it to shake dirt from grass clumps before stuffing them into their mouths. An elephant's trunk is so vital that paralysis of the trunk invariably proves fatal.

Elephants in the wild must constantly forage for food in order to fill their minimum daily requirement of at least 200 kg of food and 170 liters of water. Supplying food for each park elephant occupies the better part of a day for two men, though the bulk is reduced by feeding them an hors d'oeuvre of molasses, salt, and grain wrapped into neat football-sized bundles, just the right size for an elephantine mouth.

Each Chitwan elephant has three keepers to tend to its needs. Highest in status is the driver (phanit), who sits behind its ears and provides encouragement by constantly drumming his knees on the beast's head, with occasional thwacks of a heavy

---

and Lami Tal, then crosses the river to the small village of Jagatpur, where you overnight in a village lodge. The next day you bus up to Gitanagar, walk along a canal to the many small lakes of Bis Hajaar Tal, and return to Sauruha. Guide cost is around Rs400 for two days.

Camping in the park is allowed at designated sites for Rs300 a night and requires a much higher level of organization: porters, a cook, provisions, and supplies are all needed. As of yet, Sauruha has no trekking gear for rent so you'd have to bring your own or rent in Kathmandu.

OUTSIDE THE PARK

There are plenty of things to do around Chitwan after the two-day park entry permit expires. Bicycles rented in Sauruha considerably extend your range in the flat countryside, and things get more interesting the farther one goes from Sauruha. Cycle up to Tadi Bazaar, then turn east along the highway to explore the many side roads; or turn west to Tikauli and take it as a launching point into the countryside.

The rural areas are dotted with neatly kept Tharu villages set amid remarkably flat and fertile fields. Those villagers who live within walking distance of Sauruha are understandably a bit blasé, but further out people are remarkably friendly and open. Depending on the season, you can observe harvest, threshing, ploughing, or planting. Most fields are still ploughed with yoked oxen pulling wooden ploughs, though a few tractors can now be seen, doing the work of several days in a few hours.

Hattisaar

From Sauruha it's an easy stroll east to the Hattisaar or Elephant Camp, where the riding elephants are stationed. Visit in mid-afternoon or

goad. Due to the immensity of the elephant's skull, these mighty blows register as a dull thud. Why the huge beasts docilely submit to such treatment is a continuing mystery, rooted in an apparent fondness for humans. Certainly no elephant can be forced into doing something it doesn't want to do.

As cousins of the god Ganesh, wild elephants were traditionally exempted from being hunted in Nepal. The constant demand for hunting, parades, and ceremonial purposes was filled by annual roundups. Sometimes a lone male, excited by the sight and scent of tame females used as bait, would be lured into a pit and hauled up with ropes. An entire herd might be driven into a stockade, or a wild loner would be chased by hunters aboard tame elephants.

The captured elephant would then be subjected to a nonstop barrage of stimuli designed to break its resistance. Tied in a network of ropes, dozens of men working in shifts would climb about it day and night, pounding it with their bare feet and hands to keep it in a state of helpless panic. Later, to accustom it to noises, a brass band might play in front of it, while guns were fired from its back. This would continue with decreasing severity for several weeks, until the captive was perfectly docile and ready to be trained in the fine points of *shikar*.

elephant and phanit, *Chitwan National Park*

around sunset when they're sure to be around. It's rather a sad sight to see the beasts tightly chained to their wooden posts. Caretakers are busily at work making bundles of rice, sugar, and salt. A single elephant consumes some 400 of these bundles per day, requiring three full-time workers to tend to it.

Elephant Breeding Center

This government-run camp four km west of Sauruha has a half-dozen resident elephants and several calves, the latter being the only difference from Hattisaar, described above. With the cost of a trained elephant from India running around Rs250,000, breeding elephants is a lucrative proposition, though it's also a lengthy and expensive affair, with gestation taking 19-21 months. Babies are left with their mothers for the first few years so they become socialized into elephant ways. Around five years of age they are trained to accept a bit by means of persuasion (molasses) and discipline (a stick). By

the time they're 10 years old they can carry a howdah; most elephants don't enter working life till they're 15 or so.

The walk to the camp leads past tidy Tharu villages of mud-walled huts, in the winter overflowing with stacks of freshly harvested grass. You can also bike, jeep out, or take a dugout canoe down the Rapti River to a point near the camp and hike over, wading across a small river.

Bis Hajaar Tal

This sal forest scattered with small oxbow lakes lies a few kilometers northwest of the Elephant Breeding Center. The name "20,000 Lakes" is a bit of an exaggeration, but the grove is a favorite habitat for birds and deer. You can walk here directly from Sauruha in two hours, but without a guide, it's best to cycle to the village of **Tikauli** three km west of Tadi Bazaar, then follow a path along a canal several more kilometers to the lakes.

PARK PRACTICALITIES

ACCOMMODATIONS, FOOD, AND NIGHTLIFE

Where you stay—the luxury lodges inside the park or the budget lodges at Sauruha—makes a big difference in your Chitwan experience. The vast price differential will probably make the decision for you. Those staying in Sauruha wouldn't dream of spending US$150 a night, while guests inside the park wouldn't dream of staying at Sauruha.

If you can pay the higher bill without flinching, you won't regret it. Luxury lodges charge more because they pay hefty concessions to operate in the park. They provide not just shelter but a complete experience—activities and meals are included in their price—and their pampering is pure pleasure. On the other hand, you can replicate the experience at a more modest level for a fraction of the cost at Sauruha. Budget lodges will arrange activities at your request, though you'll be paying piecemeal for them.

Guests in luxury lodges should book in advance, as these places are not prepared for walk-ins. Travelers to Sauruha, however, would do better *not* to book the prepaid packages offered in Kathmandu, usually a three-day/two-night visit including transport, food, accommodations, and activities. Prices for these range US$50-140. It's invariably much cheaper to go on your own, which also gives you the ability to check out places before settling on one, and the option of extending your stay.

Luxury Lodges

Deluxe lodges in the park offer solar-heated showers, comfortable rooms, Western food, dinnertime drinks around the fireplace, and other unexpected luxuries. Unlike many tourist hotels in Nepal, these are built of local materials and are designed to blend into the natural setting. The typical model involves individual thatched-roof cottages set around a main dining hall. They offer a carefully planned balance of excursions on their own elephants and lectures by trained naturalists. The real appeal, though, is the feeling of total immersion in the jungle, which starts at your front door.

Booking offices are clustered on Durbar Marg in Kathmandu. Prices are quoted as package deals. Daily rates include everything but tips and the bar bill; transport can be arranged for an extra fee. While most people stay two nights, prices drop for longer stays. Don't be afraid to ask for a better rate, especially in off-season. Another option is the less-expensive but still deluxe alternative facilities offered by some operations. These usually involve roomy safari tents, as opposed to individual cottages.

Prices listed below are per night, per person on a double occupancy basis. Single supplements are high—US$75-160 per night. The per-night charges may also require government tax, park entry, and camping fees, which can add another US$30 or so to the bill.

Tiger Tops Jungle Lodge, tel. (1) 222-706, fax (1) 414-075, is the original safari camp, operating in Chitwan since 1965. **Tiger Tops Lodge** is a handsome two-story, bamboo-walled stilt building in the western portion of the park, about 40 km from Sauruha. It's expensive (US$250 per person per night on a sharing basis) but deservedly famous for its excellent service and superb staff of naturalists. Reservations are recommended 6-12 months in advance, especially for the fall season. Most visitors fly into **Meghauli,** where they're met by elephants for the two-hour ride to camp.

Tiger Tops has two other operations at Chitwan. The **Tented Camp,** with a dozen twin-bedded safari tents, is set on an island in the Narayani River a little west of the main lodge and runs US$150 per person; the schedule of activities is similar to the lodge's. **Tharu Village** is a beautifully decorated traditional Tharu-style longhouse with a swimming pool, located just outside park boundaries on the north bank of the Narayani River. Rooms with bath are US$150 per person; the program here is cultural rather than jungle-oriented, and most visitors don't actually enter the park.

The other two operations in the western end of the park are not up to Tiger Tops' standards.

Temple Tiger Wildlife Camp, Kantipath, tel. (1) 221-585, features safari tents complete with separate dressing rooms for US$150 per night. **Island Jungle Resort,** Durbar Marg, tel. (1) 216-736, is on an island in the Narayani River, a stone's throw from Tiger Tops' Tented Camp. It's getting pretty run-down and charges only US$100 (bus transport included) for a two-night package in tents, US$140 for the lodge.

Near Sauruha, **Gaida Wildlife Camp,** tel. (1) 220-940, is one of the older lodges in the park, overlooking the Dungre River. Thatched-roof cottages set in a semicircle are US$110 per person per night. Gaida's tented **Jungle Camp** (US$80) is 11 km south of this, in an excellent birdwatching region.

On the park's more remote eastern side is **Chitwan Jungle Lodge,** Durbar Marg, tel. (1) 228-918, its thatched-roof bungalows set on spacious grounds near a creek. A two-night package including car transport is US$260.

Machan Wildlife Resort, Durbar Marg, tel. (1) 225-001, has a small swimming pool and nicely decorated bungalows; at one time it even had a pet rhino on the grounds. It's in the park's far east, on the border with Parsa Wildlife Reserve. The lodge is US$154 per night; the tented camp US$70; car transport is included in package deals.

Just outside the park, **Safari Narayani Hotel,** tel. (56) 20-130, in Bharatpur operates an eight-cottage resort near the Rapti River a little east of Jagatpur. An all-inclusive package is US$300 for two nights, US$400 for three nights.

Sauruha Deluxe
These lodges fall somewhere between the luxury and budget categories. They're located in Sauruha, not in the park; but the rooms, grounds, and standard of service are distinctly superior. Theoretically most of these places accept only advance bookings: all-inclusive pack-

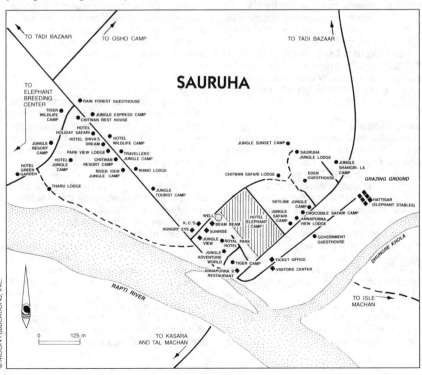

ages run around US$100 per night. In practice, though, they are often empty and you can simply show up and negotiate for a room. A double room with bath might be around US$15, a bargain considering the high standard.

Jungle Adventure World, Sanchayakosh Building, tel. (1) 225-393, is marvelously sited right on the riverbank, with fantastic sunset views. Comfortable bungalows have solar-heated showers; there's a big dining room and decent grounds. The package rate is US$120 per night.

Next door, the new **Royal Park Hotel,** Maharajganj, tel. (1) 414-939, gets top marks for its well-executed traditional decor and spacious landscaped grounds. Private cottages are exceptionally nice and there's a thatched-roof bar with river views; at the moment this is the nicest place in Sauruha. The standard rate is US$85 per night.

Jungle Shangri-La Camp, Kamalpokhari, tel. (1) 417-986, is set in a quiet garden; it's shady and private, maybe a little far down the strip, but a public grazing ground and the Hattisaar nearby make for local interest. Package tourists are charged US$40 per night.

Hotel Elephant Camp, Durbar Marg, tel. (1) 222-823, had a good reputation but outlasted its heyday and is currently undergoing reorganization. A two-night package with transport is US$180; US$230 for three nights.

Budget Lodges

On the other hand, you don't *have* to spend a lot to visit Chitwan. Sauruha has dozens of inexpensive lodges, ranging from tiny mud huts to modern brick cottages. Most establishments are slowly moving upscale, with a mix of both for now. The standard is Rs150 for a mud hut without bath, Rs400 for a simply furnished small brick cottage with private bath. Most places can offer hot water in the winter months, either solar- or wood-heated; most are clean, well-kept, and peaceful. Because there are seldom enough tourists, prices are virtually identical, and bargaining is very likely. Prices listed here are for peak season; expect a 50% discount in the off-season.

As in Pokhara, there are so many decent places to stay in Sauruha that it's difficult to single out the very best. Names and owners constantly change and new places spring up

overnight. Look for some kind of shade or garden (some lots are as bare as football fields) and, ideally, a river view.

Tiger Camp at the extreme south end of Sauruha's "strip" has regular cottages for Rs750 with bath, and a surprise: two *machaan*-style rooms with verandah, reached by ladder for Rs400. It's a better place than most, well-sited right on the riverbank and with a good restaurant. You could book in Kathmandu, but don't, as it's much more expensive.

Rhino Lodge is a tolerable place with rooms for Rs600 d with fan, Rs55 d without. Package deals from Kathmandu are no bargain at US$65 per day. Across the road, the **River View Jungle Camp** has a river view in name only. There's a big garden and cottages for Rs400 with bath, windowless mud huts without bath for Rs150. **Hotel Wildlife Camp** has a decent garden and a range of rooms for Rs300-400 with bath, Rs150 without.

Chitwan Resort Camp charges Rs400 for cement rooms with bath. **Jungle Express Camp** has a good garden and solar hot water; a decent bungalow is US$10 in season.

Hotel Holiday Safari goes against the separate-cottage grain with its single Kathmandu-style brick building, a monstrosity in sleepy Sauruha. Rooms are Rs300; there's a generator on the premises.

For very budget rooms under Rs150, try the simple **Rain Forest Guesthouse** set in a pretty garden, or the isolated and basic **Tharu Lodge** near the river. The latter is often empty, so it's very private. **Travellers' Jungle Camp** is another budget place, with a tolerable garden and concrete block bungalows for Rs120.

The road running up to the park entrance is similarly thick with budget lodges, though these are generally less pleasant. Give **Annapurna View Lodge** and **Crocodile Safari Camp** a miss; **Skyline Jungle Camp** must have been named for its lack of trees. The lodges down a side lane leading from here are a little remote but peaceful, like **Eden Guesthouse,** where rooms are Rs150, Rs400 with bath. **Jungle Sunset Camp** is popular, with pleasant grounds. The huts aren't particularly well maintained but are cheap at Rs60, Rs150 with bath. **Sauruha Jungle Lodge** next door is run by the same family and is similar in all respects.

Food

Eating is one of Sauruha's low points. Lodges do Western breakfasts of a sort and *daal bhaat* dinners; the pricier ones serve butter-drenched pseudo-Continental cuisine. The handful of tourist restaurants clustered in central Sauruha have borrowed the names of more famous Pokhara and Kathmandu establishments: thus Beam Beam, K.C.'s, and the Hungry Eye. Unfortunately the food is far below the modest standards of the originals. Overambitious menus list delights like "boneless lasagna" and "scrambled aigs." Stick with fried rice or fried noodles, which are pretty hard to mess up, and concentrate on enjoying the views from the rooftop terraces. Tiger Camp's **Annapurna II Restaurant,** a rooftop cafe overlooking the river, is presently the best of the lot.

The ubiquitous German Bakery has materialized in Sauruha, dispensing bread, rolls, and dubious-looking pastries. There are a few tea shops in the village, and snack carts parked in the shade sell *pakora* and bananas. Local shops are well-provisioned with important tourist needs like biscuits, chocolate, and toilet paper. Every cold shop here has picked up on the catch phrase "Freezing Cold Drinks."

Nightlife

Sauruha's after-dark quiet is enhanced by the lack of electricity: light comes from oil lamps, candles, or lanterns. Nightlife is limited to the bigger lodges where thatched-roof bars concoct exotic-sounding drinks, and to the handful of tourist restaurants, where travelers compare the day's wildlife sightings.

About the only real event is the overrated **Tharu stick dance** put on by groups of local men who visit two or three Sauruha hotels in a single night. If your lodge doesn't have a show, it's easy to find a performance put on for package tours—just listen for the drums. The vigorous movements are said to have been inspired by the movements of farming, or maybe hunting, or maybe efforts to scare away animals—the story is unclear. The tourist performances are pretty hokey, but have their roots in authentic dances performed at the springtime festival of Falgun Purnima.

Beyond Sauruha

If jungle Thamels get you down, be a cutting-edge budget traveler and stay at **Jagatpur** or **Meghauli.** These tiny villages west of Sauruha and just north of the park border are simple and definitely unspoiled; a few small guesthouses provide Nepali food and tea. In a year or two these are likely to be the next trendy places, as Sauruha is definitely overdone. Presently there are no elephants, boats, or jeeps available for rent, but locals can be persuaded to serve as guides. Dugout canoes ferry villagers across the river into the park. There's no formal park entrance here, but soldiers met en route will check for and issue park entrance permits.

GETTING THERE

By Air

Guests at luxury lodges usually fly into either Bharatpur (US$50) or Meghauli (US$72); the latter is the access point for Tiger Tops, Temple Tiger, and Island Jungle Resort.

By Bus

Sauruha's nearest bus stop is **Tadi Bazaar,** a small village on the Mahendra Highway about 15 km east of Narayanghat. It's a seven-hour bus ride from Kathmandu or Pokhara via Mugling, or four hours from Bhairawa or Birganj. From Kathmandu, catch a bus to Narayanghat and a local bus from there to Tadi; from Pokhara, take a Birganj bus and get off at Tadi. **Tourist buses** advertised in Thamel and Lakeside cost over double the regular fare but shave an hour off the trip. **Student Travels** in Kathmandu operates a daily minibus to Tadi Bazaar for Rs150.

From Tadi Bazaar it's a dusty six km to Sauruha, most easily traversed by the jeeps operated by various lodges (Rs30). Aggressive touts will try to get you to commit to a particular lodge, but don't feel pressured. Rumbling wooden-wheeled carts drawn by oxen charge a similar rate and are quaint but very slow; it's actually faster (around 90 minutes) to walk. If your luggage is light, you can rent a bicycle at Tadi for Rs50 a day, but be prepared to ford a river en route. A dugout canoe ferries pedestrians and bicycles across when the water is high. In dry season, even taxis can make it across.

Onward Travel: Have your lodgekeeper or a Sauruha ticket agent get an onward ticket, available from stalls at Tadi Bazaar. Tourist buses run daily from Tadi to Kathmandu. Local buses go to Narayanghat, a convenient hub for travel to Pokhara, Bhairawa, or Kathmandu.

By Car

Upscale lodges may include transport in package deals. If not, it can be arranged for sometimes outrageous prices—anywhere from US$45-140 per person for roundtrip car transport from Kathmandu.

If you're traveling independently, it's easy to rent a taxi from Pokhara or Kathmandu to Chitwan. You'll pay more if you want the driver to stay several days and drive you back; a fair price for roundtrip travel and two nights in Chitwan would be Rs3300—quite reasonable when split among three or four people. Sometimes in Sauruha you can find stray drivers willing to continue to Kathmandu or Pokhara. Travelers to or from Kathmandu might want to go via the Tribhuvan Rajpath, a little-used mountain road that is slower but offers some spectacular scenery (see "Daman and the Tribhuvan Rajpath," above).

By Raft

An increasingly popular way to kill two adventure-travel birds with one stone is to raft down the Trisuli River to Chitwan. Trips usually start at Mugling, from where it's a fairly gentle two- or three-day float down to Narayanghat. (See special topic "Rafting" for more information.) Independent rafting companies in Kathmandu run trips here for US$30-50 per day, or lodges will arrange a raft trip for a supplement. Shop around, and be sure to clarify transport arrangements from Kathmandu to the put-in point, as well as from the riverbank to your lodge.

NARAYANGHAT AND BHARATPUR

Most travelers to Chitwan pass through Narayanghat, a busy new town lying at the intersection of the Mahendra Highway and the main Kathmandu-India route, near the confluence of the Trisui and Kali Gandaki Rivers. Narayanghat sprawls seamlessly into Bharatpur, another hot, dusty new town with an airstrip. Buses to Pokhara and Kathmandu stop at the northern end of Narayanghat; Terai buses stop in the middle of town, just east of the the highway intersection, while local minibuses run from another lot a little further east.

There's no reason to stay here, but should you happen to get stuck, try the big brick **Hotel Quality** (Rs250 d with bath) or **Hotel River View** (Rs150, Rs250 with bath) in the north part of town near the Pokhara bus park. Across the river in Gaidakot is **Gaida Cottage Tourist Lodge,** tel. (56) 20-590, a simple place oriented to foreign travelers with rooms for Rs100 and river views.

Bharatpur's posh **Safari Narayani Hotel,** tel. (56) 20-130, is a spinoff of Kathmandu's Hotel Narayani. It has a big garden, swimming pool, and tennis courts: a/c rooms are US$35 s, US$45 d. The hotel also offers pricey safari packages into Chitwan. The a/c dining room, with an extensive Western menu, is by far the best place to eat in either town, though there are plenty of basic restaurants and *bhojnalaya* along the main strip.

The most interesting place around here is **Devghat,** five km northwest of Narayanghat at the confluence of the Trisuli and Kali Gandaki Rivers. Elderly Hindus retire here to follow the tradition of *sannyasin* or renunciates, considered the final stage of human life. The small village here is dotted with shrines, while people perform *puja,* and occasionally cremations, on the riverbank. It's a tranquil place that's worth a visit if you've got extra time; catch a minibus from Narayanghat's Pokhara bus park or walk one hour along the path heading upriver and cross at the footbridge. A huge festival, Tribeni Mela, is held here the new moon of Magh (usually Jan.-Feb.), and devotees flood in the following month again for the festival of Shiva Ratri.

RIVER RAFTING

With the world's highest mountains and deepest river gorges, Nepal is guaranteed good rafting. Its rivers drop some 3000 meters in altitude over a distance of 240 km—that's a lot of water rushing down at tremendous speed.

A river trip provides a different perspective on the countryside than trekking. It's less strenuous in that you float past the scenery rather than struggle across it, but there's a fair amount of upper-body work involved in paddling. Rafting trips offer the chance to enter remote areas where trekkers seldom go. There are plenty of chances to slip off and swim, and guides will alert you to "swimming rapids" that can be floated in a life jacket.

Rafting trips are organized like a trek: five or six hours a day on the river, broken by a lunch stop, then a late afternoon camp on a riverbank, with time to swim, photograph, and explore. Many of the less expensive companies encourage "participation," which means clients help with cooking and setting up camp—fortunately, most people find this enjoyable. Meals generally get high ratings, and companies provide all the gear, including sleeping bags and mattresses.

The best rafting season is fall. Rivers are excitingly high in October, a little milder and cooler in November. Winter trips are possible though a bit chilly. March-April is the next-best season, with lower waters but warm weather and longer days. By May, water levels have dropped and the rains are coming; rafting is slower and you may have to portage some stretches. Monsoon trips are limited to the tamest rivers, which can be plenty exciting at peak flow.

The Rivers

About a half-dozen of Nepal's rivers are currently considered commercially raftable; the rest are left for adventurous individuals to pioneer. Most companies run the tamer, warmer stretches below 500 meters in altitude. The rapids on these are just wild enough to be fun, but nothing to be frightened of. A handful of companies can arrange remote custom trips for a higher cost. Pick up a copy of *White Water Nepal* (see Booklist) for more information on these trips.

The **Trisuli,** named after Shiva's trident, draws 90% of all rafters: it's cheap and easily accessible from the highway running along its bank, but it's not exactly wilderness—in fact, it's getting crowded and littered. Trisuli trips generally run from one to three days, the latter being preferable. The put-in point is generally Charaudi, 80 km west of Kathmandu; the best rapids are all in the first day. It's a three-day float down to Narayanghat, which is less than an hour's bus ride to Tadi Bazaar and Chitwan National Park. Many companies offer rafting/jungle safari packages, booking clients at whichever lodge they have a connection with. It's generally better to avoid advance booking and arrange your own transport and accommodations (see "Chitwan National Park").

A less trafficked but easy and easily accessible choice for a brief trip would be a day on the **Bhote Kosi** north of Kathmandu.

The 8- to 10-day float down the **Sun Kosi** ("River of Gold") is rated among the world's best river trips. Rafters put in at Dolalghat, a two-and-a-half-hour drive east of Kathmandu. The rapids from here are Class 4 and above, with names like "Meatgrinder" and "High Anxiety." Once you've put in, you're committed—no roads come near here, which is a big part of the Sun Kosi's charm. The area is remote and unspoiled, characterized by steep gorges, followed by dense jungle strung with waterfalls. There are few villages on the riverbank, but local people materialize at stops to marvel at the big boats. The trip ends at Chatara, shortly after the Arun and Tamur Rivers have joined the Sun Kosi to form the incredibly broad Sapta Kosi. Chatara is a one-hour jeep ride to **Dharan,** which is a long, long ride back to Kathmandu. Break the return trip with a visit to **Kosi Tappu Wildlife Reserve** or **Janakpur,** or continue on to explore eastern Nepal's superb trekking regions.

Rafting Nepal's longest river, the **Karnali,** is an even more extraordinary experience. The trip begins with a flight or drive to Nepalgunj and the drive to the roadhead at Surkhet. It's a two-day trek from here to the launch site at the junction of the Karnali and Lohari Rivers. From here it's 190 km—about a week's trip—down to Chisopani, winding through unspoiled country filled with wildlife. The Karnali is colder than most rivers, with some very *rapid* rapids in the middle stretch. It would be good to have previous rafting experience before doing it, as it's a little

(continues on next page)

RIVER RAFTING

(continued)

more difficult than other rivers—another reason why it's important to find a qualified company for this trip. The trip ends up with a visit to Bardia National Park, for a big helping of unspoiled Nepal. The **Bheri River** on the park's northern border provides a milder adventure, again with an emphasis on wildlife and unspoiled country.

Trips out of Pokhara are usually pretty tame. The most popular is a gentle two-day float down the **Seti Gandaki** from Damauli to Narayanghat. The standard trip down the **lower Kali Gandaki** from Ramdi Ghat to Narayanghat is placid and smooth with few rapids. The **upper Kali Gandaki** from Kusma to Ramdi Ghat is a more exciting whitewater trip, newly accessible with the construction of the Pokhara-Baglung Highway.

Other rivers are too remote to be very popular. The **Upper Arun** is too challenging (the first expedition here lost everything in a total wipeout), while floating the **Lower Arun** in three days from Tumlingtar to Chatara is excellent—unspoiled countryside teeming with birdlife—but seldom done due to the expense of flying to Tumlingtar. The **Tamur Kosi** in east Nepal is a superb whitewater trip recommended for experienced rafters.

Arranging a Trip

Companies in the rapidly expanding rafting industry are virtually unregulated, and thus find it easy to exploit staff or rip off customers. Many of the smaller agencies haven't the faintest idea about safety concerns or professionalism. Everybody's jumped onto the latest outdoor adventure boomlet, but few do it well. Equipment may be in poor condition or missing altogether; guides may be untrained and inexperienced; and medical kits are rare—bring your own. The Nepal Association of Rafting Agents (NARA) hasn't done much to set standards except establish minimum prices.

All this means a rafting trip requires some serious shopping around. Talk to guides and check their experience as well as your personal compatibility. Ask for references, the best possible one being the opportunity to meet with a recently returned group and quiz them on their experience. Companies should have quality equipment, including self-bailing rafts for harder trips, and should provide helmets, jackets, and roll-top bags for keeping gear dry. For safety, trips should have a minimum of two rafts, three in high-water conditions.

Companies should provide tents, sleeping bags, mattresses, and all food. Also confirm transport arrangements. Cheaper companies send clients off by local bus, but will arrange a minibus for an extra fee—worth it, unless you're a fan of Nepali buses. Companies are supposed to arrange rafting permits (US$5 per person), though some skip this formality and pocket the money. Finally, realize that asking hard questions is no guarantee, because some companies will promise you anything and still not deliver.

As the above implies, low price is not the only

BEYOND CHITWAN: MORE SAFARIS

If Chitwan's rocketing popularity makes it seem too crowded and commercial, more remote national parks and reserves beckon the adventurous traveler. These are like Chitwan was 30 years ago: virtually undeveloped, seldom visited, and pristine. Wildlife doesn't reach the abundant levels of Chitwan's, but there's plenty, including exotica like wild elephants. Indigenous cultures as well are more interesting, especially the traditional Tharu villages of far western Nepal.

Luxury lodges in a handful of these parks provide the usual jeep drives, hikes with trained naturalists, canoe trips, river-rafting, and elephant rides. For independent and budget travelers it's a different story: these places are hard to get to and even harder to get around in. There are few to no facilities for visitors, though you can sometimes pitch a tent. Arranging for guides, elephants, jeeps, and such would be trailblazing of a different sort. **Note:** Park admission for individual travelers is Rs650, usually good for two days. Elephant rides, when available, are Rs650 per person per hour.

criteria in choosing a company. Even the more expensive companies are reasonable by international standards—especially considering the world-class ratings of Nepal's rivers. Prices range US$20-80 per day, averaging around US$40, and depending on the number of people in the group. Services are more or less the same among middle- and upper-range companies. Cheaper ones may skimp on the food and cut corners on safety and reliability. Avoid the real cheapies. An offer of the Trisuli for US$15 per day drew so many clients the company ran out of basics like plates and tents—and simply sent people down the river without them.

To save money, book directly with a company rather than a travel agent. It's much easier to bargain, and to get at least part of the agent's 20-30% commission in the process. The exception is if you're hunting for a scheduled departure on a less popular river, in which case it's easiest to let a travel agency do the calling around. Or put together your own group of four to six people, and ask the agency to sell spare places in order to reduce the cost.

The companies listed below are considered reliable. Smaller, cheaper companies in Thamel offer Trisuli trips for as little as US$20 a day, but it's hard to recommend any of them, partly because the quality of trips depends greatly on rafting guides, who switch jobs frequently.

Ultimate Descents in Thamel, tel. (1) 229-110. Dedicated professional staff, excellent equipment, highly recommended. Specializes in longer trips like the Sun Kosi and Karnali.

White Magic, Jyatha, tel. (1) 226-885. Good service and equipment ratings. Owner Nima Sherpa is one of Nepal's best river guides, and one of the few Sherpas involved in the business.

Karnali River Tour & Exploration, Kamaladi, tel. (1) 226-130. Experience on lesser-known rivers.

Himalayan Encounters, Thamel, tel. (1) 417-426. Less expensive, one of the "participation" companies that has clients help with camp work. Can arrange kayaking and custom trips.

Himalayan River Exploration, Naksal, tel. (1) 418-491. The old, staid, expensive standby, originally specializing in slower, less strenuous oar rafts, where only the guide paddles. Mainly older clients looking for a quieter trip, but also does cheaper participatory paddle trips.

What to Bring

Bring sunscreen, brimmed hat, and sunglasses, and tie the latter on with a cord, or they're likely to fly off into the river. Don't underestimate the burning power of the sun on water. For daytime, a bathing suit and T-shirt are fine in hot weather, but remember that shady gorges can be unexpectedly cool. Long shorts prevent the rash that may result from sitting in the rubber boat. Wear cloth shoes or securely strapped sandals, since plastic sandals get lost too easily, and bring warm clothes for the evenings. Daytime gear, like clothes and cameras, can be stowed in a plastic expedition barrel on the raft, though photography may be difficult unless you've got a waterproof camera. On the Trisuli, a vehicle loaded with gear may meet you at camp, but on other rivers everything goes in the boat, so pack light. Finally, if you've gotten good service it's a nice gesture to tip your staff.

KOSHI TAPPU WILDLIFE RESERVE

Budget travelers will find the most accessible park to be the small Koshi Tappu Wildlife Reserve, set in the floodplain of the mighty Koshi River in the eastern Terai. Some 70 km from Biratnagar and 63 km from Dharan, it's easily reached if you're passing through either town, perhaps en route to the Kangchenjunga region. "Sapt Kosi" refers to the mighty stream formed by the joining of seven smaller rivers which drain eastern Nepal. The reserve is on a peninsula projecting into the Sapt Kosi River, which turns into an island *(tappu)* in the monsoon. Its eastern side is lined by high embankments which channel water into the Kosi Barrage, a massive series of flood-control gates 12 km downstream. Built in 1964 by India to control monsoon flooding in Bihar, it has created abundant wetlands which form a highly important wildlife habitat.

The reserve was formed to protect Nepal's last herd of wild buffalo *(arnaa),* currently numbering around 200. Floods, inbreeding, and crossbreeding with domestic buffalo are threatening the *arnaa*'s existence. Birdwatching draws the park's few visitors. Huge quantities of 280 species of waterbirds stop here on their winter migrations, usually Nov.-February. There are also spotted deer, wild boar, monkeys, and a semi-legendary wild elephant known to locals as Ganesh Maharaj. *Nilgai,* or "blue bull," a beefy type of antelope once common to Terai tropical forests, is also found here. Large males can weigh up to 250 kg and are 1.5 meters tall at the shoulder. As Hindus consider it a type of cow it's not hunted, but shrinking habitat has made it increasingly rare.

There's a very simple lodge at park headquarters at Kusaha, across the river from the reserve. Dugout canoes ferry passengers into the reserve, which at 155 square km is small enough (and, being rhino-free, safe enough) to explore on foot. The park has a few elephants for rent, though they are not always available.

The East-West Highway runs along the edge of the reserve. Look for a sign 12 km east of the barrage or three km west of Laukhi pointing to reserve headquarters at **Kusaha,** which lies three km further north down the dirt road. There's a very simple lodge here, and basic food is available in the nearby village.

BARDIA NATIONAL PARK

Way out in far Western Nepal, this is the country's largest remaining chunk of Terai wilderness. Similar to Chitwan but drier and more remote, it encompasses nearly 1,000 square km of sal forest and riverine grassland. A former royal hunting preserve gazetted as a national park in 1988, Bardia is the place to go for serious wildlife watchers. The game viewing is better (there's a good chance of spotting a tiger) and it's much more unspoiled than Chitwan: only 350 tourists visited in 1991. It's also much harder to reach, being 585 km by road from Kathmandu or a US$100 flight to Nepalgunj and a four-hour drive. While there is an upscale Tiger Mountain lodge here and a single smaller, cheaper one, Bardia has no equivalent to Sauruha, and at the moment is still a difficult destination for independent travelers.

Park Fauna

Bardia's 125 Royal Bengal tigers constitute the country's second largest population. Other endangered species include a small herd of wild elephants, some swamp deer, and a tiny gharial population of less than 20. Some of the gharial raised at the Chitwan hatchery have been released in the Babai and Karnali Rivers here. Spotted deer and wild boar are plentiful in Bardia, and sambar, hog deer, sloth bear, and leopard are all commonly found. Some 350 bird species have been recorded here, including ducks, geese, cranes, and cormorants.

Bardia was a traditional haunt of rhinos, but the population was wiped out by poachers in this century. It was ridiculously easy to trap rhinos, who deposit their cannonball-like dung in the same place, approached backwards. Poachers simply found an old dung mound, dug a pit and waited for the beast to back in.

In an attempt to reestablish the population, 38 rhinos were transferred here from Chitwan in 1986-90. At least 10 calves were born to the relocated beasts, and the transition appeared to be going smoothly until well-organized gangs of armed poachers moved in. Eight of the 38 original rhinos have been found dead, all minus their valuable horns, which fetch up to Rs1.2 million per kg on the Chinese black market. Most likely even more have been killed, and their remains buried. While Bardia is protected by some 500 soldiers, their regular patrols have proven easy for poachers to outwit.

An attempt to relocate endangered blackbuck antelope into Bardia has proven even less successful than the rhino effort. The situation for the rare Gangetic dolphin *(susu)* is also grim. Some 20-30 are believed to live in the Karnali River, but construction of a hydroelectric dam at Chisapani will severely damage their habitat. The same goes for the gharial and the *mahseer,* a prized game fish which can weigh more than 13 kg.

The Chisapani Dam

Bardia has suffered from modernization despite its remote location. The East-West Highway cuts through the heart of its sal forest from Motipur to Chisapani, and the negative impact will increase as traffic grows. The giant dam and irrigation project proposed for Chisapani is among the world's largest projects, costing US$5 billion and projected to produce some 10,800 megawatts of power. This is nearly 70 times greater than Nepal's present output, far beyond its ability to absorb. The idea is to sell electricity to Indian industries, but the dam would also

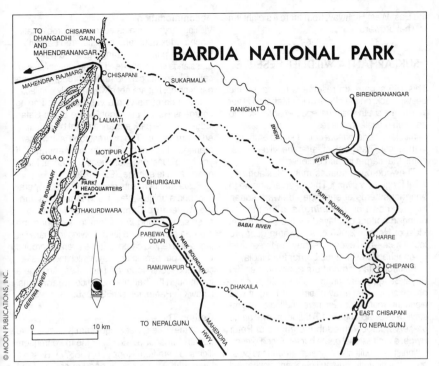

© MOON PUBLICATIONS, INC.

flood some 300 square km of land, destroying wildlife habitats and blocking fish migration.

Accommodations

Visitors can camp near the **warden's office** at park headquarters for Rs300 per night. Simple teashops provide food and will put travelers up in a pinch, but bring some supplies just in case. Guides can be hired from the warden's office. The park has 10 elephants, stabled an hour's walk south of the warden's office, which are theoretically available for rent. The single established outfit at the time of writing was **Bardia Jungle Cottage** near park headquarters in Thakurdwara, which offers lodging in thatched-roof huts, *daal bhaat* meals, and a program of activities, including elephant rides and game walks. The local contact phone number is (84) 20-124 or (84) 20-288.

Tiger Tops Karnali Lodge, Durbar Marg, tel. (1) 222-706, is run by the same operation as Chitwan's famed Tiger Tops. Standards are similarly high, but it's less expensive and less crowded, for serious nature buffs rather than jungle socialites. It's advertised as offering a much better chance of sighting a tiger than Chitwan. The lodge is US$150 per person per night, including all meals and activities; transport from Nepalgunj is US$50 extra. The lodge also operates a deluxe **tented camp** (US$120) on the bank of the Geruwa River, a particularly rich wildlife area.

Getting There

Bardia is an exhausting 585 km by road from Kathmandu. Most visitors fly to **Nepalgunj** (US$100); the park is about a two-and-a-half-hour drive from the airport. A more exciting option would be to raft three days down the Bheri River to the park; Tiger Tops can arrange this for an added fee.

On your own, it's a three-hour bus ride from Nepalgunj to park headquarters at **Thakurdwara.** More frequent buses run to **Motipur** on the East-West Highway; from there it's eight km to Thakurdwara.

SUKLAPHANTA WILDLIFE RESERVE

This 155-square-km reserve is far, *far* off the beaten track, on the plains of the Mahakali River in extreme southwestern Nepal. *Phanta* refers to an open grassland; the reserve encompasses a particularly huge *phanta* called *sukila* or "white" in the local Tharu dialect, after the silvery blossoms that carpet it each October.

The wide-open spaces make Suklaphanta ideal for game viewing. The reserve is home to enormous herds of endangered swamp deer, locally known as **barasingha,** after the 12-pronged antlers displayed by the adult male. Most of Nepal's 2,000 or so swamp deer are found here—and even here they are threatened by poachers crossing the border from India.

Suklaphanta also harbors approximately 50 Royal Bengal tigers, gharial and marsh mugger, otters, and a vast array of birds. A herd of wild elephants roams between here and India. The reserve was established in 1976 from a royal game preserve, largely through the efforts of Peter Byrne, a professional game hunter turned preservationist who built his campaign around the presence of a gigantic lone bull elephant nicknamed "Thula Hatti." Judging from his two-foot-wide footprints, this creature's height is estimated at over 11 feet at the shoulder, which would make him the biggest Asian elephant of the last 200 years. Byrne made him the selling point of the reserve, writing a book (see Booklist) and making a film on the pursuit of Thula Hatti.

Accommodations

Visiting Suklaphanta on your own is problematic, since pedestrians and cyclists aren't admitted inside the park—too dangerous. To patrol the grasslands you really need a jeep, unavailable locally. Elephants can be rented through the warden's office, but are not always readily available.

If you do come with a vehicle, the camping charge is Rs300 per night, or the Silent Safari lodge near the park entrance might be persuaded to put you up. The nearest food is in Mahendranagar, five km north of the park entrance. If you have questions, park headquarters at Majagaon has a telephone: (99) 21-309.

Suklaphanta has its own luxury safari operation, and a unique affair it is. **Silent Safari Jungle Adventure Camp** is a small family business specializing in custom trips around the area via elephant and jeep, staying in Tharu villages and tented camps. Tours average around US$150 per person per day, which includes accommodations, food, and activities. Arrange a trip through the Kathmandu office at Jawalakhel Chowk in Patan, tel. (1) 523-055.

Getting There

Catch the once-a-week flight from Kathmandu to **Mahendranagar** (US$160) or the more frequent flights to here from Nepalgunj (US$77). Reserve headquarters are barely one km south of the airstrip. Flying from Kathmandu to **Dhangadhi** (US$149) is another possible point of access: Silent Safari will arrange pickups from here, or buses take three hours to Mahendranagar. Traveling overland, it's a nine-hour bus ride from Nepalgunj to Mahendranagar. From Mahendranagar, buses depart daily to Delhi, a nine- or 10-hour drive.

JANAKPUR

This Terai city is as intense and tasty as one of its Indian sweets—as exotic as India, and more manageable. Steeped in brilliant colors and soaked in religious devotion, it's absolutely the best city in the Nepal Terai.

Janakpur is tailored for tourism, only this time it's Indians, not Westerners. Busloads of white-clad, singing, clapping pilgrims pour through here daily, more often than not making a shopping stop in Janakpur's new bazaar after their

puja. Hundreds of pilgrim hostels *(kuti)* dot the city, along with dozens of water tanks and sacred ponds which are used for laundry, swimming, water buffalo-bathing, and ritual ablutions. Supposedly over 1,000 tanks were constructed here by King Janak to accommodate the gods who came to Janakpur for Sita's wedding. It was a long and dusty journey from their Himalayan abode of Mt. Kailas, and King Janak couldn't expect the gods to *share.*

Located 128 km southeast of Kathmandu, Janakpur is a bit inconvenient to reach unless you fly directly from Kathmandu or happen to be passing through Birgunj, 165 km west. It does slot well into a journey to Eastern Nepal.

History

Janakpur is the historic capital of Mithila, an ancient North Indian kingdom that flourished from the 9th to 3rd centuries B.C., encompassing North Bihar and the adjoining Nepali Terai and foothills. Mithila's orthodox Brahmans were famed for their erudition, and its ancient written language, derived from Sanskrit, holds a rich literary tradition: it was used in the medieval courts of Kathmandu for poetry and drama, and influenced the development of Newari script. Today, some 2.1 million Nepalis have Maithili as their mother tongue, making it second only to Nepali.

Janakpur is revered as the birthplace of Sita, daughter of King Janak and beloved heroine of the ancient Hindu epic the Ramayana. While the legend is mostly fantasy, there actually was a King Janak, who reigned around 2500 B.C.

When Sita reached marriageable age, her father tested her suitors by asking them to shoot an arrow from the great bow of Shiva, which could be drawn only by the pure of heart. Dhanusa, 15 km north of Janakpur, is still visited by pilgrims who revere it as the site of this contest. Hundreds failed, then Rama stepped up to pull the string easily, shattering the bow and winning Sita's hand. The pair were idolized in the Ramayana as the ideal married couple. Rama is considered an incarnation of Vishnu, the epitome of masculine virtues, while Sita is associated with Lakshmi and is the model Hindu wife, chaste and devoted to the end. Janakpur's famous images of Rama and Sita are worshipped by Indian newlyweds hoping for a happy married life.

SIGHTS

Janaki Mandir

This massive marble shrine is less than a century old but looks timeless, its Mughal-style battlements and domes resembling a Rajasthani palace. A local queen, Brishavanu, built it in 1911 at a cost of some Rs900,000, thus the name "Nau Lakh Mandir." It's believed to be on the site where King Janak discovered Sita in the furrow of a ploughed field; the present temple is the latest in a long succession of shrines.

The 100-square-meter outer facade encloses a much smaller, exquisitely decorated main temple housing sacred images of Sita and Rama. Sita is said to have been retrieved from a holy river in Ayodhya; Rama is said to have been made by the divine craftsperson Vishwakarma in a legend described in the Ramayana. The inner sanctum is open 5-7 a.m. and again at 6-8 p.m.; priests perform elaborate daily *puja* here around 8 a.m. and 4 p.m. During the day the place is nearly deserted. Morning and evening are the times to visit, as devotees crowd inside to murmur prayers and hymns and make offerings to the images in a frenzy of devotion.

The huge plaza in front is the heart of town: here vendors sell sweets, flowers, and luridly colored religious pictures, and pilgrims congregate in groups. Just north of the temple is the **Ram Janaki Vivek Mandap,** a squat new edifice with a stacked roof which immortalizes the couple's wedding. Inside are doe-eyed images of Sita and Rama in full makeup, with red lips, blue eyelids, heavy *tika,* and golden robes.

The City

The most interesting and densely packed neighborhood lies south of the main temple, where narrow streets hold tiny shops selling traditional goods. To the east is the modern bazaar, catering to Indians looking for bargain-priced modern items. The multitiered, century-old **Ram Mandir** in the middle of town is the focus of the Ram Navami festival; beside it are the holiest of Janakpur's 24 major ponds, **Dhanush Sagar** and **Ganga Sagar.** Devotees perform early-morning religious ablutions here; during festivals they're the scene of much wet merriment.

A 10-minute walk west of Janaki Mandir is **Ramanand Chowk,** a crossroads surrounded by pilgrim *kuti.* Turn south here and a little ways further is **Hanuman Durbar,** where the world's biggest monkey, weighing 55 kg, lies in a cramped cage, a sad sight unredeemed by the steady parade of pilgims stuffing him with tidbits.

JANAKPUR

© MOON PUBLICATIONS, INC.

Around Janakpur

Janakpur is manageable on foot, and the lack of cars makes it an absolute pleasure to walk. Cycle rickshaws are plentiful and cheap as long as you bargain, and your hotel might be able to come up with a bicycle. The countryside surrounding the city is worth exploring. Brick-paved lanes lead past vistas of palm trees and onion-domed shrines set amid rice paddies and sacred ponds. The area west of town is particularly worthwhile: claimed to be "old" Janakpur, it's now more or less a village set with two ancient tanks, **Agni Sagar** and **Gyan Sagar.**

Around here you can still see the typical white-washed mud houses decorated with Maithili paintings of gods, peacocks, elephants, fish, and stick figures, protective devices painted by household women continuing an age-old tradition. The **Janakpur Women's Development Project,** tel. (41) 20-130, is an organization of local women who create and market traditional paintings on daphne paper; a newer innovation is glazed ceramic wares painted with traditional

(top) trekking staff setting up tent (Christopher Gamm);
(bottom left) chorten (stupa) at Tengboche Monastery, Khumbu (Kerry Moran);
(bottom right) trekkers in Khumbu (Christopher Gamm)

(top) valley scene near Bhaktapur (Kerry Moran);
(bottom left) Bhotia village of Thinigaon, with buckwheat fields, near Muktinath (Kerry Moran);
(bottom right) Junbesi village, Solu (Kerry Moran)

MAITHILI PAINTINGS

Janakpur's mud-walled houses display the bold, dramatic paintings that constitute an ancient Maithili art form. Centuries of tradition, myth, and legend have been condensed into highly stylized symbolic art, in which every motif carries a wealth of meaning. Women decorate walls and courtyard floors at Tihar with designs of prosperity and abundance that can be as imaginative and witty as a procession of pregnant elephants. A wedding evokes an outpouring of fertility symbolism—parrots and bamboo, bamboo entwined with lotus leaves, turtles and fish—all symbolizing richness and fecundity.

More recently, women have begun to transfer paintings to paper for use in courtship rituals. A young girl may send her betrothed paintings depicting the handsome Krishna, Shiva's terrifying consort Kali, or the legendary Maithili princess Sita, luckless heroine of the Ramayana. The accompanying decorative motifs have been refined over the centuries to near-abstractions resembling meditative mandalas.

The idea of transferring paintings to paper was inspired by an Indian drought relief project in the mid-'60s, when women were encouraged to find alternate ways of making money. Janakpur women now produce paintings for sale, marketed through the original Janakpur Women's Development Project and several smaller organizations. Like the Indian paintings found across the border, these depict big-eyed characters wearing elaborately patterned garments and carrying out everyday tasks. Intricate borders and designs fill in all the empty spaces. Styles differ depending on the village and individual women: some are black-ink outline sketches of intricate detail; others are less complex drawings tinted in bright mineral hues of red, yellow, blue, and purple. Humorous and direct, these paintings speak for women who might otherwise be too shy to speak for themselves.

a Maithili painting of Lakshmi and Ganesh

patterns. The goal is to give women a degree of independence, a small income, and a sense of self-worth in a restrictive culture. The project office is south of town, past the Janakpur Campus and Kuwa village. The office gives the women a place to work and sells the paintings and ceramics, which are also available in Kathmandu's handicraft shops. Office hours are Sun.-Fri. 10 a.m.-5 p.m.; the building itself is worth seeing as it incorporates the style of traditional houses with a fanciful portico and walls decorated with mud designs.

Festivals

Janakpur's religious significance manifests during several important festivals. Tens of thousands of pilgrims converge at Ram Mandir for **Ram Navami** in March-April, celebrating the birthday of Rama. Early December's **Biha Panchami** draws even more when it commemorates Rama and Sita's wedding with colorful processions of elephants, horses, and chariots.

During **Chath,** celebrated a few days after Tihar in October/November, Janakpur's ponds and tanks are lined with colorful offerings: brilliant powders; ritual fruits, nuts, and spices nestled in clay dishes; clay elephants; piles of sweets; tall stalks of sugarcane; and clusters of bananas. Tradition demands 60 types of offerings be presented to the Sun God, who awards devotees with health and prosperity. Women will spend all day arranging their offerings in artistic patterns, then immerse themselves in the water in ritual bathing. Worship continues after dark, when small oil lamps are floated on the still waters of ponds.

Steam Railway

Nepal's only operating railroad runs through Janakpur to the Indian railhead at **Jayanagar,** 28 km southeast. An equal distance to the northwest on a separate line is the terminus of **Bijalpur.** A tiny steam locomotive pulls the old carriages along a narrow-gauge track, past ricefields, villages, and temples. While it's scenic, it's also exceedingly slow—three hours to Jayanagar—so you'll probably just want a taste of it. Trains are crowded, so either buy a ticket early or be prepared to ride on the roof. Fare to Jayanagar is Rs9 in second class, Rs24 in first.

Trains depart Janakpur for Jayanagar daily at 7:30 a.m. and 3:30 p.m; Jayanagar-Janakpur departures are supposed to be simultaneous, which simplifies returning. You can get off along the way and wait for the return train chugging through an hour or so later (do check beforehand), or get off at the village of **Parbaha** or **Baidehi** and walk back. End of the line for foreigners, who are not allowed to cross the border, is the Nepali town of **Khajuri,** three km north of Jayanagar.

Heading north, trains depart Janakpur for Bijalpur at 2:45 p.m.; again, you can catch a return train back or get off early and walk.

PRACTICALITIES

Accommodations and Food

There's little in the way of tourist hotels. Book in advance for festival times, which are crowded. **Hotel Welcome,** tel. (41) 20-646, on Station Road is the best place in town, which isn't saying much. Dorm beds here are Rs35 and rooms are Rs75-200; air-conditioned rooms are Rs450-600. Second choice is **Hotel Rama,** tel. (41) 20-059, quieter and off the main street, where rooms with bath are Rs100 s, Rs200 d. **Hotel Holiday,** tel. (41) 20-399, on Station Road is a poor third. The government tourist office on Station Road past Bhanu Chowk, tel. (41) 20-755, might be prevailed upon to help find a hotel room.

Local food is deliciously Indian influenced, with vegetarian specialities for devout Hindus and lots of sweets. The lack of menus may reduce you to a point-and-eat system. Look across from Janaki Mandir or along Station Road for teashops, sweet shops and restaurants, or try Hotel Welcome's dining room.

Getting There

RNAC flies from Kathmandu three times weekly; airfare is US$75. Rickshaws ply the two km between the airport and the town. The RNAC office is at Bhanu Chowk on the north side of town, tel. (41) 20-185.

By "express" bus, Janakpur is 12 hours from Kathmandu and seven hours from Kakarbhitta. As it lies down a spur road 30 km south of the East-West Highway, it's not really en route to anywhere. Birgunj, 165 km west, and Biratnagar, around 200 km east, are the closest major towns, with regular bus service to Janakpur. The bus park is on the southern edge of town; again, cycle rickshaws bridge the gap. Buses depart here for Kathmandu every evening around 6 p.m. Day buses to Kathmandu, operated by the government-run Sajha cooperative, depart from the highway north of Ramanand Chowk. There are plenty of buses each morning to Kakarbhitta.

BOB RACE

TREKKING
INTRODUCTION

Nepal's unparalleled combination of natural beauty and cultural riches reveals itself only to those who walk. Practically the whole northern section of the country is untouched by roads: in order to explore it you *have* to trek. The greatest inducement is the Himalaya. With eight of the world's 10 highest peaks, Nepal is loaded with spectacular mountain vistas. Rather than gazing at them from a distance, trekkers walk and live amid the mountains for weeks at a time. The leisurely pace creates a sense of intimacy with the land that goes far beyond that of a day hike or a wilderness weekend.

Mountains may be the main lure, but there are surprises along the way. There are people amid this spectacular scenery—all sorts of people, living in a world virtually untouched by modern development. The realities of the third world can be an eye-opening introduction to how most of the world lives. Trekkers find ultimately that trekking is not just about the landscape: they learn much more about the world, about other people, and about themselves.

Reality Checks
As trekking makes the transition from cult to big business, trekkers' expectations become increasingly wilder. Herewith a few surprises many discover only on the trail.

Trekking is walking. Many organized trekkers are shocked at the effort required to trek, having been lured by seductive advertising into what they discover (too late) is a very physical enterprise. Some clients don't realize they'll be going to high altitudes, and join because "cruises are boring." Or they want to see Everest, but don't realize they have to walk three weeks to do so. If you've never hiked for a day up and down hills, try it before signing up.

On the other hand, trekking shouldn't frighten off anyone in reasonable health. It's demanding, but you can walk at your own pace, and there's an undeniable satisfaction in feeling your body do what it was made to do: walk.

Trekking is a cultural rather than a wilderness experience. You *could* choose a remote trail avoiding populated areas, but it would be a

> *As I stepped out on my first day's march in the Himalayas, a strange exhilaration thrilled me. I kept squeezing my fists together and saying emphatically to myself and the universe at large: "Oh yes! Oh yes! This is really splendid!"*
>
> —SIR FRANCIS YOUNGHUSBAND

shame to miss Nepal's people. The amount of personal interaction is dictated by the individual. Organized treks are often maligned for the limited cultural interaction they provide, but many independent trekkers have even less contact with Nepalis. More than any other factor—age, physical fitness, type of trek, money spent, route—your trekking experience depends on you.

Finally, *trekking is a process rather than a destination*. Trekking should not be a constant forced march: the best moments are time to stop and play with kids or admire a pretty stream or a cloud drifting over the mountains. It's all too easy to fall into walking-machine mode. Consciously remind yourself to stop at teashops and shady *chautaara,* admire the views, and splash in a stream. The walking is a way to link these moments, not the reason in itself. Walking and nothing but, day after day, provides illuminating insights into one's own mind and how seldom it's here in the moment. Even on the trail, thoughts race ahead to the next meal, the night's stop, the return to Kathmandu. Seldom do we delight in the pure present, but these sudden moments seem to come increasingly easily on the trail, as mind and body synchronize.

Largely for this reason, many people find their trek to be a personal watershed. Beyond the physical challenge, observing terrain and cultures completely unlike what you've ever experienced can be mind-blowing. Many trekkers find a new perspective on their own lives, and a high percentage of first-timers swear to return.

History

"Trekking" is an Afrikaans term used by Dutch settlers to describe self-sufficient bush travel across the African veldt, usually with wagons packed with gear. The word was picked up by British mountaineering expeditions in Asia, and eventually spread to Nepal. Nepal officially opened its backcountry to tourists in 1964. The following year the first trekking company, Mountain Travel, was founded by Lt. Col. Jimmy Roberts, a retired British Gurkha officer and an avid mountaineer. He believed people would pay much to see the Nepal Himalaya in style, and he was right.

The original treks were in the classic sahib fashion, with long lines of porters bearing supplies, tents, even tables and chairs. While this tradition remains in organized treks, budget travelers soon discovered it was possible to go alone, staying in local teashops and homes. Nepalis know an opportunity when they see it: they opened special tourist lodges, simple but modified to make Westerners feel comfortable, and business has been booming ever since. The number of trekking permits issued went from 13,000 in 1976 to 76,000 in 1994, and there are now nearly 250 trekking agencies in Kathmandu.

Seasons

Contrary to popular belief, it's possible to trek at any time of year. The trick is tailoring your route to the season. The main season, drawing 40%

BOB RACE

of all trekkers, begins the second week of October and runs through the third week of November. The weather is indeed divine, with minimal rainfall and crystal-clear mountain views, but the main trails are packed. Autumn remains the best time to trek if you don't mind crowds; for remote trails it's unqualifiedly superb.

The winter months, Dec.-Feb., are surprisingly undertrekked. Though it's freezing above 4000 meters and high passes may be snowbound, winter is an ideal season for a lower trek like Solu, Helambu, Pokhara-Trisuli, or the lower reaches of the Annapurna region. Late February marks the beginning of the spring trekking season, which peaks around mid-April and ends in late May. The weather grows progressively warmer, and while views are not as crisply inspiring as autumn's, days are longer and multicolored rhododendrons blossom at progressively higher elevations. By April lower elevations are steamy; by May they're practically unbearable.

Very few trekkers venture out June-Aug., but a monsoon trek has its merits, especially for those who can't visit Nepal at any other time (see special topic "The Monsoon" in the general Introduction for more details). Places like Khumbu, which appear dry and desolate in the tourist season, are gloriously green in monsoon; herders are up in the high pastures, and wildflowers and water are everywhere. The rainfall peaks in July and tapers off Aug.-September. Weather improves steadily from the last week in August, and there's still nobody on the trail. This is the time to visit high rainshadow areas: Manang, Khumbu, and the upper Kali Gandaki. Flying directly into these areas bypasses the slippery lower trails, but flights are particularly erratic in monsoon, so allow extra time.

The Walking

Anyone in reasonable shape can trek. It helps to prepare in advance—weight-lifting emphasizing the leg muscles, running, stair-climbing, or simply some good hard walks (look for hills). Somehow, nothing completely prepares you for the real thing. Muscles are inevitably sore in the beginning; expect a definite slump the third day. By the end of the first week bodies loosen up. Most first-time trekkers are amazed at the energy and strength they discover, and by visible changes as weight drops and muscles firm.

> *Over the first few days of any march it is wise to draw a veil. The things that have been forgotten are gradually remembered, and the whole organization creaks and groans like your own joints. You wonder if man was really intended to walk, whether motoring after all is not his natural mode of progression, and whether the call of the open road is as insistent as you yourself thought or as the poets sing.*
>
> —H.W. TILMAN

The pure physical pleasure of walking is reason enough to trek; finding out what your body can actually do may be the biggest thrill of all.

You learn on the trail how to gauge a hill, how to pace yourself on a long climb. Altitude figures that at first seem arcane slowly begin to make sense, as your body learns what a 1500-meter climb means, and how to adjust to it. At first the ups and downs seem endless, and you long for a level stretch. Downhill is harder on the knees, and long steep descents can be extremely tiring. After a while it doesn't matter which direction the trail is heading—you just walk it.

TREKKING STYLES

People tend to divide naturally into independent and group trekkers. Much is dictated by the time/money tradeoff: the more time/less money crowd goes alone, while the reverse case signs up for groups. Statistically the split is nearly even: 40% group, 60% independent trekkers. The major trails are surprisingly easy to do alone. Group trekking's biggest advantage is its ability to open up remote regions that are practically inaccessible without porters, tents, and supplies.

Independent Trekking

This is also called teahouse trekking, after the lodgings along main trails. Independent trekkers tend to cluster on a few of Nepal's best-known trails, but you can teahouse trek wherever Nepalis live. Even if there's no sign saying "lodge," teashops and local homes will put you up.

A QUESTION OF IMPACT

A deep chasm divides group and individual trekkers. Trekking companies are suspicious of the budget travelers they sneeringly refer to as "backpackers," and frequent articles in the local press denounce the money that's slipping away with independent trekkers. Individual trekkers, meanwhile, view group trekkers as packaged tourists missing out on the real thing; harried people who pay a lot of money to rush through Nepal, and leave.

To a neutral observer it may seem that trekkers of both styles leave nothing but trash and cultural havoc. Trekkers' support of local economies is supposed to make their presence worthwhile for villagers. Actually, the impact on local economies is minimal. According to one study, only 20 cents of the average trekker's daily expenditure of US$3 goes into the local economy (the figure is an average for group and individual trekkers).

This is more obvious in the case of organized treks, which haul everything in from Kathmandu. First off, a large chunk of money goes to the head of-

trekkers and firewood-carrying porters, Pharak

CHRISTOPHER GAMM

fice. The staff is from Kathmandu, and the porters are hired at the trailhead. Group trekkers are so well-drilled in the dangers of unclean food that they rarely buy even a glass of tea; at most the *sirdar* will purchase firewood and a few vegetables. On the other hand, he can afford to pay any price for luxuries like chickens and eggs, driving them far above the reach of local people.

Individual trekkers contribute less than they might think. Most supplies—everything from beer and toilet paper to noodles and even rice in many areas—are imported from lower regions or Kathmandu. Prices are marked up to pay for porterage, and local profits are minimal. Only a very small percentage of the local population operate shops or lodges that do business with trekkers. Local products are scarce, and few people learn to raise or make goods to sell to trekkers. Indeed, in many areas there's little to sell but the scenery.

Members of the trekking industry like to maintain their trips are environmentally correct, the main point being teahouse trekkers who stay in wood-burning lodges contribute to deforestation. They neglect to state that group treks may burn massive quantities of wood in preparing three elaborate meals a day, plus food for the staff and porters, who outnumber clients by three to one. Kerosene is supposed to be used for cooking in national parks, but cooks dodge this requirement whenever they can, and regardless of what the staff does, porters still build fires for cooking and for warmth.

The environmental impact of a group trek is thus much heavier than companies lead you to believe. Few bury their wastes sufficiently; often the toilet pits are left open, one at each campsite. Most Sherpas litter astoundingly. "Cleanup" means tossing tins and bottles into rivers or over a cliff—and there's a lot of such litter, since meals revolve around packaged food.

Individual trekkers are not much better. In season, the woodstoves burn continually as lodges produce piecemeal orders from ridiculously elaborate menus. The Annapurna Conservation Area Project (ACAP) has sensibly moved to streamline local menus and standardize prices in the Annapurna Sanctuary.

In the big picture, the amount of firewood used to feed, warm, and wash 60,000 trekkers is negligible when compared to the eight million tons consumed annually by 19 million Nepalis. Environ-

trekker with Langtang people

mental concern is fashionable nowadays, but far more serious is the cultural erosion caused by tourism. Trees can be replanted, but the loss of cultural identity is irreversible, and no amount of money can buy it back.

ACAP director Chandra Gurung is more worried about tourism's impact on local culture than anything else. In the Gurung communities of the Annapurna region, he says, "Younger people aren't interested in learning about their culture; they don't wear the clothes, they hardly speak the language anymore; they don't want to work in the fields."

ACAP is trying to emphasize the importance of cultural identity, improve local standards of living, and point out economic incentives, teaching people to use their experience in agriculture and handicrafts to sell products to trekkers. But intangibles like cultural changes are tough to influence, and this is certainly ACAP's hardest battle.

So where's the solution? Increasing numbers of people, including many in the trekking industry, are warning of environmental dangers. Some go so far as to recommend closing overused regions for a few years' respite, or limiting the number of trekkers on major trails. So far the government has brushed these suggestions aside: as a large source of foreign revenue, tourism is not to be lightly discouraged. It appears new regions will be more strictly controlled, however. Part of the impetus in restricting Kangchenjunga and Dolpo to group treks was to control the environmental impact.

Better management will help, but ultimately the greatest responsibility lies with trekkers. Most people are well-meaning but unaware of the broad environmental and social consequences of their innocent vacation. The environmental dos and don'ts are relatively straightforward: coordinating and simplifying meals; minimizing hot water use; burying waste or using local toilets as much as possible; carrying out garbage. Group trekkers can cheerfully prod and assist their staff into doing these things; a few companies are beginning to assume responsibility on their own.

Trickier are the more ephemeral issues of cultural contact: apparently innocuous things like dressing modestly (it applies to men as well as women), minimizing consumption—a good policy after the trek as well—discouraging begging, approaching people as human beings rather than photogenic objects, and realizing that every one of your actions is scrutinized and makes a far greater impression than you might think.

Independent trekking began in the tradition of mountaineers like Eric Shipton and H.W. Tilman, who pioneered the "living off the land" style. Over the past 20 years the main routes have evolved a trekking subculture of their own, supported by local entrepreneurs good at providing what people want: apple *pai,* pancakes, and cold beer. The Western food loses something in the translation, but trekking lodges suit most people. Fellow trekkers provide an international

flavor to the conversation, while Nepal is the scenic backdrop. The result is a hybrid culture that's neither here nor there.

Most individual trekkers are in their twenties, often doing the Asian or world-travel circuit with a few months in Nepal along the way. The resulting far-flung conversations mean you can learn a lot about Kenyan safaris while sitting in a Sherpa lodge, but not much about Nepal beyond how difficult the trail is and what to eat where. The blinders worn by many independent travelers, supported by a dogged by-the-guidebook mentality, are a discouraging aspect of this subculture.

The daily schedule is dictated by yourself: you can stay a few extra days in a fascinating place, conk out early by the riverside, or sprint ahead according to your mood. The routine is flexible compared to that group of trekking, but there's an equal danger of being isolated from Nepal. Most people expect trekking to be a remote and somewhat harrowing adventure, and are pleasantly surprised to find crowded trails. Social life is easy and there's almost always somebody to walk with if you want—one reason to not worry too much about starting off alone.

Independent trekking is certainly cheaper than group trekking, Rs150-300 per day, compared to US$35-100 for a group. Double that amount for a porter, and add more if you're going to a remote high-altitude region like Khumbu. Prices of goods and lodging will increase steadily the farther you get from the road, since all goods must be carried in by porter.

Drawbacks include an increased risk of getting lost and a higher hassle factor in that you'll have to arrange food and lodging yourself at every stop. Both of these problems are minimal on well-trodden main trails. You do need a certain flexibility and an ability to deal with ambiguous situations that applies to all Asian travel.

Independent travelers on a first trek should stick to a main trail. Hiring a guide and/or porter would expand the possibilities considerably. A good one will lead you down remote trails, interpret for you, and teach you a lot about Nepal in the process. Consider hiring a porter for main trails as well.

On your own and off the main trails, independent trekking is what all trekking used to be: adventurous, demanding, and very rewarding. Local people routinely open up their homes to travelers, providing the opportunity to eat and sleep in authentic circumstances—not always comfortable, but guaranteed interesting. Traveling in this fashion probably requires a de-gree of comfort with spoken Nepali, and certainly a very adventurous spirit.

Organized Trekking

Group trekking's high-employment, high-impact style is a direct spinoff of the British Raj. Organized trekkers tend to be slightly older than teahouse trekkers, generally late thirties and up. Usually they're professionals with steady jobs and limited vacation time. Going through a company saves a lot of hassles and guarantees a trek will fit within their limited free time.

Group trekkers live in comparative luxury. You still have to walk, of course, but in camp you've got chairs and tables in the dining tent, a toilet tent with paper, and staff to shepherd you down the trail if necessary. Food is Western-style and plentiful, and cooks work miracles on their wood fires and kerosene stoves, producing a different menu every evening: cakes, spring rolls, pizza. While it's not all as good as it looks, they try hard.

Accommodations are in two-person tents, cramped compared to some lodges but often cleaner, quieter, and free from smoky cooking fires. Pitched on snow, though, they're downright cold. The camping mentality of a group trek seems out of place on main trails where there are so many comfortable lodges, but it comes into its own in remote areas. For most people, especially first-time trekkers, off-the-beaten-track routes are best explored through a company.

The staff is led by a *sirdar,* an organizational wizard responsible for logistics, operations, and trekkers' general well-being. Most *sirdar* are

---

RECOMMENDED TREKKING COMPANIES

Asian Trekking
Bhagawan Bahal, Thamel
P.O. Box 3022
tel. (1) 413-732

Cho Oyu Trekking
Gairidhara
P.O. Box 4515
tel. (1) 418-890

Guides for All Seasons
Gairidhara

P.O. Box 3776
tel. (1) 415-841

Himalayan Excursions
Thamel (Hotel Tilicho)
P.O. Box 1221
tel. (1) 418-407

Himalayan Rover Treks
Naxal
P.O. Box 1081
tel. (1) 414-373

Sherpas. In larger groups he will be supplemented by a Western trek leader who acts as cultural interface, though the recent trend is to cut costs by eliminating this position. Other staff members include the cook, several "Sherpas" who serve as trail scouts, guides, and go-fers, and a few kitchen boys, the hardest-working of the entire lot. Employees are almost always enthusiastic and charming, and a good staff can make a trek. Two to three weeks gives you time to get to know people; generally your greatest cultural interaction will be with the staff.

Scheduling is strict. Trekkers are awakened with "bed tea," a vestigial Raj-era custom. Shortly after comes a basin of hot washing water. Pack your bags and stumble out to breakfast; while you dine, the staff is taking down tents, packing loads, and sending the porters along their way. The morning walk is a few hours to the lunch spot, which like the campsites is picked out in advance by the *sirdar*, who may consider the availability of firewood and water more than the scenery. Quite a few camps will be made in bare fields. Lunch is a two-hour break, followed by several more hours of walking to the evening's campsite. Dinner comes just after dark, and people are generally in bed by 8 or 9 p.m.—there's not much else to do in a cold tent. One or two rest days at scenic viewpoints vary this routine.

Drawbacks to group trekking are price (booking through a company outside of Nepal, you'll pay US$70-120 per day) and an essential lack of freedom. Many people are willing to trade this for the reassurance of being taken care of every step of the way. Internal group dynamics are unpredictable, not surprising when you consider how a group of strangers is cast into the wilderness and expected to get along for several weeks. Some groups develop a great sense of camaraderie and organize regular reunions, while others can't wait to split up.

If organized trekking sounds attractive but prices seem high, consider going through a reputable local company. Foreign trekking agencies channel their clients through local companies, charging a higher price for the privilege of signing up abroad. Services are pretty much identical for local sign-ups, but the cost can be less than half, depending on the size of your party. You can sign up in advance for scheduled group trips,

but be prepared to make arrangements up to six months beforehand.

It's simpler just to go to Kathmandu: a week is enough time to arrange most treks. Tailor a custom trek to your own specifications: go alone or with a few friends, bring your kids, indulge in birdwatching or photography, visit remote regions groups don't go to.

Choose a company belonging to TAAN (Trekking Agents Association of Nepal), which gives some recourse should something go wrong. The TAAN office in Gairidhara, tel. (1) 419-245, has a list of agency locations and numbers. Beware of rock-bottom cheap agencies, which cut too many corners and often don't know anything but the main trails. Shop around to find a company specializing in the area you're interested in. Recommendations from satisfied recent clients are a good way to choose a company.

A final reason to sign up with an organized trek is the government regulation that visitors to certain semi-restricted areas—including Manaslu, Mustang, Upper Dolpo, and Kangchenjunga—must travel with a registered company. (This doesn't necessarily mean traveling in a group; even individuals can contract with a company.) Groups must be accompanied by a liaison officer, who is supposed to make sure groups stick to the scheduled trail and oversee ecologically sound practices. L.O.s are drawn from the ranks of police and soldiers, and seldom have much experience dealing with either tourists or different Nepali cultures. Stories have emerged of L.O.s who get tired and refuse to walk any further, who insist on staying in villages so they can drink, or who expect a big "tip" at the end of a trek.

Mini-Treks

It's not necessary to hike for weeks in the mountains to get a taste of the trekking life. Those with limited time, energy, or inclination can fly or drive into a number of places and stay in a nice hotel, doing day hikes and returning to a comfortable home base at night.

Hostellerie des Sherpas in Solu is a 10-minute walk from the Phaplu airstrip. It has pleasant wood-panelled rooms, a big main dining hall decorated in Tibetan style, and a lovely garden—even a sauna! Room and board are around US$35 per person; airfare to Phaplu is US$77.

From here it's an easy day's walk to Junbesi, Chiwong Gompa, and Tragsindhu Gompa.

The trekking company Ker & Downey, Kathmandu tel. (1) 416-751, operates a series of upper-crust lodges along the lower Annapurna Sanctuary Trail, all a day's walk at most from the road. The **Sanctuary Lodge** 20 minutes' walk past Birethanti overlooks the Modi Khola. It includes a library, landscaped gardens, and luxuries like hot water bottles in bed. The **Himalayan Lodge** in Ghandruk is built around an old Gurung house which now serves as the dining room; there's also the **Basanta Lodge** in Dhampus.

The most deluxe easy option is the spectacularly located **Everest View Hotel** in Syangboche, above Namche Bazaar in Khumbu. Contact the hotel office on Durbar Marg, tel. (1) 224-271. Rooms are US$175 s, US$270 d, plus another US$35 for meals; roundtrip airfare adds another US$290 to the bill. Clients are mainly Japanese tourists who fly in for a night to see Everest. Altitude sickness is a major risk when flying into this altitude (3870 meters); oxygen cylinders are on hand to treat it.

Trekking Peaks

If trekking leaves you craving still more adventure, consider an ascent of a trekking peak. Eighteen peaks in this category can be climbed by arrangement with the Nepal Mountaineering Association. Unlike the 118 official expedition peaks, which require expensive permits and a liason officer and *sirdar,* an ascent of a trekking peak is a much simpler procedure, fairly free of red tape and fuss. Because they're fairly easy for small groups, they're a favorite for alpine-style fast and light ascents.

The "trekking" part is a misnomer: actually these peaks are shorter, lower versions of full-on ascents. They range 5687-6654 meters. Anyone planning an ascent should know the basics of ice axe, crampons, and snow-climbing; winter mountaineering experience would be a plus. Safety is an issue, especially after the death of 11 German climbers on Pisang Peak in 1994: check the experience of the company you climb with.

Khumbu has the most trekking peaks (eight), which serve as prime viewpoints for the region's array of soaring mountains. The most popular include Island Peak (also called Imja Tse, 6185 meters), Mera Peak (6476 meters), and the more difficult Kwangde (6187 meters) west of Namche Bazaar. In the Annapurna region Fluted Peak or Singhu Chuli (6501 meters) and Chulu West and East (6419/6584 meters) are popular.

Foreign trekking companies market these trips as mini-expeditions at premium prices. It's also possible to go with a few friends through local companies for a much lower fee. This gives a choice of an expedition-style ascent with Sherpas, porters, and full camps, or a light alpine-style climb made carrying your own gear. Climbing permits must be obtained through a registered trekking company from the Nepal Mountaineering Association in Nag Pokhari, tel. (1) 411-525. The fee is US$300 for the most popular peaks; a few minor ones are US$150. Bill O'Connor's *The Trekking Peaks of Nepal* provides detailed information on routes and planning for all 18 peaks.

PREPARING FOR A TREK

For more trekking practicalities, see "Conduct and Customs" in the general Introduction; and "Accommodations" and "Food" in the On the Road chapter.

Trekking Permits
You'll need a trekking permit to visit Nepal's interior, essentially any place more than a day's walk from a road. Central Immigration issues standard permits for the main trekking regions: pink for Everest, yellow for Annapurna, blue for Langtang-Gosainkund-Helambu. Officials will write special white permits for all sorts of lesser-known areas, as long as these don't fall in the restricted zone along the northern border, which was created in 1962 by the Nepali government to prevent travelers from wandering into Tibet. Police posts and checkposts are rare in these seldom-visited areas, but without a permit you could be turned back.

The trekking permit procedure is similar to that for visa extensions. Bring two passport-sized photos and a fair amount of patience. Fees for most regions are Rs250 per week for the first month, Rs500 per week thereafter. More intriguing areas are at a premium: Kangchenjunga and Lower Dolpo cost Rs500 per week for the first month, then Rs1000 per week. Upper Dolpo and Mustang cost US$70 per day. Permits for Manaslu run US$90 per week Sept.-Nov., US$75 per week other months. Humla (the Simikot-Yari region) is US$90 for one week, US$15 per day thereafter. If you are combining treks and are baffled as to what exactly you need, explain your route and let Immigration work out the details and cost of permit.

Permits are generally available the same day, but lines can be long in season, especially October, when the Dasain holiday coincides with peak trekking arrivals. Go early in the day, or do it through an agency—some trekking companies will arrange independent permits for a small fee. Remember to keep your permit handy if you're traveling by road to a trailhead, as there are often police checkposts along the way.

Overstaying your permit is usually a *ke garne?* ("what to do?") affair, though police may occa-sionally attempt extortion. You shouldn't have to pay on the trail, at any rate. Go to Immigration in Pokhara or Kathmandu directly upon returning to renew your visa, and pay a mild fine.

Trekkers to national parks like Langtang, Sagarmatha, and Rara must pay an additional entrance fee of Rs650 when obtaining permits. Annapurna trekkers are liable for an Rs650 fee that goes directly to the Annapurna Conservation Area Project, a worthy endeavor. Keep the receipts for these fees as you'll be expected to produce them with your permit on the trail.

INFORMATION

Trekking Maps
In Nepal, maps are only supplements to finding your way. The main trekking trails are such highways you could walk them without a map at all. The trail description and sketch maps provided in a trekking guidebook should be sufficient, especially when supplemented by directions from villagers and other trekkers. A map is more necessary on remote trails, but in such places you're best off with a local porter-guide. To buy maps, look in tourist bookstores in Kathmandu; see "Information" in the On the Road chapter.

The best available maps, locally known as Schneider maps, are a regional 1:50,000 series based on early '60s surveys of Eastern Nepal and published in Vienna by Research Scheme Nepal Himalaya. These superbly detailed eight-color maps depict topographic and natural features, trails and villages. The East Nepal series includes *Likhu Khola, Tamba Kosi, Dudh Kosi, Lapchi Kang, Rowaling Himal,* and *Gaurishankar;* Everest trekkers will need *Khumbu Himal* and *Shorung/Hinku* for Solu. The Schneider series also covers *Langtang/Helambu* and *Annapurna.* A bootleg copy of the latter (1:250,000) is marketed by Nepa Maps. The National Geographic Society has published a beautiful color topo map of the area immediately surrounding Mt. Everest—not very practical for trekkers, but a stunning souvenir.

PORTERS AND GUIDES

Hiring someone to carry your pack is nothing to be ashamed of—portering is one of the few means of cash employment in Nepal's Hills, and carrying a pack is a holiday compared to the 100-kg bags of cement porters haul up trails. Aside from giving you the distinct relief of getting the pack off your back, a porter can open up new avenues of communication with Nepal.

A guide, on the other hand, is really unnecessary for the major trails, which are virtual highways. A local porter will show the way if necessary, and carry your gear as well. On more remote trails a guide will serve you well, and it's all the better if he carries some of your gear.

Hiring a guide through a Kathmandu agency is the most expensive option, since you'll have to pay a higher salary (around US$12 per day, and the company takes a big cut), along with his transport to the trailhead. This is the only way to guarantee finding someone with good English, however. It's easy to find porters at roadheads and airstrips; ask your lodgekeeper to help if you don't come up with anyone yourself. Another option is to hire someone on the spot for a few rough days crossing a pass, though they may be hard to find when you need them. The current daily salary is around Rs100 per day, higher in certain regions like eastern Nepal, and during the autumn festival season when nobody wants to work. A Sherpa porter in Khumbu may get more than double that. When setting a salary, make it clear that your porter will buy his own food. It's easier and usually cheaper to pay a higher daily rate than to fund his food bill. You'll probably have to give a high-altitude supplement as food prices rise, and it's always nice to throw in a few cups of tea and cigarettes along the trail.

Hiring a porter is a matter of instinct—search for the classic honest face. Older, more traditional men are preferable to cool young dudes who may be more interested in your sunglasses and Walkman. A drawback is they seldom speak much English, which will do wonders to stimulate your Nepali. A "professional" porter will go anywhere, while a farmer trying to earn some extra cash may get homesick a few days from his village and agitate to turn back. Try to determine beforehand just how far

your porter will go, and don't be surprised if he doesn't go as far as he says he will. Women porters, usually Sherpa or Bhotia, can sometimes be hired but Nepali women are usually reluctant to travel far from home.

Don't expect your porter to cross a high pass without some help from you in terms of warm clothes, shoes, and equipment. Check in advance to see what he has, and loan, rent, or buy enough for him to make it over safely. This is a good point to keep in mind when selecting a trekking company: ask what equipment they provide porters at altitude (few give anything), and hold them to their promises by bringing it up upon your return if they haven't followed up on the matter. This is the only way to get beyond the remarkable irresponsibility many companies display in terms of taking care of their porters.

porter

CHRISTOPHER GAMM

Unless you're a map freak with a fondness for topographical lines, the Schneider maps may be *too* detailed (or expensive) for an ordinary trek; at any rate they cover only a few regions. Adequate and much cheaper color topo maps of the Annapurna region are produced by ACAP and Mandala; the former costs Rs200 and includes a wealth of regional information on the reverse side. The old standby is Mandala's cheap dyeline trekking maps covering most of Nepal. These are barely adequate for rough navigation: villages are often missing, either on the map or in reality, and the contour lines are a travesty. Still, it can be reassuring to have a piece of paper indicating the route. To buy maps try the big tourist bookstores like Pilgrims Bookstore in Kathmandu.

Trekking Information

The best sources are returned trekkers lounging in Thamel and Pokhara's Lakeside district. For up-to-date info on more remote regions, query local trekking agencies, though you may have to hunt to find a knowledgeable one. The best general sources are the **Himalayan Rescue Association,** tel. (1) 418-755, in the Hotel Tilicho building in Thamel, and the **Kathmandu Environmental Education Project,** tel. (1) 410-303, down the next dirt road in the Potala Tourist Home. Staff at both will answer questions and provide advice on trekking, transport, timing, trail conditions, or just about any aspect of Nepal. Both KEEP and HRA maintain small libraries and sponsor frequent talks on useful topics like preventing altitude sickness or ecotourism, along with occasional slide shows, videos, and lectures. Their notice boards are helpful for trekkers searching for partners (also check signboards at restaurants around Thamel). Hours for both offices are Sun.-Fri. 10 a.m.-5 p.m.

HRA's logbooks of comments from recently returned trekkers are gold mines of information, if you can decipher the handwriting. Certain themes stand out: "It was COLD up high!" (written by most travelers Nov.-March), "Many people with altitude sickness," "Be prepared with good equipment," and finally, invariably, "Great walking!" Those who have hired porters are invariably positive about the insights this provided into Nepali culture. Many people list their favorite lodges, but such ratings are highly sub-

jective, depending on the day, the trekker's mood, and the number of other people staying at the lodge. Base your decisions on personal instinct, not others' recommendations.

More generally, the rumor network along the trail will regale you with tales of frostbite and amputations, missing trekkers and dead porters, helicopter rescues and expensive expeditions, the visits of Princess Sarah or Joan Rivers or Jimmy Carter. The celebrity treks are generally true; take the rest with many grains of salt.

PACKING FOR A TREK

Some trekkers spend as much on the latest outdoor gear as they do on their plane ticket to Kathmandu. But high-tech isn't as important as comfort, and simplicity has its own virtues. Your pack is lighter, for one thing; for another, you don't appear quite as alien to local people. Keep in mind the price of a Gore-Tex jacket exceeds the average annual income of a rural Nepali family.

Most group trekkers bring far more than they need, while independent trekkers are often unprepared and underdressed for the cold temperatures encountered up high. Make sure that by piling everything on you'll be sufficiently warm and dry at the highest altitude you're going to, even in a snowstorm. Two complete changes of clothes is a basic trekking minimum but it's nice to have more, especially shirts and socks. Forgotten necessities can probably be purchased in Kathmandu, though prices for foreign goods may be higher than you're used to.

Consult special topic "Packing Checklist" in the On the Road chapter for more trekking essentials.

Clothing

Trekkers should boost their supply of clothing to deal with temperature extremes. Aside from ignoring altitude sickness, the single biggest mistake people make is to underestimate how cold it gets up high. Start with a basic layer of T-shirt or cotton shirt/blouse, plus skirt or lightweight pants. Always remember the innate modesty of traditional Nepalis and dress accordingly. Bring long underwear, either polypropylene or silk: the bottoms make warm leggings beneath a skirt, and the set can be used as sleepwear.

From here on, start thinking in layers: a heavier shirt, a nonbulky wool sweater, a pile jacket, maybe a down vest, and a warm cap. Remember that you'll usually be warm while walking, except for places like the Thorung La on a windy day. The extra clothes are crucial for evenings and chilly mornings, especially if you're staying in a tent rather than a lodge. Metabolisms vary wildly, so figure out in advance if you get cold easily and pack accordingly.

If you're going over 3500 meters or are trekking in the winter, a pile jacket is not enough; you'll need a warm coat. The best choice is a good down jacket—it's lightweight yet warm, squeezes into a small stuff-sack, and doubles as a pillow. Look for an expedition-weight jacket if you're going high for long periods. Thamel trekking shops rent down jackets for around Rs25 a day, well worth the money to save you from freezing.

Raingear depends on the season. Spring is wetter than autumn, but occasional showers fall even in Oct.-November. The lightweight minimum is a rubberized poncho with hood, which protects both you and your pack in an emergency. A supplemental virtue is its ability to double as a groundcloth or a bedbug-proof undersheet in questionable lodges. In anything more than a brief downpour, though, poncho-wearers are soon be soaked. Often you can wait out the storm in a teashop, but on more remote trails these are few. In this case, expensive raingear comes into its own; in general, though, it's nice but not necessary.

Pick up a big plastic bag or two from the bazaar to protect your load from rain. Split open, it will provide emergency shelter for you or your porter. The crowning touch is an umbrella, which doubles as a sunshade. Small collapsible ones are easy to carry; the big black Asian variety provides maximum protection and is indispensable in the monsoon. Finally, don't forget sunglasses, sunscreen, and a brimmed hat to keep the fierce sun off your face.

Footwear

Boots, well-fitting and broken in, are a vital non-rentable trekking item. Trekking shops sell used boots, mostly the outdated, clunky leather variety. New Korean-made lightweight models are also available.

Running shoes are okay on most trails—some people even trek in flip-flops—but most trekkers favor lightweight, ankle-high, lug-soled hiking boots. Stiff leather alpine boots give extra support if you're carrying an exceptionally heavy pack over rugged terrain, but generally they just add an extra half-kg to each step. Even brand-new lightweight boots may start to dissolve after 200 km or so of Nepal's rugged trails, so bring a shoe repair kit (heavy glue and thread) or even an extra pair if you're planning an intensive trek. Village cobblers can work wonders with crumbling boots, but they're not always there when needed.

Also bring an extra pair of lightweight shoes (sneakers, thongs, Chinese slippers) to change into at the end of the day and to serve as emergency backups. Use the double-sock system: thin, slick nylon or silk socks under thick woolen socks reduce friction and cushion the feet. Bring at least four pairs: clean dry socks are essential to avoid blisters and persistent fungal infections, locally known as "Sherpa foot rot."

Sleeping Gear

Every trekker needs a sleeping bag; how warm it should be depends on season and destination. If you're doing a long trek from low to high altitudes, you'll probably find the weight you'll need up high is *too* warm in the lower valleys. Sleeping with the bag unzipped and spread over you greatly reduces heat retention. Lodges seldom have pillows, so bring an inflatable one, or stuff a sweater or down coat into your sleeping bag stuff sack.

Sleeping pads are unnecessary for lodges on the Everest, Langtang, and Annapurna trails, where lodges have mattresses. Bring them on other trails or maybe just in case—they're useful as lounging pads for rest breaks and basking in the sun. Black polyurethane pads are cheap and durable; Therma-Rest air mattresses are lightweight and make sleeping on the ground an absolute pleasure. Most trekking companies provide foam mattresses; a few ask clients to bring their own sleeping pads.

Renting Trekking Gear

Everything from boots and bags to crampons and climbing ropes is sold or rented in Kathmandu's trekking shops, some of it brand-new, some extremely used. This saves travelers on the Asian circuit from having to haul cold-weather gear around various tropical countries. But in the main season of Oct.-Nov. it may be difficult to find a top-quality warm bag or coat. Check beforehand for small holes or sticky zippers; you're responsible for returning equipment in the same condition. The shopkeeper will want a significant deposit for valuable gear, either a passport, your plane ticket, or traveler's checks. The last is preferable, in case you need your passport or ticket in an emergency.

Rental prices are pretty much standardized at around Rs35 per day for a down coat or sleeping bag, depending on quality. You'll need to leave a generous deposit, or get a referral from a local friend or company. Shops once sold good used equipment at bargain prices, but no more—with the latest catalogues on hand, proprietors are now well aware of the market value. Still, barely used expedition goods are sometimes found for 20-30% off the original price.

You can also rent sleeping pads, raingear, crampons, and ice axes, though the latter two items are rarely needed. If you're heading up to Everest, heavy boots, crampons, and ice axes are available for rent in Namche Bazaar, not that you'll necessarily need them. Annapurna trekkers can rent coats and bags in Pokhara shops, though the selection isn't as good as in Kathmandu.

Photography Tips

Trekkers should pack several sets of extra camera batteries, as cold drastically reduces battery life. Preserve them by keeping them warm in your pocket or sleeping bag at night. At freezing higher altitudes you may have to put the whole camera in your sleeping bag in order to have it thawed out for early morning shots.

The intense light of high altitude makes for some stunning photos but can generate too much contrast at midday. For a more dramatic effect, shoot in the slanting light of early morning or late afternoon. The light combines with snow to really bring out the blue tint in Ektachrome; Fujichrome or Kodachrome give better, warmer results.

Automatic metering systems may fail when confronted with exceptional situations like bright snow-covered mountains. Compensate for the glare by deliberately overexposing one or two stops, and always bracket your shots up high. You can also set the meter by reading a gray rock, a friend's sweatshirt, or a nearby wall—anything that's medium-toned and in similar light.

A final tip which may sound stupid but isn't: don't move about while looking through the viewfinder. Several trekkers have died from nasty falls taken while trying to frame the perfect shot.

HEALTH AND SAFETY

Trekking places puts you in an unusual medical situation. Not only are you exposed to risks unique to the mountain environment, you're days or even weeks away from medical care. Realize this, and go prepared. It's a good idea to take out a temporary insurance policy before you leave home. Make sure it will cover the costs of medical evacuation or helicopter rescue if necessary—an unlikely but very expensive event.

There are few opportunities for medical assistance on the trail. The Himalayan Rescue Association operates **Trekkers' Aid Posts** in Pheriche (Khumbu) and Manang (Annapurna), staffed by volunteer doctors during the spring and fall trekking seasons. Government-run village health posts offer minimal and low quality services, and are frequently either closed or out of medicine. Group treks are hopefully outfitted with medical kits, but there's no guarantee the *sirdar* or trek leader will know how to use it.

Your medical responsibility extends to your porters and trekking companions. Victims of hypothermia or altitude sickness may quickly become disoriented and unable to care for themselves. Don't send anyone back down alone if you suspect these conditions; they could easily wander off and die.

Consult "Health" in the On the Road chapter for a rundown of common illnesses and basic sanitary measures, including water treatment methods, that should be followed along the trail.

Treating Nepalis

Trekkers are often besieged with requests for *aushaadi* (medicine) from villagers who may display a specific problem or simply reel off a long list of aches and pains. It's easy to feel torn between the natural desire to help and an honest

TREKKER'S MEDICAL KIT

The following are the bare-basics essentials to take on the trail. Most items are available in Kathmandu inexpensively and without prescription; an asterisk indicates items to bring from home. Don't neglect to bring medication, as an attack of diarrhea or dysentery can spoil a trek.

antiseptic cream (Betadine): for cuts and scrapes

aspirin or paracetemol: for relief of pain and fever

Band-Aid bandages (assorted sizes)

Ciprofloxacillin: for diarrhea

codeine (30 mg): for cough, pain, diarrhea

cotton gauze pads and adhesive tape

elastic bandage: for strained knees, sprained ankles

erythromycin: broad spectrum antibiotic for strep throat, skin infections, bronchitis

Jeevan Jal: oral rehydration formula for diarrhea

Himalayan First Aid Manual, The: pocket-size guide with symptoms, treatments and specific dosages, available from the HRA office in Kathmandu

moleskin or Second Skin: for blisters

Norfloxacillin: for chest, skin infections

Pepto-Bismol tablets: for upset stomach and diarrhea

thermometer, scissors, tweezers, needle

throat lozenges: for sore throat, common at altitude

Tinidazole: for giardia and amoebic dysentery

lack of knowledge. *If* you're certain of the problem and can somehow make sure your treatment is correctly understood and carried out, it's worthwhile to help, but indiscriminately handing out antibiotics, Lomotil, even aspirin can do more harm than good. A failure can undermine belief in the system of allopathic Western medicine the government is trying to establish (not that much success has been achieved yet), while a success will just encourage a villager to ask another uninformed trekker for treatment.

Help and advice can be beneficial in a few cases. Cleaning and dressing wounds and explaining the need to do so is helpful because people can then do it themselves. Similarly, it never hurts to explain about the need for sanitation, and to emphasize rehydration treatment in diarrhea cases, especially in small children.

The traditional tendency is to restrict fluid consumption in the belief it will "dry up" the problem; too often it dries up the child, who dies.

Foot Care

Rule #1: break in your boots before you start out on the trail. Tighten the laces going downhill to reduce sliding of the toes, and wear a double pair of dry socks (thin cotton or nylon under thick wool) to reduce friction between foot and boot. Rule #2: stop to treat hot spots the moment they are sensed. If you wait until the end of a day a big blister will have developed which will take days to heal. Put moleskin or Second Skin on tender spots. Blisters need to be exposed to air, not bandaged. You can protect them with corn plasters or moleskin in which a hole has been cut out. Or, drain them with a sterilized needle, then loosely bandage the site.

A common and unpleasant occurrence is fungal infection or athlete's foot, an itchy, smelly phenomenon appearing between the toes. Avoid it by wearing clean socks, frequently washing your feet, airing shoes in the sun, and using an antifungal cream or powder at the first sign. Once it's in your boots it's hard to get rid of.

Hypothermia

Hypothermia, a decrease in the body's core temperature, can occur rapidly even in above-freezing temperatures. If you're underdressed, wet, underfed, dehydrated, and/or exhausted, your body's ability to retain heat may break down, and this condition will be aggravated by strong winds or wet clothing. Mild hypothermia begins with shivering and pale skin color. Poor coordination, apathy, and disorientation signal a further drop in the body's temperature. If not properly treated, hypothermia can result in coma and death within a few hours.

Hypothermia has killed quite a few under-dressed and poorly equipped porters who have been abandoned by the trekkers who hired them. Whether you're with a group or on your own, porters are your responsibility. The victim should immediately be warmed up. Shelter plus fire or vigorous exercise works for milder cases; more serious ones may have to be stripped of wet clothing and put in a sleeping bag with another warm body, preferably naked. Severe cases are difficult to treat, so it's crucial to recognize hypothermia before it becomes severe.

Frostbite

Frozen tissues caused by impaired circulation are often associated with hypothermia and can occur whenever temperatures are below freezing. The chances of getting frostbite are low as long as you're properly dressed, adequately fed, and moving reasonably quickly. Tight boots may cut off circulation to the toes and increase chances of frostbite, or you may risk it on high passes and summits if a snowstorm sweeps in and you're unprepared. Fingers, toes, ears, or nose are first painful and white (this is frostnip), then become progressively number. A frostbitten area requires rapid rewarming in steadily hot water, a medically delicate process that can take an hour or more. Rubbing snow on the area is a useless and dangerous procedure. As with hypothermia, the best treatment is prevention.

Hyperthermia

Clambering out of a sweltering river valley can be as debilitating as crossing a frozen pass. In hot weather, drink as much water as possible. Wear light-colored, loose cotton clothing and protect your head from the sun with a brimmed hat, or, better yet, a big black umbrella. This portable shade-maker can really cool down a sweaty walk.

Heat exhaustion occurs when too much blood is at the skin surface and too little reaches the brain, resulting in faintness, nausea, and a rapid heart rate. Rest in a cool, shady place and take in plenty of salt and liquids. Heatstroke is a genuine medical emergency in which the body's heat regulation process suddenly fails. Body temperature rises rapidly to 40.6° C (105° F) or higher, and the victim rapidly becomes disori-ented and uncoordinated. Cool as quickly as possible by dunking in cold water or employing a combination of sponging and fanning.

Sun and Snow

Nepal's sun can be a real scorcher, for several reasons. The country's southerly latitude gives the sun's rays a tropical intensity. In addition, ultraviolet exposure is higher than normal at altitudes because the thinner atmosphere filters out less of the sun's harmful wavelengths (ozone depletion may be increasing the danger here). In addition to this, snow and ice reflect incident radiation, giving a near-double dose. Most of a day's UV radiation occurs 10 a.m.-2 p.m., when the sun is directly overhead. All this means that you should use a sunscreen with PABA, even on a cloudy day, and especially when traveling over snow. Don't forget lips and ears and the underside of the nose and chin. Even the inside of the nostrils can be painfully burned.

If you're traveling over snow, wear good dark glasses to prevent snow blindness, a temporary but extremely painful condition involving sunburn of the eye. There are no symptoms during the day but 8-12 hours later the eyes begin to itch, progressing to the point where they feel as though they're filled with sand. Snow blindness will heal naturally in a few days, but it can be excruciatingly painful.

Sunglasses should have side pieces to block reflected light: improvise temporary shields with cardboard and tape if you don't have glacier glasses. Your porter's eyes need to be protected too. The local method of smearing charcoal under the eyes to reduce reflection is not enough. You can fashion makeshift goggles by cutting slits in cardboard; it's better to have an extra pair of cheap sunglasses on hand.

Helicopter Rescues

For serious medical emergencies when a patient can't walk or be carried out, a helicopter rescue may be arranged. A typical rescue runs US$1200-2000 and must be paid for by the rescuee. Your embassy or trekking agency may vouch for you, but they won't pick up the tab—a good reason to arrange for comprehensive trip insurance beforehand. Registering at your embassy before a trek greatly expedites this process.

ALTITUDE SICKNESS

One of every 500 trekkers to the Everest region once died from Acute Mountain Sickness (AMS) brought on by climbing too high, too fast. Now, increased awareness has brought the rate down to one or two deaths a year across Nepal. Much of the credit goes to the Himalayan Rescue Association or HRA, a nonprofit private organization established in the early '70s to educate trekkers about altitude-related sickness. The HRA office in the Hotel Tilicho building near Central Immigration, tel. (1) 418-755, provides information on AMS prevention and treatment and holds talks twice a day in season.

Awareness has improved to the point where a counter-syndrome is now appearing: "AMS paranoia," in which healthy trekkers flinch at every cough and headache. Deaths from AMS occur when people ignore warning signals. Your symptoms will tell you how well your body is acclimatizing to altitude; all you need to do is pay attention to them and respect your personal limits.

The atmospheric composition at high altitude is the same as at sea level (20% oxygen), but a reduction in atmospheric pressure reduces the amount of oxygen taken in with each breath. At 5500 meters, as high as any trekker will reach, you're breathing roughly half the amount of oxygen you're accustomed to. Not far above this height, the human body seems to hit a natural limit, slowly deteriorating no matter what is done. But up to this height and given time, the body will adapt through a miraculous array of physiological changes, such as increasing the production of oxygen-bearing red blood cells. You're 80% acclimatized after 10 days at high altitudes, 95% after six weeks; you lose it just about as fast as you gain it.

AMS can strike as low as 2500 meters, but most commonly it hits trekkers who fly into a high region then quickly ascend even higher—typically the Everest region. The whys of altitude sickness are still being researched. Age, sex, physical condition, and prior experience at heights seem to have no effect on who gets it—some people are just naturally more susceptible, and there's no way to predict who. Well-trained young athletes have ignored the warning signs and died from AMS, while 70-year-olds breeze into Everest Base Camp.

At least 75% of high-altitude trekkers experience mild symptoms, but if the ascent is gradual these should decrease in severity after the third day. In some two percent of cases AMS becomes serious, generally because the original milder symptoms were ignored. If you feel worse after ascending, it's a sign to stay put or descend.

Initial symptoms may include headache, fatigue, mild breathing irregularities, swelling of the hands, face and feet, loss of appetite, and drowsiness and

---

Independent trekkers should have a radio message sent to their embassy through police, national parks, or local airports. The message should include the injured person's name, passport number, and location, and the name of the person supplying the information. Describe the person's medical condition so rescuers can assess the urgency, and make sure the location is specifically described. This last detail is frequently forgotten in panicky messages, engendering an expensive search.

Trekking and Safety

Leave nonessentials in your Kathmandu hotel, assuming the people seem trustworthy. To avoid problems later, make an itemized list and have them review it, and lock up the bag. Be discreet with the valuables you do take with you, as well as the considerable amount of cash required for a long trek. A very few lodges along main trails have a bad reputation for things disappearing; most likely you'll hear about them in advance, but it's good to be consistently careful.

Group trekkers may want to lock their duffel bags with a small padlock every morning, though generally porters bundle the bag with other items to make it completely inaccessible, to you as well as everyone else. Try to keep track of your possessions so you know immediately when something turns up missing. Realizing your camera has been gone since last Thursday does little good.

Security in a tent is difficult. Keep your camera out of sight and way in the back. Items left by the door, even things like shampoo and combs, may be snatched up by children overcome by sudden temptation. Usually the large number

yawning, accompanied by restless sleep and vivid dreams. None of these are necessarily serious in themselves; they're simply warning signals telling you to slow your rate of ascent until you feel more comfortable. If you're experiencing mild discomfort, once you're above 3000 meters limit your ascent to 300 meters per day. Above 4300 meters you should never go higher than 400 meters per day, no matter how good you feel. A rest day every third day is recommended above this altitude and seems to be particularly effective in reducing AMS. The old adage "climb high, sleep low" appears to have some truth in it.

A severe headache is a clear signal to stop ascending. Descend if it persists after a second night—300-500 meters is usually sufficient. Ignoring mild symptoms and continuing higher can quickly lead to more serious complications: symptoms can include bubbly breathing signifying fluid in the lungs (pulmonary edema), severe headaches or lassitude, loss of coordination, delirium or confusion, and breathlessness even at rest. Any of these signs require *immediate* descent to a point where the symptoms ease. If things seem okay after a few days' rest, you might cautiously reascend, but give it up if symptoms reappear. Those who ignore the serious AMS symptoms for several days can lapse into a coma and die within 12 hours.

To aid acclimatization, drink plenty of fluids to counter increased dehydration. Deeper, more rapid inhalation of cold dry air increases water loss through the lungs at a rate of up to four liters per day. Drinking more can also ease nausea, a common symptom of altitude sickness. Eating plenty of carbohydrates also seems to improve adaptation to altitude. You'll probably need to make a conscious effort to eat because your appetite will be reduced. Greasy foods are especially difficult to digest up high, while sweets are usually tolerated.

HRA doctors at trekking posts may treat AMS cases with a Gamow bag, a portable hyperbaric chamber that looks somewhat like a sleeping bag. A foot pump increases the air pressure inside, simulating a descent of several thousand feet. A session in one may be enough to avert serious symptoms, or it may only defer them, in which case descent is recommended.

Avoid taking sedatives at altitude, even though difficulty sleeping is a common problem. They slow breathing and can lead to AMS. The drug Diamox (acetazolamide) reduces discomfort from minor symptoms of altitude sickness, but it doesn't speed up acclimatization or prevent AMS and in fact may merely mask the warning signals. The best course—really the only course—is to plan a slow, steady ascent with rest days built in the schedule. Rest days at 3600 meters and 4300 meters appear to be crucial to adaptation.

of trekkers and staff around a campsite deters potential thieves. Don't leave your boots outside the tent—they're very valuable items in Nepal. Bring laundry in at night too, especially nifty items like blue jeans.

A few remote places in Nepal have problems with gangs of local thieves who creep up in the middle of the night to slash tents and steal items from inside. Sometimes they even make off with the toilet tent. Trekking staff will warn you about these places in advance, and will do their best to stand watch all night.

Avoiding theft is one good reason to hire porters through a reputable trekking company rather than picking them up yourself, although local village porters are usually wonderful, completely honest men. Hiring guides and porters through a company is a reasonable guarantee of their honesty, and provides some recourse if something does disappear.

TREKKING ROUTES OF THE ANNAPURNA REGION

North of Pokhara, Nepal's spectacular diversity appears at its finest. The deep valleys and high mountains encircling the giant Annapurna Himal embrace a wide range of people and terrain, from subtropical jungle to a high, dry landscape resembling the Tibetan Plateau. This is the most popular trekking region, attracting nearly 60% of all trekkers—that's more than 44,000 visitors each year. It's also among the tamest areas, with excellent lodges lining the main routes. Finding the real Nepal beneath the flood of trekkers can be difficult at times, but the scenery and culture are top-notch, and it's possible to avoid the peak-season crush and still enjoy fine weather and views.

The region's two main trails follow river valleys in relatively easy ascents: on the west side, up the Kali Gandaki River to Jomosom and Muktinath, and to the east, up the Marsyangdi River to Manang. By crossing a high but straightforward pass, the Thorung La, these trails can be joined into the classic Annapurna Circuit. As the land climbs, thatched-roof mud-walled huts are replaced by flat-roofed stone houses, and people change from farmers to herders, Hindus to Buddhists. The Annapurna region dramatically reveals the highland/lowland frontier running across Nepal, an interface that is both geographic and cultural. Mountain views are frequent and good,

though they don't equal the heart-of-the-mountains feeling of Khumbu. This is provided by another trek, the trail up to the Annapurna Sanctuary, a secluded high-altitude hollow ringed by huge peaks.

POKHARA TO MUKTINATH

This major Himalayan highway follows the gorge of the Kali Gandaki River, crossing from subtropical jungle to high-altitude desert in less than one week. It's *the* most popular trek in Nepal, especially the first few days up to Poon Hill. Lodges are the highest standard anywhere, with private rooms, foam mattresses, enchiladas, and pizzas—even a few VCRs en route. Intermixed with the stream of international trekkers are Hindu *sadhu* and jingling mule trains heading down from Tibet laden with bales of wool.

The endpoint is the ancient shrine of Muktinath, one of Nepal's holiest pilgrimage sites. Set in thoroughly Buddhist high country, Muktinath began thousands of years ago as a natural power place, later adopted by formal religions. The old animistic beliefs still influence local Buddhism. The primordial guardian of the region was the sacred mountain **Dhaulagiri,** and its massive snowy white bulk dominates much of the trek.

BOB RACE

It would be futile to describe the region, for in exclusively mountainous countries every beauty is too extreme to be conveyed by any words that I might choose. None of the books or photographs studied before leaving home had even slightly prepared me for such majesty. Truly this is something that does have to be seen to be believed, and that once seen must be continually yearned for when left behind, becoming as incurable a fever of the spirit as malaria is to the body.
—DERVLA MURPHY, THE WAITING LAND

THE ANNAPURNA REGION

© MOON PUBLICATIONS, INC.

The Kali Gandaki gorge is considered the deepest in the world. The river flows between Dhaulagiri (8167 meters) and **Annapurna** (8091 meters), which are separated by a distance of less than 20 km, and rise six km straight up from the riverbed. Walking through here, though, doesn't provide the sensation of being in a gorge—the peaks are so steep they're incredibly foreshortened.

The Basics

Figure at least two weeks to walk in and out, and allow a few extra days for exploration—the upper region in particular is lined with fascinating villages. Flying into Jomosom and walking back down is possible, but you'd have to acclimatize before climbing to Muktinath. Flying from Jomosom to Kathmandu (US$110) or Pokhara

(US$50) is more likely now that the new airlines have relieved the bottlenecks typical of trekking season, but flights are frequently cancelled due to high winds.

The trail is in good shape, except for a few landslide-prone stretches in the middle. Aside from the notorious "killer staircase" to Ghodepani (not as bad as everyone thinks), it's neither difficult nor high. The route follows the gentle uphill course of the Kali Gandaki River, with a final climb to Muktinath at 3800 meters. Above Tukche, a strong south wind blows from late morning until sunset. It will literally propel you up the trail; the return is like leaning into a wall.

The short trek up the first portion of the trail to Ghodepani and Poon Hill has achieved cult status among trekkers. Returning from here via Ghandruk makes a nice week-long low-altitude trek. For the adventurous, side trips up from the Thak Khola offer splendid mountain views—far better than the main trail—and a taste of wilder, more remote country. You'll need a local guide, plus shelter, food, and fuel for two to seven days. Or just day hike up as far as possible. Possibilities include **Tukche** to **Dhampus Pass,** the **Dhaulagiri Icefall,** and the original **North Annapurna Base Camp** near the headwaters of the remote Mristi Khola.

To vary the return route, loop back to Pokhara through Ghandruk and Dhampus, or continue down the Kali Gandaki to Beni and on to the highway at Baglung, all in all two easy days from Taatopani. Three more days downriver is the seldom-visited hill station of **Tansen.** Most trekkers exit via the usual entry point, Birethanti and Naya Phul.

Naya Phul to Ulleri

The traditional first day of this trek has been eliminated with the completion of the new Pokhara-Baglung Highway. Catch a bus from the station at the north end of Pokhara to **Naya Phul,** a collection of teastalls huddled by the roadside. It's a half-hour walk down to the pretty riverside town of **Birethanti,** complete with riverside cafes and a pleasant place to overnight if you've gotten a late start. From here, an infamous 3,767-step stone staircase leads north up from Tirkhedhunga to Ulleri (2073 meters). It continues up through beautiful dense forest, nearly deserted apart from a few small lodges, to the pass at Ghodepani.

An alternate route would be to walk a short day from Birethanti to the interesting Gurung village of **Ghandruk,** then take a relatively new trail through incredibly lush forest, passing **Tadapani,** to join Ghodepani. See the Annapurna Sanctuary trek description for more details on this route.

Ghodepani

Ghodepani (2850 meters) is perhaps Nepal's most extreme example of a trekking ghetto. Until 1978, it was a lone cowherder's hut set in a dense forest, visited only by pack trains which watered here—thus its name, "Horse Water." Now some 30,000 trekkers tromp through here annually, and at last count 37 lodges were chopping down one hectare of rhododendron forest per year. The site is overused and littered, and sanitation is a serious problem.

Don't expect much from the village—there is none, just a collection of lodges ranging from shanty to chalet. What everyone comes for are views: **Poon Hill,** one hour's climb above, is reputed to have some of the finest mountain views in Nepal. More accurately, these are the finest views within a few days' trek. The Annapurnas and Dhaulagiri are pretty but distant, and the panorama doesn't compare with Everest or even Upper Manang on the Annapurna Circuit.

From Ghodepani the trail descends to a notch with excellent mountain views and drops to **Taatopani** (1219 meters), famed for its excellent Thakali lodges and hot springs. The cement

thatched houses

water tank is often crowded, but it's wonderful to bask in the hot water with the river rushing below and the stars glittering above. In season the lodges can be crowded as well. Local people use less-visited hot springs, 15 minutes' walk south on the Beni trail at **Raatopani.** Lodges here are a quiet alternative to touristy Taatopani.

In Nepal there are no roads and few bridges—and you really should make your will before setting foot on the ones there are. You climb and descend the whole time: from the depths of the valley to the summit, from the summit to the valley two or three times a day.
—Giuseppe Tucci,
Journey to Mustang

From this point on the trail follows the Kali Gandaki, climbing past the waterfall of **Rupse Chaharo** to cross the river as it swirls through the steep gorge. The next stretch can be a real cliff-hanger if frequent landslides have wiped out the trail.

Ghasa, with its entrance *chorten* and small *gompa,* is the trail's first Thakali village. Its flat roofs are a clear signal of the region's diminishing rainfall. The Kali Gandaki soon becomes broad and tranquil, a meandering river instead of a rushing torrent. Between Ghasa and the pretty Thakali villages of **Lete** and **Kaalopani** the land changes dramatically, as dense jungle is replaced by pine forests, followed by the dry vegetation of the Tibetan Plateau. The villages themselves are more Tibetan-influenced, a shift which will become increasingly distinct. Lete is directly below Dhaulagiri, and thus at the heart of the world's deepest river gorge.

The Thak Khola

The broad valley of the Kali Gandaki is called the Thak Khola, and its people, the Thakali, are distantly related to Tibetans. The men are famed as traders; the women once operated simple teahouses *(bhatti)* on the lower trails in winter months, known for their good cooking and cleanliness. When foreign trekkers arrived, the Thakali simply transferred their *bhatti* experience to running lodges, expanded their menus, and raked in the money.

Tukche (2590 meters) is a major Thakali settlement, once a linchpin of the Kali Gandaki trade route, as demonstrated by its name, "Flat Place for Grains." Here wool, salt, and turquoise from Tibet were swapped for rice, cloth, and cigarettes from lowland Nepal. Four powerful Thakali families granted special dispensations by the government ran the trade. Since the Chinese takeover of Tibet, the enterprising Thakalis have shifted to other lucrative enterprises. Many have left their homeland for good, leaving their old houses in the hands of caretakers.

Tukche's neglected old Buddhist shrines indicate the Thakali's 19th-century switch to Hinduism in their rise to power. The oldest is the **Rani Gompa,** first built in 1621 and now on the verge of collapse. There's a small **Mahakali**

the broad valley of the Kali Gandaki near Ghasa

MUSTANG

This remote and wildly beautiful region north of Jomosom was closed to foreigners for over 30 years before its recent opening inspired a rush to "be the first" to penetrate its aura of mystery and allure. Set in a dramatic landscape, its rich Tibetan culture included several exceptional ancient monasteries and the only walled city in the Himalaya.

The kingdom of Mustang (pronounced "MOO-stahng") was founded in the 15th century by King Ame Pal, carved out from territory ruled by local warlords. Strategically located to dominate a local trade route, Mustang remained remote enough from Kathmandu to be left to its own devices, remaining a semi-autonomous kingdom into the '60s. Increased government control was provoked by the arrival of the Tibetan guerrilla fighters who settled here in Manang and in Dolpo in the 1960s and made forays into Chinese-occupied Tibet. The "inner line" created along Nepal's northern border in 1962 to prevent foreigners from contacting the rebel Tibetans put Mustang off limits to trekkers, along with much of northern Nepal. It remained an isolated and mysterious kingdom until its opening in 1992.

The government approach has emphasized re-stricted and big-bucks tourism. Trekkers must travel in groups with a registered agency accompanied by a liaison officer, and must pay a royalty of US$70 a day for the trip (usually 10 days). The original restriction of 400 permits a year has been upped to 1,000.

Groups fly into Jomosom and walk north up the Kali Gandaki, though an increasingly stark landscape. The Annapurna and Dhaulagiri massifs block monsoonal rains from this region, creating a desert environment typical of Tibet, right down to the bare open spaces and dazzlingly clear light. Permits are checked at Kagbeni, the last open village. The trail proceeds past villages like **Chele** and **Tangbe**, surrounded by little plots of wheat, barley, and buckwheat nurtured by irrigation. Lower Mustang's inhabitants call themselves Gurung, and while they are Bhotia, they are less Tibetanized than the Loba found higher up.

Further upvalley the culture becomes increasingly Tibetan, right down to the vicious chained mastiffs that should be treated with great respect. The trail crosses several passes of around 4000 meters before reaching the large settlement of **Cha-**

Gompa in the center of town; at the north end is the **Gompa Sarpa,** once a big monastery.

Less than two hours up the trail is **Marpha** (2665 meters), a fascinating collection of stone houses, prayer flags, and neatly paved streets with an elegant system of covered sewers. Marphalis are related to Thakalis and own most of the mule trains seen on the trail. They're known for apple and peach "brandy" (actually excellent *raksi*) produced from nearby orchards. Across the river, the Tibetan settlement at **Chaira** is home to the souvenir vendors seen all along the trail; there's an 18th-century *gompa* here with an image of Padmasambhava.

From Marpha on up, beginning daily around 11 a.m., a gritty wind of up to 40 kph gusts north-ward up the trail. You may want to start out earlier to avoid it, especially on the return trip.

The next town is **Jomosom** (2713 meters), a drab government headquarters with dozens of offices, a bank, and a few fancy hotels near its STOL airstrip, including a "Jimi Hendrix Restaurant." The name is the Nepali corruption of Dzong Sarpa, Tibetan for "New Fort." The old section of town across the river, with some less luxurious lodges, is mildly more interesting. Try to visit the **Jomoson Eco-Museum,** south of the airport and atop a hill. It has exhibits on the area, a good if small library, and even a video library where you can watch documentaries on the region. A Tibetan doctor practices in an office in the compound. If you've got

BOB RACE

rang with its spectacular ruins of an ancient palace and decrepit local monastery featuring some fine frescoes.

From here it's a half-day's walk to the capital of **Lo Manthang,** a unique collection of mud-walled buildings huddled within seven-meter-high walls crowned by watchtowers. The town's narrow winding streets are a timeless labyrinth. Look for the four-storied **palace** of King Jigme Paldor Bista just inside the main gate, adorned by an aluminium sign proclaiming "Hearty Welcome." A direct descendant of King Ame Pal, the king is a modern-day Renaissance man, acting as arbitrator, scholar, spokesman, and horseman. It may be possible to arrange an appointment with him: bring a *khatak* or prayer scarf as a sign of respect, and a gift like a bottle of rum or some fruit.

Lo Manthang holds two ancient 14th-century *gompa* adorned with classical wall frescoes, statues, and *thangka,* decaying but still stunning. The tall, ochre-walled **Jampa Lhakhang** features a 15-meter-high image of Maitreya, the Coming Buddha, and walls covered with elaborate mandala patterns. The walls of the nearby chant hall of **Thugchen** are covered with exquisite images of Buddhist deities. An overnight trip can be made to the abandoned *gompa* of **Luri,** though it must be written in the permit in advance. The small chapel is set in a natural rock tower eroded from spectacular cliffs, and is adorned with a unique collection of magnificent frescoes.

Mustang is a stunningly beautiful but harsh place to live in. Its 6,000 people cobble together a living from agriculture, summer grazing, and winter trade in lower regions. Residents petitioned Nepal's king to open the region to trekking in the hope this would benefit the local economy, but as only self-sufficient groups are admitted, only a few families benefit, primarily those wealthy enough to rent out horses and mules as pack animals.

More resentment was generated by the fact that the steep trekking royalties originally went straight to the central government. The highly regarded Annapurna Conservation Area Project has now been put in charge of the region and is supposed to receive a portion of these revenues. Its mission is to improve local standards of living and help people benefit from the introduction of tourism. ACAP's first plans are to help restore Lo Manthang's crumbling *gompa,* to develop alternative energy systems, and to improve irrigation systems in order to increase the availability of food.

---

time to kill here, hike two km east to **Thinigaon,** a large Tibetan-style village with an annual Yak Dance held in early fall. The *gompa* above this town is finely decorated and preserves all sorts of relics, including five terra-cotta images said to be from Samye Monastery in Tibet, one of Guru Rinpoche's slippers, and the skull of a high lama imprinted with the Tibetan vowel 'AH'. Another interesting place, some two hours' walk from Jomosom, is the secluded village of **Lupra,** site of a very old Bönpo *gompa.*

En Route to Muktinath

The trail continues upriver through desolate barren landscape to **Eklai Bhatti** ("Alone Inn") and forks, with the right-hand trail going directly to Muktinath. It's worthwhile to take the half-hour detour at the fork to **Kagbeni** (2810 meters), an old medieval fortress town on the riverside. Kagbeni was once the center of an independent kingdom, as its ruined palace testifies. With its central wall of prayer wheels and close-packed mud-walled houses bristling with stacked firewood, it's hard to find a more Tibetan-feeling town in Nepal. In the crumbling Sakya monastery here, Giuseppe Tucci found 15th-century frescoes and mounds of ancient bronzes, both probably long gone.

A checkpost here prevents independent travelers from crossing the river and continuing north into the legendary region of **Mustang,** open to groups whose members pay US$70 a day for the privilege. Gaze over the strangely eroded and colored hills folding off into the distance—"fascinatingly ugly country, the more fascinating for being so little known," wrote H.W. Tilman. Geologically and culturally, Mustang is Tibetan. China conceded it to Nepal in the 1950s on the basis of a small annual tribute paid by its king, but it remained semi-autonomous well into the '60s.

Muktinath and Vicinity

From Kagbeni a trail leads up into a lovely high valley dominated by the ruined fortress of **Jharkot.** Less than an hour further is the sacred pilgrimage site of Muktinath (3800 meters). There's no real village, but lodges around the lower portion, known as **Ranipauwa,** put up pilgrims and trekkers.

This ancient holy site is a typically confusing blend of natural, Buddhist, and Hindu beliefs. The little Newar-style pagoda to Vishnu is a relatively recent addition. Muktinath has been sacred for over 2,000 years; the Mahabharata mentions it as Shaligrama, "Place of the Shaligram," the black fossil-stones sacred to Vishnu and found in abundance in the Kali Gandaki valley. Its holiness stems from flickering blue flames of natural methane gas burning on water, stone, and earth, and now enclosed in the shrine of Jwala Mai below the Vishnu temple.

Near the pagoda a sacred spring spurts out through 108 spouts shaped like bulls' heads. Devout pilgrims bathe in the freezing water to purify their sins and earn *mukti* or spiritual liberation. The place has ancient associations for Buddhists as well: Guru Rinpoche is said to have passed through here en route to Tibet, leaving his footprints in a rock; the 84 Siddhas dropped their wooden staffs, which magically sprang up as the surrounding poplar grove. There are many old Buddhist temples around here, including an eerie, abandoned shrine filled with crumbling yet serene terra-cotta images.

The six small villages of the Muktinath Valley deserve some extra time for exploration. The magically clear light makes the area absolutely radiant in good weather. Women weaving on the flat rooftops of local homes may try to sell woolen blankets or Tibetan artifacts; most of the latter are the usual junk brought up from Kathmandu. The Pompo Yartung festival (usually the August full moon) draws locals dressed in splendid finery for a day of *chang*-drinking, singing, dancing, and daring horse racing.

The valley's head is guarded by twin peaks flanking the Thorung La. The pass is usually crossed from Manang, but this side is possible if you're well-acclimatized and in good shape. In the main season a few teashops are open slightly higher up at the foot of the moraine; overnighting here gives you a head start. See "The Annapurna Circuit," below, for a discussion of the pass.

MANANG

This trek is usually described as the first portion of the Annapurna Circuit, but it stands as a worthy destination on its own. Slightly shorter than the Muktinath trail, it offers the same combination of lowland Hindu and highland Buddhist villages, a similar cultural and geographic diversity, and even more spectacular mountain views. Upper Manang is more rugged and less populated than the upper Kali Gandaki, and even more evocative of highland Tibet. Finally, Buddhism here is much more active, and Manang's monasteries are among the most intriguing in Nepal.

Upper Manang has a fairly wild recent history. Early visitors like Tilman and Snellgrove commented on the rude reception they received from villagers here, and a starving Maurice Herzog was sent back up to Tilicho Tal without a bit of food. The region above Chame was closed to trekkers until 1977, due to Khampa guerrillas who controlled the valley for over a decade. Before that, an armed feud between Braga and Manang made it unsafe for visitors. Nowadays Manangis welcome trekkers with open arms, due more to an innate respect for trade than any sense of hospitality.

Manangis began international trading in 1784, when a royal edict exempted them from customs and gave them unprecedented freedom to travel. They began by exporting herbs and musk to Southeast Asia; eventually they were bringing back gold, semiprecious stones, and Swiss watches. Visiting Manang in the early '50s, Toni Hagen was astonished to discover a remote valley full of Nepalis wearing gold Swiss watches, who, when he pulled out his camera, pulled out their own and took photos of him!

Though their privileges have been curtailed, Manangis remain Nepal's premier traders, specializing in Asian fashions, gold, and electronic goods. Rumor is that they built a special tunnel underneath the new airport to expedite customs. Not surprisingly, this is an exceptionally cosmopolitan mountain community, where young men in jean jackets mix with farmers and herders. Increasingly, Manangis are leaving their remote district to settle in more central locations, and Tibetans, Gurungs, and Bhotias take their place as tenant farmers and caretakers.

The Basics

Two weeks would give a little extra time to spend in Braga and Manang. There's an airstrip at **Ongre,** below Manang, but flights (US$88) are generally charters. Lodges are not quite as deluxe as on the Jomosom side, but are comfortable and abundant. Be sure to pack sufficiently warm clothing if you're crossing the Thorung La (hat, gloves, thick socks, down coat).

In places, the trail adheres to the wall of a narrow gorge. Portions were once death-defyingly narrow, but blasting has expanded them into reasonably safe trails.

Any further north, above Chame snow piles up in winter, and local people start heading to lower settlements by mid-November. A late monsoon trek in the rainshadow region of Upper Manang would avoid the crowds and much of the rain, if you're lucky.

The first step is to get to the dusty little roadside town of **Dumre,** a five-hour bus ride from Kathmandu or two hours from Pokhara. Dumre is, frankly speaking, a charmless roadside dump.

Gurung girls in Bagarchhap

CHRISTOPHER GAMM

Once off the bus, most trekkers immediately buy a ticket on a local truck, jeep, or bus to Besisahar, Rs150-250. The five- to seven-hour ride up the rutted road is bone-rattling and often obscenely crowded; many trekkers consider it the worst part of the entire trip. It may be better to walk for a day and a half along the trail paralleling the road, perhaps veering off to visit the hilltop Gurung town of **Ghan Pokhari.** From Pokhara, you could walk to Besisahar in two to three days starting from Begnas Tal following a network of trails that weave east through the lowland hills. This is interesting and seldom-trekked country; either take a guide or be prepared to constantly ask directions.

Besisahar to Chame

Besisahar (823 meters) is a typically unattractive little roadhead boomtown. The first two days of walking wind through typical hill country inhabited by Gurungs and Hindu castes; this lowland portion is hot in springtime. The trail begins climbing around **Bhulbhule.** Past **Bahundanda** and **Syangje** (1072 meters) the steep trail cuts across a sheer-walled gorge. Once the route here went over wooden planks lashed to the rock wall; it's been improved but is still steep and narrow.

The water buffalo and rice paddies continue up to **Chamje** (1433 meters); then forests of huge oaks take over as the valley narrows and the scenery becomes more spectacular. The village of **Tal** is set in a broad valley at the foot of a waterfall. The trail steadily rises through cooler zones, changing from pine forest to open meadows, and finally dry rainshadow. At **Dharapani** is the first of many entrance and exit *chorten* marking Manang's Buddhist villages. **Bagarchhap** (2164 meters) is an interesting village with a newish Nyingma *gompa* with nice frescoes. Houses here are both flat-roofed stone and sloped-roof wood, the latter soon vanishing in the higher, drier country ahead.

Tucked into a side valley up from **Kotoje** is the fascinating off-limits region of **Nar-Phu,** one of the three traditional regions of Manang. There's a guard post here to make sure you don't visit it, as it falls within the government-decreed restricted zone. *Cloud Dwellers of the Himalayas* (see Booklist) provides an excellent account of life in this secluded area.

The district headquarters of Chame (2685 meters) has a police post, bank, various government offices, lodges advertising 24-hour hot showers, and the biggest shops of the entire trail. Prices are reasonable here, but they rise as you go higher. There's a shallow but good set of hot springs near the trail before Chame, and another within reach of the town.

Chame to Manang

Beyond Chame are extensive apple orchards; spectacular views of the Annapurnas begin here and remain all the way to Manang. Cross the river just before **Bratang,** which until 1975 was inhabited by Khampa rebels who virtually controlled the trail from this outpost. Ahead, the trail passes through a superb pine forest to **Pisang** (3185 meters), the first village in Manang proper. The lower town has most of the lodges, but the upper portion, 100 meters higher and across the river, is the real village, with stone houses surrounding an old *gompa.* It's worth climbing up just for the views of the Annapurnas. Above the town towers the trekking peak of Pisang.

From here on you're in the rainshadow area of Nyeshang (Manang's traditional name), a dry 20-km-long strip of land with an average altitude of 3500 meters. From upper Pisang, a trail climbs steeply through fields to **Gyaru** (3700 meters), with more great views of Annapurna, and continues on through **Ngawal** to Braga. Practically everyone skips this wonderful high route in favor of a faster, duller trail from lower Pisang, which leads past **Ongre** with its rarely used STOL airstrip. A half-hour further down the lower trail a **Trekker's Aid Post** operates out of a mountaineering school set up with Yugoslav assistance in 1980.

The two trails join just before **Braga** (3505 meters), a spectacular collection of flat-roofed houses stacked up against steep cliffs. With its ochre and white *mani* walls, prayer wheels, and *chorten,* Braga is incredibly picturesque. Chulu East rises across the river; directly behind is Annapurna III. The town is dominated by a spectacularly located **Kargyü Gompa,** the largest in Manang and over 500 years old. In the main temple, 108 terra-cotta images surround statues of Tara, Samantabhadra, and Mahakala.

Few trekkers stay in this fascinating place; the lure of nearby Manang pulls them north. There aren't many standard tourist lodges in Braga, but it's easy to find a house where you can sleep on the floor or (less smoky) on the roof. There are lots of day-trips into the mountains behind, topped by cairns crowned with prayer flags. On a ridgetop between Braga and Manang is **Bodzo Gompa,** the most active in the region and, like Braga's, over five centuries old. The marvelous old frescoes admired by Snellgrove have been touched up by a heavy hand.

Manang to Phedi

Manang (3350 meters), the unofficial capital of the region, is a half-hour past Braga, about 500 houses huddled together with plenty of lodges

Braga village, Manang

CHRISTOPHER GAMM

and shops, though it's hardly a shopping mecca and is much smaller than many trekkers expect. Mountain views are again spectacular, with a foreshortened Annapurna and Gangapurna looming over town and Chulu East and West across the river. To the south is a full-on view of the north side of the Annapurnas, including steep hanging glaciers cascading down between Annapurna IV and III. Manang's *gompa* is moderately interesting, but nothing like Braga's, though you can get a "blessing cord" here to wear when crossing the pass.

Trekkers crossing the Thorung La usually stay at least a day in Manang to acclimatize. There are lots of good day-trips: a small **glacial lake** across the river; the village of **Khangsar,** five km west; and the ridge north of town, which offers views of Annapurna IV and II and Glacier Dome. The HRA post in Manang, staffed by Western doctors, offers talks each afternoon on altitude sickness that are well worth attending.

The next stop after Manang is usually Phedi (4404 meters), a two-lodge stop at the foot of the Thorung La, which is otherwise known as the "Trekkers' Penal Colony." The main lodge is poorly managed, windy, and crowded, and a good night's sleep is virtually impossible, given the quantities of trekkers who rise noisily at 3 a.m. in order to get over the pass early. Such efforts are unnecessary, and indeed foolish—the pass is normally a four- or five-hour ascent and a three- or four-hour descent, a long but not impossible day. Many trekkers now prefer to stay at **Lattar,** an hour before Phedi. While this makes the following day slightly longer, you'll probably sleep better the night before, and there's a wider choice of lodges.

THE ANNAPURNA CIRCUIT

This classic 330-km walk combines the Manang and Muktinath treks described above by crossing the 5380-meter Thorung La. It's an extraordinary trek, one of the world's best in terms of cultural and environmental diversity, requiring at least two weeks and preferably three. It's also extraordinarily popular, and the Thorung La's limited open season crams everyone into the fall and spring months, when it is more justifiably called the "Annapurna Circus." This has its ad-

vantages—comfortable lodges, no need to take a guide, guaranteed company along the way—and its disadvantages as well.

Nearly everyone does the circuit counterclockwise, crossing the pass from Manang and exiting through the Kali Gandaki valley. Coming over the pass from the east, you're higher and presumably better acclimatized, and the net ascent over the pass is 979 meters, compared to 1578 meters from Muktinath. Too many trekkers rush through Manang, not realizing this side has the best mountain views of the entire trek. Go slow and enjoy; take a few rest days in scenic locations like Braga, Manang, Muktinath, Kagbeni, or Marpha.

The pass *is* definitely crossable from Muktinath if you're well-acclimatized and in good shape. Going in the reverse takes you out of the flow. Instead, you'll be passing trekkers the whole way—and saying "Bonjour, G'day, Namaste" all day long, which can be as tiring as traveling with the same batch of people for three weeks.

Whichever side you choose, the Thorung La deserves some respect as the highest commonly trekked pass in Nepal. Get briefed on altitude sickness, and be prepared for extreme weather, as snowstorms can roll in unexpectedly. The guy who thought it was the "Thong La" and went over it in flip-flops is legendarily foolish. You'll need good boots, warm clothing, and sunglasses. Take care of your porter as well: lowland Nepalis are usually woefully unprepared for altitude, and every year a few porters die from exposure or altitude sickness because their employers figured they knew what they were doing and ignored them. Most of these tragedies occur on the Thorung La.

The trail over the pass is steep but in good shape and not hard to follow. This is the one point of the entire circuit when you feel really *in* the mountains, which might compensate for the thin air. If altitude isn't a problem the day-long crossing is not difficult, but many people find themselves gasping for air and moving painfully slowly. Snow is a possibility, and you might find a walking stick or ski pole helpful. Coming down may prove harder than the ascent. The first lodge is just below the moraine, about an hour from Muktinath. Carry a flashlight in case you get in late.

IN ACAP LAND

The area around the Annapurna Himal is the most highly impacted trekking region in Nepal. Over 40,000 people live off the land, and the equal number of foreign travelers who trek through yearly only increases environmental pressures. Sensing the potential for ecological disaster, the **Annapurna Conservation Area Project (ACAP)** was launched in 1986 with the intent of improving local living standards, protecting the environment, and educating trekkers on what they can do to help—or at least not harm—the region. On a 1990 trek, I discovered first-hand what ACAP is doing to promote these ideas.

Two days north of Pokhara we begin hearing talk of "Yeh-Kap." It takes some time for me to equate this with the Annapurna Conservation Area Project (ACAP). The first mention is in a Landruk lodge, as our young host agonizes over raising his modest prices. He asks us earnestly why foreigners who have traveled halfway around the world at tremendous expense will argue over one or two rupees, try to bargain down the cost of a bed, always seek the cheapest lodges, and sometimes walk out on the bill. "Don't they understand that this is how we make our living?" he asks in genuine bewilderment.

Then he tells us how a lodgeowners' committee in Chomrong sponsored by ACAP has established standard prices to avoid the bitter competition common along main trails. Many lodgekeepers provide services below cost, neglecting to charge for the wood they chop, the water they haul, the vegetables and milk they produce. "Since they didn't have to buy it, they think of it as free," he says.

The next day we reach Chomrong, an idyllic village with Swiss-chalet lodges and gorgeous flowers framing mountain views. One lodge here heats its water with solar power; most others have back-boiler water heaters installed behind the wood-burning kitchen stove. This marvelously simple system uses convection to pull water through the pipes, heating it without burning extra wood. These innovations have been introduced by ACAP, which has also banned the use of firewood above Chomrong. Campers and group treks may burn only kerosene; even porters cook with it, and though they may furtively build a small fire at night for warmth, it's nothing like their usual bonfire.

Our Gurung lodgekeeper proudly shows off lami-nated certificates from an ACAP-sponsored lodge-owner's training program and a month-long English course. Discovering that lodgekeepers often had no inkling as to why tourists visit Nepal, ACAP addressed the subject directly; as a result, local people are now more motivated to preserve their environment and culture.

In town we pick up a leaflet describing more about ACAP, which deals with trekkers as well as locals, distributing brochures and selling maps and a guide to regional wildlife. In addition, ACAP collects Rs650 from each trekker in the Annapurnas. The fee is paid when obtaining a trekking permit from Central Immigration, but unlike regular permit fees absorbed by the central government, the money goes directly to the project, and the region.

Ghandruk is a tidy village of several hundred slate-roofed houses perched on a hillside high above the Modi Khola. A thin veneer of trekking culture is laid atop traditional subsistence agriculture: women thresh wheat in courtyards and boys drive water buffalo up the muddy trails.

We ask our lodgekeeper about ACAP. "Up until now, it's been good," he says, typically cautious about anything perceived as government (actually ACAP is a private, nonprofit organization). Then his eyes light up as he lists what ACAP has done in Ghandruk: built a water tap and installed a water system, brought in furniture for the village school, improved trails, installed rubbish bins, planted trees; and, he triumphantly concludes, a micro-hydropower project has supplied electricity to the town.

While he credits ACAP, all this was actually accomplished by local people. ACAP provides support and encouragement, supplies matching funds for projects, and accepts donated labor in place of cash. Villagers thus have an incentive to use and maintain what they've built themselves, and they generally do. The idea is to have ACAP motivate: the community gets to decide exactly how it wants to develop.

The next day we visit ACAP's field office in Ghandruk. By a stroke of luck program director Chandra Gurung happens to be in town for a few days and explains the beginning of ACAP. Dr. Gurung combines a local perspective (he grew up in the village of Siklis) with a Ph.D. in human geography from the University of Hawaii. He tells us project designers spent four months in the field talking with people, and soon concluded the standard National Park model would prove too disruptive to the region's inhabitants. Instead, a multiple-use approach was adopted to balance the diverse needs of local people, trekkers, and the environment that accommodates both.

Most important has been the emphasis on fulfilling local needs, unusual for a conservation project, but essential in Nepal. "Without addressing local needs, we knew there would be no cooperation," Gurung said—and without local participation, the project would fail. By repairing schools and trails and constructing water taps and health centers, ACAP built up local trust, creating a base for conservation efforts. To deal with issues like woodcutting and forestry, community groups have been formed with ACAP's encouragement and support to make decisions on their own—such as the effort to revive traditional systems of regulating forest use, which virtually disappeared after Nepal's forests were nationalized in the late '50s. These have proven remarkably effective in mobilizing local leadership abilities. The Ghandruk Forest Management Committee won the 1992 J.P. Getty Foundation award, along with a US$25,000 prize.

While ACAP is involved in a wide array of projects, its managers are careful not to spread efforts too thin. The original pilot focused on the heavily impacted 200 square km of the upper Annapurna Sanctuary. ACAP has slowly expanded to cover 800 square km, establishing more regional centers like Ghandruk's. Gurung is eloquent regarding ACAP's ultimate goal: "To create a small Utopia where all needs are available, an area that is fully protected and conserved, where people, forests, and wildlife all live together in a harmonious manner." The vision does sound Utopian, but ACAP's flexible, locally based approach holds much promise.

Sudden snowstorms can shut the pass down unexpectedly, so keep an eye on conditions and be ready to turn back if things get bad. The pass is generally uncrossable Jan.-March or into mid-April some years, though local people will often plough a yak trail through the snow. In other years the snowfall is insignificant and it's crossable, though freezing cold, all winter long.

THE ANNAPURNA SANCTUARY

In many ways this is *the* ideal trek: lovely, short, and intense, a direct route into the heart of the Himalaya compressing the best of Nepal's diversity into less than two weeks of walking. Spectacular mountain vistas and easy access—the Sanctuary is only five days' walk from Pokhara—make it among the most popular of treks. Not surprisingly, the fragile alpine environment of the upper Sanctuary is suffering from overuse. Up to 40 trekkers arrive daily in season at the upper "base camps," and the crowding is compounded by the single narrow entry-exit trail.

The Sanctuary is a hidden pocket of meadow, moraine, and glacier, ringed by magnificent sheer-walled peaks: the Annapurnas, Gangapurna, Machhapuchhare, Hiuchuli. This is the sacred land of the native Gurung people, the abode of their gods. Traditionally, no women or low-caste men were allowed past here, impure foods like meat, eggs, and garlic were forbidden, and hunting and butchering were prohibited. The Sanctuary must have been an idyllic place, a haven for wildlife and wildflowers, visited only by a few shepherds who brought their flocks up to graze summer meadows. It's shocking to see the hordes passing through here nowadays (including plenty of women and garlic). Some Gurungs darkly attribute misfortunes—anything from trekking deaths to crop failures—to their sanctum's violation. Certainly the amount of litter on the trail is enough to enrage even a god.

The Basics

A single trail enters the Sanctuary between a high-walled mountain gorge, a portal cut between Machhapuchhare and Hiuchuli. The trail rises nearly 2000 meters in the last eight km, necessitating slow going for purposes of acclimatization. Winter trekking is unlikely here as the trail is frequently slippery and the danger of avalanches in a few places lingers into early spring. Accommodations in the lower portion, especially Chomrong, are deluxe; the upper stretch is understandably simple—after all, nobody lives up here full time. Bring good boots and warm clothes for the upper portion, as you may encounter snow.

It's possible to gallop up the trail and back in 10 days from Pokhara, *if* you're already acclimatized from a previous trek. Otherwise, allot something closer to two weeks. If you don't want to go high or are short on time, an idyllic lower circuit from Dhampus-Chomrong-Ghandruk-Birethanti can be done in less than a week; add a few more days to visit Ghodepani and Poon Hill.

The Trail

From the Jomosom trail, other trails lead off from Chandrakot, Birethanti, Tirkedhunga, and Ghodepani. From Pokhara, take a bus to Naya Bazaar on the Baglung Road and walk to Birethanti, then up to Ghandruk. Or, catch a jeep or taxi to **Phedi** and climb up to the small ridgetop village of **Dhampus,** a nice place to stay if you've gotten a late start. The trail crests a pass and drops to **Landruk,** pure Gurung hillbilly, then descends to the Modi Khola.

Across and higher up is the interesting village of Ghandruk, best visited on returning in order to avoid a steep climb. Take the trail leading upriver, crossing and climbing *very* steeply for several hours up to **Chomrong** (2050 meters), a lovely Alpine-style village with a few chaletlike lodges. Chomrong is a great place to hang out for a few days, perhaps visiting the hot springs at **Jhinu Danda** on the bank of the Modi Khola—clean, deep hot water, set in lush jungle. The village of Jhinu, which has a few lodges of its own, is an hour below Chomrong.

Chomrong is the last permanent settlement, and a good place to wait if the upper trail is blocked by snow or avalanches. Until recently only shepherds went above here; now seasonal lodges line the trail. Facilities are simple, and standardized rates set by ACAP preclude competition. Unless you're coming off a high trek you'll have to go slowly to acclimatize, but the distance isn't that far—only two days' walking.

The Sanctuary's unofficial entrance is past **Dhovan,** where a small *chorten* and prayer flags honor guardian spirit Pujinam Barahar. Local men passing by will leave a little rice or strips of red cloth here, offerings for safety and good luck.

A few hours further is **Machhapuchhare Base Camp,** a fictional name, since there's been only one expedition to Machhapuchhare (described in special topic "Tail of the Fish," under "Pokhara" in the Beyond the Valley section). Two hours further is **Annapurna Base Camp** (4130 meters). Mountain views are considered slightly better at the latter, but it's not likely you'll be dissatisfied with either. To get the best out of the trek, and to ensure good acclimatization, spend a night at each. Sheer mountain peaks ring the bowl of the Sanctuary: Hiuchuli, Annapurna South, Fang, Annapurna I, Annapurna II, Machhapuchhare.

Returning, vary the route by visiting **Ghandruk** (2012 meters), several hundred tidy slate-roofed houses perched on a hillside. One of the largest Gurung towns in Nepal, it's worth an extra day to explore. From Ghandruk a relatively new route leads through lush, nearly virgin jungle and forest to Ghodepani, a long day's walk with only one stopping place en route, the lodges of **Tadapani.** Or you could continue south a few hours to **Birethanti,** a half-hour's walk from the Pokhara-Baglung Highway.

(top) thatched hut by Pokhara's lakeside, Machhapuchhare in background (Kerry Moran);
(bottom left) boys on swing, eastern Nepal (Kerry Moran);
(bottom right) sunset over the Rapti River, Chitwan National Park (Kerry Moran)

Ghandruk, as seen on the Annapurna Sanctuary trek (Kerry Moran)

TREKKING ROUTES OF THE EVEREST REGION: SOLU-KHUMBU

This classic walk through the Sherpa homeland of Solu-Khumbu is a tough trek with a clear-cut goal—to see Everest. Many people find the snoutlike Everest outranked by peaks like Ama Dablam and the Lhotse-Nuptse wall. Khumbu is the best major region in Nepal for close-up mountain views. Enshrined in **Sagarmatha National Park,** it's visited by some 14,000 trekkers yearly—a mere handful compared to the number of visitors to the Annapurna region.

Most Everest trekkers avoid the hardest walking by flying in and out of the crowded Lukla airstrip. If you've got the time and energy, the walk-in from Jiri through the traditional Sherpa homeland is worth the extra effort. It passes through the lovely southern region called **Solu** and the narrow gorge of the Dudh Kosi **(Pharak)** to reach the high mountain region of Khumbu in a little over a week. Khumbu is an exceptionally high-altitude region, with trekking routes going up to 5400 meters. Here you don't just cross a high pass and descend; you *stay* high for a week or more.

While Solu can be trekked year-round, Khumbu's season is limited. Most trekkers pour in during Oct.-Nov. and March-May, which offers festivals like the five-day Dumje celebration (usually April) and the masked Mani Rimdu dances held at several monasteries. Winters are cold, and you may not be able to go above Tengboche between mid-December and mid-February, but in some dry years little or no snow falls and higher lodges stay open. Khumbu is an excellent choice for a monsoon trek: high pastures are full of wildflowers and grazing yaks, and the people are relaxed and happy, taking a break from trekking and expedition work.

Solu-Khumbu's rugged landscape and high altitude are intimidating, and nearly half of Everest trekkers come on organized treks. The entire route is set up for teahouse trekking, however, with a full selection of lodges. Those in Namche Bazaar have electricity, hot showers, and fresh cinnamon rolls; above here, simpler stone huts predominate. Independent trekkers may actually be better off in Khumbu, since tents aren't very enjoyable above 4000 meters, and groups often end up crowding into lodges.

Namche Bazaar is the nerve center of Upper Khumbu: from here, trails branch out to explore at least four separate high valleys. It's a cosmopolitan little village, a good place to pick up tips on trails and conditions from descending trekkers. Food prices skyrocket above here, since all supplies must be carried in from a distance; budget extra for this trip.

Getting There

The approach to Everest is a classic case of the encroaching road. Originally the trail started in Bhaktapur; with the construction of the Arniko Rajmarg it moved up to Laamosanghu. Now it's been pushed to the hill town of **Jiri,** and nobody seems to miss the week of hill walking that's been chopped off. The hilly 65-km road was built by the Swiss as part of a foreign aid package of projects focused on Jiri and its surrounding hills. The district headquarters of **Charikot** lies up a short spur about halfway down along this road; an hour's walk from it is the Newar trade entrepôt of **Dolakha.**

The bus to Jiri is the longest ride to a popular trailhead, 10 hours of hell (modified if you sit on top). There are frequent reports of theft on this bus, so watch your pack: tie it down or tie it with a friend's, sit on top of the bus, or bring the pack inside. Jiri consists of a single long street with a Wild West flavor, lined with shops and lodges. Try the **Mt. Everest Lodge,** which has a top-floor restaurant overlooking the street. Ask your lodgekeeper or enquire around the bazaar if you want a porter.

Flying into **Lukla** chops nearly a week off the trek, plummeting you within a long day of Namche Bazaar. Altitude problems seem to increase with fly-ins, however, and during peak season flights are heavily booked. If you plan to fly in only one way, it's best to fly into Lukla and walk out in order to avoid hassles. Going against the flow is a good way to beat the system and miss the crowds. Most groups fly into Lukla in mid-October and in early April; thus there are plenty of flights going back empty to Kathmandu at these times, and you can often walk in and buy a ticket. Three weeks later the airport is crammed with returning groups; it's a good time to fly in, but don't count on getting out.

Helicopters fly twice a week to **Syangboche** just above Namche Bazaar—a bit too high for safe acclimatization, but an easy out from Khumbu. Another option is to fly in or out of **Phaplu** (US$77), which cuts off the first three hard days from Jiri and puts you in the best part of Solu.

The excellent **Hostellerie des Sherpa** lodge near the Phaplu airstrip makes a great destination in itself. The trail north joins the main trail at Ringmo, passing **Chiwong Gompa** en route. Backtracking a few hours to visit Junbesi is worth it if you've got the time.

Finally, increasing numbers of trekkers are taking the week-long backdoor route out to eastern Nepal, and flying back from Tumlingtar or busing back from Hille (see "Eastern Nepal" in "Off the Beaten Track"). This varies the route if you've walked in from Jiri; if you flew into Lukla, the Solu route makes a more interesting return.

THE SHERPAS

The Sherpas are probably the best known and most admired of all Nepal's ethnic groups. Sir Edmund Hillary has described their homeland of Khumbu as "the most surveyed, examined, blood-taken, anthropologically dissected area in the world." According to their oral history Sherpas migrated to the high valleys south of Mt. Everest from eastern Tibet about 450 years ago, hence the name Sharpa, "People from the East." Their language, customs, and religion reflect their Tibetan origins. Sherpas follow the Nyingma school of Tibetan Buddhism devoted to Guru Rinpoche, and ancient beliefs linger as well. The Sherpa homeland is still dominated by the old mountain gods, the most sacred being Numbur in Solu and Khumbi-lha in Khumbu.

Sherpas have long known how to maximize the potential of Khumbu's fragile mountain environment, farming on lower slopes and herding hardy yak and crossbred cattle up high. The shortfall was made up by skillful trading with nearby Tibet. This system collapsed with the Chinese occupation of Tibet, but in a stroke of fortune, foreign mountaineers were allowed to enter Khumbu at precisely the same time. Already famed for their work on British expeditions in the Indian Himalaya, Sherpas were quick to profit from new opportunities. The development of trekking has provided an added boon, a way to earn money without the danger of expedition work. Today up to 85% of households in some villages have members working in trekking and mountaineering.

Over 10,000 tourists visited Khumbu in 1992; that's one for every two of Solu-Khumbu's Sherpas. Inevitably, Sherpa life is changing with increased exposure to outsiders—Nepalis as well as tourists. Milk tea is replacing salt tea; jeans and down coats are worn instead of *chuba,* and many Sherpas now prefer rice, imported at high prices, rather than the staple potato. Expedition *sirdar* have

a Sherpa-run trekker's lodge, Junbesi

CHRISTOPHER GAMM

SOLU: JIRI TO NAMCHE BAZAAR

With its rolling hills and broad valleys covered with fields and forests, the Solu region provides a gentle counterpoint to starkly spectacular Khumbu. Moderate altitudes (2600-3200 meters) and a mild climate make even a winter trek here feasible. Prosperous Solu is as bountiful as Nepal's Hills get, and a visit here offers insights into Sherpa life you won't get in touristy Khumbu. Its impressive stone houses verge on mansions, some with private chapels as fine as any *gompa*. As an added plus, Solu is the center of a recent religious revival, with some of the finest Buddhist monasteries in Nepal.

The trail cuts across the grain of the land, heading east over north-south river valleys and ridges. Steep and seemingly endless, the ups and downs create incredible leg muscles by the time you reach Namche; it takes extra determination to walk this route. Lodges range from adequate to idyllic, with extras like apple pie and cheese factories to cheer up hedonists. Figure on at least a week to walk from Jiri to Namche, and add an extra day for exploring around Junbesi.

Trekkers cluster on the main trail to Everest, but there are many other possibilities. Study the Schneider maps or talk to local Sherpas for ideas. An alternate and perhaps more interesting route to Junbesi drops down from Bhandar to cross the Likhu Khola to the south and climb through **Goli Gompa**, along a ridge that is parallel to, but south of, the one leading to the Lamjura pass. The last settlement is the marvelously named **Ngowur** (as in "middle of"). With a tent, stove, and food you can linger on the next long day's walk, which ascends below the viewpoint of **Pike** (4070 meters) to Pangbuk, then drops through pine and rhododendron forests to Junbesi. Either the Schneider *Tamba Kosi-Likhu Khola* sheet or a guide is essential.

Jiri to Junbesi

See "Getting There" above for a description of the Kathmandu-Jiri bus trip. Jiri (1905 meters) is the homeland of the Jirels, a small ethic group of some 8,000 people with a language similar to that of the Sherpas. Set in a small valley, the town consists of a single long, wide road lined by dozens of lodges catering to both tourists and Nepalis. There a weekly *haat bazaar* is held Saturday on the field just below the police checkpost; onions and potatoes are the main commodities.

From Jiri the trail plunges straight into the hills, twisting through **Shivalaya** and climbing to

---

become the new upper class, nudging aside the old landed wealth, and plastic expedition barrels stand beside copper pots in many Sherpa homes.

These changes are cosmetic, however. Most observers agree Sherpas are adjusting remarkably well to rapid change, adopting material benefits while retaining the essence of their identity. Religion remains a focal point of society. Unlike many traditional cultures, the Sherpa cultural renaissance was quite recent. It was fueled, oddly enough, by the 18th-century introduction of the New World's potato, which supported a virtual population explosion in Khumbu. The sudden surplus of wealth and energy was channeled into the construction of Buddhist *gompa*: six have been built in Solu in the past 50 years, many now headed by active reincarnate lamas or *tulku*.

Anthropologist James Fisher feels the rapid rate of change has actually intensified Sherpa identity, forcing them to consciously determine their values. It helps that Westerners are such vociferous ad-mirers of the Sherpas' good humor, stamina, and common sense. Sherpas themselves have a slightly bemused view of their fans. Many are mystified by the expense and effort tourists make to visit Khumbu. "Don't you have mountains in your own country?" they frequently ask. Certain sayings reveal a pragmatic attitude, like one related by Fisher: "Like cattle, tourists give good milk, but only if they are well-fed." Another Sherpa told me: "You people are like eggs—white on the outside, but you must be taken care of because you break easily."

Their open, casteless society has eased the adaptation; so has a Buddhist sense of equanimity. Citing their "gaiety and friendliness, their tolerance and kindness toward each other," anthropologist Christoph Von Fürer-Haimendorf called traditional Sherpa society "one of the most harmonious I had ever known." It appears to be stronger and more resilient than that of most traditional peoples. So far, Sherpas seem to be successfully walking the thin line between tradition and modernity.

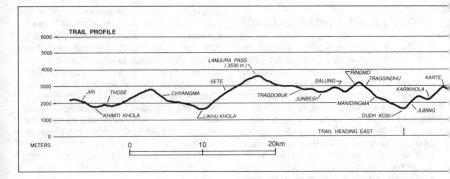

TRAIL PROFILE

LAMJURA PASS (3530 m)

RINGMO
SETE
SALUNG
TRAGSINDHU
KARTE
JIRI
THOSE
CHYANGMA
KARIKHOLA
TRAGDOBUK
JUNBESI
MANIDINGMA
KHIMTI KHOLA
LIKHU KHOLA
DUDH KOSI
JUBING

TRAIL HEADING EAST

METERS   0   10   20km

a 2713-meter pass of **Deorali.** A small cheese factory and *gompa* are about 45 minutes' walk above here. Below, the quaint village of **Bhandar,** marked with mossy *chorten,* nestles in a broad, bowl-shaped tableland. The trail passes through the riverside town of **Kenja** (1634 meters), then begins a seemingly endless climb up a huge ridge, the first of many on this trek. The little village of **Sete** (2575 meters) is the usual stopping place. It's worth a 15-minute detour to visit the nearby *gompa.* Continue climbing through rhododendron forests (and watch out for poison rhododendron honey in the lodges) to top the **Lamjura Pass** (3530 meters) and descend into Solu.

The charming village of Junbesi two hours away is an excellent place to spend an extra day or two, with good lodges and interesting sur-roundings. The **Junbesi Gompa** is quite impressive for a town this size, with imaginative frescoes and a two-story image of Shakyamuni Buddha flanked by Chenrezig and Guru Rinpoche.

Day-trips from Junbesi

A 90-minute walk up the valley is the large and active monastery of **Thupten Choling,** an authentic Tibetan establishment transplanted in the 1960s from Rongbuk Monastery on the north side of Mt. Everest. That establishment was totally destroyed by the Chinese, but the monks had time enough to make a deliberate move, bringing yak loads of books, paintings, ritual objects, silver and gold, and settling in this idyllic site.

Tulsi Rinpoche, one of Rongbuk's abbots, directed the rebuilding of the monastery. Some 150 monks and many nuns and lay practition-

Junbesi village, Solu

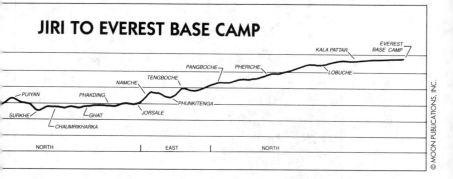

JIRI TO EVEREST BASE CAMP

EVEREST BASE CAMP

KALA PATTAR

PANGBOCHE — PHERICHE

TENGBOCHE — LOBUCHE

NAMCHE

PUIYAN — PHAKDING

PHUNKITENGA

SURKHE — GHAT — JORSALE

CHAUMRIKHARKA

NORTH | EAST | NORTH

© MOON PUBLICATIONS, INC.

ers live in small dwellings clustered around the *gompa,* monks on one side, nuns on the other. Local Sherpas gather for frequent rituals held here, when the place takes on the air of a medieval temple fair. The wall paintings inside the main shrine are lovely; this is the finest monastery in Solu-Khumbu, far more authentic than touristy Tengboche. Ask a monk for a prayer scarf *(khatak)* if you want to meet Tulsi Rinpoche.

Another day-walk is to **Chiwong Gompa,** about three hours southeast, set atop steep cliffs overlooking Phaplu. The masked Mani Rimdu dances held here every fall are less crowded than Tengboche's.

The Junbesi Valley is dominated by the white spire of **Numbur** (6959 meters) or **Shorung Yul Lha,** the "country god" of Solu. From Junbesi it's a two-day walk up to the sacred pilgrimage site of **Dudh Kund** at the foot of the Numbur glacier. Pilgrims flock here for the Janaai Purnima festival in August to perform *puja* and circumambulate the lake. This site has spectacular views of the steep, ice-covered faces of Numbur and Karyolung. A return trail ends up at Ringmo. Take tent, stove, food, and a local guide from Junbesi.

Ringmo to Karikhola

From Junbesi the trail rounds the Sallung Ridge for a first glimpse of Mt. Everest. Pass through the small apple-oriented village of Ringmo, serving pie, juice, pancakes, and cake, to cross the **Tragsindhu La** (3071 meters). Just over the pass is a thriving little religious community of some 50 monks and nuns. Exquisite murals painted by the same artists who did Thupten Choling decorate the *lhakhang.* You may have to

ask around for the key. The slightly dilapidated lodge is run by a nun who grew up here before there was even a *gompa.*

Most trekkers stay in the **cheese factory** just before the pass and down a short side trail. It's run by a Jirel family who serve homemade bread, pie, yoghurt, and cheese (sometimes a bit underdone). Trail conversations all the way from Namche tend to revolve around what to order here: raclette? grilled cheese? apple pie?

From the pass the trail descends through an idyllic forest to **Nuntala** (also called **Manidingma**) and drops down a knee-jarring 1500 meters to cross the Dudh Kosi River draining Khumbu. Next are the pastoral little Rai village of **Jubing** and the busy bazaar town of Karikhola.

From here the trail enters the region of **Pharak,** an interim zone between Solu and Khumbu following the narrow gorge of the Dudh Kosi. This area seems gloomy and slightly poorer than Solu, partly because clouds tend to gather and the sun rises late and sets early. The trail continues its steep ups and downs past minor villages: **Poiyan** is a ghetto compared to most places on this trail. Try to make it to **Surke,** a pleasant riverside stop. Namche Bazaar is one day's walk north of here; most people take longer. The side trail from Lukla joins this main trail at **Chaumrikarkha;** the remainder of the route to Namche is described below.

KHUMBU

Upper Khumbu is a land of dazzling light and immense spaces, of highland valleys ringed by soaring snow-covered peaks, including three of

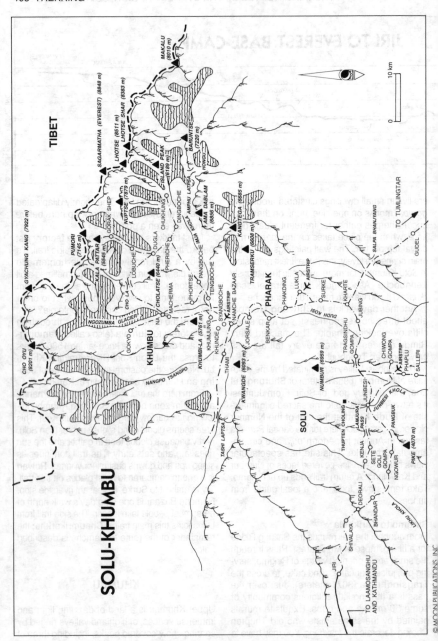

SOLU-KHUMBU

the world's seven highest mountains (Everest, Lhotse, and Cho Oyu). No other trek in Nepal equals its feeling of being in the mountains. Instead of admiring them from a distance you walk amid them, and the shifting perspectives are endlessly fascinating.

> *I felt like I could go like this forever, that life had little better to offer than to march day after day in unknown country to an unattainable goal.*
>
> —H.W. TILMAN

The Sherpas say Khumbu was once a *beI-yul,* one of the sanctuaries set aside by Guru Rinpoche for Buddhists in times of trouble. The outer valley was opened and settled hundreds of years ago, but the inner, secret one is invisible; perhaps this accounts for the magical feeling permeating this high region.

The upper Khumbu region is spared the steep ups and downs of Solu, and the walking is not particularly rugged, but as the highest of the main trekking regions, with an average altitude of over 5000 meters, Khumbu's altitude knocks many people out. Those flying into Lukla seem particularly vulnerable. Go slowly, plan rest days at strategic altitudes, and watch your body's adaptation.

The unofficial headquarters of the region is the relatively new village of **Namche Bazaar.** From here, trails fan out into four different highland valleys, each offering stunning mountain scenery and glimpses of Sherpa culture. It takes about a week to visit Everest Base Camp, Chukhung, or Gokyo separately; combining them saves some walking time. The fourth valley, and the village of Thami, is only a day's walk from Namche. Visit as many of them as possible; these high regions are the payoff for the long trek in from Jiri.

Lukla

The flight to Lukla (2850 meters) is an adventure in itself: the runway and the village are set on a small shelf halfway up a high mountain, and surrounding peaks seem to rise up rapidly to meet the descending aircraft. Passengers are plopped down in the highlands without the week's walk from Jiri, but spare a thought for those walking the tortuous switchbacks below.

Lukla life revolves around the airstrip, where a dozen flights may land daily in peak season. Trekkers stuck here waiting for a flight may go stir-crazy, but there are a few diversions: the Thursday *haat bazaar* is as interesting as Namche's—in fact, it's the same one: porters move up to Ghat on Friday and sell their goods in Namche on Saturday. Day walks include the steep trail over the **Kaalo Himal** just east of town (the beginning of the trek to Hongu), or the drop down to visit **Surke** on the main trail.

Lukla's deluxe lodges increase and improve yearly. The **Sherpa Coffee Shop** beside the airfield serves cinnamon rolls to trekkers anxiously awaiting their morning flight. All in all, Lukla has come a long way from the *luk la* or "sheep place" it was a few decades ago. The airfield was built in 1964 by local people with Sir Edmund Hillary in order to receive materials for a construction project involving a half-dozen of Solu-Khumbu's schools—his expression of gratitude to the Sherpa people who assisted his Everest ascent.

Namche Bazaar

From Lukla it's a long day to Namche Bazaar and you'd have to start early in the morning to make it. Most groups overnight in **Phakding.** The Sagarmatha National Park entrance is at **Jorsale,** where video cameras are subject to a Rs3000 entry fee. Crossing the Dudh Kosi, the trail climbs steeply to Namche Bazaar, with a glimpse of Everest halfway up to cheer you on.

Namche Bazaar (3446 meters) is the modern Sherpa capital, a collection of houses, lodges, and shops set in a horseshoe-shaped natural amphitheater facing the splendid Lumding Himal, with Tramserku and Kangtega peeking over the rim behind. Namche is the ultimate of trekking villages, its shops stocked with paperback novels, eight kinds of chocolate, and fake Tibetan jewelry from Kathmandu. Here you can rent trekking gear for higher up—convenient for walk-ins from Jiri. Some find the town overly commercialized, and many Sherpas will tell you "all Namche people do is think about money." Still, most trekkers enjoy spending an acclimatization day here revelling in the deluxe lodges, cinnamon rolls, and shopping opportunities.

The **visitor's center** at Sagarmatha National Park headquarters, atop a hill east of town, has informative displays on local life and geology. Saturday's *haat bazaar* is the week's big event, as lowland porters and local Sherpas meet to haggle over grain, Chinese goods, and fresh yak meat. By early afternoon people are drifting away to *chang* shops to catch up on the week's gossip.

Khumjung, Khunde, And Everest View Hotel

If Namche's commercialism seems too gross, take refuge in Khumjung (3780 meters), an hour's walk over the hill but a world away. Khumjung and its sister village Khunde are bastions of traditional Sherpa life, rows of stone houses nestled just below the sacred mountain Khumbi-la. The few small lodges in town are hard to find, but local families are happy to put you up if you can convince them you don't mind old houses like theirs. If you're lucky they'll cook *riki kur*, crispy potato pancakes served with yak butter and yoghurt.

The trail to Khumjung passes the **Syangboche airstrip** above Namche. Perched above it on a ridge with stunning views is the "highest hotel in the world," the Everest View Hotel (3870 meters). Reopened under Japanese management, the hotel boasts views of Everest, Lhotse, and Ama Dablam from every room and bathroom. Clients are generally flown in directly to Syangboche (US$160) and walk, or rather stagger, up to the hotel. A number have nearly keeled over from the abrupt altitude change, but the hotel now has a pressurized Gamow Bag to treat serious cases. Rooms are US$120 per person, but the surrounding area has some great views for free.

Tengboche Gompa

Most trekkers make the beautiful one-day walk from Namche to Tengboche Gompa, through a thick forest where you may spot nearly tame *danphe* pheasants. Founded in 1912 as a secluded meditation retreat, the monastery has become one of the premier tourist destinations in Nepal. Perched on a ridge and ringed by spectacular peaks, it's in an absolutely stunning natural setting, guarded by Khumbila and Kangtega, with Ama Dablam and the Everest massif rising in the northeast. The *gompa*'s dual

TENGBOCHE'S MANI RIMDU

Mani Rimdu involves a 19-day cycle of intense *puja* invoking the protection and blessings of the compassionate bodhisattva Pawa Chenrezig upon the Sherpa community of Khumbu. Held during the ninth Tibetan month (usually late October), the highlight is the masked dance-drama retelling the story of the introduction of Buddhism to Tibet by Guru Rinpoche. Good and evil clash in the meetings of costumed demons and deities, and the demons are conquered and converted into protectors of Buddhism. The story line depicts Buddhism's historical victory over the old Bön religion. It's also a richly symbolic interpretation of the psychological and spiritual growth of the mind. The dense layers of meaning would be difficult to digest were they not delivered in the colorful, dramatic form of ritual dance. Laypeople may not be able to explain the esoteric significance of Mani Rimdu, but everyone watches the familiar scenes with rapt attention, aware of their spiritual significance. Mani Rimdu is also a great social event, drawing Sherpas from surrounding villages and Kathmandu to celebrate their reunion with days of feasting and drinking.

The dance is preceded by the creation of a mandala delineating sacred space, and by the consecration of sacred *rilbu*, small "pills" distributed with blessings by Tengboche Rinpoche to the Sherpa community on full-moon day. The *rilbu* are supposed to bring spiritual blessings and wisdom as well as health and long life. The following morning the dances begin, a visual drama of 16 sequential acts, each illustrating a different chapter of the story. Dancers play the eight manifestations of Guru Rinpoche, and spiritual beings like *dakini* and protectors of the Dharma. Comic relief is provided by a skit of a yogi teaching a thick-headed novice. The dances conclude with a final purification ceremony to disperse negative influences. The next day is the Fire Ceremony. A culminating offering of *torma* or sacrificial cakes is burned on a juniper fire, the mandala is dissolved and its sand distributed as blessings, and people slowly drift back to their homes.

Tengboche Gompa after the 1989 fire

identity creates some bemusing juxtapostions: prayer flags beside a solar-heated lodge; stupas along a helicopter landing pad; and a sign atop a wall of engraved prayer stones reading "Please do not stand on the *mani* wall."

Tengboche's recent history provides a mini-moral in the dangers of rapid modernization. A small hydroelectric station funded by the American Himalayan Foundation was inaugurated here with much fanfare in April 1988. Nine months later the main temple burned to the ground, in a fire probably started by an unattended space heater. With its lama and most of its monks in Kathmandu for a religious event, few people were left on the scene to save things. About 80% of the *gompa*'s artifacts were destroyed, including irreplaceable treasures from Tibet like hand-lettered scriptures, dance costumes, images, and the magnificent frescoes adorning the interior walls.

Local and international contributions funded the construction of a new and larger *gompa* that was opened in 1992. Redesigned and enlarged

to suit its modern functions, the new *gompa* relied on traditional construction techniques and craftspeople. It will take years for the interior to attain the elaborate level of decoration of the old *gompa,* though.

Tengboche remains the cultural and religious center of Khumbu under the leadership of its abbot, the Tengboche Rinpoche, who has sponsored efforts like a *shedra* or school for 25 young monks, and a **Sherpa Cultural Center** featuring exhibits for visitors. The *gompa* suffered a slump in the '70s when most of its monks left to work in trekking, but it's now back to over 40 monks. Every autumn the Mani Rimdu dances held here retell the ancient story of Buddhism's conquest over the Bön religion, drawing hundreds of tourists and Sherpas. The same dances, less crowded but equally interesting, are held at Solu's Chiwong Gompa a month later, and at Thami Gompa in May.

Tengboche's accommodations include a glassed-in **National Park Lodge** and a slightly funkier monastery lodge where old monks cook up "yak steak" (generally buffalo meat) in the big kitchen-dining hall, and Ama Dablam and Everest peer through the windows of the dormitory.

To Everest Base Camp

The trail continues past the small nunnery of **Deboche** to **Pangboche** village, with its old *gompa* built over the hermitage of Khumbu's saint, Lama Sanga Dorje. The juniper trees on either side are said to have sprung from hair he cut off his head, while a rooflike rock projection is a piece of the mountainside he pulled out for shelter one day. Yeti relics preserved here were sent to Europe for scientific examination and pronounced to be the 200-year-old skin of a Himalayan serow.

Pheriche (4252 meters), the next stop, once existed only as a summer yak-herders settlement. Today it's a dull but crowded trekkers' huddle, as it's at just the right altitude for an extra acclimatization day. The **Trekkers' Aid Post** here gives talks on altitude sickness every afternoon in season. A day-trip up the Imja Khola to Dingboche and **Chukhung,** described below, is good recreation.

The main trail continues northwest and curves slightly to cross the terminal moraine of the Khumbu Glacier. A day from Pheriche is **Lobuche**

EVEREST

The world's highest peak was discovered in 1852, when routine calculations of the Survey of India revealed a remote mountain on Nepal's northern frontier to be something over 29,000 feet (it has been exactly fixed at 8848 meters). Peak XV, as it was labeled on the survey's map, was so isolated no local name could be found. Everest was nothing special to the Sherpas, who live surrounded by dozens of great peaks. (The Nepali—or more precisely, Sanskrit—name Sagarmatha, "Brow of the Oceans," was appended only a few decades ago.) Tibetans living on the northern side had a number of names for the mountain, though efforts to translate them ran aground. The list includes "Cooking Pan of the Queen of the Five Sister Goddesses" and "Wind Goddess." Best-known is Jomolungma, poetically rendered as "Mother Goddess of the Earth," though "Valley Goddess" would be more accurate. (One Englishman insisted the name was Jomo Langma, "Lady Cow.") Survey officials took the prudent course and named the mountain after their recently retired boss, Sir George Everest.

The first British reconnaissance expedition arrived on the mountain's north side in 1921, shivering genteelly in the tweedy outdoor wear of the era. Seeing a photo of an early Everest expedition, George Bernard Shaw commented that it looked "like a picnic in Connemara surprised by a snowstorm." They returned the following year with a full-fledged expedition, carrying among other things five mule loads of copper coins and a store of 24 Homburg hats, considered the most direct way to the hearts of Tibetan government officials.

Early expeditions resembled war rather than sport, organized like a military campaign and relying on an arsenal of equipment and an army of porters. Parties laid siege against the mountain and attempted to batter it into submission. More often, they would beat themselves into exhaustion against the frozen immensity of Everest.

Eleven major unsuccessful expeditions were mounted over the next three decades. The Chinese takeover of Tibet sealed off access to the north side, but in a masterful coincidence, Nepal had begun admitting foreign climbers only a few years before. The southern side of Everest seemed doubtful at first, but a straightforward route was soon discovered and expeditions embarked on the race to the summit. New Zealand beekeeper Edmund Hillary and Sherpa Tenzin Norgay won the prize in 1953.

Six decades of Everest attempts make for good reading, beginning with George Mallory's eloquent accounts of the first British expeditions. Members of the 1963 American Expedition were overtaken by

(4930 meters), with a few sometimes crowded lodges. A little further is the lakelet of **Gorak Shep**, with more lodges. Either place provides a base for a day hike up to **Kala Pattar** (5545 meters). This spur running from the peak of Pumori provides an incredible overview: the Khumbu glacier cascading down below, the broad snout of Everest, and Lhotse, a wedding-cake fantasy of swirling snow and ice. Sitting up here, watching distant avalanches dropping clouds of powdery snow, you feel on top of the world.

You can walk up the Khumbu Glacier to Everest Base Camp, a very long day hike from Lobuche or four hours from Gorak Shep. However, the mountain is blocked from view and there's not much to see besides expedition camps, their accompanying litter, and across the way, the dangerous **Khumbu Icefall**, scene of most fatalities on Everest—generally of Sherpa porters.

Gokyo

This alternate route heads up the Dudh Kosi Valley, crowned by Cho Oyu (8201 meters) and its companion peak Gyachung Kang (7922 meters). Gokyo vs. Kala Pattar is a favorite argument: those who have visited both seem to rate Gokyo slightly higher, as it puts Everest in true perspective amid its array of companion peaks. Despite this it gets fewer trekkers; the lure of Everest Base Camp is too strong.

You can access Gokyo most directly from Kala Pattar by crossing the 5420-meter **Cho La**, a high route which is do-able if you're fit and equipped. Intermediate lodges make it possible to travel from Gokyo to Lobuche in one long day, but don't try this route if there's too much snow; crevasses may be hidden, and the trail is unclear in portions.

The standard route is to backtrack downvalley and round the ridge through **Phortse** to enter the

darkness after a successful ascent. They miraculously survived an open bivouac at 8000 meters, though two members paid the price with their toes. The late '70s saw the first successful "climbing-style" attempt without oxygen or fixed camps by Reinholdt Messner and Peter Haebeler. In 1980 Messner returned to solo the mountain in four days without oxygen, part of his successful bid to solo all 14 of the world's 8000-meter peaks.

More recently, the advent of guide-led commercial climbing has been making things crowded atop Everest's summit. A single day in May 1992 saw 32 climbers from four expeditions reach the easy "tourist route," or "yak route," as it's disparagingly called. Nowadays, it seems, it takes only money, inclination, and a reasonable degree of fitness to summit Everest, though the amount of the former is increasing. The Nepali government has raised royalties to US$50,000 per expedition and limited numbers to one team on each route at a time.

Climbers struggle to distinguish themselves from other summiteers by using increasingly inventive methods. Everest has been done in winter, without oxygen, solo and solo without oxygen, live on television, on skis, and by paraplane. If these attempts seem contrived, consider the reaction of the locals mystified by the straightforward early expeditions. Hugh Ruttledge, the leader of an early British expedition, noted that every Tibetan they met asked what the party was doing in such a remote region. All were incredulous at the reply that they hoped to climb Everest. ("We must improve upon our story," concluded Ruttledge.) The Western view of mountains as a challenge, a test of the human spirit, is utterly foreign to people dwelling in their shadows, who respect and fear them too much to lay foot on them. Most Sherpas will privately admit they climb for the money rather than the thrill. The lama of Rongbuk met the first British expedition in 1924, and was astonished at their determination to accomplish such an odd goal. "I was filled with great compassion for their lot, who underwent such suffering for unnecessary work," he wrote in his journal, resolving to pray for their future conversion to Buddhism.

Just why humans continue to hurl themselves against Everest and other high peaks remains a mystery that has inspired countless eloquent answers, including Maurice Herzog's *Annapurna* and the quotes assembled in *Everest: The West Ridge*. It was George Mallory, who vanished high atop Everest in 1924, who gave the cryptic reply, "Because it is there!" Whether it was a veiled metaphysical observation or an impatient brush-off is still a matter of contention, but it's as articulate an answer as any.

Dudh Kosi valley. From Namche, head directly up via Khumjung, and pace yourself—it's easy to ascend too quickly. By either trail it's a three or four-day walk. Take the trail on the valley's west side, which has more lodges and teashops; the eastern side is virtually deserted. Head through small summer herding settlements to skirt the giant **Ngozumba Glacier** and arrive at a series of small lakes.

Gokyo (4750 meters), a tiny herding settlement by the third lake, has several lodges, including the deluxe **Gokyo Resort,** outfitted with a glass-walled sun room and a shop selling champagne. Climb 5318-meter **Gokyo Ri** for views of Cho Oyu, Everest, Lhotse, and Makalu, plus a host of smaller peaks. Several more lakes and **Cho Oyu Base Camp** lie north up the glacier.

Chukhung and the Imja Valley

This side valley branching off from the Everest Base Camp route is a good day walk from Pheriche. It's also a splendid and little-traveled destination in itself, with some unique mountain views. Cross the ridge east of Pheriche to **Dingboche** and continue up the steep-walled valley of the Imja Khola. Ama Dablam appears to the south with yet another bewitching perspective. A few hours later are the small lodges of **Chukhung** (4734 meters), with views of Lhotse-Nuptse and Island Peak. Overnight here and climb **Chukhung Ri** (5043 meters) to the north for breathtaking views of the Lhotse-Nuptse wall in total solitude. Further up the valley is **Island Peak** (Imja Tse, 6189 meters), climbable if you've got gear and are comfortable using an ice axe, crampons, and rope. (Of course you need a trekking peak permit, too.) With a good map, you can hike along the edge of glaciers into a wilderness of peaks. Across from Island Peak is the 5780-meter **Amphu Laptsa,** leading into the remote and wild **Hongu Valley.**

Thami

This is the easiest of all walks above Namche—warm and low, with relatively few mountain views. It takes three to four hours to reach Thami, but not many trekkers go up here. The trail heads west around the ridge behind Namche and continues north up the Nangpo Tsangpo valley through small villages. Above **Mende** is a *gompa* and retreat center associated with the Himalayan Yoga Institute in Kathmandu. Cross the river and climb steeply to Thami (3780 meters), Tenzin Norgay's hometown. **Thami**

Gompa is above the village, set in a rock wall facing several gigantic waterfalls cascading down Kongde Ri. It's a spectacular setting for the Mani Rimdu dances performed during the May full moon, an event that's as colorful as Tengboche's, and less crowded with tourists. To the west, the Thami River descends from the treacherous **Tashi Laptsa** (5755 meters) leading into the Rolwaling Valley. The valley north of Thami is also restricted: two days' walk north is the broad **Nangpa La** pass into Tibet, a virtual highway through the Himalaya.

Mani Rimdu mask

BOB RACE

TREKKING ROUTES NORTH OF KATHMANDU

Less than 30 km northeast of the capital are three relatively short yet interesting treks, ideal for trekkers with limited time. This region is generally bypassed in favor of Annapurna and Everest, which means trails are less crowded, yet there are plenty of simple lodges along the main routes to serve independent trekkers. The easy access doesn't mean you lose out on quality. **Langtang** in particular is among the finest mountain treks anyone could hope for, a high, mountain-ringed valley only four days' walk from Kathmandu. **Helambu,** a Sherpa area northeast of Kathmandu, and the sacred lake of **Gosainkund** high atop an open ridge, are admittedly more minor treks, shorter than Langtang, but worthwhile in themselves. Langtang, Gosainkund, and the northern reaches of Helambu are all included in the boundaries of **Langtang National Park.**

The regions are usually visited separately but can be combined into a trip of as little as 16 days if high passes are open. Lower regions like Helambu are perfect for winter treks, and in springtime this region's rhododendrons are especially showy. The people are a mixture of Tamang, Sherpa, and Bhotia largely unaffected by the closeness of Kathmandu. Food and lodging are easily available along the main routes. A few high passes require carrying some food and possibly shelter, but usually herders' huts and rock overhangs can be found for an overnight on the trail.

LANGTANG

This region extends north of Helambu all the way up to the Tibetan border. Langtang National Park protects a typical example of a high Himalayan valley. At minimum it's a 10-day trip, counting transportation time and a day above Kyangjin, but really you should allot more time for further explorations out of Kyangjin. The trek is entirely teahouse-able, but a tent, stove and some provisions would provide greater freedom up high or allow crossing the Gangtsa La into Helambu.

Getting There

The Trisuli road is a gut-wrenching, twisty route with one of the highest nausea rates in all Nepal—be careful who you sit next to. Buses to Dhunche leave from Kathmandu's bus park around 7 a.m. and arrive 7-10 hours later. Watch your packs, and keep your trekking permits handy as there are several checkposts along the way. It's also possible to take a different bus from Kathmandu all the way to Syabrubensi, cutting a day's walking off the trek, but adding another 90 minutes of bus ride.

The usual lunch stop is in the old trading town of **Trisuli,** unimpressive at first glance, but the quaint old stone-paved bazaar behind the main road is worth a look. If you need to overnight here, try **Hotel Trisuli,** which lies up a bumpy dirt

looking down on the Langtang River

CHRISTOPHER GAMM

road two km before the bridge to Trisuli; look for the sign on the right. Clean, sunny rooms with bath are Rs250 s, Rs300 d; Rs100 cheaper with common bath. An hour's hike uphill is **Nuwakot,** a pleasant hilltop village that's the site of the **Sat Talle Durbar,** a seven-story fortress of Prithvi Narayan Shah's.

The highway's pavement runs out after Trisuli, and the road bumps and winds through Betrawati, Ramche, and finally **Dhunche,** a nondescript little district headquarters and roadhead packed with dumpy trekking lodges. Most popular by far is **Hotel Langtang View,** with

pizza on the menu and a free trekking map showing times between places and the exact locations of teashops and landslides. The Langtang National Park entry office in Dhunche checks permits and receipts for the Rs650 entry fee payable at Central Immigration.

Dhunche to Langtang

The route begins with an uninspiring walk down the untrafficked road, then starts to climb through patchy forests and Tamang villages, "Tamang" being widely applied to a range of Bhotia people populating this region. **Syabru,** the first night's

LANGTANG, HELAMBU, AND GOSAINKUND

LANGTANG II (6571 m)

LANGTANG LIRUNG (7246 m)

YALA

DORJE LHAKPA (6990 m)

GHODE TABELA

LANGTANG

KYANGJIN

LANGSISA

SYABRUBENSI

LANGTANG KHOLA

GANGTSA LA

PHURBI CHYACHU (6722 m)

DHUNCHE

ISYABRU

SING GOMPA

GOSAINKUND

PHEDI

PANCH POKHARI

MALEMCHIGAON

GOSAINKUND

TRISULI RIVER

THAREPATI

TARKEGHYANG

HELAMBU

THIMBU

TARSA

BETRAWATI

KUTUMSANG

SHERMATHANG

TRISULI

NUWAKOT

TADE KHOLA

GUL BHANJYANG

MALEMCHI KHOLA

INDRAWATI KHOLA

BALEPHI KHOLA

LIKHU KHOLA

TALAMARANG

PATI BHANJYANG

MALEMCHI PHUL

KAKANI

BURLANG BHANJYANG

BAHUNEPATI

CHAUTARA

SUNDARIJAAL

MULKHARKA

SHIVAGHAT

KATHMANDU

PANCHKHAL

0   10 km

BANEPA

© MOON PUBLICATIONS, INC.

stop, is a moderately interesting little ridgetop town with views of Langtang Lirung and Ganesh Himal. Its spring full-moon festival, with whirling, drum-banging *jhankri* and lots of *chang,* is not to be missed.

The trail drops through dense forests of oak, maple, and alder, then climbs steeply alongside the Langtang Khola. A few hours later it crosses to continue up the opposite side of the gorge. The terrain here is similar to Colorado's, with forest and mountain streams backed by peaks—some of the nicest forest to be found along a main trekking trail. One of the few clearings in the woods is the site of the **Lama Hotel,** a formerly esteemed stopping point transformed into a literal shithole. It's much better to stay in **Rimche,** 15 minutes before.

The narrow valley begins to open out at **Ghode Tabela** (2880 meters), a grassy meadow with a Tibetan-run lodge and an army checkpost. The land rapidly changes into a drier, colder, stonier realm inhabited by Bhotia—this time more or less pure Tibetans, including many refugees who fled south in 1959. Yak-herding is the main enterprise up here, since the surrounding country is superb pastureland. The Buddhist orientation is apparent from the many *chorten* and prayer flags, and from some incredibly long *mani* walls.

Langtang (3307 meters) is the region's largest village; it's good to overnight here to acclimatize and perhaps even spend an extra day. The valley around here is a grazing paradise, rich in flowers and grass and dotted with stone huts used in summertime butter-making. Once sewn in skins and exported up to Tibet to flavor tea and fuel monastery lamps, butter remains the region's major product.

Kyangjin and Above

Two hours farther is Kyangjin Gompa (3750 meters), a little metropolis which serves as the Namche Bazaar of Langtang. Here are apple pie, chocolate cake, a small *gompa,* a cheese factory (usually closed), and a cluster of lodges, including a lavishly wood-paneled **National Park Lodge. Yala Peak Hotel** is the current favorite.

Kyangjin makes a great base for day hikes into the upper valley, where you may sight *tahr,* a long-haired goat-antelope. Ringed by impressive high peaks, Langtang is a heart-of-the-mountains valley similar to the Annapurna Sanctuary. Traditionally it was a Buddhist sanctuary where hunting and butchering animals were forbidden; rules have been bent nowadays to provide *momo* and buff steaks for trekkers.

From Kyangjin, climb up the small hill to the north (Kyangjin Ri, 4773 meters) for views of the graceful east face of Langtang Lirung, or head upvalley to climb 4984-meter **Tsergo Ri** for stunning views, including Shishapangma across the Tibetan border.

Slightly harder is the ascent of **Yala Ri** (5520 meters) to the northwest. Most climbers overnight on the backside of Tsergo Ri on a flat spot along the Yala Chu at around 4800 meters and continue from there. It's a rocky, icy climb best done with crampons and ice axe.

Not far from Kyangjin is the beautifully formed Fluted Peak christened by H.W. Tilman. The higher valley is dotted with summer yak-herding settlements; the last is **Langsisa** (4804 meters), where you can pitch a tent in one of the empty stone shelters. Above and across the river, the Langtang glacier rolls down from Tibet; a few kilometers farther are two huge rock guardians called **Guru Rinpoche** and **Shakyamuni.** Five hours' walk further up the glacier is a beautiful, if cold, camping spot; or just walk up here from Langsisa for the views.

Returning, you can vary the route by staying on the north side of the river all the way to **Syabrubensi,** which has a Tibetan settlement camp and hot springs nearby. Buses leave from here to Kathmandu.

With good weather, minimal snow, and some extra food, you could climb up to Gosainkund from either Dhunche or Syabru (the former is the main route), continuing down into Helambu or walking directly back to the Valley.

The Gangtsa La

This difficult high pass (5122 meters) linking Langtang and Helambu requires preparation, at least two days of food, and preferably a local guide, available in Langtang. The pass is more easily crossed from the Helambu side. Things have been made easier by the establishment of a rude lodge, nicknamed "Gangtsa La Base Camp," around three hours' walk up from Kyangjin at 4700 meters. The vacant herders' huts of **Keldang** are six or seven hours' walk farther up; you can overnight here with warm sleeping gear, though it's likely to be cold. A lodge will eventually open up here, making the route easier. From Keldang it's one very long day over the pass and into Tarkeghyang; water is short and you may be forced to melt snow. The pass is also the takeoff point for the 5846-meter trekking peak **Naya Kanga** immediately west, a moderately technical snow climb.

HELAMBU

The most easily accessible of all trekking regions is the upper valley of the Malemchi Khola, called Yolmu, Helmu, or Helambu by its Sherpa residents. It's temptingly close to the Valley, just three days' walk northeast over the forested ridge, yet remains remarkably untouched by trekkers. Helambu is below 3000 meters and creates few altitude problems; it's short (less than a week), and so close you can take off on a whim. There are lodges and teashops all along the way and you don't need a guide, but do ask directions frequently, as side trails meander off all over the place, and it's not a trekkers' highway.

This is a ramble rather than a distinct trek. There's no real destination besides the higher ridges with their pleasant forests, occasional mountain views, and interesting Sherpa villages. The lower valley is comparatively dull and depressingly hot much of the year, so plan to

THE FLESH TRADE

The rolling hills north of Kathmandu are a prime area for recruiters in the flesh trade, who focus on the traditionally poor districts of Kavre, Sindhupalchowk, and Nuwakot. The practice has become common within the last decade, drawing on an older tradition of concubines for the vast Rana palaces selected from among Tamang and Gurung girls of Kathmandu's surrounding countryside. Modern trafficking supplies the Indian market, where Nepali girls are preferred for their fair skin and cheerful disposition. Some 100,000-200,000 Nepali prostitutes work in India, with 30,000-40,000 concentrated in Bombay alone.

Every year some 5,000 Nepali girls and women from 10-18 years enter the flesh trade. About a third are abducted; others are lured by promises of unspecified but legitimate "work" in India. Some are sold to patrolling middlemen by parents, brothers, even husbands. The going rate can be as little as Rs150, a large sum for people who can't even afford two good meals a day. Girls as young as 13 may be sold; in one case a husband sold his pregnant wife. Getting rid of the girl or woman eliminates a mouth to feed, and also relieves parents of the burden of having to provide a dowry. All this only serves to underscore the low social value placed on girls, who are often considered as property to be disposed of. Merely having a young daughter in Nuwakot District is said to constitute a valid guarantee for lenders and local merchants, who are happy to sell parents goods on credit. They will either get payment from the daughters in Bombay, or take it out in their own personal trade.

The practice has also become more or less socially acceptable. Returned prostitutes display such wealth that they are admired rather than ostracized: parents are proud of their financially supportive daughters, and there is no shortage of marriage partners for them either. Most of the girls, who went into the trade from compulsion of one degree or another, want nothing more than a good husband and a happy family life; unfortunately chronic STDs make it difficult for many to have children.

Once in India, the girls are turned over to "trainers" who beat and rape them until they are compliant, a process which may last up to a month. A "broken-in" prostitute can earn up to 300 times her original price in a big-city brothel. Customers are willing to pay premiums for the youngest girls, as it's commonly believed they cannot contract AIDS—but of course they can. When a girl is found to be infected she is thrown out of the brothel. Often she'll return to her village continuing to support herself the only way she knows how. The sex trade thus channels HIV transmission directly from Indian brothels into rural Nepali villages, where it may not be detected for years.

Prostitution is not just limited to India, of course; there are perhaps 5,000 prostitutes in Kathmandu and more in Terai towns. Most of them work voluntarily, earning more in a night than they could in a month at an alternate job.

spend most of your time up high. The trek offers a sudden and dramatic contrast betwen high and low regions and their characteristic cultures. The comparison isn't favorable for lowland villages, which seem hot, fly-ridden, and unfriendly compared to the neat Sherpa villages above.

Sundarijaal to Kutumsang

The starting point is Sundarijaal on the northeast edge of the Valley. Hire a taxi here for around Rs250, or walk two hours up the dirt road heading north from Jorpati, the next suburb beyond Boudha; slow and crowded minibuses also run from here. The road ends at a row of teashops and lodges, also the site of the **Himalaya Rescue Dog Training Centre,** started by an enterprising Dutchman who trains dogs and handlers for mountain rescue work. Check in here for up-to-date trail information or for guides, or to register your trek.

A stone staircase ascending past the **Sundarijaal waterfall** soon transforms into a footpath, heading steeply up through scattered Tamang villages to reach **Burlang Bhanjyang** (2438 meters) on the Valley rim. The first night is usually at "Pub Pass" or **Pati Bhanjyang** (1768 meters), named for its *pati* serving homemade rice beer. Avoid Chisopani, roundly condemned by trekkers as a settlement of "creeps."

The next day the trail runs along ridges to the small village of Kutumsang. From here to Malemchigaon, a longish day's walk, there are no permanent settlements. The trail traverses high pastures seldom visited except by shepherds and woodcutters, providing a solitude rarely experienced in Nepal. Mountain views are superb; you may want to prolong the pleasure by overnighting in an empty herder's hut. About five hours from Kutumsang is **Tharepati,** a huddle of seasonal lodges. Innkeepers will point out the steep trail descending two hours through dense forests of rhodie and oak to Malemchigaon. If you stay up on the ridge, head to the single lodge at **Phedi,** then walk to **Gosainkund** and Laurabinayak (see "Gosainkund" following for more details).

Malemchigaon to Tarkeghyang

Malemchigaon (2560 meters) is Helambu's finest Sherpa village, a collection of neat houses fronted by prayer flags and surrounded by or-

boy with rhododendron

ALISON WRIGHT

chards and fields. Lodges are pretty much people's homes, a great opportunity to stay with a family. The Sherpas of Helambu are distant cousins of Khumbu Sherpas, speaking a related but distinct dialect; like Khumbu Sherpas, they emigrated from Tibet several centuries ago. According to legend Helambu was one of Guru Rinpoche's "hidden lands" or *belyul.*

The trail drops down to cross the Malemchi Khola. A project to divert it through a 27-km-long tunnel into Kathmandu to boost the water supply is currently being researched, a good example of the grandiose schemes contrived by development agencies. Climb up the exact same distance to Tarkeghyang (2560 meters), a larger and less secluded village than Malemchigaon. Poised on the main trekking route, it's more commercialized: every house sells souvenirs and instant "aged" *thangka.* There's also a large restored *gompa* here dating back to the early 18th century. Ten minutes' walk downhill is an even finer old *gompa* called **Chure Gyang.**

Out of Helambu

With warm clothes and sleeping gear, some food, and a local guide, you could walk three days north of Tarkeghyang into the Langtang Valley, crossing the difficult 5123-meter **Gangtsa La.** The pass is normally open May-Nov. but is exceptionally steep and icy. See under "Langtang" above for more details.

East of Tarkeghyang a ridge trail leads to **Panch Pokhari** (see "Jugal Himal" under "Central Nepal" in "Off the Beaten Track," below), an isolated and wild pilgrimage site. Again food, gear, and a guide are necessary; allow five or six days out of Tarkeghyang.

The main route out of Helambu heads south down the Indrawati Khola valley. From Tarkeghyang a pleasant high trail runs through the Sherpa village of **Shermathang,** then descends. Another drops directly to the river, then meanders through lowland Hindu villages, a distinct and rather depressing counterpoint to the neat Sherpa settlements. It's nine or 10 hours of walking from Tarkeghyang to the roadhead at **Malemchi Bazaar;** most people break the journey at **Kakani,** a village near Shermathang. From Malemchi Bazaar minibuses run in three and a half hours to **Banepa;** from here you can catch a bus into Kathmandu. An alternate trail, steep and rather confusing, climbs back up from **Talamarang** to reconnect with the high trail and Pati Bhanjyang, allowing you to reenter the Valley on foot.

GOSAINKUND

In itself Gosainkund is really a mini-trek, only four days' walk from Kathmandu. However, its high altitude means it's best done after a visit to Langtang or Helambu. It's easily joined with one of these regions, or can be used to link both, adding three or four extra days to a trek. If you come directly from Kathmandu, add some extra acclimatization days into the schedule.

This is the least-visited of the main trails north of Kathmandu, and until recently it was necessary to carry extra food and a tent. Simple lodges open in the main trekking season now line the entire route, and herders' huts and rock overhangs provide additional shelter. You might want to bring a little extra food to munch on

Nepali jhankri *celebrating full moon, Syabrubensi*

while walking, though. Lodges are closed when snow prevails, quite often from Oct.-March. The dominant impression of many trekkers here is how cold it is. It may be best done in the summer with pilgrims to the holy lake, or in May, when other areas are too hot.

From the Langtang side, a trail climbs steeply from Dhunche up to **Sing Gompa** (3254 meters), where a cheese factory and lodge are perched on the hillside. The cheese here is excellent, but the seller reportedly has a heavy hand on the scales. Trekkers from Syabru can either walk to Sing Gompa or take an alternate trail, slightly harder to follow, to **Cholung Pati** (3584 meters), set in a saddle. The hill just above here offers fantastic mountain views, including Langtang Lirung straight ahead.

From Cholung Pati, a clear trail climbs through rhododendron forests to reach **Laurebina** (3901 meters), a few ridgetop lodges with superb mountain views that is another popular overnight stop. As you cross over the ridge, the first of several lakes appears, each dedicated to a different deity. Don't expect crystal clear mountain lakes; these are really little more than ponds. The third, **Gosainkund** (4298 meters), is sacred to Shiva, whom devotees claim they see floating in the bottom of the lake in the form of a large rock—climb the surrounding hills for the best view of it.

According to a Hindu legend, the gods once churned the ocean to find treasure, and came up with a burning poison that threatened to destroy the entire world. They begged Shiva to drink and contain it and he did, burning his throat in the process. He fled to the high Himalaya, thrusting his trident into the rock to create the lake and taking refuge in its cold waters. The lake is said to be connected via subterranean channel to Patan's Kumbeshwar temple, and thousands of pilgrims flock here for the Janaai Purnima festival (usually the August full moon). There are no

mountain views from the lakes; climb the nearby hill to the north for excellent views extending all the way to Annapurna. Lodges here are simple and not particularly friendly.

The trail to Helambu passes the sacred lakes of Bhairab Kund and Surya Kund to reach a 4600-meter pass yielding a final set of good views. Near the single tiny lodge at **Phedi** is the site of the 1992 Thai Airways crash, macabre twisted bits of steel still scattered about. Dropping past the scattered huts of **Ghopte,** the trial meets **Tharepati** and the trail junction to Malemchigaon five or six hours from the pass. (Coming up, you could stay at Phedi, visit Gosainkund and go down to Laurabinayak the next day, a warmer solution.) From Tharepati you can drop down to Helambu, or continue along the upper ridge through Kutumsang and Pati Bhanjyang to reach the Kathmandu Valley in two more days.

TREKKING ROUTES
OFF THE BEATEN TRACK

Beyond the aforementioned "Big Three" trekking regions, Nepal is untouched by trekkers. When the main trails start to seem too crowded and tame, it's reassuring to remember all these unknown ones. Trekking off the main paths can be immensely rewarding, though it demands a sense of adventure and the capacity to deal with the unexpected. First-time trekkers are probably best off choosing a main route, though a few of the following are easy enough to qualify as a first trek. Unless you speak some Nepali or feel perfectly comfortable on your own, it's a good idea to take a guide. These treks range from teahouse treks to wilderness hikes. Frequently they combine both aspects by crossing over one or two uninhabited passes—a nice combination of company and solitude.

The main treks are popular for good reason, being the most spectacular scenery within easy reach of Kathmandu. Busing to and from trailheads in western and eastern Nepal will add three or four transport days onto your schedule unless you fly, and domestic flights are often unreliable. While you'll need extra time to get beyond the standard routes, the rewards are great— not just mountain views, but increased contact

with a wide range of Nepalis, and the chance to glimpse a completely different way of life.

EASTERN NEPAL

Overview

Lower, greener and friendlier, eastern Nepal is altogether more welcoming than the west, yet it's virtually untouched by trekkers. It's lovely, as-of-yet unspoiled country where people greet you with wholehearted curiosity and the traditional palms-together "Namaste," a nicety that's disappeared on the main trekking trails.

The lower hills are the homeland of Rai and Limbu, while Sherpa, Tamang, and Bhotia herd yak and cattle crossbreeds up higher. There are plenty of uninhabited high ridges with sweeping Himalayan vistas, including Kangchenjunga, Makalu, and Everest. Culturally, eastern Nepal is interesting too, with many local festivals and weekly *haat bazaar* where different ethnic groups meet to exchange goods and gossip, and to drink *tongba*.

Eastern Nepal bears the brunt of the monsoon; vegetation is rich, with bamboo everywhere, and in springtime rhododendrons blaze across the hillsides. A less attractive consequence is frequent snow that can block high passes, especially in spring. The plentiful water supports intensive irrigation, and though the hill regions here are the most densely populated of all Nepal's Hills, the land doesn't seem overworked.

The region is relatively prosperous and comfortable: food, lodging, and porters are easier to find and transportation is at least marginally better than in western Nepal, though it's still a long, long way to Kathmandu by bus—at least 22 hours from Basantapur. There are plenty of teahouses in lower regions, but don't expect proprietors to speak English or to serve pancakes. As usual, it's best to hire a local porter-guide if you don't speak some Nepali.

The network of lower trails is delightful, especially in the winter months. **Phidim-Taple-**

BHUTANESE REFUGEES

The plight of the 100,000 Bhutanese refugees huddled in eastern Nepal has received scant attention in the international press. Much of this is due to Bhutan's idealized image as a peaceable Buddhist kingdom, a sort of last Shangri-la. The fact remains that 10-15% of Bhutan's population now resides in eight refugee camps across Jhapa and Morang Districts. Ethnic Nepalis, they have been arriving here since 1990.

The biggest camp, Beldangi I, ranks as the world's largest Bhutanese settlement, with a population of some 45,000. Administered by the U.N. High Commission for Refugees, the camps are well-organized, with adequate housing and food and an excellent educational system for the children—even clean drinking water, tested daily. That the refugees' standard of living exceeds that of most rural Nepalis is a matter of some resentment for local people. Most refugees still hope to return to their prosperous lives in south Bhutan, but talks between Nepal and Bhutan have foundered without the participation of India, which has refused to get involved.

The roots of the problem lie in Bhutan's ethnic division into three communities. Some 20% are Ngalong, the dominant ruling class clustered in the high valleys of the north, whose Tibetan-influenced culture defines Bhutan's national identity. Another 30% are Sarchokpa or easterners, who have more in common with the tribals of Arunachal Pradesh across the Indian border. The lower hills are inhabited by Lhotsampa ("southerners") or ethnic Nepalis, many of them descendants of migrants who arrived with British encouragement at the turn of the century to work the tea plantations and logging operations of then-uninhabited southern Bhutan.

The 1988 census revealed the Lhotsampa population to be unexpectedly large, on the verge of becoming a majority. Attributing the increase to illegal immigration, the government launched a campaign to solidify national identity and crack down on illegal residents. Lhotsampas were required to prove their citizenship, while the Driklam Namsha code required the wearing of Bhutanese dress in official buildings and offices and suppressed the use of Nepali in public schools.

Heavy-handed implementation of these rules led to political agitation by the Nepali population, fueled by the success of Nepal's 1990 revolution. The ensuing crackdown led to the flight of thousands of refugees, and the panic and fear thus generated triggered an even more massive outpouring. Violence by Bhutanese security forces appears to have decreased, but gangs of refugee rebels now make forays across the border to attack villagers and local officials, trying to tip the balance further.

Most refugees say the police arrived in their village and insisted on immediate eviction. Some were paid in exchange for their land and a formal renunciation of their nationality; others were merely threatened with violence or imprisonment. The pattern appears to have been one of intimidation and panic rather than direct violence, though Amnesty International has confirmed reports of the latter.

Waters have been further muddied by exaggerated media coverage on both sides. The Nepali press makes lurid claims of "ethnic cleansing," while Bhutan insists it has simply been protecting its culture from outside influences—an astute claim. To say it was protecting the status of the dominant minority, or its monarchy, would not go down so well. Tensions are increased by Bhutan's admittedly valid fears of becoming another Sikkim, a similarly tiny Himalayan kingdom that India absorbed in the 1960s due to agitation from a growing Nepali population. India would have no qualms about gobbling up Bhutan either, should it prove necessary.

EASTERN NEPAL

TIBET

SAGARMATHA NATIONAL PARK

▲ SAGARMATHA (MT. EVEREST) (8463 m)

▲ MAKALU (8470 m)

HONGU

KHUMBAKARNA GLACIER

▲ KANGCHENJUNGA (8586 m)

NAMCHE BAZAAR

LUKLA ✈

MAKALU-BARUN NATIONAL PARK

GUNSA

TASHIGAON

TOPKE GOLA

NUM

KHEMBALUNG CAVES ■

SIKKIM (INDIA)

BUNG GUDEL

← TO JIRI

MILKE DANDA JALJALE HIMAL

KHANDBARI

SALPA BHANJYANG

CHAINPUR

TAPLEJUNG ✈

TUMLINGTAR ✈

BASANTAPUR

PHIDIM

BHOJPUR ✈

TERHATHUM

HILLE

ARUN RIVER

TAMUR KOSI

ILAM

DHANKUTA

DHARAN

KAKARBHITTA

EAST - WEST HIGHWAY

KOSI TAPPU WILDLIFE RESERVE

0   20 km

THE BORDERS SHOWN ON THIS MAP ARE NEITHER CORRECT NOR AUTHENTIC

INDIA

BIRATNAGAR ✈

© MOON PUBLICATIONS, INC.

jung-Basantapur and **Tumlingtar-Chainpur-Ilam** are easy one-week treks through unspoiled country. Much of the fascinating high country is off-limits, places like the old Bhotia trading town of **Walungchung Gola**, and the upper Arun Valley with its Bönpo villages. There's always the chance restrictions will relax, and in any case adventurous trekkers can still find many interesting routes unhampered by checkposts.

Until the recent rejection of the massive Arun III hydropower project by the World Bank, eastern Nepal faced big changes in the form of a giant dam expected to produce more electricity than the installed capacity of the entire country. Most of the power would have been sold to India. Local opposition and government inde-

cision combined to make the project unpalatable for the World Bank, however.

Originally conceived of as a counterpoint to this massive development scheme, a national park has been established to protect the unique ecosystems of the upper Arun. The 1,500-square-km **Makalu-Barun National Park** extends from the Tibetan border all the way south to the Salpa Bhanjyang trail connecting Lukla and Tumlingtar. It combines with the adjoining Sagarmatha National Park and Tibet's Qomolungma Nature Preserve to create one of the world's largest park systems.

Access point for many of these treks is **Hille**, some 13 km north of Dhankuta and 19 hours by bus from Kathmandu. The road from here continues three hours farther to end at **Basantapur.** The airstrip at **Tumlingtar** is the other main entry point; the town is a week's walk away from the Everest region to the west or Ilam in the east.

Easy East Nepal

This mellow lowland trek is great in the winter, when higher routes are too cold. From the Tumlingtar airstrip, walk up to **Chainpur,** a pleasant town with a Friday *haat bazaar* and a long tradition of metal-working. Follow the ridge up to **Siddhi Pokhari,** where mountain views emerge, then drop down to cross the Piluwa Khola and ascend along the rhododendron-rich Milke Danda to **Gupha Pokhari,** with its small lake and busy *tongba* stalls. From here it's an easy walk down to the roadhead at Basantapur, where you can bus to Biratnagar and bus or fly to Kathmandu.

Kangchenjunga

Eastern Nepal is dominated by Kangchenjunga, at 8586 meters the third-highest mountain on earth. Its name is Tibetan, and means "Five Great Treasuries of the Snows." Straddling Nepal's eastern border, it towers over Sikkim, and the excellent views of it from Darjeeling made it the best-known peak in the Himalaya a century ago. For a time it was even believed to be the world's highest mountain. Mountaineers scaled the main summit in 1955, but severe weather and avalanches continue to challenge expeditions.

A formerly restricted area, Kangchenjunga was opened in 1989, but only to organized treks. The restriction is intended to protect the region from environmental and cultural pressures (maximizing profits was another idea), but judging from the ribbons of toilet paper festooning the trail, the plan hasn't been too effective. Solo trekkers still manage to explore the region, but difficult logistics tend to place it in the realm of an organized trek. There are no settlements along the upper portion, so you have to bring food and shelter. Figure on two to three weeks from Taplejung; walking to the road at Basantapur is an extra three days.

Groups generally fly to **Taplejung** (US$110). The bus ride from Kathmandu-Dhankuta and up to Basantapur is a grueling 22-plus hours; flying to Biratnagar saves a lot of time. There is a road to Taplejung, but bus service is erratic at best; ask around. The trail heads northeast through Rai and Limbu farm country; higher up Tibetans and Sherpas graze herds of yak, dzo, and dzopkio. Cultural interaction on this trek is more limited than most; so, surprisingly, are the mountain views, at least until the end. The trail follows a high-walled valley, finally emerging onto one of the huge glaciers sweeping down from Kangchenjunga's flanks, to reveal a whole cluster of peaks above. One route goes up the Simbua Khola to **Yalung Glacier** (4890 meters); another, slightly farther west, goes through the Tibetan town of **Gunsa,** a good place to spend an extra rest day, eventually connecting to **Pangpema** (5150 meters) on Kangchenjunga Glacier. Trails over the **Lapsang La** or the lower **Sinion La** connect these two in a long loop.

Jaljale Himal

This trip leads through pleasant low farm country up onto a remote, uninhabited ridge with fine mountain views of four of the world's five highest peaks. A guide is a must in the high country, to help find water as well as to show the way. The first few days out of Basantapur are easy, pleasant, and teahouse-able, leading up to **Gupha Pokhari,** where Makalu's reflection shimmers in the waters of a pond. A trail continues up through the extensive pure rhododendron forests of the **Milke Danda** past herders' camps and onto Jaljale Himal (about 4700 meters), a rocky ridge set with a few small lakes. The high portion is often snowed in, especially in spring. For the return, several trails run down side ridges to reach **Tumlingtar** in the west or **Taplejung** in the east. Figure on at least two weeks of walking, plus travel time.

Makalu-Barun National Park

The newest of Nepal's national parks, established in 1992, Makalu-Barun protects a remote wilderness of enormous biological diversity. Only two small settlements are within the park boundaries, but the adjoining Conservation Area includes a population of some 32,000 Rais, Sherpas, and Bhotias. Unlike other national parks, Makalu-Barun doesn't rely on the Nepali Army for protection of its resources. Instead, planners are trying to involve the local population in park management.

Few trekkers visit this little-known area—only 350 in 1993. Trails are rugged, steep, and slippery, and the narrow season to cross higher passes is mid-March through April, and Oct.-November. Many trekkers are turned back by snow. The most popular route is the trek to **Makalu Base Camp.** This route is for the gung-ho only: you need to carry shelter and food for at least 10 days, and the difficult double pass is frequently snowbound. Count on two to three weeks of trekking.

From the STOL strip of **Tumlingtar,** the trail leads through the bazaar town of **Khandbari** up the increasingly deep gorge of the Arun River. Mountain views are spectacular in a few places, especially **Munche.** The trail drops down to **Num,** then descends to cross the Arun and reach **Seduwa,** where park entry permits are checked. From here it's a half-day's walk to **Tashigaon** (2060 meters), the last settlement along the trail, where you may find leftover expedition goods for sale.

Take a local guide for the rest of the journey; you may have to hire one lower down to get an English-speaking one. The route crosses the often-foggy **Shipton La** and the **Barun La** (4110 meters) to enter the isolated upper Barun Valley. Snow here is often lighter than on the passes. Trekkers are supposed to stay in designated campsites in order to reduce their impact. The trail follows the Barun Glacier to **Makalu Base Camp** set beneath the massive 8463-meter peak. A possible return route heads down the western side of the river from Num, passing near the legendary pilgrimage site of the **Khembalung Caves,** though accommodations and food are limited on this side.

Back Door to Everest
Trekkers usually do this as an escape route from overcrowded Lukla and Solu, but it could be an entry point as well. Simple food and lodging are available along the way, and the trail can go on as far as you like—less than a week to the Tumlingtar airstrip, or 12 days to Ilam at the east-

ernmost end of the country. You may want to hire a local guide, as it's not really a main route.

The turnoff from the main Everest trail is less than a day south of Lukla at **Kharte,** above the Kari Khola. (A smaller trail runs from Jubing.) The trail heads southeast over steep, forested hills, with Rai villages on the lower slopes and Sherpa villages above. H.W. Tilman passed through here en route to Khumbu in 1949. The discouraging descent and ascent between the towns of Bung and Gudel inspired this ditty:

For dreadfulness nought can excel
The prospect of Bung from Gudel;
And words die away on the tongue
When we look back at Gudel from Bung

Cross the **Salpa Bhanjyang** (3350 meters) and descend into the steamy Arun Valley to reach **Tumlingtar,** about six days from Kharte. Since a portion of the trail falls within the boundaries of Makalu-Barun National Park, trekkers are liable for the Rs650 park entry fee. From Tumlingtar, you can fly to Kathmandu, and walk two days to the road at **Hille** or continue east to **Ilam,** either via Chainpur and Terhathum or through Taplejung to the roadhead at Phidim. Ilam is a small hill town surrounded by tea gardens, a day-long jeep ride from the main East-West Highway. By now you're in the southeasternmost corner of Nepal, a two-day bus ride from Kathmandu, but very close to Darjeeling, India, which lies just beyond the border town of **Kakarbhitta.**

Hongu
This remote area southeast of the Everest massif is a tangle of high mountains, completely uninhabited and often snowbound. This trek is pure isolation, just ice, snow, and rock. The best season is April-May. You need full gear and a knowledgeable guide; an agency trek is almost a must. Flying in and out of Lukla, Hongu could be done in less than three weeks. The route heads over the steep ridge east of Lukla and continues for five or six days, crossing the 5400-meter

Tamang woman,
eastern Nepal

Mera La, with excellent mountain views. The same day you reach the Hongu Khola. Turning north, it's another few days up to **Panch Pokhari,** five small lakes that feed the river. From here you can retrace your steps to Lukla, or if conditions are good continue north, crossing over the 5780-meter **Amphu Laptsa** into the Chukhung Valley.

CENTRAL NEPAL

Pokhara to Trisuli

This lowland trek traverses classic hill country dotted with Newar and Hindu villages, huge spreading pipal trees, and good views of Himalchuli, Manaslu, Ganesh Himal, and the Annapurnas. It's a good introductory off-the-beaten-trek: the altitude is low, the ups and downs are constant but not too steep, and the hill town of Gorkha with its motor road is midway in case you change your mind and want a *really* short walk. It's short (a week at most), easily accessible, and one of those rare trails best done in the winter—in fact, it's just too hot by late spring. There are plenty of local teahouses and travelers along the way, though few trekkers.

Starting at **Begnas Tal** in the Pokhara Valley, pick one of many trails weaving east several days through Gurung country. Try to visit **Ghan Pokhari,** a lovely old trading town a few hours above the road to Besisahar. Cross the road near Tarkughat or Besisahar; the next day cross the Darondi Khola. The old fortress town of **Gorkha** is an hour's detour and well worth a visit.

From the old Gorkha Durbar the trail continues east through Khanchok Bhanjyang, dropping down to **Arughat** on the Burhi Gandaki and continuing two more days through bazaar towns to end at Trisuli, described in the "Langtang" section above. Swaying buses head down the winding 79-km road to Kathmandu. You can reach Kathmandu in two days or less on foot, avoiding the road most of the way and ending up at Balaju. If you've extra time in Trisuli, climb up to the old seven-story palace in nearby **Nuwakot.**

Dhorpatan

Few trekkers visit this broad, high valley less than a week's walk west of Pokhara. Even Nepalis from other regions are stared at by the locals; foreigners can expect to become minor celebrities. The region is manageable for independent trekkers, with teahouses and decent trails throughout, but it's wild enough to be interesting, and it's definitely off the beaten track.

Tell people in Pokhara you're going to Dhorpatan, and they'll warn of freezing temperatures and rugged trails. They tend to exaggerate, but the pass *is* generally snowed over into late spring, and in winter many local people move to lower regions.

From the end of the Baglung Highway, the trail heads to the riverside town of **Beni,** then winds along the Myagdi Khola to ascend the **Jaljala Pass** (3414 meters). The last reliable food and lodging are at **Lumsum** or **Moreni,** about three hours below the pass; from here to the first settlements above Dhorpatan there may be nothing but herders' huts and forest, so bring food for the day. The trail is obvious and frequently traveled by mule and pony trains. At the top are good views of Dhaulagiri, the Annapurnas, Machhapuchhare, and the remote peaks of Nepal's western Himalaya. Haul up water from Moreni if you want to make a high camp and wait for the mountain views to clear, which are good from the ridge north of the pass.

From here the broad Dhorpatan Valley opens out into a vista reminiscent of the American West. Dhorpatan is five hours beyond the pass, a mixture of Nepalis and Tibetans (many Tibetan refugees settled here in the '60s). There's a small Bönpo monastery here. The surrounding ridges offer excellent views; the easiest is directly south of the airport, a two-hour climb. Side trips north into nearby **Dhorpatan Hunting**

BOB RACE

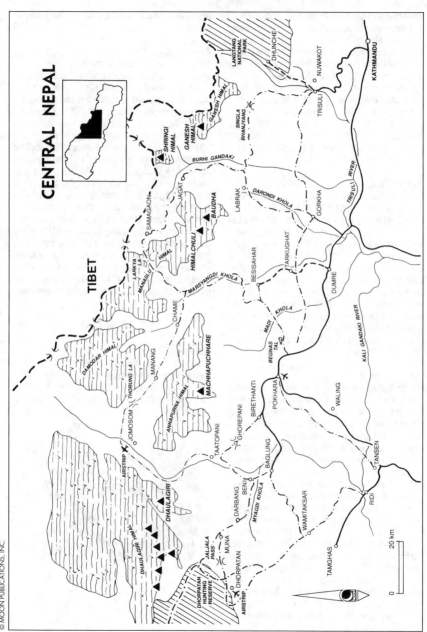

Reserve and blue sheep country require food and tents; you could continue on an even wilder trail via **Tarakot** to **Jumla,** about two weeks away. Shorter loops to the west and northwest lead through country inhabited by the Kham Magar ethnic group. Return is about five days via the same trail or heading southeast to **Tansen** through interesting hill country.

If the Jaljala Pass is snowed over, a lower, unnamed pass (2926 meters) to the south is generally open. The trail leads off from Baglung to emerge at **Wamitaksar,** a few days south of Dhorpatan on the Tansen trail.

Jugal Himal

This beautiful cluster of peaks northeast of Kathmandu is dominated by 6990-meter Dorje Lhakpa. It's relatively easy to reach, though the trail ascends steeply. Bring food, shelter, and a guide. Access is from **Chautara,** a trading village up a dirt road from Dolalghat. The trail runs up a long ridge, passing a sacred Shiva lake called **Bhairab Kund** and continuing up to the five lakelets of **Panch Pokhari** (about 3700 meters), a seldom-visited pilgrimage site. The ridge above the lakes offers spectacular mountain views. From here it's a long day's walk to the first settlement of **Helambu;** the trail eventually runs into Tarkeghyang.

Ganesh Himal

Rough and wild, this trek cuts through untraveled country south of the Ganesh Himal massif. Mountain views are good but the terrain is rugged and the local people unaccustomed to trekkers. Bring a tent and food for at least a few days; sometimes the only available food is *dhiro,* and the only tea is brewed from tree bark. A Nepali guide is a must. Even Sherpas get nervous in some of these *jungli* Tamang villages.

Several possible routes connect Gorkha and Trisuli, all taking two weeks or more. One option heads up the Darondi Khola from Gorkha to the large Gurung town of **Barpak.** Dropping down through the nasty village of **Labrak,** you cross the Burhi Gandaki via a rude cable-car, and trek up into the mountains. Two days or so are through uninhabited high territory with superb mountain views. Crossing **Singla Bhanjyang,** the trail descends to reach the roadhead at Trisuli two days later. A lower route avoids the

high pass, which is frequently snowed over in spring.

Around Manaslu

This little-known and formerly restricted trek was opened a few years ago and is being touted as the new Annapurna Circuit. Like the Circuit, it loops around a massif, this one the eighth-highest mountain in the world (8163 meters). Unlike the Circuit, permits are only issued to trekkers traveling through a registered agency. The trail begins at the old capital of **Gorkha** and heads up the Burhi Gandaki through wild and seldom-visited Gurung villages, hot and lowland at first. The terrain begins to change around **Jagat,** a Tibetan refugee settlement lined with long *mani* walls. **Samagaon** is one of the highlights of the trip, a large village with a superb *gompa.* The trail crosses the 5105-meter **Larkya La,** dropping past an intensely blue glacial lake in a steep, icy, spectacular descent revealing stunning mountain views. In a few days it enters the Marsyangdi River valley, eventually emerging at the roadhead of **Besisahar.**

WESTERN NEPAL

Overview

This is the most remote and least-known area of Nepal. When Toni Hagen came through in the '50s he met people who hadn't even heard of Kathmandu. It's safe to say many Kathman-

duites still haven't heard of Jumla or Humla. Stretching all the way from Dhaulagiri to the Mahakali River on the nation's western border, western Nepal is half again as big as the central and eastern sections, but its land is so dry and infertile that it has the smallest population of all Nepal's five zones.

Western Nepal is markedly different from the rest of the country: remote, dry, and the people dirt-poor and frequently more suspicious. The landscape is characterized by lower, less spectacular Himalayan peaks with many long, forested ridges *(lekh)* extending southwards from them. It's a food-deficit region, so bring your own supplies: you'll be lucky to be served rice, *daal,* and potatoes all in one meal. Pizza and pancakes have definitely not penetrated here, and people eat on the Nepali schedule of two meals a day. Transport and arranging porters create further challenges deterring even organized treks. If you're looking for something different, Nepal's Wild West may be it—but it's not recommended unless you've already come to terms with, and love, Nepal.

This is not a teahouse trekking region; you'll need a local to arrange food and lodging in some villages. In some places you'll be able to sleep in the potato storage shed, for a price. In others you'll find basic *bhatti* and teashops to put you up, though they may not welcome you with open arms. It may be best to contact a Kathmandu agency with experience in the region: try **Sagarmatha Trekking,** tel. (1) 417-036, **Parbat Travels,** tel. (1) 223-596, or **Api Saipal Treks,** tel. (1) 413-441.

History and Culture

Historically part of the Khasa empire, Western Nepal was the cradle of the Nepali language. Stone columns and stelae linger from the ancient Malla kingdom (no relation to Kathmandu's) which ruled the region between the 12th-14th centuries, uniting it with southwestern Tibet, Garhwal, and Kumaon.

Its hill people are predominantly Hindu castes: Brahman, Chhetri, Thakuri (a Chhetri subcaste which includes Nepal's king), and the low-caste occupational groups. Stricter Hindu mores mean people are more reserved than in other areas of Nepal. The higher hills are sparsely inhabited, mostly by Bhotia, who, free from caste restrictions, are more hospitable to foreign trekkers. You'll probably meet them on the trail, following the old trade route up the Karnali River valley through Sinja, Mugu, and Humla into Tibet. Western Nepal's poor soil and low rainfall have forced them to keep up the Tibet trade even though the exchange has become less favorable. Herds of sheep or goats serve as pack animals, carrying saddlebags loaded with salt, grain, or wool.

Western Nepal has served as a Himalayan crossroads, a mixing and meeting point for various cultures and religions. Today Hinduism dominates, and both Buddhists and Hindus worship Masta, an indigenous folk deity whose shrines are dotted across the countryside. Wooden *dok pa* figurines carved in the shapes of humans guard bridges and trails, relics of a strong animistic tradition. Every village has its long-haired *dhami* or *jhankri,* entrusted with healing and religious rituals.

> *But if one professes and practices living on the country one must take the rough with the smooth, rancid yak fat and frogs along with buckwheat cakes and raksi.*
>
> —H.W. TILMAN

Jumla

The hub of the region is the district capital of Jumla, reached by flights from Kathmandu (US$127) and Nepalgunj (US$44). The latter is used as a base for flights to the outposts of Baitadi, Chainpur, Bajura, Sanfebagar, and Dipayal; again, cancellations are frequent. One thing you need in western Nepal is plenty of time: if flights are delayed, the nearest road may be a week's walk or more away.

Jumla is a small, unwelcoming place with a minor bazaar that's the region's biggest. Temples to Bhairabnath and the mythical saint Chandannath are among the few local attractions beyond the airstrip and the abundant local apples—just about the only thing cheaply available, due to a lack of transport to outside markets. Little English is spoken, and the few hotels are very basic. A saying goes, "You need claws of steel and knee-joints of hardwood to survive in Jumla."

The unforgiving life has bred an isolated and suspicious attitude typical of the region.

Attractions in the area include the village of **Miha**, a half-hour's walk distant, with a line of stone stupas dating to the 15th century, and **Sridhuska**, 30 minutes further, with another massive ancient stupa. To the east, just past the junction of the Chaudabise and the Tila Rivers, a 4000-meter-high ridge provides sweeping views of the western Himalaya from Saipal to Dhaulagiri.

Rara National Park

If you're looking for a wilderness experience, this is the trek. This small (106 square km) park in remote northwestern Nepal protects a high-altitude mountain lake ringed by snowy peaks and pine forests, scenery reminiscent of the Rocky Mountains. It might be cheaper and easier to simply camp in the Rockies, but Rara's solitude is rare in crowded Nepal. The trek itself is relatively easy and short; a loop is possible, and it can be done in less than two weeks if you manage to fly in and out of Jumla.

From Jumla, two trails lead to Rara in three or four days. The easternmost is lower but has more ups and downs. It crosses the windy **Danphe Lagna** (3688 meters) with spectacular mountain views (if there's snow, cross the lower Khali Lagna nearby), then tops the **Gurchi Lagna** (3444 meters). Another trail passes

CONSCIOUS TREKKING

"**E**co-trekking" rolls so smoothly off the tongue nowadays it's in danger of becoming a cliché. Really, though, everyone bears the responsibility for ecologically and culturally conscious trekking, from the government down through trekking companies, lodgekeepers, and most of all, individual trekkers. Here are some suggestions for minimizing your impact on the trail:

—Eating in a lodge, consolidate food orders with others, ordering the same meals at the same time. *Daal bhaat* is often cooked and on hand already. Don't keep the cookfire burning for hours with orders for another jam pancake, another lemon tea—try to order everything at once.

—Reduce hot showers (or skip them altogether), and take them in lodges that heat water with either a backboiler system or hydro- or solar power.

—Burn or bury trash, in designated disposal sites where these exist, and encourage trekking staff to do the same. Local people are usually happy to acquire clean empty bottles, jars, and other containers. Pack out nonbiodegradable items to Kathmandu. Pick up litter on the trail yourself—why not? Don't fixate on litter as the biggest problem, though: litter is a Western concept, as is revulsion to it. Most Nepalis don't even perceive it as a problem, and in truth there are more serious aspects to pollution, for instance the horribly unsanitary water that kills 43,000 Nepali children each year from water-borne diarrheal disease.

—Group trekkers can reconsider the extravagant style of organized treks, in which staff members are trained to produce three multi-course meals daily, and to provide boiled drinking water, hot washing water, and endless cups of tea. They want to please you, and may even truly believe you can't function without these things, but if groups could agree to reduce some of the ridiculous excess everyone would be better off. This requires discussion with other members, of course, but consider these options, especially at wood-scarce high altitudes: cutting down or eliminating the heated morning and evening washing water; squelching the sahib custom of "bed tea"; iodizing drinking water instead of boiling it; having less elaborate meals.

—Make sure your group's food is cooked with kerosene (discuss this with the company in advance). In an ideal world, porters would cook on kerosene too, but as long as they continue to be underequipped and unsheltered it's hard to begrudge them a nighttime cookfire. In the same vein, make sure porters will be provided with warm clothing and shoes for high-altitude treks—necessities that most companies still consider an optional luxury. Independent trekkers are responsible for their porters' welfare as well.

—Other pointers: Use established toilet facilities, making sure they're at least 30 meters distant from any water sources. Be modest when bathing. Don't rinse soap or shampoo into streams, not even biodegradable brands. Don't give to begging children; donate funds to schools or monasteries instead.

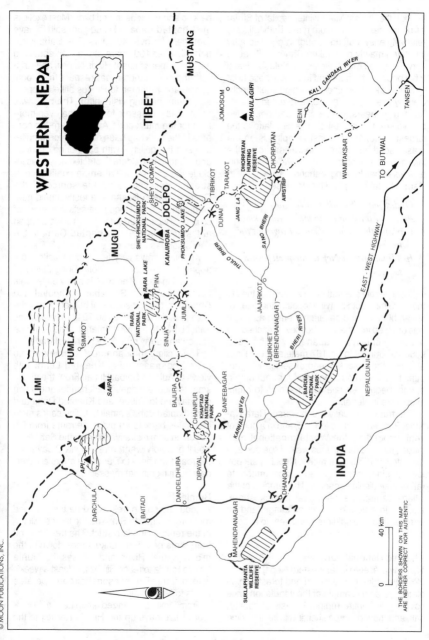

through the ancient Malla winter capital of **Sinja;** it's usually taken as a return route. Both trails are relatively easy, cutting through rugged country inhabited mainly by Thakuri Chhetris. If you're very lucky you might glimpse the elusive Rauti tribal people who hunt and forage in these hills.

Rara Lake is perched on a high shelf, encircled by gray ridges and pine-forested hills inhabited by bears, jungle cats, and deer. Five by two km, this crystal-clear alpine lake is the largest in Nepal. The best camping is on the grassy southern shore. The trail encircling the lake makes a pleasant six-hour walk: it was built as a horse trail for King Mahendra's 1964 visit to Rara. The lake inspired him to verse:

> *O, did you collect all beauty's store*
> *And pour it into Rara to make beauty more*
> *Garland the wreath of snow ranges on the*
> *neck*
> *In Himalaya, in Nepal, for pretty Rara's*
> *sake.*

Local people say that once a foreigner tried to measure the depth by tying together the skins of seven buffalos and securing them to a rock. It was dropped into the lake, but never reached the bottom. Actually, a Japanese with an echo sounder found it to be 167 meters deep. Rara also has the typical legend of selfish villagers punished with a sudden flood for snubbing a hungry beggar—a tale which seems to haunt every lake in Nepal.

The truth is actually much worse. Rara National Park was formed in 1975, and in a burst of zeal inspired by the Western national park model, two Thakuri villages were dispersed and relocated in 1978. Fortunately, Nepal's park policy has since been revised to accommodate rather than displace people. The remains of the village can still be seen near the lakeshore, along with a post office, of all things, and an army post for the soldiers who seem to accompany every Nepali national park.

Khaptad National Park

This tiny preserve in far western Nepal protects 225 square km of grassland and forested high plateau, a small sample of the vegetation once covering the entire region. Forests of conifer, oak, and rhododendron shelter wildlife, including

barking and musk deer, and birds. Most exotic is the **Khaptad Baba,** a Hindu guru said to have lived here for over 40 years. The Baba is reportedly over 100 years old, a well-educated man who speaks fluent Hindi, Nepali, and English and commands great respect from local people and Kathmandu Hindus alike (supposedly even the king visits him). The park was created as a preserve for the Baba even more than for the musk deer. A five-square-km core area in the park has been reserved for "meditation and tranquillity," with butchering, alcohol, and tobacco forbidden. Protected holy sites include the shrines of **Tribeni,** a confluence of streams believed to be the source of the Ganges. Ganga Deshara, a festival held here around the June full moon, attracts thousands of pilgrims. Two months later, Shiva is worshipped at the small lakelet of **Khaptad Daha** in the park's northeast corner.

Khaptad draws very few foreign visitors but appears to be teahouse-able. Bring plenty of food, just in case. The park is a few days' walk from three airstrips: **Sanfebagar, Dipayal,** and **Chainpur,** the last seasonal but reportedly the easiest. Airfares are US$60-70 from Nepalgunj, about US$140 from Kathmandu. The entrance station and army guard post is at **Lokhada.**

Trails climb through forest to emerge onto the rolling grassland of **Khaptad Lekh,** with views of Api and Saipal Himal. From the single small teahouse-lodge at park headquarters you can day-trip to Tribeni and Khaptad Daha and visit Khaptad Baba's small hut. The park's main trail dates back to an old trade route from **Dipayal,** an administrative town on the Seti River. You'll probably want to return via Dipayal, as the road from here to Dangadhi offers an alternate out if flights get messed up.

Humla

A good late spring trek would be the highland route from Jumla to **Simikot,** the largest village of the remote Humla district. The trail turns off from **Sinja** near Rara Lake, drops down to the mighty Karnali River, and crosses the **Munla La** into Humla to reach Simikot, at least a week's walk distant. The seasonal airport operates flights to Nepalgunj.

From Simikot, organized group treks may walk four or five days up the Humla Karnali to the

4580-meter **Nara Lagna** on the Nepal-Tibet border. A half-day's walk from here is the Tibetan border, and across it the fascinating trading town of Purang, which Nepalis call **Taklakot.** Lake Manasarovar and **Mt. Kailas,** the sacred center of the Buddhist and Hindu universe, are only a day's drive north. This route is more interesting and preferable to the long, tough overland journey by road across western Tibet.

Dolpo

The best known of the many isolated high Himalayan valleys across northern Nepal, Dolpo preserves one of the last remnants of traditional Tibetan culture. Legend says it's a *belyul,* one of the "hidden valleys" created by Guru Rinpoche as a refuge for devout Buddhists in troubled times. Surrounded by high mountains, including the Dhaulagiri massif to the southeast, and cut off by high passes closed by snow half the year, Dolpo's easiest access is Tibet, from where its people emigrated perhaps 1,000 years ago.

Upper Dolpo shelters about 5,000 people, whose lives revolve around Buddhism, barley, and yaks; their villages are among the highest settlements on earth. A large portion of Dolpo has been set aside as **Shey-Phoksumdo National Park,** at 3,555 square km Nepal's largest. Meant to preserve a complete example of the trans-Himalayan ecosystem, the park shelters blue sheep, Himalayan black bear, leopards, wolves, and the elusive snow leopard, which provided the title for Peter Matthiessen's classic book on his 1973 journey through this region.

Largely thanks to *The Snow Leopard,* Dolpo is the best-known of Nepal's forbidden northern border regions. In 1989 the government announced the opening of the trail through Lower Dolpo up to **Phoksumdo Lake;** a few years later, Upper Dolpo, a premium area, was opened to those willing to pay US$70 per day for a permit. Both routes are restricted to trekkers going through an agency, probably just as well, as food and accommodations are scarce along the way.

If you fly in and out, the trek to Phoksumdo takes less than two weeks. Longer, but highly rewarding options, would be to walk in from Dhorpatan over two high passes (about one week) or to cross the 5000-meter Kagmara pass from Jumla. Kagmara means "Crow Death," either because it's so high the birds flying over it drop dead, or because of the grisly rumor that they attack and kill victims of altitude sickness and snow blindness.

Groups generally fly from Nepalgunj to the airstrip at **Juphal,** then walk several hours to the district headquarters of **Dunai** (2100 meters). The trail follows the Suli Gad River, passing through thick conifer forests and a few Thakuri Hindu villages. The national park checkpost is one day from Dunai; two steep days later is Phoksumdo.

Phoksumdo Lake (3627 meters) is the highlight of the whole trek, a basin of unearthly turquoise blue ringed by rocky crags and forest, framed by snowcapped peaks. Veteran traveler David Snellgrove raved over its beauty: "Here we set up camp, feeling that we had come at last to the paradise of the Buddha 'Boundless Light.' The water is edged with silver birch and the gleaming whiteness of the branches against the unearthly blue of the water is one of the most blissful things that I have known," he wrote in *Himalayan Pilgrimage.*

Legend says a demoness fled here during Guru Rinpoche's conversion of Tibet's resident spirits, offering local people a gigantic turquoise to keep her passage a secret. Guru Rinpoche transformed the turquoise into a lump of dung, and the disgruntled people revealed the demoness's hiding place. In revenge she called down a flood upon their village, submerging it beneath the lake. The legend is a concise mythic summary of the ancient struggle between Bönpo and Buddhists; the latter won, but the former remain, even here at Phoksumdo.

At the lake's eastern end is the village of **Ringmo,** also called Tso. The town's entrance *chorten* has nine complex Buddhist and Bönpo mandalas painted on its wooden ceiling, described in detail by Snellgrove. "These villagers dwell in one of the most glorious places on earth without being remotely aware of it," he noted of Ringmo's 100 or so residents. Perhaps they are too busy moving around between their various settlements. In late spring they plant crops in Ringmo and at a higher settlement; in winter they descend to another town to graze their herds. The people are Bhotia and only very distantly related to Tibetans. They are gradually becoming Hindu-ized, adding Chhetri surnames to their Tibetan names.

The Bönpo monastery, **Tso Gompa,** is two km from the village, set above the lake on forested cliffs with views across to Kanjiroba. Below the village, a gigantic waterfall cascades over a series of rock steps, draining into the Suli Gad far below. A visit to the Bönpo *gompa* at **Pungmo,** two hours up a side valley to the west, is a worthwhile expedition.

The best part of Dolpo lies beyond the lake, along a difficult trail crossing a high pass into Upper Dolpo. **Shey Gompa,** named after nearby Crystal Mountain and described in *The Snow Leopard,* is several days' walk north of the lake. You may meet maroon-clad Dolpo-pa on the trail, as they drive their salt-laden yak caravans south in the fall and return to their high villages in the spring.

NEPALI PHRASES AND VOCABULARY

(See "Languages" in the Introduction for more tips on learning Nepali.)

Pronunciation

Transliteration from Devanagari into English is fairly straightforward, but there are a few waffly points. 'B' and 'v' are interchangeable in Nepali; thus Bishnu and Vishnu. The same goes for 'f' and 'ph,' leading to statements like "Puck you!"

Things get more complicated with 't' and 'd.' Different combinations of aspiration and retro-flexion make four varieties of each. These are tricky points for English speakers to pick up or even note, but they can make a big difference in meaning.

Retroflex consonants ('t' and 'd') are pro-nounced with the tongue curled up and slightly back, touching the palate. To start, listen to the way a Nepali pronounces "Kathmandu"—the 'th' is almost a 'd.'

Aspirated consonants (kh, gh, jh, ph, bh, dh, th, and chh) have an extra 'h,' signalling an extra puff of air. Don't worry too much about this subtle point, but remember 'th' is never pro-nounced as in "this"; the 'h' is simply aspirated.

The difference between 'aa' and 'a' is easily glossed over but shouldn't be. A single 'a' sounds almost like 'uh,' as in *ma* or 'I'; maa (a suffix mean-ing 'in'), is long and drawn out. Listen to someone say *chaamal* (uncooked rice) to get both.

BASIC GRAMMAR

Nepali grammar is relatively simple. The only plural is made by adding -*haru* onto the end of a noun; there's no gender, there's little future tense, and you can get by using one or two tenses for practically all subjects and times. The subtleties are endless, but picking up a basic operational framework is not too hard.

Order in a sentence is subject-object-verb: I'm studying Nepali—*Ma Nepali sikchhu.*

For **questions,** simply raise your voice at the end of the sentence:

Are you going to Namche?
Tapaai Namche-maa janne?

Pronouns

I	*ma*
you (formal)	*tapaai*
(familiar, for kids)	*timi*
we	*haami*
he/she (formal)	*wahaa*
(familiar)	*u*

For **possessives,** add -*ko* to the pronoun, name, or noun:

Ram's daughter	*Ramko chhori*
wheat flour	*gauko pitho*
whose book?	*kasko kitaab?*

Exceptions are *mero, timro, usko* (mine, yours, his/hers).

The most important postposition is -*laai,* meaning "to" or "for":

Please give it to me.	*Malaai dinuhos.*
Please tell that to him.	*Wahaalaai bhannaidinuhos.*

Nouns

Many modern words are adopted from English: *bas, tiket, motaar, hotel, reydio.* When in doubt, try the English word with a Nepali pronunciation.

book	*kitaab*
bottle	*sisi*
bridge	*pul, saanghu*
candle	*mainbatti*
chicken	*khukhura*
cow	*gaai*
cup	*gilas, kap*
dog	*kukur*

electricity	*bijuli*
fire	*aago*
firewood	*daauraa*
foot (and leg)	*khutta*
forest	*ban*
government	*sarkaar*
hill	*lekh, pahaad, danda*
house	*ghar*
inn, lodge	*laj*
kerosene	*mattitel*
knife	*chakku, khukuri*
light (lamp)	*batti*
load	*bhaari*
luggage	*saamaan*
matches	*salaai*
medicine	*aushaadi*
pass	*bhanjyang*
pen	*kalaam, dat pen*
place	*thau*
porter	*kulli, bokne maanche*
religion	*dharma*
river	*khola, kosi, nadi*
road	*baato*
room	*kothaa*
shop	*pasal*
snow	*hiu*
soap	*saabun*
sun	*ghaam*
toilet	*chharpi*
town	*gaun*
trail	*-baato*
main trail	*mul baato*
tree	*rukh*
village	*gaun*
water	*paani*
(un)boiled water	*(na-)umaaleko paani*
drinking water	*khaane paani*
hot water	*taato paani*
washing water	*dhune paani, nuhaaune paani*

Verb Survival

Some of these suggestions are unorthodox pidgin Nepali, but they're readily understood, and handier than wrestling with formal verb conjugations your hosts may not use either.

1. Take the basic verb shown below and subtract *-nu* to get the root.

2. Add *-nuhos* to form a polite command:
Chiyaa dinuhos. (Please) give me tea.
To form a negative, add *-na* as a prefix:
Tyo nachunuhos. Please don't touch that.

3. Add *-ne* to form a simple, all-purpose form indicating the present and future:
Ma janne. I'm going
Janne? You're going?

4. Add *-eko* to form the past participle:
Khaanaa khaaeko? Have you eaten?

5. Add *-yo* to indicate completion:
sakyo finished
bhayo it's over with, accomplished, past

Wahaa hijo gaayo. He went yesterday.

As in Spanish, "to be" *(hunu)* has two forms: *chha/chhaina* used for location and quality, and *ho/hoina,* a more permanent definition. If you get confused, either is generally understandable.

arrive	*pugnu*
buy	*kinnu*
carry	*boknu*
come	*aaunu*
cook	*pakaaunu*
do	*garnu*
eat (also drink)	*khaannu*
(to be) enough	*pugnu*
forget	*birsanu*
give	*dinu*
go	*jannu*
help	*madat dinu*
look for	*khojnu*
meet	*bhetnu*
need	*chaahinnu*
put	*raakhnu*
read, study	*padhnu*
rest	*aaram garnu*
return	*pharkanu, pheri aaunu*
sell	*bechnu*
sit, stay	*basnu*
sleep	*sutnu*
take	*linu*
teach	*sikaunu, padhaunu*
throw out	*phaalnu*
try	*kosis garnu* (or "try" *garnu*)

understand	*bujhnu*
wait	*parkhanu*
walk	*hidnu*
wash	*dhunu* (face, clothes), *nuhaaunu* (body)
work	*kaam garnu*
write	*lekhnu*

Useful Dual Verbs

v. + *hunchha*: to be okay to
Is it okay for us to stay here?
    Haami yahaa basnu hunchha?

v. + *sakchha*: to be possible to, able to
Can you go tomorrow?
    Tapaai bholi jaana sakchha?

v. + *parchha*: to must, have to do something
Tomorrow we'll have to go very early in the morning.
    Bholi bihanaa saberai jaanu parchha.

v. + *man laagchha*: to like doing something
I like wandering around in Nepal a lot.
    Ma Nepalma ghumna janne dherai man laagchha.

Adjectives and Adverbs

a little bit	*ali ali, ali kati*
after	*pachhi*
again	*pheri*
all	*sab, sabaai*
alone	*eklai*
always	*sadhai*
angry	*risaayo*
another, the other	*arko*
bad	*kharaab, naraamro*
before	*aghi, agadi*
big	*thulo*
cheap	*saasto*
clean	*saphaa*
closed	*bhandaa*
cold	(person, weather) *jaado* (liquid) *chiso*
crazy	*bauluhaa*
difficult	*gaarho, muskil, aaptyaro*
dirty	*pohor*
easy	*saajilo*
everyone	*sabaai janna*
expensive	*mahango*
far	*tadaa*

fun	*ramaailo, maja*
good	*raamro*
heavy	*garungo*
hot	(person, weather) *garmi* (liquid) *taato*
hungry	*bhok*
inside	*bhitra*
lazy	*alchhi*
less	*toraai*
(a) lot, many	*dherai, tupro*
more	*dherai, jyaada*
near	*najik(ai)*
new	*nayaa*
old	*purano*
only	*maatrai*
open	*kholeko, khulaa*
outside	*baahira*
quickly	*chitto*
scarce, lacking	*komti*
slowly	*bistaarai*
small	*saano*
strong	*baliyo*
stupid	*murkaa*
sweet	*guliyo*
tasty	*mitho*
very	*dherai, ekdum*
How is it?	*Kaasto chha?*
How nice! Great!	*Kaasto raamro!*
What a person! (said disapprovingly)	*Kaasto manchhe!*

Feelings

afraid	*dar laagyo*
cold	*jaado laagyo*
drunk	*raaksi laagyo*
happy	*kushi laagyo*
hot	*garmi laagyo*
hungry	*bhok laagyo*
lazy	*alchhi laagyo*
pleasant, nice	*ramaailo laagyo*
sleepy	*nidraa laagyo*
thirsty	*tirkhaa laagyo*
tired	*takaai laagyo*

Question Words

who	*ko*
what	*ke*
when	*kahile*
where	*kahaa*
why	*kina*
how (in what way)	*kasari*

USEFUL PHRASES

Accommodations

Is there a place to stay (in that town?)
(Tyo gaun-ma) baas painchha?

Is it okay if we stay here?
Haami yahaa basnu hunchha?

Please show me a room.
Kotha dekhaunuhos na.

Is there anything better/cheaper/bigger than this?
Yo bhandaa raamro/saasto/thulo chha?

One person only.
Ek janna matraai.

Two people.
Dui janna.

My friend is coming.
Mero ek janaa saathi aauncha.

Food

(Where) Is there food available?
Khaanaa (kahaa) painchha?

What do you want to eat?
Ke khaane?

Is the rice cooked yet?
Bhaat pakaeko chha?

I have to cook it.
Pakaunu parchha.

What do you have for food/snacks?
Khaanaa/Khajaa ke ke chha?

How long will it take to cook food?
Pakaaunalaai kati time laagchha?

Give me a plate of *daal bhaat*, please.
Daal bhaat ek plaat dinuhos.

Don't add chili.
Khursaani nahalnuhos.

Please make it hot.
Piro pakaaunuhos.

Bring more food.
Bhaat lyau/khaana lyau.

Please give me a little bit.
Ali-ali (thorai) dinuhos.

That's enough/that's plenty.
Malaai pugyo or *Bho, bho.*

I'm finished.
Sakyo.

Please take it.
Linuhos.

I don't eat meat.
Ma maasu khaandina.

Please give me a cup of tea.
Chiyaa ek gilas dinuhos.

milk tea	*dudh chiyaa*
black tea	*kaalo chiyaa*
without sugar/	*Chini nahalnuhos/*
with sugar	*chini halnuhos*

Another cup of tea, please.
Arko ek gilas chiyaa dinuhos.

The food is very tasty.
Khanna ekdum mitho chha.

Please give me a spoon
Chamchaa dinuhos.

It's okay; I'll eat with my hand.
Thik chha; ma haatle khaanchhu.

apple	*syaau*
banana	*keraa*
beer	*biyaar (jaar* or *chang* for local brew)
butter	*makhan*
cauliflower	*kauli*
candy	*mithaai*
chicken	*kukhuraako maasu*
chili pepper	*khursaani*
coffee	*kaphi*
cookie	*biskoot*
corn	*makai*
egg	*phul*
fish	*maachhaa*
flour (wheat)	*gahuko pitho (maida* or *atta)*
fruit	*phalphul*
greens	*saag*
lentils	*daal*
liquor	*raaksi*
mango	*aap*
meat	*maasu*
buffalo	*raangako maasu*
chicken	*kukhuraako maasu*
goat	*khaasiko maasu*
pork	*sungurko maasu*
milk	*dudh*
noodles	*chow-chow*

oil	*tel*
orange	*suntalaa*
popcorn	*murali makaai*
potato	*aalu*
relish	*achaar*
rice (cooked)	*bhaat*
(uncooked)	*chaamal*
(in the field)	*dhaan*
salt(y)	*nun(ilo)*
snacks	*khaajaa*
spices	*masalaa*
sugar	*chini*
tea	*chiyaa*
vegetables	*tarkaari, sabji*
water	*paani*
drinking	*khaane paani*
boiled	*umaaleko paani*
yoghurt	*dahi*

Meeting People

To address strangers, Nepali (like most Asian languages) uses kinship terms, a feature guaranteed to make you feel at home. To call a woman or man around your age or slightly older, say *Eh, didi/daai* (Oh, older sister/older brother).

Distinctly older than you:
Eh, baabu/amaai (Oh mother/father)

Distinctly younger than you:
Eh, bahini/bhaai (Oh younger sister/brother)

To call a shop- or lodgekeeper:
Eh, sahuji (male)/*sahuni* (female)

-ji is a polite suffix that can also be added onto given names: "Ram-ji," "Bob-ji"

Hajur is a polite term for a man (like 'sir') as well as a good way to say "Excuse me, I didn't quite catch that" (when said in a questioning tone). "Thank you" is seldom used in Nepali, though overeager Westerners have revived the Sanskrit term *dhanyabaad*. For routine thanks, it's best to use the English, or simply smile and nod.

When leaving, say "Namaste," or *Raamro sangha basnuhos* if the person is staying; *Raamro sangha jannuhos* if the person is departing.

See you tomorrow/again.
Bholi/pheri betaunlaa.

Go slowly, take it easy.
Bistaari jaanuhos/aaunuhos.

baby	*bachha, naani* (girl), *baabu* (boy)
children	*ketaa-keti* (lit. "boys and girls")
daughter	*chhori*
foreigner	*bideshi* (*ghuire* is an impolite epithet for Westerners)
friend	*saathi*
girlfriend	*keti saathi*
husband	*logne* (informal), *pati, srimaan* (most polite)
person	*manchhe*
inn- or shopkeeper	*sahuji* (m.)/*sahuni* (f.)
son	*chhora*
wife	*swasni* (informal), *patni, srimaati* (most polite)

Conversation

How are you?
Tapaailaai kasto chha? (or simply *Aaramai?*)

I'm fine, and you?
Malaai sanchai chha, tapaai ni?

I'm/It's okay.   *Thik chha.*

Ke chha?   *What's up?*

What's the matter, what's happened?
Ke bhayo?

What's your name?
Tapaaiko naam ke ho?

My name is _____.
Mero naam_____ho.

Where do you live?
Tapaai kahaa basnu hunchha?

I'm from the U.S.   *Ma Amerikaan hu.*

How old are you?
Tapaaiko umer kati bhayo?

I'm ___ years old.
Malaai ___ barsha bhayo.

Are you married?   *Tapaaiko bihaa bhayo?*

Yes I am/No I'm not.
Bhayo/Bhaeko chaaina.

Do you have children?
Bachaa chha ki chaaina?

How many? Boy or girl?
Kati jana chha? Chhora ki chhori?

What kind of work do you do?
Tapaai ke kaam garnu hunchha?

Do you speak Nepali/English?
Nepali/English (kura) bolnu hunchha?

I speak a little.   *Ma ali ali bolchhu.*

Please speak slowly. *Bistaari bolnuhos.*

I understand/don't understand.
Bujhyo/Bujhdaina.

I (don't) know.
Malaai tahaa chha(ina).

Pardon?   *Hajur?*

Excuse me.   *Maaph garnuhos.*

Let's go.   *Jaau* or *Jaam.*

Don't worry.   *Chinta nagarnuhos.*

Don't be angry.   *Narisaaunuhos.*

Go away.   *Jau, jau.*

You shouldn't beg. *Maagne hundaaina.*

I won't give anything.
Ma kehi pani dindaaina.

Don't give me trouble.
Dukhaa nadiu.

Health
I'm sick.   *Malaai biraami bhayo.*

Where does it hurt?
Kahaa dukhchha?

stomachache   *pet dukhchha*

diarrhea   *disaa laagchhha*

fever   *jwaaro aayo*

headache   *tauko dukhchha*

Shopping and Bargaining
Do you have any . . . ?
. . . chha ki chaaina?

Where can I get . . . ?
. . . kahaa paainchha?

How much is this?
Yesko kati?

How much per kilo?
Kiloko kati?

How much is the food?
Khaanaako kati?

How much for one?
Eutaako kati?

How much total?   *Jammaa kati bhayo?*

No, that's too expensive. Give it to me a little cheaper, please.
Hoina, tyo ta mahango bhayo. Ali sastoma dinuhos na.

Give me your best price.
Thik bhannuhos.

Please give it to me for Rs90.
Nabbe rupiyaama dinuhos.

Here's the money.   *Paisaa linuhos.*

Please give me change; I don't have any.
Chanchun dinuhos; mero chanchun chaaina.

Bill, please.   *Bil dinuhoss.*

Transportation
Where is this bus going?
Yo bas kahaa jaanchha?

How much is a ticket to . . . ?
. . . jaane tikat ko kati?

What time will we reach . . . ?
. . . maa kati baaje pugchha?

What time do we go?
Kati baaje jaanchha?

Taxi! Are you empty?
Yaaksi! Khaali ho?

Please go to Durbar Marg.
Darbar Margma jaanuhos.

Put on the meter.
Mitaarma jaanuhos na.

I'll give one-and-a-half times the meter.
Ma mitaarko dedhi dinchhu.

How much to go to Bhaktapur?
Bhaktapurma jaane kati paarchha?

Directions

Where is . . . ?   *. . . kahaa chha?*

Which is the trail to Namche?
Namchema pugnalaai kun baatoma jaanchha?

Which trail is the best/fastest/easiest?
Kun baato raamro/chitto/saajilo chha?

How far is it?   *Kati tadaa chha?*

How many hours to reach (the next town)?
(Pallo gaun) pugnalaai kati ghantaa laagchha?

Where are you going?
Kahaa jaanu hunchha?

Where are you coming from?
Kahaa bataa aaeko? or *Kaata pugera aaunu bhayo?*

here/there	*yahaa/tyahaa*
right/left	*daayaa/baayaa*
straight	*sidha*
north	*uttar*
south	*dakshin*
east	*purbaa*
west	*paaschim*
up	*maathi, upallo*
down	*muni, tallo*
uphill	*ukaalo*
downhill	*oraalo*
level	*samma*

"Red mud, slippery trail." (proverb)
Raato maato, chiplo baato.

Porters

I'm going to Namche, and I need a porter for one week.
Ma Namchema jaanne, ma ek haptaa ko kulli chahinchha.

How much per day?
Ek dinko kati chahinchha?

I'll give you Rs100 per day.
Ma ek dinko sae rupiyaa dinchhu.

| without food | *khaanaa nakhaaera* |
| with food | *khaanaa khaaera* |

For returning, how much do you need?
Pharkanako laagi dinko kati chahinchha?

Please come with me.
Ma sanghaa aaunuhos.

porter	*kulli, bokne maanche*
load	*bhaari*
heavy	*garungo*
light	*halungo, halaun*
salary	*talaab*
equipment, stuff	*saamaan*
let's go	*jam*
let's rest	*bhaari bisauu*

Do you want some tea?
Chiyaa khaane?

Time and Days

There is no indication of a.m. and p.m.

What time is it?	*Kati baajyo?*
It's three o'clock.	*Tin baajyo.*
It's 10:30.	*Saadhe das baajyo.*
today	*aaja*
tomorrow	*bholi*
yesterday	*hijo*
the day after tomorrow (vague future)	*bholi-paarsi*
a while ago (vague past)	*hijo-aasti*
one week	*ek haptaa*
one month	*ek mahinaa*
one year	*ek barsaa*
next week	*aaune haptaa*
last week	*gaaeko haptaa*
last year	*pohor saal*
morning	*bihanaa*
evening	*belukaa*
day	*din*
night	*raat*
eating time	*khaanaa khaane bela*

What day is today?	*Aaja ke baar ho?*
Sunday	*aaitabaar*
Monday	*sombaar*
Tuesday	*mangalbaar*
Wednesday	*budhabaar*
Thursday	*bihibaar*
Friday	*sukrabaar*
Saturday	*sanibaar*

Numbers

These are rendered difficult by the fact there's a different word for each; it's not as systematic as "twenty-five," "thirty-five," etc. Nepali numbers are frequently written in Roman, but the original system appears also. These are the same as Indian numbers, which were the original inspiration for Arabic numerals.

Another trick is adding counting particles onto numbers. Basically there are two particles: *wotaa* for things, *jana* for people. You can't say *tin kalaam,* (three pens); you need to say *tin wotaa kalaam.* Three people is *tin jana maanchhe.* Often you can drop the noun and use just the particle:

How many are in your party?
Tapaai kati jana hununhunchha?

We're only two.
Dui jana matraai ho.

Abbreviations are commonly used for lower numbers. One thing is *eutaa*, two *dui wotaa* or *duitaa*, three *tintaa*. After that add the full particle: *chaar wotaa,* etc.

1/2	*aadha*	18	*athara*
1	*ek*	19	*unais*
2	*dui*	20	*bis*
3	*tin*	25	*pachis*
4	*chaar*	30	*tis*
5	*paanch*	40	*chaalis*
6	*chha*	50	*pachaas*
7	*saat*	60	*saathi*
8	*aat*	70	*sattari*
9	*nau*	80	*aausi*
10	*das*	90	*nabbe*
11	*eghara*	100	*(ek) sae*
12	*barha*	200	*dui sae*
13	*terha*	1,000	*(ek) hajaar*
14	*chaudra*		
15	*pandra*	100,000	*(ek) lakh*
16	*sorha*	10 million	*(ek) crore*
17	*satra*		

GLOSSARY OF NEPALI AND TIBETAN TERMS

agam—temple to the guardian deity of a family or lineage

ajima—fierce Newar mother goddesses who must be placated with sacrifices to avoid sickness and misfortune

apsara—celestial nymph of Hindu mythology

Ashta Mangal—the "Eight Auspicious Symbols," frequently used in Indian and Tibetan designs

Ashta Matrika—the "Eight Mothers," a collection of fierce goddesses representing different aspects of Durga

aushaadi—medicine

bahal—former Newar Buddhist monastery complex, now inhabited by families

baksheesh—a tip given in advance to expedite service

bayul, belyul—"hidden valleys" created by Guru Rinpoche to provide refuge for Buddhists in troubled times

Bhagwati—the great goddess Durga

Bhairab—a fierce manifestation of Shiva

bhajan—religious hymns sung by Newar men

bhakku—see *chuba*

bhang—sticks and stems of marijuana, usually brewed into a potent tea

bhanjyang—pass

bhariya—porter

bhatti—trailside inn serving food and drink

bhoj—a ritual feast

bhojnalaya—a local restaurant, generally serving *daal baat*

Bhotia—general term for the Tibetan-influenced northern border peoples of Nepal

bindi—stick-on *tika* worn as part of a woman's makeup

bodhisattva—a buddha-to-be who has renounced individual enlightenment to help other beings attain liberation

Bön—the old indigenous religion of Tibet, preceding Buddhism

Brahman—the highest Hindu caste

Buddha—a spiritually enlightened being

chaarpi—toilet

chaitya—a Buddhist monument; a smaller version of a stupa

chang—Tibetan barley beer

charas—hashish

chautaara—trailside resting place with stone supports for porters to rest their loads

Chhetri—the second-highest Hindu caste, like Brahmans considered "twice-born" or ritually pure

chillum—vertical clay pipe for smoking hashish

chorten—the Tibetan version of a stupa, appearing in different styles

chowk—courtyard or road intersection

chuba—Tibetan coatlike garment, belted and with long sleeves. Women wear a sleeveless, wraparound variation, tying in the back.

crore—10 million

daal bhaat—the Nepali national dish, boiled rice with lentil sauce and curried vegetables

dakini—female spiritual beings who protect the Buddhist Dharma

danda—a hill or ridge

danphe—Nepal's national bird, the Impeyan pheasant

Dasain—Nepal's biggest holiday, a 10-day festival celebrating Durga's victory over the buffalo demon

Das Avatara—the 10 incarnations of Vishnu, a favorite subject for artists and storytellers

Devanagari—the script used to write Nepali, Hindi, and Sanskrit

dhaka—handmade cloth woven in colorful geometric patterns

dhami—see *jhankri*

dhara—a water tap, anything from a simple spigot to an elaborately carved series of spouts set in a sunken enclosure

dharamsala—a public shelter and resthouse used by travelers and pilgrims, usually an open-sided building

Dharma—the Buddhist faith

dhiro—cooked mush (generally corn), the staple of those who can't afford *daal bhaat*

dokko—a wicker basket used for carrying loads

Durbar Square—the temple-studded plazas opposite the old royal palaces of the Kathmandu Valley's three main cities

Durga—The Great Goddess who appears in many manifestations (Kali, Taleju, the Ashta Matrika, the Kumari), often fierce, to defend good and defeat evil

gainey—wandering minstrels who sing topical ballads and play the four-stringed fiddle (*sarangi*)

gandharva—celestial musicians; companions of Ganesh

Ganesh—the roly-poly elephant-headed god of luck, son of Shiva and Parvati

ganja—marijuana

Garuda—the winged man-bird who serves as Vishnu's mount

Gelug—one of the four main sects of Tibetan Buddhism, this one ruled by the Dalai Lama

gharial—a rare, long-snouted crocodile found in the Terai

ghat—stone steps lining the banks of sacred rivers, used for laundry, bathing, and cremation

ghee—clarified butter used in Indian cooking (*ghiu* in Nepali)

gompa—a Tibetan monastery-temple complex

guirey—impolite word for Westerners

Gurkha—regiments of Nepali soldiers in the Indian and British armies, famed for their fighting ability

Guru Rinpoche—Padmasambhava, the 8th-century Indian tantric magician and teacher who established Buddhism in Tibet

gush—a bribe

guthi—informal Newar social organization which fulfills religious and social obligations

haat bazaar—weekly regional markets popular in eastern Nepal

Hanuman—the "Monkey King" appearing in the Hindu epic the Ramayana

himaal—snow mountains

hookah—water pipe generally used for smoking a mixture of tobacco and brown sugar

ihi—a Newar rite of passage. Young girls wed the fruit of the *bel* tree, symbolizing Vishnu, thus avoiding the stigma of widowhood if their human husband dies early.

jaatra—festival

jhankri—shamanistic healer widely consulted for both physical and mental diseases

jungli—wild, uncouth

jutho—ritually contaminated or impure

Jyapu—Newar peasant subcaste

Kali—the Dark Goddess, wild and terrifying, an emanation of Durga

Kargyü—a sect of Tibetan Buddhism

karma—the Hindu-Buddist principle that what goes around, comes around

Ke garne?—"What to do?" Nepal's national slogan, recited whenever reality overwhelms one's plans or intentions

khat—a palanquin carried on men's shoulders, used in festivals and celebrations

khatak—Tibetan prayer scarf, a length of white cloth presented at meetings and leave-takings as a token of respect and good intentions

khola—river

khukri—curved Nepali knife

kichkinni—a supernatural being, a beautiful young woman who seduces men and saps their strength

kot—hilltop fort

Krishna—Blue-skinned god of love, one of the 10 incarnations of Vishnu

Kumari—a young virgin Buddhist girl worshipped as an embodiment of the Hindu goddess Durga. Of the Valley's 11 Kumari, the most famous is Kathmandu's Royal Kumari.

kund—small lake or pond

la—pass (Tibetan)

lakh—100,000

Lakshmi—the Hindu goddess of wealth and abundance, consort of Vishnu

laligurans—rhododendron, Nepal's national flower

lama—a Tibetan Buddhist spiritual teacher

lekh—a long ridge, generally a spur running off higher mountains

lhakhang—Tibetan Buddhist shrine

Licchavi—Hindu dynasty that ruled the Valley from A.D. 300-879

linga—ancient Hindu symbol associated with Shiva, among other things a phallic symbol of masculine generative power

lungi—long piece of printed cotton wrapped around the waist and worn as a skirt

maanaa—unit of volume used to measure grains, cooking oil, etc., and equalling about two cups

machaan—treetop game blind

Machhendranath—"Lord of the Fishes," rainmaking patron deity of the Kathmandu Valley. Buddhist Newars worship him as an emanation of Avalokitesvara, bodhisattva of compassion.

madal—hand drum

Mahabharata—an ancient Hindu epic poem interweaving philosophy and ethics with the mythical great battle between the Pandava brothers and their cousins

mai—one of the "mothers" of Newar religion, bloodthirsty nature goddesses who are remnants of ancient animistic beliefs

Maithhili—belonging to the ancient kingdom of Mithila or Videha, centered around what is now the city of Janakpur in the eastern Terai

makara—a sea serpent of Indian mythology, often depicted spouting jewels and pearls

mala—Hindu prayer beads or rosary

Malla—the medieval dynasty that ruled the Kathmandu Valley from A.D. 1220-1768

mandap—roofed rectangular platform; pavilion

mandir—temple

mani **wall**—prayer wall made of flat stones carved with mantras, a Tibetan Buddhist tradition

Manjushri—the sword-wielding bodhisattva of wisdom who drained the Valley's waters and opened it for settlement

mantra—mystic formula of Sanskrit syllables, chanted as meditative device or to work magic

masan—cremation platform, usually round, found on the banks of sacred rivers

math—Hindu priests' residence

matha—an old Hindu monastery. Like Buddhist *bahal,* they are now inhabited by private individuals and families.

mela—temple fair; a religious celebration held at a temple or holy site

momo—a Tibetan dish, little steamed dumplings usually stuffed with minced meat (fried *momo* are *kothey*)

Mughlai—a rich, spicy style of Northern Indian cooking, influenced by Persian cuisine

naan—disc-shaped Indian bread cooked in a tandoori oven, chewy and delicious

naga—serpent deities that dwell underground, guardians of wealth, bringers of water, and senders of illness. Particularly important in the mythology of the Kathmandu Valley

Nandi—the name of the bull who serves as Shiva's vehicle

Newar—the indigenous people of the Kathmandu Valley

Nyingma—the "old sect" of Tibetan Buddhism, which especially reveres Guru Rinpoche

paisaa—generally, money; more specifically, small change

panchayat—a system of "partyless democracy" followed in Nepal from 1959-89, now discredited

Pancha Buddha—the Five Buddhas (also called Jina or Dhyani Buddha), especially important in Newar Buddhism. Each is assigned a particular direction, color, emotion, symbol, etc.; together they symbolize the varied aspects of enlightenment.

paubha—a Newar-style scroll painting (see *thangka*)

pipal—*Ficus religiosa,* a spreading tree with heart-shaped leaves often found shading *chautaara.* Often called the "Bodhi tree," as it's said to be the tree beneath which the Buddha gained enlightenment.

puja—an act of worship, offerings presented to honor a deity

pujari—priest who tends to a specific deity or temple

Punjabi—woman's garment, a two-piece ensemble of drawstring pants and a long shirt slit up the sides

pukka—proper, real, genuine

raksi—Nepali firewater, distilled from grain or potatoes

radi—handmade felt carpet

Ramayana—Indian epic tale of the adventures of Rama (an incarnation of Vishnu), whose wife Sita has been abducted by an evil king

Rana—the aristocratic Chhetri family that ruled Nepal for nearly a century, controlling the office of prime minister

rinpoche—literally "precious one," a title of respect used for lamas

rudraksha—the furrowed brown seed of the *Eleocarpus* tree, used in Hindu rosaries

sadhu—Hindu ascetic or holy man who's renounced family and caste to wander, beg, and pray

sahib—Term of respect used to address Westerners, despite its connotations of the Raj. Pronounced "saab," for women "memsaab."

Sakya—one of the four main sects of Tibetan Buddhism

sal—a hardwood tree found extensively in Nepal

Saraswati—Hindu goddess of speech, music, and learning, often depicted holding a lute and a book

sattal—a roadside resthouse

sati—the custom, now banned, that a Hindu wife throw herself on her husband's funeral pyre

Shah—the ruling dynasty of Nepal, descendants of the 18th-century king Prithvi Narayan Shah

shakti—the essence of female power which permeates the universe

shaligram—ammonite fossils embedded in black stones found in the valley of the Kali Gandaki, considered an emblem of Vishnu

Sherpa—an assistant trekking worker, regardless of his or her ethnic group

shikara—style of temple consisting of a tapered cigar-shaped tower set over a square shrine

Shiva—the Hindu god ruling over transformation and destruction, a powerful being with many names and forms, including Mahadev (the "Great God") and Pashupatinath, the protector of Nepal. His consort is the beautiful goddess Parvati, who is a pleasant variation of Durga.

shraddha—offerings made to satisfy the spirits of deceased ancestors

siddha—magical powers gained by intensive spiritual practices or asceticism

sindhur—vermilion powder used as a religious offering and to make *tika*

sirdar—leader of a trek or expedition, in charge of organization and logistics

stupa—Buddhist monument based on the form of ancient burial tumuli, a hemispherical mound topped by a conical spire

sukunda—small oil lamp used in worship

tal—lake

Taleju—patron goddess of the Malla Dynasty, a form of Durga

tantra—a mystic philosophy developed in ancient India that has influenced both Hinduism and Buddhism

Tara—benevolent female bodhisattva

tempo—a three-wheeled motor vehicle serving as an inexpensive taxi

Terai—the narrow, fertile strip of land along Nepal's southern border, an extension of India's Gangetic Plain

thaali—a metal plate with compartments for separate dishes

Thakuri—high Chhetri subcaste that includes the royal family and the Ranas

thangka—a Tibetan scroll painting of religious subjects; Newar *thangka* are called *paubha*.

Tharu—aboriginal tribal people, among the original inhabitants of the Terai

thukpa—Tibetan noodle soup

tika—an auspicious mark made on the forehead as part of worship, usually with red powder or *sindhur*

tirtha—Hindu pilgrimage site

tol—neighborhood or quarter

tola—a unit of weight used for precious metals and hashish, approximately 11 grams

tongba—hot Tibetan beer, made from boiling water poured over fermented mash (usually millet) and sipped through a bamboo straw

topi—hat worn by Nepali men, a brimless, slightly lopsided cloth cap

torana—semicircular tympanum mounted over the doorways and windows of temples, carved or embossed with images of mythological characters and the deity inside

tsampa—a Tibetan staple, roasted barley flour generally eaten mixed with tea

tso—lake

tulku—a reincarnate lama

Tundikhel—the central parade ground found in many Nepali towns

Uma-Mahesvara—Shiva with Parvati on his knee, a favorite theme of sculptors

Varja—the "thunderbolt H" symbol of the absolute nature of reality, symbol of Vajrayana Buddhism

vahana—the vehicle or mount of a deity

Vishnu—one of the main gods of the Hindu religion, Vishnu the Preserver is benevolent and beneficent, worshipped in 10 main incarnations including Narayana, Rama, and Krishna. His symbols are the conch, lotus, disc and mace; his consort is Lakshmi; his mount the winged man-bird Garuda.

yaksha—graceful nymph of Hindu mythology popular in Nepali art, especially woodcarving

yatra—pilgrimage

yeti—also known as the "Abominable Snowman," a hairy man-ape said to inhabit Nepal's remote highlands

BOOKLIST

DESCRIPTION AND TRAVEL

Choegyal, Lisa, ed. *Nepal Insight Guide*. Hong Kong: Apa Publications, 1994. A lavishly illustrated all-Nepal guidebook. Apa's *Kathmandu Insight City Guide* covers the Valley in more detail.

Forbes, Duncan. *The Heart of Nepal*. London: Robert Hale, 1962. Well-written account of a visit to Kathmandu and a trek through Helambu and Langtang; interesting for its glimpses of a newly opened Nepal.

Giambrone, James. *Kathmandu Bikes and Hikes*. Hong Kong: Apa Publications, 1994. Pocket-sized illustrated guide with itineraries for day hikes around the Kathmandu Valley and a range of best mountain-biking trips.

Greenwald, Jeff. *Shopping for Buddhas*. San Francisco: Harper & Row, 1990. Western consumers in hot pursuit of spirituality; a sometimes edifying, often funny look.

Gurung, Harka. *Vignettes of Nepal*. Kathmandu: Sajha Prakashan, 1980. A Nepali geographer's travels across Nepal, incorporating history, geography, and culture. Great for descriptions of remote regions.

Holle, Annick. *Kathmandu: The Hidden City*. Kathmandu: Hill Side Press, 1994. Detailed little guide to the backstreets of the old city, complete with precise maps to lead you into otherwise invisible nooks and crannies.

Iyer, Pico. *Video Night in Kathmandu: and Other Reports from the Not-so-far East*. New York: Alfred A. Knopf, 1988. A look at East-meets-West clashes along the world travel circuit, with a single chapter on Kathmandu; somewhat weak on content, but slick.

Kasajoo, Vinaya Kumar. *Palpa As You Like It*. Tansen: Kumar Press, 1988. A locally produced guide, full of information on obscure Tansen.

Matthiessen, Peter. *The Snow Leopard*. New York: Viking, 1978. Sensitively written account of a journey into Dolpo in pursuit of the elusive snow leopard. Vivid descriptions of the land, interwoven with perceptive insights into the mind. A classic.

Murphy, Dervla. *The Waiting Land*. London: John Murray, 1967. Well-written as all Murphy's books are, this is the adventurous Irishwoman's tale of working in a Pokhara Tibetan refugee camp in 1965. The descriptions and insights still apply.

Snellgrove, David. *Himalayan Pilgrimage: a Study of Tibetan Religion by a Traveller through Western Nepal*. Oxford, Bruno Cassirer, 1961. A Buddhist scholar's 1956 journey through Dolpo, the Kali Gandaki, and Manang, this book mixes anecdotes and observations, permeated with dry humor. In the process, it painlessly teaches a lot about Buddhism.

Tucci, Giuseppe. *Journey to Mustang*. Kathmandu: Ratna Pustak Bhandar, 1977. Local reprint of the Italian Tibetologist's description of his 1952 journey up the Kali Gandaki into Mustang, his practiced eye deciphering history and culture along the way. Fascinating reading for the trek to Muktinath.

FICTION AND LITERATURE

Han Suyin. *The Mountain is Young*. London: Jonathan Cape, 1958. Love story set in "Khatmandu," as the author prefers to spell it, interweaving romance, schmaltz, and local color on an epic scale.

Hutt, Michael James. *Himalayan Voices*. Berkeley: University of California Press, 1991. Vivid survey of Nepal's rich and vital literary tradition, focusing on poetry and short stories.

Robinson, Kim Stanley. *Escape From Kathmandu*. London: Unwin Hyman Ltd., 1990. An amusing romp through clichés, as the heroes rescue yetis, save a hidden valley, and climb Everest with a mountaineering lama.

COFFEE-TABLE BOOKS

Bubriski, Kevin. *Portrait of Nepal*. San Francisco: Chronicle Books, 1993. Haunting black-and-white portraits of Nepali villagers at work, play, and prayer, photographed with extraordinary intimacy and respect.

Doig, Desmond. *My Kind of Kathmandu*. Delhi: Indus, 1994. A personal account of life in Kathmandu circa 1965 through the eyes of this journalist/artist/designer; wonderfully readable and lavishly illustrated with sketches and watercolors.

Hagen, Toni. *Nepal—the Kingdom in the Himalayas*. Bern: Kummerley and Frey, 1980. The first photo book on Nepal, written by a Swiss geologist who walked 14,000 km across the country in the 1950s. Especially interesting for the text.

Kelly, Thomas L., and Patricia Roberts. *Kathmandu: City on the Edge of the World*. New York: Abbeville Press, 1988. An insider's look at the intricate patterns and cultures of the Valley.

Kelly, Thomas L., and V. Carroll Dunham. *The Hidden Himalaya*. New York: Abbeville Press, 1987. A loving, detailed examination of life in the remote Humla region.

Lloyd, Ian, and Wendy Moore. *Kathmandu: The Forbidden Valley*. New Delhi: Times Books International, 1990. One of the best-written and -photographed of the large-format books; among the lowest-priced, too.

Valli, Eric, and Diane Summers. *Dolpo: Hidden Land of the Himalayas*. New York: Aperture Foundation, 1987. An inside look at the Dolpo-pa, whose lives revolve around "Buddhism, barley, yaks, and barter."

ibid. *Honey Hunters of Nepal*. New York: Harry N. Abrams, 1988. Spectacular photos of the Gurung men who retrieve honey from cliff-side hives while dangling from rope ladders.

ETHNIC GROUPS AND CULTURES

Bennett, Lynn. *Dangerous Wives and Sacred Sisters: Social and Symbolic Roles of High-caste Women in Nepal*. New York: Columbia University Press, 1983. An exploration of the lives of Brahman/Chhetri women in a central Nepal village, revealing the frequent conflicts of traditional family life.

Chorlton, Windsor. *Cloud-dwellers of the Himalayas: the Bhotia*. Amsterdam: Time-Life Books, 1982. Excellent photo essays documenting life in the remote region of Nar-Phu, north of Manang; applies to many Bhotia peoples.

Coburn, Broughton. *Nepali Aama: Portrait of a Nepalese Hill Woman*. New York, NY: Doubleday, 1995. Black-and-white photos of the life of an old and very spunky Gurung woman, combined with quotes from Vishnu Maya herself, provide rare insights into a Nepali life.

Downs, Hugh R. *Rhythms of a Himalayan Village*. New York: Harper and Row, 1980. A sensitive evocation of Sherpa life in Junbesi, expressed through black-and-white photos, narrative, and masterfully selected quotes.

Fisher, James. *Sherpas: Reflections on Change in Himalayan Nepal*. New Delhi: Oxford University Press, 1990. Insightful observations on changing Sherpa society over the decades (the author's first visit to Khumbu was in 1964), including an amusing section on how Sherpas and Westerners view one another.

Hartsuiker, Dolf. *Sadhus: Holy Men of India*. London: Thames & Hudson, 1993. Striking photos and detailed text illuminating the rituals and beliefs of *sadhu*, Hinduism's "living idols."

Macfarlane, Alan, and Indra Bahadur Gurung. *Gurungs of Nepal*. Kathmandu: Ratna Pustak Bhandar, 1990. Slim but comprehensive volume detailing modern Gurung life; good reading for the Annapurna region.

Nepali, Gopal Singh. *The Newars*. Bombay: United Asia Publications, 1965. The standard review of Newar culture.

Peissel, Michel. *Mustang: a Lost Tibetan Kingdom.* London: Collins and Harvill Press, 1968. Well-written account by a Tibetan-speaking French adventurer who visited Mustang in 1964.

Shepherd, Gary. *Life Among the Magars.* Kathmandu: Sahayogi Press, 1982. Personal story of a linguist who lived with his family in a northwest Nepal village for 12 years.

Shrestha, D.B., and C.B. Singh. *Ethnic Groups of Nepal.* Kathmandu: Mandala Book Point, 1992. Comprehensive rundown of customs and cultures of various ethnic groups.

Tucci, Giuseppe. *Tibet, Land of Snows.* London: Elek Books, 1967. Good survey of Tibetan traditions and religion, which also permeate northern Nepal.

von Fürer-Haimendorf, Christoph. *Himalayan Traders.* London: John Murray, 1975. Examination of Bhotia trading communities across Nepal and how their lives have changed.

LANGUAGE

Clark, T.W. *Introduction to Nepali.* Kathmandu: Ratna Pustak Bhandar, 1989. Comprehensive survey of the language, with lots of good sample sentences.

Karki, Tika B., and Chij Shrestha. *Basic Course in Spoken Nepali.* Kathmandu. Basic lessons on various aspects of Nepali using the situational approach.

Matthews, David L. *A Course In Nepali.* London: School of Oriental and African Studies, 1984. As comprehensive as Clark's book; later lessons are in Devanagari.

Meerdonk, M. *Basic Gurkhali Dictionary.* Singapore: Straits Times Press, 1959. Over 16,000 English-Nepali and Nepali-English definitions crammed into a pocket-sized book.

Schmidt, Ruth L., editor-in-chief. *A Practical Dictionary of Modern Nepali.* New Delhi: Ratna Sagar, 1993. The definitive listing: 70,000 entries, complete with idiomatic sample sentences.

HISTORY AND CULTURE

Anderson, Mary M. *The Festivals of Nepal.* Calcutta: Rupa & Co., 1988. The standard compendium of the Kathmandu Valley's multitude of festivals: descriptions, legends, what happens when and where.

Avedon, John. *In Exile From the Land of Snows.* New York: Alfred A. Knopf, 1984. The emotionally wrenching saga of Tibetan refugees in exile. It deals mainly with settlements in India, but provides essential background for anyone interested in Tibetans in Nepal.

Burbank, Jon. *Culture Shock! Nepal.* Singapore: Times Editions, 1992. Insightful discussion of Nepali customs and etiquette which goes far beyond the trite "dos and don'ts" of most cultural guides. Useful briefings on the caste system, "Nepali ways of seeing," and working with government counterparts.

Brown, Percy. *Picturesque Nepal.* New Delhi: Today & Tomorrow's Printers, 1984. Reprint of the 1912 work by an art historian; quaint by now, but some pertinent observations on Valley culture.

Farwell, Byron. *The Gurkhas.* London: Allen Lane, 1984. From the 1815 skirmish with the British to the Falkland Islands, the story of the Gurkhas, the "world's best infantrymen."

Landon, Percival. *Nepal.* London: Constable, 1928. Reprinted by Ratna Pustak Bhandar, these two volumes contain a thorough rundown of the Valley's history, marred only by obsequious praise of the Rana Maharaja who commissioned the work.

Levy, Robert. *Mesocosm: Hinduism and the Organization of a Traditional Newar City in Nepal.* San Diego: University of California, 1990. Massive anthropological study of the way Bhaktapur's traditional society interweaves individual and social lives.

Oldfield, H. Ambrose. *Sketches from Nepal.* New Delhi: Cosmo Publications, 1974. Reprint of the 1874 observations of a British Residency surgeon, including elephant hunting with Jung Bahadur and tidbits on Valley customs and religion.

Slusser, Mary Shepherd. *Nepal Mandala: A Cultural Study of the Kathmandu Valley.* Princeton: Princeton University Press, 1982. At Rs5000 for the two-volume set (plates and text), this will be taken home by few, but it's an extremely detailed and well-written study of the complex world of the Valley's Newars, interweaving art, architecture, religion, and history.

Smith, Warren W., ed., and Mana Bajra Bajracharaya, trans. *Swayambhu Purana: Mythological History of the Nepal Valley.* Kathmandu: 1978. Well-rendered version of the classic 16th-century text relating the Buddhist myth of the Valley's origin.

Stiller, Ludwig F. *The Rise of the House of Gorkha.* Kathmandu: Ratna Pustak Bhandar, 1973. One of many scholarly works produced by Jesuits in Nepal, this is the story of Prithvi Narayan Shah's rise to power.

Whelpton, John. *Jang Bahadur in Europe.* Kathmandu: Sahayogi Press, 1983. An entertaining account of the Nepali prime minister's 1850 visit to England and France, including a translation of a narrative written by one of his party.

Wright, Daniel, ed. *Vamsavali: History of Nepal, with an Introductory Sketch of the Country and People of Nepal.* Cambridge: University Press, 1877. Reprinted locally, this is a translation and commentary on the historical chronicles, the traditional history of the Kathmandu Valley.

DEVELOPMENT AND POLITICS

Bista, Dor Bahadur. *Fatalism and Development: Nepal's Struggle for Modernisation.* Madras: Longman, 1990. Provocative examination of how caste hierarchy and a fatalistic attitude, among other factors, hamper development in Nepal, by a respected Chhetri anthropologist.

Blaikie, Piers, John Cameron, and David Seddon. *Nepal in Crisis.* New Delhi: Oxford University Press, 1980. Taking the construction of roads as a starting point, the authors examine the complex problems of "development" in Nepal. Heavy going, but interesting.

Hancock, Graham. *Lords of Poverty: The Power, Prestige and Corruption of the International Aid Business.* New York: The Atlantic Monthly Press, 1990. Often shrill denunciation of the foreign aid business, which seems to benefit only its own bureaucrats and the ruling classes of the countries it's meant to assist.

Pye-Smith, Charlie. *Travels in Nepal.* London: Aurum Press, 1988. Combining travel writing with analyses of foreign-aid projects, this book is a palatable way to dive into development issues and myths. The author examines little-known subjects like outcastes, the poverty-stricken Chepangs, and the possibility that Nepal isn't sliding into the ocean from erosion after all.

Shah, Rishikesh. *Politics in Nepal: 1980-1990.* Kathmandu: Ratna Pustak Bhandar, 1990. Essays on the contemporary political scene, an updated edition of a formerly banned book. Good summary of the 1989 democracy movement.

Thapa, Manjushree. *Mustang Bhot in Fragments.* Lalipur: Mirral Books 1992. Daughter of a Nepali diplomat, Thapa grew up in the U.S. and returned to Nepal as both insider and outsider. This slim volume records her observations on two visits to the newly opened Mustang region.

Tutig, Ludmilla, and Kunda Dixit, eds. *Bikas/ Binas: Development-Destruction.* Kathmandu: Ratna Book Distributors, 1986. Snappy compendium of articles on environmental and cultural issues in the Himalaya, focusing mainly on Nepal. Examines the links betweeen ecology, development, and tourism, and deals with cultural as well as environmental pollution.

ART, CRAFTS, AND ARCHITECTURE

Aran, Lydia. *The Art of Nepal.* Kathmandu: Sayahogi Prakashan, 1978. Remarkably relevant study of Nepali art, focusing on the Kathmandu Valley and doubling as a study of religion.

Bernier, Ronald. *The Nepalese Pagoda—Origins and Style.* New Delhi: S. Chand and Co. Ltd., 1979. Scholarly yet readable unveiling of the complex symbolism of the pagoda; adds much depth to Valley sightseeing.

Dunsmore, Susi. *Nepalese Textiles.* London: British Museum Press, 1993. Color and black-and-white photos record the techniques and history of the ancient tradition of weaving.

Gajurel, C.L., and K.K. Vaidya. *Traditional Arts and Crafts of Nepal.* New Delhi: S. Chand and Co. Ltd., 1984. Details the production techniques of arts and crafts: metalworking, brickmaking, weaving, and dyeing paper—even food. Well-organized and written.

Hutt, Michael. *Nepal: A Guide to the Art and Architecture of the Kathmandu Valley.* Gartmore, Scotland: Kiscadale Publications, 1994. Lucid, comprehensive overview of the Valley's cultural treasures, complete with color plates and detailed maps. An excellent buy.

Kuloy, H.K. *Tibetan Rugs.* Bangkok: White Orchid Press, 1982. Over 260 color illustrations of antique rugs, with commentary.

Macdonald, Alexander W., and Anne Vergati Stahl. *Newar Art: Nepalese during the Malla Period.* New Delhi: Vikas, 1979. Architecture and paintings of the Kathmandu Valley examined in the context of classical Newar culture.

Pal, Pratapaditya. *Art of Nepal.* Los Angeles/Berkeley: Los Angeles County Museum of Art/University of California Press, 1985. A lovely collection of sculpture and paintings from the Los Angeles County Museum.

RELIGION

Anderson, Walt. *Open Secrets: A Western Guide to Tibetan Buddhism.* New York: Viking, 1979. An accessible introductory book to Tibetan Buddhism, placing it in a modern psychological context.

Bernbaum, Edward. *The Way to Shambhala.* Garden City, NY: Anchor Books/Doubleday, 1980. Fascinating overview of the Tibetan tradition of "hidden valleys," and a good explanation of the many levels of Tibetan Buddhism.

Locke, John K. *Karunamaya.* Kathmandu: Sahayogi Prakshan, 1980. A scholarly study of the complex cult of Machhendranath, with many insights into Newar Buddhism.

O'Flaherty, Wendy Doniger, ed. *Hindu Myths.* New York: Viking Penguin, 1975. Introductions to the major gods in their many moods, a good way to soak up the riches of the Hindu pantheon.

Sen, K.M. *Hinduism.* London: Penguin, 1961. Standard overview of the social and historical development of Hinduism.

NATURAL HISTORY

Byrne, Peter. *Tula Hatti: the Last Great Elephant.* London: Faber and Faber, 1992. Describes the conversion of a "Professional White Hunter" from game-stalker to game protector in his quest to protect Suklaphanta Wildlife Reserve in remote southwestern Nepal.

Cameron, Ian. *Mountains of the Gods.* London: Century, 1984. An interesting illustrated survey of the entire Himalaya: history, geology, ecology, peoples.

Fleming, Robert L., Sr. *The General Ecology, Flora, and Fauna of Midland Nepal.* Kathmandu: Tribhuvan University Press, 1977. A thorough overview of the environment of Nepal's Hills, with an emphasis on the Kathmandu Valley.

Fleming, Robert L., Sr., Robert L. Fleming, Jr., and Lain Singh Bangdel. *Birds of Nepal.* Kathmandu: Nature Himalayas, 1976. This masterpiece illustrates over 1,000 individuals of 753 species in color, with descriptions on facing pages for easy identification. Fascinating even if you aren't a birdwatcher.

Grewal, Bikram. *Birds of India.* Hong Kong: The Guidebook Company, 1993. Photographic book that serves as a good substitute if *Birds of Nepal* is out of print.

Gurung, K.K. *Heart of the Jungle: The Wildlife of Chitwan Nepal.* London: Andre Deutsch, 1983. An extremely well-written overview of the natural history of Chitwan National Park.

Hillard, Darla. *Vanishing Tracks: Four Years Among the Snow Leopards of Nepal.* London: Elm Tree Books, 1989. Written by a woman who spent four seasons in remote northern Nepal tracking the snow leopard. Enjoyable descriptions of the Himalayan mountain environment and the local Bhotia people, in their own way an endangered species as well.

MOUNTAINEERING

Gillman, Peter, ed. *Everest.* Boston: Little, Brown and Co., 1993. Compilation of photographs and writings detailing the history of humanity's relationship with Everest, "the ultimate symbol of human endeavor."

Herzog, Maurice. *Annapurna.* London: Jonathan Cape, 1952. The classic account of the conquest of the first 8000-meter peak, told with enormous dignity—Herzog dictated the book from a hospital bed where he was recovering from frostbite that claimed most of his fingers and toes. A gripping story capturing the essence of mountaineering.

Hornbein, Thomas F. *Everest: The West Ridge.* Seattle: The Mountaineers, 1980. Written by a member of the giant 1963 American Expedition, this book rises far above the usual mountaineering saga, matching exquisite photos with meditative quotes.

Tilman, H.W. *The Seven Mountain-Travel Books.* Seattle: The Mountaineers, 1983. Only *Nepal Himalaya* deals directly with Nepal, covering the first reconnaissance of the Langtang, Annapurna, and Everest regions, but 886 pages of wry humor by the best expedition writer ever will have you rolling on the floor.

TREKKING AND RAFTING

Armington, Stan. *Trekking in the Nepal Himalaya.* Victoria, Australia: Lonely Planet, 1982. While it leans toward group trekking, there's a lot of practical information—the author has been in the business for 20 years.

Bezruchka, Stephen. *Trekking in Nepal.* Seattle: The Mountaineers, 1991. The standard guide, a masterpiece of extremely detailed trail descriptions covering all major regions and a few minor ones. Thorough and sincere, with appendices on cultural and natural history.

Knowles, Peter, and Dave Allardice. *Whitewater Nepal.* U.K: Rivers Publishing; U.S.: Menasha Ridge Press, 1992. The first guide to river rafting in Nepal, with introductory chapters on the country, detailed descriptions of trips, and advice on selecting a company; packed with anecdotes and drawings. Not necessary for a float down the Trisuli, but indispensable for more serious rafting.

McGuiness, Jamie. *Trekking In the Everest Region.* Hindhead, Surrey: Trailblazer Publications, 1993. Detailed guide devoted exclusively to Solu-Khumbu; a lengthy introduction to Kathmandu and trekking, followed by step-by-step trail descriptions complete with times, altitudes and sketch maps, right down to the locations of lodges. May be *too* detailed for those who prefer an element of adventure in their trek. The same company publishes Bryn Thomas's *Trekking in the Annapurna Region.*

O'Connor, Bill. *The Trekking Peaks of Nepal.* Ramsbury, Marlborough: The Crowood Press, 1988. Descriptions of all 18 peaks, including trekking approaches and climbing routes.

ibid. *Adventure Treks: Nepal.* Ramsbury, Marlborough: The Crowood Press, 1990. Personal accounts of various treks, followed by brief itineraries. Lively armchair reading rather than a guide, but the chapters on remote regions like Hongu, Ganesh Himal, and Jugal Himal could be useful.

Swift, Hugh. *Trekking in Nepal, West Tibet and Bhutan.* San Francisco: Sierra Club, 1990. In contrast to Bezruchka's hour-by-hour trail descriptions, Swift's enjoyable approach is to take a broad overview, leaving you to discover the details yourself. Great coverage of remote regions.

Wilkerson, James A. *Medicine for Mountaineering.* Seattle: The Mountaineers, 1985. The best medical book for trekking, detailed yet simple enough for laypeople, though a bit bulky to carry around.

ACCOMMODATIONS INDEX

Page numbers in *italics* indicate information found in charts or special topics. Accommodations beginning with "Hotel" are indexed by the second word; e.g., find Hotel Eden under Eden, Hotel.

RESTAURANT INDEX

GENERAL INDEX

Page numbers in **boldface** indicate the primary reference. *Italicized* page numbers indicate information in charts, maps, photos, or special topics.

ABOUT THE AUTHOR

Kerry Moran received a Bachelor of Journalism degree from the University of Missouri-Columbia in 1981. Following a year in Paris and a stint as a newspaper editor in Northern California, she moved to China in 1984 with her husband Chris Gamm to teach English at Zhongshan University. From there she traveled overland through Tibet to Kathmandu, where she's lived since 1985, working as a freelance writer and a sometimes trek leader. Her articles have appeared in *The Asian Wall Street Journal* as well as a number of inflight and travel magazines.

She speaks Nepali, Tibetan, and Chinese, and her extensive travels in Nepal and Tibet include 18 treks in Nepal and two journeys to Tibet's holy Mt. Kailas. With photographer Russell Johnson, she's the author of *Kailas: On Pilgrimage to the Sacred Mountain of Tibet* (Thames & Hudson, 1989). Her other books are *Odyssey Illustrated Guide to Nepal* (The Guidebook Company, 1995) and *Hong Kong Handbook* (Moon Publications, 1995).

MOON TRAVEL HANDBOOKS
THE IDEAL TRAVELING COMPANIONS

Moon Travel Handbooks provide focused, comprehensive coverage of distinct destinations all over the world. Our goal is to give travelers all the background and practical information they'll need for an extraordinary travel experience.

Every Handbook begins with an in-depth essay about the land, the people, their history, art, politics, and social concerns—an entire bookcase of cultural insight and introductory information in one portable volume. We also provide accurate, up-to-date coverage of all the practicalities: language, currency, transportation, accommodations, food, and entertainment. And Moon's maps are legendary, covering not only cities and highways, but parks and trails that are often difficult to find in other sources.

Below are highlights of Moon's Asia and Pacific Travel Handbook series. Our complete list of Handbooks covering North America and Hawaii, Mexico, Central America and the Caribbean, and Asia and the Pacific, are listed on the order form on the accompanying pages. To purchase Moon Travel Handbooks, please check your local bookstore or order by phone: (800) 345-5473 Monday-Friday 8 a.m.-5 p.m. PST.

MOON OVER ASIA
THE ASIA AND THE PACIFIC TRAVEL HANDBOOK SERIES

"Moon guides are wittily written and warmly personal; what's more, they present a vivid, often raw vision of Asia without promotional overtones. They also touch on such topics as official corruption and racism, none of which rate a mention in the bone-dry, air-brushed, dry-cleaned version of Asia written up in the big U.S. guidebooks."

—*Far Eastern Economic Review*

BALI HANDBOOK
by Bill Dalton, 428 pages, **$12.95**
"This book is for the in-depth traveler, interested in history and art, willing to experiment with language and food and become immersed in the culture of Bali."

— Great Expeditions

BANGKOK HANDBOOK
by Michael Buckley, 221 pages, **$13.95**
"Helps make sense of this beguiling paradox of a city . . . very entertaining reading."

—*The Vancouver Sun*

FIJI ISLANDS HANDBOOK
by David Stanley, 275 pages, **$13.95**
"If you want to encounter Fiji and not just ride through it, this book is for you."

—Great Expeditions

HONG KONG HANDBOOK
by Kerry Moran, 347 pages, **$15.95**
"One of the most honest glimpses into Hong Kong the Peoples Republic of China would like never to have seen."

—TravelNews Asia

INDONESIA HANDBOOK
by Bill Dalton, 1,351 pages, **$25.00**
"Looking for a fax machine in Palembang, a steak dinner on Ambon or the best place to photograph Bugis prahus in Sulawesi? Then buy this brick of a book, which contains a full kilogram of detailed directions and advice."

—Asia, Inc. Magazine

"The classic guidebook to the archipelago."

—Condé Nast Traveler

JAPAN HANDBOOK
by J.D. Bisignani, 952 pages, **$22.50**
Winner: Lowell Thomas Gold Award, Society of American Travel Writers
"The scope of this guide book is staggering, ranging from an introduction to Japanese history and culture through to the best spots for shopping for pottery in Mashie or silk pongee in Kagoshima."

—Golden Wing

"More travel information on Japan than any other guidebook."

—The Japan Times

MICRONESIA HANDBOOK
by David Stanley, 342 pages, **$11.95**
"Remarkably informative, fair-minded, sensible, and readable . . . Stanley's comments on the United States' 40-year administration are especially pungent and thought-provoking."

—The Journal of the Polynesian Society

NEPAL HANDBOOK
by Kerry Moran, 466 pages, **$18.95**
Winner: Lowell Thomas Gold Award, Society of American Travel Writers
"This is an excellent guidebook, exploring every aspect of the country the visitor is likely to want to know about with both wit and authority."

—South China Morning Post

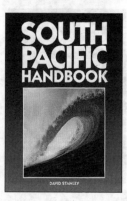

TAHITI-POLYNESIA HANDBOOK
by David Stanley, 243 pages, **$13.95**

"If you can't find it in this book, it is something you don't need to know. "

—*Rapa Nui Journal*

THAILAND HANDBOOK
by Carl Parkes, 800 pages, **$19.95**
"Carl Parkes is the savviest of all tourists to Southeast Asia."

—*Arthur Frommer*

TIBET HANDBOOK
by Victor Chan, 1,103 pages, **$30.00**
"Not since the original three volume Murray's Handbook to India, published over a century ago, has such a memorial to the hot, and perhaps uncontrollable passions of travel been published. . . . This is the most impressive travel handbook published in the 20th century."

—*Small Press Magazine*

"Shimmers with a fine madness."

—*Escape Magazine*

VIETNAM, CAMBODIA & LAOS HANDBOOK
by Michael Buckley, 650 pages, **$18.95**
The new definitive guide to Indochina from a travel writer who knows Asia like the back of his hand. Michael Buckley combines the most current practical travel information—much of it previously unavailable—with the perspective of a seasoned adventure traveler. Includes 75 maps.

STAYING HEALTHY IN ASIA, AFRICA, AND LATIN AMERICA
by Dirk G. Schroeder, ScD, MPH, 197 pages, **$11.95**

"Read this book if you want to stay healthy on any journeys or stays in Asia, Africa, and Latin America."

—*American Journal of Health Promotion*

MOONBELT

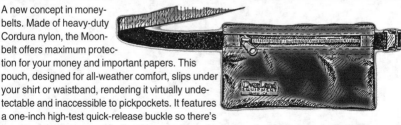

A new concept in money-belts. Made of heavy-duty Cordura nylon, the Moon-belt offers maximum protection for your money and important papers. This pouch, designed for all-weather comfort, slips under your shirt or waistband, rendering it virtually unde-tectable and inaccessible to pickpockets. It features a one-inch high-test quick-release buckle so there's no more fumbling around for the strap or repeated adjustments. This handy plastic buckle opens and closes with a touch, but won't come undone until you want it to. Moonbelts accommodate traveler's checks, passports, cash, photos, etc. Size 5 x 9 inches. Available in black only. **$8.95**

PERIPLUS TRAVEL MAPS

Periplus Travel Maps are a necessity for traveling in Southeast Asia. Each map is designed for maximum clarity and utility, combining several views and insets of the area. Transportation information, street indexes, and descriptions of major sites are included in each map. The result is a single map with all the vital information needed to get where you're going. No other maps come close to providing the detail or comprehensive coverage of Asian travel destinations. All maps are updated yearly and produced with digital technology using the latest survey information. **$7.95**

Periplus Travel Maps are available to the following areas:

Bali	Ko Samui/
Bandung/W. Java	Lombok
Bangkok/C. Thailand	S. Thailand
Batam/Bintan	Penang
Cambodia	Phuket/S. Thailand
Chiangmai/N. Thailand	Sabah
Hong Kong	Sarawak
Indonesia	Singapore
Jakarta	Vietnam
Java	Yogyakarta/C. Java
Kuala Lumpur	

Travel Matters

Travel Matters is Moon Publications' free quarterly newsletter, loaded with specially commissioned travel articles and essays that get at the heart of the travel experience. Every issue includes:

Feature Stories covering a wide array of travel and cultural topics about destinations on and off the beaten path. Past feature stories in *Travel Matters* include Mexican professional wrestling, traveling to the Moon, and why Germans get six weeks off and Americans don't.

Transportation tips covering all forms of transportation by land, sea, and air. Transportation topics covered recently have included driving through Baja California, new Eurail passes, trekking in Tibet, and biking through Asia.

Health Matters, by Dirk Schroeder, author of *Staying Healthy in Asia, Africa, and Latin America,* focusing on the most recent medical findings that affect travelers. Learn about hepatitis A and B, critical travel supplies, and how to avoid common ailments.

Book and Multimedia Reviews providing informed assessments of the latest travel titles, series, and support materials. Recent reviews include The Rough Guide to *World Music, Passage to Vietnam* CD-ROM, and *I Should Have Stayed Home: The Worst Trips of Great Writers.*

The Internet page, which provides updates on Moon's WWW site, online discussions, and other travel resources available in cyberspace. A wide range of topics have been covered in this column including how to go online without going crazy, the Great Burma Debate, and details on Moon's *Road Trip USA* project.

Fellow Traveler, a reader question and answer column for travelers written by an international travel agent and world traveler.

To receive a free subscription to *Travel Matters,* call (800) 345-5473,
e-mail us at travel@moon.com, or write to us at:

Moon Publications
P.O. Box 3040
Chico, CA 95927-3040

Please note: Subscribers who live outside of the United States will be charged $7.00 per year for shipping and handling.

MOON TRAVEL HANDBOOKS

NORTH AMERICA AND HAWAII

Alaska-Yukon Handbook (0161)	$14.95
Alberta and the Northwest Territories Handbook (0676)	$17.95
Arizona Traveler's Handbook (0536)	$16.95
Atlantic Canada Handbook (0072)	$17.95
Big Island of Hawaii Handbook (0064)	$13.95
British Columbia Handbook (0145)	$15.95
Colorado Handbook (0447)	$18.95
Georgia Handbook (0390)	$17.95
Hawaii Handbook (0005)	$19.95
Honolulu-Waikiki Handbook (0587)	$14.95
Idaho Handbook (0617)	$14.95
Kauai Handbook (0013)	$13.95
Maui Handbook (0579)	$14.95
Montana Handbook (0498)	$17.95
Nevada Handbook (0641)	$16.95
New Mexico Handbook (0153)	$14.95
Northern California Handbook (3840)	$19.95
Oregon Handbook (0102)	$16.95
*Road Trip USA (0366)	$22.50
Texas Handbook (0633)	$17.95
Utah Handbook (0684)	$16.95
*Washington Handbook (0455)	$18.95
Wyoming Handbook (3980)	$14.95

ASIA AND THE PACIFIC

Bali Handbook (3379)	$12.95
Bangkok Handbook (0595)	$13.95
Fiji Islands Handbook (0382)	$13.95
Hong Kong Handbook (0560)	$15.95
Indonesia Handbook (0625)	$25.00
Japan Handbook (3700)	$22.50
Micronesia Handbook (3808)	$11.95
Nepal Handbook (0412)	$18.95
*New Zealand Handbook (0331)	$19.95
*Outback Australia Handbook (0471)	$18.95
*Pakistan Handbook (0692)	$22.50
Philippines Handbook (0048)	$17.95

Southeast Asia Handbook (0021)	$21.95
South Korea Handbook (3204)	$14.95
South Pacific Handbook (0404)	$22.95
Tahiti-Polynesia Handbook (0374)	$13.95
*Thailand Handbook (0420)	$19.95
Tibet Handbook (3905)	$30.00
*Vietnam, Cambodia & Laos Handbook (0293)	$18.95

MEXICO

Baja Handbook (0528)	$15.95
Cabo Handbook (0285)	$14.95
Cancún Handbook (0501)	$13.95
Central Mexico Handbook (0234)	$15.95
Mexico Handbook (0315)	$21.95
Northern Mexico Handbook (0226)	$16.95
Pacific Mexico Handbook (0323)	$16.95
Puerto Vallarta Handbook (0250)	$14.95
Yucatán Peninsula Handbook (0242)	$15.95

CENTRAL AMERICA AND THE CARIBBEAN

Belize Handbook (0307)	$15.95
Caribbean Handbook (0277)	$16.95
Costa Rica Handbook (0358)	$19.95
Jamaica Handbook (0129)	$14.95

INTERNATIONAL

Egypt Handbook (3891)	$18.95
Moon Handbook (0668)	$10.00
Moscow-St. Petersburg Handbook (3913)	$13.95
Staying Healthy in Asia, Africa, and Latin America (0269)	$11.95

* New title or edition, please call for availability

PERIPLUS TRAVEL MAPS
All maps $7.95 each

Bali	Indonesia	Phuket/S. Thailand
Bandung/W. Java	Jakarta	Sabah
Bangkok/C. Thailand	Java	Sarawak
Batam/Bintan	Kuala Lumpur	Singapore
Cambodia	Ko Samui/S. Thailand	Vietnam
Chiangmai/N. Thailand	Lombok	Yogyakarta/C. Java
Hong Kong	Penang	

WHERE TO BUY MOON TRAVEL HANDBOOKS

BOOKSTORES AND LIBRARIES: Moon Travel Handbooks are sold worldwide. Please contact our sales manager for a list of wholesalers and distributors in your area.

TRAVELERS: We would like to have Moon Travel Handbooks available throughout the world. Please ask your bookstore to write or call us for ordering information. If your bookstore will not order our guides for you, please contact us for a free title listing.

> Moon Publications, Inc.
> P.O. Box 3040
> Chico, CA 95927-3040 U.S.A.
> tel.: (800) 345-5473
> fax: (916) 345-6751
> e-mail: travel@moon.com

IMPORTANT ORDERING INFORMATION

PRICES: All prices are subject to change. We always ship the most current edition. We will let you know if there is a price increase on the book you order.

SHIPPING AND HANDLING OPTIONS: Domestic UPS or USPS first class (allow 10 working days for delivery): $3.50 for the first item, 50 cents for each additional item.

EXCEPTIONS: *Tibet Handbook* and *Indonesia Handbook* shipping $4.50; $1.00 for each additional *Tibet Handbook* or *Indonesia Handbook*.

Moonbelt shipping is $1.50 for one, 50 cents for each additional belt.

Add $2.00 for same-day handling.

UPS 2nd Day Air or Printed Airmail requires a special quote.

International Surface Bookrate 8-12 weeks delivery: $3.00 for the first item, $1.00 for each additional item. Note: Moon Publications cannot guarantee international surface bookrate shipping. Moon recommends sending international orders via air mail, which requires a special quote.

FOREIGN ORDERS: Orders that originate outside the U.S.A. must be paid for with either an international money order or a check in U.S. currency drawn on a major U.S. bank based in the U.S.A.

TELEPHONE ORDERS: We accept Visa or MasterCard payments. Minimum order is US$15.00. Call in your order: (800) 345-5473, 8 a.m.-5 p.m. Pacific standard time.

ORDER FORM

Prices are subject to change without notice. Be sure to call (800) 345-5473 for current prices and editions or for the name of the bookstore nearest you that carries Moon Travel Handbooks • 8 a.m.–5 p.m. PST. (See important ordering information on preceding page.)

Name: _____ Date: _____

Street: _____

City: _____ Daytime Phone: _____

State or Country: _____ Zip Code: _____

QUANTITY	TITLE	PRICE

Taxable Total_____

Sales Tax (7.25%) for California Residents_____

Shipping & Handling_____

TOTAL_____

Ship: ☐ UPS (no P.O. Boxes) ☐ 1st class ☐ International surface mail

Ship to: ☐ address above ☐ other _____

Make checks payable to: **MOON PUBLICATIONS, INC.**, P.O. Box 3040, Chico, CA 95927-3040 U.S.A. We accept Visa and MasterCard. **To Order**: Call in your Visa or MasterCard number, or send a written order with your Visa or MasterCard number and expiration date clearly written.

Card Number: ☐ **Visa** ☐ **MasterCard**

☐ ☐ ☐ ☐ ☐ ☐ ☐ ☐ ☐ ☐ ☐ ☐ ☐ ☐ ☐ ☐

Exact Name on Card: _____

Expiration date:_____

Signature: _____